The
Pound
Era

The Pound Era

By HUGH KENNER

UNIVERSITY OF CALIFORNIA PRESS

BERKELEY AND LOS ANGELES 1971

University of California Press
Berkeley and Los Angeles
California

Copyright © 1971 by Hugh Kenner

ISBN 0-520-01860-5
LCCC No. 72-138349

Printed in the United States of America
Designed by Dave Comstock

IN MEMORIAM M.J.K.

In signo fidei praecedentis

CONTENTS

ILLUSTRATIONS

ACKNOWLEDGMENTS

Ezra Pound, to start with. When I first met him he was 62. As these words are written he approaches 86. Mine was the third generation he had taught, and owes him its testimony. So this book was planned as an X-ray moving picture of how our epoch was extricated from the *fin de siècle*.

It led me long journeys. And having sat in a Venetian noon at the behest of three words—

mermaids, that carving

—waiting for the doors of Santa Maria dei Miracoli to be unlocked, having then seen the mermaids ("sirenes") Tullio had carved "in the tradition," and watched the custodian's wooden pick pass behind the minute stonework of their frieze to demonstrate its cunning detachment from its base; having visited Rimini drawn by a few more words, and Montségur ("sacred to Helios") on account of words still fewer, I cannot but endorse the accuracy of perception that set in array the words that drew me on.

No one knows enough to undertake a book like this, but generous help has made good much ignorance. For information and shafts of specialized judgment the reader and I are indebted to Ezra and Dorothy Pound, Mr. Omar S. Pound, Miss Olga Rudge, Prince Boris and Princess Mary de Rachewiltz; Eva Hesse and her husband Mike O'Donnell; Guy Davenport (*polumetis*); Mr. R. Buckminster Fuller, Miss Marianne Moore, Robert Lowell, Charles Tomlinson, Samuel Beckett, George and Mary Oppen, Louis and Celia Zukofsky; Mrs. T. S. Eliot, Mrs. Wyndham Lewis, Mrs. William Carlos Williams; Fred Siegel, Christine Brooke-Rose, Geoffrey and Joyce Bridson, Mr. Joseph Bard, William Cookson, Christopher Middleton, Richard G. Stern, Joan Fitzgerald, Walter Michaels; my colleagues Herbert N. Schneidau, Alan Stephens,

Marvin Mudrick, Mary Slaughter, David Young, Immanuel Hsu, Wai-Lim Yip and Chalmers Johnson; Mrs. Alice Leng and Miss Anne Freudenberg; Donald Davie, John Frith, Laurence Scott; Mr. James Laughlin, Mr. Harry M. Meacham; Mr. Reno Odlin and his anonymous correspondent; Mrs. Gatter of Wyncote, Pa.; Mrs. Gay of Excideuil (Dordogne); Prof. D. S. Carne-Ross, Prof. Leon Edel, Prof. A. Walton Litz, Prof. David Hayman; Mr. Fritz Senn; Rev. Walter J. Ong, S.J.; Miss Barbara Tuchman; Mr. David E. Scherman; Mr. Peter du Sautoy of Faber & Faber Ltd., Mr. August Frugé, Director of the University of California Press; my diligent editor Mr. Joel Walters; and—for getting me in touch with Ezra Pound in the first place—Marshall McLuhan and the late Felix B. Giovanelli.

Many who helped and whom I had hoped to please are dead: T. S. Eliot, William Carlos Williams, Wyndham Lewis, Henry Rago, Miss Agnes Bedford, Mr. Frank Budgen, Mr. John Cook Wylie. It was my tacit understanding with the late W. K. Rose that our projected books would complement one another, but his, on the personal interactions in the days of the London Vortex, will never be written now. And I was too late to discuss Social Credit with the late Gorham Munson, or Chinese History with the late Joseph Levenson, and have had to be content with learning from their books.

A letter from Mr. John Reid catalyzed the book years ago, though it is not the book he suggested. Mr. William F. Buckley's logistical resourcefulness was indispensable. So was the help of the Guggenheim Foundation, the American Philosophical Society, the Committee on Research of the University of California, Santa Barbara, the library staffs there and at the Universities of Virginia, Texas, Chicago, Buffalo and Wisconsin (Milwaukee), and the New York Public Library. And finally, the patience and advice of my wife Mary Anne; there are no fit words.

Portions of this book, often in earlier versions, have appeared in *Agenda, Arion, Canadian Literature* (and the reprint of its articles, *Wyndham Lewis in Canada*), *College English*, Eva Hesse's *New Approaches to Ezra Pound*, *Kentucky Review*, *National Review*, *Poetry*, *James Joyce Quarterly*, *St. Andrews Review*, *Shenandoah*, *Sou' Wester*, *Spectrum*, *Stony Brook*, *Sumac*, *Texas Quarterly*.

Quotations from the writings of Ezra Pound appear through the courtesy of Dorothy Pound, Committee for Ezra Pound, New Directions Publishing Corp., and Faber & Faber Ltd. Unpublished Pound material is used by Mrs. Pound's courtesy and is fully protected by copyright. Mrs. Pound owns the Gaudier-Brzeska panther drawing that appears on the title-page and elsewhere; it is reproduced with her permission. Quotations from William Carlos Williams' poems are used by permission of New Directions Publishing Corp. and Laurence Pollinger Ltd. The quotation from *Success and Failure of Picasso* by John Berger (Penguin Books) is used by permission of Hope Leresch & Steele.

References to the Cantos

Commencing with the 1970 printing, the American (New Directions) collected edition of the *Cantos* was paginated continuously, as the British (Faber) edition had been since 1964. I give references to the *Cantos* in the form (74/447:475). This means Canto 74, page 447 of the repaginated New Directions edition, page 475 of the Faber.

The reader who wishes to locate a passage in the earlier New Directions edition, which is paginated by separate volume, may subtract from the New Directions page number in the reference the corrections from the following table:

	subtract
Cantos 1–30	0
Cantos 31–41	150
Cantos 42–51	206
Cantos 52–71	254
Cantos 74–84	422
Cantos 85–95	540
Cantos 96–109	648
Cantos 110–end	770

Thus the example given, 74/447, is on page 25 of the old edition (447 minus 422). Though eight different pages are numbered "25," the Canto number will indicate which one is meant.

The Cantos subsequent to 109 have not, as of 1971, been incorporated into the British collected edition. In the very few references to these Cantos, the second (Faber) number refers to the separately published *Drafts and Fragments*.

The reader who finds such complication annoying may reflect that publishers' costs are governed by the accounting system C. H. Douglas described.

Part One

TOWARD
THE VORTEX

GHOSTS AND BENEDICTIONS

Toward the evening of a gone world, the light of its last summer pouring into a Chelsea street found and suffused the red waistcoat of Henry James, lord of decorum, *en promenade*, exposing his Boston niece to the tone of things.

Miss Peg in London, he had assured her mother, "with her admirable capacity to be interested in the near and the characteristic, whatever these may be," would have "lots of pleasant and informing experience and contact in spite of my inability to 'take her out'." By "out" he meant into the tabernacles of "society": his world of discourse teems with inverted commas, the words by which life was regulated having been long adrift, and referable only, with lifted eyebrows, to usage, his knowledge of her knowledge of his knowledge of what was done. The Chelsea street that afternoon however had stranger riches to offer than had "society." Movement, clatter of hooves, sputter of motors; light grazing housefronts, shadows moving; faces in a crowd, their apparition: two faces: Ezra Pound (quick jaunty rubicundity) with a lady. Eyes met; the couples halted; rituals were incumbent. Around them Chelsea sauntered on its leisurely business. James to play:

3

"Mr. Pound!..." in the searching voice, torch for unimagined labyrinths; and on, to the effect of presenting his niece Margaret; whereafter Mr. Pound presented to Mr. James his wife Dorothy; and the painter's eye of Dorothy Pound, née Shakespear, "took in," as James would have phrased it, Henry James. "A fairly portly figure"—

Fifty years later, under an Italian sky, the red waistcoat seemed half chimerical—"that may be imagination!"—but let us posit it; Gautier wore such a garment to the *Hernani* première, that formal declaration (1830) of art's antipathy to the impercipient, and James would have buttoned it for this outing with didactic deliberation.

Fifty years left nothing else doubtful. The voice now given body was part of her world's tone, effusing from pages read in her mother's house: fictions wherein New World impetuosity crossed the Atlantic on journeys of sanctification. They came as pilgrims or they came as shoppers; as passionate antiquaries or as seekers-out of inconceivable sensations. Some of them amused their creator hugely: the young woman from Bangor who knew, she said, what she wanted and always went straight for it, and preferred to spend her money "for purposes of culture"; or the young man from Boston who proposed that the great thing was to *live* ("I don't want any second-hand spurious sensations; I want the knowledge that leaves a trace—that leaves strange scars and stains, ineffable reveries. . . . But I'm afraid I shock you, perhaps even frighten you"). Grotesque though might be its assertive manifestations, the allure of Europe for the American psyche was in James's awareness the dominant American fact; and "an ear for stilled voices," a responsiveness to "the scrutable, palpable past," were talents occasionally possible to American intensity, even to an intensity so inexperienced as to think the European experience a wetting of lips at the origins of romance.

America, here, had imaginative advantages, being unencumbered by the worldliness with which Europe had learned to inhabit the European world. It was Whistler, not anyone English, who had known how to make Turner's heritage fructify, and crossed that heritage with what was assimilable from the vogue for Japan. It was another American settled abroad, and not some congener of

Thackeray's, whose multiform consciousness of "felt life" had shaped the most intricate registrations of nuance in human history: subdued the taxonomic pretensions of epithets and vanquished the linear rigor of linked sentences: indeed composed *The Ambassadors* and *The Golden Bowl*. Now on Dorothy Pound the eyes of the author of *The Golden Bowl* were bent, intent dark eyes, as he paired off Dorothy with niece Peg and sent the two young women walking ahead; then side by side with Dorothy's husband Ezra (encountered by him at hospitable hearths just sufficiently often to ratify public rites of amiability) he fell into step a deliberate distance behind them.

The young women strolled and talked; their talk is forgotten. After 50 years, though, one scrap of the master's survived. For James's fierce need to "place" and categorize spurred root curiosities, and Dorothy heard from behind her, addressed to her husband of two months, in the slow implacable voice the great expatriate's overwhelming question, as who should ask, animal, vegetable, or mineral: "And is she a com- păt- riot?": the syllables spaced, the accented vowel short.

*   *   *

Which is all of the story, like a torn papyrus. That is how the past exists, phantasmagoric weskits, stray words, random things recorded. The imagination augments, metabolizes, feeding on all it has to feed on, such scraps. What Sappho conceived on one occasion on Mitylene is gone beyond reconstitution; the sole proof that she ever conceived it is a scrap from a parchment copy made thirteen centuries later; on an upper left-hand corner learning assisted by chemicals makes out a few letters; in *Berliner Klassikertexte*, V-2, 1907, pp. 14–15, type stands for those letters with perhaps misleading decisiveness:

.*P 'A[* . . .

ΔHPAT .[. . .

ΓOΓ 'ΓΥΛΑ .[. . .

. . . plus the beginnings of a dozen more lines: very possibly, so modern editions indicate, the first aorist of the verb *to raise* (conjecturing ἦρ' ἀ), and a word unknown, and the name of a girl of Sappho's. Or you can remember from Alcaeus and Ibycus ἦρ, the contraction for *springtime*, and derive the unknown word from δηρός, *too long*, and write

Spring . . . .
Too long . . . . . .
Gongula . . . . . .

heading the little witticism "Papyrus" and printing it in a book of poems called *Lustra* as an exemplum for resurrection-men. And wait decades for someone to unriddle it.

*   *   *

To continue. "Is she a compatriot?" What part did she play— that of Innocence or Experience—in the International Theme? Her provenance, as it happened, was South Kensington, but her legal citizenship by marriage American, a distinction on which liberty would one day turn. War grinds an edge on legalities. Somewhere, as the four of them walked, picked officers were arranging the forage of British horses in France once German troops should violate Belgian neutrality, and European life was never to be tranquil again. Though not even Asquith's cabinet really knew about it, or wanted to, this staff had been at work for three years, denominating in hermetic secrecy a role for England in the first European war to be planned by typewriter. They had very little more to see to, and still a few weeks to work in, the last weeks of what was to seem in retrospect a nearly immemorial expansiveness, bobbing parasols, barbered lawns, when one could walk through Europe without passports, tendering behind any border one's 20-franc pieces. A standing order provided for the sharpening of every British officer's sword on the third day of mobilization. It was 1914, June.

They sharpened the officers' swords on August 7, for brandishing against an avalanche. "The wind of its passage snuffed out the age of unrivalled prosperity and unlimited promise, in which even poor mediaeval Russia was beginning to take part, and Europe descended into a new Dark Age from whose shadows it has yet to emerge." Within three weeks Louvain's 15th-century Library had been rendered blackened stone and its thousand incunabula white ash, in a gesture of admonitory *Schrecklichkeit*. ("Palace in smoky light . . .", begins the fourth Canto, glimpsing such an event refracted through the smoke of Troy; ruins enter Pound's poetry with the war.) By the following summer his hundred million compatriots' obstinate neutrality, as of voyeurs, had exacerbated Henry James to his own last admonitory gesture: a change of citizenship. It was no more understood than *The Golden Bowl* had been. The next January he was dead of apoplexy, and to Ezra Pound not only a life but a tradition seemed over, that of effortless high civility. Not again ... not again ..., ran an insisting cadence, and he made jottings toward an elegiac poem on the endpapers of a little book of elegies called *Cathay*. "Not again, the old men with beautiful manners."

—piling up the beautiful phrases ...

—Gone – gone – they will
      come not again   The
old men with beautiful
       manners

—The "Great Mary"
     (Mrs. Ward—)

"Mr Pound is shocked
    at my levity"

James remained thereafter his synecdoche for "custom indicating high culture," to be distinguished from an unhabitual outlay of effort. "Men of my time" (he recalled in 1937) "have witnessed 'parties' in London gardens where, as I recall it, everyone else (male) wore grey 'toppers'. As I remember it even Henry James wore one, and unless memory blends two occasions he wore also an enormous checked weskit. Men have witnessed the dinner ceremony on flagships, where the steward still called it 'claret' and a Bath Oliver appeared with the cheese. (Stilton? I suppose it must have been Stilton.)"

They had met but seldom, nowhere but in gardens and drawing rooms. "... have met Henry James again and like him still more on further acquaintance," Pound wrote in March 1912 of perhaps their second encounter. Presumptuous though it seems to calibrate one's liking for the portentous Master, even brash to allow his person and the verb "like" to coexist in one's thoughts, the young guest may be trebly excused; he had not been bred to the constraint of Jamesian proprieties, and was 26, and writing to his mother. He liked James, he wondered at James, as at a narwhal disporting. What was to be made of his immutable disregard of Latin, of Greek, of all the distinguishings formally called thought? What of his *blague*, the shameless mischievous hyperboles, the trifling with aesthetic consecrations? The young Ezra's perplexities were not always totally concealed:

> And he said:
>   "Oh! Abelard!" as if the topic
> Were much too abstruse for his comprehension,
> And he talked about "the great Mary,"
> And said: "Mr. Pound is shocked at my levity,"
> When it turned out he meant Mrs. Ward.

There survives a photograph of little Ray Pound, bright as a pippin, peeping eagerly from among more stolid faces in a class grouping at the Cheltenham Military Academy, Pennsylvania. That alert little boy never died, but after a time coexisted with a brittler, more severe persona, whose Pentateuchal capacity for moral outrage was to bewilder acquaintances for decades (". . . stupidity carried beyond a certain point becomes a public menace . . ."). The fervor of the one, the other's generous eagerness, were blended finally into a fascinating public construct called "E. P.", who was to attempt the rectification of 20th-century letters. But in 1912 "E. P." was barely invented, the boy and the moralist still unsynthesized, and the quick Jamesian eye may have caught the moralist's expression slipping unbidden across the innocent's face "when it turned out he meant Mrs. Ward": Mary Augusta Ward, author of *Millie and Ollie* and *The Marriage of William Ashe*: niece to Matthew Arnold and once caricatured by Max Beerbohm in the act of upbraiding her grinning uncle: British so-cultured nullity. The great Mary! "Hyperbole carried beyond a certain point . . .": but it slipped back into focus, entertaining hyperbole: "my levity."

A world of entertainments, unbetterable for displaying cosmologies in impingement; a world (pre-war London) of exiles. Thus Lydia Yavorska, whirligig of importunate energy, dabbler in anarchy, light of the non-Imperial Russian stage, wife of the

Little "Ray" Pound, Cheltenham Military Academy, Pennsylvania, ca. 1897.

indolent Prince Bariatinsky and now in England in political exile:
Lydia was remembered

> holding dear H. J.
> (Mr. James, Henry) literally by the button-hole ...
> in those so consecrated surroundings
> (a garden in the Temple, no less)
> and saying, *for once*, the right thing
> namely: "Cher maître"
> to his chequed waistcoat, the Princess Bariatinsky,
> as the fish-tails said to Odysseus, ἐνὶ Τροίῃ
>
> (79/488:520)

—playing the Siren in short ("Cher maître" for the "renowned
Odysseus," πολύαιν' 'Οδεσεῦ, of *Odyssey* XII-184) and implying
that she comprehended the sentiments of exile, knowing as she did
the wearing things that happened in such wild lands as he and she
had left behind them, where men spoke of the Town Executioner:

> ... no, your body-guard is not the
> town executioner
> the executioner is not here for the moment
> the fellow who rides beside your coachman
> is just a cossack who executes ...
>
> (79/488:520)

And James, as bound to a mast by his decorum. . . . Did she suppose
that such goings-on characterized Massachusetts, of the savage
name? Encounters like that, which seem as though staged for your
enlightenment, you can savor for decades: Pound fitted to it the
elucidative Homeric phrases when he first set it down thirty years
after he witnessed it, in a compact American enclave with an
executioner among its personnel.

*   *   *

It was to be hard eventually for Pound to realize that he was
older than Henry James had been the day they met: in such terms
he addressed himself to the fact of being 70. The Washington heat
wilted his visitors' stamina but not his ("It's the cold that agonizes

grampa") and the talk they had come to hear between 1 and 3 coursed on, sudden *gascon* phrases, long formally built sentences, stating and arranging elements of a civilized world ("not again . . .") from before two wars. He was readily prompted: James's talk had been like his writing?—"Exactly–ex*act*ly"—and hunching his shoulders forward, clasping his hands between his knees, he became for 90 seconds Henry James, eyes fixed on a point in space some yards past a ghostly auditor—some young Mr. Pound in some vanished person's drawing room—as he mimicked what had magnetized his attention at 26:

> . . . the massive head, the slow uplift of the hand, *gli occhi onesti e tardi*, the long sentences piling themselves up in elaborate phrase after phrase, the lightning incision, the pauses, the slightly shaking admonitory gesture with its "wu-a-wait a little, wait a little, something will come". . .

He mimicked, moreover, an impish deferring and deferring of climax: the lifting, after an intent showman's pause, of some unforeseen syntactic shell to disclose not the pea last glimpsed but ("Mr. Pound is shocked at my levity") an auk's egg on the point of hatching (with patience) yet further wonders. To what Keatonian risks did James not commit himself, risks of immobilization in mid-chaos, as he essayed for the thousandth time yet one more construction; and with what wit each impasse becomes a node, as the arrested line strikes out of it in an unforeseeable direction, seeking new points of suspension! Suitably paced, after such hints, with hesitations and onrushes, how alive a Jamesian text becomes. Thus the scarcity of congressmen in social Washington, James once wrote,

"kept down the political . . .   [here the savoring pause]
permeation,   [a *trouvaille*!]
and was bewildering, if one was
able to compare, in the light of
the different London condition,
the fact   [what a labyrinth!]
of the social . . .   [!]
ubiquity there of the . . . accept-
able M.P. and that of the social

... frequency   [nicely nuanced]
even of his ...   [what can conceivably emerge
                                   from this trembling mountain?]
more equivocal hereditary col-
league."

So under the slowly raised pile driver a Peer is squashed flat (in a time of bought Peerages), by way of finishing off the didactic exercise. It was explicitly to a pile driver, slowly cranked up, with many pauses, laborings, and diversions, that Pound that day compared the Jamesian spoken sentence.

That a language functions in time, ideally in a vast leisure, disclosing sequentially its measured vistas, this was the convention Pound in turn most clearly imposed as he attended to the enlightenment of his callers in the 1950's. "So Mr. Eliot came to London, with all the disadvantages of a ... sym*m*etrical education ... and dutifully joined the Aristotelian Society [*Aristotelian*—a porcupine of tongued consonants] ... And he took me to a meeting. And a man with a beard down to here ... spoke for twenty minutes on a point in Aris*to*tle; and another with a beard down to *here* rose up and refuted him. ... And I wanted *air*. So we were on the portico when old G. R. S. Mead came up, and catching sight of me said 'I didn't expect to see *you* here'; whereat Eliot with perfect decorum and suavity said,

'Oh, he's not here as a phil-*os*-opher;
He's here as an an-thro-pologist.'"

A bird-boned Hindu, in America on a Fulbright ("that is spelled with an *l*, not an *r*," was the Poundian gloss) smiled throughout the recital; across the lawn drifted blank figures; Pound from the depths of his deck chair dosed the air with an aerosol insecticide. A black-robed Minerva smiled from an adjacent chair: Dorothy Shakespear Pound, so little a compatriot that on disembarking she had felt dissolve beneath her feet (she later said) the shores of Muzak, Howard Johnson, and Jefferson; and, yes, Henry James, whom she read intermittently with Voltaire. On a park bench ten yards away a man reclined rigid as though spitted from skull to ankles, his entire weight supported on one elbow and on his heels, his body a taut hypotenuse: catatonic: the place was a mad-house.

"What Confucius has to say about style is contained in two characters. The first says 'Get the meaning across,' and the second says 'Stop'." And on being asked what was in the character "Get the meaning across," "Well, some people say I see too much in these characters"—here a good-natured glance at ambient lunatics—"but I think it means"—the Jamesian pause—"'Lead the sheep out to pasture.'"

For one visitor a detail of the *Pisan Cantos* was suddenly clarified; he exclaimed as much; Mrs. Pound was amused; Ezra took no notice. Let the green grass nourish, with transmuted solar energies, whoso would browse.

*   *   *

The pause in time resembles a disjunction in space: a line having been arrested before its direction grows obvious, the intent eye is confronted by a sudden node, unforeseeable, a new structure, new directions. Frank Lloyd Wright placed concentrations and epitomes so, to terminate a cumbrous line that repeated the massy low line of the earth, and would not hear them called ornament. In a sentence some four words can impart a direction—"kept down the political"—; a fifth word, "permeation," resolves what we might not have known was suspense did not the voice linger: completes the syntax with the noun it requires, and designates a way to imagine the subject, a witty way, a judgment of the subject. (The political permeates the social, an unbidden damp.) By contrast copybook sentences, a fly's crawl over the obvious, appease the drowsing mind with redundancies. And "kept down" is colloquial, indeed American colloquial; "permeation" nearly scholastic. There is social comedy, as well as intellectual energy, in such transitions from diction to diction.

.   .   .

Celebrities from the Trans-Caucasus will belaud
    Roman celebrities
And expound the distentions of Empire

.   .   .

> For the nobleness of the populace brooks nothing
>   below its own altitude.
> One must have resonance, resonance and sonority
>   ... like a goose.
>   .   .   .
>
> My little mouth shall gobble in such great fountains
>   .   .   .

Such lines, applying devices learned from James, locate their subject in a mode of thought habitual with him: the steady generosity of response to things happening, alert with its epithet when the happening veers toward unsatisfactoriness. The *Homage to Sextus Propertius* (1917) was achieved by a mind filled with James's prose, the entire canon of which Pound reread between the Master's death (January 1916) and *The Little Review* memorial issue (August 1918). Not only the ghost of the Latin elegiac couplet presides over its way of dividing discourse, but the great ghost also, "phantom with weighted motion," that drank (he wrote thenabouts) "the tone of things," and spaced its discourse with suspenseful deliberateness.

*　*　*

They say, among the many things they say, that some thousand years before Trojans founded Rome a scholar named Tsang-kié was commanded by his emperor to invent Writing, and took his inspiration from bird tracks in the fluvial sand, by whose print we know what songs were heard here. Whence men write today as birds' feet do, in little clustered lines. And a man may write 工 , which means *doing things properly* and looks as if it ought to, and may draw the sleeves ⺄⺄ of the shamaness dancing in a ritual to summon the spirits to descend, and combine the two signs 巫 to mean *ritual* or *witchcraft*, as you will, though the sign of propriety ensures that it will be acceptable witchcraft. This is called *wu*. And we may draw the rain falling from clouds, 雨 the top horizontal stroke being heaven from which the clouds hang, and set underneath three rain-drops ☐☐☐ , thus denoting the word *ling* 霝 which means *fall* as the big drops fall on a parched day. Then set *wu* under *ling*, 靈 and out of all the *lings* that chime through

Chinese speech, and mean in different tones and contexts a multitude of unrelated things, you have designated the *ling* which means the spirit or energy of a being, in harmony with the invisible and by ritual drawing down benefice: we may say, *sensibility*. It is used of the work of poets, denoting their reach into the realm of the natural (and the drops look like mouths; hence Pound's "under the cloud / the three voices" 104/740:766); and is used in the History Classic of the Emperors of Chou, whose virtue, an attunement with the invisible, won them their commission to execute heaven's decree. "Our dynasty came in because of a great sensibility" (85/543:579) ran Pound's gloss on this context, meditating the History Classic in the Chestnut Ward of St. Elizabeths Hospital. China had lost hold of *ling* and fallen to barbarian ideologies, Chiang's western or Mao's Stalinist, according to your system of disapprovals. The military governor of Sinkiang province had (1949) jumped to the winning side; such things had happened before; one lives through them. At first he thought the poet Mao possessed *ling*, but before long Mao's men were harassing Confucians. In the State Department a few miles from the poet's cell the winning side had persuasive American spokesmen. Like the I Ching's divining sticks, the ideogram, being part of a system of archetypes, should govern such bewildering facts had we but the wit to apply it. For 30 years it had been Pound's Sisyphean lot to read and misread newspaper facts in the light of the archetypes with which his mind vibrated, never willing to concede a shift of dimension between crystalline myth and the polymorphous immediate. In St. Elizabeths he continued this habit.

Meanwhile another part of his mind ran back on James, whose effort to constate, in every nuance, the present ("... where we have, in a manner of speaking, got to") is juxtaposed on the last page of Canto 87 with the sign for the Point of Rest: 止 , but thence (by association) with the great *ling*, its propriety, its spirits, its clouds and celestial voices. James knew much of spirits, James celebrated rituals, James's great sensibility brought in a generation.

* * *

But for that sensibility *Prufrock* is unthinkable, *Mauberley* and the *Cantos* are unthinkable: not that one can imagine James reading any of these. The *Prufrock* situation is stated in a story James published just before the poem was begun: "Crapey Cornelia." A decade later *Hugh Selwyn Mauberley* was "an attempt to condense the James novel." There are unlikelier derivations: what William Carlos Williams says when he opens one of the best-known poems in *Spring and All*—"The pure products of America / go crazy"—is like a Wittgensteinian extrapolation from "The Jolly Corner." The poem called "Poetry" about "hands that can grasp, hair that can dilate," the long poem called *Paterson* and the short one in which

> the reddish
> purplish, forked, upstanding, twiggy
> stuff of bushes and small trees

connotes energies and eschews verbs—they all carry his genetic material inseparable from that of their identified authors, Miss Moore and Dr. Williams. His geomancer's response to impalpabilities—tones and airs, surfaces and absences—inaugurated a poetic of the mute ("And sawdust restaurants with oystershells"), a poetic of eschewals and refrainings, working round the margins of a voiceless theme, a theme voiceless because not yet public, not yet specified, not resolved by its apperceivers to agent, action, acted-upon. That one cannot say, or else may not blatantly say, just who did what to whom, is the premise of the kind of situation that fascinates him. A writer with a different temperament need not share the fascination to find the procedures useful ("Blocked. Make a song out of that concretely," wrote Williams). James's effort to articulate such matters within the shape of the formal English sentence yielded the famous late style, where subject and verb are "there" but don't carry the burden of what is said. Other syntactic structures do that. And subject and verb, in a poem, need not always even be stated.

> ... To lead you to an overwhelming question. ...
> Oh, do not ask, "What is it?"
> Let us go and make our visit.

Behind such lines, as behind

Drifted ... drifted precipitate,
Asking time to be rid of ...
Of his bewilderment; to designate
His new found orchid. ...

persists the voice that pursued so intently so many refusals and
eschewals, and built so magisterially suspensions and resolutions
out of things only half-named, only present by way of analogy.

* * *

Henry James too had known the Washington heat. He had
visited all the America Pound had known, all but Idaho. *The
American Scene*, a book of eloquent absences, ghosts unfulfilled,
where buildings and landscapes have long speaking parts and people
are rarely more than apparitions, recounts his last survey, 1904–5,
of "a society trying to build itself, with every elaboration, into some
coherent sense *of* itself, and literally putting forth interrogative
feelers, as it goes, into the ambient air." The hero of *The American
Scene* is the scene, inhabited space dwelling on its long tale of
frustrations, while persons whose lungs fill and bodies clash dis-
qualify themselves from participating in this most prolonged, most
intimate of séances. James attended (he did!) a Harvard intercollegiate football game, and derived "an impression ... so documentary, as to the capacity of the American public for momentary
gregarious emphasis, that I regret having to omit here all the
reflections it prompted." To so abstract a psychic knot—"momentary gregarious emphasis"—were some two tons of milling players
and the exertions of all the spectators reducible. But a landscape of
failed farms in New Hampshire, ravished and discarded by the
success that on the other side of the continent goes "insolently"
forward, can speak at such length as might Desdemona's shade:

> The touching appeal of nature, as I have called it therefore, the
> "Do something kind for me," is not so much a "Live upon me
> and thrive by me" as a "Live *with* me somehow, and let us make
> out together what we may do for each other—something that is
> not merely estimable in more or less greasy greenbacks. See how
> 'sympathetic' I am," the still voice seemed everywhere to proceed,

"and how I am therefore better than my fate; see how I lend myself
to poetry and sociability—positively to aesthetic use: give me that
consolation."

And under the cone of Chocorua, in which he saw a minor Matter-
horn (and Pound—in memory: Pisa—an American Taishan
thronged with gods), he found that autumn many thousand little
apples:

> They have "run down" from neglect and shrunken from cheapness
> —you pick them up from under your feet but to bite into them, for
> fellowship, and throw them away. . . .

"Our dynasty came in because of a great sensibility": for fellowship!

When Eliot characterized (in *The Egoist*, Jan. 1918) James's
"mastery over, his baffling escape from, Ideas" (". . . a mind so fine
that no idea could violate it") he was employing a criterion refined
by long study of Bradleyan Idealism, for which the Idea, subject–
verb–predicate, is always the tempting shortcut: is the aphorism
which the imagined case sharply illustrates, or the topic sentence
from which the paragraph derives. The mind unviolated by an
idea holds converse with particulars (bites them "for fellowship"):
mute particulars, mute mental particulars, the act of perception and
the act of articulation inextricably one. ("Say it, no ideas but in
things," we read in *Paterson*.) The perceiving mind of *The American
Scene* unites itself with that eloquent space around objects which
impressionist painters have taught us to think inseparable from the
objects. (In *La Grande Jatte* Seurat expended one unifying technique on the figures, the trees, the shadows, and the air.)

So James rode, like a new Magellan, the Jersey ferry, his
fierce dark eyes distended. "It was an adventure, unmistakeably, . . .
to be learning at last, in the maturity of one's powers, what New
Jersey might 'connote'," and to his mature powers the New Jersey
shore houses answered:

> "Oh, yes; we were awfully dear, for what we are and for what we
> do"—it was proud, but it was rather rueful; with the odd appear-
> ance everywhere as of florid creations waiting, a little bewilderingly,

for their justification, waiting for the next clause in the sequence, waiting in short for life, for time, for interest, for character, for identity itself to come to them, quite as large spread tables or superfluous shops may wait for guests and customers.

But

... the most as yet accomplished at such a cost was the air of unmitigated publicity, publicity as a condition, as a doom; ... nothing, accordingly, no image, no presumption of constituted relations, possibilities, amenities, in the social, the domestic order, was inwardly projected.

Hence

The pure products of America
go crazy,

as a man was to write who at the moment of James's visit to his Jersey was away studying medicine at Penn, and the day James visited the Penn campus, to spend an hour in the "clustered palaestra" and wonder whether the aesthetic note sounded muffled or shrill ("I scarce know what fine emphasis of modernism hung about it too") was perhaps somewhere in a dissecting room. If by any chance he did glimpse the great *revenant*, W. C. Williams had no reason to know him. And Williams' intuition of "the basis of privacy" was anyhow not Jamesian; in 1958 he asked whether it were possible to talk to Mr. Eliot "animal to animal."

James missed him, missed intuiting his proximity; missed or rather was missed by Ezra Pound, who had left the University of Pennsylvania for Hamilton College 12 months before James sailed from England, and would return to Penn two months after James sailed home. Anglo-Saxon and Provençal were engrossing him. Marianne Moore did not hear him lecture at Bryn Mawr on "The Lesson of Balzac" in January 1905; she was not to arrive on campus till that fall. Anyhow her chief passion was biology. Nor was there a grazing encounter with Tom Eliot. Turning, in the company of ghosts, Lowell's and Longfellow's, from the Stadium's "more *roaring*, more reported and excursionized scene," James meditated in Harvard Yard on Lowell's fancy that Harvard was too artlessly given to its gentle privacies; he noted "the recent drop in her of any outward sign of literary curiosity"; affirmed that "the muses had fled"; and asked "in what produced form, for instance," if Lowell had been right about Harvard civility, "was now represented the love of letters of which he had been so distinguished an example?" The Smith Academy in St. Louis could not at that moment have taken up his challenge, but the answer was to be found there. And Ernest Hemingway? Aged five, he was up in Michigan, the youngest member of the Agassiz Club and able to count to one hundred. And Wallace Stevens? Practicing law in New York. And Louis Zukofsky? He had just been born, on a street James mentions in a ghetto where James marvelled at the fullness of fervent life.

So in his apostrophizing of absences there is a double meaning, one we can savor though he had no means of guessing at it: an immensely ceremonious benediction completed, through some slippage of the gyres, just before the arrival of the congregation. And always his mind dwells on intelligences not in evidence, intelligences the thwarted scene ached to produce: a scene pervaded, he saw more and more clearly, with money: with usura. In one of the two novels he left unfinished the American Girl, that heiress of the ages, is named Aurora Coyne.

*   *   *

Yet when we collect 1904's memorabilia it is James who seems to be absent. *The Great Train Robbery* had been filmed the year before, the Ford Motor Company had been founded, and Orville Wright had been airborne for 12 seconds. In St. Louis, just 30 days after James sailed from Southampton, the International Congress of Arts and Science heard Henri Poincaré formulate a "principle of relativity" and call for a new dynamics postulating the ultimacy of the speed of light. Albert Einstein, then 25, was to oblige within nine months. In Washington, seven weeks after James' ship reached New York, Theodore Roosevelt, the biographer of Thomas Hart Benton, was chortling over his record presidential majority (two and a half million). The previous year, one evening after dinner at the White House, he and a visiting lecturer, Ernest Fenollosa, had recited in unison "The Skeleton in Armor." Salient Parisian happenings were less public. On a washerwoman's barge near the Rue Jacob, Pablo Picasso, 23, was coming to terms with his new city and commencing to specialize in blue. In the Rue Mouton-Duvernet Wyndham Lewis, 22, about to ship laundry to his mother in England, was fussing about the customs documents ("must I declare them dirty?"). In what was still St. Petersburg Ivan Pavlov received word of a Nobel Prize for his work on the physiology of digestion, and Igor Stravinsky the judgment of Rimski-Korsakov that his talents were less well suited to law than to music. *The Psychopathology of Everyday Life* appeared that year in Vienna (and *Peter Pan* in London). In Dublin there was much action. The Mechanics' Institute Playhouse and what had been the adjoining city morgue were connected and at year's end opened as the Abbey Theatre. On June 16 a man who never existed wandered about the city for 18 hours, in the process sanctifying a negligible front door at 7 Eccles Street. The night of October 8 James Joyce, 22, about to flee to the continent with a woman, arranged to be met at 7.10 outside Davy Byrne's by a friend with a parcel containing such necessaries as tooth powder and black boots ("I have absolutely no boots"). At the dock, to forestall interferences, he boarded the ship as though alone and trusted (rightly) that the lady would follow.

These events did not solicit the Jamesian seismograph, which was recording that fall an absence of sensibility in New Hampshire ("The immodesty"—of a loud youth and two loud girls—"was too colossal to be anything but innocence—yet the innocence, on the other hand, was too colossal to be anything but inane"). And New York, the great city, typified, he divined, the "artless need" of young societies "to get themselves explained": a need most felt, he went on, by those parts "that are already explained not a little by the ample possession of money." He thought this subtle bewilderment "the amiable side of those numerous groups that are rich enough and, in the happy vulgar phrase, bloated enough, to be candidates for the classic imputation of haughtiness. The amiability proceeds from an essential vagueness; whereas real haughtiness is never vague about itself—it is only vague about others." Into that vagueness his imagination later moved ghosts, his age's handiest convention for the impalpable ("A ghost / Is that part of your feeling / You don't see"). Four years later the first number of Ford Madox Hueffer's *English Review* presented "The Jolly Corner": a house in New York where James's surrogate corners a ghost with a ravaged face and missing fingers: his own face, yet a stranger's ("the bared identity was too hideous as *his*"): himself had he remained in the New World and consented to be "explained by the ample possession of money": that, and also the Novelist, normally of a Flaubertian invisibility, cornered by vigilance where he is always in residence, in the House of Fiction.

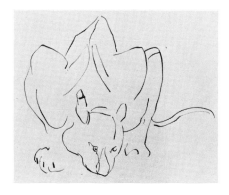

SPACE-CRAFT

The devotion of Henry James was to the literary form most elaborated by the 19th century: the prose fiction, which is to say, the enigma. In his Prefaces he hugs secrets, talking round that overwhelming question, what the story may be *for*. Even in his Notebooks as he ponders his theme or works out his tale we detect him flushed with orgies of reticence, divulging even to himself no more than he must know to get on with the job. This is not his perversity, but his deepest response to the nature of the craft he practiced. Always, the "story" has been a hermetic thing. Of the first hearers of the Parable of the Sower, it was those closest to the Parabolist who wanted afterward to know what it meant.

The words in the Parable are very simple: a sower went out to sow his seed, and as he sowed some fell by the wayside, and it was trodden down. . . . "What does it mean?" asks not What did you say? but To what end did you say it?, a question the storyteller's closing words have solicited: "He that hath ears to hear, let him hear." Part of the primitive fascination of a story is this, that we often cannot be sure why it has been told. Often we can: it may say, I am Odysseus, this happened to me: share my self-esteem; or, This may happen to you, King Pentheus, be prepared; or, This happened here in Athens: know how to feel. Or often: You will wish this might happen to you. But devoid of arteries from *me*, or *you*, or *here*, why does that tale's heart beat? A sower went out to sow his seed . . . ; or, A governess went to Bly, where there had been servants named Quint and Jessel, undesirable people, and the two children. . . . Why are we being told *that?*

—To offer me an hour's diversion?

—When you read it you will find the sentences too long for diversion.

Hence 80 explicative articles.

*   *   *

"Why am I reading this?" is a different question. The post-Romantic answer was apt to be, "In order to savor the romance of *time.*" Antiquarian passions, vulgarizing romantic ones, sponsored numerous exhumations, Donne's for instance or Fra Angelico's, and whatever such passions admired was set at a great distance. The Kelmscott Chaucer his admirers gave Yeats on his 40th birthday was not a book to read in but a sacred object, the text rendered handsomely inaccessible by William Morris's typography. This was in keeping, since if you did not journey back to him through time, making the effort, breaking off some golden bough and essaying some labyrinth, Chaucer was not Chaucer but simply "stories." An unreadable text corresponded with this respectful remoteness. Such sentiments were not reserved for a few connoisseurs. People with 2/6 a month to spend could buy the *Morte D'Arthur* as the installments appeared, with Aubrey Beardsley designs modelled on Morris's to encumber it with a neurasthenic remoteness, thought "mediaeval." And Homer? *Very* remote; to represent the feel of his text in a time of brick chimneys, his Victorian translators adduced Biblical obfuscations. Donne? Donne, a fantastick. (Never mind that the author of *Hamlet* would have known him.) Fantastic old great men loom in time's mists; as we edit and annotate them (for the Early English Texts Society perhaps) we funnel time's romance through the very printing houses whence newspapers issue. And meaning gives way to glamour. Our effort is not to understand but to respond. All idiosyncrasies of diction and syntax, or (if it is a

picture we are reading) whatever catches the eye, a flattened perspective, a simple brilliance of color, these are simply the automatic
writing of some age. Art is the opportunity for time travel.

Browning, magician, gestured: "Appear, Verona!" Browning
asks only our faith (Christ asked no more) and "Sordello compassed
murkily about / With ravage of six long sad hundred years" will
step into Melbourne's England.

> Only believe me. Ye believe?
> Appears
> Verona

—and with a Faustian rending of time's curtains:

> Lo, the Past is hurled
> In twain: upthrust, out-staggering on the world
> Subsiding into shape, a darkness rears
> In outline, kindles at the core, appears
> Verona.

Or you could give your artifact what James called the Tone
of Time. Because they thought that the old masters, rather than generations of curators, had applied that varnish now brown to near-
opacity, Academicians varnished their pictures to make them look
like "old masters." One put "Hist!" and "eftsoons" into one's
poems. As for one's stories, one was apt to be sardonic about
modernity. Henry James often was, and a novel he left unfinished
when he died is about a man who changes places with a man in an
old picture. It was called *The Sense of the Past.*

*   *   *

A picture is an object in space, enigmatic but somehow
(somehow) eloquent. The instinct that applied brown varnish was
setting the object at a distance to make it interesting. The instinct
that as the 19th century progressed drew writing and painting
closer and closer together was enacting a massive bafflement at the
question, how to go about *meaning* anything. For objects are even
more enigmatic than stories. What are they doing here? Why do
broken rims crumble here in the desert? What is the wind doing?
I will show you fear in a handful of dust. . . . When objects have

invaded the universe the sage grows mute, as did Newton, who does not enlighten us with sayings but with silent symbols. And when a sensibility has grown attuned, as had Wordsworth's, to the domain of quiet objects (no motion have they now, no force), then a man may seem like a huge stone, or like a sea-beast, or like a cloud, and when he commences to speak our first awareness will be physio-logical—

> His words came feebly, from a feeble chest,

and our next stylistic—

> But each in solemn order followed each
> With something of a lofty utterance drest—

and man and speech, between our acts of attention to his meaning, will dissolve into that unreality within the skull where phenomena are classified:

> But now his voice to me was like a stream
> Scarce heard; nor word from word could I divide;
> And the whole body of the Man did seem
> Like one whom I had met with in a dream; ...

(1802: Poe would be born in seven years.) Keats in a similar way interrogates an urn, and answers for it, and its last utterance, about Beauty and Truth, may seem almost intolerably enigmatic. And a novelist born half a century after Keats was to give fiction its characteristic 20th-century turn, inventing a protagonist who knew how to interrogate bloodstains, walking sticks, footprints, "clues." (What great issues, Watson, may hang upon a bootlace!)

The incompatibility Wordsworth had discovered between *speech* and *people who seem to be things* is the special case of some radical incompatibility between language and the silent world where things appear (and unlike the spirit of Hamlet's father, the apparitions of Peter Quint and Miss Jessel, or of the ravaged figure in "The Jolly Corner," are silent). The silent world has of course its icon-ography, exploited by the visual arts for many ages. It has parallels with the four-level exegesis of stories.

So it is unsurprising that Henry James, who did not care greatly for pictures, nevertheless was mesmerized by "artists," a caste of men who in places called studios, with brush, pigment, sponge, and varnish-bottle, practiced a mystery which entails a gift they call "rightness of touch" (touch: the blind man's sense). Inspired by their analogy, James made not stories but "things," and did not write them but "did" them. They took "doing." And he put in "touches," just the right touches. (You cannot touch words.) He was helped by conceiving that he did not tell but *make*: making objects, substantial as statues and heavy framed pictures are substantial. The story enters the mute world and partakes of the enigmatic silence of objects, though attention may discern "the figure in the carpet." So a whole generation felt, deaf to words' duration, blind to their transparency; and we still talk as though fictions existed in three-dimensional space.

We say that a novel has *structure*, being more like a building than a statement; we talk of *surfaces* and *depths* and *insight* which suggests peering into a window, and *outlook* which suggests gazing out of one. We accept Mr. Forster's distinction between *round and flat characters*, the latter like cardboard impostors in a third dimension. And though in the time of discourse, as distinguished from the space of architecture, there are no points of view, we talk of the novelist's management of *point of view*. The word *perspective* comes in handy, and *foreground* and *background*, not to mention *levels of meaning* (though "a poem should not mean but be"). It was Henry James himself, with his curious penchant for elaborating a figure, who gave us in the days of Edwardian country houses and the grotesquely gigantic mansions at Newport the concretion to which all these terms will attach themselves, when in the preface to his *Portrait of a Lady* (that painterly title) he spoke of The House of Fiction. At about the same time he wrote "The Jolly Corner," about one's house being haunted by oneself.

"Above all to make you *see*," wrote Joseph Conrad, his mind's eye fixed in some ideal space. Space, with its talk of structures, was whelming verbal art, its dominance encouraged by the possibility, not available to an extemporizing bard, of retrieving a page from the growing pile for revision; encouraged also by the sheer bulk of the manufactured objects book-factories ship out. Quickened by some voice, Lawes's setting of "Go, Lovely Rose" is a transience of breath, but *The Ambassadors* is a hundred cubic inches of wood pulp. Whole histories were compressed as we compress junked cars: plays, for example, into dramatic monologues where Browning's reader becomes Sherlock Holmes to reconstruct a scenario of murdered naivete from 28 couplets imagined to be spoken in front of a woman's picture, painted in one day, "looking as if she were alive." That picture epitomizes the inscrutable brevity to which Browning has brought two hours' stage time, and the spoken poem, which he would surely have made still shorter had he been able, is the exegesis of the picture.

*   *   *

On the wall, the mute *Gioconda*. Before it, Walter Pater. He soliloquizes: "The presence that thus rose so strangely beside the waters, is expressive of what in the ways of a thousand years men had come to desire. ... She is older than the rocks among which she sits; like the vampire, she has been dead many times, and learned the secrets of the grave; and has been a diver in deep seas, and keeps their fallen day about her; ... and all this has been to her but as the sound of lyres and flutes, and lives only in the delicacy with which it has moulded the changing lineaments, and tinged the eyelids and the hands. ..." That is not Leonardo's statement but Pater's, who does not claim that Leonardo would have endorsed it: only that Leonardo made the *mantram* to which this fantasy answers. The connoisseur has his own thoughts. And this picture and not another convokes these especial fantasies: why? No one can say. When Yeats edited the *Oxford Book of Modern Verse* he printed Pater's paragraph as his first selection, as though to concede that writing came to this, in a world defined by impenetrable objects, an elaborate verbal structure generated where alone no objects can intrude: within the mind.

*   *   *

But (1917):

Though my house is not propped up by Taenarian columns
   from Laconia (associated with Neptune and Cerberus),
Though it is not stretched upon gilded beams;

My orchards do not lie level and wide
>   as the forests of Phaeacia
>   the luxurious and Ionian,
Nor are my caverns stuffed stiff with a Marcian vintage,
My cellar does not date from Numa Pompilius,
Nor bristle with wine jars,
Nor is it equipped with a frigidaire patent;
Yet the companions of the Muses
>   will keep their collective nose in my books,
And weary with historical data, they will turn to my dance tune.

Something has happened; the tone of time has vanished, and aerial perspective. There is no "point of view" that will relate these idioms: neither a modern voice ("bristle"; "frigidaire patent"; "collective nose") nor an ancient one ("Phaeacia"; "Marcian") can be assigned this long sentence; moreover "Laconia" has acquired what looks like a *sotto voce* footnote, while the modernisms ("frigidaire," "data") sound plausibly Latin. In transparent overlay, two times have become as one, and we are meant to be equally aware of both dictions (and yet they seem the same diction). The words lie flat like the forms on a Cubist surface. The archaizing sensibility of James's time and Beardsley's has simply dissolved.

Which is a crucial fact: it did dissolve, though not quickly, at the touch of several interrelated events. One—we shall be discussing it at leisure—was the growing awareness that since about 1870 men had held in their hands the actual objects Homer's sounding words name. A pin, a cup, which you can handle like a safety pin tends to resist being archaized. Another, which may one day seem the seminal force in modern art history, was the spreading news that painted animals of great size and indisputable vigor of line could be seen on the walls of caves which no one had entered for 25,000 years. They were not "primitive" in Fra Angelico's way; their vigor might have been put there yesterday. The first response was that they were surely fakes, and put there yesterday morning, but by 1895 physical evidence had disposed of any such notion, and a wholly new kind of visual experience confronted whoever cared. The shock of that new experience caused much change, we cannot say how much; we may take it as an emblem for the change that followed it.

The shock lay in this, that the horses and deer and aurochs brought the eye such immediacy of perception, though a disregard of *up* and *down* and *through* made them inconceivable in today's canons: and yet they seemed not to rely on yesterday's canons either. They simply existed outside of history. No felt continuum reached back to them, with dimming aerial perspective, as it did for instance to the age the Pre-Raphaelites favored. Time folded over; *now* lay flat, transparent, upon *not-now*. Devoid of information about those artists, the spectator could nowise take a time machine to their world. Nor would any evolutionary curve pass through them.

Here was a lost visual mode thrust into the present, undimmed. No one could begin to imagine how it had felt to draw such things; one could only look at the confident lines. Picasso came from Barcelona to Altamira to look at them in 1902, at the threshold of a long career of being unabashed by the past. Their existence launched Leo Frobenius on a 40-year career as an anthropologist to whom African antiquity spoke today. Henri Gaudier by his 20th year had learned to catch in instantaneous lines the autonomy of a panther or a stag; he and a Dordogne draughtsman were thenceforth co-equals. In 1919 T. S. Eliot stood in a cave in southern France, experiencing the revelation that "art never improves," and soon afterwards wrote of how all art enters a simultaneous order. When Wyndham Lewis writes (*Tarr*, about 1914) that "the lines and masses of a statue are its soul" (art has *no inside*, nothing you cannot *see*), he tells us that we may confront any art as we must confront that of the Upper Paleolithic; by 1927 he had elaborated in *Time and Western Man* a mode of contemporary experience from which the romance of time travel is excluded. (After a 20-year time lag this filtered into academies as "The New Criticism.")

The young Ezra Pound had been susceptible to the magic of time, and had archaized accordingly. This only meant, as he came to see, a bad style, which he worked to discard. When it was gone, all times could lie on the same plane, "in the timeless air." To see gods was a way to see nature, not to use an antique way of talking. Near Pisa (1945) he could watch sunbeams disperse fog and write with perfect naturalness,

Heliads lift the mist from the young willows.

He could also read Hermes' remarks in a Homeric Hymn, and write corresponding words not remotely dead but as if spoken this morning:

"Is it likely Divine Apollo
That I should have stolen your cattle?
A child of my age, a mere infant,
    And besides, I have been here all night in my crib."

And he could see that Chinese written characters are neither archaic nor modern. Like cave paintings they exist now, with the strange extra-temporal persistence of objects in space.

*   *   *

Any object in space is a memory system. They understood this in the 15th century, but made no romantic pother about memory, about ghosts and mists and gulfs. Unlike Pater, Lorenzo de Medici knew quite well what pictures memorialized: first of all, craft. After he had commissioned the *Venus* or the *Primavera* he would have been free to visit Botticelli's studio and watch successively the application of gesso, the priming, the drawing of forms in mono-chrome, the undermodelling done in greenish brown, then heightened in white or grey; and where flesh is to appear, green underpainting slowly made unobtrusive by the layer on layer of transparent color it vivifies: color painstakingly applied during many months, mixed in the yolks of eggs. And gold last; the aerial flowers in the *Venus* have gold leaf-veins. And when the pictures were accepted and hung it was easy for members of the Medici circle to see likenesses of Simonetta Vespucci (died of rapid consumption, 1476) and Lorenzo's brother Giuliano (murdered near the altar rail, 1478); and (especially in the *Primavera*) a neo-Platonic allegory of great intricacy, and (in the *Birth of Venus*) an illustration of three stanzas from the young Politian's poem in honor of Giuliano, through which stanzas (derived from Hesiod and from a Homeric Hymn) it reaches back to reconstruct an *Aphrodite Anadyomene* of Apelles, destroyed under Nero, of which treasure Pliny, Ovid, Strabo, and Cicero have left us hints and glimpses. It was Ovid for instance who

instructed Politian and Botticelli to have one of the goddess' hands
hold her wet tresses.

A lost picture of 18 centuries ago recreated, young persons
just dead resurrected and transfigured, eternal doctrine allegorically
illuminated (but only for the discerning): these and the craftsmanship too, that many-layered building-up through which Lorenzo
would have known he was looking as the Platonic eye looks through
appearance, all seeing a seeing-into: so much did a Renaissance
secular picture contain, else it had been just paint.

Similarly, in the early 20th century, artist after artist, art after
art, escapes from the locked perspective that has only an opaque
present to offer the mind, an opacity Pater's reverie before *La
Gioconda* can evade only at the cost, we now feel, of utter irrelevance.
Visual analogies, when they govern writing, now foster openness,
not inscrutability. Moments of insight, moments when "painting
or sculpture seems as if it were 'just coming over into speech',"
abound in the multi-faceted *Cantos*, whose principles their author
most vividly formulated with his mind on a sculptor (Gaudier) and
a painter (Lewis). Such work implies space, yet Wyndham Lewis
was not radically wrong to associate Ezra Pound with time, for the
drive toward fragmentation of what had been temporal narrative
was undertaken because narrative itself had disclosed its tendency
toward static constructs. The fragments, the moments, shattering
that block, recover time: through each of them rushes process.

Or stories become tableaux, "epiphanies." "Pulcra sunt,"
quotes Joyce, "quae visa placent," denoting an intellection as if
visual, and proceeds to stories that give the effect of culminating
not in static enigma but in static insight: Eveline clutching the
barrier, unable to go and unwilling to stay; Little Chandler rocking
a terrified child. Innumerable paintings of the Epiphany at Bethlehem, that moment of transcendent stillness, underwrite the
analogy to the disappointed epiphanies of his stories.

*   *   *

As, looking at the *Primavera*, we see Botticelli's craft, and
looking at his *Adoration of the Magi* in the Uffizi we see Botticelli
himself in the right foreground, so release from the prison of late

19th-century pictorial analogies came when the teller was let back into the tale.

Flaubert had wanted the artist, lonely as God, to be somewhere outside his work, which is impossible: impossible because words are said by somebody; because—at the furthest remove from the intimacies of breath—a bicycle saddle and handlebars, even when no sculpturing hand molests their shapes, denote by their power to combine into a bull's head a possibility some human eye has seen (Picasso saw it, 1943). Art does not "happen." The vision that made it is part of it. The eye of vision sees systems of connectedness; this may not *be* that, but it has the same structure. A bull's form, some drawn lines, are so similar that we "recognize" a picture of a bull, but part of the picture is the mind that conceived it. Henry James twisted and turned his contrivances to make them seem to begin, unfold, and come to rest without violating the convention that all becomes known as if to a single center of awareness, who must only acquire, page by page, such information as might plausibly have been given him. This is a way of suppressing the mind that conceived, and to Pound's generation it seemed no more than an elaborate game, yet another means of devising an enigma. For all versions of the same plot, whatever the "viewpoint," have the same system of interconnectedness. We may borrow a term from the topologist and call them *homeomorphic*; Joyce saw that the plot of the *Odyssey* and that of *Hamlet* were homeomorphs, one concentrating on the father, one on the son, but comparable in their structure of incidents. All ways of telling the same story are homeomorphic, even the way that ingeniously lets us suppose that the teller has been removed.

Pound's generation, Joyce's, Eliot's, exploited the possibilities of this fact. Pound makes no effort to vanish; he is quite frankly a character in the *Cantos*: "I sat on the Dogana's steps," commences the third Canto, "I" meaning the person who is elsewhere called "*ego scriptor cantilenae.*" Or not quite that person but his homeomorph; that person, rather, in his public role, "E. P.," homeomorphic to Ezra Loomis Pound, as various caricatures are homeomorphic to a portrait. This is called a *persona*. A poem Eliot finished in 1911 exploits his memories of yellow St. Louis fogs, his desire to imitate

Jules Laforgue, his youthful agonies of shyness, his taste for a somewhat deliquesced "mighty line," and his reading of James's "Crapey Cornelia." Yet it does not confess these matters, though it is so nearly homeomorphic to a confessional poem that it is written in exactly the words a confessional poet would use. It is headed, however, "The Love Song of J. Alfred Prufrock," that name's gravitational warp having been nicely calculated to bend every psychic line into the semblance of a different person. Eliot eight years later was the theorist of "impersonality." And Joyce, though his Stephen Dedalus gave the Flaubertian aloofness its definitive formulation ("The artist, like the God of the creation, remains within or behind or beyond or above his handiwork, invisible, refined out of existence, indifferent, paring his fingernails") made Stephen and a dozen other characters out of homeomorphs of himself. He had already begun to do this in 1904, when Henry James was buying his steamship ticket. And he carried the principle further: since several stories may be homeomorphic, it is possible to tell them simultaneously. The point of the telling may be that people live by stories, but different ones.

*   *   *

So at 22 Joyce published in the *Irish Homestead* (which paid him twenty shillings) some 1800 words about intersecting fictions. Eveline, whom we first observe with her head against the window curtains "watching the evening invade the avenue," has a fiction in her head which arranges for her the very little she knows of a man named Frank. People bully her now, "But in her new home, in a distant unknown country, it would not be like that. Then she would be married—she, Eveline." That is the essence of the fiction. It owes nothing to observation, since the marriage she has been privileged to observe, her mother's, merely shaped "a life of commonplace sacrifices closing in final craziness." (But "She would not be treated as her mother had been": an act of faith in the fiction.) She restates the fiction: "She was about to explore another life with Frank. Frank was very kind, manly, open-hearted. She was to go away with him by the night-boat to be his wife and to live with him in Buenos Ayres."

Where she works, judgments are guided by a different fiction, one with a moral: "What would they say of her in the stores when they found out she had run away with a fellow? Say she was a fool, perhaps. . . ." She calls it, this hypothetical event, going away with him to be his wife. They call it, running away with a fellow.

Her father's fiction is simple and lurid: "'I know these sailor chaps,' he said." In his tavern conversation, clearly, they have a girl in every port. Her father's fiction defines the word "sailor."

Fictions in general define words. We are shown Eveline's at this work. It has defined "marriage." It defines "Frank." "Frank was very kind, manly, open-hearted." None of these attributes is in turn definable except by reference to the short story in which she imagines herself and Frank playing leading parts, a story in which it is necessary that Frank be named "Frank," a daydream of escape.

"How well she remembered the first time she had seen him": a quotation from the very words of that story, cunningly spliced into Joyce's story. "It seemed a few weeks ago. He was standing at the gate, his peaked cap pushed back on his head and his hair tumbled forward over a face of bronze." That is our only look at him. Joyce may have amused himself with the notion that a few *Irish Homestead* readers would remember seeing "Frank" around Dublin, in his yachting cap and tennis shoes. He had even been photographed, quizzical, self-contained, in the act of wondering if the man with the camera (young C. P. Curran) would lend him five shillings. Unlike most backyard snapshots, this one has become widely known, from being reproduced with the caption "Joyce in 1904." "Frank" is Joyce's first Portrait of the Artist, standing near the periphery of the canvas like the young Botticelli, in a cool exchange of gazes with the viewer.

Eveline's glimpse—vision, rather—of the unsurnamed Frank is as ineradicable as a snapshot, and as inscrutable. The next words are, "Then they had come to know each other": words without content, except as her fiction invests them. He was persistent. He met her regularly to escort her home. He took her to *The Bohemian Girl*. After a while "she had begun to like him." This may be explained by the next sentence, or it may merely precede the next sentence, which is, "He had tales of distant countries." These consist

"Frank," i.e. James Joyce in 1904. (Photo by Constantine P. Curran, courtesy of Mrs. Josef Solterer and the National Library of Ireland.)

of: his beginning as a deck boy at a pound a month; the names of ships; the names of the different services; the allegation that he has sailed through the Straits of Magellan; and "stories of the terrible Patagonians." We may reflect that he is a laconic Othello. And the following sentence runs: "He had fallen on his feet in Buenos Ayres [comma] he said [comma] and had come over to the old country just for a holiday." Ah so. And her father ("of course") had forbidden her to have anything to say to him.

Now "fallen on his feet" is one more inscrutability. So cunningly have we been drawn into Eveline's reverie that we may not think to doubt whether her circumscribing world of dusty curtains, clacking footsteps, little brown houses, people with Dublin names— "the Devines, the Waters, the Dunns, little Keogh the cripple"—is also a world in which sailors who talk of terrible Patagonians "fall on their feet" in Buenos Aires, maintain there "a home" which is "waiting" for a bride, and "come over to the old country just for a holiday." That latter world belongs to fictions of a different order, shopgirls' romances printed in magazines, romances on which Eveline has founded her sense of the possible. Frank understands her sense of the possible, which is why in Joyce's private extra-aesthetic game, the game to which the survival of one photograph gives us a clue, Frank's stance is modelled on Joyce's.

We may say that these two worlds are verbally incompatible; in Joyce's careful reconstructions of normal reality people do not "fall on their feet"; the substance of achievement or non-achievement is gone into. Or we may appeal to realities outside literature: to the implausibility of "where he had a home waiting for her," or to any *Irish Homestead* reader's knowledge that no boat sails from Dublin to Buenos Aires. That boat from the North Wall is bound for Liverpool, and given Frank's show of easy prosperity we may wonder what will happen to Eveline there. Can she count on a boat for Argentina the next day? Frank, it is clear, understands fiction too, but also certain facts, which may include Irish girls for hire in English seaports.

However that may be, she cannot break away. Frank stands beside her in the dockside crowd "saying something about the passage over and over again," as though the reality of a booked passage to Buenos Aires were the main thing to insist on. Eveline feels sudden panic mount. She asks God to direct her. Then she clutches at the barrier, "passive, like a helpless animal," as he rushes through to board the Liverpool boat. In the story's final sentence "Her eyes gave him no sign of love or farewell or recognition"; and we may write for ourselves unwritten additional sentences, specifying that Frank, who had said he had a home waiting for her in Buenos Aires, did not return to her side but got on the boat, accepting with chagrin the waste of a trip's gambit, but no doubt expert enough to envisage, in other times, other opportunities.

*   *   *

> The heroine of "Eveline" longs to escape from her drab Dublin life and she has her chance. But, on the very point of embarking for Buenos Aires with the man who loves her . . ..
> —Anthony Burgess, *Re Joyce*, 1965.

So runs a handbook summary, typical of dozens. In missing half Joyce's point they still speak truth. Eveline has rejected that home in South America, though as an act of choice, not of judgment. Her refusal remains refusal whether or not there is any home there for her. We are to imagine the rest of her life ("of commonplace sacrifices," like her mother's) embittered by the remembered panic. She refused, though not from insight; and if her father was right about sailor-chaps, he had no right to be; and at the Stores they would have been right about folly, without right either. She has not sufficient sense of reality to be able to feel that she acted virtuously: a virtuous refusal is a refusal of recognized evil. She will never so much as know that Frank may have been less than Frank, but will live out her life in the consciousness of her onetime immobilizing terror.

"A chapter in the moral history of my country," wrote Joyce of *Dubliners*; in the same letter he wrote of Irish paralysis. It is also a chapter in the history of fiction. "Eveline" has been designed to be homeomorphic to several other stories one can imagine. It follows James's rule about the unified point of view, but James does not expect that we may imagine the other tellings. "Eveline" could have been told as a story about Frank, who has just missed a conquest. It could have been told as a story about Eveline's father, whose daughter's quiet constancy one day gave way to fits of weeping and withdrawal, and was never really restored. Or an omniscient authority might have plotted its vectors, Frank's and Eveline's and her father's, each vector changed after the encounter but Frank's the least, a real Dublin enclosing the place of intersection and a fictitious Buenos Aires exerting its attraction from the lower left of the diagram. All these stories are the one story rotated. The version Joyce chose to write maximizes her ignorance and her pathos, and emphasizes his earliest and most constant insight, that people live in stories that structure their worlds. Eveline lives in a story that must contain a Frank; a febrile unreal story she got from somewhere. Whoever can give his people better stories than the ones they live in is like the priest in whose hands common bread and wine become capable of feeding the very soul, and he may think of forging in some invisible smithy the uncreated conscience of his race.

*　　*　　*

It was to give his race superior stories that W. B. Yeats thought with passionate intensity on Diarmuid and Grania, Cuchulain and Emer, and wrote plays which require the spectator to feel as if he knew, in the way Aeschylus' audience knew the Atreid genealogies, stories that in the cold street he did not in fact know at all. He and Joyce both took seriously the epigram of another Dubliner, that life imitates art.

The Irish Ministry of Agriculture understood how the art on the coins men glance at daily may permeate life, when they required the design for the bull on the Republic's new one shilling piece to be altered "because it might have upset, considered as an ideal, the eugenics of the farmyard." The new bull, Yeats wrote as chairman of the Coinage Commission, was fortunately as fine, in a different way. "I sigh, however, over the pig, though I admit that the state of the market for pig's cheeks made the old design impossible. A design is like a musical composition, alter some detail and all has to be altered. With the round cheeks of the pig went the lifted head, the look of insolence and of wisdom, and the comfortable round bodies of the little pigs. We have instead querulous and harassed animals, better merchandise but less living." What had been a paradigm of insolent wisdom became an instigation to superior pork chops, but Yeats ceded in good humor, for the Ministry was postulating the paradigmatic force of art. Ten years later, near death, he was applauding the power of Michelangelo's Adam to get a lady tourist in heat; for an office of art is to have the cradles filled aright.

Joyce was never on a coinage commission, nor ever, in the Yeatsian way that entranced his Stephen Dedalus, the forger of conscience hitherto uncreated. Instead he worked to illuminate from within the actual fictions by which Dublin lived. His stories contain not only stories he might have written but did not, they contain also the stories people tell themselves: that there exists for instance on the other side of the world happiness with a man named (properly) Frank. They contain also ghosts of stories that have been more majestically told. Frank with his narrative of "terrible Patagonians" passes through the role of the Shakespearean Moor whose wooing talk was

> Of Anthropophagies, and men whose heads
> Do grow beneath their shoulders,

and Frank in his yachting cap, as though come from the sea, enters Eveline's life as did a Greek seaman (notorious for lies) enter that of the Princess whom Homer called Nausicaa.

RENAISSANCE II

"Where we have, in a manner of speaking, got to," constated on behalf of a court society in 1630 (Carew, Jonson) or a civil society in 1790 (Adams, Jefferson) would be unintelligible without a point of reference concerning the location of which, as of its nature, Henry James was hazy: the literary culture of Greece and Rome: the classics. Allusion to a body of wisdom all men shared could invest with authority and sometimes grandeur what would otherwise be a writer's mere remarks. ("Remarks," said Gertrude Stein, a non-Classicist, "are not literature.") Buoyed by shared allusion, the writer could even afford to remain anonymous. Thus in 1738 the *Gentleman's Magazine* printed "London: a Poem" by a young author still unknown, in confidence that gentlemen would be knowing enough to refer "Slow rises Worth, by Poverty depress'd" to at least schoolroom memories of ". . . res angusta domi."

Having no such points of reference, Henry James "excessively cobwebbed, fussed, blathered, worried about minor mundanities"; Pound complains that he explicitly had not, at just this cost, "read his classics, the better Latins especially." And yet this disability did not disable his presentation of his time's most conscious people, for the classics in James's lifetime were simply not part of the visible social world.

They were part of a change invisible to that world, which did not see everything. Schliemann had been to Troy, and a cosmos had altered.

There had been such a city. It had been destroyed, and by fire. Stones, as well as fables, persisted. And "golden Mycenae": it had indeed worked gold, and its tombs (bee-haunted; ringed with huge red poppies) yielded golden cups and a mask of gold which Schliemann thought Agamemnon's, as Troy yielded jewelry he called Helen's when he hung it on his wife Sophie for a photograph. (A photograph! It is like a photograph of the True Cross.) So Marion Tweedy Bloom in 1904 (the phrases set down about 1921) was to don and doff garments we are to think of as Penelope's: ". . . a pair of outsize ladies' drawers of India mull, cut on generous lines, redolent of opoponax, jessamine and Muratti's Turkish cigarettes and containing a long bright steel safety pin"—with no less of a cataloguer's exactness, now, could Achaean splendors be plotted.

Opoponax, a Greek word ("all-healing juice"). It is not Homeric; we find it in Dioscorides' *Physicus*. *Jessamine*, an Arabic word, from a Persian. Though both words are Homerically sonorous, Mrs. Bloom could have bought scents derived from jasmine and from a gum resin grandly miscalled Opoponax at Sweny the Chemist's, 1 Lincoln Place, Dublin. The long bright steel safety pin transposes to 1904 a different order of Achaean reality. Thanks to Schliemann, we now keep under glass golden dress-fasteners from Penelope's time, though all Penelope's dresses have long been dust. And Homer's περόνη now designates a palpable object.

"Troy" after Schliemann was no longer a dream, but a place on the map. As his discoveries persisted, more and more Homeric words came to mean something producible, something belonging to the universe of the naturalistic novelist. Each such word is salvage from the vortex of mere lexicography, where of words we learn chiefly what company they keep. When Alice in Wonderland's father Henry George Liddell, D.D., collaborated on the Greek Lexicon in the reign of Victoria, the word *euknēmides* meant only "well-greaved," which is not really English, and nothing more could be said about it except that another word *Achaioi* (of comparably uncertain scope) tends to draw it into the text, as "sea" draws the word they render "wine-dark," and "Hera" draws "oxeyed." So "oxeyed Hera," we read in the Butcher and Lang translation, and "wine-dark sea," and "goodly-greaved Achaeans." But by the reign of the second Elizabeth *euknēmides* has acquired particularization from a painted vase, a stele, two sherds of pottery, a frieze from the megaron of Mycenae, a fresco at Pylos and an ivory relief from Delos, "all of the third late Helladic era": whoever encounters the word in Homer today has reason to know that it designates something in particular, shin guards, of unspectacular appearance, leather perhaps, and distinctively Achaean, never Trojan; one more reality retrieved from amid a din of words.

. . . Words, words: a Swinburne's *materia prima*: intoxicating or edifying nullities. For Matthew Arnold it had seemed urgent business to find some vernacular cadence adequate to the Homeric moral qualities: Homer is rapid, Homer is plainspoken, Homer is plain-thinking, Homer is noble, so Arnold affirmed in 1860 with no real certainty (ever since Wolf's *Prolegomena*) that there ever was a Homer, let alone a Troy. Like the Victorian God, the Victorian Homer may well not exist, but it does us good to talk as if he did. Did Hector and Achilles exist, or Troy, or its walls, or the river Scamander? As well ask (but not aloud, in Arnold's presence), did Adam and Eve? Hush, be responsive to the rapid, the plain, and the noble. (Though if you must go into its origins, the story has very likely crystallized out of a primitive solar myth.) Biblical rhythms, a powerful charm against unsettling questions, were soon serving Butcher and Lang to hold immune from the ironmonger's kind of attention a ritual for cultivated Victorians. The ironmonger is apt to ask what "greaves" are, and such a language as Butcher and Lang contrived—

> . . . unless it so be that my father, the goodly Odysseus, out of evil heart wrought harm to the goodly-greaved Achaeans, in quittance whereof ye now work me harm out of evil hearts . . .

—such a language has the power to arrest that question unformulated.

They were behindhand. Schliemann had dug through Troy

and moved on to Mycenae by the time they were at work, and when their *Odyssey* appeared in 1879, with its prefatory bow to Arnold's authority, their Homer and Arnold's was already a ghost. By 1900 Schliemann's successor Dörpfeld was rapping his staff on the soil, he affirmed, of Ithaca, with a persuasiveness pilgrims (German professors and schoolmasters) tended to remember. "Few things were as convincing as a piece of Greek landscape . . . when Dörpfeld explained it to you," recalls Sir John Myres, and "It was probably . . . to Dörpfeld's 'troubling of the waters' that we owe the very copious output of literary criticism of the *Odyssey* in the years from 1903 to 1910." In those years Victor Bérard's readers were being convinced that Odysseus' whole voyage had been at last mapped out, among real rocks, real shores. His *Les Phéniciens et l'Odyssée* (1903) was a book James Joyce found useful.

For Joyce's was the archaeologist's Homer. As a boy, not long after Schliemann's death, he had responded to Lamb's retelling of the story. By 1906 he wanted to write a story of his own, set in Dublin and called "Ulysses." Eight years later he was seriously at work on what he had rethought as a larger project, a book whose hero should move around a single city as Homer's had moved around the Mediterranean. During his young manhood archaeology had been turning Homer into just such an organizer of information as the novelist had also become, and this Homer, unsuspected by Butcher and Lang, the Homer trust in whose text had led Heinrich Schliemann to the very spot where his spade struck a Trojan wall, presented a world as real as Dublin's bricks.

*   *   *

And not later than 1910 on a Paris *quai*, Ezra Pound with four francs to spend and two four-franc books to choose from, a Renaissance Latin *Iliad* or *Odyssey*, laid his hand on the *Odyssey*, we can now say on the future of the *Cantos*, and does not record having hesitated. Homer in most times has been the poet of the *Iliad*. That *Odyssey* decade was an historical anomaly.

The *Odyssey* is the novelist's book of the two, and Joyce and Pound both saw a novel in its workings: a grip on detailed actuality. If Telemachos after jumping out of bed, Pound was to write, "reached for his six-shooter before puttin' on his boots, *that* is a point to be made, as highly illustrative of the era. A guards officer wdn't. But I reckon in Idaho in the 80's Blue Dick or Curly might have." His noting of the order, sword then boots, was schooled by modern narrative technique; a generation earlier it would have gone unremarked. He objected to literary diction in translations partly because it concealed these accuracies. Behind the Greek words stood the real, even behind the formulaic epithets, for instance Athena's *glaukōpis*. "With gleaming eyes," say Liddell and Scott, who also inform us that the owl is called *glaux* "from its glaring eyes," and that *glaukos* ("gleaming, glancing, bright-gleaming") is applicable to the olive, the willow, and the vine, though they say it then becomes an adjective of color. Allen Upward had ventured to correlate this information, as Pound remembered with Dr. Rouse's draft of *Odyssey I* in front of him: ". . . The property of the glaux, and olive leaf, to shine and then not to shine, 'glint' rather than shine. Certainly a more living word if one lives among olive yards." And Rouse printed, "Athena answered him, her bright eyes glinting," trusting Pound's daily experience of the olive groves below Sant' Ambrogio as Pound trusted Rouse's feel for marine actualities, derived from sailing the Aegean in a small boat. The Homer of this new Renaissance could concentrate all that one knew of the real.

*　　*　　*

Should Dublin be destroyed, said Joyce foreseeing a Schliemann, his book would supply the evidence for its reconstruction: so short, in the few decades since Butcher and Lang, had the distance become between Homer and Joyce's purposes. Homeric scholars concerned themselves with maps and *periploi*, with stickpins and headgear, with lost coins, broken dishes, cutlery, kitchen debris. The Achaeans were turning very domestic in men's imagination, and it is not surprising that domesticity is the note of Joyce's equivalents. He catalogued for future scholars the furniture of a Dublin house and the contents of a Dublin kitchen cabinet (not omitting the moustache cup) and two Dublin dresser drawers. These pages might some day be key to a kitchen midden, as other pages, indicating which street intersects with which, might afford the clues to an excavator's map.

He was especially careful with the interior of Bloom's house: the arrangement of the rooms and their use, the placing of the furniture and the cooking facilities, the location of the area railing outside, and the measurement of the drop from its crosspiece to the area paving below. Here again he was on up-to-date ground: the layout of the house of Odysseus had been disputed since 1886, when Schliemann published his account of the palace he excavated at Tiryns. Literature in the subsequent decades was filled with floor plans, as proponents of the old "Hellenic" and the new "Mycenaean" archetypes arranged and rearranged doors, hearth, courtyard, women's quarters. One such floor plan in particular there is reason to think Joyce studied carefully. It is on page 16 of the book with which Samuel Butler accosted scholarship in 1897: *The Authoress of the Odyssey*.

Butler derived it, he said, directly from the poem, to each word of which he insisted on assigning a definite meaning, thought out in the process of making a new kind of translation which appears abridged in the *Authoress* and was published intact in 1900. It is the first translation to reflect the new view that Homer knew what he was talking about, and one of only two translations Stanislaus Joyce was to recollect his Greekless brother using.* Its plain prose is not simply of the surface; Butler's rule was to deduce the underlying fact, and then put *that* plainly. And pondering one adjective (*hypselos*, lofty) near the end of the first book (1-426) when Telemachus goes to his bedchamber, he perceived a difficulty which had eluded everyone, not least Butcher and Lang.

Butcher and Lang, who replace Greek words with English ones from the lexicon, tell us that the chamber was "builded high up in the fair court, in a place with wide prospect." But Butler insisted on imagining such things clearly, and having reconstructed the "court" as no more than an open space surrounded by a cloister,

---

* The other was Cowper's. He also used Butler's *Authoress of the Odyssey* and Bérard's *Les Phéniciens et l'Odyssée*, and consulted the treatments of Ulysses' career in "Virgil, Ovid, Dante, Racine, Fénelon, Tennyson, Phillips, d'Annunzio and Hauptmann." It was W. B. Stanford who had the wit to ask Stanislaus this question. See his *The Ulysses Theme*, second edition, 1964, p. 276, note 6.

he saw the need to specify a structure for Telemachus' room to be at the top of. He places it, therefore, "in a lofty tower," and marks "the tower in which Telemachus used to sleep" on his plan. He has more to say about this tower; it has, for instance, a trap door through which one could get out onto the roof. And on the first page of *Ulysses*, Stephen Dedalus, the Telemachus of Joyce, mounts to the top of the tower within which he has been sleeping.

It is true that Joyce built experiences of Stephen's on his own, that he had himself lived in the Martello Tower, and that he had also in mind the opening of *Hamlet*, high on the battlements of Elsinore. But only with Butler's help can we discover a clear Homeric correspondence at the very beginning, where the correspondences ought to be plain if they are going to work. And Butler has more for us than this one interesting detail. It is tempting to think that his book helped suggest Joyce's whole enterprise.

For theirs were the first and second creative minds to take the post-Schliemann Homer seriously: to imagine what it might mean to believe that the *Odyssey* was composed by a real person in touch with the living details of real cities, real harbors, real bowls and cups and pins and spoons, real kings, real warriors, real houses. Horace had believed in a real Homer, making things up; there were slips because he sometimes nodded. Wolf had believed in a number of bards, making things up; there were inconsistencies because they didn't check one another's work. Butler, in the age of the novel, worked from a different psychology of creation: the poet using knowledge of an immediate and experienced world, and making errors when he got beyond that knowledge and had to guess. He noticed for instance an Odyssean ship with the rudder at the front, and concluded that the writer was guessing about the sea. About other details the writer was clearly not guessing, and Butler concluded that the poem had been composed by a Sicilian city-dweller familiar with courts and noble houses.

His thoroughness commands confidence. He even visited Hissarlik to photograph the actual Trojan walls uncovered by Schliemann. In quest of likely sites for Odysseus' voyagings he pored over Admiralty charts, and having fixed on Sicily went there twice to inspect likely details. In his eighth chapter he describes what he found there once he had identified the Scherian harbor with that of Trapani on the west coast of the island. We can imagine the effect of that chapter on a man perhaps already thinking, or perhaps about to think, about Ulysses in Dublin. For not only is Scheria, where Nausicaa lived, drawn from Trapani; Ithaca as well, where Penelope waited, is drawn from Trapani, and the Ionian islands of the *Odyssey* are simply islands off Trapani. The very Cyclops' cave can be found near Trapani (Butler photographed it and shows us the photograph). All the poem's urban topography, in short, has been elaborated from familiarity with a single city, and all its rural topography and all its nautical from the country and the waters around that city. There is one remote place, Pylos, in Homer's book, and one remote place, Gibraltar, in Joyce's. Otherwise both Joyce and the Butler Homer create an illusion of epic sweep and scope while contriving to stay closely in touch with the author's home. Trapani and its harbor and environs; Dublin's streets, Dublin strand, Dublin bay. It is attractive to guess that Joyce related the Homeric world to one city after Butler's example; for what had been built out of the town of Trapani could be concentrated once more into the town of Dublin: like Trapani, a seaport on an island.

Butler's Homer, the archaeologists' Homer brought to a first focus, proves a very Joycean Homer indeed: an observer and ingenious transposer of actualities, a writer whose useful experience was that of a single city. The characters, Butler thought, had been drawn from known people (as were Joyce's), and though he detects evidence of the poet's inexperience, Butler in the age of the novel finds it natural that a masterpiece should have been produced by someone who (like Joyce) "did not like inventing," but was "richly endowed with that highest kind of imagination which consists in wise selection and judicious application of materials derived from life." For "no artist"—here Joyce would have explicitly concurred—"can reach an ideal higher than his own best actual environment. Trying to materially improve upon that with which he or she is fairly familiar invariably ends in failure. It is only adjuncts that may be arranged and varied—the essence may be taken or left, but it must not be bettered." That was written not when Joyce was 45, by a commentator on *Ulysses*, but when Joyce was 15, by a commentator on Homer. Schliemann's discoveries, meditated by an active mind which knew at first hand about novel writing, compelled such a characterization of the mind from which the *Odyssey* proceeded: a mind like the one that drafted the letter of 5 May 1906 about *Dubliners*, remarking that "he is a very bold man who dares to alter in the presentment, still more to deform, whatever he has seen and heard."

* * *

Samuel Butler, alas, allowed his intelligence, as did later Ezra Pound in other connections, to be guided, not merely quickened, by disdain for established authorities: men who claimed minute knowledge of the text, yet could not even say, when he examined them *viva voce*, whether or no Odysseus had a sister, and if so what her name was.* And overvaluing the fun of outraging them, he put himself forever beyond their serious consideration. The author of the *Odyssey*, he claimed, was a woman, and herself the model for the Princess Nausicaa. He could have been a Bentley or a Wolf, inventor of the Homer of his age. Instead he chose to be the man with the silly bee in his bonnet about a poetess, and that his most serious reader should have been James Joyce was perhaps more than he deserved to expect. Joyce with his usual thoroughness acknowledged the mad idea by putting his Nausicaa episode into the idiom of a lady novelist, and tied knots in it when he allowed readers of *Ulysses* to conclude that its author in turn had modelled on himself a different secondary character, Telemachus, and then had his Telemachus explain, at 2 p.m. in the National Library, Dublin, that the author of *Hamlet* was not to be discovered in the Prince but in the Ghost.

Invented Homers range through three millennia, and as one chapter of *Ulysses*, "The Oxen of the Sun," is a museum of styles, so is the whole of *Ulysses* a museum of Homers. The Homer of Joyce's own time, a Homer of molecular actualities, is as pervasive as the air, or as Dublin: the hardest to recognize until he is pointed

---

* Ktimene. (*Od.* xv. 363)

out, because Homers, like styles, are the more discernible the more remote they are in time. (And *Ulysses* in the year of its publication seemed styleless.) The next most recent Homer, the one of comparative mythology, is easier to see, though not being very distant he presents very large outlines, as throughout Joyce's book the *Odyssey* and two later works, *Hamlet* and *Don Giovanni*, turn out to be homeomorphs of the same story. (The text has even one reference to solar myths, in the inventory of the World's Twelve Worst Books; and the Dublin Odysseus, it may be half-remembering his earlier incarnation in the brain of Max Müller, goes in for astronomy and keeps noting the position of the sun.) Behind him we find Wolf's Homer of multiple authorship, who corresponds to the fact that *Ulysses* would seem on stylistic grounds to have a number of different authors, one of them a woman. The Homer of Stoic exegesis moreover has obviously been at work, strewing the pages with systematized lore, not only the treatise on how water reaches Bloom's tap or the mnemonic for the colors of the spectrum, but also appropriate Arts, appropriate Symbols, appropriate Bodily Organs, a compendious ordering of the various sorts of things the Educator of Greece was once supposed to have known. The way they are worked into Joyce's text has been called arbitrary, but it corresponds to the way exegetes once got them out of Homer's. And these Homers are visible, all of them, through the Homer that had been invented in Joyce's early lifetime by men who read kitchen middens as Sherlock Holmes or Flaubert could read a room and as Joyce's readers are expected to read his book.

*   *   *

Greek manuscripts dispersed from Constantinople, so we used to be told, catalyzed the Quattrocento Renaissance. The materials of the Second Renaissance—pins, cups—came from underground: from Hissarlik, from Mycenae. And other materials from dry Egyptian sands, where (while small Ezra Pound in Pennsylvania was learning the use of words and the look of words) strips of used papyrus, the Alexandrian equivalent of old newspapers, were being unwound from the pasteboard sheaths of middle-class mummies, or uncrumpled from the interior of mummified crocodiles, or rescued from scrap heaps which it hadn't been worth the flint to set light to. "Used" meant that somebody had once copied something on them, thus spoiling the surfaces; had copied, for instance, the choral odes of Bacchylides (exhumed 1896). Or papyrus, after its practical use, i.e. for farm accounts, had been salvaged from the bailiff's waste basket for Aristotle's *Constitution of Athens* to be copied on the backs of the sheets because some man wanted it to study. That man dead, the papyrus was abandoned as totally useless, but in 1890 the British Museum was glad to acquire it.

All the Menander we have is from such sources, all the Herodas, half the Sappho, most of the Archilochos; and as Agamemnon from being his "wisdom" had become his relics, so poets ceased to be their Castalian gush but rather their utterly idiosyncratic way of joining six words, the only words some mangled scrap affords. Yet we know how to feel sure whose words they are. Fragments compelled a new kind of detailed attention from minds already prepared by Poe and *Symbolisme* to find virtue in brevity, or by Pater to find it in the fleeting glimpse. A phrase of Sappho's, lacking all the rest of the poem, is really no more mysterious than a line of Mallarmé's. And in Pound's youth American boys pored over machinery catalogues, absorbed in (Saint-Gaudens would have thought) barbaric detail, in the fit of gears, "commenting on machines that certainly they would never own and that could never by any flight of fancy be of the least use to them," abstractly excited by intimate rightness of interaction, as analogous sensibilities by the diction of *brododaktylos* (rosy-fingered) *selanna* (moon).

There was virtue in scraps, mysterium in fragments, magical power in the tatter of a poem, sacred words biting on congruent actualities of sight and feeling and breath. This sensibility lasted one poet's lifetime. "Oak leaf never plane leaf," (87/573:609) we read at one point in the *Cantos*, and at another,

> Le Paradis n'est pas artificiel
> but spezzato apparently
> it exits only in fragments unexpected excellent sausage
> the smell of mint for example,
> (74/438:465)

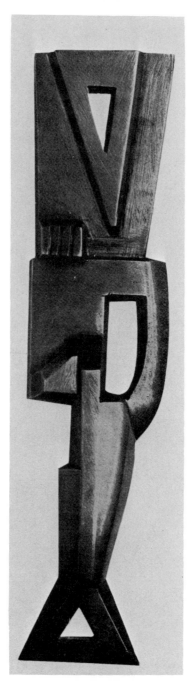

Henri Gaudier-Brzeska, Brass Toy.

and at yet another,

> Le Paradis n'est pas artificiel
>> but is jagged,
> For a flash,
>> for an hour.
> Then agony,
>> then an hour,
>>> then agony,
> Hilary stumbles, but the Divine Mind is abundant
>> unceasing
>> *improvisatore*
> Omniformis
>> unstill;

>>> (92/620:653)

which latter passage next excoriates the overlookers of detail who sink to concern with "mere dynamic": as still another detail has it, *panourgia*.* God himself, evidently, did nothing but shape interdependent details, fleas and corollas and the unfolding wonders a microscope offered to Agassiz' attention but not, it would seem, to others with similar microscopes. God is concentrated attention; a work of art is someone's act of attention, evoking ours; there have been great feats of attention.

Ahead lay Cubism and *collages*, and H. D. cutting bits of Greekness full force into *vers-libre* poems; and Gaudier about 1913 cut (did not cast) a brass figure that embodies in its four inches several hundred formal decisions: that two triangles, one fish-tailed, shall have open centers and bevelled edges, that four finger-like rectangularities shall prolong but displace the downward thrust of a straight vertebral gesture, that next to that descent in high relief shall lie a concavity, its far side curved. . . . T. E. Hulme used it for a pocket toy to occupy his restless fingers. It is a sacred object, elusively anthropo- and ichthymorphic, with no god but its own vigor. I do not know what has become of it.

---

* Athletic wit: the etymology is *pan ergon*, all-doing, as it were Freud's id and paperback psychology's "drives": but the Greeks used *panourgos*, ready to do anything, "mostly in a bad sense," and for *panourgia* (whence Rabelais' Panurge) the Lexicon gives "villany, knavery, trickery." Pound withholds this word till Canto 99, where attention to detail must correlate it with the passage quoted above.

THE MUSE
IN TATTERS

The Sapphic fragment concerning
Gongyla, which in 1916 yielded Pound his "Papyrus," is actually
parchment, one of three such parchment scraps torn by good fortune
from a book destroyed centuries ago, the kind of book into which
especially precious things were transcribed because papyrus disintegrates. They were salvaged from among masses of illegible
papyrus scraps that came to Berlin from Egypt in 1896. Professor
Schubart six years later published in a German journal the letters
he could then make out, bits of three poems of Sappho's, and in
1907 a reconsidered deciphering which by two years later (*Classical
Review*, July 1909) J. M. Edmonds had reconsidered yet more fully.
There we may find

$$\mathring{\eta}\mathring{\rho} \; \mathring{a}[\ldots \ldots$$
$$\delta\hat{\eta}\rho\alpha \; \tau\bar{o}[\ldots \ldots$$
$$\Gamma o\gamma\gamma\acute{\upsilon}\lambda\alpha \; \tau[\ldots \ldots$$

. . . plus parts of a dozen more lines, nine of which, the parchment
scrap growing suddenly wider, contained enough more words
and bits of words to tempt Prof. Edmonds' skill as an ancient Greek

poet. He diligently "restored" them, and offered a confident translation into Wardour Street. ("I would fain have thee set me in the
dewy meadow whither aforetime. . . .") Half the Greek words he
was rendering were his own. In subsequent versions he grew still
more confident, and the incautious user of his Loeb Classical
Library Sappho (*Lyra Graeca*, Vol. I, 245) has been likely to suppose
the poem substantially intact. It is not; and a half-century later
Pound's dry rendering of three words in the upper left corner
Edmonds left untinkered with still displaces in the memory Edmonds'
tushery. Which was part of what Pound meant.

*   *   *

Pound was alerted to the new fragments of Sappho by some
verses Richard Aldington gave him not long after they first met in
1912. Aldington had rendered a poem "To Atthis (*After the Manuscript of Sappho now in Berlin*)," working from an Edmonds restoration in the June 1909 *Classical Review*, the issue before the one that
offered Gongula. Pound sent the version to Harriet Monroe for her
new magazine, but though she used three Aldington poems in the
second number of *Poetry* she did not use "To Atthis," having taken
the odd precaution of checking with the head of the Greek Department at the University of Chicago, almost as if she'd known the
translator was a scant nineteen. And Paul Shorey, she wrote Pound
(9 Nov. 1912), "wouldn't stand for it," and she thought it advisable
not to antagonize the scholars. She considered Shorey "no mere
dry-as-dust." Pound replied that the Greek was so mutilated no
man living could talk of it in absolutes. "I'd like to see Shorey's
translation of the sense of the thing as it stands. I don't agree with
R's translation—but it is quite beautiful scholarship or no scholarship." Harriet did not budge. She believed Chicago scholars. Seven
years later her belief in W. G. Hale was to terminate Pound's connection with the magazine. Pound for his part anthologized "To
Atthis" in *Des Imagistes* (1914), and later reaffirmed his admiration
in *The Egoist*: "Aldington's version of the Atthis poem, from J. M.
Edmonds' conjectural restoration, will, I think, take its place in any
'complete' English 'Sappho' in the future." Aldington never reprinted it. It remains part of the story. It took Pound to Greek

fragments, to the files of the *Classical Review*, so to Gongula, and most important, to the poem Aldington had translated.

Of this poem, from the same ruined book as the Gongula scrap, a larger piece of parchment preserves much more: a torn beginning, a torn ending, and in between them five stanzas entire: a very notable addition to the Sapphic canon, in which one poem of seven stanzas, the "Poikilothron'," and four stanzas of another, the "Phainetai moi," had hitherto been the only substantial exhibits.

And its tone is elegiac. For a thousand years no more than four lines of Sappho's on such a theme had been accessible to anyone. To Pound, then intent on a poiesis of loss, it came punctually: a sustained lament for an absence, for the absence of a familiar of Sappho and Atthis, now among the girls of Lydia and remembered across the sundering sea. What we have of it is built around a long "Homeric" simile, separately elaborated and keyed by the Homeric word βροδοδάκτυλος, unique outside of Homer and unique in being applied to the moon, not in Homer's way to the dawn: "rosy-fingered." *Brododaktylos* is Sappho's spelling, the initial *b* a mark of her dialect; the word so spelled lodged itself in Pound's mind, not to be touched for 30 years, but in Pisa one day to help unlock word-hoards. The whole poem became, as soon as he discovered it, a nexus for the nuanced elegiacs he had been concerned

The Berlin Parchment of the "brododaktylos" poem, reproduced from *Sitzungsberichte der Akademie der Wissenschaften*, 1902.

with since he wrote *Cathay* and turned 30. Its few dozen words disclose Sappho who longs for a distant girl, and imagines her in turn longing for the Atthis whom Sappho's words address though she too may be absent, while a moon rosy-fingered, as pre-eminent among the stars as the distant girl among the girls of Lydia, shines on the salt sea at dusk and on the flowers. Most of the words concern the moon's remote lustrations; like "The Jewel Stairs' Grievance" of the 1915 *Cathay*, "the poem is especially prized because she utters no direct reproach."

Aldington's version ran:

> Atthis, far from me and dear Mnasidika,
> Dwells in Sardis;
> Many times she was near us
> So that we lived life well
> Like the far-famed goddess
> Whom above all things music delighted.
>
> And now she is first among the Lydian women
> As the mighty sun, the rose-fingered moon,
> Beside the great stars.
>
> And the light fades from the bitter sea
> And in like manner from the rich-blossoming earth;
> And the dew is shed upon the flowers,
> Rose and soft meadow-sweet
> And many-coloured melilote.
> Many things told are remembered of sterile Atthis.
>
> I yearn to behold thy delicate soul
> To satiate my desire. . . .
> . . . .

"The mighty sun" mangles a phrase meaning "after sunset" (deriving δύντος from δυνατός instead of from δύνω), and Atthis has become the absent girl rather than the girl addressed, and toward the end a Gordian tangle which Edmonds explicates for half a column has been most arbitrarily cut. And so on. It is clear why Professor Shorey "wouldn't stand for it." The point in Pound's letter to Miss Monroe remains valid: all editions from Schubart's of 1902 to Lobel and Page's of 1955 wrestle in their fine print with the fact that once we have passed the word "melilote" the parchment offers impenetrable riddles from which only rough sense is to be gleaned. This part is worth examining; it will occupy us again. Edmonds' text read:

> πόλλα δὲ ζαφοίταισ' ἀγόνας ἐπι-
> μνάσθεισ' "Ατθιδος, ἱμέρω
> λέπταν ϝοι φρένα κῆρ ἄσαι βόρηται

which with some grammatical forcing he took to mean:

> And oftentime when our beloved, wandering abroad, calls to mind her gentle Atthis, the heart devours her tender breast with the pain of longing.

The Greek words do, in a general way, hang together, though no one is really sure what some of them are, nor, whatever they are, how to parse them. At one point everyone has read ἀγάνας, "gentle," except Edmonds, who read ἀγόνας but assumed it stood for ἀγάνας ("it may well be the Aeolic form"); Aldington's "sterile" ignores this assumption, supplying the dictionary sense of the word Edmonds printed. (So later, in Canto 5, we find "Atthis, unfruitful.") Then there is ἱμέρω, a Lesbian form of ἱμείρω, "I yearn." What part of speech is it? We are in a syntactic quagmire whatever we decide. Edmonds makes ἱμέρω a genitive, at the price of a postulated syntax Sappho herself might have had trouble following. Aldington took it at its dictionary value, as an indicative verb with λέπταν φρένα for its object: "I yearn for thy delicate soul." That leaves all the preceding words to be trowelled into another independent clause. And of the verb form βόρηται one could only suppose in Edmonds' day that it had something to do with eating: hence Aldington's ingenious "to satiate my desire," reinforced by his assignment of ἄσαι to ἄω, satiate, instead of ἀάω, hurt. (Usages in later papyri make it possible to derive βόρηται differently, and talk of the heart being laden.)

So the words in the Aldington version are generally referrable to *something* in the Greek he was working from. Of course he was trying to write a poem, not resolve paleographic austerities. How far these were from resolution as late as 1955 we can learn from the

700 words of erudite shadowboxing on pages 91–2 of Professor Page's *Sappho and Alcaeus*.

* * *

To take from Sappho what one can use for one's poems was a tradition understood by Catullus and practiced by English poets ever since, in the 19th century, there were accessible collections of her work to take from. The edition Pound was used to, Wharton's of 1885, illustrates both the range of Romantic and Decadent indebtedness, and the slightness of the canon before 20th-century work with papyri more than doubled it. Wharton's book commences with what were in the year of Pound's birth the only two substantial poems of Sappho, each attended by a small cloud of English translations and imitations, from Ambrose Philips to John Addington Symonds; whereafter Wharton can do no more than display the thin scrapings of generations of scholars: a few other single stanzas, some portions of stanzas, and many stray lines, stray phrases, single words, cited by Alexandrian commentators in passing illustration of meters, or of Aeolic forms (so that we know how she would have spelled the word for carbonate of soda), or of semantic oddments like *barmos* and *barbitos*, names of musical instruments. Tiny though they are, these Sapphic details can rub off on other writings like bits of red dye; Wharton gives dozens of instances, and we can easily extend his citations. Thus the barbitos, and the "Pierian roses" an anthologist preserved in the 6th century along with 27 words of their context, were both to find their way into Pound's *Mauberley*; her "golden-sandalled dawn," from a line quoted only to show how she misused an adverb, is fused with a glimpse of Pavlova in his "The Garret": her distich on Hesper the bringer-home, which we owe to one word a grammarian wanted to annotate, stirred successive chords a hundred years apart in *Don Juan* and in *The Waste Land*.

In glimpses as brief as these her presence lingers, like the afterimage of a face. Of one song there survives one line, as quoted by Hephaestion of Alexandria to exemplify a meter: ʼΗράμαν μὲν ἔγω σέθεν, ʺΑτθι, πάλαι ποτά: "I loved you once, Atthis, long

ago": only that, but its pauses, its run of sounds, its tautly paced disclosure running through seven overlapping words—so slow is the
rose to open—roused Swinburne into eight lines of slow-motion
re-enactment:

> *I loved thee,*—hark, one tenderer note than all—
> *Atthis, of old time, once*—one low long fall,
> Sighing—one long low lovely loveless call,
> Dying—one pause in song so flamelike fast—
> *Atthis, long since in old time overpast*—
> One soft first pause and last.
> One,—then the old rage of rapture's fieriest rain
> Storms all the music-maddened night again.

This is surely the champion expansion, a document of the sensibility
to which Pound's generation fell heir: a whole rhapsodic strophe
on how it felt to read one Greek line. Would Dr. Johnson have
carried on so? Yet although the rhapsode was Swinburne, who was
never at a loss for more words, the Greek is shaped by an impassioned craft antiquity as well as Romanticism found exceptional;
and its theme, an evoked regret, will glow without circumstance,
as will gold in the gloom, sumptuous, for attention to prolong;
and the art of attending to radioactive moments, "simply," in Pater's
phrase, "for those moments' sake," had preoccupied two English
generations. A central tradition of 19th-century decadence, a
hyperaesthesia prizing and feeding on ecstatic instants, fragments of
psychic continuum, answered a poetry time had reduced to fragments and endorsed the kind of attention fragments exact if we are
to make anything of them at all, a gathering of the responsive
faculties into the space of a tiny blue flame.

Having collected its attention, however, the impulse of this
tradition was to dilate on attention's object: to reduplicate, to
amplify, to prolong; to transcribe as for Wagner's orchestra.
Observe, analogously, the Pre-Raphaelite cumbrousness of detail
generated (1830) in Tennyson's mind by a Shakespearean name,
"Mariana," and a Shakespearean phrase, "moated grange."

*   *   *

Pound's pedagogic bent was against such consequences of hyperaesthesia. In the summer of 1916 he had reduced "the whole art," for Iris Barry's benefit, to

> *a.* concision, or style, or saying what you mean in the fewest and clearest words.
>
> *b.* the actual necessity for creating or constructing something; of presenting an image, or enough images of concrete things arranged to stir the reader.

He also admitted "simple emotional statements of fact, such as 'I am tired,' or simple credos like 'After death there comes no other calamity'." But he left no room for rapture's fieriest rain to storm the music-maddened night again, and had Swinburne's verses been submitted anonymously he would very likely have cut them back to the phrases on which they dilate. He prized Sappho for just the concision Swinburne obliterated, and to illustrate the chisel-edge of exactness drew Miss Barry's attention to "the gulph between TIS O SAPPHO ADIKEI, and Pindar's big rhetorical drum TINA THEON, TIN' EROA, TINA D'ANDREA KELADESOMEN," misspelling words with the freedom of one who has them by heart. Τίς ἀδικήει: "Who wrongs you?": the question Aphrodite is to ask, in the "Poikilothron'," when she comes to Sappho's aid: the sharp words of the goddess. (They are quoted in the *Pisan Cantos* and directed toward Athena, in a curious detail (76/461:490) which glimpses the descending Aphrodite in the guise of a butterfly that changes its mind and goes back out the tent's smoke hole.)

In the months in which he was writing to Iris Barry he was struggling to make Elkin Mathews print intact the sharp words of *Lustra*, and one of the poems at which Mathews and his printer balked was "Ἰμέρρω,"* an extrapolation from a detail in the poem

---

* Since the folk of Lesbos dropped their aitches this word takes a smooth breathing, and did in three *Lustra* printings. The rough breathing it acquired in the 1926 *Personae* and wore through four decades of reprints is traceable to a misprint in the Concise Liddell and Scott *Lexicon*, where Pound had the bad luck to check it. There are endless pitfalls in printing single Greek words; one must imagine a compositor matching mirror images from an unfamiliar font against queer things handwritten into a typescript: hence, throughout the Pound canon, a tendency of accents to get reversed, and of similar shapes—Υ and γ, ζ and ξ, to get confused. And Pound generally did not use modern editions, but the 18th-century ones he could pick up on bookstalls. And in Pisa he quoted from unreliable memory.

Aldington had translated. It says what it means in the fewest and clearest words, and was eventually omitted from the British trade edition of *Lustra*. It extrapolates not by pouring Swinburne's hot fudge over crystals of ice but by growing a larger crystal: supplying a phrase with a structure. The phrase is "Ἀτθίδος, ἱμέρρω: for Atthis, longing. Pound's expansion is

Ἰμέρρω
Thy soul
Grown delicate with satieties,
Atthis,

O Atthis
I long for thy lips.
I long for thy narrow breasts,
Thou restless, ungathered.

—a corrective to the music-maddened night, which Pound certainly knew because Wharton's *Sappho* puts it on display.

He drew hints from two lines of Aldington's:

I yearn to behold thy delicate soul
To satiate my desire.

And since φρήν designates the breast as well as the passion therein, he may have gotten the hint for "narrow breasts" from the same phrase that suggested Aldington's "delicate soul." In the course of inventing a poetic structure anything in the penumbra of the poet's attention may suggest a word: even a page of the *Classical Review* looked at sideways.

In *Lustra*, moreover, this is not an isolated poem but one of a suite of five poems. So we discover the point of "Papyrus," which Pound never printed by itself, for "Papyrus"—

Spring . . . .
Too long . . . . . .
Gongula . . . . . .

—is the first poem of the suite, its authentic (mock authentic?) keynote. It is followed by

"IONE, DEAD THE LONG YEAR"

Empty are the ways,
Empty are the ways of this land
And the flowers
        Bend over with heavy heads.
They bend in vain.
Empty are the ways of this land
           Where Ione
Walked once, and now does not walk
But seems like a person just gone.

The flowers and the absence are from Sappho, the girl's name from Landor, who devised it as a fine pseudonym for a Miss Jones. The third poem is "Ἰμέρρω." The fourth, which abandons the classical key, is

SHOP GIRL

For a moment she rested against me
Like a swallow half blown to the wall,
And they talk of Swinburne's women,
And the sheperdess meeting with Guido.
And the harlots of Baudelaire.

—another girl now remembered in absence, but one never properly present: molecule of the merest encounter, "like a swallow half blown to the wall": yet a muse as were the women in other poets' perhaps imaginary encounters: and she was real. And nearly non-existent: and granted no favors: and granted the stuff of a tiny poem, to set beside Guido Cavalcanti's five strophes—*E tanto vi sentio gioi' e dolzore*. . . . Likewise in *Mauberley* a few years later the eyes of the eternal Aphrodite will look through the blank face of a London girl, being painted by Burne-Jones as a beggar-maid.

From a scrap of parchment with Gongyla's name on it the sequence has traced modes of passion declining to this. For coda it paraphrases Catullus' estimate of a comparable decline, which ends:

And they call you beautiful in the province,
And you are even compared to Lesbia.

O most unfortunate age!

Pound has fitted Sappho, as he fits everything that interests him, into an historical process, complicating the ancient tradition of poetic *aemulatio* with his own concern for cultural gradations. It is 1916. The *Cantos* will before long be working in this way, setting like beside almost like, to delineate losses and gains, new delicacies, lost intensities.

*   *   *

In 1919, working on Canto 5, he returned to the poem about Atthis and the absent girl, and once more spun filaments toward the world of Catullus. The theme is passion, passion eventually flowing (Borgia, Medici) into ideology and toward murder. The canto opens with the bride awaiting the god's touch (Danaë, showered with gold) and spirals through modes of love barely recapturable from time's phantasmagoria:

> The fire? always, and the vision always,
> Ear dull, perhaps, with the vision, flitting
> And fading at will. Weaving with points of gold,
> Gold-yellow, saffron . . .

—from which shower of discriminated yellows (modulation of the golden shower) a Roman wedding party emerges, Aurunculeia's, the one celebrated by Catullus (*Carmen 61*), with its saffron shoe crossing the threshold, its flung nuts ("Da nuces"), its Hymenaeus:

> . . . The roman shoe, Aurunculeia's
> And come shuffling feet, and cries "Da nuces!
> "Nuces!" praise, and Hymenaeus "brings the girl to her man."

From this marriage we are carried to Sapphic love via two other poems, Catullus' other epithalamion (*Carmen 62*) which begins "Vesper adest" and proceeds under the sign of that star, and the distich of Sappho's that begins "(H)espere panta pherōn" and has left its impress on work of Byron's, Tennyson's, Eliot's. Pound specifies only the link, the name of the star:

> and from "Hesperus . . ."
> Hush of the older song:

—and the "older song" is then paraphrased from words on the Berlin parchment.

Yet its most memorable feature is absent, its rich center, the Homeric simile Sappho built from the phrase about the rosy-fingered moon. Pound denied himself even the splendid word *brododaktylos*, apparently because it bespoke Homer too insistently to be usable. Catullus and Sappho were his terms of reference, and later privations and troubadors, but nothing epic. So he worked his way around *brododaktylos*, recalling that moons of that color, like the apparition of Hesper, occur at dusk, and gathered with Aldington's encouragement from *phaos* in the tenth line and *thalassan* in the eleventh the elements of

"Fades light from sea-crest

In the seventh and eighth lines he found

νῦν δὲ Λύδαισιν ἐμπρέπεται γυναί-
κεσσιν

—"now she stands out among Lydian women"—and was very likely misled by the -ιν termination of an Aeolic dative plural in which, perhaps distracted by a note of Edmonds' on νῶιν, he fancied he saw a dual:

"And in Lydia walks with pair'd women
"Peerless among the pairs, . . .

Then . . .] Σαρδε [. . . (the last letter conjectural) from the very top of the parchment, the sole surviving token of its line if we disregard Edmonds' contributions, prompted a reticent ellipse:

. . . that once in Sardis

—haunting poetry though obscure geography, since Sardis is situated in Lydia, not here where Sappho stands. And finally the sixteenth and seventeenth lines, where Atthis is mentioned—

πόλλα δὲ ζαφοίταισ' ἀγόνας ἐπιμνάσθεισ' Ἀτθιδος, ἰμέρω

gave him, not without effort his summation. To the troublesome declension and wide idiomatic applicability of the first of these words Liddell and Scott devote two columns; on the possible syntax of the third Edmonds (1909) expended some 300 words and Page (1955) twice as many, to the effect that the sense is "often going to and fro, she remembers gentle Atthis with yearning." Aldington had already made ἱμέρω begin a new sentence. Pound plunged in, and, prompted by Aldington, began by taking πόλλα not as "often" but as a neuter plural, "many things." Given this assumption ζαφοίταισ' (= διαφοιτάω, to roam about continually) yielded no sense; whereas two words later the *Lexicon* supplies διαφορέω, to spread abroad, which given the peculiarities of the Lesbian dialect he may have thought a plausible emendation. Then ἐπιμνάσθεισ' yielded "brought to mind," whence:

> ... and many things
> "Are set abroad and brought to mind of thee."

And to this result:

> Titter of sound about me, always.
>   and from "Hesperus ..."
> Hush of the older song: "Fades light from sea-crest,
> "And in Lydia walks with pair'd women
> "Peerless among the pairs, that once in Sardis
> "In satieties ...
>   Fades the light from the sea, and many things
> "Are set abroad and brought to mind of thee,"
> And the vinestocks lie untended, new leaves come to the shoots,
> North wind nips on the bough, and seas in heart
> Toss up chill crests
>   And the vine stocks lie untended
> And many things are set abroad and brought to mind
> Of thee, Atthis, unfruitful. ...

"Hush of the older song," and here first audible in English: the first considerable poem of Sappho's to be recovered since the printing of Longinus' treatise in 1554 put in circulation the "Phainetai moi" Catullus had imitated. Only a few of its words are used as seed-crystals in *Lustra*, a few of its other words in Canto 5. Fragments of a fragment grow into radiant gists; it is in keeping with the kind of attention Sappho's Greek commands of an early 20th-century intelligence that Pound nowhere presents what we have of the poem entire.

*   *   *

Swinburne's scholarship was incomparably more exact (he could correct Jowett: "Another howler, Master!") but his sense of diction less highly developed. That is one measure not simply of the difference between two poets but of a change in characteristic sensibility between Swinburne's time and Pound's. When Eliot speaks of Byron's "imperceptiveness to the English word—so that he has to use a great many words before we become aware of him" he posits his own time's criteria.

In any age how to read and how to write are complementary terms, and the reading of the Pound Era, like its writing, discerns patterns of diction and gathers meaning from non-consecutive arrays. We can tell one page of *Ulysses* from another at a glance; to our grandfathers they would have seemed as featureless as pages from a telephone directory. The Joyce of a famous anecdote spent hours rearranging fifteen words, but knew from the start what each of the words was to be. Sensitivity to detailed sculptured forms makes tolerable—cherishable—in our museums fragments a former generation would have eked out with more plaster than there is marble. "Points define a periphery," wrote Pound in 1950, and in 1965 a translator of Sappho offered, where parchment is wholly ruined, neither a despairing blank nor a mosaic of conjectures but this:

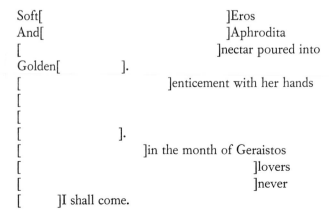

```
Soft[                              ]Eros
And[                              ]Aphrodita
[                                ]nectar poured into
Golden[          ].
[                        ]enticement with her hands
[
[
[            ].
[                    ]in the month of Geraistos
[                              ]lovers
[                              ]never
[        ]I shall come.
```

That the name of a month, and "lovers" and "never," and the resolve to come are discoverable in each other's neighborhood is to us an expressive fact, helping to characterize the ruined stanza. Similar skills brought to bear on torn pages would assure us that

]banyan, frangipani or
]s; or an exotic serpent
]and snake-skin for the foot, if you see fit,
]cats, not cobras to
]he rats. The diffident   [

is by Marianne Moore and not Ezra Pound, and that

] make price[
]teste leopard   [
]Taormina   [
]   high cliff and azure beneath it[
]in the lute's neck, tone is from the b[
]s alone over Selloi   [
] This wing, colour of feldspar   [
]   phylotaxis   [

is by Ezra Pound and not Marianne Moore, and that neither can be a scrap of William Carlos Williams.

Pound's attention, similarly, tended to fix on the constellated words in ancient texts, not on their syntactic connections. He has even suggested that preoccupation with reproducing syntax may get in the translator's way, that Aeschylus' Greek is nearly agglutinative. In 1912 he conjectured that Arnaut Daniel might have evolved Moncli and Audierna, two lovers of whom nothing else is known, from two passages misread in Vergil's ninth eclogue, Moncli being Menalcas glimpsed through scribes' contractions, and Audierna a form of the verb *audio* mistaken for a name, and the whole translated "without too much regard for Latin syntax, with which Arnaut would have been much less familiar than he was with the Latin vocabulary." Pound has gone through such processes himself, not always unconsciously.

It is tenable that he saw diction rather than syntax because not having learned declensions accurately he could not follow the syntax. This is very likely often true, but does not itself explain why a man who was never lazy, and had an appetite for old poems, did not feel an incentive to perfect his grammatical knowledge. That he was impatient with people who possessed such knowledge is not an explanation but something else to explain. What did he know that they didn't? Which means, since a man will not willingly pore over what is opaque to him, what was he responding to when he read Greek? To rhythms and dictions, nutriment for his purposes. Especially in Greek lyrics he is sensitive to the boundaries of individual words, and apt to discern a talismanic virtue in relevant English words of his discovery. In the rare plural "satieties" he found a Sapphic quality concentrated. It appears in "*'Ιμέρρω*," it is cherished and carefully laminated into the fifth Canto, and we learn nothing of its virtue from knowing that it was prompted by Aldington's misreading of *ἄσαι*. It suffices that Pound came upon it in the rich field of his English vocabulary, and cherished it as affording a mysterious glimpse into intensities important to Sappho.

The five poems in *Lustra*, the lines in Canto 5, may be taken in this way detail by detail as exempla of the disciplined attention at work, attention disciplined not only by fragments of Greek but by a time's aesthetic, an aesthetic of glimpses. For the second Renaissance that opened for classicists in 1891 with a shower of papyri was a renaissance of attention. Perhaps nothing else ultimately matters in the arts. And like the Grand Renaissance it was long preparing before anyone suspected it was happening. Degas and Toulouse-Lautrec show us glimpses, comparable to

> For a moment she rested against me
> Like a swallow half blown to the wall.

The eye's shutter captures faces and gestures of the café or the street, so composed as to seem casual. Elsewhere Rossetti—

> A sonnet is a moment's monument,—
> Memorial from the Soul's eternity
> To one dead deathless hour

—and Pater—

> Who, in some such perfect moment, . . . has not felt the desire to
> perpetuate all that, just so, to suspend it in every particular circum-

stance, with the portrait of just that one spray of leaves lifted just so high against the sky, above the well, forever?

—adumbrate the metaphysics of the glimpse. Arthur Symons, the art of whose ideal poet Verlaine was "a delicate waiting upon moods," describes himself (1905)

> as one who devoutly practiced "the religion of the eyes," looking into every omnibus, watching faces in the crowds which passed him in Piccadilly lest he miss a sudden gracious gesture, a beautiful face. . . . This was also the pleasure that the music-halls gave him: back-stage especially he enjoyed, like Degas, the vision of a world in flux—moving shapes and shadows; sudden unreal glimpses of the dancers on stage; profiles of the spectators. And if he watched carefully, the flux might momentarily resolve itself into an arrangement.

To fix the last fine shade, said Symons, "to fix it fleetingly; to be a disembodied voice, and yet the voice of a human soul . . ."; and Pound accordingly not only preserves things glimpsed "In a Station of the Metro" or "Dans un Omnibus de Londres"—

> Les yeux d'une morte
> M'ont salué,
> Enchassés dans une visage stupide
> Dont tous les autres traits étaient banals,
> Ils m'ont salué

—but also echoes the presiding doctrines in "Horae Beatae Inscriptio"—

> How will this beauty, when I am far hence
> Sweep back upon me and engulf my mind!

—or in the little epigraph to *Lustra*:

> And the days are not full enough
> And the nights are not full enough
> And life slips by like a field mouse
> Not shaking the grass.

He echoes them however not in weariness, the note of Symons and Pater, but in a passionate generosity of attention; they were not canons of living but criteria for poems. When "each moment," as Pater wrote, "some tint grows more perfect on land or sea," then not to fix such perfections is "to sleep before evening." Let us die finely; our life is a long dying, amid which to be conscious is to capture melancholy satisfactions. No, let us write finely, Pound's concern rather ran, if it is our vocation to write, and seize moments in our writing, seize glimpses, there to seize, real: meanwhile

> Nothing but death, said Turgenev (Tiresias)
> is irreparable.

*   *   *

Pound was most deeply entangled in the aesthetic of glimpses in the *Lustra–Mauberley* period, the years when the elements of his mature method were being worked out. It is a period of looking back a little wistfully, a period of laments for departed experience, the period inaugurated by *Cathay*. Sappho, her fragments, her crystalline single words, remained bound up in his mind with this time, and with its end she drops out of his zone of preoccupation. By 1920 the fifth canto was in print, and the aesthetic of Paterian elegy which its first page recalls, the aesthetic he had exorcised in *Mauberley*, was replaced by the studied aesthetic of "hard squares" worked out under the sign of Fenollosa. In the 1920's, making reading lists for young students, he cited "of the Greeks, Homer, Sappho," and in the 1930's he set Mary Barnard to writing Sapphics ("have a care against spondee too often for second foot"), but the explicit use of Sappho in his work remained confined to those late London years and their cultivated regrets: *Lustra*, Canto 5, *Mauberley*.

Then suddenly after a quarter-century circumstances changed the tone of the *Cantos* once more to elegy, and Sappho returned.

Irreparable death hung over the poet's head, and there were no books but Legge's Confucius and a Bible, and no sights but guards and prisoners and a sky and mountains and dust, and the *Pisan Cantos* invoked memory, seizing moments from the past "for those moments' sake." It was then that, reaching back to the time when Pound had pored over Greek fragments, memory yielded up, strangely, the splendid word of Sappho's that Canto 5 had skirted: *brododaktylos*. The word presented itself amid a sense that his own personality was dissolving into recollections. "To such a tremulous wisp constantly reforming itself on the stream, to a single sharp impression, with a sense in it, a relic more or less fleeting, of such moments gone by, what is real in our life fines itself down": so Pater had written in 1868, and so Pound felt in the summer of 1945. His mind ran on devouring Time, on the dead Ignez da Castro who brought the phrase "time is the evil" into the *Cantos*, on a woman's face remembered as though "dead the long year," on Mauberley's effort to memorialize such glimpses, working as Pisanello had worked on medallions in the Greek manner "to forge Achaia"; on new-made Aphrodite blown upon by winds; and on Aubrey Beardsley, doomed. And did he remember that Beardsley had designed the cover for the third printing of Wharton's *Sappho?*

> Time is not, Time is the evil, beloved
> Beloved the hours βροδοδάκτυλος
>   as against the half-light of the window
>   with the sea beyond making horizon
> le contre-jour the line of the cameo
> profile "to carve Achaia"
>   a dream passing over the face in the half-light
>   Venere, Cytherea "aut Rhodon"
>   vento ligure, veni
> "beauty is difficult" sd/ Mr Beardsley . . .
>   (74/444:472)

So Canto 74; and though the lament for a lost woman in a lost time accords with Sappho's theme, and the vocation of Beardsley and H. S. Mauberley with the sensibility of a time when fragments had seemed especially radiant, though Sappho's word thus bridges the two motifs of this passage, the fact should be recorded that in 1949 Pound could not say why he had used the Aeolic rather than the Homeric form of the word "rosy-fingered." No matter: memory at the time of writing had supplied what was appropriate, and supplied it again in Canto 80 when amid memories of those London days Aubrey Beardsley's saying again drew up with it the Greek polysyllable:

"With the veil of faint cloud before her." Diana, by Agostino di Duccio, Tempio Malatestiana.

La beauté, "Beauty is difficult, Yeats" said Aubrey Beardsley
    when Yeats asked why he drew horrors
    or at least not Burne-Jones
    and Beardsley knew he was dying and had to
    make his hit quickly

hence no more B-J in his product.

    So very difficult, Yeats, beauty so difficult.

    "I am the torch" wrote Arthur "she saith"
in the moon barge βροδοδάκτυλος 'Ηώς

with the veil of faint cloud before her
    Κύθηρα δεινά as a leaf borne in the current
pale eyes as if without fire.

                                     (80/511:546)

    It is a poignant cluster: Beardsley; Arthur Symons, whose
"Modern Beauty" began,

        I am the torch, she saith, and what to me
        If the moth die of me?

Κύθηρα δεινά, remembering perhaps Yeats' "terrible beauty"; her
as-if-fireless pale eyes those of the moon (and perhaps of Agostino
di Duccio's triumphant Diana in the Tempio at Rimini); the moon
like Sappho's moon rosy-fingered, and rosy fingers specifying
Homer's dawn.

    The writer of those lines was living like Beardsley in the
shadow of death, like Symons and Pater in the consciousness of
a transience whose term is death, and as never before in his life
was building with precious fragments, conserved by memory as
the letters on parchments were conserved by chance: conserved for
imaginations quickened by transience to scrutinize and irradiate.
When he used Sappho's fragment on Atthis in 1916 it was as a
means of writing elegiac poems, the elegy being the poetic genre
his time gave him, a gift that corresponded to one of the moods
of youth in that decade. When she returned to him in 1945, as it
were anonymously, so that later he did not know that it was she

and not Homer who had brought him a magical word, she re-enacted a rite celebrated by Symons and Yeats, assuming the guise of eternal Aphrodite who visits poets and whose gaze confers a sad ecstasy. Aphrodite comes in mean vestments, the myth runs: in the rags of the girl who posed for Burne-Jones's beggar-maid, or in a scrap of parchment.

MOTZ EL SON

Some things were current once that are current no longer. A public for an inexpensive bilingual Dante—Italian text, notes, and a facing version in unpretentious prose—was once discoverable in England in sufficient numbers to circulate thousands upon thousands of elegant pocket-sized volumes, price one shilling. Rossetti, not Milton, had prepared that taste, and J. M. Dent began the Temple Dante with the *Paradiso*. With its gravure frontispiece "after Botticelli," it was issued in 1899 and reprinted 1900, 1901, 1903, 1904, 1908, 1910, 1912. ... An afternote cites a Dante Primer also priced (1899) at one shilling. *Inferno* and *Purgatorio* followed, then the *Convivio*, then the *Latin Works*. By 1906 *The Vita Nuova and Canzonieri* completed a six-volume set. It was not presumed that the reader knew Italian, but that, "possessing some acquaintance with Latin or one of the Romance languages," he would welcome a prose guide "to the very words of the master in the original." Pound's 1910 bilingual Cavalcanti (not published till 1912) had similar aims, if more ambitious translations, and perhaps hoped for a similar market. (He had no luck. Within six months the publisher was in liquidation; four years later fire destroyed the sheets.)

That taste sustained much that is now dug for in research

collections. In 1902 the numerous students of Dante (where are they now?) could buy H. J. Chaytor's *The Troubadours of Dante*, which offered as much "as any one is likely to require who does not propose to make a special study of Provençal." This meant working through 46 poems with a glossary, a grammar, and notes, unassisted by translations. People with Latin and French, who had been sipping at old Italian, seem not to have thought this formidable. Atop Pound's 1908 "Na Audiart" a note on the story of Bertrans' "borrowed lady" begins "Anyone who has read anything of the troubadours knows . . ." That was not swank: it was easy then to read something of the troubadours. The story had been accessible for 30 years in Dr. Francis Hueffer's book on these poets. When Dr. Hueffer's eldest son Ford Madox accepted for his *English Review* Pound's resurrection of the bloodthirsty Bertrans ("Sestina: Altaforte"), he could assume a readership that had known Bertrans since 1900 as a character in a novel (Maurice Hewlett's *Richard Yea-and-Nay*) popular enough to have drawn favorable reviews as far afield as Indianapolis. Another solid novel, Edward Hutton's *Sigismondo Pandolfo Malatesta, Lord of Rimini,* had been current since 1906. And when, in 1909 and 1910, a course was offered at the Polytechnic in Regent Street, largely concerned with Dante and Daniel and Troubadours, the registrants were not academic folk as we now understand them, but included Mrs. Olivia Shakespear, novelist, wife to a London solicitor, and her daughter Dorothy, designer in watercolors. Miss Shakespear, as is well known, subsequently married the lecturer. After the war they walked to the troubadour shrines, and she found a five-leaf clover at the summit of Montségur, within the walls of the broken Temple of Light.

The collapse of that public, its supersession by folk absorbed in introspection and politics, is an unwritten story. The printing history of the Temple *Paradiso* affords an informal graph. The 13 years up to 1912 required eight printings. After a wartime hiatus demand began to slack off: five printings in 11 years. The copy from which I take these data was printed in 1930, not sold until 1946. Similarly, by the time (1923) the Malatesta Cantos were written their subject had been erased from literate consciousness. Pound nowhere tells his reader who Sigismundo is: his mind lingered in a time when people knew. R. P. Blackmur in 1934 thought the subject most recondite. And all that half-century university registration was swelling.

*   *   *

Concurrently, Provençal scholarship peaked and declined. Prof. Shepard in 1905 taught Pound the rudiments from current books. Carl Appel's *Provençalische Chrestomathie*, a magnificent self-contained textbook with a grammar and as elaborate a glossary as one might require, was in its second edition with a third in preparation, Levy's eight-volume Dictionary was half published, Bertrans had been edited by Stimmung (1879), Arnaut by Canello (1883), Sordello by de Lollis (1896). Such things were as current as Chomsky and Wittgenstein now. When in London Pound talked of troubadours to anyone who would hear him, or when he lectured on Cavalcanti in Oxford at the invitation of T. E. Lawrence's brother, his subject if not his judgments stood validated by the most intent European philologists: there was no more active front. But 1915 saw the last of the monumental editions, Appel's of Bernart de Ventadorn; nine years later the posthumous final volume of Levy's great work closed off a labor no successor has renewed; an age had ended.

Philological interest, for one thing, is self-liquidating. Confronted by the chaos of manuscripts, a 19th-century editor could engage such large questions as sustain a career of esteem: in what world had Arnaut lived, what words had he arranged, what did they mean? By the 1930's philology had used up these questions and abandoned the field to makers of bilingual anthologies to nourish French chauvinism. In very large universities one can still find a Provençal man doing guard duty, but the front is dormant. For many decades Ezra Pound's interest in that literature has seemed a youthful freak, like the green shirt with glass buttons he wore to Giessen when he was 25.

*   *   *

He went there to present to Ford Madox Hueffer a copy of his *Canzoni*, which opened with five poems in Provençal forms: fit homage to the man who had printed four of them in such company as Hardy's and Conrad's, and from whose father's worktable had come the first book in English on those forms' inventors. By 1911, six years out of Shepard's seminar, Pound felt confident of having at last assimilated Provençal to poetry. He had left behind the use of troubadour lives or troubadour poems as subject matter; had pieced their formal rituals, and literary London's blessed-damosel diction, and mediaevalism and "Spirits Terrene" and other aesthetic stuff into a unity worthy of a poet's vocation, and had come to think of the Canzone as "the high mass of poetry," whose elaborate stanzas "serve that love of Beauty [capitalized] . . . which belongs to the permanent part of oneself"—to one's fine Pre-Raphaelite soul, in short—in poems as ceremoniously dated as the Villanelle of a Temptress Stephen Dedalus composed on waking one morning with his soul "all dewy wet." Behind "high mass of poetry" (a phrase he later deleted from the proofs) there was no very exact notion of a high mass, except that censers sway. This inexactness could not be deleted. It pervaded the book, where a panoply of Incense and Light and Glamour and Angels comported with such inchoate work as a poem salvaged from Wyncote (Pa.) adolescence and now minimally retouched:

> . . . But archèd high above the curl of life
> We dwelt amid the ancient boulders
> Gods had hewn and druids turned
> Unto that birth most wondrous, that had grown
> A mighty fortress while the world had slept . . .

So his mind soared.

Giessen boasted a Grand Duke, also a university, also furnished rooms richly stocked with ornaments "ranging from bits of coral like human brains to gilded busts of Lohengrin." Ford was there on a fool's errand—to wait out, in his 38th year, a German divorce before marrying a *domna jauzionda* who was daughter to Tennyson's "Margaret" and half a hundred years old. A skilful *Rechtanswalt* picked his pocket regularly in exchange for Sibylline documents in law-German that never quite spelled Divorce. (Later, despairing, he sort-of-married her. It lasted a few years.) Between sessions with the lawyer, in that dreadful room, he wrote: among other things, at a novel about the middle ages (*Ladies Whose Bright Eyes*) which proposed that ages do not really differ unless in convictions and cuisines and smells. His weary lucidity (save touching Miss Violet Hunt) was irradiative. The summer was the hottest since 1453. And into these quarters marched jocund Ezra Pound, tendering his new book that chaunted of "sprays [to rhyme with 'praise' and 'rays'] of eglantine above clear waters," and employed such diction as "hight the microcline." Ford saw that it would not do. The Incense, the Angels, elicited an ultimate kinesthetic demonstration. By way of emphasizing their hopelessness he threw headlong his considerable frame and rolled on the floor. "That roll," Pound would one day assert, "saved me three years."

That roll, and perhaps a "Canzone a la Sonata: for E. P." which Ford dashed off to show how neutral a diction the intricate forms might accommodate.

> What do you find to boast of in our age,
> To boast of now, my friendly sonneteer,
> And not to blush for later? . . .

For to offer Rossettian tosh as poetry 1911 was not to stride into eternal realms but to misconceive 1911. Pound had spent his time mastering not the speech proper to exalted things but what he was to call in 1934 "the common verse of Britain from 1890 to 1910," "a horrible agglomerate compost, not minted, most of it not even baked, all legato, a doughy mess of third-hand Keats, Wordsworth, heaven knows what, fourth-hand Elizabethan sonority blunted, half-melted, lumpy." Ford's vigorous critique terminated all notion of refining the common verse. It wanted abolishing. It was a civic menace.

We can reconstruct Ford's discourse that hot day from the preface he wrote the same summer for his own poems. Aureate diction was a civic menace because "the business of poetry is not sentimentalism so much as the putting of certain realities in certain aspects," and "poetry, like everything else, to be valid and valuable, must reflect the circumstances and psychology of its own day. Otherwise it can be nothing but a pastiche." And as to the use of the past, "study every fragment of Sappho; delve ages long in the works of Bertran de Born; ... let us do anything in the world that will widen our perceptions. We are the heirs of all the ages. But, in the end, I feel fairly assured that the purpose of all these present travails is the right appreciation of such facets of our own day as God will let us perceive."

And Pound left Giessen (summer, 1911) to become a modern poet: the figure we have known ever since: the revolutionary.

*   *   *

It was not as though a disciple of Mallarmé's had been swung 180 degrees by meeting Zola. Pound had known Ford for more than two years, and Ford had hammered on the diction and syntax of natural speech: "nothing, *nothing*, that you couldn't in some circumstance, in the stress of some emotion, *actually say*." Pound's habit was to temper him with Yeats, seeing Ford in the afternoons, Yeats in the evenings, and Yeats' horror of the baldly mimetic would have helped inhibit adoption of "natural speech" as panacea in the early Masefield's way. Ford, moreover, was not Zola, but "the last Pre-Raphaelite," a fixer of nuances, and a man conversant with the troubadours. When, that day in Giessen, what Ford had said over and over suddenly registered, it came with humane, not journalistic, authority, and was received by a mind already sufficiently dubious about the *Canzoni* to have suppressed the afterword about poetry's high mass: a mind, moreover, that (perhaps at Ford's prompting) had already begun to experiment with natural diction: as witness the latter pages of *Canzoni* itself. There we find the versions from Heine—

> Is your hate, then, of such measure?
> Do you, truly, so detest me? ...

and "Au Salon"—

> I suppose, when poetry comes down to facts,
> When our souls are returned to the gods
>   and the spheres they belong in,
> Here in the every-day where our acts
> Rise up and judge us; ...

and "Au Jardin," which dismisses Yeats' "Cap and Bells" and calls up to the lady at the casement,

> O you away high there ... !

He had meant to segregate these as "Leviora," but changed his mind during the same proofreading at which he deleted the "high mass." His light verse, he conceded by that act, was continuous with his weighty. Then might passion and modern diction be fused? And Arnaut had once been modern, as Tennyson had never been.

So he did not throw the troubadours over. That autumn in London he proceeded to re-examine the interest in Provençal that had washed him up a blind alley; to work once more through Arnaut Daniel, word by word; and to restate his interest in the technique of sound. He had been Daniel's enthusiast. He became Daniel's pupil. "Let us do anything in the world" ... Ford, 1911 ... "that will widen our perceptions." Forget pastiche. What might a poet *learn* from these remarkable poets?

*   *   *

He might learn, to begin with, what lift and *élan* a mind's saturation in music brings to words.

> —When the nightingale sings ...

> —Quan lo rossinhols escria

(es-cri-a; three syllables, the last instantly echoed:)

> Ab sa

(and echoed again:)

> par la nueg e·l dia

And not the metronome but the musical phrase, two in the first line, three in the second, groups these rapid syllables. By 1918 Pound had an equivalent:

> When the nightingale to his mate
> Sings day-long and night late

—his assonance of *day* with the vowel of *mate* and *late* placed exactly where the anonymous lyricist placed *sa*. Marking [/] the points where the initial rhyme-sound moves inward, we may inspect the whole poem:

> Quan lo rossinhols escria/
> Ab sa/ par la nueg e·l dia,/
> Yeu suy ab ma bell' amia/
> 　　Jos la flor
> Tro la gaita/ de la tor
> Escria/: drutz, al levar!
> Qu'ieu vey l'alba/ e·l jorn clar.*

Flor and *tor* introduce a new sound to modulate that predominant short *a* into the *ar* of *levar* and *clar*. Across the final caesura the two vocalic motifs, *a* and *or*, confront one another, *alba* and *jorn*, as it were to simulate the sweet conflict of dawn (time to love) and day (time to part); thus *escria* sounds twice, from the birds of dawn, from the watchman of day. Pound's imitation, though it never satisfied him, is a miracle of analogous virtuosity:

> When the nightingale to his mate
> Sings day-long and night late
> My love and I keep state
> 　　In bower,
> 　　In flower,
> 　　'Till the watchman on the tower
> Cry:
> 　　"Up! Thou rascal, Rise,
> 　　I see the white
> 　　　　Light
> 　　And the night
> 　　　　　　Flies."

His *Light* is an auditory modulation of *late* as *clar* modulated *dia*, and as *flor* and *tor* prepare the ear for *jorn* so *Cry* imitates the sound of *rise* and *flies*.

* Semantic map:
> When the nightingale sings
> To his own, night and day,
> I am with my beloved
> 　　Under the flowers
> Till the guard of the tower
> Cries, lovers, arise!
> I see the dawn and the clear day.

A binding, a having-to-do-with, that joins in likeness, in difference and in modulation all the poem's materials, through which interactive web the syntactic movement flows, abandoning nothing: this is the deepest, the most persistent Provençal intuition. This intricate patterning within the explicit pattern offered a way of holding short poems together without recourse to fulfillment of a metrical contract. Pound waited three decades to use it overtly: in the 1951 Montanari translation, for instance—

> A swallow for shuttle, back,
> Forth, forth, back
>   from shack to
>   marsh track:
>   to the far
>   sky-line that's fading now

—not only the explicit virtuosity of the shuttling swallow, but the modulation from *marsh* to *far* to *fading*. Or in the choruses of the 1953 *Women of Trachis*—

> The great weight silent
>   for no man can say
> If sleep but feign
>   or Death reign instantly.

Or in a hundred details of the 1954 *Confucian Odes*—

> ... birds of the air
> flashed a white wing while fishes splashed
> on wing-like fin in the haunted pool. ...

—Provence brought time and again to the service of China.

A strategic inhibition against bringing details in a long poem to so intertextured a finish keeps such devices unobtrusive in the *Cantos*, until the last ones where all is detail, but, muted, they are everywhere present:

> Behind hill the monk's bell
> borne on the wind.   (Canto 49)
>
> Wine in the smoke-faint throat   (Canto 25)
>
> and in the boughs now are voices
> grey wing, black wing, black wing shot with crimson
>   (Canto 90)

*   *   *

One notes the monosyllables, and notes next that a Provençal poem when it interests Pound is a parataxis of sound. The language seems to welcome separations. Its words clip, bounding the clear distinct syllables modern French has slurred with terminal consonants modern French omits. *L'alba e·l jorn clar* zones its sounds as *l'aube et le jour clair* blurs them. In London, 1912, such examples were pertinent. To make English words new meant to make them once more separately audible: *Pallid the leash-men* as against *immemorial elms* and against a taste "all legato ... Elizabethan sonority blunted" that slurred and fused the separate words and syllables.

This led to a reconception of what he meant by music. His muse when he was 22 had been a pianist, Katherine Ruth Heyman. But by late 1914 he had at last heard Dolmetsch instruments, their pluck and wiry percussion, and by then he was prepared to understand what they meant. He bought a Dolmetsch clavichord with "Plus fait Douceur que Violence" inscribed inside the lid and learned to pick out tunes on it; he became (1917) the *New Age* music critic and described with astonishment what a London which thought the Dolmetsches faddish would put up with in concerts dominated by an instrument he came to abominate. "A 'song' is words set to py-ano music. It doesn't matter what words." "The Pye-ano, Ge-entlemen, the PYE-ano is the largest musical instrument known to man." "At its birth the forte-piano seems to have turned people's heads; even so sensible a man as Thomas Jefferson ordered a forte-piano." And in *Mauberley*, composed in a head full of London musical goings-on, he reminds us of the quality words assume when their counterpart rumbles among left-hand piano chords, writing

> Go, dumb – born book

for us to set against crisp *motz el son*, against for instance the delicate timing of his 1945 homage to Dolmetsch—

> Has he tempered the viol's wood
> To enforce   both the grave   and the acute?
> Has he curved us the bowl of the lute?

(The sibilants in that final line—Tennyson's "geese"—run counter to a pianoforte aesthetic; the lute welcomes them, as in Waller—

> How *s*weet and fair *s*he *s*eem*s* to be.)

And no sound, not even the sound of the piano, nothing but artisticness gathering up its skirts, could be said to sponsor the verse all England's flatbed presses were emitting, 1890, 1910, *et seq.*

> A frail hand in the rose-grey evening
> Kisses the shining keys that stir,

wrote Arthur Symons; and it is as much an effort to attend to the words one by one as to pronounce them one by one.*

*   *   *

Greek was one cure for this (*poikilothron' athanat' Aphrodita,* Pound shouted in the Greek theater at Siracusa, attempting to convince Yeats that "English verse wasn't CUT"). Arnaut Daniel's Provençal was another:

> Autet e bas entrels prims fuoills
> Son nou de flors li ram eil renc . . .

A man who begins a song with the phonemes *autet e bas,* or puts *prims* between *entrels* and *fuoills,* expects us to take pleasure in the separation, not the blending, of syllables, and in sound relieving, not prolonging, sound. Tennyson would not have been pleased. Not Daniel but Jaufre Rudel of the fulsome assonances would be the troubadour to interest a Tennysonian—

> Lanquand li iorn son lonc en mai
> m'es bels douz chans d'auzels de lonh,
> e quand me sui partitz de lai,
> remambra·m d'un'amor de lonh. . . .

---

* But the poem of Symons' that Pound printed in *Profile* and quoted in the *Pisan Cantos* opens with clipped monosyllables:

> I am the torch, she saith, and what to me
> If the moth die of me? I am the flame . . .

Pound was interested in this in 1910, when he cited it in *The Spirit of Romance*. But Rudel's effects appeal to a taste stark consonants offend—one modern commentator is reminded of de Vigny's "son du cor" echoing "au fond des bois"—and the Pound of 1912, who was soon to think that such taste led straight to the Pye-ano, noted that whereas Daniel does not pull words out of shape, Rudel's word-joinery will liquefy: "Dou-ou-ou-ous cha-ans da-u z-e-els d-e-e-e-e lo-o-o-onh," ran his pedagogic mockery, "Sw-e-e-eet so-ong o-of bi-i-irds a-a-a-a fa-a-a-ar." By way of contrast he exhibited two songs of Daniel's, "Autet e bas" and "L'aura amara," both making audible the sweet song of birds but neither one miming bird-song with ambient mellifluousness. In "L'aura amara" we have (as he put it still later) "the chatter of birds in autumn, the onomatopoeia obviously depends upon the '*utz*, -*etz*, -*encs* and -*ortz*' of the rhyme scheme, seventeen of the sixty-eight syllables of each strophe there included." In "Autet e bas" "Arnaut breaks the flow of the poem to imitate the bird call in '*Cadahus en son us*'," and repeats for six stanzas with different words but the same sounds this notation of their rising cadence, their isolated sharpness of attack.

F our separate times Pound has cited and praised these instances, in no case eliciting much show of response. Have his readers supposed he was dusting gadgets in a language museum? But he had reasons for being tenacious, and his fourth exposition (1935) of

> Cadahus
> En son us
>
> Mas pel us
> Estauc clus

("That again for six strophes WITH the words making sense") reached a comprehending reader. The following year Marianne Moore published "Bird Witted," which tells in straightforward sentences of something observed in Brooklyn, a mother bird feeding her young and then driving off a cat. (Arnaut, Pound had written late in 1911, derives from life as it is: he has "no gardens where three birds sing on every bough.") Miss Moore's birds inhabit no imaginary garden, nor is her diction smoothed off to accommodate felicities:

> Toward the high-keyed intermittent squeak
>   of broken carriage-springs, made by
> the three similar, meek-
>   coated bird's eye
> freckled forms she comes; and when
> from the beak
>   of one, the still living
>   beetle has dropped
> out, she picks it up and puts
> it in again.

Through this perfectly formal prose sentence the little birds clamor: *squeak . . . meek . . . beak. . . .* And the words are clinkered with consonants. To keep both the words' identities and the syntax intelligible, tongue and lips must separate word from word. We read "meek//coated/ /bird's eye//freckled/ /forms/ /she comes," the pause after *eye* enforced by a rhyme, the other pauses by consonantal impact or syntactic structure; and a line-break enforces the fledglings' fumble with a beetle which "has dropped/ /out."

    To find these effects felicitous we must take as our unit the whole stanza, and its syntax as well as its rhyme schemes; must hear it moreover in conjunction with the previous stanza, where the little birds sit "feebly solemn" and the salient rhymes are not on *eek* but on *ee*, and with the stanza following, where they preen feathers in silence and the rhymes fall silent likewise, so that one must trace the pattern to learn that "dressed" rhymes with "surfaced." The fourth stanza recalls mating-time, when the parent bird sang variations on *ute* and *ote*:

> . . . What delightful note
> with rapid unexpected flute-
> sounds leaping from the throat
>   of the astute
> grown bird, comes back to one from
> the remote
>   unenergetic sun-
>   lit air before
> the brood was here?

But now "How harsh / the bird's voice has become": harsh, as in
the sixth stanza the cat is assaulted with a jabbing of shrill sounds,
chills . . . fills . . . half kills . . . :

> and half kills
>   with bayonet beak and
>   cruel wings the
>   intellectual cautious-
> ly creeping cat.

"Bird Witted" is the closest approximation in English to one
quality of Arnaut's, an intricate refusal of prettiness, working close
to the bone. Its six stanzas, arrayed on the page, even look Daniel-
esque. And when we derive its technical felicities from its whole
structure (for in isolation most of the adept details seem either
awkward or accidental) we find ourselves stationed at the proper
distance to grasp its meaning as well, a meaning which runs from the
"bird witted" birds of the title to the "intellectual" cat of the
conclusion, articulating a parable of two forms of intelligence, a
parable the understanding may disengage from words that never
deign to discuss it. The cat, a foreseer of objectives, a cautious
strategist, is repulsed; the birds, always enwrapped in immediate
necessities, live in mustering at every instant their whole energies,
making in the process the various sounds of which poetic convention values only

> rapid unexpected flute-
> sounds leaping from the throat.

And cat-like human enterprise, we are sure, made the poem, to
simulate the bird-like functional vigor; incidentally to extend our
notion of what a poem can be, as did Arnaut when he set aside all
the Provençal precedents for melodious scene-setting and let twelve
rhymes on *-us* punctuate a refusal to be conventionally eloquent.
That poem ends,

> Arnaut loves, and ne'er will fret
> Love with o'er speech, his throat quaileth,
> Braggart voust's not to his fancying.

*   *   *

For many years the texture of such poems challenged Pound, a texture inseparable from their exploitation of consonantal boundaries, their sharp discrimination of word from word. The "word" is perhaps the most artificial element in prosody; one normally does not hear words; the junctures one hears are between phrases. Anyone who has listened in vain to foreign speech for the separate words he memorized in a classroom understands how alien to normal speaking is a cutting between word boundaries. And except when they handle things and name them, are a people without writing aware of "words"? The space was among the last written symbols to be invented; for centuries it seemed sufficient to set down a phonemic tune from side to side of the parchment, unbroken. And today's descriptive linguistics, reasonably comfortable with morphemes as units of meaning, nearly rejects the concept of the word.

With abrupt variations of pitch the careless ear may mistake for pauses, line after line of verse can run nearly unbroken—

> Let us go then, you and I . . .

> Only at nightfall ethereal rumors . . .

> Here I am, an old man . . .

The space enters this orthography for convenience, not as notation of how the lines are spoken. Ezra Pound by contrast typewrites

```
Pull   down   thy   vanity
                    Pacquin   pull   down     !
   The   green   casque   has   outdone   your   elegance,
```

striking the space bar not once but at least twice, and meaning by this gesture something intrinsicate to his feeling of how the lines sound and of how meanings are built up. And he does this whenever he types anything, the final text of a poem or the hastiest note, and did it the day he first possessed a typewriter, circa 1913, reproducing on the machine a gesture his hand always performed when it held a pen and marked with wide spaces the initial stroke of the new word. "Dissociate . . . ," said Remy de Gourmont, earning his homage.

"With usura"—with any decadence—"is no clear demarcation." A rare but recurrent temperament owns such zest for demarcation as a life-pattern. William Blake did not daub but engraved, driving the burin through the metal; it could go wrong or right, but could not approximate. And Blake saw decadence in any muddling about with line ("The beauty proper for sublime art is lineaments, or forms and features that are capable of being the receptacles of intellect") and the golden rule of art as of life in the "distinct, sharp, and wirey" bounding line, to efface which (Correggio, Rembrandt) was "to leave out life itself." "What is it that distinguishes honesty from knavery, but the hard and wirey line of rectitude and certainty in the actions and intentions?" And, "How do we distinguish the oak from the beech, the horse from the ox, but by the bounding outline?"

And Pound, whose own handwritten signature is a pattern of disjunctions,

> In nature are signatures
> needing no verbal tradition,
> oak leaf never plane leaf.
> (87/573:609)

"Oak leaf never plane leaf": five words with consonantal boundaries. For the moral virtue Blake the engraver attributed to outlines Pound the poet associated with bounded sounds, and preferably bounded terms. Enunciation had its morality. Discussing French decadence, he said that he had heard French *spoken* by Cocteau, and heard vigorous regional dialects full of humanity, but "most of the rest of the denizens wheeze, sniffle, and exude a sort of snozzling whnoff whnoff apparently through a hydrophile sponge." On another occasion he used very nearly the same phrases to describe decadent concert singing. On the other hand (citing Binyon—"a very courageous statement, and a sound one"): "melodious smoothness is not the characteristic of Dante's verse." Dante's!

Nor of Arnaut's. The need for elements, dissociable elements, was from student days the characterizing note of Pound's psyche, lost a while but recovered after Ford's roll. We need not wonder that he ultimately made it a moral criterion, nor that his poiesis welcomes ideograms, voiced as monosyllables and affirming semantic boundaries by their integrity of design on the page. In the late Cantos the Chinese monosyllables wear their tone indications (*motᵢ el son* driven into lexicography), whole pages devote inspection to bits of Byzantine semantics, and the lyric passages put on display discrete elements, phrases, single words:

<blockquote>
the great algae
color prediletto
the crystal body of air
deep green over azure
Sirenes σῆραγξ as crystal Σειρήν
dark hippocampi θελκτήριη
god's antennae.
(107/762:786)
</blockquote>

And this is the outcome of a process running from 1911, at an early stage of which an aborted book on Daniel's importance commenced by exhibiting a "Seafarer" with consonantal structures like rocks—

<blockquote>
May I for my own self song's truth reckon
Journey's jargon . . .
</blockquote>

putting *self*//*song's*//*truth* into its opening line and compelling us to hear them, craggy monosyllables, one at a time.

*   *   *

In Japan in the eighth century they "listened to incense"; "some arbiter burnt many kinds and many blended sorts of perfume, and the game was not merely to know which was which, but to give each one of them a beautiful and allusive name, to recall by the title some strange event of history or some passage of romance or legend. It was a refinement in barbarous times, comparable to the art of polyphonic rhyme, developed in feudal Provence four centuries later, and now almost wholly forgotten."

There are subject-rhymes, two sensibilities may rhyme, there are culture-rhymes. The Homeric simile rhymes some narrative event with a vignette; snow fills ten lines of *Iliad* XII to rhyme (alike, yet different) with hurtling missiles, and the reader of the snowfall passage at the end of Joyce's "The Dead" may detect a rhyme with the *Iliad*. Henry James rhymed Fellowship with the gesture of biting a neglected apple, and Ovid a scarlet curtain with the skin of Atalanta. The ceremony of Yeatsian rhymed stanzas renders rhymes audible or inconspicuous according as congruences are being ensheaved or simply iterated, and a Japanese poet without rhyming his sounds may rhyme a crow with the night.

The pine-tree in mist upon the far hill looks like a fragment of Japanese armour.

The beauty of the pine-tree in the mist is not caused by its resemblance to the plates of the armour.

The armour, if beautiful at all, is not beautiful *because* of its resemblance to the pine in the mist.

In either case the beauty, in so far as it is beauty of form, is the result of "planes in relation."

The tree and the armour are beautiful because their diverse planes overlie in a certain manner.

—So Pound, 1915, assaying a visual rhyme. Arnaut distributed concords the length of *canzoni*, sounds in each stanza rhyming with sounds in the next because the matter, stanza by stanza, accords. The *Cantos* affords a thesaurus of subject-rhymes. Many heroes rhyme with Odysseus, and a house of good stone rhymes with mountain wheat, strong flour, the mind of Agostino di Duccio, and the proportions among the plain arches at St. Hilaire in Poictiers.

THE INVENTION
OF LANGUAGE

Pisa, 1945, retrospect:

"forloyn" said Mr Bridges (Robert)
"we'll get 'em all back"
meaning archaic words and there had been a fine old fellow
named Furnivall and Dr Weir Mitchell collected

(80/507:541)

Despite Bridges' ambition, the *Cantos* is very likely the one
modern work in which the word *forloyn* can be found. The poem
also contains *rathe*, the lost positive of *rather*, and *Witte me thurh
crafte* borrowed from Layamon, and *trine* in a sequence with
duality and *tetrad* (with a nod to John Heydon, "Secretary of Nature"); also *dreory* and *bever* and *bikini* and *contraption*, and a note
on military philology:

the army vocabulary contains almost 48 words
one verb and participle one substantive ὕλη
one adjective and one phrase sexless that is
used as a sort of pronoun
from a watchman's club to a vamp or fair lady

(77/471:501)

94

—moreover judicious borrowings from the Greek, Latin, Chinese, Italian, French, Provençal, Spanish, Arabic and Egyptian Hieroglyphic languages; this list is not complete. And as for *The Waste Land* . . . ; and as for *Ulysses* . . . ; and one shrinks from a linguistic inventory for *Finnegans Wake,* where even Swahili components have been identified. The province of these works, as never before in history, is the entire human race speaking, and in time as well as in space: Sappho of Mitylene putting the signature of her dialect on Homer's *rosy-fingered* centuries after Homer, or the ambience of a Harvard philosophy seminar in the great days of German idealism evoked by Thos. Eliot M.A., amid careful abstractions, by the single word *Erhebung.*

This aplomb amid the multitudinous tongues of the world, moreover amid testimony to their constant change, has been possible for only a few decades, and is still not accessible to all readers. If we no longer think, with Swift and Johnson, that languages ought to be stabilized, we still feel that their proper condition is stability. The admission of *ain't* to a large American dictionary provoked newspaper hysteria in 1961–2. That in Canto 53 the same emperor appears indifferently as Tcheou Kong and Chao Kong causes many readers uneasiness outweighing the instruction the Canto affords, and a scholarly convention in citing the word *ideogramic* is to tag it [*sic*], meaning "not so in my dictionary." Words, since the 18th century, have seemed fixed upon a rigid and authorized grid, each little violation of which incites the Great Anarch.

Behind such feelings lies the notion of a stable shared world in which all men's senses participate and the features of which have been labelled by agreement, though different agreements obtain in Italy and in Sweden. *Gatto,* say the Italians for some reason, and *katt* the Swedes; it would be simpler if they said the same thing, but anyhow cats are cats. The linguistic contracts, being arbitrary, are fragile, and only the code book, Webster's or Larousse's, wards off unspeakable disorder. An alternative notion, that names should be left in place because they are somehow *right*, is traceable in theory to Plato's *Cratylus* but in practice to costive notions of correctness. Both positions were still seriously defended in the early 19th century. Both linger in the average literate psyche. Both were rendered obsolescent by the slow discovery of *language*, a complex coherent organism that is no more the sum of its constituent words than a rhinoceros is the sum of its constituent cells, an organism that can maintain its identity as it grows and evolves in time; that can remember, that can anticipate, that can mutate. Latin is not a dead language; everyone in Paris speaks it, everyone in Rome, everyone in Madrid. The poetic of our time grows from this discovery.

*   *   *

In January 1922, a matter of days before *Ulysses* was published, bookstore browsers could turn for the first time the pages of Otto Jespersen's *Language, Its Nature, Development and Origin*, a pioneer summary for non-specialists of the kind of understanding out of which Joyce worked. Five decades later the principles are familiar. We are to think not of babelized languages but of Language, a mesh of filaments uniting all human beings, binding all Frenchmen in one web of understanding, all Spaniards in another, between which webs, as between them and the webs that unite all Germans or all Englishmen, numerous sympathies of structure exist—

> The cat is brown
> Le chat est brun
> Die Katze ist braun

and thousands of nodal similarities—

England	*Sweden*	*Germany*	*Spain*	*Italy*	*France*		
cat	katt	Katze	gato	gatto	chat	. . .	. . .
moon	måne	Mond	luna	luna	lune	. . .	. . .
fish	fisk	Fisch	pez	pesce	poisson	. . .	. . .
flower	blomma	Blume	flor	fiore	fleur	. . .	. . .

The filaments run back in time likewise, binding us all to our dead ancestors. As we trace them back, such similarities merge, to become identities or to suggest them. ("The cords of all link back," Joyce wrote in an episode of *Ulysses* whose "art" is Philology, "strandentwining cable of all flesh," and did not omit to mime the process by fusing words, "strandentwining.") We are joined—this is the theme of Comparative Philology—as much to one another as to the dead by continuities of speech as of flesh. Twenty years after

Joyce died the analogy he intuited had grown so pervasive that exegetes of the ribonucleic acids were speaking of the DNA Code, genetics linked formally to Information Theory.

Cords are distinguishable within that cable: language families, to explicate which was a major intellectual achievement of the 19th century. What had once seemed unintelligible mutations—so that Johnson (1755) worked back from *fish* to the Saxon *fisc* but could make no connection with the Latin *piscis*—were seen to be so consistent they characterized for instance Romance and Teutonic strands, and so orderly one could talk, like Newton, of Laws. Thus between *piscis* with its Romance progeny *pesce, pez, poisson*, and the Teutonic *fisc* or *fish* or *Fisch*, there had intervened a massive slippage from *p* to *f* (*pater/father*; *plenus/full*; *pes/foot*) so uniform that along with eight other such modifications it helped isolate long ago the languages we call Teutonic. These nine consonantal transformations were neatly tabulated in 1822 by Jakob Grimm. The Great Consonant Shift ("Grimm's Law") was a new kind of historical event, different in quality from the Dorian Invasion or the building of Stonehenge: something a whole people had done without knowing they were doing it, controlled by their need to keep understanding one another, and so sharpening a familial identity they were not aware of possessing.

As such events differentiated languages out of the *Ursprache*, peoples came to share ways of experiencing the world. "How can you have 'PROSE'," Pound was to ask, "in a country where the chambermaid comes into your room and exclaims: 'Schön ist das Hemd!'" One senses that Hegel was possible only in German, and finds it natural that Locke in a language where *large* and *red* precede *apple* should have arrived at the thing after sorting out its sensory qualities, whereas Descartes in a language where *grosse et rouge* follows *pomme* should have come to the attributes after the distinct idea.

And history creates subtler alienations. "That was the real way to work things out": could any Englishman have composed that clause? Henry James wrote it. Its shading of *real* is not in the *O.E.D.* "Quiet fields, Anglican sainthood, accuracy of thought," wrote Ford Madox Ford, Englishman; "heavy-leaved, timbered hedge-rows, slowly creeping plough-lands moving up the slopes." All these are saturated with moral feeling, and *accuracy* draws virtue from its etymology, *ad* + *curare*, signifying the taking of care. "As far as I have gone it is accurate," wrote William Carlos Williams, American, signifying dogged persistence, and *accurate*, closing its mind to its etymology, denotes a flat absolute achieved. We tell which sentence is British, which American, by the cadence, and know accordingly what scope of feeling to accord the words, and do this so well we do not know we do it, do not even know, until someone makes us see, how much of what we suppose a dictionary can sort out (it cannot) is controlled by our sense of the voices cadence imitates. Dr. Williams' concern for "the American idiom" and his shaping of a metric that can flatten lilt—

> So much depends
> upon
>
> a red wheel
> barrow

—are interdependent functions in his poetic.

An un-English English was also discernible in Dublin, where Stephen Dedalus heard the Dean of Studies speak of a funnel.

—What funnel? asked Stephen.
—The funnel through which you pour the oil into your lamp.
—That? said Stephen. Is that called a funnel? Is it not a tundish?
—What is a tundish?
—That. The . . . the funnel.
—Is that called a tundish in Ireland? asked the dean. I never heard the word in my life.
—It is called a tundish in Lower Drumcondra, said Stephen laughing, where they speak the best English.

. . . As they do; for *tundish*, tun + dish, is an old English word, for some reason preserved in Ireland, whereas *funnel* entered England by way of Old French **founil* with Provençal cognates, from a Latin root, *infundibulum*. One need know none of this (as the dean does not) to sense with the dean that *tundish*, like any Saxon word beside a Romance synonym, sounds picturesque and "low" ("A tundish, said the dean reflectively. That is a most interesting word. I must look that word up. Upon my word I must. His courtesy of manner rang a little false.") And Stephen senses with a smart of dejection that he is speaking to a countryman of Ben Jonson, and thinks,

> —The language in which we are speaking is his before it is mine. How different are the words *home*, *Christ*, *ale*, *master*, on his lips and on mine! I cannot speak or write these words without unrest of spirit. His language, so familiar and so foreign, will always be for me an acquired speech. I have not made or accepted its words. My voice holds them at bay. My soul frets in the shadow of his language.

And Stephen Hero—by safe inference, James Joyce—read Skeat's *Etymological Dictionary* by the hour. We are told in the same sentence that his mind "was often hypnotized by the most commonplace conversation." "People seemed to him strangely ignorant of the value of the words they used so glibly," and when the dean said "I must look that word up. Upon my word I must," a dictionary entry and his sacred word lay stunned beneath adjacent mouthings of the same blank syllable.

In Skeat's *Etymological Dictionary* "the cords of all link back," woven by phonetic laws clearly understood and firmly stated. His Introduction popularized the subject for Joyce's generation. Though *care* resembles the Latin *cura*, he writes, we can see if we understand Grimm's Law and *ablaut* that they have no genetic connection. Other attractive analogies will not seduce us if we reflect that peoples who exchange words must be in touch (keep in mind realities: peoples). Behind every sound we utter extends a history of ordered changes and remote cultural transactions, traceable into a prehistory where research can discern some 461 relevant Aryan roots. (And beyond the roots? Perhaps such sounds as thunder? The future author of *Finnegans Wake* is attending.)

And Skeat's leisurely entries are civil to overused words, liberating the mind from the supposition, for instance, that Victorian custom invalidates the Anglo-Saxon credentials of *swoon*, a verb in which Joyce's interest has been noted. Joyce belonged to the first generation of young authors who could study their own language as historic process by browsing in such a work. Previous lexicography, deriving from Augustan norms, had taught not roots and developments but distinctions and discriminations. Pope's

> View him with scornful, yet with jealous eyes

is an exercise in distinguishing cognate vices, as his

> Blest with each talent and each art to please

is careful to distinguish endowments from skills. His

> ... were there one whose fires
> True Genius kindles, and fair Fame inspires

remembers that Fame is a speaking, hence a breath, inspiration a breathing into, hence directed breath, and Genius a power pro-creative, hence warm; and arrays these knowledges around its evocation of a kindled and insufflated flame. And Pope's

> ... vindicate the ways of God to Man

proposes, by alluding, an ambition cognate with Milton's

> ... justifie the wayes of God to men,

but stipulates, by differentiating *vindicate* from Milton's *justify*, a different procedure from Milton's and a different tone. *Justify* contains *jus* and *facere*, law and willed activity; Milton will catch hold of our minds and cause us to see that God's ways are compatible with law. *Vindicate* contains *vindex*, one who stands surety; Pope will map God's dispositions against the orderliness of neat language, and let us draw reassurance from their unemphatic niceness of fit, comparable to that of his rhyme-words, *can* and *Man*.

Latin roots in this way govern the best Augustan usage: not remote ancestors of our words but their present active monitors. Since Latin was in use when Johnson made his *Dictionary*, its Latin etymologies tell us not so much where the word came from as what norms ought still to be guiding it. Any other etymologies, Saxon for instance, are antiquarian; they offer to identify the frontier the word last crossed, by way of accounting for its presence among us. With no grasp of language families, with no hint that linguistic morphology follows laws, and with only a few thousand years since

Babel to contain all the borrowings and derivations that have ever occurred, ingenious people etymologized at whim. Johnson derived *crocodile* from Greek words meaning *saffron-fearer*, he did not say why, and was uncertain whether the peacock was named from its "peak" of head-feathers or from the French *beaucoq*. (He had the Latin *pavo* at hand, but no way of perceiving how Old English had made it into *pāwa* which became *pēa*.)

By contrast, the strandentwining cables of Skeat reach into a foretime Johnson could not guess at, and Skeat's father's generation thought impious. Converging evidences, geological, archaeological, biological, had but lately accustomed men's minds to a nearly immeasurable prehistory, wherein whole languages whose descendants we speak had perished. With room for the unrecorded, what was recorded grew intelligible, and the processes Skeat could document reflect not mysterious and arbitrary corruptions, but the migrations of peoples, and minds adopting new themes. "Tigers mourn Sikandar" (87/576:612) because Alexander reached India. Sheep and cows, tended by Saxons, receive French names, mutton and beef, in the conquering Normans' kitchens. Danish words come off Dublin tongues today in consequence of a 10th-century invasion (and when the young Joyce studied Ibsen's language he felt him a foster-father, a near-compatriot). And as one can hear to this day the words *gadzooks* and *forsooth* (sounded gadsoot, forsoo) in the speech of certain Panamanian Indians with whose ancestors the buccaneers consorted, so Joyce could hear obsolete English (*tundish, disremember*) in the speech of the Irish provinces, and Gaelic syntax ("She asked me was I going to *Araby*") in the sentences of people with no Gaelic. To open one's ears was to wander in a language museum. Later he lived in Trieste and in Zürich, assaulted by the living voices of half Europe.

Skeat's *Dictionary* appeared in four parts, 1879–82; this last date was also the year of Joyce's birth. In January 1884, when he was almost two, the first part of the *New English Dictionary* (A–Ant) was published. By the time he had commenced *Ulysses* it had reached the S's and T's. Its 125th and final fascicle is dated April 1928; several installments of the polyglot *Wake* were by then in print.

The insight behind the great Dictionary is that meanings, arrayed in chronological sequence, display a seamless intelligible continuity. To assist its sub-editors (among them W. M. Rossetti) hundreds of readers gathered hundreds of thousands of dated instances. One of the readers in later decades was W. H. D. Rouse, in whose *Classical Review* Ezra Pound was to find new texts of Sappho about 1912, and whose English *Odyssey* he was to correct in 1935. The slips poured in for decades; as early as 1879 they bulked 1¾ tons; the preliminary sub-editing of the verb *set* took one valiant man 40 hours, the final entry 40 days.

On his very different enterprises Joyce too worked from thousands of paper slips the words on which he checked off in coded colors as he distributed them through his pages. Like the *New English Dictionary*, the *Wake* was virtually a collaborative process; there survives a card—

> Dear Mr. Joyce
> The text is:
> ἐκπορενόμενον
> παρα πατρος
> The infinitive:
> ἐκπορενέσθαι
> The substantive
> το + Infinitive
>
> Sincerely yours
> Sam Beckett

This touches on Trinitarian relationships; if or how Joyce used it remains unascertained. Other friends meanwhile "prepared notes from books which interested the writer, although not more than a word or two might be included in the text." The complete *Wake* was published in 1939, when the complete *Dictionary* was just 11 years old.

More than coincidence brought Joyce's work and the Oxford lexicographers' within the compass of one lifetime. Skeat's *Dictionary* helped prepare Joyce's mind. An elder colleague of Skeat's, Richard Chenevix Trench, "gave the first impulse" to the *N.E.D.* by a paper read before the Philological Society in 1857, and this same

Trench (later Anglican archbishop of Dublin) had defined in 1851 the state of awareness, at length transmitted to Joyce by philological tradition, within which such a thing as *Finnegans Wake* was conceivable: "Many a single word ... is itself a concentrated poem, having stores of poetical thought and imagery laid up in it." Trench also reflected on the *signatura rerum*, the second scripture, Nature, which has evolved like language and asks to be read like a book. "Signatures of all things I am here to read," thinks Stephen at the beginning of the *Ulysses* episode whose title is Proteus, polymorphous nature, and whose art is Philology; and Pound writes in a late Canto,

> ... In nature are signatures
> needing no verbal tradition,
> oak leaf never plane leaf. ...
> (87/573:609)

*   *   *

Arcane interlude:

Oak leaf never plane leaf. And every oak leaf is a natural signature, signature of "the kind of intelligence"—Pound, 1950—"that enables grass seed to grow grass; the cherry-stone to make cherries." DNA transmits that writing. Ten years earlier he had been trying to persuade Santayana that it was in fact a kind of intelligence, and that it bore out the possibility that a language might be a system of natural signs: 人 man, 木 tree. When he found in Morrison's Chinese Dictionary the sign of the sun above the horizon, 旦 dawn (a Chinese says *tan*) he wrote beside it, "Magnificent ideogram—phanopoeia": his word for the casting of images on the visual imagination, and here a visual image of a thing visible.

> They who are skilled in fire
> shall read 旦 tan, the dawn
> Waiving no jot of the arcanum
> (91/615:649)

—for though *tan* has a natural sign that sign for its full interpretation still needs resonance with perhaps arcane experience. "All men," said Confucius, "eat and drink; few distinguish the flavors." So they who are skilled in olive-groves shall read γλαύξ (*glaux*).

Gaudier, skilled in forms, could read the primitive forms of many Chinese radicals at sight. Is a natural poetic language conceivable, based on such natural signs? Did the first men know what most clearly pertains to men? Pound once drafted an essay, "L'uomo nel Ideogramma," which began by noting the contents of the first men's world, earth, plants, sun, sky, moon, and went on to note the dominance of the human body in radical after radical. At Brunnenburg in 1958, returning once more in his last months of full vitality to Ernest Fenollosa's notes on Professor Mori's turn-of-the-century lectures, he paused over an anecdote "as old as the characters themselves," about how their inventor "struck the very chord of the elements so skilfully" that Heaven caused a rain of grain to fall, and the demons of night to whine. For the characters have a "very deep essence in them, in touch with the very spirit of the universe," and "men by their use may cause prosperity, or, on the contrary, may fall with great misfortune." He transcribed this into a sheaf of typed notes, where he also improved Fenollosa's glosses on an ancient gnome. It remains amid the scraps of an unwritten book, Ezra Pound's last apologie for poetry:

> Poetry speaks phallic direction
> Song keeps the word forever
> Sound is moulded to mean this
> And the measure moulds sound

*　　*　　*

The vision of Trench, gazing into the single word as if into a concentrated poem, had been trained by a half-century's revaluation of etymology, which no longer sought idle parallels but traced continuities of meaning from some root, always sensuous (earth, plants, sun, sky, moon, man) to which by metaphoric process all subsequent applications are referrable. As early as 1839 a two-volume *Dictionary of the English Language* had been dedicated to this principle. "To *spark* and to *speak* (D. Spreck-en), I consider to be the same word," wrote its compiler, Charles Richardson, "and to mean,—to throw out, to emit, to utter. We call a small particle of *light thrown out*, or emitted,—a *spark*: we call vocal, articulate sounds, *thrown out*, emitted, uttered,—speech. But *spark*, or *speech* means (anything) *thrown out*: all other respective applications, are consequential or metaphorical. ...." Richardson guessed right, though the root sense (cf. Lat. *spargere*) is rather to sow than to emit. Even when, as commonly, he relates words modern scholarship disjoins ("May not the *blue*, formerly *blewe* skye, be the *blew*-en or blown skye; the sky from which the clouds are *blown*, dispersed?") he has hold of a sound principle, that where morphologies are continuous so are meanings, but his knowledge did not permit an adequate critique of morphologies. "To Etymology, then, the lexicographer must first resort. ... When the intrinsic meaning is fixed, every lexicographical object is firmly secured." This is overbold (*buxom* is no longer secured to its ancestor *buhsum*, obedient) but the impulse is sound. Richardson's most fanciful etymologies, like those of his master Horne Tooke, undertake to make language intelligible, an interrelated organism which mind and experience have bred. ("And if that be etymology," wrote Tooke, "barely to find out a similar word in some other language, the business of the etymologist is perfectly idle and ridiculous." He might have been thinking of Johnson's crocodile, "saffron-fearer").

* * *

Horne Tooke's *Diversions of Purley*, a great compilation of willful inspired guesswork from which all English insight into etymology came to derive, was borrowed from the Boston Library Society by the 26-year-old Ralph Waldo Emerson on 26 February 1829, and returned nine days later. In 1844 Emerson wrote in "The Poet" of language as "fossil poetry," a phrase Trench quotes to reinforce his own remark that the single word is a concentrated poem. Trench instigated the *N.E.D.* And we shall see Emerson inspiring another willful genius, Ernest Fenollosa, the Horne Tooke of sinology, for whom all poetry "was once in the language itself, and still underlies the dry bones of even our dictionaries."

Every word, a metaphor, perhaps several degrees deep, still has the power to flash meaning back and forth between apparently divergent and intractable planes of being. The prehistoric peoples who created language were necessarily poets, since they discovered the whole harmonious framework of the universe and the essential interplay of its living processes. We should find the whole theory of evolution (which our selfcentered Aryan consciousness afterwards forgot) lying concrete in our etymologies.

"Give examples from Skeat," he reminded himself in the same notebook, working out his presentation of the Chinese Written Character which was to encourage Ezra Pound (1914) to describe the poetic image not as a thing called by another thing's name but rather as "a radiant node or cluster": a knot, we shall also later see, in an invisible cable.

*   *   *

The etymological cable runs back, for "our" family at least, to Indo-European ancestors and pre-Sanskrit roots. And to what beginning? A question for a Romanticist. Herder (*Ursprung der Sprache*, 1772) imagines the first vocabulary collected from the sounds of the world: "From every sounding being echoed its name." Hence Stephen Dedalus: "Listen: a four-worded wavespeech: seesoo, hrss, rsseeiss, oos. Vehement breath of waters amid seasnakes, rearing horses, rocks. In cups of rocks it slops: flop, slop, slap." And hearing the speech of all things and reading their signatures, the bard composes on their behalf utterances pervaded by their rhythms:

> Under the upswelling tide he saw the writhing weeds lift languidly and sway reluctant arms, hising up their petticoats, in whispering water swaying and upturning coy silver fronds. Day by day: night by night: lifted, flooded, and let fall. Lord, they are weary: and, whispered to, they sigh. Saint Ambrose heard it, sigh of leaves and waves, waiting, awaiting the fullness of their times, *diebus ac noctibus injurias patiens ingemiscit.*

In composition rich with ceremony, thought the Symbolists, lies a poet's vocation. Mysterious, sacerdotal psychic rituals, transcending science, can blend our vocables with the remote impulses which licit speaking no longer satisfies.

For Stephen and Saint Ambrose, as for Mallarmé,

> Le Maître, par un oeil profond, a, sur ses pas,
> Apaisé de l'éden l'inquiète merveille,
> Dont le frisson final, dans sa voix seule, éveille
> Pour la Rose et le Lys le mystère d'un nom.

Mallarmé's Master, capitalized like Christ, is the "priest of the eternal imagination," composing the trouble leaves and waves have sighed to enunciate since Eden's loss terminated their radiant declarations. He gives voice on behalf of the voiceless flowers, and common words, rose and lily, acquire in his utterance "le mystère d'un nom," the value of each word discriminated and released. So the word finds speech. So *speech* finds speech. Common expressions are transubstantiated: Joyce found no more eloquent metaphor for the artist than the priest, in whose hands "the bread and wine of common experience" alter nothing of their appearance but nevertheless are changed, to afford spiritual as well as bodily food.

When Pound noted (1913) among the poetic kinds certain passionate simplicities "beyond the precisions of the intellect"— Guido's

> Perch' io non spero di tornar già mai
> Ballatetta, in Toscana

—common Italian words from which Eliot in turn was to make

> Because I do not hope to turn again

using only eight of the commonest words in English—or Yeats's

> The fire that stirs about her, when she stirs

—his attention, with less ceremony than Mallarmé's, was upon just such a mystery, the rare cooperation of genius with common speech: neither the laconic expertise of a Flaubert ("Comme elle était très lourde, ils la portait alternativement") nor the adoption of that "real language of men" which is but another persona, but the power to charge simple vocables with all that they can say. He was to labor all his mature life to bring the *Cantos* into the domain of such intensities, and achieve the way of it finally—

> So slow is the rose to open
> (106/752:777)
>
> .   .   .
>
> but the light sings eternal
> (115/794:24)
>
> .   .   .
>
> over Amazon, Orinoco, great rivers
> (106/753:778)

—only when midway through his eighth decade the whole poem seemed to be falling apart in his hands.

If such power, as experience suggests, is latent (though rarely released) in the simplest words, one would like to characterize the words more exactly. Are they the oldest? They ought to be somehow the core of a language, identifiable by tracing its history backward. Mid-19th-century England abounded in amiable enthusiasts for Saxon roots. The "fine old fellow / named Furnivall" (1825–1910) whose repute is alluded to in the *Pisan Cantos* (and who was editor-in-chief of the *N.E.D.* for a while) made a point of writing Fore-words rather than Pre-faces to the Early English Texts he edited; Bridges (who said of the old words "We'll get 'em all *back*") admired Doughty, much of whose *Dawn in Britain* Pound read aloud to Yeats one wartime winter; Doughty in turn was indebted to the *Speechcraft* (i.e. Grammar) of William Barnes, who proposed *sunprint* or *flameprint* to replace *photograph, sleepstow* for *dormitory*, and *pitches of suchness* for *degrees of comparison*, drawing always on the "wordstores of the landfolk." The time's enthusiasm for Anglo-Saxon studies was transmitted to Pound by Professor Ibbotson at Hamilton; it led in 1911 to his *Seafarer*

> (Bitter breast-cares have I abided,
> Known on my keel many a care's hold)

—eloquent eccentricity of diction akin to Hopkins', though protected by the convention of a translation; used once again, explicitly *as* archaism, in Canto I

> (Circe's this craft, the trim-coifed goddess)

and thereafter abandoned. There were less quirky ways, he had decided, to purify English.

* * *

The Romantic quest for purity, the one Pound's generation inherited, took the form of a tracing backward. Wordsworth went back to a pre-urban diction, still accessible in strata of society not yet (1799) urbanized, whose denizens "hourly communicate with the best objects from which the best part of language is originally derived." More daring speculation, for instance Herder's, had wondered about that original derivation; he imagined early man naming sounding things with the sounds they made, and naming non-sounding things with cries prompted out of some *sensorium commune* where all senses intertwine. Though "lightning does not sound," it can be expressed by "a word . . . that gives the ear, with the help of an intermediary sensation, the feeling of suddenness and rapidity which the eye had of lightning": a less plausible suggestion in England than in Herder's Germany, where the word is *Blitz*. And was this first language, asks Herder, "eine Sammlung von Elementen der Poesie?"—"A Dictionary of the Soul, at once mythology and wondrous epic of the actions and voices of all being! Thus a stable mythopoeia for the passions and the mind!— What more is poetry?"

This first language, as Herder understood better than his elder contemporaries the Universal Grammarians, would have been an affair of sounds, not of ideas (the affinities of ideas are with writing); and as to what these sounds may have been like, there was already available the analogy of Sanskrit, being investigated as were so many remote tongues in those days by French Jesuit missionaries. Herder had been told enough about it to believe in 700 basic Bengalese roots corresponding to the elements of reason. By 1788 the resemblances among Sanskrit, Greek and Latin had suggested to Sir William Jones the common source we now call Indo-European, to which is ascribed for instance the root lexicographers write *DA. In *The Waste Land*, whose author (1921) was less than ten years out of a Sanskrit classroom, DA is the voice of the god in the Brihadaranyaka Upanishad speaking thrice out of thunder, as though dictating elements in Herder's Dictionary of the Soul. DA becomes *Datta*, give, *Dayadhvam*, sympathize, *Damyata*, control: an etymology which makes sympathy and control not a sentiment and an interference but forms of giving. Primitive wisdom; and we can sense how *Datta* of the heavenly injunction has ravelled from language to language, culture to culture, by way of a Latin past participle to an English noun: the mere "data" beneath which minds perish. And by appending to the three Sanskrit thunderclaps a medley of the subsequent tongues of Europe, Eliot invokes some two centuries' philological effort to recover the deepest memories of the tribe. It was with the example of a scholarship committed in that way to finding the immemorial energies of language that he perceived how the most individual parts of a poet's work "may be those in which the dead poets, his ancestors, assert their immortality most vigorously," and also how in language used with right attention "a network of tentacular roots" may reach "down to the deepest terrors and desires."

*   *   *

The voices of *The Waste Land* agitate a Romantic darkness where crazed women drown, ruined kings wait on their thrones, and questers for the Grail ride among perilous rocks. The poem's philology rhymes with such occasions. A romantic quest for the primitive, for early man giving tongue to impassioned communion with thunder and falling water, had united with romantic Orientalism (Xanadu) to draw the philological imagination back through Sanskrit to Indo-European roots. Men engaged on research commonly suppose they are doing it because it is there to be done, like housecleaning; but the intuitions that drive them have frequently been divined by poets, the ventriloquists of social need. Thus amid the 19th century's dark sensuality there stirred, first in France, then in Germany, the appeal of a corrective sensibility, long ago lost with the Provençal language, and again to be had at the cost of disengaging, like sword from stone, Arnaut's and Sordello's craft from the look of degenerate Latin and misspelt French. In that effort the morphology of the Romance languages was set in order. Friedrich Diez (1794–1876), whose *Grammatik* (1836–44) and

Etymologisches Wörterbuch (1853) did for the Romance tongues what Grimm had done for the Teutonic, had commenced by writing two books on the troubadours at the instigation of Goethe.

Old Goethe, when Diez at 24 paid him a visit of homage, had just perceived virtue in the newly published *Choix des Poésies des Troubadours* of François J. M. Raynouard, where he saw clarities worth German attention. But

> Doutz brais e critz
> Lais e cantars e voutas
> Aug del auzels qu'en lor latins fant precs

—what a jargon! Latin, Italian, French and Spanish we know; this seems all four and yet none. And does "Doutz brais . . ." even represent Arnaut's language correctly? "Moutz braills . . .", says another manuscript; "Motz braus . . .", another; "Los braid . . .", a third. Raynouard himself was driven to compiling a Comparative Grammar of the Latin languages of Europe and collecting the materials of a six-volume *Lexique Roman* to aid in underwriting textual decisions and penetrating meanings. His persistence, like Diez's, like Goethe's, like Robert Browning's (who struggled in the 1830's with the songs of Sordello in virtual philological darkness) attests to a conviction, reinforced by Dante's authority, that some lack of the mind, obscurely felt as one feels a protein deficiency, was assuageable there: a need for mental landscapes in full sunlight, for sound not muffled by Venusberg drapery but cutting across concordant sound, for flowers and trees clearly seen, for unpowdered hair, for will not trammelled by *la politesse*. To recover these poems from what seemed almost random scribal markings, like combing a faint message out of static, entailed for Diez finally a *chef d'œuvre* of linguistics, displaying with the aid of laws stated by Grimm and others the gradual differentiation of Latin into seven or eight tongues, texts registering this process century by century as fossil bones the differentiation of phylae.

Such achievements were in a way like Arnaut's own: they educed and defined intricate order; and early in our century young Ezra Pound, who did not suffer pedantry gladly, carried from his classrooms not only what W. P. Shepard and Hugo Rennert could tell him about Provençal poems but the habit of thinking that the Romance tongues, "Provençal, Italian, Spanish, French, Portuguese, Catalan, Roumanian and Romansch," were at first simply "ways of speaking Latin somewhat more corruptly than the Roman merchants and legionaries spoke it": a paradigm of complex, orderly change held in the mind. Soon, in *The Spirit of Romance*, whole literatures were being examined on that principle, differentiation yielding occasion for novelties and new masteries.

Inheriting a century's work, young students thought no longer of fixed and authorized languages of which dialect and degenerate versions annoy the litterateur. But to think of languages in constant change means to think of people speaking them, singing them, thinking in them: one reason the *Cantos* resonate with so many hundred voices. It means to think also of coherence, not "correctness": Provençal is a *patterned* variation from Latin, not a clot of random misspellings, and a canzone is a still more tightly patterned integrity discernible within the Provençal: sounds and words and images and affirmations unfolding, refolding, answerable to the unity of one man's thought. Patterns of thought, moreover, have their morphologies and affinities, and the 20th Canto, opening its constatation of Provençal quality with the word "Sound," bounds that quality by adducing Homeric, Catullian, Propertian detail:

> Sound slender, quasi tinnula,
> Ligur' aoide: Si no'us vei, Domna don plus mi cal,
> Negus vezer mon bel pensar no val.
> Between the two almond trees flowering,
> The viel held close to his side;
> And another: s'adora.
> "Possum ego naturae
> non meminisse tuae!" Qui son Properzio ed Ovidio.

Five languages here, a thread of clear song, clear sight, clear passion running through them. "Sound slender" is not "slender sound," but a willed patterning, against usage, as music patterns random sonorities: an aural patterning, moreover, the consonant structure (s/nd) repeated, the vowel modulated, a new syllable reaching forward to "quasi tinnula" which comments ("little bell") on the percussive double ictus the line began with. "Quasi tinnula" in turn resumes the liquids and nasals of "sound slender," and inblends a memory of the "voce carmina tinnula" of Catullus' epithalamion (*Carmen 61*, 13). Then the bride of the epithalamion—this is also a nosegay of women—is set off by the Odyssean Siren of the "sharp song" ("Ligur' aoide"); the words are not quite in Homer just as "quasi tinnula" is not quite in Catullus, but Homer's words float above these words, their persistent *n*'s an unwritten counterpoint:

ἐγγύθεν ὀρνυμένη, λιγυρὴν δ' ἔντυνον ἀοιδὴν

[XII-183]

Then bride and siren become a Provençal *Domna* as Bernart de Ventadorn sings the words a later Canto will render

> "And if I see her not,
> no sight is worth the beauty of my thought."
> (92/612:652)

Then the flowering trees frame a glimpse of the singer with his viel; Cavalcanti's voice speaks in Italian of adoration

> (Una figura de la donna mia
> S'adora, Guido, a San Michele in Orto, . . .
> La voce va per lontane cammina: —*Sonetto XXXV*)

Propertius proposes that the lady's nature ("naturae tuae": not her face or figure) cannot be effaced from the mind, its "bel pensar"; and a modern Italian voice, to answer the modern English the passage began with, utters syllables still close to the sounds Ventadorn heard daily, identifying the quality we have encountered as Propertian and Ovidian.

That, grown here like a few clear crystals on a thread, was the quality so many minds in the previous century had toiled after, relating and sorting out languages to disengage it from. Pound's patterning of sound ("the vi*el* he*l*d c*l*ose" for instance reaffirming liquid sounds from "a*l*mond trees *fl*owering," which liquids in turn restate Ventadorn's ca*l*, be*l* and va*l*) has an intricacy learned from Arnaut: craft hard won, and won by understanding that Arnaut made music also, and by visiting the Ambrosiana (Milan) in quest of the only two settings of his we have. There, under the eye of Achille Ratti the librarian (later Pope Pius XI*) he copied from the two sides of a 14th-century page the music to the second canzon ("Chansson do'ill mot son plan e prim") and the eighteenth ("Lo ferm voler q'el cor m'intra"), staves with square notes that clarified pitch intervals though he did not know how to sing them. Canto 20 preserves the shelf mark: *71 R sup.*

It was the summer of 1911; he was 25, *en route* to Giessen and Ford. He took the copied music to Freiberg on a visit of homage to Emil Levy, "old Levy" (then 56), the only man, Professor Rennert had said in Pennsylvania, who "knows anything about Provençal." The Canto continues:

> And he said: "Now is there anything I can tell you?"
> And I said: "I dunno, sir," or
> "Yes, Doctor, what do they mean by *noigandres?*"
> And he said: "Noigandres! NOIgandres!
> "You know for seex mon's of my life
> "Effery night when I go to bett, I say to myself:
> "Noigandres, eh, *noi*gandres,
> "Now what the DEFFIL can that mean!"

For Levy had inherited Diez and Raynouard's responsibilities; his eight-volume supplement to Raynouard's *Lexique* had been appearing since 1892. (The last volume, which Carl Appel finished up, is dated 1925, seven years after his death.) And what the devil *noigandres* may mean is a characteristic scholar's perplexity. Pound encountered the word in Canello's edition of Arnaut (1883), the 13th canzon, the final line of the first stanza. Arnaut had commenced the stanza,

> Er vei vermeills, vertz, blaus, blancs, gruocs
> Vergiers, plans, plais, tertres e vaus

* Hence
> "I knew but one Achilles in my time
> and he ended up in the Vatican"
>   (80/502:536)
and
> "and the Pope's manners were so like Mr. Joyce's,
> got that way in the Vatican, weren't like that before"
>   (38/187:194)

—a parataxis of sharp-cut perceptions, one word apiece:

> Vermeil, green, blue, peirs, white, cobalt,
> Close orchards, hewis, holts, hows, vales,

—so Pound rendered it about 1917, tessellating a handful of the "old words" Robert Bridges prized. Wordsworth's landscapes are not offered in that staccato way. Arnaut alliterates the perceptions into groups but preserves their identity as separate acts of the mind, mapped onto separate words and lute-notes. He goes on:

> Eil votz dels auzels sona e tint
> Ab doutz acort maitin e tart

(*Tint* ... *tart*, half rhyme the bird-songs, quasi tinnula; and *tart* with *acort* and *tint* with *maitin*: Pound's English describes an effect it couldn't imitate:

> And the bird-song that whirls and turns
> Morning and late with sweet accord).

Daniel proceeds:

> Som met en cor qu'ieu colore mon chan

These things, the landscape and the birds, staples of Provençal song but here seen afresh though for the thousandth time, all these bestir his heart, he says, to color his song with (we may say) a rhyme to the birds and fields and hues, rhyme fetched not from the scene before him but from the mind: a magical "flower of which the fruit is love"—

> D' un' aital flor don lo fruitz sia amors

—whereupon, alas, we collide with the incomprehensible word:

> E jois lo grans, e l'olors de noigandres.

—"and joy its seed, and the perfume"—? —*de noigandres.*

A vexing anticlimax: one wants to follow the fine orchestration of sight and thought and sound to its close, and is made to taste seminar perplexities. Such a word is the lexicographer's despair. If it exists at all it exists here only, as for Greek lexicographers do many of the words in Sappho, so all we can do is guess at its meaning here. And it may not exist at all; the manuscripts chatter a dissident babel: nuo gaindres, nul grandes, notz grandres . . . ; and comparing a later display of variants, Toja's of 1960, we find even these transcriptions disputed, the scribes' very letters shifting about under inspection. Signor Canello in 1883 speculated for half a page of fine print; leaning on Raynouard's *Lexique*, he fancied some kind of nut, nutmeg or walnut, and conjured up cognate forms of which a French correspondent in turn doubted the existence. And Levy's job was emending and extending Raynouard. One sympathizes with his bedtime ritual.

And some years before the young American's visit Levy had solved the problem, divining (after six months, the Canto bids us realize) that the second part of *noigandres* must be a form of *gandir* (protect, ward off); then *enoi* is cognate with modern French *ennui*; and the word comes apart neatly into *d'enoi gandres*, wards off ennui; and the line reads,

> e jois lo grans, e l'olors d'enoi gandres

—"And joy is its seed, and its smell banishes sadness." He entered this triumphant emendation, complete with Arnaut's reconstructed line, under *gandir* in his great *Provenzalisches Supplement-Wörterbuch*, page 25, Vol. IV (G–L), 1904, where it would have eluded Pennsylvania inquirers await for the volume that should treat of N. But one member of Prof. Rennert's seminar was rewarded with the solution he went to Freiburg for (we are not to suppose that Levy spoke that day only of his six months' bafflement); and Pound's text and final translation, first published in *Instigations*, concur with Lavaud's 1910 edition (which he cites) in following Levy's reading:

> . . . Bestir my heart to put my song in sheen
> T'equal that flower which hath such properties,
> It seeds in joy, bears love, and pain ameises.

Arnaut has conjured into existence, or evoked from "quasi-allegorical descriptions of the tree of love," a lover's pharmaceutical flower, the color of which (and what would its colors be?) he will emulate by the color of his song (what are music's colors?).

Continuing the 20th Canto, Pound stated a corresponding ideal landscape—

> Wind over the olive trees, ranunculae ordered
> By the clear edge of the rocks
> The water runs, and the wind scented with pine
> And with hay-fields under sun-swath.

("Sun-swath" might be Hopkins: the band of sunlight changing the field's colors as mowing does.) He peopled it with ideal personnel, the stone-carver of the Tempio Malatestiana, sundry painters of Venus, men whose visual sensibility rhymes with the Provençal *motz el son*; he is emulating Provence in the very act of discriminate subject-rhyming:

> Agostino, Jacopo and Boccata.
> You would be happy for the smell of that place
> And never tired of being there, either alone
> Or accompanied.

Happy and *smell* and *never tired* reconstellate components of Arnaut's line, lifted now from philology and from gardens of allegorical trees to natural delight: *jois, olors, d'enoi gandres*. And the Canto's opening word, "Sound," recurs, transsensualized:

> Sound: as of the nightingale too far off to be heard

—a conception to fascinate a neo-Platonist. The dance proceeds:

> Sandro, and Boccata, and Jacopo Sellaio;
> The ranunculae, and almond,
> Boughs set in espalier,
> Duccio, Agostino; *e l'olors*
> The smell of that place—*d'enoi gandres.*
> Air moving under the boughs,
> The cedars there in the sun,
> Hay new cut on hill slope,
> And the water there in the cut
> Between the two lower meadows; sound,
> The sound, as I have said, a nightingale
> Too far off to be heard.

"Sound/ the sound/ as I have said": three echoes; and "as of" has now vanished from the construction: we are hearing this

inaudible sound in the three words "too far off," words here
accessible to the ear as they were not when they first filled a dropping
cadence in mid-line. Then sound yields vision, the anthology of
ladies the Canto began with blending into that ideal woman the
Cantos so often allow us to glimpse as lyric ecstasies terminate. One
word asserts that another canzon of Arnaut's produces her:

> And the light falls, *remir*,
> From her breast to thighs.

*   *   *

That single word—it is characteristic of alien words in the
Cantos—governs concentric fields. It is first of all two musical
syllables, their pure sound played against the surrounding lexical
texture. It is second, in a Provençal dictionary, a verb of seeing,
germane to the evocation of revealing light. Its affinities, third,
are with the Latin *mirari*, to wonder at, and the Vulgar Latin
mirare (whence Old French *mirer*), to look at with attention:
there is more than a simple inspection here, there is rapture. And
fourth, a master has transubstantiated it for the wonder of the
elect, as the dawn-sign is for those who are skilled in fire. The
reader of Arnaut Daniel, or of the second chapter of *The Spirit of
Romance*, will recognize in

> the light falls, *remir*
> from her breast to thighs

elements from the end of the fourth stanza of Arnaut's twelfth canzon—

> Quel seu bel cors baisan rizen discobra
> E quel remir contral lum de la lampa,

Pound's dealings with which, in three separate translations he has
printed, amount to asserting that Arnaut by linguistic alchemy
elicited a re-mirroring from *remir*, her flesh as if luminous.

E quel remir contral lum de la lampa. Referred to a dictionary,
the words say "And look at her against the lamplight," the *quel*
being pronominal, object of the looking. Pound took the *quel* as
subject to the verb, not object, denoting her body which puts
forth a re-mirroring of the lamplight. His 1909 version has "her

fair body, with the glamor of the lamplight about it"; his 1912
version, "glamor of the light reflected"; his last, catching some of
the glancing intricacy,

> Yes, that she kiss me in the half-light, leaning
> To me, and laugh and strip and stand forth in the lustre
> Where lamp-light with light limb but half engages.

In *The Spirit of Romance* he finds a parallel effect in Juan Mena's
line "Y dar nueva lumbre las armas y hierros": "And the arms
give forth new (or strange) reflections." "Nueva lumbre" was a
phrase he saved until Canto 106, where it radiates in apposition to
"deep waters reflecting all fire."

*　　*　　*

"But the great thing to remember is that all this poetry was
once in the language itself, and still underlies the dry bones of even
our dictionaries. Every word, a metaphor, perhaps several degrees
deep, still has the power to flash meaning back and forth between
apparently divergent and intractable planes of being."—Fenollosa.

E quel remir.

*　　*　　*

E quel remir. Earlier in that canzon she (perhaps the wife of
Guillem de Buovilla?) had thrown over Arnaut her indigo mantle,
to shield him from vulgar eyes the day they kissed. This perhaps
reminds the seventh Canto to rhyme her skin's luminous glamour—
remir—with the translucence of Ovid's scarlet curtain—

> cum super atria velum
> Candida purpureum simulatas inficit umbras:

which is a simile for the running Atalanta's naked skin, the flush
suffusing the white:

> Eleanor!
> The scarlet curtain throws a less scarlet shadow
> Lamplight at Buovilla, e quel remir
> And all that day
> Nicea moved before me
> And the cold grey air troubled her not
> For all her naked beauty, bit not the tropic skin. . . .
>   (7/26:30)

—joining Arnaut Daniel's visionary world with Ovid's and with a modern possibility (in foggy London). And the troubadour is present only by the grace of three Provençal words.

*   *   *

For language creates its characteristic force fields. A whole quality of apprehension inheres in its sounds and its little idioms. If Arnaut enjoyed an aesthetic of "clear sounds and opaque sounds," his language afforded and differentiated them. That a mind thinking in Provençal corresponds with the quality of vision that relates with imagined flushed skin the less scarlet shadow of a scarlet curtain, this one may sense without being instructed in the unstated system of allusion that joins these details in the seventh Canto. Words characterize languages; languages are discriminated phases of Language; Language is the total apprehension, in time and space, of the human mind, that labyrinthine marvel. Philology, in sorting out such matters—not always knowing what subtleties it sorted— permitted Pound's generation the vision of languages as inter- textured, cognate systems of apprehension, to each its special virtù.

"Very often," we read in *The Spirit of Romance*, "a Romance or Latin word stands between two English words, or includes them: thus in the *Pervigilium Veneris* 'nemus resolvit comam' can scarcely be translated 'the grove unbinds its hair'; yet the Latin phrase is more picturesque than 'puts forth its foliage'; the word *coma* is used for hair, foliage, standing corn, grass, indifferently:—thus in Gaelic 'RUN' means 'mystery' or 'the beloved'."

Such complexities, such characterizing spreads of meaning, in 1910 are welcomed; in 1750 one tried not to think of them, so scandalously did they violate the convention of things plainly labelled.

And Pound's next stop was into the domain of radiant gists we call ideograms.

WORDS SET FREE

As language changes something happens to old poems, the range of whose words changes. That is one reason why "what happens when a new work of art is created is something that happens simultaneously to all the works of art which preceded it." How do words found in 1611 stir us now?

> Fear no more the heat o' the sun,
>   Nor the furious winter's rages;
> Thou thy worldly task hast done,
>   Home art gone, and ta'en thy wages;
> Golden lads and girls all must
> As chimney-sweepers, come to dust.

"Golden lads": fine words to caress our post-Symbolist sensibilities. English lads, perhaps, with yellow hair; "golden," because once precious when they lived; "golden," touched with the nobility and permanence of gold (that royal metal, colored like a cold sun, in which wages are paid), as now, gone home, they receive the wages of immortality; "golden," in contrast to "dust": a contrast of color, a contrast of substantiality, a contrast of two immemorial symbols, at once Christian and pagan: the dust to which all sons of Adam return, the gold by which human vitality braves time; dust, moreover, the environment of chimney-sweepers, against whose lot is set the promise of shining youth, *la jeunesse dorée*, who may expect to make more of life than a chimney-sweeper does, but whom death at last claims equally. "Golden," magical word, irradiates the stanza so that we barely think to ask how Shakespeare may have found it.

Yet a good guess at how he found it is feasible, for in the mid-20th century a visitor to Shakespeare's Warwickshire met a countryman blowing the grey head off a dandelion: "We call these golden boys chimney-sweepers when they go to seed."

And all is clear? They are shaped like a chimney-sweeper's broom. They come to dust when the wind disintegrates them. And as "golden lads," nodding their golden heads in the meadows around Stratford, the homely dandelions that wilt in the heat of the sun and would have no chance against the furious winter's rages, but need never confront winter because they turn to chimney-sweepers and come to dust, would have offered Shakespeare exactly what he needed to establish Fidele's death in *Cymbeline* as an easy, assimilable instance of nature's custom.

Death as the blowing of a common flower: that is how he seems to have understood what he was writing. Then very early in the play's career, perhaps on the afternoon of the first performance if there were no Warwickshire ears in the Globe to hear that Warwickshire idiom, the dandelions and their structure of meaning simply dropped out. Yet for 350 years no one has reported a chasm. Even in the great age of conjectural emendations no editor emends "golden" to some more assimilable word. Also no one remarks upon its beauty. Hanmer or Theobald may have thought it "incorrect" but authentic, scribbled without pause for a second thought, in one of the thousand lines Ben Jonson wished his great colleague had blotted. One sign of Augustan dissatisfaction is detectable: in 1749 William Collins felt moved to rewrite the entire song, omitting among many other words the word "golden."

But we, the heirs of Mallarmé and Valéry and Eliot, do not simply pass over "golden" but find it richly Shakespearean, its very indefiniteness interacting as though chemically with the other words in the poem.

Hanmer or Theobald, with Dr. Johnson, supposed that words denoted things. A language is simply an assortment of words, and a set of rules for combining them. Mallarmé and Valéry and Eliot felt words as part of that echoing intricacy, Language, which permeates our minds and obeys not the laws of *things* but its own laws, which has an organism's power to mutate and adapt and survive, and exacts obligations from us because no heritage is more precious. The things against which its words brush are virtually extraneous to its integrity. We may want to say that Shakespeare wrote about happenings in the world, the world that contains mortal men and sunlight and dandelions, and that a post-Symbolist reading converts his work into something that happens in the language, where "golden" will interact with "dust" and "wages" and "lads" and "girls" and "chimney-sweepers," and where "dust" rhymes with "must," mortality with necessity. Thus the song seems to us especially fine when we can no longer say what the phrase "golden lads" was meant to name. (And "genuine poetry," wrote Eliot in 1929, "can communicate before it is understood.")

We can have no idea how often or on what a scale such meanings have dropped out of sight. (Much of Yeats, it may be, or much of the *Cantos*, is already beyond recall.) We should not know it had happened here in *Cymbeline* had not the Warwickshire saying chanced to survive and to be reported. Very likely, page after page, we have not the slightest idea what was present to the mind of Homer, the sheer authority of whose melopoeia holds together impenetrable remarks about ox-eyed goddesses who for all we know may have been ox-faced, since the Greek word permits that understanding, and may even have come to the Hellenic mind from Egypt, cow's head and woman's body. There is no way to tell. Sometimes we can tell something. A line that survives to this day in Bartlett's *Familiar Quotations* as a very touchstone of the Romantic Indefinite—

A rose-red city half as old as time

—was made, in the course of putting together an entry for the Newdigate Competition, by John William Burgon, who simply joined a *fact* (that Petra contains a temple hewn out of red rock) with a *quotation* ("Many a temple half as old as time") from Samuel Roger's *Italy*, a customary bedside book for young romantics.

Though romantic, Burgon was being workmanlike. To his generation the age of Time was quite definite; for since Adam was created in the year 4004 B.C. on October 23, Time in the year Burgon wrote, 1845, was exactly 5849 years old, going back through half of which we locate the founding of Petra at 1080 B.C. Once again the effect to which we respond today replaces something that has dropped out, the chronology Burgon's age inherited from Archbishop Ussher and Vice-Chancellor Lightfoot. In the absence of some convention about the age of Time, "half as old as time" is perfectly meaningless. But again the chemistry of Language supersedes meaning, and we do not think to apply the Ussher convention. It is against our own feeling of indefinite, measureless Time that "half as old" expends itself and dissolves, carrying with it into unfathomable mists the sunset connotations of "rose-red," a phrase we are just as unlikely to attribute to hard reality. Yet Burgon felt behind every word in his line an exactitude nearly neo-Classical.

Again: a poem that used to be attributed to Sappho, and though now removed from her canon remains perhaps the best-known of Greek quatrains—

> Δέδυκε μὲν ἀ σέλαννα
> καὶ Πληῒαδες, μέσαι δὲ
> νύκτεσ, παρὰ δ' ἔρχετ' ὦρα,
> ἔγω δὲ μόνα κατεύδω.

> The moon has set, and the Pleiades,
> It is the middle of the night
> Hour follows hour. I lie alone.

Guy Davenport, who made this translation, remarks that two lines of Robert Burns seem to answer the Greek as though from beneath the same moon but by another sea in another age:

> The wan moon is setting behind the white wave,
> And Time is setting with me, oh.

And W. B. Yeats raised Burns' lines (slightly misquoted) to current fame in perceiving in them the supreme efficacy of the Symbolist aesthetic:

> Take from them the whiteness of the moon and of the wave, whose relation to the setting of Time is too subtle for the intellect, and you take from them their beauty. But, when all are together, moon and wave and whiteness and setting Time and the last melancholy cry, they evoke an emotion which cannot be evoked by any other arrangement of colours and sounds and forms. We may call this metaphorical writing, but it is better to call it symbolic writing. . . .

Yeats might equally well have been explaining how men can respond as they do to 17 Greek words that appear to say such unrelated things: that the moon and the Pleiades have set, that time flows, that I lie in my bed alone. *Mona*: alone: we may recall its resemblance to the other Greek word for moon, the one not used in the poem, *mēnē*. *Egō de mona kateudō*: and my loneliness comports with that of the cold moon and the remote stars, now gone, borne on their great circles down under the horizon: a loneliness to fill the dark empty sky. So we read it, forgetting once again how much has dropped out. For what Greek forgot that the moon sleeps nightly with Endymion, or that the Pleiades visit the bed of Ocean? They go to their appointed partners, but I have no one; and "alone" means "unlike them."

The word "golden," the word "time," the word "alone": three words set free for chemical interaction: set free, however, from explicit structures we happen to be able to reconstitute, a folk idiom, a chronology, a habit of apprehending the heavens through myth. Restored to those structures, they act as schoolteachers assert words normally act, naming things, making comparisons, completing rational squares by means of paraphrasable sentences.

But if we continue to expect the paraphrasable once these structures have dropped away we shall find that bits of nonsense confront us; for what is a golden lad or a golden girl, and where do we place the halfway point in the unmeasurable, and what have two propositions about my lack of company and about the location of eight heavenly bodies to do with one another?

But we do not discern nonsense. We locate each such detail in a structure of another kind, a structure of words, where the words exchange dynamisms in the ecology of language.

* * *

Ecology—dynamisms interchanged—is the 19th-century's intellectual achievement and characterizing paradigm, as that of the 18th century is System. In a System nothing happens; nothing can happen except the system's decay, like that of a satellite's orbit. Thus on 18 April 1783, "Mr. Walker, the celebrated master of elocution," asked Dr. Johnson, the lexicographer, whether there were any perfect synonyms in any language, which is to say, any wholly superfluous words, and was told, "Originally there were not; but by using words negligently, or in poetry, one word comes to be confounded with another."

"By using words negligently, or in poetry": the poet, a negligent opportunist, always forcing the word that will *fit* into the office of the right word, ministers to linguistic decay (change is decay). But when Mallarmé a century later defined the poet's office—*Donner un sens plus pur aux mots de la tribu*—to give a purer sense to tribal words—he understood that language lives in usage, usage to which memorable specializations, as when Yeats transfigured "slouch" with the aid of "beast" and "Bethlehem," may impart a second youth.

For the norm is now Speech, which binds men, which flows through minds and cultures. (The Augustan norm was Silence, as the Newtonian norm was the state of rest; and Augustan language needs to be defended against the people who speak it, and against poets.) But we know the words we join have been joined before, and continue to be joined daily. So writing is largely quotation, quotation newly energized, as a cyclotron augments the energies of common particles circulating. The Formulaic Homer of modern scholarly fashion, a bard never out of touch with hallowed units of expression, is the West's archpoet understood in such a way; each age's Homer epitomizes its poetics.

"Really it is not I who am writing this crazy book," said Joyce of *Finnegans Wake*. "It is you, and you, and you, and that man over there, and that girl at the next table."

And "I am less alarmed," wrote Eliot, "about the decay of English when I read a murder story in the appropriate paper, than when I read the first leader in 'The Times'."

And "Poetry"—Pound—"must be *as well written as prose*. Its language ... departing in no way from speech save by a heightened intensity (i.e. simplicity). ... no book words ... no hindside-beforeness, no straddled adjectives (as 'addled mosses dank') ... nothing—nothing that you couldn't, in some circumstance, in the stress of some emotion, actually say."

And Wyndham Lewis, than whose ear for speech there was no more voracious, listened in his times of poverty, hour by hour, to the talk in pubs.

"The speech of Polish mothers," said Dr. Williams of his poetic idiom: mothers listened to on obstetric house-calls, or on deathbeds:

> Has
>
> she eaten anything yet?
>
> Has
>
> she eaten anything yet!
>
> Six oysters—she said
> she wanted some fish and that's
> all we had. A round
> of bread and butter and a
> banana
>
> My God!
>
> —two cups of tea and some
> ice-cream.
>
> Now she wants the wine
> Will it hurt her?
>
> No, I think
>
> nothing will hurt her.
>
> She's
> one of the wonders of the world
> I think, said his wife.

> (To make the language
> record it, facet to facet
> not bored out—
>   with an auger.
>
> —to give also the unshaven,
>   the rumblings of a
> catastrophic past, a delicate
> defeat—vivid simulations of
> the mystery ·)

—1949. Against which, 1713: "What oft was *Thought* but ne'er so well *Exprest*," offering to clean the blackboard, to supersede the mere spoken tongue's inadequate expressions: to build what must be said into immutable aphorisms, and around them restore the silence.

*   *   *

Language on living tongues is the word's environment; in silence the word has no environment. Ecology—interest in trans-actions with an environment—is a romantic discovery, in poetics as in biology. (Thoreau was an ecologist.) *Symbolisme* was poetic ecology made scientific: whole poems existing as systems of linguistic interaction. The Imagist recall of poetic diction to speech was more profound than Wordsworth's, because speech in 1913 was better understood; Wordsworth had simply thought rural diction "pure" by nearly Augustan canons. But the process which led to *Symbolisme*, thus to Symons and Yeats, to Eliot and obliquely to Pound, is already stirring when Keats closes a cadence with

> . . . perilous seas in faery lands forlorn,

not omitting to distinguish "faery" from "fairy," and then invites us to notice the sound his closing word has made:

> Forlorn: the very word is like a bell
> To toll me back from thee to my sad self.

The very word, we may be persuaded, it like a bell, in a language where the syllables of *forlorn* can enact a grave equable tolling, and where *bell* rings clear with the *l*-sound on which *forlorn* turns. But

"Perdu: l'expression même est comme une cloche"? It simply isn't; which is merely to remark that in another language that particular interactive potential is not available. For the century Keats inaugurated made its poetic effects more and more out of elements so inherently linguistic they will not pass through translation at all. It seems to be about the time of Coleridge that we begin hearing poetry identified with what cannot be translated, a notion which would have puzzled Chaucer and Dr. Johnson alike. Nor were such interests confined to English; Keats' contemporary Alfred de Vigny was hearing in "son du cor" an echo of "au fond du bois," the sound of the horn and the deep of the woods responding to one another as they only can in French.

These poets were paying language a new kind of attention. They were manifesting the Romantic interest in the vernacular, in the homemade, in the idiosyncrasies of the local. They were partaking in the century's concern with languages as living organisms, every cell responsive to any sensation one cell undergoes, all language "fossil poetry." And they were responding to the sheer weight of literary history: to the distance, now, and strangeness (thus *faery*, not *fairy*) of so much earlier poetry (in writing *faery* Keats remembers Spenser, for whom in turn the word was an archaism). Out of such earlier poetry for one reason or another semantic structures had faded, so that phrases which work as "golden lads" will work when we do not know about the dandelion had come to seem the very essence of poetry. (And inspecting such principles as these, and their pathology, Eliot conceived *The Waste Land.*)

* * *

For the Romantics, harking back to foretime, discovered literary history. The English poets, when Johnson wrote their lives, were all men alive so recently that readers still understood the world as they did, and time's dissolution of their conscious meanings had not begun. Earlier poets, Donne and Chaucer for instance, concealed with their linguistic habits matter reclaimable by diligent modernization: thus Dryden retold Chaucer's stories, and Pope "versified" certain satires of Dr. Donne. Shakespeare was a disadvantaged genius, for whose inability to be everywhere clear one made allowances. And the Greek and Latin classics were archives of observation and moral reflection, baffling in their immunity to change. With all the poets who mattered drawn in so close, one presumed full understanding (Johnson does). If the relation of adjective to noun was unclear, or the relation of stars to loneliness, that was a fault. There could be no question of linguistic affinities replacing vanished meanings. But to the Romantics a generation later, all poetry stretched serially in time clear back to Homer, and Homer was very ancient. The remoter poetry in particular was replete with *effects*, an effect being something hypnotic we cannot quite understand, whiteness of moon and wave related to the setting of Time in a manner "too subtle for the intellect." And all over Europe, by the late 19th century, poets had decided that effects were intrinsic to poetry, and were aiming at them by deliberate process.

Effects, then, "too subtle for the intellect." By the end of the century, in France, whole poems have been made "too subtle for the intellect," held together, as effects are, by the extra-semantic affinities of their words. Picking up a name that was once thrown at their authors, we have learned to call them "Symbolist" poems. In the Symbolist poem the Romantic effect has become a structural principle, and we may say that Symbolism is scientific Romanticism, thus an effort to anticipate the work of time by aiming directly at the kind of existence a poem may have when a thousand years have deprived it of its dandelions and its mythologies, an existence purely linguistic, determined by the molecular bonds of half-understood words.

Certain remarks of Mallarmé's, as that poetry is made not of ideas but of words, that the poem can convey "for example, the horror of the forest, or the silent thunder afloat in the leaves, not the intrinsic dense wood of the trees," or that the things words seem to name are non-existent, since there is no thing the word "flower" names: all these seem to us now self-evident, and we read them back with profit into the work of poets who never heard of them. And certain practices of Keats, endeavoring to layer into his Odes a history of which he was largely ignorant except as he could sense its presence in language (*faery*, pointing to Spenser; *Tempe*

and *Arcady*, names merely; *Provençal song*, something fine he had
heard of, associated not with *trobar clus* but with sunburnt mirth)
seem to us so normal as to be hardly worth remarking. Poems are
structures of words.

*   *   *

Seven words, then, too subtle for the intellect:

Let us go then, you and I . . .

Three clear vowels, *o, u, i,* zoned by intervening nasals. As natives
whose ancestors heard buccaneers are still saying *gadʒoot* ("Gadzooks!") in Panama, so might some future Finn or Lapp or Lett
pleasurably mouth that run of seven monosyllables with no meaning
whatever attaching to any portion of it.

And what meaning do we attach to it, for instance to *you?*
"You" is potentially an auditor *in* the poem, but no such auditor
appears again; or is possibly the reader, but if so then we have silent
overheard speech aware it is being attended to; or is possibly some
other part of that "self" which the title suggests we call J. Alfred
Prufrock; or is possibly, by extension from the poem's Italian
epigraph, Dante or some analogue of Dante's, come to interrogate
this locked soul in its locked world. Transposing the Italian to
English,

> . . . *But since no one ever goes back alive out of this gulf (if what I hear
> is true), without fear of infamy I answer you.* Let us go then, you and
> I . . .

But we cannot, it soon appears, be in Dante's hell, not here in this
city of "half-deserted streets." Perhaps some other hell?

Not to make heavy weather, it is a typical Eliot line, symptomatic in that it now causes no difficulty, but at one time seemed to
direct the Love Song and its readers into anxiety deepening to
confusion. Those Georgian readers need not have been immediately
anxious:

When the evening is spread out against the sky

Ah yes, the mahogany feel: iambic pentameter and a gratifying
rhyme. Then:

Like a patient etherized upon a table.

—sheer nonsense. Yes, as much so as "half as old as time." Eliot's line does differ from Burgon's in two particulars. (1) *Old* and *time* and *rose-red city* lie on the same continuum, along which we are borne past sense without noticing, whereas *evening* and *sky* carry feeling in one direction, but the *etherized patient* in another. We may choose to anaesthetize this fact by speaking of counter-romantic irony. (2) Burgon's line, if we care, can be restored to sense with the aid of Ussher's lost structure, which is to say that Burgon did not intend, possibly did not intuit, a potential for nonsensical glamour; but Eliot's line has no lost structure to restore, as the searcher after "meaning" eventually discovers. Eliot's line aimed from the first at its "effect," "too subtle for the intellect," the intellect being unable to build much of value on the physicist's association of *ether* and *sky*. On:

> Let us go, through certain half-deserted streets
> The muttering retreats
> Of restless nights in one-night cheap hotels
> And sawdust restaurants with oyster-shells . . .

Is *streets*, as the line suggests, in apposition to *retreats?* and then *nights* with *restaurants?* Or *restaurants* with *hotels?* One soon forgets to ask. This poem had been finished by 1911. It marks, after Symons' and Dowson's poetic of atmospheric slightness, a new beginning for post-Symbolism in English. Harriet Monroe, when she received it from her Foreign Editor in October 1914, shifted from haunch to haunch, bombarded by Ezratic objurgations for eight uneasy months before printing it.

The Foreign Editor's breadth of sympathy was remarkable. He detected the authority of Eliot's language, and did not think it faulty though his own is never obscure in Eliot's way.

> Only at nightfall, aethereal rumours
> Revive for a moment a broken Coriolanus

and

> Pull down thy vanity,
>   Paquin pull down!
> The green casque has outdone your elegance

will both communicate before they are understood, yet no knowledge about Coriolanus will lock Eliot's lines neatly together as the information that Paquin was a Paris dressmaker will lock Pound's. Pound omits, omits, but knows what he is omitting and can restore on demand, but behind Eliot's resonances there is frequently nothing to restore (how centrifugal are the Notes to *The Waste Land*!).

*   *   *

Yet the Symbolist revolution lay behind them both. It allowed Pound to know that there would still be poetry for the reader who could not fill the ellipses back in, who literally, therefore, did not know what many words meant. Or even for the reader who filled them in wrong. Paquin, mused an American classroom handbook, possibly from Pasquino, on whose statue in Rome anonymous satirical verses used to be fixed; which error did not impede the editors' response to Pound's eloquence. "Shall two," Canto 93 asks, "know the same in their knowing?" By contrast, the characteristic mistake of Eliot's annotators is to annotate at all.

One poet moved out of Symbolism, one deeper into it. Commencing from the post-Symbolist nineties, Pound worked his way clear of systematized suggestiveness until his chief point of contact with 19th-century French verse was Théophile Gautier of the direct statement ("Carmen is thin") and his most Symbolist procedure an isolating of single words, not necessarily English. Eliot after some years' infatuation with a peripheral Symbolist poet, Jules Laforgue, worked more and more deeply into the central Symbolist poetic, translated Perse, sponsored the reputation of Valéry in England, and wrote his last principal work, the *Four Quartets*, under the sign of Mallarmé himself and with a title that remembers Verlaine ("De la musique avant toute chose"). The Dante each man carried in his mind is an index to their radical difference of temperament. Pound's was Pre-Raphaelite, miniaturist of detail exactly perceived. Eliot's, distilled in Harvard classrooms, fulfilled a New England ideal in discriminating moral tonalities, apprehensible even before the words were quite understood. On 22 September 1914 these two traditions of Dante scholarship confronted one another for the first time. That is a way of putting it.

*   *   *

"The form in which I began to write, in 1908 or 1909, was directly drawn from the study of Laforgue together with the later Elizabethan drama; and I do not know anyone who started from exactly that point": so Eliot, 1928. Laforgue he encountered (*aetat.* 20) in Arthur Symons' *The Symbolist Movement in Literature*, where in a quoted description of a poet who had died at 27 he would have seen, or perhaps foreseen, himself portrayed: "Strictly correct in manner, top-hatted, soberly cravatted, given to English jackets and clerical overcoats, and in case of necessity an invariable umbrella carried under his arm." That is the Possum; Laforgue was first of all a *role*. And Laforgue's verse, Symons goes on, "scrupulously correct, but with a new manner of correctness," serves "an art of the nerves," which is "distressingly conscious of the unhappiness of mortality, but plays, somewhat uneasily, at a disdainful indifference." ("*I am aware of the damp souls of housemaids.*") And "In Laforgue, sentiment is squeezed out of the world before one begins to play at ball with it"; a sentence in which Eliot even then may have heard the perhaps unintended echo of Marvell. ("*To have squeezed the universe into a ball.*")

But in Symons' account, this art is an art of *dwindling*. "The old cadences, the old eloquence, the ingenuous seriousness of poetry, are all banished," and if we choose to detect behind "Restless nights in one-night cheap hotels" a distich quoted by Symons from Laforgue—

> Hôtel garni
> De l'infini

—we cannot help noticing what a difference the later Elizabethans have made. They commanded—helped Eliot command—a more portentous rhetoric than was discoverable in Laforgue's French generation or in the English post-Symbolist derivations from Verlaine. Their iambic pentameter eloquence ("Prufrock" is not *vers libre* but iambic pentameter) allowed shortish poems to hint at mighty themes

> —Do I dare
> Disturb the universe?—

and their catachrestic figures offered a formula for Mighty Lines aware of Henry James.

> ... Though I have seen my head (grown slightly bald)
> Brought in upon a platter

remembers not only Wilde, Mallarmé, Gustave Moreau, but Webster.

Laforgue was the first of a succession of poets whom Eliot does not so much imitate as face toward, by way of locating his own structures of words set free, liberated in magnificent but sober nonsense, which however beaten upon will not disclose "meaning." It is obscurely helpful to discern Gautier (examined at Pound's instigation) in the vicinity of his 1917 quatrains, but the Gautier of "perfectly plain statements" ("Perfectly plain statements like his 'Carmen est maigre'," Pound wrote in 1916, "should teach one a number of things") does not betray Eliot into perfectly plain statements but remains part of his teasing implication of meaning.

> The couched Brazilian jaguar
> Compels the scampering marmoset
> With subtle effluence of cat;
> Grishkin has a maisonette.

The word is "couched," in a rare usage cognate with the heraldic *couchant*, but its rarity does not arrest us, being protected by affinity with "crouched" and with the habitat of a reclining Grishkin. And the parallel between jaguar and Grishkin, so elaborate yet (the laconic words imply) so simple: though a line seems drawn as though accounts had been balanced, nothing we are told of the one really tallies with what we are told of the other.

And after Gautier, a time of equivocal vision (*Waste Land, Hollow Men*) closer to Ernst and Chirico than to anything literary; then Dante's mode, likewise transferred to a plane of verbal suggestion—

> Here are the years that walk between, bearing
> Away the fiddles and the flutes, restoring
> One who moves in the time between sleep and waking, wearing
>
> White light folded, sheathed about her, folded

—with which contrast the optical certainty of

> una donna soletta, che si gia
> cantando ed iscegliendo fior da fiore,
> ond' era pinta tutta la sua via.*

And finally, in the *Four Quartets*, Mallarmé, who receives in these considerable poems perhaps his most elaborate homage in any language other than his own. Not only is "garlic and sapphires in the mud" a fusion of "Tonnerre et rubis aux moyeux" and "boue et rubis", and "to purify the dialect of the tribe" a homage to the line in the sonnet to Poe, "Donner un sens plus pur aux mots de la tribu," not only are these and other details borrowed, but the unseen eyebeam falling on flowers that seem looked at seems derived from "le regard diaphane" which in *Toast Funèbre* rests on unfading because verbal flowers, and the intent insistence on silence into which "words, after speech, reach" (for "that which is only living / Can only die") reflects the arch-Symbolist's best-known preoccupation.

The details, however many we identify, are less important than the way of conceiving poetry. Mallarmé, approached with such diffidence after so long, is the austere codifier of Eliot's difficult art, the art of creating with an air of utter precision the feel of concepts one cannot localize. To name is to destroy, thought Mallarmé; and as we will never know what is happening in "Sweeney Among the Nightingales," where

> Branches of wisteria
> Circumscribe a golden grin

and a geometrician's verb half-enjoins us against visualizing, so at the end of "Little Gidding" a condition of complete simplicity is to cost "not less than everything."

Like the Symbolists, he is not there, but has withdrawn in favor of the language. "The pure work," wrote Mallarmé in a passage cited by Symons, "implies the elocutionary disappearance of the poet, who yields place to the words, immobilized by the shock of their inequality; they take light from mutual reflection, like an actual train of fire over precious stones, replacing the old

---

* "A lady alone, who went along singing and plucking flower after flower from the flowers that colored all her path."—*Purgatorio.* xxvii, 40–2.

lyric afflatus or the enthusiastic personal direction of the phrase."
We are familiar with this doctrine now because ten years after
Eliot read of it in Symon's book he gave it classic expression in his
testament to the poet's impersonality, "Tradition and the Individual
Talent," where the materials of the poem, its feelings, its emotions,
its very words, are like chemicals ready to combine, and the poet's
mind not the enthusiastic personal director of phrases but simply a
catalyst. And it is with our own post-Symbolist sensibilities, finally,
that we receive the final meditations of "Burnt Norton," which
talk about words but never about their meanings:

> ... Only by the form, the pattern
> Can words or music reach
> The stillness, as a Chinese jar still
> Moves perpetually in its stillness. ...

And

> ... Words strain
> Crack and sometimes break, under the burden,
> Under the tension, slip, slide, perish,
> Decay with imprecision, will not stay in place,
> Will not stay still. Shrieking voices
> Scolding, mocking, or merely chattering
> Always assail them. The Word in the desert
> Is most attacked by voices of temptation,
> The crying shadow in the funeral dance,
> The loud lament of the disconsolate chimera.

Did he mean by his "chimera" anything as exact as Shakespeare
meant by his "golden lads"? Very likely not. Is any of us learned
about the meanings of "chimera"? Not necessarily. But time and
the Symbolist poetic set words free; they have set "chimera" free,
to work on us as do those Shakespearean words which we need not
know were about dandelions.

   Pound retained misgivings about the entire enterprise. Remembering a time when his inscrutable colleague, making lines as
if for actors to speak, had experimented with perfectly direct
statement—

> Well he kept her there in a bath
> With a gallon of lysol in a bath

—he used to remark to callers at St. Elizabeths that Eliot hadn't developed since the *Agon*.

*   *   *

Pound had commenced poet by mouthing the wonderful words of others until he got satisfaction from something theirs yet his own:

> Lord God of heaven that with mercy dight
> Th' alternate prayer wheel of the night and light
> Eternal hath to thee, and in whose sight
> Our days as rain drops in the sea surge fall . . .

One can tell what kind of thing he has been reading, as in portraits by the very young Picasso one can identify passages paraphrased from Velásquez, Manet, Degas.

But as realities, and pictures, will come apart into shapes, so poems will come apart into words; and as one can take bits of a still life—a carafe's hip, a bit of newspaper, the neck of a guitar, the checks of a tablecloth—and substituting the designer's structure for that of the perspective-box make on a flat space a "cubist" arrangement through which intimations of past still-life traditions are glimpsed, so one can take apart (1915) a Greek poem into its words and rearrange them to make a new poem that discards everything of the old but its diction.

Thus a scrap in the Dorian dialect of Ibycus, 6th century B.C.—

> Eri men hai te Kydoniai
> malides . . .

might tempt creative fancy. The authorized glosses run

> Though it's in spring that the quinces and . . .

Yet approached via the abridged Liddell and Scott, the words dissolve into mystery. *Cydonia*, says the Lexicon, a Cretan city; *malon*, Doric of *mēlon*, an apple or any tree-fruit; put together, a *Cydonian mēlon*, the Cretan Fruit, i.e. the quince. (In the same way a *mēlon Persikon* is a peach, a *mēlon Mēdikon* an orange, a *mēlon Armeniakon* an apricot.) Yet the word in the text is not *mala*, the expected plural of *malon*, but *malides*, which we find in the Lexicon under *malis*, "Doric for *Mēlis*, a nymph who protects the flocks."

῏Ηρι	μὲν	αἵ τε	Κυδώνιαι	on the one hand,
{ Early In spring		the	Cydonian	on the other hand

both . . .

μαλίδες	ἀρδόμεναι	ῥοᾶν	and
{ nymphs fruits	are watered	streams	

ἐκ ποτάμων	ἵνα	Παρθένων
from the rivers	where	of the maids

κᾶπος	ἀκήρατος	αἵ τ'	οἰνανθίδες
garden	fresh	the	first shoot of the vine

αὐξόμεναι	σκιέροισιν ὑφ'		ἔρνεσιν
grow, wax	shady	under	shoots

οἰναρέοις	θαλέθοισιν ἐμοὶ		δ'	Ἔρος
vine-leaves	flourish	for me		Love

οὐδεμίαν	κατάκοιτος	ὥραν
no	asleep	time, season

⟨ἀλλ' ἅ⟩θ'	ὑπὸ	στεροπᾶς	φλέγων
but	with	lightning-flash	burning

Θρηΐκος	Βορέας	ἀΐσσων
from Thrace	north wind	rushing

παρὰ	Κύπριδος	ἀζαλέαις	μανίαισιν	ἐρεμνὸς	ἀθαμβὴς
from	the Cyprian	with parching	frenzies	black	fearless

ἐγκρατέως	πέδοθεν		σαλάσσει
masterful	from the	{ ground bottom of heart	shakes

ἀμετέρας	φρένας.
our	heart.

So a word here seems two-faceted. But syntax is a one-way street, its principals and subordinates guiding us with sometimes misleading ease through a sentence or a poem. In the same way perspective (small means distant; lacuna means overlap) tells us how to relate the members of a picture. Disregard, then, the faceted *Malides*, fix your mind on the structure determined by the little words *men* ("on the one hand") and *de* ("but on the other hand"), which gives "[these things] happen in Spring, but Love ravishes me at all seasons," specify the spring happenings, waterings and burgeonings, with an eye on such aspects of the Greek words as will fit, and you get (J. M. Edmonds, *Lyra Graeca*, II, 84)—

> 'Tis but in Spring the quince-trees of the Maids' holy garden grow green with the watering rills from the river, and the vine-blossoms wax 'neath the mantling sprays of the vines; but for me Love's awake the year round, and like the Northwind from Thrace aflame with lightning, comes with a rush from the Cyprian, with shrivelling frenzies baleful and bold, and with masterful power shakes me to the bottom of my heart.

No apple-nymphs, and *eremnos*, black, becomes "baleful," and Cydonia in the south, having vanished into an idiom for "quince," no longer counterpoises the Thracian wind.

But lay out, instead, the elements all on one plane, each sharp, each bright, each of comparable importance; disregard their syntactic liaisons; make a selection, and arrange them anew, as the cubists arranged visual elements so that one cannot say what is theme, what is detail:

THE SPRING

Cydonian Spring with her attendant train,
Maelids and water-girls,
Stepping beneath a boisterous wind from Thrace,
Throughout this sylvan place
Spreads the bright tips,
And every vine-stock is
Clad in new brilliances.

And wild desire
Falls like black lightning.
O bewildered heart,
Though every branch have back what last year lost,
She, who moved here amid the cyclamen,
Moves only now a clinging tenuous ghost.

Not, good Lord, a translation: a poem made out of words from another poem, with three lines (the last three) added to supply a new plot. Cydonian spring puts forth as formerly her transfiguring power, but she I lament returns only as a ghost. Against loss and regret (now: London) the world of the gods: it is Pound's familiar theme in those years. But the gods' world is likewise *now*; the diction, firm, blithe, immediate, sets these realities not at the far end of millenial perspectives but in just such a foreground as sensual realities occupy:

. . . Spreads the bright tips
And every vine-stock is
Clad in new brilliances. . . .

This overrides chronological as well as syntactic perspective; time is ignored. Literary history as the Romantics apprehended it, today's poems near, yesterday's far, the year before yesteryear's yet farther, Greek things exceedingly remote: this romance of temporal distance is simply absent. As in *The Lives of the Poets* all poets are contemporaneous, though not merely the poets a common idiom unites: the poets, of whatever date or language, whose clean perception sets realities before the mind.

*　　*　　*

Let us compare a Cubist painting of a chair with a Fra Angelico altarpiece.

The differences may at first be startling, but there are also similarities. In both paintings there is a delight in clarity. (Not necessarily a clarity of meaning, but a clarity of the forms.) Nothing comes between you and the objects depicted—least of all the artist's temperament: subjectivity is at a minimum. In both paintings the subject and texture of the objects is freshly emphasized—as though everything was just newly made. In both paintings the space in which the objects exist is clearly very much part of the artist's concern, although the laws of that space are very different: in the Fra Angelico the space is like that of a stage-set seen from the auditorium; in the Picasso the space is more like that of a landscape seen from the air. Lastly, in both paintings there is a simplicity and lightness, a lack of pretentiousness, which suggests an almost blithe confidence. One might think that one could find the same qualities in paintings from any period, but this is not the case. There is nothing comparable in the five centuries between.

—John Berger, *Success and Failure of Picasso*, 48–9.

Pound of course rearranges elements drawn from Ibycus, whereas Picasso's chair is not derived from anything in Fra Angelico. Many Picasso paintings do derive from earlier paintings, as many more Pound poems than "The Spring" derive from other poems, but the comparison though tempting is not close. Picasso tends to destroy his exemplar, saying "This is what it comes to." Pound's restructurings do homage to work that remains undisturbed, unreplaced. Which is perhaps to say that Picasso ceased being a cubist, whereas Pound's work, say from *Lustra* to the last Cantos, is the longest working-out in any art of premises like those of cubism.

*   *   *

Of certain Symbolist premises as well: the Symbolist willingness to lift words out of "usage," free their affinities, permit them new combinations. Cydonian Spring, not Cydonian fruits which are quinces, and *malides* nymphs, not apples, apple-nymphs moreover, not the flock-nymphs of the Lexicon, and with an invented name, Maelids, which John Quinn in the American proofs of *Lustra* tried to correct to Meliads but Pound in *Personae* and in Canto III retained in the form he preferred, a word that ought to exist. (A number of his words ought to exist, as a number of the poems he translates ought to have been written: for instance the Heine "So hast du ganz und gar vergessen" where he misread *Leid* [pain] as *Lied* [song] and would not have been interested had he read correctly.) This passage from the third Canto ought to be a Latin Renaissance poem:

> Gods float in the azure air,
> Bright gods and Tuscan, back before dew was shed.
> Light; and the first light, before ever dew was fallen.
> Panisks, and from the oak, dryas,
> And from the apple, maelid,
> Through all the wood, and the leaves are full of voices,
> A-whisper, and the clouds bowe over the lake,
> And there are gods upon them,
> And in the water, the almond-white swimmers,
> The silvery water glazes the upturned nipple,
>   As Poggio has remarked.
>   (3/11:15)

The Panisks, little rural Pans, are from Cicero's *De Natura Deorum*, the dryas, oak-spirits, *passim* from the Greek heritage, the maelids from Ibycus, the gods upon the clouds from Poliziano; the lake is Garda, gazed on by Pound from his magical place, Sirmio; and Poggio Bracciolini, papal secretary, observed, A.D. 1451, bathers in a German pool. This is *collage*, another cubist strategy, and the absence of dew, twice stated, denotes the hazeless light that abolishes planes of distance. Myth, language, poetry, fact, lie disposed in a common reality, and Poggio's remark, cited as one cites in a work of scholarship, is literature and the validation of literature by a living eye, and the sharpening of that eye in turn by other literature: Roman erotic poetry, which taught the papal secretary to see. Its ultimate source is Catullus 54:18—*nutricium tenus exstantes e gurgite cano*. Poggio's phrase has not been located.

*   *   *

This readiness to lift single words out of history, as the *Kydoniai malides* have been lifted out of the tradition by which Ibycus' poem is normally understood, underlies the famous dealing with ideograms, which afforded him such erudite amusement in Pisa, that long dreadful summer. Thus looking at the ideogram *hsien* (to manifest, to be illustrious; #2692 in Mathews' *Dictionary*) where it appears in a quotation from the 267th Ode near the end of the Confucian *Chung Yung* (Pound's "Unwobbling Pivot"), he spied in its upper left corner 日 the sun, and below that 絲 silk (in its primitive form a cocoon); these two gave him the "tensile light" of the Pivot's penultimate sentence, and of the 74th Canto (74/429:455) and in Canto 91 the *hsien* ideogram, far removed from its Confucian context, appears in a setting of Italian folk custom, the sole link being the silkworms that were once cultivated near Rapallo:

> The peasant wives hide cocoons now
>
>   under their aprons
>   for Tamuz
>
> That the sun's silk
>
>   hsien 顯   tensile
>
>   be clear
>   (91/612:646)

Any sinologist is entitled to protest that this is like finding *iron* in *irony*; but Picasso by analogous process found a baboon's head in the shape of a toy car.

*   *   *

And in this verbal kaleidoscope, what abides? What is Shakespeare's or Ibycus' song, if the words mutate? A patterned energy: as follows:

KNOT AND VORTEX

Of patterned energies; and first,
Buckminster Fuller on knots. He grasps and tenses an invisible
rope, on which we are to understand a common overhand knot, two
360° rotations in intersecting planes, each passed through the
other:

Pull, and whatever your effort each lobe of the knot makes it
impossible that the other shall disappear. It is a *self-interfering
pattern*. Slacken, and its structure hangs open for analysis, but
suffers no topological impairment. Slide the knot along the rope:
you are sliding rope through the knot. Slide through it, if you have
them spliced in sequence, hemp rope, cotton rope, nylon rope. The
knot is indifferent to these transactions. The knot is neither hemp
nor cotton nor nylon: is not the rope. The knot is a *patterned
integrity*. The rope renders it visible. No member of Fuller's audience
has ever objected (he remarks) that throughout this exposition he
has been holding no rope at all, so accessible to the mind is a
patterned integrity, visible or no, once the senses have taught us its
contours.

Imagine, next, the metabolic flow that passes through a man and is not the man: some hundred tons of solids, liquids and gases serving to render a single man corporeal during the seventy years he persists, a patterned integrity, a knot through which pass the swift strands of simultaneous ecological cycles, recycling transformations of solar energy. At any given moment the knotted materials weigh perhaps 160 pounds. (And "Things," wrote Ernest Fenollosa about 1904, are "cross-sections cut through actions, snapshots.")

So far Buckminster Fuller (1967). Now Ezra Pound (1914) on the poetic image: ". . . a radiant node or cluster; . . . what I can, and must perforce, call a VORTEX, from which, and through which, and into which, ideas are constantly rushing." A patterned integrity accessible to the mind; topologically stable; subject to variations of intensity; brought into the domain of the senses by a particular interaction of words. "In decency one can only call it a vortex. . . . *Nomina sunt consequentia rerum.*" For the vortex is not the water but a patterned energy made visible by the water.

*   *   *

A patterned energy made visible by the water. Pound did not chance on such a conception lightly. Patterns made visible had occupied him when he wrote in 1912 of "our kinship to the vital universe, to the tree and the living rock," having "about us the universe of fluid force, and below us the germinal universe of wood alive, of stone alive": man being "chemically speaking . . . a few buckets of water, tied up in a complicated sort of fig-leaf," but capable of having his thoughts in him "as the thought of the tree is in the seed." "Energy creates pattern," he was writing three years later, explaining "Imagisme." "Emotion is an organizer of form." A magnet brings "order and vitality and thence beauty into a plate of iron filings," their design expressing "a confluence of energy." Thirty years later, in Pisa, he closed the 74th Canto with a double image of patterned energy: the magnet's "rose in the steel dust" and the fountain's sculptured flow through which passes renewing water, tossing a bright ball. The same passage mentions the winds Zephyrus and Apeliota, moving energies so stable they have names, and cites Verlaine's comparison of the soul's life to the fountain's, and a phrase of Jonson's uniting Charis and swansdown, and Dante's adduction of the souls of the blessed composing in space a great rose: poetic images, patterned energies.

"Energy creates pattern." Like molecules of water in fountain or vortex, particulars of the pattern mutate; the pattern is stable, an enduring integrity, shaped by the movement, shaping it. This is a whole time's way of thinking. "Art never improves," wrote T. S. Eliot in 1919, "but the material of art is never quite the same": an Eliot aware, while they were dismembering Europe in the Hall of Mirrors, of the mind of Europe persisting like the Cumaean Sibyl's, "a mind which changes" but "abandons nothing *en route*": not Homer, nor Shakespeare, nor the rock drawing of the Magdalenian draughtsman. A patterned integrity, the mind of Europe, or equally the poet's imagination where the greater mind is active here and now: where (suitably catalyzed) new objects of attention enter into new combinations ("really new") while the mind's identity (called Tradition) remains.

In Zürich James Joyce was drawing the 18 hours of Leopold Bloom through a patterned integrity defined by Homer: a tough self-interfering pattern through which, he discerned, Shakespeare had already drawn the skein called Hamlet (Telemachus, Stephen), and Mozart his Don Giovanni (Antinous, Boylan) and even the elder Dumas his Monte Cristo, returned avenger (Odysseus at Ithaca, the stone guest at the banquet, the ghost at Elsinore). Time, place and personnel alter; the pattern remains.

* * *

To specify: what is Homer's *Nekuia?* A tale of visiting the dead, which archaic bards, it is now orthodox to believe, rendered audible through somewhat different words every time they recited it. Pound wrote in 1935 that it seemed *older* than the rest of the *Odyssey*: foretime: a remembering of rites already ancient when the tale came to Homer. Some time after 700 B.C. one set of wordings was (somehow; by Homer?) fixed with a newfangled visual aid, the alphabet: which event stabilized the *Nekuia* but did not fix the speech, for the Greek language continued to change its sounds (would Plato have understood Homer's recitations? would we understand Chaucer's?), and the Greek sensibility continued to alter its values (pernicious fables, Socrates decided, banning Homer from the Republic of the Guardians), and copyists no doubt modified the text repeatedly.

For centuries, from the 8th B.C. to the 20th A.D., the Greek language has slid through a knot called *The Odyssey*. Late in the third millenium since Homer, a modern Greek gives to every word the modern pronunciation he brings to his newspapers.

But long before Greek had become modern Greek the mind of Europe had commenced an interior monologue in Latin, a Latin partly shaped by Vergil, who impressed on his native locutions much of his understanding of Greek epic; and into Latin accordingly in the early 16th century the *Nekuia* was transposed by one Andreas Divus Justinopolitanus: *Et postquam ad navem descendimus, et mare . . .* : the self-interfering patterned integrity still apprehensible though not a word of Homer's remains. The knot had been slipped onto a different rope.

And "in the year of grace 1906, 1908, or 1910" Ezra Pound acquired on a Paris *quai* Divus' book, and a few years later set keel to breaker, pen to paper, to ringing effect:

> And then went down to the ship . . .

Pound had inherited, and learned in detail, a language called English, Englysshe, English, American, impregnated with Saxon vigors he had already reinforced in transposing *The Seafarer* from an ancestral form of this tongue into a modern. Now, discerning an autochthonous knot resembling Homer's, he brought the appropriate emphases to the surface of his 1917 English:

> . . . Heavy with weeping; and winds from sternward
> Bore us out onward with bellying canvas

in imitation of, for instance,

> bitre breostceare   gibiden hæbbe,
> gecunnad in ceole cearselda fela,

to emphasize the pattern's analogy.

And Canto I (as it eventually became), with its thudding alliteration, its Saxon vocables (*swart, mead, dreory*), its Anglo-Norman compounds (*sea-bord, trim-coifed*), its Greek survivals (*pyre, Kimmerian*), its prevalent monosyllables ("And we set up mast and sail on that swart ship"), its Homeric narrative and its injunction to Divus, recapitulates the story of a pattern persisting undeformable while many languages have flowed through it and many more pronunciations in the thousands of years it has been a property of the Western mind. Is it our oldest such pattern? It may be. And in 1917 our newest poetry. And fifty years later still cavilled at, as was doubtless Homer.

* * *

The Canto is not simply, as was Divus' Homer or Chapman's or Pope's, a passing through the knot of newer rope. It is also *about* the fact that self-interfering patterns persist while new ways of shaping breath flow through them. It illustrates that fact, and its subject is in part that fact. It is what mathematicians call a second derivative, a function of a function, an inspection of what is happening derived from its way of happening. "Lie quiet Divus," are its operative words:

> Lie quiet Divus. I mean, that is Andreas Divus
> In officina Wecheli, 1538, out of Homer

—as suddenly Divus, from whose Latin text we are to understand Pound to be working, becomes one of the ghosts to whom, in the narrative taken from Divus himself, blood is being brought that they may speak in the present. With these words we are suddenly watching rope flow through the knot, particulars rushing through the "radiant node or cluster"; and the Canto is no longer a specimen "version of Homer" but an exhibition of "Homer" as a persistent pattern, "from which, and through which, and into which" flow imaginations, cultures, languages.

As the rope makes the knot visible, the language makes Homer's imagined realities apprehensible. The poem is not its language. It exists, just here and now, in *this* language, this niceness of linguistic embodiment, inspection of which will tell us all we shall ever know about it.

The poem is not its language. Hence Pound's reiterated advice to translators, to convey the energized pattern and let go the words. To tie the knot you need not simulate the original fibers. "I'd like to see a 'rewrite' [he wrote W. H. D. Rouse] as if you didn't know the *words* of the original and were telling what happened." And to Michael Reck, about a proposed Japanese *Trachiniae* (from Pound's English, from Sophokles' Greek), "Don't bother about the WORDS, translate the MEANING." And even, to his German translator, "Don't translate what I wrote, translate what I MEANT to write." But the language is responsible to the poem: hence the moral obligation laid on technique, which alone can disclose the persistent patterned energy. ("A bust of Mozart carved in a sausage," he said of Bruno Walter's conducting.) In the vicinity of poems, the word "technique" tends to arouse animosity: from minds, Pound once wrote, "too trivial to believe that any subject could be worth the labor of exact presentation."

*   *   *

It seems to have been about 1911 (*aetat.* 26) that Pound came to think of translation as a model for the poetic act: blood brought to ghosts. ("He can only translate," cavilled the school of Blackmur years later; and when the dog in the story walked on water, his inability to swim was remarked on.) In 1911 Pound was drafting a book on Arnaut Daniel, never published because one publisher went broke in 1912 and another (for whom 20 years later he made a retouched version) in 1932. The draft survives as a series of 12 articles published in A. R. Orage's weekly *New Age*, 30 Nov. 1911– 22 Feb. 1912: *I Gather the Limbs of Osiris*. "Under this heading," ran the standing rubric, "Mr. Pound will continue expositions and translations in illustration of the 'New Method in Scholarship.'— ED." The "New Method" began with his title, for as we may learn from the *Oxford Companion to Classical Literature*, it was Osiris, "the male productive principle in nature," who became when his scattered limbs had been regathered the god of the dead (of Homer, of the Seafarer poet, of Arnaut Daniel), but also "the source . . . of renewed life. The Greeks identified him with Dionysius." The limbs' reunited energies assert themselves; Pound's book, by a young man at the threshold of great renovations, was about patterned energies.

The first installment confronted its readers not with preliminary remarks but with an opening gesture, simply and solely *The Seafarer*, called "A Translation from the early Anglo-Saxon text," and accompanied by a note on textual degeneracy. "It seems most likely that a fragment of the original poem, clear through about the first thirty lines and thereafter increasingly illegible, fell into the hands of a monk with literary ambitions, who filled in the gaps with his own guesses and 'improvements'." To recover the patterned integrity, we thus have to strip off "improvements"; "I have rejected half of line 76 ['against the Devil'], read 'Angles' for angels in line 78, and stopped translating before the passage about the soul and the longer lines beginning 'Mickle is the fear of the Almighty,' and ending in a dignified but platitudinous address to the Deity: 'World's elder, eminent creator, in all ages, amen'."* Files of the *New Age* are scarce, this note appears nowhere else, and Pound's "remain 'mid the English" for "live among angels" has long been pointed to as a prize howler, but he did it deliberately.

His purpose was to untrammel the poem's energies, which he took (as for that matter do many scholars) to be pre-Christian. Its first arraying he thought gone beyond recall: "The groundwork may have been a longer narrative poem, but the 'lyric,' as I have accepted it, divides fairly well into 'The Trials of the Sea,' its Lure and the Lament for Age." Out of the wreck of structures the essential rises, unkillable; later Canto I will distill Homeric narrative to 67 lines of essential vigors.

And explaining in a later installment *The Seafarer's* place at the head of an exposition largely concerned with Arnaut, he had recourse to a chemical metaphor: "I have ... sought in Anglo-Saxon a certain element which has transmuted the various qualities of poetry which have drifted up from the south, which has sometimes

---

* So his text ran to the terminal "Amen," line 124, which means it was not, as one would otherwise suppose, from Sweet's *Anglo-Saxon Reader*, where the poem is cut off at line 108. What text Pound did use, how it was punctuated, what glosses accompanied it, remains an unsolved problem. A multigraphed sheet from the Anglo-Saxon course he took a half-dozen years previously? And it seems impossible that he had at his elbow Cook's 1902 prose translation, or for that matter a crib of any kind.

enriched and made them English, sometimes rejected them and refused combination." For vigors have their affinities, notably national vigors in national languages; it is reasonable to show English readers through what warps in their perceptual field they will be apprehending the Provençal. In the rich chord that opens the *Cantos* as *The Seafarer* opened *Osiris*, we discern once more the insistent English element.

"The New Method in Scholarship," furthermore, turns out to be "the method of Luminous Detail," used intermittently "by all good scholars since the beginning of scholarship," and hostile both "to the prevailing mode of today, that is, the method of multitudinous detail, and to the method of yesterday, the method of sentiment and generalization." Luminous Details are the transcendentals in an array of facts: not merely "significant" nor "symptomatic" in the manner of most facts, but capable of giving one "a sudden insight into circumjacent conditions, into their causes, their effects, into sequence, and law." History is full of facts that tell us nothing we did not already know: in the year ———— a revolt against ———— was led by ———— with the result that ————. With perfect indifference these blanks will accommodate Egyptian, Greek, Roman, American names, telling us in no case anything arresting about Egypt or Greece or Rome or America. The Pattern is not self-interfering.

> But when in Burckhardt we come upon a passage: "In this year the Venetians refused to make war upon the Milanese because they held that any war between buyer and seller must prove profitable to neither," we come upon a portent, the old order changes, one conception of war and the state begins to decline. The Middle Ages imperceptibly give ground to the Renaissance.

The Seafarer in the same way is such a fact: not simply poetry-of-exile but a self-interfering identity, its specific characteristics not discoverable in China or Tuscany among the laments in exile of Li Po or Cavalcanti.

> In the history of the development of civilization or of literature, we come upon such interpreting detail. A few dozen facts of this nature give us intelligence of a period—a kind of intelligence not to

be gathered from a great array of facts of the other sort. These facts are hard to find. They are swift and easy of transmission. They govern knowledge as the switchboard governs an electrical circuit.

The *Cantos* undertake to make a poem-including-history out of such facts:

> That T'ang opened the copper mine
> (distributive function of money)
> (88/580:616)

or

> the state need not borrow
> as was shown by the mayor of Wörgl . . .
> (74/441:468)

or

> So he said, looking at the signed columns in San Zeno
> "how the hell can we get any architecture
> when we order our columns by the gross?"
> (78/480:512)

And the well-known list of "inventors" in "How to Read" offers to control literary history with no more such facts than will fit on a half-sheet of notepaper.

*   *   *

Luminous Details, then, are "patterned integrities" which transferred out of their context of origin retain their power to enlighten us. They have this power because, as men came to understand early in the 20th Century, all realities whatever are patterned energies. If mass is energy (Einstein), then all matter exemplifies knottings, the self-interference inhibiting radiant expansion at the speed of light. Like a slip-knot, a radioactive substance expends itself. Elsewhere patterns weave, unweave, reweave: light becomes leaf becomes coal becomes light. The universe (Fuller, 1967) "is the aggregate of non-simultaneous, only partially overlapping, transformational events." Its rhythms, knowingly exploited, will support geodesic structures. Esoteric traditions, early in the century, were surfacing at the same time as such insights. "And that the universe is alive . . .", thought Apollonius of Tyana, a sage the *Cantos* cited in 1955, a half-century after Pound's old friend G. R. S. Mead devoted a book to him. "As we, or mother Dana, weave and unweave our bodies," said Stephen Dedalus, mimicking Irish esoterism in 1904, "from day to day, their molecules shuttled to and fro, so does the artist weave and unweave his image. And as the mole on my right breast is where it was when I was born, though all my body has been woven of new stuff time after time. . . ." So, in the first decade of our century, artists abandoned forever the Newtonian universe which had yielded a Pope his jauntiest effects and a Wordsworth his most stoical. "Shakespeare" became not "Elizabethan poetry" but a unique force moving among Elizabethan poetic conventions, and criticism was free to talk about conventions without assuming that they can only immobilize. An acorn was no longer six cubic centimeters of "matter" but an encapsulated pattern that can guide metabolic energies for many decades; glancing at its achievement, we say "oak tree." Yeats saluted the "great rooted blossomer" and thought of the dance as a normal mode of being.

In London, 1912, sober men alive to living thought inhabited a universe of ordered dynamisms. Marconi was in England, filling the ether with patterns that could be intercepted in Newfoundland (1901) or Buenos Aires (1910). The discovery of Mendel's writings in 1900 incited biologists to explore the power of latent patternings in mammal, bird and insect over remote descendants; by 1909 a textbook of genetics at last existed. In the Curie laboratory across the channel the metal called radium, which transforms itself into energy, had been known since 1898 and isolated by 1910. "*La virtù*," wrote Pound in that very year with his mind on Cavalcanti, "is the potency, the efficient property of a substance or person. Thus modern science shows us radium with a noble virtue of energy." And his writings of 1910–14 touch on all these themes in passing, as illustrative facts too thoroughly "in the air" to require explication. For instance, in 1913,

> We might come to believe that the thing that matters in art is a sort of energy, something more or less like electricity or radio-activity, a force transfusing, welding, and unifying. A force rather like water

when it spurts up through very bright sand and sets it in swift motion. You may make what image you like.

Newton's universe—a mental, not a physical entity—was gone: gone too the objects strewn through it in a state of "rest," awaiting the impingement of causality: the metals waiting to be oxidized, the water to be pumped, the poets to be "influenced." When Picasso first dissected a mandolin the stability of painted objects ended, and it was natural for Pound in 1911 to compare a room full of pictures by Fra Angelico, Velásquez, Hokusai, Whistler, or a shelf of books by Homer, Dante, Guido, Chaucer, Shakespeare, to an array of engines each designed "to gather the latent energy of Nature and focus it on a certain resistance. The latent energy is made dynamic or 'revealed' to the engineer in control, and placed at his disposal." Electric engines, steam engines, gas engines all do this, "all designed for more or less the same end, none 'better,' none 'worse,' all different. Each perhaps slightly more fit under certain conditions, for certain objects minutely differentiated." (In that year part of the London transport system ran by electricity, and part ran by steam.) And as one cannot hope to understand such engines by calling some ugly and some pretty, but only by attending to their way of gathering and concentrating the latent energy of Nature, so one can begin to understand painting or literature by knowing "at least, a little of the various stages by which that art has grown from what it was to what it is," and attending to the moments when new dispositions of vital energy become available.

For if there are "symptomatic" works, resembling "significant" fact in being "what one might have expected in such and such a year and place," there are also "donative" works, resembling "Luminous Details" in patterning anew the energies of living speech.

> The donative author seems to draw down into the art something which was not in the art of his predecessors. If he also draw from the air about him, he draws latent forces, or things present but unnoticed, or things perhaps taken for granted but never examined.

For "the air about him" is alive with invisible dynamisms; whence (1945)

> To have gathered from the air a live tradition
> or from a fine old eye the unconquered flame
> This is not vanity;

$$(81/522:557)$$

and when Pound in 1934 called artists "the antennae of the race" he was thinking not only of the mantis but of Marconi.

The latent forces art brings before the senses, like the latent energies the engine reveals and places at man's disposal, filled the knowable if not the known world before the engine was conceived or the artist born. Intelligence draws them out of common experience, as intelligence first differentiated steel out of stone, and then tensile and compressive factors out of steel. The artist himself, however, a patterned integrity, manifests his own spectrum of forces, called his *virtù*.

> It is by reason of this *virtù* that a given work of art persists. It is by reason of this *virtù* that we have one Catullus, one Villon; by reason of it that no amount of technical cleverness can produce a work having the same charm as the original, not though all progress in art is, in so great degree, a progress through imitation. . . .
>
> It is the artist's business to find his own *virtù*. . . . It may be something which draws Catullus to write of scarlet poppies, or orange-yellow slippers, of the shaking, glorious hair of torches; or Propertius to
>
> > Quoscumque smaragdos
> > Quosve dedit flavo lumine chrysolithos.
> > —"The honey-coloured light." . . .

And his *virtù*, a patterned energy, we find reasserting itself in his disposition of stone or pigment or language: the unique energetic signature of all he does, the knot he alone ties, the radiant node "from which, and through which, and into which, ideas are constantly rushing"; and the experience will rush, too, of some man come in a much later age, to open a book bought on the Paris quais and confront (an alien, reading a dead alien tongue)

> Et postquam ad navem descendimus, et mare,
> Nauem quidem primum deduximus in mare diuum,
> Et malum posuimus et vela in navi nigra: . . .

—And we set up mast and sail on that swart ship: Homer's *virtù*, indefatigable.

*   *   *

Patterned integrities. "A true noun," wrote Ernest Fenollosa, "an isolated thing, does not exist in nature. Things are only the terminal points, or rather the meetingpoints of actions, cross-sections cut through actions, snapshots. Neither can a pure verb, an abstract motion, be possible in nature. The eye sees noun and verb as one, things in motion, motion in things. . . .

"The sun underlying the bursting forth of plants = spring.

"The sun tangled in the branches of the tree sign = east. . . . No full sentence really completes a thought. The man who sees and the horse which is seen will not stand still. The man was planning a ride before he looked. The horse kicked when the man tried to catch him. . . . And though we may string never so many clauses into a single compound sentence, motion leaks everywhere, like electricity from an exposed wire. All processes in nature are inter-related. . . .

"All truth has to be expressed in sentences because all truth is the *transference of power*. The type of sentence in nature is a flash of lightning. It passes between two terms, a cloud and the earth. No unit of natural process can be less than this. . . . Light, heat, gravity, chemical affinity, human will, have this much in common, that they redistribute force. . . ."

And "the whole delicate system of speech is built upon sub-strata of metaphor. Abstract terms, pressed by etymology, reveal their ancient roots still embedded in direct action." And language, said Ralph Waldo Emerson, is fossil poetry: "the etymologist finds the deadest word to have been once a brilliant picture." And in Nature, said Emerson, there are no terminations; and Nature's processes, Emerson affirmed repeatedly, constitute a system of analogies for the mind to incorporate: "Things admit of being used as symbols because Nature is a symbol, in the whole and in every part." And Fenollosa again: ". . . Nature furnishes her own clues. Had the world not been full of homologies, sympathies, and identities, thought would have been starved and language chained to the obvious."

From Emerson's lectures on "The Poet" (1844) and on "The Method of Nature" (1841) we can collect without trouble a body of propositions indistinguishable in import from the statements about reality out of which Fenellosa's great Ars Poetica is educed. For "He that would bring home the wealth of the Indies" (Emerson, quoting a proverb) "must carry out the wealth of the Indies," and Ernest Francisco Fenollosa (1853–1908), born in Salem and educated at Harvard, took with him to Japan in 1878 as Professor of Philosophy (Hegel, Herbert Spencer) the treasures of Transcendentalism, and brought back with him from Japan on his last journey in 1901 that same Transcendentalism, seen anew in the Chinese Written Character and set forth in what Pound, who acquired the ms. twelve years later, was to characterize as the "big essay on verbs, mostly on verbs." There were several drafts, none final. Fenollosa had meant it, quite in Emerson's way, for a public lecture, and four pages of a 1901 notebook list lantern slides he intended to have made: "Photograph of a man doing something, as 'Man leads horse'," and

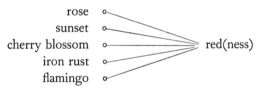

rose   ○
sunset   ○
cherry blossom ○————→ red(ness)
iron rust   ○
flamingo   ○

CHERRY IS RED

cherry reddens itself
cherry silvers (its) bark
cherry angles (its) branches ——→ cherry
cherry bunches (its) blossoms

photograph of a cherry tree in pink blossom
Character for cherry (tree)
same char. for all parts of speech at once
giving a function of something that lives.

Such reminders of patterned energy came promptly. Except for *The Seafarer* and the resolve some day to make decent versions of Arnaut Daniel, Pound had left the *Osiris* series behind him. By the summer of 1913, when he sent the ms. of *Des Imagistes* to

Alfred Kreymborg, the hygiene of Imagism, its clean words and its eschewal of reduplication, had occupied him for about a year, almost to the exclusion of dynamism and *virtù*. Imagism had drawn him to Chinese motifs, glimpsed through the rhymed translations in Giles's *History of Chinese Literature*, but even the inspired addendum to his paraphrase of one of the Chinese poems—"A wet leaf that clings to the threshold"—illustrates his flirtation with a poetic of stasis. Then late in 1913, through the Fenollosa mss., China itself appeared to be declaring the needful truth to liberate Imagism, the truth that words pattern process, and that Nature, from which language comes, is patterned process. "The forces which produce the branch-angles of an oak lay potent in the acorn," wrote Fenollosa; and again, "The development of the normal transitive sentence rests upon the fact that one action in nature promotes another; thus the agent and object are secretly verbs." And what does the Chinese writer set on his page? Why, a picture of an active thing.

We write in ideographs "Man sees horse," and we set down "a vivid shorthand picture of the operations of nature. . . . First stands the man on his two legs. Second, his eye moves through space: a bold figure represented by two running legs under an eye, a modified picture of an eye, a modified picture of running legs, but unforgettable once you have seen it. Third stands the horse on his four legs." And similarly, when we write "Sun rises (in the) east,"

日 昇 東

"the overtones vibrate against the eye." He goes on:

The wealth of composition in characters makes possible a choice of words in which a single dominant overtone colors every plane of meaning. That is perhaps the most conspicuous quality of Chinese poetry. Let us examine our line. The sun, the shining, on one side, on the other the sign of the east, which is the sun entangled in the branches of a tree. And in the middle sign, the verb "rise," we have a further homology; the sun is above the horizon, but beyond that the single upright line is like the growing trunk-line of the tree sign. This is but a beginning, but it points a way to the method, and to the method of intelligent reading.

*   *   *

For the ideogram, Fenollosa does not tire of repeating, sketches a process, seizes some continuous happening—the movement of attention through an eye, the flow from roots to branches within a tree—and fixes it, like Buckminster Fuller's knot, with three or four minimal vigorous spatial gestures. Thus the word, freed from evanescent sound, transcends the moment of utterance and reutters itself in a vibrating field of force where, augmented by neighboring words, particulars rush *from* and *through* and *into*. The Chinese poet given a choice of expressions chooses, Fenollosa thought, with an eye for dominant overtones. Pound had groped in 1912 for a clumsy analogy, and imagined words like great hollow cones "charged with a force like electricity." Thinking perhaps of how magnetic fields can augment or neutralize one another, he had postulated a care in placement whereby the forces hidden in the steel cones could not merely augment but multiply. ". . . Thus three or four words in exact juxtaposition are capable of radiating this energy at a very high potentiality; mind you, the juxtaposition of their vertices must be exact and the angles or 'signs' of discharge must augment and not neutralize each other. This particular energy which fills the cones is the power of tradition, of centuries of race consciousness, of agreement, of association; and the control of it is the 'Technique of Content' which nothing short of genius understands."

And now it seemed that China had understood all this for centuries, with the aid of a script that would let no man with an eye forget what energy it is that fills words: the energy of process in nature. Take the last line of Li Po's poem that is called in *Cathay* "Taking Leave of a Friend":

簫	簫	班	馬	鳴
hsiao	hsiao	pan	ma	ming
(hsiao	hsiao	parting	horse	neigh)

The first two words are simply onomatopoeic, though "centuries of race consciousness, of agreement, of association" caused the scribe to select from all the characters pronounced "hsiao" one that confirms an allusion to the 179th Confucian Ode. And the third looks like a parting (its central dividing stroke is a knife), and the fourth, the horse with his four legs, has an eye-rhyme in the fifth, though the radical changes to bird, the mouth to his left denoting bird-talk, but in juxtaposition as here with horse, horse-talk. Horse plus bird-talk denotes a clear neigh; for raucous neighing the character would be different.

Here is the perfect analogy, to replace Pound's clumsy supposition of steel cones. In a few months the Image became the Vortex; in the late spring of 1914 pages were added at the bindery to sheets of *Blast* already printed, to introduce the term "Vorticism" and claim *Blast* as the organ of the Great English Vortex; a poet's eye educated in ideograms had seen in Gaudier's sculpture the emotive force of "planes in relation"; Gaudier himself had spent a fortnight in the British Museum studying Chinese characters, discovering he could read the radicals and many compound signs "almost at pleasure," and had also displayed on sheets of drawing paper how a horse or a cock could be metamorphosed into something ideographic; by 1915 Imagism had been redefined as corollary of the proposition that "energy creates pattern"; by 1917 the long poem Pound had hankered to write for years was at last under way. Its elements shook free from connectives. "Nature herself," wrote Fenollosa, "has no grammar."

* * *

The appeal to Nature, mainstay since Wordsworth of poetic reformers, had in Fenollosa's mind the peculiar transcendentalist torque. Another mind similarly energized was soon to detect in Nature an equally significant reticence. In 1917, while Ezra Pound in London was extracting *virtù* from *The Seafarer* to make what would be *Canto* I, a seafarer ten years his junior, great-nephew of Emerson's collaborator Margaret Fuller, was watching the bubbles boiled up in the wake of a Navy ship, and concluding from those millions of changing spheres that nature did not use *pi*. For *pi* will only describe a sphere once formed, and a sphere moreover idealized because static. But the generation of forms is described by vectors ("Vectors represent energy events, and they are discrete"), and Buckminster Fuller proposed to make it his business to find nature's energetic geometry. Just 50 years later the bubble behind the ship had become in Montreal a geodesic skybreak bubble 20 stories high, enclosing 7 million cubic feet of air, as free as a water bubble of internal supports, and weighing a hundredth of what former technology dictated that such a structure should weigh. The load on its foundations was less than the weight of its materials, and had it been a mile wide it would have floated away. Outlining the first principles of the universe whose differentiation by mind can yield such a marvel, its designer spoke of knots.

And in 1920, within earshot of guns near Minsk, a Red Army poster artist shared freight-car lodgings with a former instructor of Japanese. The teacher talked; the artist applied himself with passion, and learned 300 ideographs: knife-and-heart, "sorrow"; water-and-eye, "weep." His name was Sergei Mihailovitch Eisenstein. He envisaged an orientalist's career, drifted amid economic chaos into the theater instead, and by 1925 was applying ideographic principles to an art of blended snapshots: *The Battleship Potemkin*.

To such dynamic vigors from Chinese poetry is both a long way and a short one, and reviewed from the end of the way, the starting point alters. Mind applied fire to stone, and we, knowing of iron, can see stone with a different eye. A Russian mind, applied to ideographs in a time of Revolutionary propaganda, in conceiving *montage* has altered our understanding of ideographic potentialities. An American mind, brought to ideographs by an art historian of Spanish descent who had been exposed to Transcendentalism, derived Vorticism, the *Cantos*, and an "ideogrammic method" that modifies our sense of what Chinese can be. Buckminster Fuller adduces a general law: "Heisenberg said that observation alters the phenomenon observed. T. S. Eliot said that studying history alters history. Ezra Pound said that thinking in general alters what is thought about. Pound's formulation is the most general, and I think it's the earliest." Where, when, in what connection had Pound said that? Fuller couldn't remember; he'd read it long ago; it would take weeks to find it. No matter: such a self-interfering pattern does not derive its power from its credentials. To think of Pound in that way alters Pound.

TRANSFORMATIONS

"The forces which produce the branch-angles of an oak lay potent in the acorn."—Fenollosa, about 1904.

". . . the pattern-making faculty which lies in the flower-seed or in the grain or in the animal cell. . . ."—Pound, 1915.

What else, besides an oak-tree, grows from a kernel by controlled transformational process? According to Zellig Harris (1952) and Noam Chomsky (1957) a sentence of any intricacy you like: hence the mid-century emergence of generative grammar, which asks how it is possible for the first sentence of *Paradise Lost* to be grown out of normal English constituents, and moreover to be acknowledged as grammatical by readers who have never heard such a sentence before. Descriptive linguistics does not ask this kind of question, just as Euclidean geometry does not ask Fuller's kind. Fuller wanted to know how all those spherical bubbles came to be generated: what equilibrium of vectors kept them spherical. The pursuit of *pi* starts from a different question, pertinent to a static universe: how many times a thread long enough to gird a bubble would be measured by its diameter. This question is not posed by nature, and we should probably not be surprised that its answer is a patternless number, 3.141592653589793. . . .

Or you may ask why a dancer does not topple, and get no answer unless you postulate motion as her norm. Yeats intuited this ("O body swayed to music, O brightening glance") and in the same movement of thought adduced a tree, which is none of its parts and also none of its states. "Great-rooted blossomer"; and a public man of 60 has no more than a scarecrow's reality, a tattered coat upon a stick,

unless
> Soul clap its hands and sing, and louder sing
> For every tatter in its mortal dress . . .

To be is a verb. "Sailing to Byzantium" moreover is a transformation wrought on two Odes of Keats, about a bird not born for death and about a Grecian artifice of eternity.

The generative grammarians say that language itself, doing infinite things with limited means, works by transformation. At the heart of the process they trace lies the "kernel sentence," identical with Fenollosa's natural grammatical unit, the transference of power. Though ingenuity could no doubt derive any syntactic structure from any other, "When we actually try to set up, for English," wrote Chomsky, "the simplest grammar that contains a phrase structure and a transformational part, we find that the kernel consists of simple, declarative, active sentences (in fact, probably a finite number of these), and that all other sentences can be described more simply as transforms."

"Nature does not use *pi*" means that nature does not measure bubbles but generates them.

"Nature has no grammar" means that nouns and qualifiers are not part of creation's paraphernalia (we feel the warm air move on our morning walk; we cannot experience an adverb), and it also means that people without formal instruction in the rules they are said to be following generate without forethought (as Henry James did) very intricate utterances, grown, we are now told, out of kernel sentences, as Yggdrasil grew from its acorn. Nature's way and mind's way rhyme; mind is the regenerative part of nature. Fenollosa would want to add that the germ of the kernel sentence is its verb, and that subject and object are also verbs, though considered without reference to time, and *to* and *from* and *above* have verbal force, and all the qualifiers are verbal *ways*. "Blue" is not a taxonomy; it is the sky's and the robin's egg's way of showing.

Like all truths this can become naive but need not, so profoundly does it typify 20th-century thought. Niels Bohr like Picasso was a student of metamorphoses. Matter, thought Bohr's generation of physicists, is energy tied into self-interfering patterns: when such a knot is untied the mass becomes energy, expanding with the speed of light. Dr. Williams was to perceive the relevance of the Curies to poetics, and the engines of Pound's 1912 paragraph which "gather the latent energy of Nature and focus it on a certain resistance" had 30 years later been generalized into the cyclotron.

And Pound seems always to have thought of poetry as the controlled use of energy attendant on just such a transformation. The elements, for instance Homer's *Nekuia*, can be detected in history and listed. All other literary history is a chronicle of (1) transformations, where energy is released; (2) derivations, where energy is dissipated; (3) simulations, where it was never present.

As to simulations: "There are few fallacies more common than the opinion that poetry should mimic the daily speech. Works of art attract by a resembling unlikeness. Colloquial poetry is to the real art as the barber's wax dummy is to sculpture. In every art I can think of [1912] we are dammed and clogged by the mimetic; dynamic acting is almost forgotten; the painters of the moment escape through eccentricity."

As to transformations and derivations: "If a book reveal to us something of which we were unconscious, it feeds us with its energy; if it reveal to us nothing but the fact that its author knew something which we knew, it draws energy from us."

Paul Valéry's poetry concerns itself with the mind making poetry, in part out of past poetry: a concern we can free of its decadent tinge by noting that since past poetry has occurred in time, a poetic of transformation will assimilate history to a present moment, and glimpse Persephone in a station of the Metro.

"For order to persist after the supervention of novelty" (Eliot, 1919) "the *whole* existing order must be, if ever so slightly, altered." The alteration, as when the domain accepts a new electron, occasions a release of energy. Just that release is the poetic effect.

"My God, why hast thou forsaken me?" was quoted from the Psalms, on an occasion the Psalmist did not foresee. And the simplest lyric—"When icicles hang by the wall" or "The winter evening settles down"—is a quotation from Language. And "This music crept by me upon the waters" is Eliot quoting from Shakespeare, who himself may be imagined as quoting from Homer, and by way of a Renaissance crib.

*   *   *

Marianne Moore's "Novices" (1923) closes with a sheaf of quotations:

> "... an abyss of verbs full of reverberations and tempestuous energy"
> in which action perpetuates action and angle is at variance with angle
> till submerged by the general action;
> obscured by "fathomless suggestions of colour",
> by incessant panting lines of green, white with concussion,
> in this drama of water against rocks—this "ocean of hurrying consonants"
> with its "great livid stains like long slabs of green marble",
> its "flashing lances of perpendicular lightning" and "molten fires swallowed up",
> "with foam on its barriers",
> "crashing itself out in one long hiss of spray."

Four authors, none aware of the others, contributed to this: the author of *The Poets of the Old Testament*, the author of *Christ on Parnassus*, the author of *The Expositor's Bible*, and Leigh Hunt in his *Autobiography*. We are being sent to none of these books; the poem is assembling their phrases for its own purposes. And as "the forces that produce the branch-angles of an oak lay potent in the acorn," so the force that produced verbal integrities this *assemblage* can use lay potent in the absorption of four minds with perceived realities. Minds so absorbed write with pith and concision. Such qualities, engendered by intercourse with a subject, persist in the writing even when we do not know what its subject was, and the phrases have a *virtù* Miss Moore can put to her own uses. Not all writing can be used in Miss Moore's way: only attentive writing. Idiosyncrasy of language derives from attention: such attention as Louis Agassiz paid to nature's minute realities. "Agassiz" (Pound, 1954, private letter) "could teach a litteratus to write." In one Paradisiac Canto (93/625:658) we encounter him in the heaven of the fixed stars. Agassiz was enabled by perception:

> ... vesicles almost entirely cover the wall of their parent, simulating, by their clearness and roundness of contour, drops of dew lining a glass globe.

> ... snapping in the same fierce manner as it does when full-grown, at a time it was a pale, almost colorless embryo, wrapped up in its foetal envelopes, with a yolk larger than itself hanging from its sternum, three months before hatching.

> ... the grasses, in which the leaves are placed alternately on opposite sides of the stem, thus dividing the space around it in equal halves.

The British biologist D'Arcy W. Thompson was attentive in the same way:

> The cells are stellate, and the tissue has the appearance in section of a network of six-rayed stars, linked together by the tips of the rays, and separated by symmetrical, air-filled intercellular spaces, which give its snow-like whiteness to the pith.

(He also proved that a style energized by perception can accommodate "hearken" and "oftentimes" in the same sentence.) The English lexicographer Samuel Johnson was attentive to taxonomies:

> HORSE: A neighing quadruped, used in war, and draught and carriage.

> DRAKE: The male of the duck.

And the French novelist Gustave Flaubert, attentive to the rhetoric of furniture:

> Un vieux piano supportait, sous un baromètre, un tas pyramidal de boîtes et de cartons. Deux bergères de tapisserie flanquaient la cheminée en marbre jaune et de style Louis XV. La pendule, au milieu, représentait un temple de Vesta. . . .

And the fine phrase Stephen Dedalus "drew from his treasure-house," "A day of dappled seaborn clouds," he had found in a book called *The Testament of the Rocks*, by the Scottish evangelical geologist Hugh Miller.

Natural sciences formed on minute attention produced in the 19th century a new order of descriptive exactness, obligated by the fact that there was no accurate way to reproduce a picture. Eschewing the Johnsonian "grandeur of generality," writers "numbered the streaks of the tulip," whose number mattered. In the Pound Era poets learned that the energy concentrated in exactness was a poetic resource. "An anthology of transit," said Dr. Williams, attentive to Miss Moore's way of collecting and spacing such verities. He did not say, an anthology of phrases; he perceived that the poetic energy, something new on the poet's page, was discernible in the unstated connections between them. The quotations concentrate idiosyncratic energy; the poem's tensile energy, equally idiosyncratic, pulsates between them. Analogous patterns of compression and tension have been discerned in the universe itself:

> Therefore when nature has very large tasks to do, such as cohering the solar system or the universe, she . . . has compression operating in little remotely positioned islands, as high energy concentrations, such as the earth and other planets, . . . while cohering the whole system by comprehensive tension:—compression islands in a non-simultaneous universe of tension.
> —Buckminster Fuller, *World Design Science Decade* Document #2.

No one can see tension. Newton called one form of it *gravity*. Another form keeps bicycle wheels from collapsing, and another inhabits the clear spaces on a Japanese scroll.

*   *   *

In 1917, the year of the *Homage to Sextus Propertius* which transforms

> aetas prima canat Veneres, extrema tumultus:
> bella canam, quando scripta puella meast

into

> The primitive ages sang Venus,
>   the last sings of a tumult,
> And I also will sing war when this matter of a girl is exhausted,

D'Arcy Wentworth Thompson published the first edition of his *On Growth and Form*, a study of economies and transformations, where by systematic warping of rectangular frames into circular "a typical Scaroid fish"

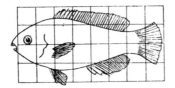

yields "a very good outline of an allied fish, belonging to a neighbouring family, of the genus *Pomacanthus.*"*

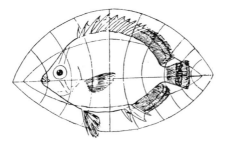

They correspond point for point, as Pound's phrases correspond to the Latin word by word, but directions and emphases alter. "This case is all the more interesting, because upon the body of our *Pomacanthus* there are striking colour bands, which correspond in direction very closely to the lines of our new curved ordinates," quite as though nature had chosen to emphasize an aesthetic of deformations.

This principle is very general. Poems cohere, as do fish, and yet are derivable from other poems, as *Lycidas*, via Vergil, out of Moschus and Theocritus. "Influence" is no longer the relevant metaphor: we are dealing not with inflow but homeomorphism, the domain of topology, systems of identical interconnectedness. Thus Joyce discerned homeomorphic structures in the *Odyssey*, *Hamlet*, *Don Giovanni*, *The Count of Monte Cristo*, and his own

*Figures 519 and 520 from D'Arcy W. Thompson, *On Growth and Form*, by permission of Cambridge University Press.

life. This suggests a grammar of generative plots. In a lecture of 1914 (how fascinating were transformations in those years!) Gilbert Murray presented Hamlet as a homeomorph of Orestes. *The Golden Bough* and Jane Harrison's *Themis* enabled him to find a kernel plot in the ritual of the King-Slayer, sprung from "that prehistoric and world-wide ritual battle of Summer and Winter, of Life and Death, which has played so vast a part in the mental development of the human race." Thus *Hamlet* could resemble the *Oresteia* without Shakespeare knowing why, or even knowing the *Oresteia*. But *Ulysses* resembles the other books it resembles because Joyce knew them, and the *Homage* resembles selected passages of Propertius because Pound had Müller's edition (1892) open in front of him. Transformation, translation, their systematic deformations, are themselves in the Pound Era foci of attention.

Pope could fit poems about the current scene very comfortably into the structure of poems by Horace, conforming line by line to the Roman structure of tropes. His triumph is in making Horace virtually disappear, discernible (once the title tells us to look) not as an idiosyncratic poet but as a pervasive impersonal common sense, the very *form* of articulate common sense, to validate Pope's way of commenting on today. Pound, too, was pleased by his own snug fit into the words of Propertius ("almost thirty pages with nothing that isn't S.P., or with no distortion of his phrases that isn't justifiable by some other phrase of his elsewhere") and insisted too that his subject was contemporary ("certain emotions as vital to me in 1917, faced with the infinite and ineffable imbecility of the British Empire, as they were to Propertius some centuries earlier, when faced with the infinite and ineffable imbecility of the Roman Empire") but Pound's language, unlike Pope's, is so conspicuous, his transformed Propertius so vivid a Yankee-in-England persona, that we catch not only the cultural subject-rhyme but the striking system of bent coordinates. Here once more the subject of poetry is partly poetry; and "a resembling unlikeness" obtains between two ages which differ so in the act of being similar.

*   *   *

Self-interfering patterns again, reconstituted. The pattern is an abstraction, not the rope but apprehensible only on some rope, bristly or sleek or thick or slim, lending itself to compact or loose or heavy or suave patterning. No poem is an end product. Each is a controlled transformational process. As the cables of a suspension bridge graph a system of stresses, the words on the page plot stabilized energies.

Rare single words can imply, like seeds, whole energy systems. "Anaxiforminges," in the fourth Canto, belongs to Pindar, "Aurunculeia" to Catullus. Three cantos later "Smaragdos, chrysolithos" say "Propertius," and "e quel remir" says "Arnaut." "Quel remir" also says "sexual radiance," and says too that a poet once transubstantiated a common word. Such a word becomes "Gestalt seed," implicit with *maestria*. So writing in the 52nd Canto of the Emperor's duties toward the first month of summer, Pound with his eye on French phrases in Père Couvreur's *Li Ki*, page 354, "la voiture rouge" and "des pierres de prix de couleur incarnate," wrote "In red car with jewels incarnadine / to welcome the summer," bidding us remember how Shakespeare found an unforgettable word to be spoken by a king with bloody hands.

* * *

Potent in a rough bluish-brown capsule the size of an acorn lie the forces that know how to shape an Australian Gum Tree and send it rapidly to great heights in a dry climate. In the late 19th century Australia's climate reminded someone of Italy's, and today the gum trees grow here and there by the Mediterranean. A rhymer of climates planted one on a hillside above Rapallo, just where the long steep *salita* down from Sant' Ambrogio turns sharp left for its final descent to the town. Its material, like that of most artifacts, is local: Italian water and Italian air, clasped in a cellulose tension network of which the patterned integrity alone is Australian. (Canto I bears the same relation to Homer.) The tree has thrived and become a point of rendezvous. Every spring its seeds drop to the path. On the second of May, 1945, Ezra Pound, coming down the *salita*, he thought for the last time, a pirated reprint from Shanghai of Legge's Confucius in one of his coat pockets and a dictionary of ideograms in the other, two men with Tommy-guns flanking him, stopped to pick up one pip. It was all he expected to take with him from Italy (if he lived to go). Looked at endwise, it had a cat face; Gaudier would have read it so, and remembered the Vortex of Egypt. The tree's red flower before it opens being covered with a sort of cap, it is named *eucalyptus*, well-hidden. Like himself, it had come to Italy from halfway round the world. The pip he dropped into his pocket was synecdoche for his dearest landscape, and for the Greek language, where its name has the same root as Calypso, Odysseus' protector. In Pisa he put it where prowling cats could not get at it, and wrote ". . . eucalyptus that is for memory." He has it yet, a kernel, a memory, a word, an exotic great-rooted blossomer's Gestalt-seed.

IMAGISM

A divagation here.

From the directed force and constellated *virtù* of the "Osiris" articles (November 1911 to February 1912), through the pulsating universe of Fenollosa's essay (acquired late 1913) to the Vortex of 1914, and thence into the *Cantos*, runs a steady preoccupation with persistently patterned energies. Lodged in that current, an enigmatic stone called "Imagism" (mid-1912 to mid-1913) created and continues to create its distracting turbulence.

Involving as it did many minds, Imagism received much attention. *The Egoist* ran a "Special Imagist Number" as late as May 1915. Several factors moreover—Amy Lowell's secessionist group, which kept using the name; Pound's effort to incorporate the Imagist terminology into the Vorticist; the printer's delays that held up *Des Imagistes* until March 1914 though the mss. had gone to America the previous summer—have made Imagism seem to occupy Pound's mind much longer than it did. Even the stones and squares and hard edges and sculptured forms in the *Cantos* have helped perpetuate this confusion, though such detail is more plausibly traced to his time with Gaudier.

* * *

Nomina sunt consequentia rerum: "Imagisme" (in pseudo-French) was a name coined to describe a quality of H. D.'s verse: by one account in the British Museum tearoom, where Pound with a slashing pencil made excisions from her "Hermes of the Ways" and scrawled "H. D. Imagiste" at the bottom of the page before sending it off (October 1912) to Harriet Monroe at *Poetry*:

> The hard sand breaks
> And the grains of it
> Are clear as wine.
> Far off over the leagues of it
> The wind,
> Playing on the wide shore,
> Piles little ridges,
> And the great waves
> Break over it. . . .

"It is in the laconic speech of the Imagistes," ran his covering letter. "Objective—no slither—direct—no excess of adjectives. etc. No metaphors that won't permit examination.—It's straight talk—straight as the Greek!" He also noted that H. D. had lived with the things she wrote of since childhood, and "knew them before she had any book-knowledge of them."

They were old friends. He had called her "Dryad" since Pennsylvania days, when a crow's nest high in the Doolittles' maple tree had been one of their adolescent trysting-places, and the little apple orchard in the Pound's back garden at Wyncote another. He had brought her Balzac's *Seraphitus,* and Ibsen and Shaw, and Whistler's *Ten O'Clock* ("We have then but to wait—until, with the mark of the Gods upon him—there come among us again the chosen—who shall continue what has gone before"), and William Morris ("The Gilliflower of Gold" and "The Haystack in the Flood"), and under the apple trees read to her

> Gold on her head, and gold on her feet,
> And gold where the hems of her kirtle meet,
> And a golden girdle round my sweet,
> *Ah! qu'elle est belle, la Marguerite.*

He wrote her sonnets and verses ateem with labile archaisms, and gave her 26 of them in blue typescript, bound with thongs into a little four- by five-inch parchment chapbook: "Hilda's Book." One still leads off *Personae*: still called "The Tree."

"Tall, blond, and with a long jaw but gay blue eyes": so William Carlos Williams recalled her 40 years later. "Ezra was wonderfully in love with her." Williams associated her with storms, as Pound with trees; each saw half. "'Come, beautiful rain,' she said, holding out her arms. 'Beautiful rain, welcome.' And I behind her"—on a country walk—"feeling not inclined to join in her mood. And let me tell you it rained, plenty. It didn't improve her beauty or my opinion of her—but I had to admire her if that's what she wanted." Or in June 1906, after another storm, "without thought or action she went to meet the waves, walked right into them. I suppose she could swim, I don't know, but in she went and the first wave knocked her flat, the second rolled her into the undertow. . . . They dragged her out unconscious, resuscitated her. . . ."

Her father, Professor of Astronomy at Pennsylvania, made "studious careful measurements of the earth's oscillation on its axis in turning." She studied Greek, not eagerly.

Her grown life was a series of self-destructions, her poetic discipline one of these. Speech is held down, held back; the "breathless impatience" Williams remembered is checked by the application of sculptural analogies to language: not in Gautier's way ("Vers, marbre, onyx, émail") making opulent little miniatures, but cutting, arresting, limiting, permitting no flow. In her average work one is more aware of rhythmic constriction than of images. But in the first words of "Hermes of the Ways" perception slides over perception, each line the natural unit of the process:

> The hard sand breaks
> And the grains of it
> Are clear as wine.

—one line of statement, its narrative implication (feet crushing salty dried shore) compressed to the uttermost; one line of microscopic attention, discerning the grains; one line of arresting comparison, visual and evaluative (like wine, this shore is welcome; like sand, the benison is equivocal). "H. D. Imagiste": the personal statement is made without stating. When the 54-line poem ends—

> Hermes, Hermes,
> The great sea foamed,
> Gnashed its teeth about me;
> But you have waited,
> Where sea-grass tangles with
> Shore-grass.

—a psychic relief, sea's gnashing teeth exchanged for this place of tangled grasses, has been articulated but never specified. We do not mistake the poem for the imagined utterance of some Greek, nor do we hear a modern saying "I feel as if. . . ." Nor have we simple homecoming after seafaring: a stanza which gratefully discriminates the shadow of apple boughs here from the shadow of masthead and torn sails, nevertheless stresses that the apples are hard and small and the boughs twisted. Wherever we turn our attention in the poem we find H. D. thinking through its images, exclusively through them, and presenting no detail not germane to such thinking, no detail obligated merely by pictorial completeness.

(In France, meanwhile, where *-isme* crowded *-isme*, they were arranging and rearranging the diction of Mallarmé and of Baudelaire.)

The poem is "about" her taut state of mind, a wried stasis like a sterile homecoming, and a homecoming not to a person but to a mute numinous ikon. That was to be, over and over, the story of her life. Ahead lay marriage, childbirth, desertion, bisexual miseries, and Freud's couch. Her verse never speaks except obliquely, addressing not persons but things, things of unstable menace, playing the safe game of attributing to them volition:

The sea:

> Whirl up, sea—
> . . . cover us . . .

A pool:

> Are you alive?
> I touch you.
> You quiver like a sea-fish. . . .

A storm:

> You crash over the trees,
> you crack the live branch: . . .

And of "the 'Imagist' movement" Pound wrote (17 Sept. 1915), "the whole affair was started not very seriously chiefly to get H. D.'s five poems a hearing without its being necessary for her to publish a whole book. It began certainly in Church Walk with H. D., Richard and myself."

Richard Aldington, who married H. D. and later ran off with another member of the Pound circle (he called his autobiography *Life for Life's Sake*) has this importance, that his presence helped confer the look of a "movement." He had little patience with art, but a parodist's quick sense of mannerism. He had arrived at *vers libre* in all innocence, he said, by imitating "a chorus in the Hippolytus of Euripides." This is probably true. He was 19 when he wrote the poems he gave Pound in 1912. He reported Pound as saying on that occasion, "I don't think you need any help from me," which may be glossed, having learned little, he had little to unlearn. What one was apt to learn in those days was post-Impressionism, and someone fresh out of school but untouched by that would have looked hopeful. Thus the Sappho version Pound so admired simply stuck to the Greek words as far as Aldington understood them, which was a sound way to work when Professor Edmonds was causing the rosyfingered moon to spread her light "o'er briny sea and eke o'er flowery field." With his "Choricos" in *Poetry* that November appeared a note identifying him as "one of the '*Imagistes*,' a group of ardent Hellenists who are pursuing interesting experiments in *vers libre*; trying to attain in English certain subtleties of cadence of the kind which Mallarmé and his followers have studied in France." By 1915 it was clear to Pound that he was "a pig-headed fool," though he had his "occasional concentrations," for which reason "it is always possible that he will do a fine thing." This possibility remained more or less latent.

In January 1913 *Poetry* contained three poems signed H. D., *Imagiste*. In the March number an article by the taxonomist of French schools, F. S. Flint, protracted the illusion that a movement was gathering. Flint drew his information from one "Imagiste," Pound, and did not specify that there were only two others. He mentioned their models—Sappho, Catullus, Villon, very spare poets—and set forth the famous three criteria:

"1. Direct treatment of the 'thing,' whether subjective or objective.

"2. To use absolutely no word that did not contribute to the presentation.

"3. As regarding rhythm: to compose in sequence of the musical phrase, not in sequence of a metronome."

He also mentioned a "doctrine of the image" about which his informant, he said, was reticent.

The criteria prescribed a technical hygiene. They were also a screen through which some contemporary work could pass. That summer a bundle of poems so screened—23 by the founding trio, five by Flint, and one apiece by seven other contributors, including Amy Lowell and James Joyce—was shipped to New York, under the title *Des Imagistes*, to constitute the first number of a periodical called *The Glebe*. This collection was delayed till the following spring, by which time the trio could no longer pretend to much in common. H. D. was repeating herself, Aldington was indulging his talent for pastiche, others were going their ways or dropping out of sight. By mid-1914 the "movement" was loose enough for Amy Lowell to appropriate it. It had come to mean very little more than a way of designating short *vers libre* poems in English.

But the "doctrine of the Image" about which Pound didn't talk that day to Flint remained (remains) vital.

*   *   *

As to the name "Imagisme": "I made the word—on a Hulme basis—and carefully made a name that was not and never had been used in France ... specifically to distinguish 'us' from any of the French groups catalogued by Flint in the P[oetry] R[eview]": on a "Hulme basis" because Hulme used to tell his 1909 associates that images were essential, not decorative; in a French form because French post-Symbolist softness seemed to Pound at that time an active menace.

Flint's 60-page "Contemporary French Poetry" in the August 1912 *Poetry Review* delineated on behalf of Symbolism a contempt for Romanticism, a reaction against Parnassianism, a disgust with Naturalism; then after some remarks on the rationale of *vers libre* it sought to make numerous current -isms seem different from one another: Néo-Mallarméisme, the school of L'Abbaye, Néo-Paganisme, Unanimisme (*aliter* Whitmanisme), L'École de Grâce, Le Paroxysme, L'Impulsionnisme, Le Futurisme. It contained the judgment that Emile Verhaeren (Yeats then 47) was "perhaps the world's greatest living poet," and was otherwise unlucky in its dealings with individuals, the refractive indices of whose souls it tended to estimate: "[Georges Périn's] verse is limpid water seen through a crystal vase, wherein the words like rose petals—pink, crimson, cream and yellow—fall; but he is anxious, a little, and timid; his breath troubles the surface of the water; and the perfect harmony of the colours glows through the crystal refracted into a slow flight of assonances. Or it is the music of an April morning..." [etc.] Flint was happier characterizing movements, since he could draw on their manifestoes. Thus for the Paroxystes "poetry is a lyric and inspired state; it is a faith, a religion, giving to life the value of an absolute—a passionate desire to exteriorize the manifestations of the inner ego. ...," while for the Impulsionnistes (who boasted a *Revue Impulsionniste* and had formed a Fédération Impulsionniste Internationale) "the man whose sensitive system and cerebral organization are such that not only is he prone to meditation and knows the psychic instinct, but also feels the impulsion which urges him to fix his dreams, to realize his thought, he is the Poet, the creator." Friendship drew the poets to this or that Movement, or else physiology ("M. Hertz ... is healthier than Laforgue"; M. Spire's "heart has been wrung by the spectacle of life.")

Against which, we observe that Imagisme was named for a component of the poem, not a state of the poet, and that its three principles establish technical, not psychic, criteria.

Psychic criteria, vainly hoping to distinguish poet from poet, are invoked in the decadence of a tradition, when "poetry" has become as homogenous as taffy. Everywhere in the miniature anthology which comprises the value of Flint's essay we find the same thing, post-Symbolism, vertiginous, *cherchant des sentiments pour les accommoder à son vocabulaire*. Now post-Symbolism had already come into English, and had already undergone a local mutation. It had become pictorial. *That* was something to work from.

*   *   *

In 1912 Arthur Symons, aged 47, was conspicuously part of literary London. He and other men born in English-speaking places in the 1860's—Dowson, Lionel Johnson, John Gray, "Fiona Macleod"—men who underwent the experience of the "new" French poetry in their youth, had once been at the forward edge of their time. On a foggy island, in an ambience prepared by James McNeill Whistler, they had defined a new convention for the short poem; a pictorial rather than a syntactic space holds its elements in relation: fog, half-dawn, grey rain, in which highlights, rings of lamplight, silhouettes, are indistinctly visible. Symons called his 1892 book *Silhouettes*, Gray the next year called a book *Silverpoints*: collections of poems probably for the first time titled as if they were pictures. But the problem of what to do with one's word picture, unless "interpret" it, remained unsolved. A poem from *Silhouettes* will begin with "direct presentation of the 'thing'," but then lapse:

ON THE BEACH

Night, a grey sky, a ghostly sea,
The soft beginning of the rain;
Black on the horizon, sails that wane
Into the distance mistily.

The tide is rising, I can hear
The soft roar broadening far along;
It cries and murmurs in my ear
A sleepy old forgotten song.

Softly the stealthy night descends,
The black sails fade into the sky:
Is not this, where the sea-line ends,
The shore-line of infinity?

I cannot think or dream: the grey
Unending waste of sea and night,
Dull, impotently infinite,
Blots out the very hope of day.

We notice that the stanza has come from *In Memoriam*, as the sanctified vehicle for minor melancholies; that the poem's unity is wholly pictorial; and that the diction worsens as it proceeds. "The shore-line of infinity" does not convince. "Night, a grey sky, a ghostly sea," three phrases that lay elements before the mind, belong to one technique, language creating content. "Softly the stealthy night descends" belongs to a different technique, an intrusive *idea* (the idea of comparing night to a human intruder) governing the language and filling out the line. Behind the first technique lie Whistler Nocturnes and those eerily enigmatic poems of Mallarmé that fill a space where little is clearly visible with elements of a still life. Behind the second technique lies the magazine verse that must have something to *say* about everything it handles. The poem goes on from there by an overt saying.

Or the saying need not be overt: Ford Madox Hueffer's "On a Marsh Road: Winter Nightfall" (1904) commences:

> A bluff of cliff, purple against the south,
> And nigh one shoulder-top an orange pane.
> This wet, clean road; clear twilight held in the pools,
> And ragged thorns, ghost reeds and dim, dead willows.
>
> Past all the windings of these grey, forgotten valleys
> To west, past clouds that close on one dim rift—
> The golden plains; the infinite, glimpsing distances,
> The eternal silences; dim lands of peace. . . .

"Dim lands of peace": "Don't use such an expression as 'dim lands *of peace*'," Pound wrote in *Poetry* (March 1913). "It dulls the image. It mixes an abstraction with the concrete. It comes from the writer's not realizing that the natural object is always the *adequate* symbol." In laying his finger on the point where even Hueffer's presentation failed (he did not name Hueffer) Pound was diagnosing the whole English post-Symbolist genre.

This verse does not so much blend several traditions as compromise them. It draws from Symbolism the mysterious discovery that word laid beside word will create a mental landscape; but uneasy with the indefiniteness of mental landscapes, it seeks to reinforce them with the conventions of an indefinite, atmospheric painting, the whole in turn allied with a gentle melancholy pertinent to a spectator amid mists and twilights. Then wanting to characterize the spectator's soul, it draws on, say, Tennyson for the mode of appropriate statements, telling us for instance that the waste of sea and night blots out the very hope of day. And behind the whole we may detect the program of sensitivity enunciated in the 1860's by Walter Pater.

When Pater wrote of choice moments streaming by, each with some form or tone or mood to be cherished, cultivated "simply for those moments' sake," he implied what minor talents are always apt to want, a recipe for being an artist. The art toward which it leads is a passionate attention to transient effects, and an attention which, rescuing them from the flux of time, will render them static, hence pictorial. The power of these formulae over a whole generation is not hard to understand. "Simply for those moments' sake" rhymes with Gautier's more famous formula, art for the sake of art, and to enjoy, with a little trouble taken over words on a sheet of paper, the stature, the aloofness, of someone who has learned with great difficulty how to go about painting a picture, this is very attractive. And minor poem after minor poem in the generation after Pater's impact suggests notes for a painting that would not be worth the very great trouble of painting. Symons calls one of his shortest poems "Pastel":

The light of our cigarettes
Went and came in the gloom:
It was dark in the little room.

Dark, and then, in the dark,
Sudden, a flash, a glow,
And a hand and a ring I know.

And then, through the dark, a flush
Ruddy and vague, the grace
(A rose!) of her lyric face.

This is a moment seized simply for the moment's sake; a moment as transient as a cigarette, a face revealed in the sudden glow of a cigarette drawn upon. No claims are being made for it, least of all by the poet; it is an inconspicuous poem. It is made of details.

Mallarmé made poems of details too, with a fierce enigmatic rigor, whereas Symons is using the darkness as an excuse for leaving things out, as on other occasions he and his allies used mist or twilight. What was a technical discipline in France has become a pictorial discipline, easier to comprehend and much easier to do. And life, we understand with pages and pages of such poems to turn over, is an affair of quiet moments quietly cherished.

Such had been the English domestication of Symbolism: a way of making poems converted into a way of living, so as to gather materials for poems. We find the poet watching faces in Piccadilly, alert for some beautiful impression; we find him haunting stage doors, and observing backstage shapes and shadows. We find him slipping off to the very fringes of existence, a shy looker-on; and we may note that the language of poetry likewise, in getting clear of sundry rhetorics, is dropping so low in key, giving itself to combinations so unobtrusive, that barely a line stays in the mind: a strange destiny for a movement which was inaugurated by admiration for the Verlaine of "Clair de Lune."

But the aesthetic of glimpses contained possibilities: for note that Symons' "Pastel," but for being rhymed, corresponds exactly to what Imagist poems are often supposed to be. It presents something visual, and does not ruminate nor interpret. Yet it solves, in its inconspicuous way, the problem of what to do about a visibility once you have presented it:

> And then, through the dark, a flush
> Ruddy and vague, the grace
> (A rose!) of her lyric face.

Not an interpretative comment, but three happenings, have entered the domain of the pictorial: an abstract noun; an unexpected un-pictorial adjective; and, interpolated, ("A rose!") another image fetched from elsewhere by the mind, something else to see but not present in the scene, present only in the poem. We are coming close to "Petals on a wet, black bough."

For it was English post-Symbolist verse that Pound's Imagism set out to reform, by deleting its self-indulgences, intensifying its virtues, and elevating the glimpse into the vision. The most famous of all Imagist poems commenced, like any poem by Arthur Symons, with an accidental glimpse. Ezra Pound, on a visit to Paris in 1911, got out of the Metro at La Concorde, and "saw suddenly a beautiful face, and then another and another, and then a beautiful child's face, and then another beautiful woman, and I tried all that day to find words for what they had meant to me, and I could not find any words that seemed to me worthy, or as lovely as that sudden emotion."

The oft-told story is worth one more retelling. This was just such an experience as Arthur Symons cultivated, bright unexpected glimpses in a dark setting, instantly to melt into the crowd's kaleidoscope. And a poem would not have given Symons any trouble. But Pound by 1911 was already unwilling to write a Symons poem. (And Ford's didactic roll of August 1911 lay some weeks in the future. Pound was nearly ready for that lesson.)

He tells us that he first satisfied his mind when he hit on a wholly abstract vision of colors, splotches on darkness like some canvas of Kandinsky's (whose work he had not then seen). This is a most important fact. Satisfaction lay not in preserving the vision, but in devising with mental effort an abstract equivalent for it, reduced, intensified. He next wrote a 30-line poem and destroyed it; after six months he wrote a shorter poem, also destroyed; and after another year, with, as he tells us, the Japanese *hokku* in mind, he arrived at a poem which needs every one of its 20 words, including the six words of its title:

IN A STATION OF THE METRO

The apparition of these faces in the crowd;
Petals on a wet, black bough.

We need the title so that we can savor that vegetal contrast with the world of machines: this is not any crowd, moreover, but a crowd seen underground, as Odysseus and Orpheus and Koré saw crowds in Hades. And carrying forward the suggestion of wraiths, the word "apparition" detaches these faces from all the crowded faces, and presides over the image that conveys the quality of their separation:

Petals on a wet, black bough.

Flowers, underground; flowers, out of the sun; flowers seen as if against a natural gleam, the bough's wetness gleaming on its darkness, in this place where wheels turn and nothing grows. The mind is touched, it may be, with a memory of Persephone, as we read of her in the 106th Canto,

> Dis' bride, Queen over Phlegethon,
> girls faint as mist about her.
> (106/752:777)

—the faces of those girls likewise "apparitions."

What is achieved, though it works by way of the visible, is no picture of the thing glimpsed, in the manner of

> The light of our cigarettes
> Went and came in the gloom.

It is a simile with "like" suppressed: Pound called it an equation, meaning not a redundancy, *a* equals *a*, but a generalization of unexpected exactness. The statements of analytic geometry, he said, "are 'lords' over fact. They are the thrones and dominations that rule over form and recurrence. And in like manner are great works of art lords over fact, over race-long recurrent moods, and over to-morrow." So this tiny poem, drawing on Gauguin and on Japan, on ghosts and on Persephone, on the Underworld and on the Underground, the Metro of Mallarmé's capital and a phrase that names a station of the Metro as it might a station of the Cross, concentrates far more than it need ever specify, and indicates the means of delivering post-Symbolist poetry from its pictorialist impasse. "An 'Image' is that which presents an intellectual and emotional complex in an instant of time": that is the elusive Doctrine of the Image. And, just 20 months later, "The image ... is a radiant node or cluster; it is what I can, and must perforce, call a VORTEX, from which, and through which, and into which, ideas are constantly rushing." And: "An *image* ... is real because we know it directly."

That is pure Pound. It is validated by the fact that he wrote numerous poems to which it applies before he had formulated it, that H. D. wrote "Hermes of the Ways" as if she understood it, and Joyce "I Hear an Army. . . ." There is no sign that Aldington ever had a glimpse of it, though his poems of those years frequently present an image directly, with no unnecessary word, to the rhythm of the musical phrase. The same is true of the rest of the poems in *Des Imagistes*. All the confusion about Imagism stems from the fact that its specifications for technical hygiene are one thing, and Pound's Doctrine of the Image is another. The former, which can be followed by any talented person, help you to write what may be a trivial poem. The latter is not applicable to triviality.

And an Image (this is Pound again) may be some "Luminous Detail" out of History, such as the column in San Zeno signed by its maker: "lord over fact" to this considerable extent, that pondering it we perceive so much of the mind of the 13th century. This principle, when he had digested it, opened the way to the *Cantos*.

* * *

It was the post-Symbolists of the 1890's who brought pictorial images into short poems: theirs was the dead end we are frequently told Imagism was. Imagism on the other hand made possible the *Cantos* and *Paterson*, long works that with the work of T. S. Eliot are the Symbolist heritage in English. The minor poets of Symons's generation brought the necessary elements into English verse, but lacked the intellectual energy to break, as could Imagism, into some realm beyond the mood or the impression.

For Pound's Imagism is energy, is effort. It does not appease itself by reproducing what is seen, but by setting some other seen thing into relation. The mind that found "petals on a wet, black bough" had been active (and for more than a year on that poem, off and on). The "plot" of the poem is that mind's activity, fetching some new thing into the field of consciousness. The action passing through any Imagist poem is a mind's invisible action discovering what will come next that may sustain the presentation—what image, what rhythm, what allusion, what word—to the end that the poem shall be "lord over fact," not the transcript of one encounter but the Gestalt of many, from the Metro traveller's to that of Koré in the underworld.

* * *

This setting-in-relation is apt to be paratactic. "In a Station of the Metro" is not formally a sentence; its structure is typographic and metric. Words, similarly, without loss of precision, have ceased to specify in the manner of words that deliver one by one those concepts we call "meanings." "Apparition" reaches two ways, toward ghosts and toward visible revealings. "Petals," the pivotal word, relies for energy on the sharp cut of its syllables, a consonantal vigor recapitulated in the trisyllabic "wet, black bough" (try changing "petals" to "blossoms"). The words so raised by prosody to attention assert themselves *as words*, and make a numinous claim on our attention, from which visual, tactile and mythic associations radiate. Words set free in new structures, that was the Symbolist formula. And as we move through the poem, word by word, we participate as the new structure achieves itself.

Consider the best-known of all the poems Symbolism claimed, Verlaine's "Clair de Lune" of 1869. "Your soul," it begins: "Votre âme." (Do we know the meaning of either of these words? But let us go on.) Your soul, we are told, is like an elect landscape where mummers play lutes, and dance, and seem sad beneath their disguises. Singing though they be (and in a minor key) of conquering Love and a life where the moment is there to seize, they seem not to believe in their happiness. . . . So far so good; the sad pierrots of convention; we can even make out what it may mean to say that they people the landscape of a soul. But what are we to make of the final clause about their song, which leaps without syntactic interruption into a new stanza and furnishes that stanza with wonder after wonder, each springing into existence at need because a rhyme or a cadence or a grammatical construction seems to require it, each harmonizing with each, and leaving us far from rustic landscapes or masquers, to contemplate moonlight, sleeping birds, great fountains, great fountains that sob with ecstasy among marble forms: marble forms, we may tell ourselves, white in the pallid moonlight, white as the leaping water? —

> Et leur chanson se mêle au clair de lune,
>
> Au calme clair de lune triste et beau
> Qui fait rêver les oiseaux dans les arbres
> Et sangloter d'extase les jets d'eau,
> Les grands jets d'eau sveltes parmi les marbres.

Did some subject, some envisaged reality, precede this writing? We cannot say so with any confidence. We *can* say that before our eyes a reality is created ("direct treatment of the 'thing' whether subjective or objective") by the most formal means, in obedience to the most formal demands. They do not believe in their own happiness, and their song mingles with the light of the moon: "clair de lune" completing the rhyme with "la vie opportune," and by suddenly making the landscape nocturnal effecting just that reversal of mood, that darkness circumvolving antic brightness, that the poem has twice specified. So far we move within a logic of poetic correspondences. But great formalities, silent as physical laws, now take charge: "clair de lune" is repeated and amplified—

> Au calme clair de lune triste et beau

and a new stanza now has two obligations: to manage a structure of grammar sufficiently elaborate to justify the sentence's unexpected prolongation, and to supply a rhyme for "beau." The structure is a pair of parallel verbs governed by "moonlight": which causes to dream, which causes to sob. Which causes to dream:

> Qui fait rêver les oiseaux dans les arbres

Birds dreaming in the trees, these are not unexpected. But the rhyme on "beau" is still to be accomplished. The next line, with the next parallel verb, accomplishes it:

> Et sangloter d'extase les jets d'eau

Makes the birds dream, and makes sob with ecstasy the jets of water. But is the poem starting to wander? Complying with a necessity of syntax and a necessity of rhyme, it has introduced jets of water, and it has only one line left in which to make us believe in something more than their expediency: in their necessity. And we have meanwhile incurred a new obligation; we need a rhyme for "arbres." And we must not let our poem seem to be unravelling; it has already moved sufficiently far from the mummers' landscape. At this moment of tension a new and emphatic formality gives the air of termination, repeating "les grands jets d'eau" as just previously the phrase "clair de lune" had been repeated:

> Les grands jets d'eau sveltes parmi les marbres.

"Marbres"—marble forms, marble statues—seem probable enough, in a realm of great fountains; and "arbres" has its rhyme, and the sentence its termination, and the syntax its neo-Classic symmetry, snatched from the brink of free association.

Whether Verlaine's mind worked that way is irrelevant; it is how our minds work, as the poem achieves itself line by line before us, not so much *referring to* the things in the triumphant last stanza as *creating* them, word by word, as necessity exacts. One can see why the word "symbol," once journalists had discovered it, seemed so welcome: it gave an air of system to the otherwise baffling fact that poems were producing things that had not preceded them, that were not part of a pre-existing array called "the subject of the poem," the array of things one supposes a poem to be "about," as a statement about a horse is "about" some horse whom we understand to have stood or walked or grazed before the statement was thought of.

Vers libre came after "Clair de Lune." *Vers libre*, which exacts "composition in the sequence of the musical phrase" (though certainly Verlaine does not compose "in sequence of a metronome") deprives poets of the suspense Verlaine exploits (how can this pattern possibly be completed?) but affords them a means, which may supplement or even replace syntax, for holding the poem's elements firmly in relation to one another. Thus in Pound's "The Return" (1912), in which every line has a strongly marked expressive rhythm but no two lines are alike, it is actually the rhythm that defines the meaning.

THE RETURN

See, they return; ah, see the tentative
Movements, and the slow feet,
The trouble in the pace and the uncertain
Wavering!

See, they return, one, and by one,
With fear, as half-awakened;
As if the snow should hesitate
And murmur in the wind,
         and half turn back;
These were the "Wing'd-with-Awe,"
         Inviolable,

> Gods of the wingèd shoe!
> With them the silver hounds,
>   sniffing the trace of air!
> Haie! Haie!
>   These were the swift to harry;
> These were keen-scented;
> These were the souls of blood.
> Slow on the leash,
>   pallid the leash-men!

No two lines are *quite* alike; but at exactly the halfway point a single and emphatic rhythmic figure

$$|\,'\,\text{o}\,\text{o}\,|\,'\,\text{o}\,|\,'\,|$$

enters and so asserts itself as out of nine consecutive lines to dominate six. Here it is three times in succession:

> Góds of the / wíngèd / shóe!
> With them the / sílver / hóunds,
>   sniffing the / tráce of / áir!

And the section of the poem this figure dominates is characterized by verbs in the past tense: here is how it *was*, this is how they once were. But in the present tense we have,

> See, they return; ah, see the tentative
> Movements, and the slow feet,
> The trouble in the pace and the uncertain
> Wavering!

—an explicit statement that the gods, returning now, do so in unstable meters. The poem is about the mode of divine apparitions in poetry. Not only the sharp meters but the sharp images, the wingèd shoe and the silver hounds, belong to their past state. Yet the past state is itself being recreated now, and the final lines, though they specify slowness and pallor, are both imagistically sharp and metrically cut:

> Slów / on the léash,
>   pállid the / léash-mén!

A shift of tense, a change of rhythm, and a termination that contains no tenses but draws pallor and slowness into sculptured stasis: these are the devices by which the poem encompasses a long historical span, as from Sappho's time to H. D.'s. But no kernel sentence makes a statement of this kind. The sentences of which the poem is made are syntactically very simple—"See, they return"; "These were the souls of blood"—while no syntax specifies the coherence of the whole poem. The fragmentary effect ("as if he were translating at sight from an unknown Greek masterpiece," thought Yeats, who never understood *vers libre*) corresponds to a feeling we may have that a statement of some length has been made but that important syntactic members of this statement have dropped out, as they have dropped through rents in the ruined papyri of Sappho. And yet nothing has dropped out. We have, thanks to the rhythmic definition, every necessary element, held in place in the poem's continuum so exactly that alterations of tense will specify everything.

None of this is visual, nor sculptural, though we may speak by analogy of "sculptured stasis" at the conclusion. It is wholly linguistic. The Imagist propaganda merged into the Vorticist, and in *Blast* #1 (June 1914) we read,

> Every concept, every emotion presents itself to the vivid consciousness in some primary form. It belongs to the art of this form. If sound, to music; if formed words, to literature; the image, to poetry; form, to design; colour in position, to painting; form or design in three planes, to sculpture; movement, to the dance or to the rhythm of music or verses.

"I defined the vortex as 'the point of maximum energy,' and said that the vorticist relied on the 'primary pigment,' and on that alone." The Vorticist was the more general formulation, including sculptors, painters and musicians with poets in a time that seemed trembling on the brink of a Renaissance.

There was one more reason for the change of terminology. A Movement in part defines one's company, and Imagism, invented to launch H. D., soon entailed negotiating with dim and petulant people: Fletcher, say, or Flint, or Aldington, and eventually Miss Lowell. It is folly to pretend, in the way of historians with books to fill, that they were of Pound's stature. Vorticism implied his alliance with his own kind: Gaudier, Lewis.

THE INVENTION
OF CHINA

"... it must be pointed out that Pound is the inventor of Chinese poetry for our time."
                                        —T. S. Eliot, 1928

On 22 August 1901, late in the last weeks he was ever to spend in Japan, Ernest Fenollosa smoothed a fresh page of his notebook and filled with black ink his calligraphic brush. He had been paraphrasing Kainan Mori's discourse on Chinese poetry in the rapid hand of one whose pencil has filled a great many books. Now onto four consecutive unruled pages he transcribed the 50 ideographs of a ten-line poem, chosen by Mori to illustrate an historical point. The characters, decisively stroked after years of practice, ran according to his custom in horizontal lines from left to right, to facilitate a Westerner's exegesis. Under each ideograph he pencilled the Japanese sound by which he and his instructor designated the words: *sei . . . sei . . . ka . . . han . . . so. . . .* Under each sound in turn went an English word or two, glossing nodes in the structure of meaning. And having mounted and labelled the exhibit, he resumed his scribbling of interpretative notes.

This notebook, in brown mottled binding, labelled "Prof. Mori's Lectures: Vol. II," came 12 years later into Ezra Pound's keeping, having crossed two oceans and the American continent *en route*, one of some 16 from which Pound first chose, as literary executor, to extract the notes on Noh drama. Late in 1914, in his odd-shaped flat in South Kensington, he turned at last to the poem above which Fenollosa had pencilled "(no name)." Below the characters stood the merest glosses, but sufficient:

blue	blue	river	bank, side	grass
luxuriantly	luxuriantly	garden	in	willow
fill	fill	storied	on	girl
full	full	house		
in first bloom of youth				
white brilliant luminous	(ditto)	just face	window	door
beauty of face	(ditto)	red	powder	toilet
slender	slender	put forth	white	hand
in former times	was	courtesan	house	girl
now	is	dissipated	son's	wife
dissipated	son	go away	not	return
empty	bed	hard	only one, alone	keep

Six lines present her situation, four more explain it. To mark off this structural division, like a sonnet's, each line in the first section of the poem begins with a reduplication: blue, blue; luxuriantly, luxuriantly; ... slender, slender. Pound judged his English needed some less obtrusive principle, and though the version he published in early 1915 commences, to strike the keynote, by reduplicating—

> Blue, blue, is the grass about the river

it modulates at once into a less obvious pairing:

> And the *will*ows have over*fill*ed the close garden.

The third line relies on paired m's and clustered short i's:

> And with*in*, the *mi*stress, *in* the *mi*dmost of her youth

The fourth line returns to reduplication:

> White, white of face, hesitates, passing the door.

The fifth line of the Chinese he omitted, taking from it only a title, "The Beautiful Toilet." From the sixth he made another reduplication, its members gracefully separated:

> Slender, she puts forth a slender hand.

A pairing, an internal rhyme, an assonance, a pairing, a split pairing: without recourse to anything insistent the structure of the poem's first lobe has been shaped into cohesion, aided by the opening of two consecutive lines with "And," aided too by the delicate pathos of her white face and her slender hand put forth. Then imitating the structural division, Pound contracted his line to utter a quiet quatrain:

> And she was a courtesan in the old days
> And she has married a sot,
> Who now goes drunkenly out
> And leaves her too much alone.

A former year's study of Giles's *History of Chinese Literature* had brought before his eyes a version which begins

> Green grows the grass upon the bank,
> The willow-shoots are long and lank;
> A lady in a glistening gown
> Opens the casement and looks down,

and it seems a fair guess that he now turned this up to verify that he had indeed reworked the same poem. Certainly he got from Giles the poet's name (Mei Sheng, the only name in *Cathay* not in Japanese form) and the date, 140 B.C.; and reinspecting as he did so Giles's empty couplets, he was entitled to reflect that a China of the mind existed at last.

Implying, syllable by syllable, with cunning governance of pace, an alien poetic which works by nuance even when iterating its monosyllables, such artistry deserves better than one sinologue's dismissal of "so-called 'free verse'," or another's pidgin fumbling with the same poem, published in implied rebuke three years later:

> Green, green,
> The grass by the river bank,
> Thick, thick,
> The willow trees in the garden.
> Sad, sad,
> The lady in the tower . . .

This version (yes, it is Waley's) closes lamentably:

> Now she is a wandering man's wife
> The wandering man went, but did not return.
> It is hard alone to keep an empty bed.

This is a resourceless man's verse; the resourceless man wrote but did not transmute; it is hard alone to wring song from philology.

*   *   *

Waley was but one of many who rushed in as word of the two-shilling pamphlet, *Cathay*, got around. *Vers libre* with an Oriental décor looked easy, like the automatic writing of the Zeitgeist. In those years writers dabbled in *vers libre* if they were alive in the present, and *chinoiserie* had been floating about for some decades. John Gould Fletcher has recalled the power of Lafcadio Hearn, Giles's *History*, and Judith Gautier's *Le Livre de Jade* over a young imagination first quickened by the treasures in the Oriental Wing of the Boston Museum of Fine Arts, circa 1905. (He may never have known that the collection had been assembled by

Fenollosa, whom Boston chose to forget after his 1895 divorce.)
Fletcher cites a poem—

> The lanterns dangle at the ends of long wires, the breeze bobs
>   them to and fro.
> My soul is in love with that lazy lantern dance.
> Oh how the autumn gusts through the dark gardens
> Rattle them together, rending their crimson sides

—which he entitled, in 1913, "From the Chinese," though it
actually recalled "a far-off garden party I had witnessed as an ex-
tremely young man in Arkansas." For, "Its substance was no more
taken from any particular Chinese poem than was the substance of
certain other experiments in the same book, labelled 'From the
Japanese,' actually taken from that language. I knew nothing of
either." Composition *à la mode chinoise* was one of the directions
the *vers-libre* movement, guided by current intuitions of beauty,
was fated to explore had there been no Fenollosa and no Pound.
And someone, surely, would have attempted *vers-libre* versions of
actual Chinese poems, as inevitable corrective to post-Symboliste
nostalgias. Someone in fact had; Pound himself had, with no
Chinese to draw on but only Giles's couplets. Giles's *History* for
instance contains this version of the Han emperor Liu Ch'ê's
threnody for a harem favorite—

> The sound of rustling silk is stilled,
> With dust the marble courtyard filled;
> No footfalls echo on the floor,
> Fallen leaves in heaps block up the door. . . .
> For she, my pride, my lovely one, is lost,
> And I am left, in hopeless anguish tossed.

And early in 1913 Ezra Pound, beater on impossible doors, had
rewritten this (this!) with a graver decorum:

> The rustling of the silk is discontinued,
> Dust drifts over the courtyard,
> There is no sound of footfall, and the leaves
> Scurry into heaps and lie still,
> And she the rejoicer of the heart is beneath them:
>
> A wet leaf that clings to the threshold.

This was meant for inclusion in the first "Imagiste" affirmation, and "A wet leaf that clings to the threshold" simply applies Imagist canons, the mind's creative leap fetching some token of the gone woman into the poem's system. No wet leaf clings in the Chinese, and there is no indication that Pound supposed one did; he simply knew what his poem needed. In the same way he condensed 12 lines from Giles—

> O fair white silk, fresh from the weaver's loom,
> Clear as the frost, bright as the winter snow—
> See! friendship fashions out of thee a fan,
> Round as the round moon shines in heaven above . . . [etc.]

to the masterly

> *Fan-Piece, for her Imperial Lord*
> O fan of white silk,
>   clear as frost on the grass-blade,
> You also are laid aside.

This is contemporary with "In a Station of the Metro," which early in 1913 he had instructed Harriet Monroe to print thus:

> The apparition   of these faces   in the crowd:
> Petals   on a wet, black bough.

—two lines, five phases of perception. Later typesetters, thinking this queer, have closed up the spaces. There is no indication that he was thinking of Chinese characters when he grouped sensations that way, but he was clearly ready for the gift Mary Fenollosa made him during that year, prompted, it appears, by the command of idiom displayed in that poem and in 11 others of the *Contemporania* group in the April 1913 *Poetry*.

They met under the roof of Sarajini Naidu, a Hindu nationalist poetess. In the five years since her husband's sudden death Mrs. Fenollosa had been occupied with his masses of manuscript material. By 1912, after a special trip to Japan and a spell at the British Museum, she had brought his *Epochs of Chinese and Japanese Art* into publishable form, a handsome two-volume work. There remained hundreds of pages on Japanese plays and Chinese poetry, which demanded not an editor but a poet; Fenollosa himself had written that "the purpose of poetical translation is the poetry, not the verbal definitions in dictionaries."

The notebooks record his five years' furious quest for the facts which should underlie a grasp of the poetry. Three sessions with a Mr. Hirai in September 1896 yielded detailed if sometimes vague glosses on 22 poems by Wang Wei and Li Po ("Omakitsu," "Rihaku"; all the proper names in the notebooks are in Japanese form). With a Mr. Shida two years later he studied T'ao Ch'ien ("To-Em-Mei"). Then in February 1899 he commenced two years' intensive work with Professor Mori (1863–1911), a distinguished literary scholar and himself a practitioner of the delicate art, called in Japan *kanshi*, of writing poems in Classical Chinese. Mori spoke no English, and though Fenollosa's Japanese was adequate he often brought with him to their private sessions his own former philosophy student Nagao Ariga, who had at one time written out for him texts and translations of early Chinese poems. Ariga, one surmises, helped Fenollosa be sure he understood Mori's discourse when the talk got technical.

For a year and a half they worked through "Rihaku"; two very large notebooks contain cribs, glosses, comments, scholarly apparatus for 64 poems. (These furnished the backbone of *Cathay*.) Toward the end of this time Fenollosa was also working at early and Taoist poems with another teacher. Finally, on his last sojourn in Japan (April–September 1901) he commissioned from Mori a course of systematic lectures in literary history, commencing with the legendary invention of the written characters. A Mr. Hirata interpreted. They filled three notebooks; the last entry (19 Sept. 1901) is dated just days before Ernest Fenollosa left Japan for ever.

And the record of all this study, eight notebooks in all, plus the volumes of notes on *Noh* drama, plus the books in which he was drafting his lectures on Chinese poetics, plus a sheaf of loose sheets, all these his widow in late 1913 transferred to Ezra Pound, some in London, some later by mail from Alabama. So it came about that the opportunity to invent Chinese poetry for our time fell not to some random modernist but to a master. The 14 poems in the original *Cathay*, selected from some 150 in the notebooks, were the first *vers-libre* translations not derived from other translations but from detailed notes on the Chinese texts.

No follower profited by the mastery. *Cathay* encouraged subsequent translators of Chinese to abandon rhyme and fixed stress counts. It also inaugurated the long tradition of Pound the inspired but unreliable translator. In the subsequent half-century's sniffling and squabbling its real achievement went virtually unnoticed.

*   *   *

Its real achievement lay not on the frontier of comparative poetics, but securely within the effort, then going forward in London, to rethink the nature of an English poem. It consisted in maximizing three criteria at once, criteria hitherto developed separately: the *vers-libre* principle, that the single line is the unit of composition; the Imagist principle, that a poem may build its effects out of things it sets before the mind's eye by naming them; and the lyrical principle, that words or names, being ordered in time, are bound together and recalled into each other's presence by recurrent sounds.

These things had been done before but not simultaneously. In Pound's earlier work we can point to a *vers libre* that proceeds line by line but allows the lines to seem disconnected gestures

> (Lo! this thing is not mine
> Nor thine to hinder
> For the custom is full old . . .);

and to an imagism of things named that names them as though arbitrarily

> (I have known the golden disc,
> I have seen it melting above me.
> I have known the stone-bright place,
>   The hall of clear colours);

and to a craft of sound only languidly attentive to denotations

> (My love is lovelier than sprays
> Of eglantine above clear waters,
> Or whitest lilies that upraise
> Their heads in midst of moated waters).

Much of the work of Pound's twenties, including work he later chose not to reprint, was a search for poems that should have some structural principle other than the writer's mood or the strophe's requirements. He tried turning the mood into a mask, an exiled troubadour, a Ninevite bard; he built strophes into canzones or sestinas ("Altaforte") and dissected other strophes down to their ossature ("The Return"). He iterated elementary syntactic members ("Commission") and dissolved syntax in iridescences of diction ("The Alchemist"). And in his thirtieth year, in *Cathay*, guided by notes that plotted the nodes of meaning and obligated by their concision and clarity, he managed for the first time to articulate numerous extended poems in a *vers libre* not confoundable with cut-up prose, answerable to no overt system of counts or assonances, but held together from within by so many filaments, syntactic, sonoric, imagistic, that any change, as surely as change in a verse of Pope's, will be change for the worse. Thus:

> Light rain is on the light dust
> The willows of the inn-yard
> Will be going greener and greener . . .

—three lines of a tiny vignette worked up from a quatrain Fenollosa studied with Hirai, noting that in Japanese transcription it rhymed like an Omar Khayyám stanza.* Pound used it as epigraph to "Four Poems of Departure," and contrived for it a delicate formality. Each line has its own entelechy.

> Light rain is on the light dust

* The notes, omitting the Japanese sounds, run:

I   castle   morning   rain   wets   light   dust
The castle on the I river, i.e. a walled city

Guest   house   blue   blue   willow   color   new
in the inns where you will stay thereafter, the new color of the willow trees will be green green

Advise   you lord   newly   annihilate   one   cup   saki
I advise you, however, to put an end to a cup of wine

West   departure   Yo   gate, barrier   not   original, old   man
Going westward through the Yo gate there will not be any old friend.

The pencil scribble lays frequent traps. It is easy, as Pound did, to misread *Yo* as *Go*. The poem is by Wang Wei ("Omakitsu").

—square symmetry of phrasing; symmetry of metrical emphasis, the three little words slung between two spondees; a word that recurs in two senses;

> The willows of the inn-yard

—again three little words and two spondees, but the first spondee ("willows") blunted and moved one step into the line, and the sounds of the two of them this time quite dissimilar;

> Will be going greener and greener

—a triple alliteration; a doubling, "greener" repeating "greener" as "light" previously echoed "light"; an assonantal linking, the sound of "willows" repeated by the sound of "will," and this assonance, now that three instances rule out accident, clearly a carrying forward through all three lines of the liquid syllable introduced by "light."

More: the terminal syllable of "greener" sponsors a line keyed by r's—

> But you, Sir, had better take wine ere your departure;

and here, just as the second person enters the poem, we realize that every line has featured a word in "n"—rain, inn, greener, wine—to recur, sure enough, in the "friends" of the next line also—

> For you will have no friends about you

—and to initiate the last line of all as (echoing the "no" of "no friends") alliterated gates clang with an eerie finality:

> When you come to the gates of Go.

On its page in *Cathay* the whole poem is scarcely larger than a postage stamp. Its sonoric intricacies would have delighted Pope.

And it has another claim on our attention; it documents the year it was written in more than one way. Dating from the first winter of the war, it is like a poem abstracted from the departure of troop trains. For *Cathay*, April 1915 (which did not, we should remember, include the last four of the poems now gathered under that title) is largely a war book, using Fenollosa's notes much as Pope used Horace or Johnson Juvenal, to supply a system of parallels and a structure of discourse. Its exiled bowmen, deserted women, levelled dynasties, departures for far places, lonely frontier guardsmen and glories remembered from afar, cherished memories, were selected from the diverse wealth in the notebooks by a sensibility responsive to torn Belgium and disrupted London; and as "The Jewel Stairs' Grievance" is "especially prized because she offers no direct reproach," so *Cathay* essays an oriental obliquity of reference to what we are to understand as its true theme. In the same way, two years later, Pound was to handle the plight of the poet in wartime by way of a transposed Propertius; and much as the title alone connects "In a Station of the Metro" with its occasion, so the date on the title page connects *Cathay* with the privations of the Expeditionary forces across the channel. "I keep the book in my pocket," Gaudier-Brzeska wrote from the Marne of the little two-ounce pamphlet. "Indeed I use [the poems] to put courage in my fellows. I speak now of the 'Bowmen' and the 'North Gate' [i e. 'Lament of the Frontier Guard'] which are so appropriate to our case." He had had typescripts of these two poems and a third—presumably "South Folk in Cold Country"—four months previously in the marshes of the Aisne ("a sight worthy of Dante, there was at the bottom [of the trenches] a foot deep of liquid mud in which we had to stand two days and two nights"), and "the poems depict our situation in a wonderful way."

Parts IV and V of *Mauberley* paraphrase a genre of war poem that was to come out of the trenches later on—

> hysterias, trench confessions,
> laughter out of dead bellies.

The *Cathay* poems paraphrase an elegiac war poetry nobody wrote (though "Exile's Letter" is like an elegant "Tipperary"). Perfectly vital after 50 years, they are among the most durable of all poetic responses to World War I. They say, as so much of Pound's work says, that all this has happened before and continually happens. He even interpolated his 1911 version of *The Seafarer* between "Exile's Letter" and "Poems of Departure," noting that "Rihaku" and the Anglo-Saxon poet were approximately contemporaneous, and allowing the reader to find parallels between

> Not any protector
> May make merry man faring needy. . . .
> Moaneth always my mind's lust
> That I fare forth, that I afar hence
> Seek out a foreign fastness.

and

> And if you ask how I regret that parting:
> It is like the flowers falling at spring's end
> Confused, whirled in a tangle.
> What is the use of talking, and there is no end of talking.
> There is no end of things in the heart.

—to which we may join another letter of Gaudier's:

> The rain has stopped for several days & with it keeping the watch in a foot deep of liquid mud, also sleeping on sodden ground. The frost having set it we have the pleasure of a firm if not a warm bed & when you have turned to a warrior you become hardened to many evils. . . . like the chinese bowmen in Ezra's poem we had rather eat fern shoots than go back now. . . . If you can write me all about the Kensington colony the neo-greeks and the neo-chinese. Does the Egoist still appear? What does it contain?

*   *   *

Vers libre, then, carried to new articulation; and new propaganda for a poetic of images (facts); and oblique war poems written in war time. But as a place to get what is in the Chinese? Consult an expert, and in ten minutes he will be spluttering, amid indignant asides on the Fenollosa–Pound theory of the Chinese Written Character, the "sheer nonsense" of which is usually presumed to underlie *Cathay's* derelictions. Of these there is virtually a canonical list. Thus in "Separation on the River Kiang" (where "kiang" by the way means "river" and is not the name of some river) a single line treats "Ko-jin" as a proper name, which it is not, and has him go west when he should (of course) go east; and in "The River Song" we have two poems conflated, the lines "And I have moped . . ." down to "aimlessly singing" being actually the title of the second, unrecognized as such and submerged in the continuum.

Such misadventures confirm what we already knew, that Pound did not bring to the notebooks a prior scholarly grasp of canonical Chinese poetry, and often made wrong decisions when he was unaware of making a decision at all. Their etiology is easily retraced. Thus in "Separation on the River Kiang" we find

ko	jin	sei	gi	Ko	Kaku	ro
old	acquaint-ance,	west	leave	...	.....	..

An old acquaintance, starting further West, takes leave of KKR

That "west leave" means to leave the west, not to go west, as in German "halb sechs" means half past five, not half past six, Fenollosa did not understand. Pound in turn picked up this misunderstanding; discarded, as overly picturesque, an earlier gloss on Ko Kaku ro, which was just as well since it was erroneous anyhow; and declining to open a poem with so bleak a periphrasis as "old acquaintance," turned "Ko jin," apparently with his eyes open, into a proper name. Hence the line in *Cathay*,

Ko-jin goes west from Ko-kaku-ro.

Chaucer in much the same way, perhaps misled by a scribe, mistook Boccaccio's "Fu mondo" for "Fumando," and instead of stating that the temple was clean, presents Emelye in *The Knight's Tale* "Smokynge the temple."

And as for the notorious conflation of two poems and one title into "The River Song," this came about because Fenollosa kept the left-hand pages of the "Rihaku" notebooks for comments by Professor Mori. Three right-hand pages of "River Song" face three left-hand pages of comment; then a blank left-hand page faces the long title of a new poem about Li Po in the garden full of spring softness. Pound mistook this for more of "The River Song," and the blank left-hand page, which signals a new poem, for absence of comment by Mori.

A surprisingly large number of the "errors" are quite deliberate. Chinese poets, practising an art which thrives, as did Pope's, on minimal variations within a tradition, summon up the tradition by constant allusion. Mori's notes normally explicated such matters. Pound, whose readers would see only 14 poems, very deftly worked his way round them, avoiding notes. Thus "Poem by the Bridge at Ten-Shin" omits a reference to mandarin ducks which highlighted the extravagance of the courtiers by alluding, says Mori's note, to an old song about the décor of a rich man; Pound has only "the dance of the seventy couples." At the end of the same poem whole ganglia of allusion have been cut. "Rihaku" had accomplished his rebuke to the riotously ornamental courtiers with (1) a gnomic distich on the folly of hanging around, for instance at court, when one's job is done; (2) example of this: a minister who did not retire at the death of his emperor and was executed by the next emperor; (3) further example: a minister whose concubine caught the eye of a prince, whence the minister's execution and her suicide; (4) contrasting example: a man who on completing his service to the state had the wisdom to slip away. Pound's problems commenced with the distich, which as glossed and explained in the notebook is simply incomprehensible. He omitted it. This left the three exempla with nothing specific to exemplify. Moreover, none of them has torque unless we are well instructed. As to English readers a telescope and a blind eye will denote Nelson, so to literate Chinese the luckless Li Ssu is specified by sighs and a yellow dog; on his way to execution he wished he could go rabbit-hunting with his dog again. But from "Yellow dog useless lament," which is all the text provides, nothing intelligible can be done for an occidental. As for the second minister, the text gives only his concubine's name and the fact that there was tragic animosity; and as for the third, we are given only his name and the fact that he went off, with loosened hair, by boat. Mori's comments lay before Pound, explaining all these matters. He pushed them aside and ended the poem his own way:

> ... Night and day are given over to pleasure
> And they think it will last a thousand autumns,
> Unwearying autumns.
> For them the yellow dogs howl portents in vain,
> And what are they compared to the lady Riokushu,
> That was cause of hate?
> Who among them is a man like Han-rei
> Who departed alone with his mistress,
> With her hair unbound, and he his own skiffsman!

The yellow dog, pluralized, has become an omen; lady Riokushu, no longer typifying the snares of court life, shames today's courtiers with the decisiveness of her existence; and Han-rei has become a man who valued passion properly, the unbound hair (which he would have let down to improve his incognito) transferred to a mistress Pound borrowed from Mori's commentary; every detail feels intelligible without notes.

And every detail is misrepresented. One can sympathize with the exasperation of anyone whose intimacy with the Chinese original gives those bare names potency: such potency as Ezra Pound, on his home ground the most allusive of poets, conjures with in for instance the 80th Canto:

> Mallarmé, Whistler, Charles Condor, Degas
> and the bar of the Follies
> as Manet saw it, Degas, those two gents crossing 'La
> Concorde' or for that matter
> Judith's junk shop
> with Théophile's arm chair
> one cd/ live in such an apartment
> seeing the roofs of Paris
> Ça s'appelle une mansarde
> (80/504:538)

What might some translator in China do with that?

*   *   *

Instances could be readily multiplied: errors of Fenollosa's, errors of Pound mistaking the local intent of Fenollosa, who was not writing for publication but scribbling in a tutorial to aid his own recollection; deliberate alterations made by Pound to keep the poems in English either uncluttered or self-sufficient. Of the accuracy of his versions Pound was to claim only that they were "closer than the Rubaiyat," which is correct. And the first vial of expert derision to break on his head was occasioned by almost his only venture in trusting authority. When it printed "Exile's Letter, from the Chinese of Rihaku (Li Po)," the April 1915 *Poetry* carried for the edification of Chicago a little note on Li Po, "usually considered the greatest poet of China." Three years later Arthur Waley found this judgment ridiculous. But Pound was simply transcribing from Giles's *History of Chinese Literature*, page 151: "By general consent Li Po himself (A.D. 705–762) would probably be named as China's greatest poet," and historians who say otherwise are not quarrelling with a brash interloper but with another historian.

*   *   *

Cathay has more instructive deviations to exhibit: the ones to which Pound was driven when the notes sagged. On one occasion we can follow him as he virtually invents a poem, an accretion of small deflections steering melancholy toward metaphysics, and the poet, unguided, conniving.

"With Mr. Shida Feb. 5 1899," Fenollosa had written, and Mr. Shida had not Mori's kind of authority. "From 'To-Em-Mei Shio' Work of Toemmei   Both prose & poetry.

" 'Teiwun' *Fixed* (not moving) *Cloud* the subject of 4 connected poems"

Each poem contained eight lines of four characters each. Fenollosa did not copy the ideographs from the anthology they were using. He jotted down line by line the Japanese sounds dictated by Mr. Shida, beneath them the meaning of the separate words, beneath these in turn the running sketch of a provisional English syntax.

| *ai* | *ai* | *tei* | *wun* |
| gathering | gathering | fixed | clouds |

The fixed showers gather & gather

| *mo* | *mo* | *ji* | *u* |
| pattering | pattering | temporary | rain |

& the intermittent showers patter & patter

| *Hachi* | *hiŏ* | *dŏ* | *kon* |
| eight | surface | same | dark |

The earth in all directions is equally dark

| *Hei* | *rŏ* | *ĭ* | *lan* |
| flat | road | this | wide & flat |

The level road stretches out into the flat distance . . .

These notes, and similar notes on 28 more lines, were what Pound had before him when he made the poem called "To-Em-Mei's 'The Unmoving Cloud'," one of the four poems he added to

Cathay when the sequence was reprinted in *Lustra*. It is the only one of six poems by the same author that tempted his skills, in a notebook containing some 30 of which he used only two. He began by devising a rhetoric, of some interest since it controlled the subsequent course of the poem. He discarded, as conducive to fussiness, the antithesis between fixed clouds and intermittent rain, and commenced,

> The clouds have gathered, and gathered,
> and the rain falls and falls

Then coming to "The earth in all directions is equally dark," he sensed that having expended 12 words on rainfall his poem demanded a second impetus. The words "eight surface" in the gloss supplied his hint:

> The eight ply of the heavens
> are all folded into one darkness,
> And the wide flat road stretches out.

Whether or not he recognized in "eight" a designation of Chinese compass points is neither ascertainable nor important. "Eight ply" gave the stanza what it needed, a focal strangeness at the center of its imitation of unyielding sameness, interminable rain, impenetrable flatness. Four Chinese lines have suggested five English, and these five cunningly built. Seven short a's and a parallel syntax unite the two opening lines, a shift from feminine stresses to masculine contrasts them, three thudding syllables mime the relentless rain. The spondaic "eight ply" in the third line echoes the spondaic "rain falls" in the second, while a longer fourth line imitates a longer first; the metric has reversed its direction. Yet the stanza does not reverse its structure but repeat its structure, the structure each time of two declarative clauses linked by "and." Repetition, however, is not mechanism. The first member of the pair is in one case a single line, in the other case two lines; the single line tells us that the clouds have gathered and gathered, the two lines re-examine this fact and tell us how the eight ply of the heavens are folded, statement now reinforced with image. The first "and" joins effect to cause, clouds therefore rain. The second "and" joins perception to perception, dark heaven, empty road. The five lines constitute

one sentence, an overbalanced quatrain, ceremonious, self-terminat-
ing, grown, by way of Fenollosa, Mr. Shida, and some textual
tradition anterior to Shida, out of 16 Chinese monosyllables never
heard nor seen by Pound.

This verse is free in one respect only, that it does not agree
to count stresses and then repeat that count. Its syllables are tied
by more complicated laws. We accept the division into lines because
it follows the divisions of the syntax; we allow each of the five lines
so isolated to take up the same time, though no two have the same
number of syllables nor even the same number of stresses. And as
the lines alter their pace, the imagination permits metric to seem
mimetic: the stresses seem expressive because nothing but natural
emphasis seems to dictate their fall.

> And the ráin fálls and fálls

mimes a redoubled downpour;

> And the wíde flát róad strétches óut

mimes a prolonged monotony. Meanwhile across lines innocently
parallel, innocent of enjambment, cuts a syntactic ordering as cunningly simple as a diagonal brace, supporting the passage from
within. Other translators of Chinese, marvelling at Pound's trans-
lucency but deploring his want of scholarship, have supposed
themselves to have learned his lesson when they have kept the syntax
simple and the line-length irregular, and have composed nothing it is
possible to remember.

> The lingering clouds, rolling, rolling,
> And the settled rain, dripping, dripping,
> In the Eight Directions—the same dusk.
> The level lands—one great river.

—so Mr. Waley, whose principle is to represent each ideogram by
a stress (hence here a four-stress line): "but between the stresses
unstressed syllables are of course interposed."

> Lowering, lowering, the lingering clouds,
> Drizzling, drizzling, the seasonal rains.
> The Eight Directions are all alike in twilight,
> The level roads all but impassable.

—So Mr. Acker, who does not disclose his principles.

> How fair, the lingering clouds!
> How misty, the seasonal rain!
> Darkness fills the universe,
> Blurring the level pathway.

—So Lily Pao-Hu Chung and Marjorie Sinclair, pooling, in Honolulu, their taste for the indefinite.

> The clouds have gathered and gathered
>   and the rain falls and falls,
> The eight ply of the heavens
>   are all folded into one darkness
> And the wide, flat road stretches out.

—So *il miglior fabbro*.

The question of fidelity remains, adjuring us to interrogate three separate transactions: Mr. Shida's with the Chinese, Fenollosa's with Mr. Shida, Pound's with the Fenollosa notes. The first two are now inextricable; though the notes did go wrong more than once, there is no way of being sure how. The third, Pound's way of dealing with what confronted him, may profitably hold our attention a little longer. The way of a mind creating is more interesting than a record of inattentions.

"Eight ply," we have seen, was a *trouvaille*, obligated by the rhetoric; Pound had Fenollosa's syntactic guide in front of him and preferred to disregard it. The rhetoric has also obligated subjects, verbs, numbers and tenses, of which the notes (like the originals) are innocent. In Chinese, the language accretes processes—

> Lowering, lowering, the lingering clouds

In Pound's English, a man makes affirmations—

> The clouds have gathered and gathered

—affirmations, moreover, about a universe structured by western preoccupations with time and causation. "Have gathered ... falls": the logic that small alteration of tense imports was eventually to take charge of Pound's poem, when the notes left him in difficulties.

The notes showed no difficulties just yet. Pound completed the first section of the suite in four more lines, omitting nothing and adding nothing except a doubled adjective:

> I stop in my room toward the East, quiet, quiet,
> I pat my new cask of wine.
> My friends are estranged, or far distant,
> I bow my head and stand still.

The second section opens with the same three lines as the first, but with the order of the ideograms slightly altered. Pound accordingly alters the order of his words, compressing three lines into two as he does so—

> Rain, rain, and the clouds have gathered,
> The eight ply of the heavens are darkness.

—and continues with his mobile variably stressed line, following the sense of the notebook scrupulously. But in the third part the sense of the notebook suddenly turns banal. After four lines about boughs, Fenollosa has written,

jin	*shaku*	*yu*	*gen*
man	again, too	is	speak

Men often are saying

jitsu	*getsu*	*kan*	*sei*
sun	moon	have	turn

The sun and moon have their turning

An	*toku*	*soku*	*seki*
tranquil	get	place	seat

Setting my mat where I can be at ease

Setsu	*hi*	*hei*	*sei*
to be glad	his, its	flat	born

natural or customary

Let me take joy in this course of nature.

This is hopeless; for the poem so far has projected an unwavering elegiac mood that can no more effect a *volte-face* than can a smooth river. What went wrong we can look at later; our attention is claimed by Pound's problem, which was to sustain the poem of

which he had now written 19 lines, a poem in which a sudden decision to take joy in the course of nature will seem fatuous. His
solution was ingenious. Rejecting the obvious meaning of the line
about sun and moon—that seasons come round, that dawn succeeds
darkness, sunshine rain—he concocts a decorous piece of folk
wisdom;

> The trees in my east-looking garden
>   are bursting out with new twigs,
> They try to stir new affection,
>
> And men say the sun and moon keep on moving
>   because they can't find a soft seat.

The syntactic guide has been jettisoned, "tranquil" associated
with "seat" and seat with sun and moon, and a Chinese proverb
originated in South Kensington. And the rescription firmly continues. Having lost all parallelism with the first two sections, section
three must make the most of affinities with section four. (They are
both about Nature.) Pound simply amalgamates them, and proceeds;

> The birds flutter to rest in my tree,
>   and I think I have heard them saying
> "It is not that there are no other men
> But we like this fellow the best,
> But however we long to speak
> He cannot know of our sorrow."

This terminal episode, conflating the original's third and fourth
parts, has an ingenious unity of concept; the trees "try to stir new
affection," the sun and moon seek for rest, the birds yearn for
communion with man, and all in vain. The rain-beaten estrangement of the poet, solacing himself with wine during an interminable
solitude through which no one comes, is absorbed into a cosmic
estrangement, all nature suffused with dumb longing. "To-Em-
Mei," as transcribed by Fenollosa, contains nothing of this; his
third section speaks of being cheered up by burgeoning nature,
his fourth of being sung to by the birds (who cannot of course
speak his language). Pound has unified the poem, obligated by a
diction and a movement that expect unity, and done so by imposing
on the notes just three distortions. He has slipped a stressed "try"

into the passage about the twigs, he has allotted to the birds incommunicable sorrow, he has given sun and moon no place of rest. Each time he has built on something in the text. The trees in the notebook "vying to make the most of their new beauty, with this they appeal to my affection"; "vying" has suggested "try." The birds in the notebook "hold deep sorrow in [their] minds," not out of *Angst* but because their favorite man cannot understand their speech; Pound has moved their sorrow into the speech itself. The sun and moon in the notebook are mentioned in conjunction with a tranquil seat, but for "To-Em-Mei," not for them.

These are what are normally called mistranslations, in one case grotesque mistranslation. Let us be quite clear that they are deflections undertaken with open eyes. There is no question of seduction by half-understood ideograms; no ideograms are in evidence on these pages of Fenollosa's. There is no question of misunderstanding; the notes are unambiguous. It is a question, purely and simply, of taking all necessary measures to protect the course of a poem, which having begun as it did (and brilliantly) could only finish in accordance with the mood of its beginning; meanwhile making contact, for as many words as possible, with the notes in front of him. Pound's poem is not one "To-Em-Mei" would have recognized, despite his familiarity with its components. It is newly invented in an unrelated language, almost as much so as the "Come my Celia" which Ben Jonson wrote, with Catullus in mind, for the insidious Volpone to sing.

What caused the troubles from which we have watched Pound rescuing his poem? The short answer is that Fenollosa's notes at several points are not such as a better-guided scholar would have made. Scholarship more amply endowed with works of reference has no difficulty in identifying "To-Em-Mei" with T'ao Ch'ien (A.D. 365–427), and "The Unmoving Cloud" with his "T'ing-yün" (T'ao Yüan-ming 1 1.1b); and knowing that Chinese nouns (if one may speak of nouns) do not indicate number, other translators have enjoyed the luxury of deciding whether the poem laments the absence of someone special or of friends in general, tradition indicating the former view. Scholarship tends also to agree that the tranquil mat (Pound's "soft seat") in the third stanza is to be imagined as set vis-à-vis the longed-for visitor, not as a coign of vantage for looking at the buds; thus Mr. Acker has,

> People also have a saying—
> "The days and months are on the march"
> Would that I could sit face to face with you
> And settle the problems of our daily life.

Scholarship would assert, in short, that the line which drove Pound to invent a proverb about the restless heavens, Fenollosa's "Let me take joy in this course of nature," does not correspond at all to T'ao Ch'ien's ideograms; for the first character, which Fenollosa glossed "to be glad," refers to discourse, and the last two, the "flat born" which he glossed as "natural or customary," are less misleadingly combined to mean something like "whole life," and the whole line says "Talking about each other's lives." Did Mr. Shida misunderstand the Chinese, or did he misunderstand what Fenollosa understood him to be saying? Whatever happened, Pound had little chance of making an orthodox guess.

There is a similar tangle earlier in the third stanza, and a subtler one in the fourth from which there is more to be learned. Orthodoxy finds in the last four lines of the poem not the plaint of the birds but the poet's wish for one friend more than any other.

> 1 Fluttering, fluttering, the flying birds
> 2 Settle on the branches in my courtyard
> 3 Gathering their wings they stop at leisure,
> 4 And harmonize together tunefully.
> 5 Surely many other people
> 6 Are thinking of you constantly,
> 7 But when I cannot have you with me
> 8 Oh, how resentment burns my heart.

So Mr. Acker. Fenollosa's transcriptions of the last six lines give us these words to work with;

3	Folding	wings	quietly	stop
4	Lovely	voice	each other	to be familiar
5	(negative)	not	other	man
6	love	you	truly	much
7	wish	speak	not	reach
8	bear in mind	deep sorrow	like	what

Mr. Acker takes the last word of line 5 as plural in intention, and combines the double negation into a "many." I am told that there is no philological reason for not glossing the first negative (a different character from the second) by "why," and making the line read "Why is there no one else [to talk with me]?" Fenollosa's note runs, "It is not that there is no other man than he," and determines that "he" means the poet, to whom the birds are speaking, a decision that follows naturally from his dealings with line 4. For his gloss on line 4 runs, "as with sweet voice they speak thus with each other," and he sets lines 5 to 8 in quotation marks. His "thus" and his quotation marks are interpretative additions, which Pound followed.

Familiarity with Chinese poetry and with the work of T'ao Ch'ien may encourage the decision that this is improbable. So may an intuition that the four episodes are parallel in structure, the first half of each establishing a setting against which the second half laments the absence of a friend. A developed sense of probabilities, often an inherited consensus of probabilities, guides our understanding of all verse; notably so when the verse is in a language to which indications of number, of tense, of gender are foreign, in which "parts of speech" are barely to be distinguished, in which doings are commonly named without specification of the doer.

In the field specified by a cluster of ideograms, the mind of a western reader supplies whatever syntax he assumes responsibility for, and small errors impose strange deflections. In a prose poem where a character meaning "palace" turns up next to characters pronounced "Lan t'ai" (Orchid Terrace), Fenollosa under his teacher's eye transcribed the Japanese pronunciation, Ran-tai, and then left open the supposition that he was dealing with a proper name. For in his gloss he wrote "palace of Ran-tai," as who should say, "Castle of Windsor." That small word "of" was taken by Pound as turning Ran-tai into a person, hence the owner of the palace, hence the king; and in Canto 4 we read of "Ran-ti, opening his collar" (4/15:19).*

And syntax, imported by the mind of a western translator, imposed on "The Unmoving Cloud" a subtler deflection still;

* The 1970 New Directions printing corrected "Ran-ti" to "Hsiang."

for syntax, an apparatus of verbs with discriminated tenses, implied for Pound what it naturally does imply, a mind making affirmations and setting them into relation. That is finally why, when the notes faltered and Pound had to impose a direction, he imposed the direction he did, making "To-Em-Mei" affirm a cosmos saturated with solitude to give his own solitude context. Had tradition guided him toward what appears to be the traditional reading of the poem, four glimpses of the world paired with four plaints of the lonely heart, he would very likely not have found it sufficiently interesting to translate.

*   *   *

Time and again the only meaning of "correct" is "traditional." We can sometimes say that a word cannot possibly mean what a translator has written in response to it; more often we can say that he has not written what readers of the original usually understand. The poem called by Pound "The Beautiful Toilet" opens in *Cathay*

Blue, blue, is the grass about the river

but in all other translations "green, green." The character in question is Ch'ing, Mathews 1168, the 174th radical, glossed in Mathews' *Chinese–English Dictionary* "The color of nature, green, blue, black," and in Karlgren's "Green; (various kindred colors;) blue, azure, greyish." It is a component in compounds meaning "green grass," "blue sky," "young foliage." In Mei Sheng's poem (if it is Mei Sheng's; the usual citation is to a collection called "Nineteen Old Poems") custom seems to demand the reading "green," no doubt because grass is present, but Fenollosa has only "blue, blue," and one can perfectly well imagine a light in which river grass is bluish. Was Ariga's mind's eye on such a light when he told his pupil to write the English word "blue"? Or was Ariga uncertain of the demarcation between the English words "blue" and "green"? The Chinese mind sees one color as a shade of the other. When the same character occurs at the beginning of the poem Pound calls "Taking Leave of a Friend," his "blue mountains" is more plausible than "green mountains," yet an expert gloss by Professor Roy E.

Teele again elects "green." Does either "blue," or one of them, reflect Kainan Mori's poetic judgment? Is there a traditional way to understand either poem? If so, did Mori know it, or not?

Consider, by way of analogy, what would happen if all existing translations of Homer were destroyed, leaving us to confront in a sceptical spirit the epithet which he applies 17 times to the sea and twice to oxen, and which Sophocles at one point applies to a human forearm. We find it in Liddell and Scott's *Lexicon* under a nominative singular form which occurs in no ancient text but has had to be invented to keep the lexicons consistent, and this invented form contains the judgment that the word is compounded from *oinos*, wine, and *ops*, eye or face. Wine-eyed? wine-faced? and of the sea, of oxen, and of a forearm? W. H. D. Rouse surmised that the etymology was false and the word simply an ancient blunder which there is no chance any longer of unstitching. Tradition instructs us to understand that the sea, modified by this epithet, shall be understood to be "wine-dark," and the oxen "deep red" or perhaps "brown." About the Sophoclean forearm tradition leaves us free to guess. But one can imagine, unguided by this tradition, some Mori instructing some Fenollosa to etymologize, "wine-faced," and think of the sheen of the sea and write "shining sea," and some Pound perhaps improving "shining" to "lucent," and scholars complaining of inaccuracy.

Lexicography is compendious illusion; words are strangely inexplicit; they "mean" here, here, here. And traditions of what we are to understand here and here, lacking which we often find modern poetry difficult, guide us so constantly that we are only aware of them when they lapse, as they often do in classrooms. Mr. Auden has described an entanglement with Keats' lines,

> The wakeful bloodhound rose, and shook his hide,
> But his sagacious eye an inmate owns;

two meanings, "inhabitant" for "inmate" and "accepts" for "owns" having dropped out of the current vernacular, a student with only the vernacular to guide her postulated a lunatic who had removed the dog's eye. Glossaries admonish us that the devotion of Chaucer's Knight was not given to truth and honor, freedom and courtesy, but to fidelity (*trouthe*), chivalrousness (*honour*), magnanimity (*freedom*) and the knightly code (*curteisie*); by ignoring the glossaries we alter this line completely, as the meaning of the *lewed observances* of lovers (*Troilus and Criseyde*, I, 198) is altered when nothing prompts us to understand "lewed" as "ignorant." A text, a word, means what has been continuously understood by it, and systematized understanding has sometimes come late and perpetuated guesswork (hence the plausibility of "winedark sea"). There are words in Homer that Hesiod misunderstood; we depend for our understanding on Alexandrian conjectures framed some 600 years after the Homeric world of discourse had vanished. Certain abstractions in Aristotle (what is *hybris*? what is *hamartia*?) remind us how we depend, for most of the Greek vocabulary, on a long tradition of interpretation, surely not always accurate. The first word in Sappho's second most famous poem is almost impenetrable: *poikilothronos*, on a rich-worked throne, say Liddell and Scott, evading the undecidable, for what did Sappho mean us to see? An upholstered throne? carved? studded? "Variegated," we guess from the etymology; but in color? in texture?

We know most of Sappho's words, and that knowledge steadies our guesses when we must guess. At the furthest extreme, where there is no tradition at all, we may learn humility from the luckless scholar who saw reason to approach the Linear B script by way of Basque, and eventually derived elegiac poems from what are now taken to be storehouse inventories. His book was published, in 1931, by the Oxford University Press.

Classical Chinese need occasion no such desperation. Yet today's understanding of what many details in many poems may mean is steadied by glosses that come down with the texts, and perhaps did not always come to Fenollosa's instructors in Tokyo. Mori, Ariga, Hirai, Shida, are not seldom acceptably philological, where tradition would have them wrong; and are sometimes, to judge by Fenollosa's notes, simply wrong; and in the main, it seems, right. Small or large errors committed in Tokyo cast shadows on *Cathay's* page.

*   *   *

But the major deviations from orthodoxy represent deliberate decisions of a man who was inventing a new kind of English poem and picking up hints where he could find them. Thus in the second movement of "Sennin Poem by Kakuhaku" he has transformed Fenollosa's

> Green vines hang on and twine the high forest
> Darkly they cover the whole mountain
> In it there is a silent and solitary man

by glancing at the literal dissections:

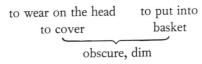

—from which he derived the verb "weave," and

> silent (lit. dark
> sometimes used in
> shutting the eyes)

—from which he made a striking locution; Hence—

> Green vines hang through the high forest,
> They weave a whole roof to the mountain,
> The lone man sits with shut speech . . .

For when the single line is the unit of composition it must contain some minute torsion, something to justify its separate existence.

Each line a little strange, yet each line clear; and when clarity lay before him he did not tamper. "Song of the Bowmen of Shu" departs hardly at all from a version written out by Mr. Ariga himself, ideographic text, English paraphrases and notes, in his clear hand and quaint English. When Pound made the "tied" horses "tired" it is hard to know whether his eye failed or his dramatic sense prompted an improvement; presumably the latter, since the writing is very clear. The other two battle poems he tightened and reshaped, guided not only by local canons but by the structure of his book. The third battle piece was to go at the end of the sequence; so he made it terse and stark, the least decorative poem in *Cathay*, the most "Attic." The notes from which he worked are worth inspecting entire, as a measure of his way of transforming them. Fenollosa made them with Mori on 10 December 1899. Pound finished his version on 21 November 1914, nearly four months into the war. Louvain was in ruins, Belgium overrun; there had been three waves of slaughter at Ypres; the lines were stalemated.

Dai	horse	not	think of	Etsu
(place in				in the south
north)				

The horses of Dai, tho taken to Etsu, care nothing for Etsu

Etsu	birds	not	love	En
				-a north region

So the Etsu birds have no love for an alien En

Emotion	nature	has	that which is	habituated

Human emotions & natures are things that spring from habit

local	manners	of course	that	(ly) adj.
(earth)	(mind)			ending

The powers which local manners have on our mind are so—necessarily thus.

(ancient)	separate	wild goose	gate	fort
former			name of gate	
yesterday				

Yesterday one has left the wild geese Tartars. (This is in the Northern province of Dai. Why called wild geese? Because believed to come from north.)

now	garrison	dragon	yard	before
	(verb)	name of locality—desert		

Today one has already come so far as the Dragon yard deserted front. (What sort of life do we live here? is supplied)

surprised	desert	turmoil	sea	sun
	sand-sea			

Sands surprised by wind cover in their turmoil the desert sea sun.

flying	snow	wanders	northern	heaven
		errs	barbarian	
			Tartar's	

(When once winter comes) the flying snow lets go astray the Manchurian heaven—one loses sight of the sky.

ants   fleas   grow on   tiger   (a kind of
ants like   lice   (part of   bird famous
lice (many)   armor)   for bravery)
                                                        fight till death.
                                                        Soldiers wear
                                                        their feathers on
                                                        their helmets
                              on armor
(Such life continuing for long) swarms of lice grow on the accoutrements.

mind   spirit   drive   banner made   banner made
                                    of feathers   of silk
(And yet under such difficulty can one's mind be easy? No!) Because
our mind and spirit must drive upon (keep close attention to) the
motion of the banners.

hard   fight   merit   not   reward
Although one fights so hard his merit is not rewarded. (The whole
intent of this is that to let soldiers undergo such distant hardship is
inhuman for an Emperor.)

loyalty   faith   difficult   to   tell-express
[as one is not a horse or a bird] so if one were allowed to express all
he feels of loyalty & faith he would be satisfied) "There is no
chance to express one's loyalty and faith."

who   will be   (General)   flying   general
            sorry for   Ri   of quick motion
Who is sorry for flying general Ri. (History: in Kan Dynasty was
famous Ri Shogun who fought more than 74 battles with the northern barbarians who called him the Flying Shogun. So skilful, he was
constantly sent out for some expedition, and was never recalled—so
he died in old age in one of the border battles.)

white   head   lost   three   outside provinces
                                                outskirt
                                                border regions
Ri[haku] is expressing the soldier's feelings. "The fate of Ri Shogun
is probably mine too." "Whose white head was lost (died) in the
three frontiers" Who died of old age. "Who will be sorry for the
fate of Rishogu?"

Having made what he can of this, the reader may examine what the poet made of it:

SOUTH-FOLK IN COLD COUNTRY

The Dai horse neighs against the bleak wind of Etsu,
The birds of Etsu have no love for En, in the north,
Emotion is born out of habit.
Yesterday we went out of the Wild-goose gate,
To-day from the Dragon-Pen.
Surprised. Desert turmoil. Sea sun.
Flying snow bewilders the barbarian heaven.
Lice swarm like ants over our accoutrements.
Mind and spirit drive on the feathery banners.
Hard fight gets no reward.
Loyalty is hard to explain.
Who will be sorry for General Rishogu,
          the swift moving,
Whose white head is lost for this province?

Pound went to great labor; the notes often put him to it. Was he deterred from seeking expert advice by the supposition, based on the frequent state of the notes, that Chinese poetry was an entity as barely comprehended as Linear B today? The acknowledgment page speaks of the *decipherings* of the Professors Mori and Ariga. These decipherings in turn he was often forced to decipher. Yet he never shirked his great debt to Fenollosa, nor concealed the devious chain of transmission. Though he knew the name of Li Po he let the Japanese form "Rihaku" stand when the little book went to press, content to leave it on record that the Chinese had come to him by way of Japan, as "Jupiter" comes from "Zeus" by way of Rome. That Li Po should reach Kensington by way of Tokyo, through the intercession of a Harvard-educated enthusiast of Spanish descent, was but a global recapitulation of the steps by which the Arabs transmitted Aristotle to 12th-century Paris, or Francesco da Bologna was set to work cutting Greek dies for Aldus' printing house as a consequence of the fall of Constantinople.

THE
PERSISTENT EAST

The Chinese Written Character caught Francis Bacon's attention before 1605, when he stated as "now well known" the proposition that "in China and the more Eastern provinces they use at this day certain real, not nominal characters, to express, not their letters or words, but things and notions; insomuch, that numerous nations, though of quite different languages, yet, agreeing in the use of these characters, hold correspondence by writing." For it seemed clear, from Jesuit intelligence even then filtering back to Europe, that the characters registered things, not the mere sounds men emit in things' presence; and as to their notorious multiplicity—

Sun   Moon   Mountain   Man   Horse

... and on, into many thousands—this was evidently due to their being exactly as numerous as were the classes of things created by God. Such notions were to polarize western speculations about language for many decades: "so many things, almost in an equal number of words," ran (1667) the formula according to which dozens of 17th-century savants, each one aware of ideographs and several fascinated by them, attempted to construct ideal languages which should promote orderly thought and be comprehensible everywhere. The supposition, itself Chinese, that the ideographs were bestowed by a single innovating emperor, lent plausibility to such projects.

And all such projects, though Newton and Leibniz were among the projectors, foundered on their own unwieldiness. The stubborn conviction remained, that symbols ought to correspond with things, the ideal language thus a system of nouns and modified nouns, a taxonomy of objects. (In Lagado Lemuel Gulliver encountered savants who saved breath by holding up the objects themselves, and a peripatetic conversation was as wearisome to the back as to the arms.)

The ideal language, and subsequently the written vernacular language when notions of ideality began to stylize it, was embarrassed by verbs, which it took for specializations of the copula, and scandalized by metaphor. A verb is not a thing, and in a universe of things we must take "John runs" to mean that John is included in the class of running objects. And a metaphor is not a proposition, for to say that my love is a red red rose is merely to publicize an error of classification, no doubt understandable when emotion beclouds perception, but scarcely admissible in discourse meant to detain cooler heads. The man who first called *hippopotamus amphibius* a river-horse, ἵππος + ποταμός, made a taxonomic mistake (it is not a horse) and also yielded to a false economy (a new species wants a new name, not an effort to make do with old ones). When *so many things* are at last represented by *an equal number of words*, then everything will have its own name, and metaphor (whale's acres, breast-cares) will be not only unneeded but excrescential.

So ideograms during their first Western incursion presided over what was to become an anti-poetic. The Descartes who (Boileau complained) had "cut the throat" of poetry, and the Locke who made poetry a diversion of relaxed or enfeebled minds, lived among learned men whom the rumors of Chinese analogy had encouraged to think of words naming things, and words as many as there were things, and language a taxonomy of static things, with many an "is" but ideally no verb. And it was just such notions, mistakenly by him styled "mediaeval," that Ernest Fenollosa, encouraged by ideograms, set out to refute, on behalf of "the language of science which is the language of poetry," unaware, certainly, that their prevalence had been sponsored by a 17th-century misunderstanding of Chinese as fecund as his own.

He warred on the copula: "There is in reality no such verb . . . , no such original conception; our very word *exist* means 'to stand forth,' to show oneself by a definite act." In the Chinese "is" he found "a splendid flash of concrete poetry": "to snatch from the moon with the hand." He assailed negation as parvenu ("*we* can assert a negation, though nature can not"), and derived a Chinese sign for non-existence from "to be lost in the forest," not a non-being but a specifiable plight. And the sentences that turn on "is" and "is not," and became in Boole's hands the algebra of classes, he referred to "the tyranny of mediaeval logic," "mediaeval" being a trusty polemic gesture though the focus of the infection was locatable not in Abelard's century but in Locke's. For behind Boole stood the *De Arte Combinatoria* of Leibniz (1666), which expressed comprehensive indebtedness to Chinese analogies; just as behind the language of today's computers, which do nothing but shift symbols very rapidly into and out of categories, lay Leibniz' invention of binary arithmetic, encouraged by yet another sinological misunderstanding. Leibniz thought he was fleshing out a Mandarin discovery enshrined in the *Book of Changes.*

Ideographs, supposed to correspond with things, had sponsored the very habits Fenollosa was to refute by positing that ideographs corresponded with actions. His great, his unassailable originality stemmed from his conviction that the unit of thought was less like a noun than like a verb, and that Chinese signs therefore denoted processes ("the ideograph meaning 'to speak' is a mouth with two words and a flame coming out of it"). Metaphor so seen was a centrality, not an embarrassment ("Metaphor, the revealer of nature. . . . The known interprets the obscure, the universe is alive with myth.")

But the Chinese written language, like any other, is entoiled in the sounds of speech: a fact Fenollosa could resist as sturdily as did any Royal Society projector. In the course of lectures he was drafting about 1901–4, his remarks on Chinese sound have so little to do with the thrust of his argument that Pound when he extracted the great Essay for publication imposed no distortion in simply omitting them.*

*   *   *

Give it time, and Pound's flywheel always restored a balance. "The whole Occident is still in crass ignorance of the Chinese art of verbal sonority": 1935, footnoting a reprint of the essay he had then known more than twenty years. He went on to pay Chinese sound his supreme compliment: "I now doubt if it was inferior to the Greek." He was to work on Chinese sound in the tolerant madhouse, where his fame attracted informal instructors; the *Confucian Odes* (1954, ninth year of incarceration) display results, and the Chinese in *Rock-Drill* (1955) and *Thrones* (1959) is as likely to appear in phonetics as in ideographs. This is simply to say that Pound was always interested in *melopoeia*, and eventually brought it into touch with his sinological pursuits. But there is no sign of such an interest in the published version of Fenollosa's essay, where of Chinese sound we find remarked only its paucity.

*   *   *

The author of *Epochs of Chinese and Japanese Art* of course lived through his eyes, and naturally regarded ideographs as visual registrations of things seen. Moreover, studying Chinese with Japanese instructors, he was impressed by what had impressed Bacon three centuries before, the fact that one could read it without knowing what sounds a Chinese reader makes, or in the knowledge

---

* One bee in Fenollosa's bonnet deserves notice: his idea that primitive Chinese sounds are less well represented by modern Mandarin ("this barbarous guttural dialect") than by modern Japanese: so that in transcribing in Japanese syllables a poem such as that attributed to the Emperor Shun (2255 B.C. if he existed) he could claim to be offering "for the first time an approximation to the old sounds." That is probably why Shun's poem appears among primeval things in Canto 49 not in Chinese but in the sounds—Kei men ran kei . . .—Fenollosa wrote down at Mori's dictation, 4 June 1901. (And *men* should be *wun*, but Fenollosa's rapid pencil is unclear and Pound mistranscribed.) Scholarship now tends to concur with Fenollosa.

that in different regions they make different sounds entirely: hence his nearly inevitable supposition that the characters imitated not speech but Nature. And in being willing to suppose that human speech is peripheral to orderly communication he exposes his inheritance from those 17th-century theorists of System whose antipoetic legacy dismayed him. Their mark is on all linguistic theory from their time to his and beyond: long after Fenollosa's essay was current we find I. A. Richards, another amateur of Chinese (whose sinology—see *Mencius on the Mind*—has a pleasant 17th-century flavor) supposing that metaphor does not blaze with process but unites two *things*, called tenor and vehicle.

Fenollosa was interested, as Bacon and Leibniz had been, in a relatively small class of characters, the ones that are totally independent of speech, either depicting something

or else uniting depictions

明   [Sun + moon; originally window + moon]

bright

信   [man + word]

sincere

In 17th-century Europe it seems not to have been suspected that these, the "ideographs" proper, are both ancient and frequent but not numerous. They comprise perhaps a tenth of the written language. They are learned so early by foreigners, their mode of formation so pleases the systematizing intellect, and they encompass such persistent and elementary ideas, that they crowded out of the polymaths' attention the characters, nine times as numerous, that simply specify a sound and then tell us which of its homonymous meanings to select. Thus the right side of the character 訪 , tells us to say *fang*, a syllable with many different significances: "square," "district," "spin," "ask," "room," "kettle," "board." The other half of the character, 言 , "speak," says that we are dealing with the meaning of *fang* appropriate to speech: in short, "ask." If to *fang* we join the "earth" pictogram we get "district"; if we join the "silk" pictogram we get "spin"; if the "door" pictogram, "room," and so on. The *fang* radical by itself means "square." But in these compounds the squareness is never relevant, only the sound.* And Fenollosa had this omnipresent principle clearly explained to him, no doubt many times but certainly on 28 May 1901, in Prof. Mori's very first discourse on the scripts, and he didn't want to believe it. Later Ezra Pound marked the notebook entry for attention with a blue crayon, but didn't want to believe it either.

Yes, yes, it is true that the pronunciation varies endlessly through uncountable dialects, none primary; that many homophones when the characters were formed are homophones no longer; that one can understand the characters and understand written pages without learning to pronounce them at all. The point is that random similarities of sound have determined which elements are common to many sets of characters, so that they are not graphed metaphors as Fenollosa thought.

By the time he was drafting "The Chinese Written Character as a Medium for Poetry" he had decided that the pictorial clues to such characters had merely been lost ("Many of our own etymologies have been lost. It is futile to take the ignorance of the Han dynasty for omniscience.")

Ingenuity can go a long way toward sustaining such a case, so adept is a mind seeking relevance. That a district is a square of earth, that a room is the square beyond the door, that a board is squared wood, these would be the plausible conjectures of anyone etymologizing the *fang*-words by eye. Only the most detailed philological learning, of a kind for which no one in 1904 was equipped, could carry conviction at last of their unsoundness. The bone inscriptions from which we now know the most primitive forms had been discovered only five years previously, and were

---

* That the main business of characters should be to distinguish among homophones is unsurprising when we began to grasp how many homophones there are; in the Mandarin dialect of Peking the entire spoken language comprises not more than 420 syllables, some having dozens of unrelated meanings.

just beginning to be worked on.* Fenollosa pressed on: "It is not true, as Legge said, that the original picture characters could never have gone far in building up abstract thought. This is a vital mistake. We have seen that our own languages have all sprung from a few hundred vivid phonetic verbs by figurative derivation. A fabric more vast could have been built up in Chinese by metaphorical comparison. No attenuated idea exists which it might not have reached more vividly and more permanently than we could have expected to reach with phonetic roots. Such a pictorial method, whether the Chinese exemplified it or not, would be the ideal language of the world."

"The ideal language of the world": Leibniz in the 1670's had been one of dozens pursuing a similar notion. It is difficult not to conclude that Fenollosa, so sensitive to poetic sound, was scandalized by semantic sound, mere usage, which will not lock down meanings but leaves the people on whose tongues language lives to remember what their words mean: as they tend not to do with any tenacity. Thus *buxom* once meant *obedient*, its root being the verb to bow; an ideograph preserving that bowing might have inhibited the subsequent drift toward generosity of figure. Latin etymologies, being referable to a static system, anchor meanings as would pictures, for people who remember them. When Dr. Johnson writes of a radical idea branching into parallel ramifications he is relying on *radix* and *ramus* for the tree that sustains his metaphor. Once Latin goes out of mind *radical* commences its vernacular slide toward *extreme*, and *ramification* toward *entanglement*.

*   *   *

Mallarmé learned English that he might read Poe (Poe!), and then supposed the subtleties alembicating in his brain to have boiled up out of Poe's depths: as they did, when Mallarmé was the

---

* And today's learning does not cancel the seduction. The single example of a phonetic compound given in James J. Y. Liu's *Art of Chinese Poetry* (p. 5) joins the phonetic *chung* with the determinant "heart," hence the meaning of *chung* relevant to the heart, hence "loyalty." But when he sees the graph *chung*,   中   "middle," the non-sinologue is not easily convinced that *chung* is merely a phonetic, and eleven pages later Mr. Liu is conceding that "It would not be out of place to think of 'loyalty' as 'having one's heart in the middle,' though this is etymologically unsound."

reader. Dante's coda to the *Odyssey* was made possible by his not having read it; he was able to suppose therefore that Odysseus was driven by lust for knowledge. Is the life of the mind a history of interesting mistakes?

More pertinently: is the surest way to a fructive western idea the misunderstanding of an eastern one? Fenollosa's rejection of phonetic characters not only did his literary studies no harm (since he wrote down simply his instructors' orthodoxies concerning poem after poem), but by encouraging him to universalize his intuition about verbs and processes freed him, as more scrupulous learning could not have, to compose the *Ars Poetica* of our time. For he needed to suppose that all ideograms followed one principle so that by gazing into them as into living monads he could expound, miraculously concentrated, the Emersonian organicism he had brought to Tokyo from Cambridge. He was teaching Emerson to his best Japanese students at the time he began looking closely into ideograms, there to find confirmation of Emerson's etymologist who "finds the deadest word to have been once a brilliant picture." More: the universe is alive, and the live mind part of the universe, and each one of these brilliant pictures made by some live mind is a living cell, specializing the life of the totality. And this, which he saw in the ideograms with an eye Emerson had trained, enabled Fenollosa for the first time in centuries to restore metaphor, "the swift perception of relations" (Aristotle's "hallmark of genius"), to the heart of a poetic process not peripheral to but concentric with the most intent working of the focused mind.

And that Emersonian organicism had known Chinese affinities before Fenollosa. In his Journal for 7 October 1863, Emerson copied passages from a copy of the same Confucius (Legge's, then newly printed) that Pound carried with him on the jeep into Pisa; and the Mailla *Histoire Générale de la Chine* that underlies nine consecutive Cantos was in the Boston Athenaeum, its presence bruited among the Transcendentalists; and the Confucian anecdote that opens Canto 13, with its talk of swimming in a pond and playing mandolins, exists on loose pages in the Harvard College Library, in a translation made, as was Pound's, from Pauthier's French version, in the handwriting of Henry Thoreau. Which is to say that

Transcendentalism was aware of its own affinities with the Far East; and Transcendentalism's other affinities are with Whitehead and Darwin and Frazer, and Gestaltists and field physicists, and the synergism of Buckminster Fuller: with the coherent effort of 150 years to rectify Newton's machine by exploring hierarchic inter-dependences in nature and in history and in myth and in mind, detecting wholes greater than the sum of parts, organisms not systems, growth not accretion: process and change and resemblance and continuity.

And behind that effort? Behind it, preparing for it, a chain of philosophers, a chain which "leads back through Hegel, Lotze, Schelling and Herder to Leibniz (as Whitehead constantly recognized), and then it seems to disappear": seems to disappear because we are looking for European predecessors, and Leibniz was indebted to China. So runs Joseph Needham's remarkable hypothesis, which attributes European organicism, via Leibniz' Jesuit friends of the China Mission, to neo-Confucian *Li* and the school of Chu Hsi: the same Chu Hsi (A.D. 1130–1200) who created the text of Confucius translated by Legge and Pauthier and Thoreau and Pound, and of whose *Thung Chien Kang Mu* Mailla's *Histoire Générale* is an 18th-century translation. These works, the argument might run, were congenial to the minds of Emerson and Fenollosa and Ezra Pound because of Chu Hsi's part in preparing their minds.

If so, then Fenollosa's sinological mistakes, rectifying 17th-century sinological mistakes, owed their right intuitions (brought with him from Massachusetts) originally after all to China: as though the east, with centuries-long deliberation, were writing the macro-history of western thought.

VORTEX LEWIS

In the summer of 1912, *annus mira-bilis*, the Imagist year and the year of the magazine *Poetry* and the book *Ripostes*, the year Duchamp painted *Nude Descending a Staircase* and Apollinaire wrote *Les Peintres Cubistes*, Wyndham Lewis, about to turn 30, felt suddenly rush into his schooled sense of design the impulse that had previously evaded design and yielded grotesques. A grotesque is an energy which aborts, as if to express its dissatisfaction with available boundaries, as a dwarf may be nature's critique of the tailor's dummy. Lewis's earlier pictures announce an energy art cannot accommodate. That summer Art and Energy moved into sudden conjunction; forms filled his spaces, not forms arrested in grotesquerie but forms locked in passionate stases; oblique lines sprang from points of radiation to reverse the thrust of traditional perspective which tapers or dwindles toward a point of vanishing, but they bounded forms such as traditional perspective bounds, and so could capitalize on traditional principles of design. (Tradition is the artist's stock of capital; it can tap impulses "older than the fish.")

He was in France, making drawings for an edition, never produced, of Shakespeare's *Timon of Athens*. The drawings have nearly all disappeared. We have them in reproductions made two

The grotesque as a trammelling of energy: *Smiling Woman Ascending a Stair*, Wyndham Lewis, 1911. (Courtesy Mr. R. W. T. Vint.)

years later by an *ad hoc* firm called The Cube Press, which disappeared likewise. The portfolio of prints is itself excessively scarce. Not being on the market where there is a vested interest in enhancing prices by talking up repute, the enterprise has dropped out of Art History, which in modern times has been written chiefly by dealers and clever collectors. (The Cubist enterprise in Paris had no such misfortune.) Lewis got beyond cubism. The fact is virtually unknown; yet one design in the Timon series, the one called "Alcibiades," has been called "arguably the greatest single manifestation of artistic energy in the whole of English painting."

It is one of history's great feats of attention, attention to an uncountable array of elements, all interacting. Being pure lines, the elements have no survival power of their own, save by virtue of the interaction that attention guarantees. In a canvas crowded with naturalistic figures, Frith's *Derby Day* for instance, much anecdotal detail can be left for the all-too-human recognizing eye to find it and perk up, cheered. Not so here. The calmest things on which Lewis lets the eye rest are a bowl and a carafe, and these are enclosed in an equivocal semicircular space whose perspective snaps in and out at whim. They are cubist props, relegated to accessory status. The rest is lightning, clouds, spears, posturing figures, Renaissance helmets, a pneumatic woman, a screaming head, all fixed in a slow-motion explosion whose next centimeter's expansion will occupy all eternity. A harsh light, falling from some source in the upper right, bathes their grimaces. They radiate downward and forward from a generating node at the upper left. The perspective seeks equilibrium between these points, where at upper center a quadrangular darkness, stood upon its corner, half-obscures a quasi-solar geometry.

Far in the foreground, vigorous glances meet across the center of the picture: a tension of human antagonism to which no drawn line corresponds. For much of the "Alcibiades"' energy depends on the interaction of human figures, whose vectors of attraction and repulsion overlie and counter the thrust of all those hundreds of lines a hand has traced. Twenty-five years later Lewis was painting portraits of men aware that a painter is in the room.

For the cubist, however, a man is a still life.

Cubism, that great revolution of vision, had simplified its

The "Alcibiades" design, *Timon of Athens*, 1912.

effort by banishing the human to that plane of sentiment where wine, violins, newspapers, tablecloths are cherished. Coy forms, in a cubist *collage*, invite relaxed recognition: beneath so much strangeness, the ikons of coziness dream. There is even a corresponding primitive appeal in the flattening of perspective. Le Douanier, of the eternally touching incompetence, was a less unlikely cubist recruit than he seems.

*   *   *

Pound had known Lewis since about 1910, the time when

> there were mysterious figures
> that emerged from recondite recesses
> and ate at the WIENER CAFÉ,
> (80/506:541)

near the British Museum. Pound was the protégé ("bull-dog," he says rather) of Laurence Binyon (1869–1943) of the Department of Oriental Prints and Drawings, and Lewis the admirer (also "bull-dog") of T. Sturge Moore (1870–1944), designer of Yeatsian title pages, whose *The Vinedresser and Other Poems* he disliked being without. These gentlemen ("BinBin" and "Old Neptune" respectively) enjoyed setting their bulldogs scuffling. Ford Hueffer, who had published both bulldogs in 1909, presided over other encounters. Pound was a Beerbohm cartoon of the salon artist, beard, earring, green velvet, Lewis the black-hatted anarchist in a cape. Yet they became friends. It was after the *Timon* and *Ripostes* breakthroughs of 1912 that they became allies. Each had come in the same year, independently, to a security in the management of his art. By 1913 Lewis was setting out to organize a movement and a review, and Pound, to whose Imagist perceptions the visual arts were becoming important now that there was non-Impressionist visual art, perceived analogies to his own hard verse in the Timon designs and in the stone carvings of Gaudier. About 1 April 1914 he could write to Joyce that Lewis was "starting a new Futurist, Cubist, Imagiste Quarterly ... mostly a painter's magazine with me to do the poems." And *The Egoist* for April 1 and April 15 carried a full-page advertisement:

"Discussion of Cubism, Futurism, Imagisme": there was no indication of the standpoint of the discussion except that the words "WYNDHAM LEWIS" were in 24-point capitals. Then, in a backstage transaction whose details are lost to history, Ezra Pound labelled the standpoint; the review was held up some weeks while Lewis had sheets added at the printer's to sheets already printed; and in June *Blast* proclaimed itself the organ of the Great English Vortex.

Cubism, Futurism, these names came reasonably close, but Vorticism was *le mot juste*. It is traceable to Pound's figure, in the ninth "Osiris" article of early 1912, of words as electrified cones, charged with "the power of tradition, of centuries of race consciousness, of agreement, of association," an image (simplified by Lewis

to *Blast's* emblem a cone and a wire) for all that the artist does not invent but must know. It assimilates also his "Osiris" term, *virtù*, for the individuating energy by reason of which "we have one Catullus, one Villon." And as for "centuries of race consciousness," they localize in capitals, and in 1913 he had likened London to Rome, "a vortex, drawing strength from the peripheries." The Vorticists disowned Futurism because it denied tradition, and were wary of Cubism because it seemed indifferent to personality.

To sort out these interfused meanings: Vorticism denoted first of all the Great *London* Vortex. The Future has no locale, an Image or a Cube may turn up in anyone's pocket, but any Vortex is somewhere on the map. And this was the English, not the French or the Russian, version of abstract art. Behind Parisian Cubism one may see café tables, behind Italian Futurism a horde of museum-keepers bedazzled by zip; behind London Vorticism, English ships and London buildings, and the intent detached passion of the countrymen of Charles Babbage and Lord Kelvin.

Second, a Vortex is a circulation with a still center: a system of energies drawing in whatever comes near ("Energy creates pattern"). So you could have a National Vortex, likewise, when it came to *virtù*, a personal Vortex ("Vortex Lewis": "Vortex Pound"; "Vortex Gaudier-Brzeska"). And the personal Vortex, since "we do not desire to cut ourselves off from the past," will draw into the artist's personal dynamism his usable arraying of past Vortices.

Thus, as John Cournos noticed, Gaudier's "Vortex" was an idiosyncratic history of sculpture. Each civilization had its individuating system of forms, the system, more profound than "style," by which we know Egyptian work from Assyrian. Gaudier postulated a metamorphosis of characterizing sculptural forms: the sphere drawn up into the Egyptian pyramid, pulled lengthwise into the Oceanic cylinder, compressed into Assyrian "splendid squatness," the sculptural vortex in each place ingathering the natural forms—cats, phalli, bulls—that Greek decadence was content to measure and copy. By formal allusion a 1914 sculptor could draw on these reservoirs of power; Gaudier's "Hieratic Head of Ezra Pound" is Oceanic/Egyptian.

So written, art history is neither a catalogue nor a chronicle of passive craftsmen flopping from derivation to derivation at some Zeitgeist's behest. The ambition to write it so was not peculiar to Gaudier. Ernest Fenollosa in the summer of 1906 had unfolded "a universal scheme or logic of art," which "as easily subsumes all forms of Asiatic and of savage art and the efforts of children as it does accepted European schools." Streams of diffusing energy, he surmised, accompanied the worldwide migration of peoples. Two of these streams, he thought, had met in China. The concentrating of such a stream—the characterizing energies of some place, some civilization (as Falls and Whirlpool characterize Niagara)—he might very well have been willing to call a Vortex. An anthropologist with a similar vision, Leo Frobenius, meant what Gaudier meant by a Vortex when he spoke of a Paideuma. Frobenius's reports, because they synthesized all that a people did, were much on Pound's mind in the 1930's.

*   *   *

And the word "Vortex," almost as a fringe benefit, succeeds in implying what was most notable about Wyndham Lewis's designs: their energy of the diagonal. (The directions of French abstraction tended to be horizontal and vertical, like water and trees.) And the arch-Vorticist was Lewis unmistakably. Without him, the movement is inconceivable; without him, those months would have contained no promise of a gathering Renaissance. His *Timon* iconography linked today's energies with the Renaissance of Italy, to which Pound had sensed an analogue gathering as long ago as 1910. One man cannot make a Renaissance, but one man may be indispensable to it. Lewis had the will, the sureness, the skill at organization and polemics. Ten words, when he put them together, bore his signature: "Caruso tenor-instincts of inflation, of tiptoe tirade" (Lewis on Marinetti); "Throats iron eternities, drinking heavy radiance, limbs towers of blatant light" (Lewis on the stars). He could comprehend Chinese Geomancy and Cézanne in one act of vision. He could collect the essentials of a head in five drawn lines. He was writing a novel. His talk ran long in the night.

He had the painter's special understanding of the *use* of movements, easily explicated. Movements bear on the painter's place in a market economy, where the writer's situation is a little less anomalous. In proportion as his book attracts attention, and then for so long as it pleases, the writer draws money from its sale, but the maker of a picture is paid only once. Expensive resales profit only the resellers. And what he is paid bears no necessary relation to his effort and intelligence, but only to his fame. Fame may be fortuitous; in the 1940's Grandma Moses commanded better prices than Lewis. It may also be a stock as carefully tended as that of a holding company. What the buyer of a Picasso purchases is just that "a Picasso": a share in Pablo Picasso's reputation. Picasso shares command high prices. To make a living therefore, such a man incurs the obligations of a dual career: the painter's, the publicist's. The painter makes pictures. The publicist shapes *nothing*—bubble reputation—into "Picasso" or "Braque" or "Warhol": the heady entity in which people will buy shares in the act of acquiring one of the signed artifacts. Whistler understood this necessity: he invented

"Whistler." So Lewis welcomed Pound's invention of "Vorticism": something in which the potential purchaser, who literally cannot *see* a picture, might yet buy shares if it proved its staying power ("A little Vorticist thing for the pantry wall"). His remark 32 years later, "Vorticism ... was what I, personally, did, and said, at a certain period," was in two senses perfectly accurate; his was the primal energy, and "The Vorticist," albeit a mere name, was a persona invented for his use. (But the war drained it of usefulness.)

In Pound's experience, as in the world's, Lewis was a phenomenon without precedent. He stood outside the human race, or more exactly outside what it had made of itself through letting its energies lapse. (All was energy.) Mind was energy, and "matter that has not sufficient mind to permeate it grows, as you know, gangrenous and rotten": mind was the vital process itself. He launched polemic missiles, massive, compact:

> Our Vortex is fed up with your dispersals, reasonable chicken-men.
> Our Vortex is proud of its polished sides.
> Our Vortex will not hear of anything but its disastrous polished dance.
> Our Vortex desires the immobile rhythm of its swiftness.
> Our Vortex rushes out like an angry dog at your Impressionist fuss.
> Our Vortex is white and abstract with its red-hot swiftness.

No one understood better the trap of the mimetic. Though all his long life he worked almost exclusively with the human figure, just after *Timon* he abstained from the figure for three years to test his conviction that, in "doing what Nature does," the mind generates forms.* The Vorticist, who is "at his maximum point of energy when stillest," "lets Life know its Place in a Vorticist Universe!"

What Life's place is we may gather. A 1914 puppet of Lewis's enunciates one extreme expression: "Anything but yourself is dirt." Three years later, with a more Nietzschean richness, anything but yourself was the Herd, and the Herdsmen have a Code, of which the 10th article reads,

---

* Through chronological accident this has come to be called his Vorticist period, though pure abstraction is not at all entailed by Vorticist thinking.

... Do not allow yourself to imagine "a fine herd though still a herd." There is no *fine herd*. The cattle that call themselves "gentlemen" you will observe to be a little cleaner. It is merely cunning and produced with a product called *soap*. ...

By 1917 a remarkable piece of writing, "Inferior Religions," had codified these dicta. ("It makes Bergson look like a gnat," Pound wrote in a covering letter to *The Little Review*.) Though we shall not "make material existence a peer for our energy," a mind making forms can freeze suggestions of such forms as its *virtù* would inhabit gratefully were they habitable. "Perfection is not in the waves or houses that the poet sees":

> Beauty is an icy douche of ease and happiness at something *suggesting* perfect conditions for an organism: it remains suggestion. A stormy landscape, and a pigment consisting of a lake of hard, yet florid waves: delight in each brilliant scoop or ragged burst was John Constable's beauty. Leonardo's consisted in a red rain on the shadowed sides of heads, and heads of massive female aesthetes. Uccello accumulated pale parallels, and delighted in cold architecture of distinct colour. Korin found in the symmetrical gushing of water, in waves like huge vegetable insects, traced and worked faintly, on a golden pâte, his business. Cézanne liked cumbrous, democratic slabs of life, slightly leaning, transfixed in vegetable intensity.

But "Napoleon was harried with Elbas, moments of vision are blurred rapidly, and the poet sinks into the rhetoric of the will." Such defeat, like Timon's, is preferable to "success." Success is predictability, a function of the habit into which energy most often lapses.

"The habit-world or system of a successful personality," such as Boswell's Johnson, becomes a circulating monument to laziness, before which, so comforting is its clockwork grotesquerie, we incline as to a fetish. ("That Johnson was a sort of god to his biographer we readily see.") Thus "a comic type is a failure of a considerable energy, an imitation and standardizing of self," and such beings "are illusions hugged and lived in, little dead totems." It follows that the calmest statements concerning such beings will be, as textbooks say, "satiric."

"The chemistry of personality," to sum up, "(subterranean in a sort of cemetery whose decompositions are our lives) puffs up in frigid balls, soapy snowmen, arctic carnival masks, which we can photograph and fix." (Hence his Portrait of Edith Sitwell. Dozens of his pictures depict such a cemetery-world, a world of stases, masks, and postures.) "Upwards from the surface of existence a lurid and dramatic scum oozes and accumulates into the characters we see. . . ." Such images did not waver. Thirty-seven years after "Inferior Religions" was published, the hero of Lewis's penultimate novel ends his life in the academic "cemetery of shells." "And the Faculty had no idea that it was a glacial shell of a man who had come to live among them, mainly because they were themselves unfilled with anything more than a little academic stuffing."

*   *   *

Lewis operated from (did not necessarily hold) a view of life, coherent however it may displease you and me (are we shells?). It fed his polemic vitality. Not surprisingly, that vitality fascinated Pound, who may not have thought about how it was incompatible with his own characteristic benevolence and patience. By late 1912 his letters to Harriet Monroe are oscillating between belief in the public's native intelligence and a willingness to "save the public's soul by punching its face" ("the public can go to the devil"). His polemics for *Blast* are almost wholly unfortunate:

> Let us deride the smugness of "The Times";
> GUFFAW!
> So much for the gagged reviewers,
> It will pay them when the worms are wriggling in
> their vitals . . .

Lewis's vehemence is creative, this is not. It is a glacial contempt remote from that central *virtù*. Triangulating the impotent vituperation into which Pound kept lapsing in the 1930's and 1940's and over Rome Radio, we may use as base line the *Blast* contributions in which he is trying to shout as loud as the next man, and make a fix on another incident that involved *Blast*. On 22 October 1914, G. W. Prothero, editor of *The Quarterly Review*, wrote that he would accept no more contributions from Pound. "Of course, having accepted your paper on the *Noh*, I could not refrain from publishing it"; but otherwise the *Q.R.*'s columns must remain closed "to any one associated publicly with such a publication as *Blast*. It stamps a man too disadvantageously." Good God.

Abstract and remote though the contents of *Blast* might be, the establishment had bared its fangs and invoked its ultimate weapon, the boycott. To men who lived on what they could pick up from articles and reviews, the ultimate weapon implied more than lack of a showcase: it implied starvation. It cost Pound "at the lowest estimate about £20 per year," half as much as he was able to earn in the next 12 months, or, at that year's prices in an Italian restaurant, 200 dinners for two.* Prothero was snarling like a guilty thing surprised. Of what was he guilty? Of reverence for death, or perhaps decorum. And there is nothing like the weapon he used to induce lethal thoughts. *Blast* should have been a great lark. (It was.) The long-term psychic damage Pound underwent is beyond calculation. On the continent men were soon killing each other. A third of a million Frenchmen died in the first five months. "Never have machine-gunners had such a heyday."

*   *   *

How did one make a living? Pound had driblets from his father's thrift, and modest fees from periodicals. Orage's *New Age*, for which by the end of the war he was the Art and the Music critic under pseudonyms, at four guineas a month was "the sinews, bi gob the sinooz." ("And give up verse, my boy," said his "Mr. Nixon," "There's nothing in it.") Eliot taught school (French, mathematics, history, geography, drawing, and swimming), delivered extension lectures, then worked in Lloyds Bank, where it has been intimated that if he had stayed he might have aspired to a Branch Managership. Lewis decorated a fireplace for Violet Hunt (who also had a Ruskin washstand), and made decorations for the Countess of Drogheda's house, and for the Tour Eiffel restaurant, and painted Vorticist designs on furniture, and talked money out of compliant

---

* In a frequent routine, as Dorothy Pound described it, Ezra would ride the threepenny bus from Kensington toward Holborn to see Orage; she would save a penny by riding only to Piccadilly. They met for 1/6 dinner and spent 2d. apiece to get home: total cost 2/3, and "it got him off the typewriter."

women; Kate Lechmere financed the Rebel Art Centre (spring-fall, 1914) and put up £100 toward the printer's bill for *Blast*. Gaudier "obtained a clerkship in the city, studied in museums in the evenings and on Saturday afternoons and spent half the night drawing. Then he broke down." And there was no mechanism to translate into food and lodging what these men gave to the life of the mind.

* * *

But (June 1914) the Vortex was massively circulating. "We will convert the King if possible. A VORTICIST KING! WHY NOT?" On June 15, five days before *Blast* went on sale, Grant Richards published *Dubliners*. *The Egoist* of that date offered the tenth instalment of its Serial Story, *A Portrait of the Artist as a Young Man*, which the author was mailing from Trieste as fast as he could copy it, and an article by Pound on Wyndham Lewis which threw "at the spectator" two small designs "with the same confidence and with the same indifference that Giotto sent back his circle to the pope or whoever it was who wanted a sample of workmanship." ("And we will sweep out the past century as surely as Attila swept across Europe.") *Des Imagistes* had been in print since March, and copies of the May *Poetry* had arrived in London with the text of the Noh play "Nishikigi" from Fenollosa's notebooks—

> How glorious the sleeves of the dance
> That are like snow-whirls!

—and the notebooks were pregnant with other treasure. Ireland was moving into the Vortex via Trieste, Japan and China via Massachusetts and South Kensington, Henri Gaudier called Gaudier-Brzeska was chipping stone under the Putney railway arch (and had studied Chinese, and could synthesize Egypt), Dolmetsch was reviving music "of a lost dynasty." Renaissance dawned. Genius might turn up at any moment. (And in fact T. S. Eliot was *en route* to Marburg, whence war deflected him to England and to publication in *Blast* #2.)

English poetry was being freed from painting, English music from "literature," painting from anecdote, sculpture from sentiment. Each art was starting forth sharp and distinct, all simultaneously released from the mimetic. At 28 Pound was immersed in the orchestration of the new sensibility, decisive and blocked and faceted, a vortex of vortices, in touch with Li Po and Provence and Chou bronzes and Uccello and Flaubert and *Feng Shui*, the Chinese geomancer's art of detecting the rhymes and unrhymes of the local cosmos. Unimpeded by fussy "tradition," *virtù* free as light in space could intersect (with precision, with immediacy) any tradition it chose. As a raised eyebrow can subsume declamation, the art of laconic quotation (a Greek phrase quoted, or a form, as the beard on Gaudier's "Hieratic Head" quotes Pharaohs' beards) could summon arrayed masteries. Our Vortex was "proud of its polished sides." And the vorticists were young: ready, as Lewis remembered it decades later, "to go to live in the unwatered moon," a world the imagination had never inhabited before, such a world as lies before the times of great innovators.

Nearer to the end of the century than to those times, we think that imagined world of theirs old hat: a strange illusion since it was never colonized. A landing party or two set down, no more. Then the supply ships were scuttled, the effort faltered, some pilots were killed, others devoted long lives to catechizing a bitter lesson, each in an isolation from the others that 1914 could not have foreseen. Have we studied the manifestoes too often, and the flight plans that were never used? Or are we dulled by loudspeakers, or have we lost the capacity to participate in a hope? "The 20th century's early modernism," we yawn respectfully or indifferently. There have been so many modernisms. *That* period, we feel sure, played itself out. But it never played; its energies separated, some were cancelled by lead, its synergies faded amid the roar of field guns. What we feel so used to in retrospect, nearly convinced that we were *there* and found it meager, is like the memory of a TV program we cannot be bothered to interrogate.

A new copy of *Blast*, puce, the size of a telephone directory lettered from corner to corner, lay on an aristocratic garden table. The summer day darkened. The rains commenced to fall. No one rescued it. Through a spattered pane wide aristocratic eyes saw in a sudden blazing lightning-flash the shocking pink cover start forth, the five fierce black letters, B L A S T. Darkness recomposed. The dull rain fell and fell.

Six weeks after *Blast* was published Europe was at war.

*   *   *

End of a Vortex, though it was 1919 before Pound fully realized this bitter fact. By then he had a theme to animate what was to have been the Vorticist epic and became instead a poem on vortices and their fate: shapings of characterizing energies, and the *bellum perenne* that dissipates them. The Provençal vortex of poetry, music, and architecture ended after the Montségur massacre. The Tuscan vortex of painting and poetry thickened from greed as did the Venetian vortex. In Rimini a vortex of architecture and sculpture did not outlast the one man responsible for it, whom bigotry and jealousy pulled down. *That* one had been made, as had the London vortex, against the time's currents of power, and true to the nature of a vortex had gathered in everything movable: the best architect and the best stonecutter in Italy, and a poet (Basinio) who "kept his melodic sense active" by using Greek phrases as *mantrams*, and Pisanello the maker of medallions, and Piero della Francesca, and even a craftsman to make dies to impress a profile and monogram on a wafer of wax to be "caught, as was the custom, between two surfaces of paper in a letter from the young Salustio Malatesta." Pound owned a seal made by Edmund Dulac, and a clavichord made by Dolmetsch, and when Yeats deflected $200 toward him bought not only a typewriter but two carvings by Gaudier. One could still do something.

THE STONE

Henri Gaudier, called Gaudier-Brzeska, "maçon"; 4 Oct. 1891–5 June 1915: twenty-three years and eight months.

Only months remained to him when Wyndham Lewis had a glimpse, not quickly forgotten, of excited eyes in the carriage window of the boat train, a train full of volunteers who would be hustled into uniform and into trenches within weeks.

> We left the platform, a depressed, almost a guilty, group. It is easy to laugh at the exaggerated estimate "the artist" puts upon his precious life. But when it is really an artist—and there are very few—it is at the death of something terribly alive that you are assisting. And this little figure was so preternaturally alive.

By April he commanded 30 men, to whom he read out of *Cathay* to put courage in them. It was a two-ounce book, no burden in his pocket.

> Who has brought the flaming imperial anger? . . .
> Barbarous kings.

And:

> Imagine a dull dawn, two lines of trenches and in between explosion upon explosion, with clouds of black and yellow smoke, a ceaseless crackling noise from the rifles, a few heads and legs flying, and *me*

standing up among all this like to Mephisto—commanding "Feu par salve à 250 mètres—joue—feu!" then throwing a bomb, and again a volley. . . .

"A few heads and legs flying." And:

Today is magnificent, a fresh wind, clear sun and larks singing cheerfully. The shells do not disturb the songsters. . . . I respect their disdain.

[Seven days to live.]

*   *   *

There is little of his work, small stones mostly, scattered in four countries. Had he lived it would all be interesting juvenilia. Nevertheless,

He was the first sculptor in a thousand years to work in modes that had been all that Homer, Ptahotep, Confucius and Sappho knew as beauty in stone.

—Guy Davenport, 1965.

Henri Gaudier-Brzeska, Marble Cat. (Courtesy Mrs. Dorothy Pound.)

"It was done" (Pound remembering) "against the whole social
system in the sense that it was done against poverty and the lack
of materials." He used oddments of stone left over from other
people's—for instance monument cutters'—hackings. The "Cat"
emerges from one side of a broken chunk of marble, "of no shape"
save that Gaudier saw the cat lying tensed in it. "The Embracers"
was elicited from a tapering balustrade-shaped block. "He was
definitely a visionary," Pound records, "and 'saw' both in waking
vision and in sleep." He saw what forms inhabited a time's rejected
stones, impish figures, cats, stags, dwarfed energies, the ignored
gods. Lines of verse in which the sculptor sees the form in the air.

> before he sets hand to mallet
> and as he sees the in, and the through,
>   the four sides
> not the one face to the painter
>   (25/117:122)

and other lines where Dionysius' great cats grow manifest when the
god has been wronged and asserts himself—

> Lifeless air become sinewed,
>   feline leisure of panthers
>   (2/8:12)

were conceived in a mind accustomed to the company of the aloof
cat Gaudier saw in the contours of a marble fragment, and saw so
exactly that to release it into permanent life there was very little he
had to cut away.

And he could see the horse in brushstrokes not yet squared by
convention: "Can't they see it's a horse?"—reading the 187th
radical—and many another—at sight. This from Morrison's seven-
volume Chinese–English Dictionary, leafed through in the Pounds'
flat. Dorothy had bought it in the Tottenham Court Road.

(And as the horse persists in the ideogram, so we hear the
birds persisting in a violin part which Gerhart Münch made from
Francesco da Milano's lute reduction of Clement Janequin's choral
arrangement of perhaps some Provençal tune descended from some
remote act of invention inspired by the form of bird-song. And
vortices intersect like geodesics, for Gerhart Münch in Rapallo two

Forms of the Horse Ideogram, Morrison's *Dictionary*.

decades later leafed through that same dictionary. To use his violin setting as the heart of Canto 75 was the inspiration of a later day, in a dusty square place around which birds sat like notes on a five-wire fence, under the guns.)

Thus (1934) "Cubism has not decayed. Concepts do not decay, but inferior minds and inferior artists waddle about in dilutions of concepts." Concepts do not decay. Vorticism remains, though the Vorticists diverged.

And as to where those stones came from, the "Cat" and "The Embracers": the sculpture for which people would pay money in 1913 included three-dimensional marble copies of Victorian pictures, done with the aid of a drill. (The drill marks are still on "The Embracers.") Large lumps had to be knocked out of the marble, as for instance beneath a sculpted chair, and Gaudier acquired two of these lumps, detritus of so to speak some private Albert Memorial (commissioned by "some one with a large house full of plush furniture.") The same sculptor also made clay models for gas fixtures. John Ruskin, only a dozen years dead, had excoriated his kind.

In a brick mansion on Melbury Road, W. 14, financed by the Victorian taste for large paintings, one can see at the topmost floor the vertical slot through which monstrous canvases still on their stretchers could be passed for lowering to the ground and the waiting van, with the eminent and opulent R.A.'s brushwork still wet.

:Whereas Gaudier once slept on his studio floor, "and woke up to find himself inundated with rain and lying in several inches of water." The floor was normally mud. Trains rushed overhead. The address was Railway Arch 25, being one half of an arch under the Putney Viaduct, not far from where Swinburne died. One measured one's wealth in pence. When Ezra Pound first roomed in Hammersmith for 3/6 per week, so small a matter as the threepenny bus fare "cut off anything in the nature of economy." A smallish block of marble, not someone's debris but a prism three feet high, cost all of three pounds, with a flaw in it. Gaudier therefore begged fragments. In his life he had just one such fair-sized piece. Ezra Pound bought it for him. God knows where Ezra Pound found "three quid, or three guineas." It weighed half a ton and Gaudier spent two months cutting at it, wearing out chisels he had forged from old steel spindles and repeatedly reforging them. In the process he reinvented Egyptian sculpture. The subject was Pound, sitting in a twelvepenny chair, reflecting that if he had lived in the Quattrocento he should have had "no finer moment and no better craftsman to fill it. And it is not a common thing to know that one is drinking the cream of the ages."

*   *   *

In the Quattrocento marble came by water to Rimini, and other marble by land, bootlegged from Classe, for Agostino di Duccio to incise with incomparable reliefs. That stone too was gotten against the time's currents of power, as was the money the stonecutters were paid with, their patron at one time drawing his pay in a squabble "over a ten acre lot." Those were barbarous times, all Italy embroiled, government conducted by assassination, and a prince of the church dealing in stone he had no title to, for the men from Rimini to cart off by night. But San Francesco in Rimini, also known to the distress of its clergy as the Tempio Malatestiana, contains carving after carving, relief after relief, a stone tomb supported by stone elephants, Diana on her moon barge clutching the crescent, "pale eyes as if without fire," stone musicians incised as if breathing, stone *putti* playing in water (Gemisthus Plethon having "stemmed all from Neptune"), a tranquil vivid astonishment of stones. Pass through five centuries' refinement of values, five centuries' synergetic augmentation of communal wealth, and observe Henri Gaudier vaccinated against smallpox, and enfranchised if that pleased him, and the railway train and the fountain pen placed at his disposal, and to effect the renovation of sculpture some broken

Sigismundus Pandolphus de Malatestis, relief by Agostino di Duccio in the Tempio, Rimini.

"Gemisto stemmed all from Neptune/hence the Rimini bas reliefs"
Detail of carving by Duccio in the Tempio, one of many that feature water.

Intertwined initials of Sigismundo and Isotta, displayed by altar-rail cherub in the Tempio.

chunks of marble no one else wanted, plus just one stone a child could not have lifted: this latter thanks to a poet living by journalism who had seemed worth sculpting because he had written "Altaforte" ("Damn it all . . ."), and had then spent two months' income rather than be sculpted in what Gaudier could afford, plaster. And the gift of a bullet, finally. This was the sort of thing that made Pound feel that something was wrong with the system.

The subject was 28, the sculptor 22. Gaudier's eye explored the high temples, the long straight nose; the intent still eyes, whose color (green) did not concern him; the broad slash of a mouth, a little turning downward; the forelock and jutting beard; the fine cheekbones. Some hundred drawings with a little flat pliable stick dipped in ink worked out defining contours. (They were mostly torn up; two or three that have survived are calligraphic; Pound salvaged one and made it his hallmark.) And doodlings in Gaudier's copy of *Ripostes* hint at a tenuous association between Ezra Pound and Egypt: a design with cats and stone blocks for "The Tomb at Akr Çaar," then a cat-faced stele, clearly a sketch for the bust, a few pages later in the margin of "An Immorality."

* * *

And why Egypt? The shape of the stone, for one thing, a blunt vertical shaft; and the vertical, Gaudier knew and Sigfried Giedion confirmed 50 years later, was an Egyptian invention. In "Egypt, the land of plenty," Gaudier wrote,

> Man succeeded in his far-reaching speculations—Honour to the divinity!
> Religion pushed him to the use of the VERTICAL which inspires awe. His gods were self made, he built them in his image, and RETAINED AS MUCH OF THE SPHERE AS COULD ROUND THE SHARPNESS OF THE PARALLELOGRAM. . . .

That sphere, he thought, had been man's primary formal intuition, "the fruitful sphere," expressing a paleolithic preoccupation with animals. Egyptian verticality was its first modification: fruitfulness fused with knowledge of the gods, the invisible. Thus, the Hieratic Head. And the vertical when cylindrical becomes, Gaudier held, the African and Oceanic VORTEX OF FECUNDITY.

The fruitful (cerebral) sphere upwelling from the shaft's thrust yielded (in Wyndham Lewis' succinct description) "Ezra in the form of a marble phallus." Eight years later Ezra was reflecting on a career of driving ideas into "the great passive vulva of London," and speculating on the brain as a localization of seminal energy, notions Gaudier's image may have catalyzed.

The incised narrow eyeslits gaze, without pupils, on the invisible; the asymmetric rhombic nose carries its flat thrust upward to the plane of the brow, overlapped by a flame-like forelock; the broad mouth is calm; the formalized goatee, as if clapped on, is from Egypt, as are the truncated shoulders rising as through illimitable sand. There is no constriction of scale, no adequation of size to the size of living bone and tissue, because no notation for such tissue. The Hieratic Head geometrizes structure not impression. The bleak masses, the unadorned planes, the massiveness of even such a passage of detail as surmounts the right eye, suggest a three-foot maquette of something fully realizable only in 40: a minatory colossus to dominate some world that did not "waste good stone" in such places as the cemetery that adjoins the bus-route between Kensington and Putney.

*　*　*

"You understand it will not look like you, it *will* ... *not* ... *look* ... like you. It will be the expression of certain emotions which I get from your character." And in a notebook rejection of Michelangelo, dated "20 Avril 1911,"

> dessiner dans les plans majeurs les masses principales
> „　　„　　„ masses 　„　　„ plans mineurs
> „　　„　　„ plans mineurs „ masses 　„
> et rendre fermes ces masses mineurs par l'étude correcte
> et vraie de tous leurs plans. ...

For "line is a purely imaginary thing, entering the design only to contain the planes of the mass, receiving light and creating shadow; the planes convey the whole artistic effect and the line serves only to bound them." And (in the trenches) "I SHALL DERIVE MY EMOTIONS SOLELY FROM THE ARRANGEMENT OF SURFACES, I shall present my emotions by the ARRANGEMENT OF MY SURFACES, THE

Henri Gaudier-Brzeska, Hieratic Head of Ezra Pound, 1913.

PLANES AND LINES BY WHICH THEY ARE DEFINED": as he had always done, for he is affirming that his views on sculpture are absolutely unchanged by the experiences of war.

So not only does the bust express, by surfaces and planes, "certain emotions which I get from your character," those emotions were themselves derived (we may take "solely" as rhetorical concentration) "solely from the arrangement of surfaces": the surfaces of a head that fascinated Wyndham Lewis, who drew it time after time and later memorialized it for the Tate, and that Cocteau drew in spiky profile, crowned with laurel, and that in the chaos of another war received the definitive critique of the Tirolese with heavy rifles who took Pound into custody near Gais but concluded the planes of so noble a head were not meant for bullets. (The father of their spokesman had carved madonnas.)

Shape, Gaudier thought, manifests psychic intent. The shape of a Mauser rifle "swamped me with a powerful IMAGE of brutality," an effect derived, he was at pains to emphasize, not from his knowledge of what the Mauser was for, but "FROM A VERY SIMPLE COMPOSITION OF LINES AND PLANES." He broke off the butt and reformed it with his knife "to express a gentler order of feeling, which I preferred." All shape was eloquent; and such a sensibility, moving among London's shapes—taxicabs, door-knockers, fan-lights, headgear, footwear, flowerpots, railway engines—undergoing at every conscious moment the cacophony of their planes which his quick eye intercepted as he walked; douched in their relentless chitchat of boredom and fussiness and assumed importance and stark insensibility, of which that polychrome banana split the Albert Memorial is the culminating statement, as it were an anti-Tempio: such a sensibility could not but conceive its own least aggressive artifacts as points of counter-radiation, their planes and masses projected outward from Putney into Kensington and into Knightsbridge and St. John's Wood and still darker places. If he had been able to do the Hieratic Head in granite, as high as Selfridge's, to be erected . . . where? In Hampstead Heath? Or on Dover Cliffs, to demark a new Easter Island? . . . He was never a maker of little things for dealers to traffick in. He made little things with the little stones he could get.

And the ultimate insipidity, he conceived, was the Hellenic: "pretty" works of "a people to whom instinct is secondary to reason": a people picking up the Egyptian influence from across the middle sea, and using it to delineate their admiration for themselves. ("An ideal for super-aesthetes and matinee girls," wrote Pound of Greek sculpture after exposure to Gaudier's conversation; and again, "the Greeks ... the caressable ..."; and again, after 14 years, "... plastic moving toward coitus, and limited by incest, which is the sole Greek taboo": whereas the Egyptian stone has the god inside it.) Nevertheless caressable Greek ninepins, in the Louvre or the British Museum, not to mention the Vatican, constituted in wartime much of the official inventory of Culture: that, to defend the values of which, men died, a myriad. Gaudier whose excited eyes Lewis had remembered, peering through the window of that boat train, was to become for Pound the archetypal war casualty; hence the special bitterness of the lines in *Mauberley*,

> Quick eyes gone under earth's lid
> For two gross of broken statues ...

—quick eyes capable of seeing, had they lived, better sculpture by far in better stones than fortune had ever allotted him. Surely John Quinn would have staked him to some marble.

*   *   *

The donation remained: a few pieces, of which the Hieratic Head is the most ambitious; an orientation toward sculptural history that encouraged the reading of whole civilizations in their masses and planes and the very equating of civilization with stone, cut stone; and among many memories the memory of a time when the carver of planes in relation had addressed himself to that one decent stone, a memory to cast huge shadows on the screen of the *Cantos*, whose first full-length hero derived from wars as petty as London journalism the money for stone for Agostino di Duccio. That hero's bones rest in his Tempio, and Pound was one day to complete the analogy by directing that the Hieratic Head should stand over his grave in Idaho.

*   *   *

The Hieratic Head came from England to Rapallo and to a rooftop, whence its eyes gazed seaward. It gleamed in the moonlight, and in the 1940's was required to be shrouded for fear of night raiders homing in on a town where nothing else, one might suppose, was so bright. Years later, in the castle garden among the Tirolean mountains, it faced the dawn like the Sphinx, when one day Pound decided it ought to face the West, and several men managed to turn it. He looked by then much more like it than he had when it was carved, Gaudier's eye having seen in a young face what only five more decades of living would realize, but he was occupied still as he had been at twenty with the pre-dawn he had celebrated in *A Lume Spento*, a light seen before there is anything eastward-gazers can see, beheld by a lone man facing the westward air the unrisen sun illumines. So the stone eyes, narrowed as though to penetrate distance, temporal distance and spatial, perceive every morning the first gleam visible anywhere, suffusing the mountains along the Upper Adige. The eyes face the peak called Ziel (purpose), just left of the one called Mut (courage). So Pound long before had seen Gaudier, while the east-watchers were expecting some caressable Renaissance.

*　*　*

Had he seen into the future in 1915, when he was writing his memoir *Gaudier-Brzeska*, he might have glimpsed seven years thence a man of 24, as though just the age to take up Gaudier's dropped life, reading it and turning over its plates: a man of slacker and more cumbrous but persistent *virtù* who had wanted to make sculpture since he was in his teens (when Gaudier had been alive, but unheard-of), but had had to settle for schoolteaching and then soldiering, and then a scholarship bringing undirective years at art schools. And in 1922 his mind was suddenly unclouded by Gaudier's "Vortex" ("Sculptural energy is the mountain . . ."), and immediately thereafter he made his first direct carvings in stone and in wood: Henry Moore.

Part Two

INTERREGNUM

PRIVACIES

And who were they?

Longfellow's grand-nephew, Pound was said to be. That is one taxonomy, an unimportant one, though Lawrence ("of Arabia") professed to think the effort to live it down explained some of Ezra's conduct. He belonged, with Eliot, to the last generation in whose early education Latin and Greek were normal: not necessarily rigorous Latin and Greek, but enough to take fire from the shaping of

> ... *para thina poluphloisboio thalasses*

His mother (remembered by an acquaintance walking "as though in ermine") had ambitions for her son, and when 4% of the nation's college-age youth were in college (it is 40% today) he was one of them. Comparative literary studies—unsystematic and redundant to be sure—had replaced the old classical curriculum. They would later in turn be replaced by watertight "departments," notably of "English," whence incomprehension radiates. In his day one acquired languages; it was normal.

He had always wanted "to be a poet," which meant in part to assume a special role, in part to acquire the language-lord's *maestria*. The role put people off; Bill Williams in the Penn medical school was especially irritated. The *maestria* excused the role, and quickened early. There was a Miss Summer or Sommer ruling one classroom he sat in—was he ten or thereabouts?—his ode to whose departure lingers in oral tradition—

> O Summer time, O Summer time
> The winter time is here.
> No longer doth the yardstick bend
> Beneath thy sway;
> > O happy day
> When Summer time is gone away.

An internal rhyme is detectable even so early. He teemed with energy. He thought, like George Boole, in dichotomies. His perception of rhythm was subtle, strong, innate.

He was taken from Idaho at 18 months (in a blizzard, behind the first rotary snowplough) to New York City where his mother's aunt kept a "too large" hotel. Its guests and personnel peopled his earliest memories—

> . . . the voice of Monsieur Fouquet or the Napoleon 3rd
> barbiche of Mr Quackenbos, or Quackenbush
> as I supposed it,

and a city of "white-wash and horse cars" with its excitements,

> . . . a fellow throwing a knife in the market
> past baskets and bushels of peaches

and himself, small and precocious,

> playing checquers with black Jim
> on a barrel top where now is the Ritz-Carlton.

To live was to observe variety, after he was six the variety of estates and barbered lawns spread out around Wyncote, where his parents bought a tall frame house with colored glass in parlor windows and an apple tree in the backyard. Packing-case tree houses were improvised in the apple tree, and Ezra's incessant tennis practice cracked a stained glass pane. His tennis, like his reading, was a triumph of will and skill over lifelong presbyopia. By maturity he was carrying various glasses to be pulled on and off at need, and some of his notorious misreadings are attributable to imperfect perception of the

print. His father Homer, who had assayed ore in Hailey, was assistant assayer to the United States Mint at Jupiter and Chestnut
Streets, Philadelphia. (Homer, Jupiter, Chestnut: a charming public
syncretism, part of the old American weather. Every small town had
its State Street, also its Euclid Avenue, and a mind nourished on
such easy congruences was to sum up a Pisan landscape, light on
grainfields, a cone-shaped mountain,

> Zeus lies in Ceres' bosom,
>> Taishan is attended of loves
>>> under Cythera, before sunrise

—Greece, Rome, China, separate but indivisible.)

Peering over the banister, little "Ray" could inspect dinner
guests: their neighbor Cyrus Curtis, for instance, of the *Ladies'
Home Journal*. Or George Horace Lorimer of the *Saturday Evening
Post*, taking his routine shortcut through the Pounds' backyard,
would outline his latest *coup* while Homer hoed corn (81/519:554).
Publishing executives and other Philadelphia *nouveaux riches*—
Widner, Elkins, Stetson, Wanamaker—filled the surrounding
countryside with Renaissance palaces. Ezra could skate on Wanamaker's pond, and once helped rescue pictures from a Wanamaker
fire: all fakes he was to learn.

The Pounds' parlor bric-à-brac was not uncultivated: a sequence of tranquil scenes for instance that some Oriental had painted,
and adorned with poems in ideograph. The edges were gilded, and
the tablets hinged together to stand up like a zigzag screen. When it
came to Rapallo with his parents in the 1930's he drew the Seven
Lakes Canto from it.

He grew to middle height; five feet ten a passport says.
Translating vigor and carriage into stature, everyone seems to
remember him as tall.

Who was he? A naif, thought undergraduates, who dunked
him in a lily pond. The first poem he has chosen to have us read, a
poem of his adolescence which he once gave Hilda Doolittle
whether or not he wrote it for her, is about how it feels to become a
tree and thus understand many a thing "that was rank folly to my
head before." The next poem in *Personae* imagines how it feels to

be Tristram and beyond passion because dead; the next, "La Fraisne," imagines how it feels to be a "gaunt, grave councillor" who need not be hurt by women any more because he has decided to be an ash tree and love a dogwood; the next, "Cino," imagines how it feels to be a trecento poet who need not be hurt by women any more because he does not sing of them now but of the sun and white birds and clouds; the next, "Na Audiart," imagines how it feels to be Bertrans de Born who had been hurt by two women at least, and is contriving in homage to one of them an ideal lady whose torso is the other's; and when Audiart of the torso, who wishes him ill, shall have grown old, she will soften, remembering his homage.

His susceptibility to women (and theirs to him) was lifelong; so was his sensitivity to their slights; so was his knack for roles. At 70, telling stories in the Chestnut Ward, he would imitate voices, James's, Eliot's, "Old Krore"'s, not phonographically—his own Philadelphia idiom was ineradicable—but with minute attention to mannerisms. At 80, like the gaunt councillor who became an ash tree, he had elected silence but not torpor; an arc runs from 1908

> She hath called me from mine old ways
> She hath hushed my rancor of council,
> Bidding me praise
> Naught but the wind that flutters in the leaves

to 1960 circa:

> I have tried to write Paradise.
> Do not move.
> Let the wind speak.
> That is Paradise.

His silent old age was didactic still. Brancusi's bird, in Peggy Guggenheim's loggia, reached by a back gate, was juxtaposed with Carpaccio's St. Ursula sequence, firm outline with firm outline, as fast as the old man with his rapid walk could lead friends through Venetian back streets to the *Accademia* and its second floor. No word was spoken in this final persona, though in 60 years he had spoken several million didactic words; his second impulse, never really disjunct from the poetic, was always to teach, to share, and that impulse like the poetic entailed a problem of role.

Teaching is sharing, a function of generosity. One role, patience and affable expostulation ("Expect to be carried up Mt. Helicon in an easy chair?") engaged much of himself but took time. The Lewisian "Wipe your feet" (". . . any change in any art has had to be pushed down the public throat with a ramrod") was not in character but could mobilize a sliver of his character from which appalling forces might sometimes radiate. It was during the war years, the years of imprisonment in beleaguered England, that a surface of implacable irony, imitated in part from the Encyclopaedists, united patience and impatience behind the convention that a man serves his intelligence, to which truth is self-evident. The self-evidence of truth is a facet of American optimism; Pound came to play, and nearly to become, a stage-Yankee to whom virtue is knowledge, and action at variance with the norms I know, once I have laid them before you, is sheer bad faith, sheer evil. In the note printed with "La Fraisne" from 1908 to 1920 he had spoken of being "freed of the weight of a soul 'capable of salvation or damnation'," which meant freed from a provincial Christianity that kept one anxious. A chief irony of his life was the fashioning during that war of a persona that could damn so much and so many.

All his early work asks, "Who am I?" He was Bertrans ("Damn it all"), he was the Seafarer bard and the inditer of the Exile's Letter, he was Sextus Propertius bidding empire go hang, and Mauberley (aesthetic, ". . . unable . . ."), and the E. P. ("wrong from the start") whom Mauberley buries with "all his troublesome energies" but who gets the very war into an epigram ("Quick eyes gone under earth's lid"). Finally, life being an experiencing and a knowing, he was Odysseus concerning whose epithet *polymechanos* the scholia "give a long list of his various accomplishments, as ploughman, shipwright, carpenter, hunter, steersman," since "Homer clearly admires this kind of versatility." Odysseus has a near-monopoly on the Homeric epithets in *poly-*.

The Renaissance poet was expected to possess poetic omnicompetence built on wide practical experience; thus Milton's time as Cromwell's Latin Secretary counted toward his preparation for writing his epic. The American, whom frontier conditions forced to play Odysseus, prized versatility likewise. Perhaps it was inevitable that some day an American should fuse the epic bard with the epic subject, Renaissance poet with Homeric hero, so clearly do all the specifications converge: poet as musician, as sculptor, as economist; hero as traveller, as role-player, as observer of "many men's manners." And all the while, underneath, ran a mystical conviction, shyly divulged in poems never reprinted, that one might actually be possessed, beyond role, by the actual *virtù* of the great dead whom one has much pondered: a conviction that near Pisa, his passport identity nearly swept away, sustained many pages of poetry.

*   *   *

And Lewis? "Yourself," he said, "must be your caste"; and "Why try and give the impression of a consistent and indivisible personality?" and "I have allowed these contradictory things to struggle together, and the group that has proved the most powerful I have fixed upon as my most essential ME." "What an entangled Absalom!" wrote Yeats to Lewis's old protector Sturge Moore, developing a fancy that should correlate genius with hair. By contrast Bertrand Russell, Yeats thought, had been bald the whole of his life. Though logic has its own snares, it does not get entangled Absalom-wise in trees.

If a Russell's energies were wholly cerebral, Lewis's quickened the painting animal. Perfusing his musculature, running down the arm from ganglia and cortex, localized in his fingers like the quickening power of the Michelangelo Jehovah, ran the pattern-generating faculty which reason could not articulate but from which mind might not abdicate: bidding the arm swing from the shoulder, the forearm from the elbow, the stylus hook and hatch in the grip of a bony compass now pivoted at the wrist and now modulated by contracting finger muscles, miraculously correlated with the promptings and stern satisfactions of the eye to make an "Alcibiades," a "Red Duet," a "Timon," an "Ezra Pound." This was Lewis's profoundest sense of himself, and there was little his discursive mind could say about it, except that it was a faculty "older than the fish." The few centuries that separate the artist from the savage "are a mere flea-bite to the distance his memory must stretch if it is to strike the fundamental slime of creation."

The creation of a work of art is an act of the same description as the evolution of wings on the sides of a fish, the feathering of its fins; or the invention of a weapon within the body of a hymenopter to enable it to meet the terrible needs of its life.

This did not mean, he was careful to specify, "The music of *Carmen*, the *Prince Igor* ballet, all the 'savage stuff' that always gets the audience": *that* order of genteel savagery ("clash of cymbals, howl of clansmen, voluptuous belly-dance") was merely a feeble and fashionable creativity's self-congratulation at having taken the very first tiny step into the first and closest circumvolving zone, the zone of the barbaric. The noises made by folk arrested in this zone helped convince the public that artists were wild men "loaded with Spanish knives, sombreros, oaths, . . . archpriest[s] of the romantic Bottle." A Cézanne's moving hand derived none of its power from such role-playing; it simply *created* at the prompting of forces like those that have generated forms since form began. "As to the wing mechanism that first lifted a creature off the ground, and set it spinning or floating through the air, you must call Shakespeare in to compete with it," but Shakespeare at work doing something comparably wonderful felt no need to grimace nor swill gin nor retrogress from 1601 back as far as he could toward Caliban.

Lewis wrote, of course, in the presence of several knowledges unavailable to Shakespeare. One was knowledge of the cave paintings, first discovered only in 1879 and not at all "barbaric" in their austere draughtsmanship. Eliot went to look at some in June 1919, the year Lewis wrote the sentences we have been quoting, and returned to write "Tradition and the Individual Talent" and to discern in Wyndham Lewis "the thought of the modern and the energy of the cave man." Another was Creative Evolution, potent for all Lewis's polemic dislike of the way Professor Bergson romanticized it. And Fabre had described beetles which could "grow out of their bodies menacing spikes, and throw up on top of their heads sinister headdresses, overnight"; not a profound invention but certainly a creative feat, and "any art worth the name is, at the least, a feat of this description." And the chemists, the physicists, the biologists, were everywhere discovering a pattern-making faculty inherent in nature. Salt was crystalline, bubbles were vectorial

equilibria, Marconi's pulses patterned the very ether, D'Arcy
Thompson in 1917 explained how the bird's skeleton and the
cantilever bridge utilize identical principles. To divide like Bergson
the vital from the mechanical seemed mere romance—"life, simply,
however vivid and tangible, is too material to be anything but a
mechanism, and the seagull is not far removed from the hydroplane"
—and stones were quite as wonderful as birds: "Whether a stone
flies and copulates, or remains respectably in its place, half hiding
the violet from the eye, is little matter. It is just as remarkable to be
so hard and big as to be so busy and passionate." If there was a
functional division, therefore, it fell between two kinds of intelligence: the kind that manifests, like nature, the power to create,
and the kind that chooses to keep itself outside, and "arrange"
and "compose" and also "appreciate." That was the true antithesis
between death and life, and it consigned the official art-world,
merchants, tastemakers, connoisseurs, to the category of death.

One humored them, one saved oneself trouble, by assuming
the costumes they provided for genius. They believed in cloaks and
sombreros, and Lewis assumed these; for that matter did not T. S.
Eliot, the shaman who dressed like a banker, behave the more
eccentrically of the two? One did not trust them an inch. (Lewis
was once called briefly away while a young woman was deciding
which picture to buy, and to safeguard the pictures locked her in
with them; *that* was a caveman gesture.) One opposed them, and
called one's periodical, and oneself, The Enemy. One affected to
hang in the midst of one's personae, operating them "with detachment," much as, long ago, one had consulted one's mother by frequent post about the difficulty of managing one's laundry and one's
mistresses, sharing an amusement with all roles including the
bohemian.

Young energies diminish, notably the energies of attention
you need for discerning hour after hour where a role's usefulness
stops. "Do not send yourself to sleep with the rhythm of the passes
that you make," Lewis admonished the élite in 1917. In the 40
years that followed he was never asleep, but not seldom flypapered
by his own defense against flies. Intermittently the intelligence he
guarded, "older than the fish," came to full assertion: as late as

1938 he was making his most remarkable pictures, the great portraits: "burying Euclid deep in the living flesh," notably in Ezra Pound's, depicted dreaming before a painted ocean. He had a sharp eye for the personae of others. All of them had.

*   *   *

Joyce we know best, and least. "Stephen Dedalus" modulating into the Fabulous Artificer was the show he managed to stage; yet his letters, year after year, three thick printed volumes of them, do little but complain, complain, an interminable tenor solo. ("My Dear Job," Pound commenced an answer to one of them, "You will establish an immortal record.") And he sang "Let me like a soldier fall" in a way that mocked his own keening, and recorded ("Mr. Chairman, ladies and gentlemen") the speech from *Ulysses* about intransigent Moses in tones that both meant that eloquence and mocked it; and every time he was photographed the camera seemed to pick up a different man. Defining Stephen, he defined by reflection a counter-Stephen, a Dublin intellectual milieu which the last survivor of his college generation, publishing a memoir at 84, showed to be patently untrue (Joyce was not surrounded by clodhoppers, nor was he the only student who took an interest in languages and philosophy; and as for his breadth of learning, much of it emanated from college anthologies.) He was the president of his sodality in the years when, the *Portrait* would have us believe, he was wallowing in brothels and being terrified by a sermon: a sermon he confected, for the *Portrait*, out of a pamphlet called "Hell Opened to Christians," having once perhaps heard something of the kind delivered, or perhaps not. And Anglo-Irish Dublin, so vivid to visitors or to readers of Yeats, is absent from his books. Yet anyone who goes to the physical Dublin from *Ulysses* is haunted, passing the windows of Brown Thomas, silk mercers, or walking under Waterhouse's clock, by the eerie conviction that he was once there before. It is enough to make one believe in parallel universes, as did Joyce, almost.

Almost. *Ulysses* takes as if literally the talk of Yeats and his friends about metempsychosis. As Maud Gonne was Helen with no second Troy to burn, so Bloom is Ulysses with no sea to sail, committed however to a circuitous wandering through the to him known world. And Yeats is quoted, midway through *Ulysses*, burbling of "The most beautiful book that has come out of our country in my time. One thinks of Homer." One does, though Yeats was talking of another book. Not a "parallel," *Ulysses*, but a simple identity, though with differences, and a great joke on the Yeatsians, who loathed naturalism. And Dublin reconstructed by naturalist methods is not parallel to the Dublin men inhabit but identical with it, though different; for instance frozen in a single day in time, which it re-enacts forever, unable to escape the wheel of fiction. The fictional Dublin is reading the real Dublin's newspapers of that day, though with trifling discrepancies; for instance a funeral the real papers did not notice has slipped in, and a list of the mourners one of whom has a misprinted name (L. Boom). The fictional Dublin's stores and streets coincide with those survivors might remember, and the City Directory shows 7 Eccles Street to be vacant, though in the fiction Mr. Bloom lives there. Could the census taker somehow not see Bloom, or are we being told that Bloom like Ulysses is Noman? And Oliver Gogarty inhabits the fictional Dublin much as Dubliners may remember him, though his name has somehow altered to Mulligan; and that, a denizen inspecting the book's mocking mirror might exclaim, is surely Jimmy Joyce, but what is he called now? Dedalus? What kind of a name is that?

What kind of a name is that indeed; it is the sole incredibility in the Joyce canon. Mulligan, Bloom, even Cashel Boyle O'Connor Fitzmaurice Tisdall Farrell, these one will credit, but a Dublin that incorporates someone named Dedalus is surely a strange Dublin. Dedalus the aeronaut-artificer, Stephen the first martyr (whom they stoned when he reported a vision): was that name not almost certainly modelled on the name another Dubliner fabricated on similar principles to cover his anonymity in exile, a martyr Sebastian, a fabulous wanderer Melmoth (from Charles Maturin's novel *Melmoth the Wanderer*): Sebastian Melmoth, the last persona of the fallen Oscar Wilde? Joyce seems to have begun what was finally the *Portrait* just after Oscar Wilde died; was it to have offered a lower-class Catholic analogue to Wilde's upper-middle-class Protestant career, "the artist" being not altogether the man who signed the portrait, but more importantly the artist-type?

For Joyce was in so many ways so nearly Stephen, as he was nearly Eveline's Frank, and nearly the Mr. Duffy of "A Painful Case," and nearly Gabriel Conroy with his pince-nez and his wife from the west country, and nearly Bloom even, so nearly all of these that he might nearly have become any one of them. It is only by a long series of small accidents that anyone becomes what he does become, and though he can only be what he is, he can look back along the way he has come at branching-points now cancelled.

If the differences between Stephen and Joyce are small, all differences are small, and it is always small differences that are decisive. One has only to refuse a casual opportunity, and the curve of one's life commences a long slow bending away from what it would have been. Such an argument is not only Aristotelian, but obvious to a man brought up like Joyce in a climate of clerical exhortation. From the time he could first remember hearing human words he must have listened to hundreds of homilies, ruminations, admonitions, declaring how the little sins prepare the habit great sins will later gratify, or how the soul's destiny is prepared in early youth, so that there is nothing that does not matter. And a very few small changes, in the same way, would have made Dublin (1904, by the Liffey) the Dublin of *Ulysses*.

Something not produced by little changes, but something a few little changes might have occluded, was his enormous verbal gift, more than the endemic Irish flow of language because responsive to accuracies of moral perception. His life, as soon as he was aware of his genius, became a series of stratagems to safeguard it, as he imagined the boy in "Araby" bearing his chalice through a throng of foes.

And much chance enters into such purpose. As he is said to have let typists' errors stand when they were good ones, so he shaped his fortunes' caprice into what seems the most rigorously planned *oeuvre* of modern times. We see a man write 15 classic stories, then at 28 put the brief narrative forever behind him to complete in turn an autobiographical novel and then a *magnum opus* to which the novel leads and which the stories authenticate:

each of these works unique in its excellence, *Dubliners*, *Portrait*, *Ulysses*, the whole accomplished by his fortieth birthday, and the whole then counterpoised by a huge shaping of literary anti-matter: *Finnegans Wake*. Yet he had thoughts of a second book of stories which he might have written had anyone published the first book; and the loose autobiographical novel he tossed off in 1904–5 occupied him instead and became the austerely finished *Portrait* in part, it seems, because stories were unsalable and he had no other materials for a novel; and *Ulysses*, conceived as one of the unwritten stories, grew inordinately for seven years and to 700 unmarketable pages as he gave up leaving things out and began putting things in; and the *Wake*, which he also thought to finish more quickly, entailed a new kind of language he hadn't foreseen and took 17 years, very nearly all the rest of his life. What if there had been a ready market, about 1908, for all the stories he could write? That was another thing he might have become, a writer of *contes*.

Censorship, which regarded literature as a dangerous nuisance, and years of miserable grinding poverty during which his teeth rotted and his eyesight failed, these iron walls shaped his career. And had poverty not driven him to exchanging endless empty practice sentences with language pupils in Trieste, searching the English vocabulary for its simplest bases and its starkest syntax, would his unique feel for the unspoken have developed, or his unique response to the eloquent fragment?

Pound misconceived him for years, imagining that the man he knew only through stories and letters was like himself an un-committed free lance ("It has always struck me that you could do a unique series of 'portraits', 1000 to 2000 words, Priests in Padua, Students in Dublin, etc. God knows where you have been and what you have gazed upon with your microscopic, remarkable eye.") Instead he was the slave of a literary monster, and of his own will that would not leave a thing unfinished.

*   *   *

And Eliot, Thomas, last comer to the Vortex, *que faisait-il dans cette galère?* Elegant, shy, shy from great sensitivities and

great gifts, the youngest of eight children, he came, by way of
several Academies, from a birthplace by Twain's Mississippi in
Twain's lifetime, of a family of some local prominence, connected,
moreover, with the Massachusetts Eliots. His grandfather founded
Washington University, his grandfather's third cousin once re-
moved was president of Harvard for 40 years and edited the
Five-Foot Shelf of Classics. Insofar as inheritance can make you
Somebody, he was fit to be Somebody.

He acquired like an inheritance from the Eliots his sense of
responsibility to the Language: Henry James for instance uses far
more Americanisms. It was not that Eliot wanted his language to
be English instead of American; he wanted it to be neutral, and in
this he was very Augustan, equating reason and order with the internal structure of the language itself, which should consequently be
purged of incompetences and quirks. He was also in this way post-
Symbolist, the *Symboliste* poem being meant to seem as though
no one had written it: as though generated by the autonomous
language.

He quietly furnished his tenacious, subtle mind, and wrote
some poetry, some of which he thought good. It seemed as if no
one had written it. It was more like a private agony than a role; he
has described the poem struggling to get itself written, and the
struggle to write it so as to be left in peace. As both Mallarmé and
Edward Lear had in different ways understood, poetry walked on
the borders of the nonsensical;

> I grow old, I grow old
> I shall wear the bottoms of my trousers rolled.

—a rich nonsense, especially when the first words remind you of
fat Falstaff's "There lives not three good men unhang'd in England;
and one of them is fat, and grows old." They reminded Eliot of
Falstaff's words, he once said; they may not remind another; and
it is probably more true to say that they reminded Eliot of Falstaff's
words as he wrote them down, than that writing them down recorded
his decision to make Prufrock allude to Falstaff.

In the echo chamber, Tradition, one's words often pass through
forms other men have used. Who is the poet? A medium? To some

extent words use him; in his mind diverse things, linguistic included, are perpetually entering into new combinations. Sometimes, turning the tables, he can make words other men wrote sound like words he might have written himself:

> Here, said she,
> Is your card, the drowned Phoenician Sailor.
> (Those are pearls that were his eyes. Look!)

So he taught us that the separation between art and the event is always absolute; that the poet enters the poem not as an ingredient enters a chemical reaction, but only as a catalyst does; that "Poetry is not a turning loose of emotion, but an escape from emotion; it is not the expression of personality, but an escape from personality." He taught us, almost by that one sentence, to look at his poems, not at him; and so effectively that for half a century nobody noticed the next sentence: "But, of course, only those who have personality and emotions know what it means to want to escape from these things." For there were strong emotions from which he wanted to escape. During 32 years, almost from his first appearance in the Vortex, his life was bounded by the conditions of a miserable marriage, to a gifted woman of whom it was soon evident that her emotions were deranged, and hopelessly so.

And as words in a poem may coincide with some dead poet's words, unnoticed unless memory or a note alert us, so they may coincide with a living poet's actualities, unnoticed unless biographers apprise us.

> Or when, under ether, the mind is conscious but conscious
>   of nothing—
> I said to my soul, be still, and wait without hope
> For hope would be hope for the wrong thing; . . .

—words effective as symbols, words he literally meant in his private capacity, remembering a flat in which Vivien Eliot indulged her penchant for ether-sniffing. The words recall not only the ether but, with bitter honesty, the hope that kept offering itself to him, hope for her death: an honesty that confronts unflinching from the page readers who had thought this a casual *exemplum*. After his death the poetry is transfigured, as Eliot must have known it would one day be: under that fine smooth skin, so shocking a skull. All his life he felt akin to Donne, a great churchman who had wrecked his first career by an imprudent marriage.

He toyed with thoughts of her death by water, and seems not to have cared that we should one day know this. In *The Waste Land* a deranged voice (remembered?) speaks of being the Hyacinth Girl; a moment later the soothsayer hints at drowning and hanging, and someone else at a buried corpse; then a lady ("My nerves are bad tonight. Yes, bad. Stay with me. Speak to me") offers to rush out with her hair down and is suddenly metamorphosed into the mad Ophelia. And *Ash-Wednesday*, renouncing the blessed face and renouncing the voice, letting us know that he cannot drink "there, where trees flower and springs flow, for there is nothing again," in being a homage to Dante is the most agonized, most personal poem of all, and does not forget that Dante's ideal lady too once walked an earthly street. A lady watches with unnerving calm while three beasts dismember him, and though "She honors the Virgin in meditation" she is later "withdrawn / In a white gown, to contemplation, in a white gown," as it were in a nursing home; whereupon a litany hails her as "Lady of Silences" and as "end of the endless / Journey to no end."

Such was the poetry that for two generations made the 20th century seem habitable because accessible to language. His miseries, in that iridescent verse that seems as particular as something seen and yet as omnipresent as sound, changed scale and shape after his marriage and filled a world apt for expressive symbiosis with misery. Yet has anyone, unaware of the private facts, ever suspected how many lines of *Ash-Wednesday* simply meant what they said? Nothing is so unbelievable as exact truth told in a calm voice, and the friends who tell posthumous tactful truths about his life betray nothing.

*   *   *

Multiple men each one of them, not double men as were the great Victorians, the personnel of the Vortex so people a movement that we hardly miss allies. Eliot's strange case is in one way paradigmatic: all of them, though they had not his misfortune, could speak a time in speaking their own lives, having been born each one in that decade, the 1880's, which came to maturity just before the War, and could therefore remember afterward what had been lost. An Auden (born 1907) was too young to manage stereoscopic vision: the world of which he became conscious was wholly post-war. A Ford (born 1873) or a Yeats (born 1865) was too old; after the war Ford lived on his memories, and Yeats as if nothing had occurred but Irish troubles.

Their destiny should have been to people the Vortex. Instead it was to maintain continuity. Civilization is memory, and after 1918 effective memory was almost lost.

SCATTER

BLAST (June 1914), announced as a quarterly, managed one more issue (July 1915); whereupon the woman who had grubstaked #1 made it known, through her solicitor, that she regarded her £100 as an investment, and, the enterprise seeming solvent, expected it back. Lewis replied that the next two or three numbers might be expected to pay off the costs of the first. He did not divulge his plans for financing these future numbers. They never appeared.

Gaudier's death was announced in the second *Blast*. Since manifestly such lunatics had never existed, one journalist felt this was carrying a joke too far.

The Egoist, which had been *The New Freewoman*, "ended with 185 subscribers and *no* newsstand or store sales." It was better than nothing. It had room for a "Serial Story": Remy de Gourmont's *Horses of Diomedes*, then *A Portrait of the Artist as a Young Man*, then Lewis's *Tarr*, and even had a try at *Ulysses* till printers balked absolutely. The jejune Aldington had many opinions in its pages, which, as the Correspondence columns indicate, were read chiefly by cranks, feminist and other.

Eliot turned up late in September 1914, having gone to Germany to study philosophy and been shipped out when Germany went to war. He was mannerly and intelligent and had a poem called "Prufrock" that no one would publish. After eight months' hammering Miss Monroe published it in Chicago, at the back of her June issue. Five months later Elkin Mathews published *The Catholic Anthology*, and Arthur Waugh in the *Quarterly Review* mentioned "anarchy" and "red ruin." He recalled the "classic custom" of instilling morality in young men by displaying a drunken slave; such, he thought, might be the use of "Prufrock" and the other poems in the anthology. Waugh's concern for family tone is understandable. He had a son Alec and a son Evelyn.

Such were the fortunes of the Vortex.

*   *   *

In August 1910, during the visit to America when he had conceived that a Renaissance might stir, Pound had spent an evening with W. B. Yeats's father and the old painter's patron the New York lawyer John Quinn. At Coney Island Yeats *père* sat on an elephant "smiling like Elijah in the beatific vision," while Quinn plugged away in the shooting gallery. They also ventured on the Shoot-the-Chutes, "and a very good day it was." Early in March 1915 the mail brought a letter from that lawyer. Did Pound remember that day? And did he not think it unjust to lash out, as he had in *The Egoist*, at American collectors as if they bought nothing but "faked Rembrandts and faked Van Dykes," when he, John Quinn, sought eagerly for the living and owned more Augustus Johns than anyone alive? And where could he buy some Gaudiers?

Here was Maecenas. Pound to Quinn:

> ... If a patron buys from an artist who needs money (needs money to buy tools, time and food), the patron then makes himself equal to the artist: he is building art into the world; he creates. ...
> ... If you can hammer this into a few more collectors you will bring on another cinquecento.

Quinn bought Gaudiers, notably the cat that had been educed from scrap marble (it found its way back to the Pounds' hands after his death). He bought Lewises. He offered *The Egoist* money to improve it, but the editors rejected a Poundian incursion. He rallied in emergencies:

Dec. 20 '15 Lewis enlisted needs money debts = Pound.
Dec. 20 '15 Quinn Washington requests cable how much Lewis needs will cable money receipt reply = Quinn.
Dec. 22 '15 Thirty pounds = Pound.
Dec. 22 '15 Cabling you thirty pounds for Lewis = Quinlex.

By May 1916 he was agreeing that a new *Blast* would be better than burial of good stuff in *The Egoist*; and "I think it would give it distinction if I could get Roosevelt to write an article." (Teddy in *Blast #3*: the mind boggles. Yet he had recited "The Skeleton in Armor" in unison with Ernest Fenollosa.) A new *Blast* did not materialize. What materialized, with a subvention from Quinn, was a complex scheme. It amounted to buying space in two magazines, *The Egoist* (London) for argument, *The Little Review* (New York) for art. Eliot was installed as sub-editor of *The Egoist*. Eliot, Joyce, Lewis, Hueffer—whoever Pound could recruit—would appear in *The Little Review*, up to 5,000 words per issue chosen by Pound, and the magazine would gain the new subscriptions they drew. Quinn's subvention was to go to Pound for distribution to contributors. Eventually more Quinn money went direct to the review as well, and by May 1917 Pound's "magazine within a magazine" was launched, and Quinn found himself transmitting and retrieving mss., attempting legal recourse when the proprietors were indicted for printing Lewis and Joyce, and subjecting himself to the tedious bohemianism of one editress, Jane Heap, out of admiration for Margaret Anderson, the other. Pound for his part transmitted long lists of people to receive sample copies (Phyllis Bottome, R. B. Cunningham-Grahame, Henri de Regnier, Sir Thomas Beecham)—people who would "talk about it" rather than subscribe—and shorter lists of subscribers he had solicited. And he forwarded copy, and advice on spacing it out, and cursed the lack of proofreading. He arranged the French Number; he reread all of James for the James number; he fussed about Eliot's "undependable volition."

He also mailed off a long prose manuscript, *This Generation,* to a New York publisher who disappeared; and a manuscript of Arnaut Daniel translations to a clergyman in Ohio who never received it; and Fenollosa's "Chinese Written Character" to a periodical in Illinois which would neither use it nor return it, and had Quinn look into all these *contretemps*. And with fragments of his attention he tried to get on with his real work.

*   *   *

This was to have included more Chinese poems and Noh plays, but he never got around to them. The plays he had extracted from Fenollosa's *Noh* notebooks were published in the first weeks of 1917. They required none of the prodigies of re-creation he had expended on *Cathay*; the *Kakitsubata* for instance was made from a prose gloss Fenollosa had written out on the right-hand pages of a small notebook, as a guide to the performance notes he later scribbled on the left-hand pages in the theater. It was June 1901; he was by then an experienced *Noh* spectator; the gloss is fluent:

> . . . But the world has glory once—soon it fades; and this came upon him too. To seek his place of living, he went toward Adzuma, wandering like a piece of cloud. Looking on the waves of the sea at Ise and Owari, he was longing so much for his year of glory —"Why do the waves, the breakers return? (but not my glory) So thinking, he stood on the foot of Asama in Shinano—and he saw the evening smoke curling up—
> *Shite* – This is the smoke curling up from the peak of Asama in Shinano. . . .

With minimal alteration Pound extracted poetry:

> The world's glory is only for once,
> Comes once, blows once, and soon fades,
> So also to him: he went out
> To seek his luck in Adzuma,
> Wandering like a piece of cloud, at last
> After years he came
> And looking upon the waves at Ise and Owari
> He longed for his brief year of glory:
>   The waves, the breakers return,

> But my glory comes not again,
> Narahira, Narahira,
> My glory comes not again.
> He stood at the foot of Asama of Shinano,
> and saw the smoke curling upwards.

LADY

> The smoke is now curling up
> From the peak of Asama.
>
> Narahira, Narahira,
> My glory comes not again.

Once he turned back a few pages to consult a note on a place name: "Here it is called Yatsubashi because there are 8 bridges on the streams of Kumode—"spider hand' (web crossing)." With the aid of this he transformed "the Kakitsubata swelling itself (blooming) on the marsh of that famous Yatsubashi" into

> ... the flowers Kakitsubata
> That flare and flaunt in their marsh
> By the many-bridged cobweb of waters.

In another place he resolved an uncertainty of Fenollosa's quite arbitrarily, reading, beside transliterated Japanese,

> No moon! The spring is not the spring of old days—my
> person only is as ~~it was~~ and final body being. (old)

and writing:

> No moon!
> The spring
> Is not the spring of the old days.
> My body
> Is not my body
> But only a body grown old.

But in general he could work rapidly, "arranging," as he put it, "beauty into the words." When there was doubt about getting the dialogue about Poggio done in time for the July 1917 *Little Review*, he felt able to promise, "If I don't finish in time, I'll use a Noh play."

But no more *Noh* plays were done. Notably he never got round to the *Takasago*, though when he sent the three Ur-Cantos to Miss Monroe he had said that his long poem's theme was ("roughly") *Takasago's* theme: twin pines, to whose spirits distance is no barrier; people metamorphosing into trees; trees emblematizing the proposition that all things speak, all things are poems, and that the diligent quester may behold a tree become a dancing god. He thought of incorporating the story into a later Canto. Instead after 40 years its hymn to vegetal powers became the whole of *Rock-Drill*. Canto 4 preserves one allusion to the play:

> The pines at Takasago
> grow with the pines of Isé!

And *Cathay* as augmented in the 1916 *Lustra* contains four more Chinese poems, and *The Little Review* for November 1918 two others, never collected. And that ended that.

*   *   *

For, exasperated, isolated, overworked, Pound was shifting toward a mask of ironic superiority, largely derived from French prose writers. He spent a guinea on Pierre Bayle's *Dictionnaire historique et critique* and dragged the four volumes three miles home in a burlap sack ("cubic capacity 10 by 16 by 10 1/2, weight uncertain, and no busses running"). He translated twelve urbane dialogues of Fontenelle, the deceptively gentle tolerance of which, analogous to the quality he admired in Remy de Gourmont, was subversive of Anglo-Saxonry ("He who would paint for immortality must paint fools," says Molière at the end of the last of them). From Voltaire's *Dictionnaire* he extracted "Genesis, or, The First Book of the Bible ('Subject to Authority')." ("It seems probable that God was not attempting to educate the Jews in philosophy or cosmogony.") He sent "Three Cantos" off to *Poetry* with a note expressing "extreme diffidence" toward the elect, "amiable respect" for the non-elect willing to leave the poem alone, and "contempt for those few who, incapable of comprehension, rush in with their ubiquitous malevolence to meddle with what is not for them." He had written "Religio, or the Child's Guide to Knowledge" ("Do we know the number of the gods? —It would be rash to say that we do. A man should be content with a reasonable number").

Monogamy did not convince him, nor the Christian sanctions. He contended intolerantly for tolerant scepticism. He praised de Gourmont who "carried his lucidity to the point of genius," and for whom "the multitude of men thinks only thoughts already emitted, feels but feelings used up, and has but sensations faded as old gloves." And he made his *Homage to Sextus Propertius*.

> And it was morning, and I wanted to see if she was
> alone, and resting,
> And Cynthia was alone in her bed.
> I was stupefied.
> I had never seen her looking so beautiful . . .

"I was stupefied" will attach itself to either the proposition that precedes or the one that follows. That is one kind of witty scepticism.

> And in the mean time my songs will travel,
> And the devirginated young ladies will enjoy them
> when they have got over the strangeness,
> For Orpheus tamed the wild beasts—

That is a scepticism directed at Latin professors, who take *tacta* not as the opposite of *intacta* but as meaning that the ladies were touched by poetry.

> If any man would be a lover
> he may walk on the Scythian coast,
> No barbarism would go to the extent of doing him harm,
> The moon will carry his candle,
> the stars will point out the stumbles,
> Cupid will carry lighted torches before him
> and keep mad dogs off his ankles.
> Thus all roads are perfectly safe
> and at any hour;
> Who so indecorous as to shed the pure gore of a suitor?!

That declines to believe that all the world loves a lover; and as for

> Oh august Pierides! Now for a large-mouthed product.
> Thus:
> "The Euphrates denies its protection to the Parthian and apologizes
> for Crassus."
> And "It is, I think, India which now gives necks to your triumph,"

And so forth, Augustus. "Virgin Arabia shakes in her inmost
  dwelling."
If any land sink into a distant seacoast,
  it is a mere postponement of your domination.
And I shall follow the camp, I shall be duly celebrated,
  for singing the affairs of your cavalry.
May the fates watch over my day.

—it declines to accord bombast any reality (in the third year of the
war).

It is the great unknown poem of our time, Pound's triumph of
logopoeia, the fruit of a creative exasperation he never regained (his
later exasperations yielded invective). Harriet Monroe declined to
exhibit it whole; she would use the first three sections and the sixth.
"All right," Pound wrote her (December 1918), "print the left
foot, knee, thigh and right ear of my portrait of Propertius. We
remember that when the Whistler 'Irving' arrived in Chicago the
canvas was cut in this manner, reassembled, and only restored to
its original form on reaching Pittsburg." In her March number she
printed the four excerpts; in her April number she printed a letter
from Professor W. G. Hale, who found the poet "incredibly ignorant of Latin,"* alluded to "about three-score errors," and found the
bit about devirginated young ladies "peculiarly unpleasant." She
did not print Pound's letter of April 14, addressed "Editor, *Poetry*"
and commencing "Cat-piss and porcupines!!" ("The thing is no
more a translation than my 'Altaforte' is a translation, or than
Fitzgerald's Omar is a translation. ... [Hale] misses a number of
avoidances of literal meanings. ....") But on November 1 she wrote
formally accepting this outburst and Pound's subsequent silence as
his resignation from the foreign editorship of *Poetry*. Which was
the end of *that*.

*   *   *

* "Were Pound as 'incredibly ignorant of Latin' (in Hale's words) as to
make *unintentionally* the bloomers Hale accuses him of, he would not have been
able to read Propertius at all or get anything like the sense out of his elegies that he
actually does."—J. P. Sullivan, *Ezra Pound and Sextus Propertius*, 1964, 5. Sullivan's
is the definitive discussion.

Whereafter, 1919–20, disengaging himself from his own past and from London, Pound composed *Hugh Selwyn Mauberley*, an elegy for the Vortex.

Citing classical tags and picking its way through phrases, a British voice pronounces "E. P." dead. He was born "In a half savage country, out of date"; he had striven

to maintain "the sublime"
In the old sense. Wrong from the start;

he fussed with "factitious" aestheticism; and no one has paid any attention to him since *l'an trentiesme de son eage*, when he published *Cathay*. For one cannot afford to be "unaffected by 'the march of events'."

(Crosslight:

The primitive ages sang Venus,
the last sings of a tumult.
—*Homage to Sextus Propertius*, v.)

Whereupon another voice (E. P.'s) constates what "the age demanded": mimesis: the respect for "fidelity" that pronounced Gaudier's work not lifelike, and the Propertius not accurate.

Better mendacities
Than the classics in paraphrase!

The "age demanded" chiefly a mould in plaster,
Made with no loss of time,
A prose kinema, not, not assuredly, alabaster
Or the "sculpture" of rhyme.

And Samothrace went, and the Christian beauty is going; "The pianola 'replaces' / Sappho's barbitos"; the beautiful is what will sell; and as to "the march of events," the men who went marching have marched home now, "home to old lies and new infamy"; and Gaudier is dead ("quick eyes gone under earth's lid") and "a myriad" likewise,

For two gross of broken statues,
For a few thousand battered books.

And the Pre-Raphaelites came to little, and the "nineties" to little, and "Mr. Nixon" says "Follow me, and take a column." ("If any man will come after me, let him . . . take up his cross, and follow me. . . . For what is a man profited, if he shall gain the whole world, and lose his soul?"—*Mat.* XVI, 24, 26. Mr. Nixon has gained a steam yacht.) And "the stylist" lives beneath a sagging roof, and patronage is trivial, and the Fleet Street for which Dr. Johnson forsook patrons is venal.

And in these times, as for the "sensitive," as for Hugh Selwyn Mauberley, his delicacies are uncertain, his life eschews and refrains, and he leaves one poem, "Medallion," a *collage* of optical analogies. For sights stroke his retina, he is confined in the "now" of merely physiological vision, and the "now" brutalizes so that one guards against it, cherishing one's porcelain and one's perception of Minoan ornament in the British Museum, perceptions "selected" "by constant elimination."

Set off by italics, E. P.'s "Envoi" stands against the "Medallion": a time tunnel clear back to Sappho's roses and Chaucer's "Go litel bok," a self-interfering pattern "from which, and through which, and into which" rush Waller's rose, Lawes's music, Raymonde Collignon's singing, other times' diction, and ours; an art of the Vortex, by and large hopeless here, where energies have failed.

*   *   *

For despite Quinn's generosity and *The Little Review*, despite the installments of *Ulysses* arriving by post, there had been no Vortex really since 1914. The war years had seen much printed that was written earlier, and much written in desperate haste for the sake of getting it printed, and appalling energies expended against appalling obtuseness. But the Vorticists who remained had been elbowed into crank papers nobody saw, and besides they had to stay alive. Lewis was kept alive by the war machine, which periodically threatened to kill him; Pound spilled out his mind into dozens of factitious articles for which he could get a few shillings; Eliot worked in a bank, and delivered extension lectures, *au bout de ses forces*. In mid-1917 Mrs. Eliot reported to Pound that her husband had done no work of the kind that augments vortices, not for weeks. He returned daily from the bank and fell into a leaden slumber until bedtime.

冐 MAO⁴,
OR PRESUMPTION

Notes, drafts, outlines for a course
of lantern lectures on Chinese poetry cram page after page of notebooks Ernest Fenollosa kept during his period of American lecturing
(1901–6). Certain themes recur: that language springs from creative
metaphors in which "man and nature come to brotherhood," these
intertwined with mythologies and primitive poetries; that all words
act, enact, verbwise—the very prepositions channellers of force; that
ideograms show forth this energy, which in our languages we must
uncover by etymologizing; that (nature being in metamorphic
process) the transitive sentence partakes of and imitates nature, and
ideograms in succession mime vital processes with "something like
the vividness of a moving picture."

The Vitascope, the first practical projector, dates only from
1901, so viewing moving pictures had just become possible. Can we
recover the freshness of Fenollosa's pioneer analogy? In "things" he
saw "cross-sections cut through actions, snap-shots"; likewise in
single ideograms and single cinema frames. Both exist for the sake of
their blended succession, the moving picture, the sentence, the poetic
line.

When "The Sun Rises in the East,"

日　昇　東

and we see the sun in each character, or when "Man Sees Horse"

人　見　馬

and running legs carry each character, we should imagine them as if on the screen in visible metamorphosis (as nature works; as for instance trees grow and species evolve), the recurrent element like that constancy from frame to frame that confers on the projected happening an intelligible identity. To make happenings run through words, not to join static categories with copulae, the writer might, as "perhaps his finest training," "compose a page that contained no single use of the copula." (You have just read such a page.)

Metamorphosis—identity persisting through change—gives the rationale of "artistic unity"; in music, the key; in painting, the harmony within which "the farthest and faintest influence of each potent tint melts into the enormous sum of the influences of all," and "every color modifies every other"; in poetry, the control of metaphorical overtones, the "halos of secondary meaning" which vibrate "with physical wealth and the warm wealth of man's nature," and yet must "blend into a fabric as pure as crystal." Flagrant cases of failure, he says, we call "mixed metaphor," and (words being polyvalent) the best poet will find it almost impossible to avoid "the crossing and jarring of some of the vibrations." Shakespeare time and again does the impossible:

> . . . Death, that hath suck'd the honey of thy breath
> Hath had no power yet upon thy beauty.
> Thou art not conquer'd. Beauty's ensign yet
> Is crimson in thy lips and in thy cheeks,
> And death's pale flag is not advancèd there. . . .

We can imagine an ideographic script that might point up such coherences, and for the best Chinese poems Fenollosa claims simply that to their technique of sound (which his notes discuss at length) they add both visual grace and visual reinforcement of the metaphors everywhere flashing. "The elements of the overtones vibrate against the eye" (whereas in such a line from the 18th century as Thomson's torrent "tumbling through rocks abrupt," the overtones of *abrupt* [cf. *rupes*, rocks] come only to the etymologizing mind), and "the frequent return of the same element into new combinations makes possible a choice of words in which the same tone interpenetrates and colors every plane of meaning."

Hence as in the new century we "enter into [the] new conception of 'Comparative Literature'," we must understand oriental poems, commonly thought trivial, "as a true part of the world's poetry, but as a new species of it."

About 1904 (probably) he pulled everything into a draft for the first lecture: "The Chinese Written Character as a Medium for Poetry." It lay in his notebooks, presumably never delivered, until in the winter of 1914–15 Ezra Pound extracted, shortened, polished, and typed it.

And where, in wartime London amid the Georgians, did one publish such a piece of exotica? "The adamantine stupidity of all magazine editors delays its appearance" (Pound, June 1915). In the same letter he calls it "a whole basis of aesthetic." And to a poetess who had used "become" where an active verb might have glistened, "You should have a chance to see Fenollosa's big essay on verbs, mostly on verbs. Heaven knows when I shall get it printed." (June 1916) He even tried *Seven Arts* in Greenwich Village. Hope dawned eventually still further west, where in La Salle, Illinois, a saturnine journal called *The Monist* had printed two philosophical essays of Eliot's. The typescript crossed the torpedo-infested Atlantic, got accepted in early 1917, and commenced a long sojourn in a "pending" basket in La Salle. Only Pound and an unknown number of editors had read it.

*   *   *

Meanwhile, in a crystal cloud above Brookline, Mass., far-darting Apollo was preparing to smite with an illumination Amy Lowell, the "hippopoetess," to argue with whom, Carl Sandburg once remarked, was "like arguing with a big blue wave." The lady in whose company she received the revelation was to undergo seven years' nagging rather than argue. Moreover illuminations ran in the family. Thus her brother Percy ("a fine chap," Pound once remarked, "and she is delightful") had suddenly grasped the rationale of the newly discovered Martian "canals"—intelligent efforts to irrigate a dying planet—and founded an observatory to follow the matter up. Thus Amy, on 21 October 1902, had suddenly, aged 28, sat down and "with infinite agitation" written her first poem. "It loosed a bolt in my brain and I found out where my true function lay." In 1913, concurrent with the arrival of the January *Poetry*, another bolt was loosed: "Why, I too am an *Imagiste*." She hied her twice from Massachusetts to the Imagist headquarters in London, crossing like a big blue wave or like Daisy Miller, in 1913 to join the movement and in 1914 (with maroon-clad chauffeur and matching auto) to appropriate it since she had not been properly accepted. As against *Des Imagistes* which displayed only one of her poems, she proposed to sponsor a new book with equal space for each poet, selection of the poems by vote of all, and freedom from the decisions of a tiresome man who supposed that impersonal standards were accessible to his judgment. Democracy in the arts was her credo, with herself as chief democrat. The Aldingtons, Richard and H. D., were soon at her feet. By September Aldington had reported encouragingly that Ezra looked "terribly ill." It had been a model campaign. She had ended his reign, and neatly separated him, she thought, from everyone who mattered: Richard and H. D. and Flint and Lawrence and J. G. Fletcher. He was nothing, clearly, without this betyrannized crew; for (Amy wrote) "he does not work enough, and his work lacks the quality of soul, which, I am more and more fain to believe, no great work can ever be without." (Soul was a Lowell commodity.) She relayed hints that he was tuberculous, and that the bacilli had attacked his brain. "This is merely surmise. The fact remains"—she was tipping off Harriet Monroe, his one American editor—"that where his work is concerned he is failing every day." September 15, 1914; signed, Amy Lowell.

But in 1915 he had the impertinence to publish *Cathay*, in 1916 *Certain Noble Plays of Japan*, and in 1917 *Noh, or Accomplishment*.

Now the Orient was Amy's by right of Lowellship. Her

brother Percy when Pound was in his cradle had travelled there and written four books, one of which lured Lafcadio Hearn to Nippon. Percy had sent back photos and copious curios, and once returned with a Mr. Miyaoka who talked to the pinafored Amy on his lap about fox-sprites and spider-demons. "From those days," recalled an admirer she had coached, "Japanese prints and wood-carvings became an intimate part of Amy Lowell's entourage, and books on Japan always lay upon her table." This heritage for some reason lay fallow until Macmillan published the Pound-Fenollosa *Noh*; whereafter, "becoming more and more absorbed in Japanese literature," Miss Lowell dashed off some "Lacquer Prints" and a long poem on the opening of Japan by Commodore Perry. Its account of hara-kiri has been called "blood-curdling in the white heat of its vigor and restraint." Still her daemon went unassuaged. "In this poetry business," she once avowed, "there are rings of intrigue." Might one not "knock a hole in Ezra Pound's translations"?

A hole seemed knockable; clearly his weak flank was Fenollosa, whose name Miss Lowell did not always manage to spell. For "he having got his things entirely from Professor Fenolosa, they were not Chinese in the first place, and Heaven knows how many hands they went through between the original Chinese and Professor Fenolosa's Japanese original." But being no more a sinologue than Pound, Miss Lowell was hardly in a position to assail what she took Fenollosa's ignorances to be. Then in the autumn of 1917 an old acquaintance, Florence Wheeler Ayscough, came to Brookline for a long visit. She brought some Chinese scrolls of which she had made rough versions to illustrate lectures. (One had culture? One spread it.) Moreover she had been born in Shanghai. "Miss Lowell was immensely interested." They began working up translations. And the lightning descended. Miss Lowell seized the bolt: it was just what could be hurled at E. P. Mrs. Ayscough recorded the Apollonian moment:

> We were at work upon a poem, and I read aloud the character *Mo*: "It means 'sunset'," I said, and then added casually, "The character shows the sun disappearing in the long grass at the edge of the horizon."
> "How do you mean?" asked Miss Lowell.

"Why, what I say," I replied, and forthwith showed her the character or pictogram in its ancient form. . . . She was more enthralled than ever.

"I have made a discovery," Amy later exulted. No one out of China had realized it before. *The key to Chinese poetry lay in the overtones imparted by the written character.*

Aha! And so much for dependence on Japanese intermediaries. This was just what Fenollosa could not have known: just what would knock that desirable hole in *Cathay* (where, it may be, she did not notice "flowers that cut the heart," nor guess that it was based on a notation of *knife* and *gizzard* components). And poetic justice should be administered in *Poetry.* The two of them set to work to vivify *vers libre* with "split-ups," Amy's nickname for dissociated roots. The catalytic sun-behind-grass proved intractable: only "sunset" would fit. Nevertheless they had made a great discovery. Florence was put to work etymologizing every character. In June eleven poems were in the hands of Harriet Monroe, whose first response, that the lines were rather cut up—

> My son is ill and neglects to water
> the flowers

—Miss Lowell deflected with some bluff about cadence. "You see I have made an awful study of cadence. . . . No such study has been made by any other of the *vers libristes* writing in English. Even Ezra has felt and announced his convictions, rather than tabulated, measured, and proved." ("I wrote back and sounded as learned as if I really knew something," she confided to Florence. "It is always well to take a high hand with Harriet.") But cadences were a side issue. More important, the expert hand was transforming poor Florence into what the age needed, the hyper-sinologue *de nos jours.* "I also gave her a great song and dance as to your qualifications as a translator. I told her you were born in China, and that it was, therefore, in some sense your native tongue (Heaven forgive me!) . . . I explained that in getting you she was getting the *ne plus ultra* of Chinese knowledge and understanding; it being assumed, of course (though not by me expressed), that in getting me she was finding the best Englisher there was going." One longs for the finesse with which Henry James would have here suffered to emerge a salient datum about Florence: that in China she spoke only "Shanghai pidgin to her servants."

And on, to the construction of the torpedo: a prose statement by Florence of "that root theory of ours." ("Oh, I am certain of it; it is a great discovery." It was also "ours" whenever Florence was to sign for it.) "It will make Ezra and the whole caboodle of them sit up, since it will prove that their translations are incorrect, inasmuch as they cannot read the language and are probably trusting to Japanese translators, who have not the feeling for Chinese that you have. I tell you we are a great team, Florence, and ought to do wonderful things." So Amy to Florence, 28 June, 1918.

*   *   *

By now the Fenollosa typescript had gathered Illinois dust for more than a year. Since February demands for its dislodgment, on John Quinn's legal letterhead, had assailed Mr. Carus of *The Monist*. Space was waiting in *The Little Review*, with 64 pages per month and a guaranteed printing bill (guaranteed by Quinn). *The Monist* continued neither to print the manuscript nor to return it.

*   *   *

As words, T. S. Eliot had remarked, flew obediently from trope to trope at Amy Lowell's bidding, so persons were disposed in whatever postures of incompetence or expertise she required. Florence, greatness thrust upon her, had commenced struggling with a Chinese primer. ("I will only try to conceal the extreme shallowness of my knowledge.") Back in China she hunted out a teacher, a Mr. Nung who could barely understand what they were driving at, in part because he understood no English whatever. He bewildered her with explanations. For years, as Amy drove the mad enterprise through another ten dozen poems, Florence was to complain what a fool she felt, how stupid. "Oh, dear me, I wish I knew more!! I read *so* slowly, and the whole thing is so dreadfully difficult." She forwarded misinformation, found it was wrong, prostrated herself with apologies. Amy was unperturbed, except when Mr. Nung's dicta conflicted with her intuition ("perfectly foolish; it is what is known in literary technique as the 'pathetic fallacy' and is considered one of the very worst things to do in literature.") Her contempt for Mr. Nung, eventually for Waley and for all the sinologues, served to keep up to the end her assurance in what she had told Harriet Monroe about Florence.

Florence in the early months even doubted if it were wise to proclaim "our grand discovery" about roots. Nonsense, replied Amy, it must be divulged, and for a good reason: "it is simply and solely to knock a hole in Ezra Pound's translations." ("It would be most impolitic to come out and criticize Ezra in so many words; I do not think you had better mention him at all." Suffice it to mention the utter impossibility of getting "the real Chinese effect through a Japanese translation.") "Dearest Amy," Florence replied, "please don't think that I am shirking"; but "I feel utterly incapable of saying anything that would 'knock a hole' in Ezra Pound's translations. You know I am very diffident of my own powers, and I know that *you* could say something *so* apt." No, Amy wired, "it must be over your signature, not mine"; for "being a rival of Ezra's, and in some sense his enemy," words of mine would be put down for pique. "I obey," Florence replied, feeling, she said, like the ruler of the state of Shang who "with fear and trembling" knew he must save the country whose king was "a degenerate idiot." She prepared a draft. Amy wished it stronger. She strengthened it, though not with conviction.

*   *   *

It was now August 1918. At *The Little Review* Miss Anderson had Pound's instructions to notify him if by September 1 the Fenollosa essay had not arrived from La Salle. "I will in that case have the damn pencil scribble recopied and get it to you by Nov 1st or thereabouts." By 20 August it had arrived ("Thank GOD"). There is no record of its exciting Miss Anderson. She announced it for the January 1919 issue, but then delayed.

*   *   *

So Fenollosa was nowhere in print to give anyone pause when the "Written Pictures" rendered by Florence and Amy, together with Florence's little essay, appeared in *Poetry* for February 1919.

Cadenced according to Amy's "awful study," the verse was often preposterous:

> I am sick,
> Sick with all the illnesses there are.
> I can bear this cold no longer,
> And a great pity for my whole past life
> Fills my mind.
> The boat has started at last. . . .

Nor is the essay's hemoglobin conspicuous. Florence wrote it, Florence's caution suffuses it. She did, under duress, mention the need for analysis of the ideographs, of which each element "plays its part in modifying either the sense or sound of the complex," and did also gently protest that Chinese poems "translated from Japanese transcriptions cannot fail to lose some of their native flavor and allusion." This was hardly the Big Bertha of Amy's desire, but a deed was nevertheless done: the disclosure of the great principle, and eleven poems. The acid could be imagined eating through Ezra, whose *Cathay* had been unadvantaged by any such insight. "Poor Ezra," Amy wrote Harriet Monroe in July, "he had a future once, but he has played his cards so badly that I think he has barely a past now."

*   *   *

In September "The Chinese Written Character as a Medium for Poetry," cut up into four installments, commenced running in small type at the back of *The Little Review*. Nowhere in Miss Lowell's correspondence with Mrs. Ayscough do we find any mention of it. Their discourse ran on about the "split-ups."

This great idea, on which they never ceased to congratulate one another, worried poor Florence all the years they worked on at *Fir-Flower Tablets*, in part because she was never sure how much Amy meant her to claim for it. Was it quite the omnipresent indispensable key it had seemed? Amy exacted analyses of every character out of simple lust for the blood of a rival poet whose mentors must not have known the characters mattered. Florence, in Shanghai, stuck with this appalling labor, needed support no one would give her. Were Chinese readers, for instance, aware of the character elements? Not at all, said whatever English sinologists she could get at; 東 means "east," and never mind the sun in the tree. That generation's sinologues were in China for missionary and for consular purposes, with little more interest in etymological niceties than a ward boss in the connection between "candidate," "candor," and a toga's whiteness. One Britannic Commissioner "was very angry" after she had argued with him for two hours. Yet a poet was one day to write, in the way of poets,

> what whiteness will you add to this whiteness,
>   what candor?

and a Chinese poet, Florence suspected, may on similar principles discriminate among synonyms. She had no poets to call on. One scholar did sound promising; he was interested in archaic forms of the characters, and had translated a 13th-century treatise on their history. In 1921, just before their book appeared, she sounded him out. But his lack of interest was radical. He could not see why people ever wrote poetry. "It is the poorest way of saying things." His name was L. C. Hopkins. His late brother Gerard Manley (d. 1889) had been raised three years previously to some poetic notoriety by the editorial attention of the Laureate.

And Florence Ayscough's distress was all to no purpose. After those thousands of hours etymologizing, perhaps "a baker's dozen" of the etymologies ended up in Amy's text. Not a mistaken theory, not a theory ridden too hard, not even "inaccuracy," makes *Fir-Flower Tablets* unreadable today, but Amy Lowell's impregnable vulgarity: the bluntness of mind that decked a Li Po farewell with phonetic bellyaching—

> ... I bid good-bye to my devoted friend—Oh-h-h-h-h—now
>   he leaves me
> When will he come again? Oh-h-h-h-h—When will he
>   return to me?
> I hope for my dear friend the utmost peace. ...

—and needed informing by Florence, in one of the last letters to pass between them, that when lecturing before huge audiences on one's new *métier*, Chinese poetry, one ought not to use the word "Chinamen" ("For some reason or other the Chinese resent this very much.")

Part Three

TOWARD NOW

DOUGLAS

Clifford Hugh Douglas (1879–
1952) spent half a lifetime confronting the material needs engineering
can help resolve; and as Chief Reconstruction Engineer for the
British Westinghouse Company in India, as Deputy Chief Engineer
for the Buenos Aires and Pacific Railway Company in South America, as Railway Engineer for the London Post Office (tube) Railway,
he was frequently in a position to be told that "there was no
money" to do something useful. Then he noticed that during the
war—he was Assistant Director of the Royal Aircraft Works at
Farnborough—money could apparently be found for any project
however wild.

And during the war, while production useful to consumers was
enormously reduced, the standard of comfort was "more uniformly
high than ever before." If comfort could increase in the face of curtailed production, there was obviously no difficulty about producing
enough.

Yet in peacetime money seemed to go into hiding, and millions
were unable to purchase what there was manifest capacity to produce.

Moreover "competition for foreign markets" had helped to
bring about the war itself (and untold misery, and nine million
violent deaths). "Competition for foreign markets" means that not

all that is produced can be distributed at home, though Englishmen in uncountable numbers were badly sheltered and shabbily clad and less well fed than horses. They had no money.

Ezra Pound met him in 1918, when he had come under the tutelage of Pound's old sponsor A. R. Orage. And "Orage taught Douglas how to write," Orage who by patient criticism of their submissions had taught so many litterateurs to put one declarative sentence after another until they had set forth their matter, and then to stop. In June 1919 *Economic Democracy* commenced serial appearance in Orage's *New Age*, where readers might also find excerpts from *Homage to Sextus Propertius* and a series of articles mailed by Pound from Toulouse.

Orage was keeping Pound alive in those times. One of the few paid contributors, he was not only writing whole series of signed articles (the series he began from Toulouse ran to 18 parts) but as "B. H. Dias" column after column of Art Notes and as "William Atheling" biweekly music criticisms. They were years of intense overwork. His bibliographer lists 71 periodical items for 1917, 117 for 1918, 89 for 1919, 89 more for 1920. Much—too much—had to be done because the landlord wanted paying or the soupbone replenishing. What endures in today's collections—the poetry, the "Translators of Homer," the "Notes on Elizabethan Classicists," the "Henry James"—was donated to *The Egoist* and *The Little Review*. More than once he complains that he cannot afford to write such things properly, needing time in which to do the writing that should pay the rent. And the writing that paid the rent and the grocer was ephemeral.

Many years later, rereading the lot, he observed that "what I had written as free agent . . . was the solidest; what I had written at a guinea a shot for Orage was worth gleaning; but no article for which I had been paid three to five guineas was worth a hoot": this despite the fact that "I could recall no occasion on which I had written anything against my belief and conscience."

His job was supplying an ambience with mental *formae*. They endure still. And the ambience offered a financial mechanism that would feed him only insofar as he did something else.

Gaudier's job was the creation of forms. And he could have

eaten regularly had he manufactured vendible bric-à-brac embodying forms already long accepted. There existed random cognoscenti like Olivia Shakespear to give him money for the few forms he had a chance to create. For a few months in Munich his talents had been employed by a masterpiece factory which retained among its specialists a man who conferred on the new canvasses the tone of time. The artist who paints and carves what a market is ready for is doing something not always distinguishable from that.

The Sitwells helped feed Lewis in the 1920's. In the 1930's he lived chiefly on advances for books he would not otherwise have chosen to write, though having signed up he punctiliously wrote them. The books seem seldom to have repaid these advances.

Eliot worked in a bank.

And books? *Prufrock and Other Observations* was published (though with an anonymous subvention) at the expense of Harriet Weaver. So was *A Portrait of the Artist as a Young Man*, so was *Tarr*, and so was the volume called *Quia Pauper Amavi*, which contained the *Sextus Propertius*. *Ulysses* was serialized at the expense of John Quinn, and finally published at the risk of an American lady who had opened a bookshop in Paris. And year after year a standing donation from Miss Weaver kept Joyce somewhat extravagantly alive.

These are not conditions of freedom.

*   *   *

Economic Democracy, some 25,000 words, appeared in book form (London, 1920) not many months after its *New Age* serialization. On page 65 its author speaks of "useful effort." The effort of converting one thing into another—leather into shoes, seed and sun into grain; one may add, English vocabulary into *The Seafarer*— may or may not have a money value attached to it. Yet "if this effort is useful effort—'useful' in the sense that a definite, healthy and sane human requirement is served—the wealth of the community may thereby be enhanced. If the effort is aimless or destructive, the money attached to it does not alter the result."

When Douglas spoke of "aimless or destructive" effort, he had in mind the production of pointless artifacts that seem economically justified because people can be gotten to buy them. Novelty firms find plastic back scratchers worth stocking. But his words allow us to say that *The Seafarer* enhances the wealth of the community while two hours of wide-screen cinematic trash does not, and that the money attached to the latter does not alter this result. "Waste is not less waste because a money value is attached to it."

"If by wealth we mean the original meaning attached to the word: *i.e.* 'well-being,' the value in well-being to be attached to production depends entirely on its use for the promotion of well-being, and bears no relation whatever to the value obtained by cost accounting."

And as for riches, far from paid employment bringing riches to a man, employment takes riches away: for your riches are reckoned by your store of time and energy, and are diminished by any encroachment upon these. (So Pound was impoverished by his three-guinea articles, as we are the poorer today for lack of what he might have done with the time they took.)

We are the poorer today: this is metaphor? In Douglas's mind it is not metaphor. The quality of our lives, and our freedom, these are our wealth. If cost accounting instead values plastic back scratchers, and once valued buttonhooks, cost accounting is an art erected on false premises. And these premises, since cost accounting determines how frequently a seamstress shall eat (what is her "worth" to somebody?) keep us entrapped and anxious and distracted, and kept Gaudier under the Putney railway viaduct cadging scrap marble from the man in the next cubicle, a man who could buy large blocks because he had an employer the quality of whose life was served by marble replicas of historical paintings. (The "fittest," the economic survivors, noted Douglas, are not necessarily those who ought to have the power economic survival confers.)

Douglas's work attacks the premises of cost accounting, notably the premise that the world's books balance, so that the work men do earns them the money that will buy the goods they produce. For while we produce more and more goods, and even seek foreign markets in which to sell them, the number of citizens who cannot afford to buy them—who must beg, or else are merely always anxious—seems not to diminish. (And machines, which augment production, put people out of work and so diminish consumption, as the Luddites had protested.)

The Luddites smashed machines. The machine is the evil symbol of romantic poetry; mills are dark and satanic; "mechanical" is Blake's ultimate pejorative adjective, and a hundred years later is still Yeats's. "Sabotage" was named from the wooden shoes French weavers threw into mechanical looms. Ruskin shrieked at machines; William Morris's prescription for a happier England meant learning to take one's satisfactions anew from the old handicraft economy. Thoreau supposed that machines did no more than rearrange one's stock of energy; we can walk from Concord to Boston, he thought, in the time it takes us to earn the price of a railway ticket. Today we do not need an economist to persuade us that the machine, far from rearranging our advantages, multiplies them, and so augments, inconceivably, the stock of wealth.

The economist, in the course of his remonstrance with all such early critics of the machine, will invoke his first principle, the division of labor. They were moralists first, he avers, and dabbled in economics afterward, and ought to have left these activities divided. That is what specialists are for, to avoid mistakes.

Douglas thought not. Sane economics, he thought, is bound to perceptions of what men are trying to achieve, and the purpose of a monetary system is to abet their efforts. So commencing as did Morris and Thoreau from moral assumptions, he perceives that it is foolish to inveigh against the machine. For "there is absolutely no virtue in taking ten hours to produce by hand a necessary which a machine will produce in ten seconds, thereby releasing a human being to that extent for other aims."

> (. . . a buzz-saw,
> And he put it through an ebony log: whhsssh, t ttt,
> Two days' work in three minutes.)
>
> (18/83:87)

But, Douglas adds at once, it is essential that the human being *shall* be released; and "'labour-saving' machinery has only enabled the worker to do more work." And the work is dehumanizing and monotonous (to that extent Ruskin was right); "and the ever-increasing

complexity of production, paralleled by the rising price of the necessities of life, is a sieve through which and for ever out go all
ideas, scruples and principles which would hamper the individual
in the scramble for an increasingly precarious existence."

As these words were being printed, unemployment was increasing; somewhat later "an orthodox economist" in the hearing
of Douglas and Pound attributed the high cost of living to "shortage
of labour" when there were two million men out of work; in 1925
England suffered a general strike; in 1929 the bottom dropped from
the whole world's economy; in the 1930's Americans starved while
"surplus" food was destroyed to get the price up so farmers could
survive. Industrialization had brought the world's productive plant
to undreamed-of capacity, and there was a worldwide shortage of
money. And Douglas seemed to have shown how this came about.

It came about, he will tell us, from our supposing that the value
of necessities is still determined by the market, as it was when
necessities were scarce (but they are scarce no longer). The market
sets price, not value; moreover, only the upper limit of price (by
making grain scarce you can increase its price, and hence raise
farmers' incomes). But the lower limit of price is set not by the
market but by costs: all the costs bread has incurred on its way
from sun and soil to the shop counter (thus a glut will only reduce
the price of grain to the point where every farmer is thoroughly
miserable, his selling-price barely balancing his costs.) Thus costs
will ensure that American toilet paper, on the *pharmacien*'s counter in
Rapallo, shall be priced higher than another paper artifact, *The
Divine Comedy*: "Costa più della *Divina Commedia*," the "epitaph,"
Pound wrote, "on Anglo-Saxon civilization." Cost, which supply-
and-demand cannot reduce, is the rock on which economies are
wrecked; and cost, said Douglas, however accurately the cost
accountant adds his figures, is artificially high because some of the
figures he adds do not belong there. The cost of the goods which an
accountant's system distributes will always exceed the money which
the system also distributes; and—Canto 38, written 1933—

> . . . there is and must be therefore a clog
> and the power to purchase can never
> (under the present system) catch up with

prices at large,
and the light became so bright and so blindin'
in this layer of paradise
that the mind of man was bewildered.

(38/190:198)

*   *   *

Total cost exceeds total purchasing power: that is Douglas's central and most controverted claim.* "The sum of the wages, salaries and dividends distributed in respect of the world's production, even if evenly distributed, would not buy it, since the price includes non-existent values." Repeat. "The sum of the wages, salaries and dividends distributed in respect of the world's production, even if evenly distributed, would not buy it, since the price includes nonexistent values."

"Even if evenly distributed": but of course they are not evenly distributed; and "the unequal distribution of wealth is an initial restriction on the free sale of commodities;" even Croesus could not eat more than two dinners a day, nor the senior Rockefeller, bestower of dimes, wear more at one time than one single pair of shoes.

"Since the price includes non-existent values": hence an emptiness, a nothing, is costed:

> And from the stone pits, the heavy voices
> Heavy sound:
> "Sero, sero . . .
> "Nothing we made, we set nothing in order,

* It was called "the A + B theorem." Costs comprise (A) salaries, wages, and dividends, which flow into the economy as purchasing power, and (B) plant and bank charges which do not; and "A will not purchase A + B." It was quickly and repeatedly objected that since every payment is made *to* somebody the B costs enter the economy likewise, to which Douglas' exegetes were less quick than they might have been to respond that rates of flow, not totals, were at issue. Gorham Munson's exposition is unbetterable: "For generations economists have taught that every cost entering into the determination of price was at some time or other somebody's income, . . . and they have neglected to note the bearing of the phrase, 'at some time or other.' It is as though in the field of vital statistics they argued that since every person born also dies and since the number of births equals the number of deaths, the birth rate therefore equalled the death rate, and therefore the population is stationary." As early as his second book (*Credit Power and Democracy*, 1920) Douglas's expositions were focused on rates, not totals, but never with sufficient emphasis.

"Neither house nor the carving,
"And what we thought had been thought for too long;
"Our opinion not opinion in evil
"But opinion borne for too long.
"We have gathered a sieve full of water."
                                        (25/118:123)

The previous page reminds us to distinguish carefully this nothing
from the nothing into which a *forma* is cast:

"as the sculptor sees the form in the air
          before he sets hand to mallet
"and as he sees the in, and the through,
                              the four sides . . .
                              (25/117:122)

Consider that such a formed nothing is wealth, and comfort
some future Gaudier; and as for the nothing, *vanus*, that false
accounting has reared into a solemn edifice,

          Pull down thy vanity
                    How mean thy hates
          Fostered in falsity
                    Pull down thy vanity
          Rathe to destroy, niggard in charity,
          Pull down thy vanity
                    I say pull down.
                              (81/521:557)

(And "The real unit of the world's currency"—Douglas—"is
effort into time—what we may call the time-energy unit"—

          But to have done instead of not doing
                    this is not vanity . . .

                    To have gathered from the air a live tradition
          or from a fine old eye the unconquered flame
          This is not vanity.
                    Here error is all in the not done,
          all in the diffidence that faltered,

—"the not-done," ". . . since the price includes non-existent
values.") The lyric parts of the *Cantos* are not about Douglas's

economic perceptions but always rhyme with them and frequently brush against them. The "pull down thy vanity" commences by examining the analogy between what is well loved and what is measured in gold.

*   *   *

What nonexistent values? Costs amortized over and over again, but still carried on the books; and all waste; and all inefficiency; and all bank charges. And as we mechanize, the hire and keep of the machines entails more and more overhead which either has escaped into the surrounding community and been spent long before our factory's goods are offered for sale, and so is not around to help buy them, or else never escapes into the community at all because it goes to service bank loans. The machines cheapen our product, which is a palliative, but decrease real purchasing power at the same time, and decrease it faster than they cheapen the product. They thus defer a smash they help render inevitable; 1929 seemed a validation. In 1929 everyone was suddenly reminded of the central symbol of oppression in the *Cantos*, which is not the machine but gold.

"The real unit of the world's currency is . . . the time-energy unit." The banks say otherwise. They say it is gold. "The quantity of currency in circulation was at that time [1919] rigidly determined by the amount of gold held by the Bank of England." The biographer of Orage who wrote that sentence betrays no detectable bias toward Douglas's ideas, Orage's acceptance of which rather puzzles him; yet he adds firmly, "A more absurd basis of currency issue cannot be conceived." Quite so, since currency has a distributive function; while the amount of gold held by the Bank of England is determined by no estimate of the need to distribute, but by men's success in digging it out of the earth and by the Bank's success in cornering what it can. This is good for gold merchants and gold speculators. Wheels turn, and in 1968 England once more felt its poverty intensify as the price of gold altered in Zürich.

The banks, while talking about gold reserves, issue credit, more credit than there exists gold, much more. This means that they create money, a fact nearly everyone is reluctant to believe until it has been explained to him several times. Let us posit it. The banks create money (and charge interest on it, payable in more money). On Douglas's showing it is the consumer who needs more money, since when he comes to buy, his wages, dividends, and salaries cannot unaided buy what is produced; but the bank will not create money for the consumer, since consumption is not something to invest in.*

They will create it for a potential producer, someone who wants to build a factory or acquire a productive machine. And his factory, once more, will incorporate the bank's charges in those mounting, anfractuous "costs," the costs that always exceed the wages, dividends, and salaries his factory distributes.

(Those charges were levied on money that did not exist till it was loaned: "Nothing we made, we set nothing in order.")

So bank credit alone is what creates the illusion of a functioning money supply. And bank credit consists of interest-bearing debt.

*   *   *

Intermission.

Said Paterson:

> Hath benefit of interest on all
> the moneys which it, the bank, creates out of nothing.
>
> (46/233:243)

That was a prospectus to shareholders in the Bank of England, 1694. And:

> Bank creates it ex nihil. Creates it to meet a need,
> His est hyper-usura. Mr. Jefferson met it:
> No man hath natural right to exercise profession
> of lender, save him who hath it to lend.
>
> (46/234:244)

And:

> Mr Marx, Karl did not
> foresee this conclusion . . .
>
> (46/234:244)

---

* So 1919. Fifty years later consumer credit—at high interest—had become a major banking activity.

Mr. Marx, Karl, alias Charlie Mordecai, supposed that the discrepancy between costs and wages was explained by profits. But Douglas's equation is not unbalanced by profits; the man who founds or organizes or supervises performs, Douglas saw, economically useful service, of which the so-called "profit" is the wage. And Mr. Marx also supposed that values are "masses of congealed labor time."

*   *   *

The unit of money, said Douglas, is time-energy, but the value of a product is not labor-time. Imagine one man tending a machine that prints circuits: is the value of the printed circuit his labor-time? The value of the printed circuit is design value: the design of the circuit, the design of the machine. Men turn out resistors and capacitors and transistors: these would be utterly worthless curiosities did not designs exist for television sets and computers and amplifiers. Or a Boeing 747 carries twice the load of a 707, but the crew works no harder. What has multiplied the value of their work is design done once and for all. Douglas called it the cultural heritage. It includes many esoterica: the results obtained by mathematicians long dead, the formulae of anonymous metallurgists, even, we may hazard, Brancusi's sense of form, which in a time of motorized box kites anticipated the aluminum cylinders we fly in today.

Not only does the "cultural inheritance" confer value, it abridges effort, allowing Douglas to designate "the fallacy that labour produces all wealth, whereas the simple fact is"—he spoke as an engineer—"that production is 95 per cent a matter of tools and processes, which tools and processes form the cultural inheritance of the community." Of the community, moreover, "not as workers but as a community." What men gain by not being isolated from one another he was later to call "the increment of association." Like the cultural inheritance, it has demonstrable economic worth. The two constitute the greater part of our capital, and they back, to anticipate a term coined some years later, our Social Credit.

To build Stonehenge took 1.5 million man-days. Its builders' cultural inheritance included knowledge of tree-felling and of raft-poling, and of the use of deerhorns ("picks") and the shoulder bones of oxen ("shovels") to dig into chalk. Their increment of association permitted 80 men to move a five-ton stone perhaps a mile a day; one man in a lifetime could not have budged it. If we could duplicate Stonehenge rather easily now, it is because we have inherited so much.

The cultural inheritance—tools and processes—can be represented by sheets of specifications. It is sweatless and, Buckminster Fuller would add, weightless. It is made up of *formae mentis*, as much so as the *Paradiso* or Gaudier's *Dancer*. Written in ink, $E = mc^2$ weighs about $\frac{1}{10}$ milligram; it guarantees electric power to whole cities, for their surgical lamps and electric typewriters and drill presses. Once think of the cultural inheritance in this way, as a pattern of energies to govern the energies whereby men are fed and satisfied, not as "two gross of broken statues . . . a few thousand battered books," and a *Divina Commedia* acquires economic worth surpassing that of toilet paper, and a Wyndham Lewis has a claim to be fed. Douglas was never more prescient than in divining (though he was thinking mainly of tools) that sheer mind, sheer intellection of self-interfering patterns, was the guarantor of all values.

*   *   *

And no one understands any of this, and yet the system keeps running, after a fashion. It keeps running, Douglas thought, thanks to constant diversification. Encountering a clog in houses, the economy diversifies into back scratchers, golf carts, scented dog-bones, and so long as it can generate new demands it can postpone the Damoclean stasis. But creating newer and ever newer sets of insurmountable costs, drawing on more and ever more bank credit (some day to be called), "misdirected effort which appears in cost forms a continuous and increasing diluent to the purchasing value of effort in general." Hence the paradox (1969) of a recession threatened by record prosperity: employment nearly full, the Gross National Product at a record high; the President preaching austerity, the Federal Reserve Board contracting the money supply; new housing money nearly unobtainable.

For it is a mistake to suppose that whatever can be sold is economically valuable. "The whole argument which represents a manufactured article as an access of wealth to the country and to everyone concerned, so long as by any method it can be sold and wages distributed in respect of it, will, therefore, be seen to be a dangerous fallacy." We entertain this fallacy because anything that moves in the market keeps the market moving, and so helps distribute necessities. In wartime the battlefield was a guaranteed market, and everything delivered there was destroyed. The resulting economic velocity benefitted everyone left at home, and since consumers did not need to buy the exploded shells and the crashed aeroplanes, their wages did suffice to buy what remained, food and clothes and cottages. The community, to be sure, paid to have shells and aeroplanes produced, but then it pays to have everything produced. Relief occurs precisely when we need not buy all the product back again (as we cannot).

More generally, "if production stops, distribution stops, and as a consequence, a clear incentive exists to produce useless or superfluous articles in order that useful commodities already existing may be distributed." Useless products—as back scratchers—are a form of beneficial sabotage. So is "making work," a specialty of unions. So is planned obsolescence. So is useless supervisory and bookkeeping effort. So is war; and World War II terminated the Great Depression (American unemployed, 1940, 8.1 million; late 1942, 1.5 million). About 1943 a Canadian economist proposed on empirical grounds a Permanent War as panacea. Antarctica might have been a suitable adversary, but the Cold War and the War on the Moon have served nearly as well.

That "clear incentive to produce useless or superfluous articles," likewise the incentive to do less with more, accounted, Pound thought, for much he had observed. "The tawdry ornament" (Douglas, 1919), "the 'jerry-built' house, the slow and uncomfortable train service, the unwholesome sweetmeat, are the direct and logical consummation of an economic system which rewards variety, quite irrespective of quality, and proclaims in the clearest possible manner that it is much better to 'do' your neighbour than to do sound and lasting work." And Pound, 1936,

With *Usura*
With usura hath no man a house of good stone
each block cut smooth and well fitting
that design might cover their face,
with usura
hath no man a painted paradise on his church wall
harpes et luthes
or where virgin receiveth message
and halo projects from incision,
with usura
seeth no man Gonzaga his heirs and his concubines
no picture is made to endure nor to live with
but it is made to sell and sell quickly . . .

(45/229:239)

"Gonzaga his heirs and his concubines," fresco by Mantegna in La Camera degli Sposi, Palazzo Ducale, Mantua, ca. 1465.

Mantegna painted Duke Gonzaga and his family in fresco on the wall above the fireplace of the Camera degli Sposi in the palace in Mantua, and there is no way to detach and sell a fresco. For a certain portable Wyndham Lewis portrait £2000 was recently being asked. Lewis received for it perhaps 1/20 of that. Three of its intermediate purchasers have been dealers, and one of these dealers bought it from another dealer. Long ago, Pound to a dealer:

> what art do you handle?
> "The best" And the moderns? "Oh, nothing modern
> we couldn't sell anything modern."
>
> (74/448:476)

"Best" means "salable." But of course Lewis is dead.

*   *   *

To provide that an artist shall be fed as his pictures are bought is to acquiesce in a system of piecework, as when nailmakers were paid by the nail; and Douglas noted that piecework, among its other defects, entails the fallacy that value is related to demand. But one should not offer to pay a Lewis for his piecework. He should be paid for "nutrition of impulse," as the farmer for nutrition of muscle. "How to Read," nine years after *Economic Democracy*, contains Ezra Pound's effort to fit the arts into the cultural inheritance of the community beside its aircraft designs and its machine tools.

Far from having "a refining influence on the student," which tends to keep him inactive, like Mauberley, Pound thought that "the function of literature as a generated prize-worthy force"—in short, as patterned energy—"is precisely that it does incite humanity to continue living; that it eases the mind of strain, and feeds it, I mean definitely as *nutrition of impulse*."

And insofar as the writer's work is exact, "so is it durable and so is it 'useful'; I mean it maintains the precision and clarity of thought, not merely for the benefit of a few dilettantes and 'lovers of literature', but maintains the health of thought outside literary circles and in non-literary existence, in general individual and communal life."

Paying a man by piecework, said Douglas, we pay him insofar

as he is not free, insofar as he ties up his time-energy, and thus expect millions of noses to reckon their prosperity in grindstone-hours. But surely the easing of strain, the maintenance of health, the extension of freedom, surely these are what we should mean to reward? And Douglas proposed that whoever sets men a little freer, for instance whoever decreases a little the time some process takes, should be rewarded for that, since he has augmented the communal stock of unmortgaged time-energy.

And nourishing impulse—this is what Pound had in mind in "How to Read"—augments that stock as much as does shortening factory time, and the painter or writer, as much as the industrial designer, augments the cultural heritage, but in ways present cost accounting does not know how to get at. The best present cost accounting can suggest is payment to the sculptor per piece, and to the writer per word. But "Tous mes choses datent de quinze ans," said Brancusi; and Binyon, "Slowness is beauty."

Money is not a commodity but a measure. Labor is not a commodity but a levy to be abridged. Possibly three hours a day for adults between 18 and 40, were they not working for the banks, or to write off overhead, or to make the back scratchers that keep the system moving, would (Douglas' estimate, 1919) supply all men's necessities. Rewards should accrue to whoever could abridge this; technical progress might be expected to abridge it. "It must be perfectly obvious . . . that the State should lend, not borrow." Pound was to find examples: the Athenian State financed the fleet at Salamis; Alexander paid the debts of his soldiers. And "real credit is a measure of the reserve of energy belonging to a community," whose members are therefore corporate shareholders in its economy. "Production" is "a conversion, absorbing energy," and the share-holders—all of us—should receive something representing this absorption. This is the State Dividend.

Expounded in *Economic Democracy* with none of the fuss over administrative detail that was to clutter it later, Social Credit seemed to Pound not one man's panacea but a time's culmination: an ordered view of what mankind is doing. For the next 40 years its Pisgah-sights were never out of his mind. They gave meaning to the present and the past alike, and relieved art from the impasse of aestheticism by absolving it of the need to demonstrate its immediate utility. The artist had only to refrain from curling up with his dreams, and set about patterning the air with forms. "Hugh Selwyn Mauberley" (1919–20) was the first fruit of this insight, and Pound's first work to contain the word "usury."

*   *   *

The right to life, liberty, and the pursuit of happiness—Douglas began from this proposition, and from Jefferson's words—entails economic freedom, to be had by "co-operation of reasoned assent, not regimentation in the interests of any system, however superficially attractive." (The Fabians proposed regimentation.) And economic freedom would put at everyone's disposal the benefits of science and mechanization, so "that by their aid he is placed in such a position of advantage, that in common with his fellows he can choose, with increasing freedom and complete independence, whether he will or will not assist in any project which may be placed before him."

Against which, *usura*. And by 1933 it seemed possible to suppose that Benito Mussolini understood these notions. Perhaps he did, in a way.

THE SACRED
PLACES

American soil requiring a more
energetic furrow, Jefferson designed a New World plough, so
specifiable that any blacksmith could duplicate it. Thus every
smithy would become one cell in a diffuse invisible plough factory.
On trial designs for Charlottesville buildings he computed wall by
wall the numbers of bricks that would have to be fabricated one by
one by hand: a figure to minimize. Garden walls two bricks thick
being uneconomical, he made thinner ones stand up by curving
them, serpentine. Not brute materials but only mind, designing,
could render the great continent quickly habitable. By the 1860's
diverse instrumentalities—machines to make cheap nails in quantity,
power saws to slice tree trunks into thin structural members, railways
to move stacked lumber across the plains—were orchestrated by
anonymous designing genius to yield the first thoroughly American
structures: houses whose toothpick frames could support a roof
before the walls were closed up, in a self-sustaining lightness
Buckminster Fuller's geodesics would one day geometrize. They
were called (at first in derision?) balloon frames. The walls were

simply windbreaks, clapped on later. American craft works by structure, not accretion, and an American poetic is unembarrassed by open spaces between the members (hence Whistler's and Fenollosa's hospitality to an oriental aesthetic of intervals). How few words Zukofsky needs to lay on the page:

> Not the branches
> half in shadow
>
> But the length
> of each branch
>
> Half in shadow
>
> As if it had snowed
> on each upper half

Or,

> The lines of this new song are nothing
> But a tune making the nothing full
> Stonelike become more hard than silent
> The tune's image holding in the line.

—complete poems both. Delight in spareness, and (as Dr. Williams wrote of Miss Moore) "a distaste for lingering, as in Emily Dickinson." One may be leaving for Terre Haute tomorrow.

But never forgetting Europe. In troubled conscience, perhaps? After having read the course of human events as sanction to swing shut the eastward door? It was not triple-barred; the letter-slot stayed open; lists of necessities were ordered. Jefferson procured European skeletons for the Virginia medical school by competitive bidding, and John Adams enjoined Otis to print for colonial enlightenment his work on Greek prosody.

> He said there were no Greek types in America
> and if there were, no typesetters cd/ use 'em,
>   (71/420:442)

recalls Canto 71, rhyming this occasion with the "die-cutter for greek fonts and hebrew" brought by Hieronymous Soncinus to Fano before 1503. (That was in Canto 30, which ends one block of the poem as 71 ends another; and at 82/524:559 a mere pairing of names serves to make the parallel explicit: "Otis, Soncino."

Structure, spareness, spaces.) The parlor game—which books for a desert island?—was played by America in earnest. Homer's book was not just *there*, as in London or Leyden; one decided to bring it along, or to send for it, or decided not to. Yale University was founded with a gift of books. The contents of American libraries have been selected (but who knows what is in the Bodleian?). Curricula are debated (do we need *Hamlet?* Hesiod?). President Eliot nominated five linear feet of indispensable books, Professor Adler somewhat more; could I devise "a portable substitute for the British Museum" —Pound, 1929—I would do it "like a shot, were it possible." Though he added, "It isn't," the impulse endured; the *Cantos* fit into one volume.

Combinations as well as elements were optional. Jefferson writing his University's curriculum founded the study of English on Anglo-Saxon, as radical a gesture in its time as Pound's Chinese, and lined three sides of the campus with a teaching anthology of architectural orders, doubling as useful buildings; its Library was a brick Pantheon. In New England they decided the culture needed an epic and elected Dante's. Longfellow commenced to profess the *Commedia* in 1836. Though Margaret Fuller disapproved because Dante was high and transcendental and not for classrooms, James Russell Lowell continued the practice at Harvard after 1855, Charles Eliot Norton after 1877, Dr. Grandgent after 1896. The students plunged in with or without Italian grammar. In this tradition T. S. Eliot puzzled out meaning with the help of the Temple Classics crib, and used to recite aloud whole cantos of Paradise he did not know how to pronounce, "lying in bed or on a railway journey," say from Cambridge home to St. Louis. Going lightly, in the native way, one incorporated Europe (whence Jefferson had also fetched ice cream; America devised the freezer).

And in the balloon-frame houses old-world artifacts accumulated:

> Towers of Pisa
> (alabaster, not ivory)
> coloured photographs of Europa
> carved wood from Venice venetian glass and the samovar
> (74/447:475)

ran Pound's remembered (1945) impression of his great aunt's
spoils: by the time of Henry James, who complained of a thinness
of New World experience, the passionate pilgrims were taking ship
for the old world. Aunt Frank went every June, and took young
Ezra along when he was 12—

> Cologne Cathedral
> the Torwaldsen lion and Paolo Uccello
> and thence to Al Hambra, the lion court ed el
> mirador de la reina Lindaraja
> orient reaching to Tangier, the cliffs the villa of Perdicaris
> Rais Uli, periplum
>
> (74/447:475)

—and again when he was 16. Both times they came to Venice. She
believed that travel broadened, had danced with General Grant, and
made up tissue-paper packets of green tea to be "distributed throughout her multifarious luggage," one for each day of the summer's
three-month trip. A photo survives of her riding a mule in Tangier.
She accumulated experience.

*　　*　　*

Aunt Frank belonged to the Baedeker generation: one "did"
Venice, Pisa, Lucerne, Cologne, the Uffizi. Later her great-nephew's
Baedeker was Justin Smith's *The Troubadours at Home* (1899), two
volumes using the new zinc-block process to instruct America with
photographs of ruins. Prof. Smith had travelled with the kind of
camera you hired a native to carry. Ezra Pound travelled on foot
with a pocketful of small coins, and later remarked on his advantage
over Henry James, whose Europe tended to be a succession of the
authorized sights because he got about it by train. One major expedition (1912, the summer after Ford Heuffer's didactic roll) took
him as far south as Foix and Rocafixada in the Pyrenees. And what
did he see? The authorized sights of the troubadour country are
dumb.

In winter 1914, while reading Charles Doughty to Yeats, he
reflected on his own travels in "Provincia Deserta." The poem
evokes today's customs—

At Chalais
        is a pleached arbour;
Old pensioners and old protected women
Have the right there—
        it is charity

and unchanged landscapes—

        I have seen the fields, pale, clear as an emerald,
        Sharp peaks, high spurs, distant castles

—amid which, in one's knowledge that one is on this or that very
spot, one can recall the age that is gone:

        I have said:
                "Here such a one walked.
        "Here Coeur-de-Lion was slain.
                "Here was good singing.
        "Here one man hastened his step.
                "Here one lay panting."

We do not learn from the ruins, to which Ezra Pound did not have
the romantic response; we learn what an instructed mind may con-
jure up. In "Near Perigord" the instructed mind conjectures that
Bertrans, his castle located as it was, had strategic reason to arouse
the lords of just these other castles, a hypothesis that later in that
poem disappears into the realm of the unprovable.

        There were other such journeys, to the birthplaces of the major
Latin poets, and the places sacred to Dante and Cavalcanti, none of
whom, any more than the troubadours, has left a trace unless the
Grotte di Catulle at Sirmio be authentically named. Thus Cavalcanti
and Catullus would have drawn him to Verona, where, he later
confessed, his reliving of Guido's life was mostly "a pleasant lie":

                        Shall I claim;
        Confuse my own phantastikon
        Or say the filmy shell that circumscribes me
        Contains the actual sun;
                        confuse the thing I see
        With actual gods behind me?

But Verona, on further reflection, was more than the occasion for
pleasant lies; for there, in 1911, he and Edgar Williams found the
signed column.

*   *   *

It is inconspicuous in the semidarkness, on the left as you
descend to the crypt; a double shaft with a common capital, shaped
from one block, and inscribed as though in proud afterthought with
ornate freehand letters,

ADAMINUS
DESCO
GIORGIO
ME FECI
T

and Williams, who was in Italy on an architectural fellowship, asked
how the hell *we* could have any architecture when we ordered our
columns by the gross. It was a Luminous Detail, with the capacity to
admonish the present. Mind focused here once, it says, a person
knew this stone and the stone proclaims the person. (Pride in the
work: Ruskin stirs, who had lived until Pound was 14 and had taught
Europe to measure the craft by the craftsman's involvement.)

    Here was an autonomy, more than an allusion, more than the
fact that "Cavalcanti lived here." Here was a detail to go into an
American structure, a poem made of details, with a balloon frame.
Just as lightly, on a trip in the 1950's, Louis Zukofsky appropriated
butterfly details to glint in his weightless structure—

> . . . In germ
>   the ribbed vault
> on a sarcophagus
>   also a tiny
>
> Fan vault—
>   so proportioned
> as not to excite
>   later doubts of lavishness.
>
> So the unribbed
>   vault at
> San Vitale
>   hints at the rib

San Zeno, Verona, the signed column.

But remains
>   where
the eye can take in
>   gold, green and blue:

The gold that shines
>   in the dark
of Galla Placidia,
>   the gold in the

Round vault rug of stone
>   that shows its
pattern as well as the stars
>   my love might want on her floor . . .

Alertly seen, acknowledged, left in place, barely touched by being named, they pass down a firefly page like clavichord notes, freighted by no rhetoric of "history." A moving mental structure leaves them free. The Age of Byron ("Stop!—for thy tread is on an Empire's dust!"), the age of travellers ateem with *sententiae*, is gone.

Pound's structures, like Jefferson's plough, were meant to be useful: to be validated therefore not by his opinions but by the unarguable existence of what exists. No more than Zukofsky, then, does he expatiate, in many passages that tend to set annotators scribbling. Rather he constellates Luminous Details, naming them, as again and again in the *Cantos* he names the signed column. For the column exists; what it proves about forgotten possibilities it proves by simply existing. And five hundred more such columns would not intensify the proof. Again and again in the *Cantos* single details merely prove that something lies inside the domain of the possible. It is not necessary to prove that the possibility was ever widely actualized; only that it exists. What was done at Wörgl—once, by one mayor, in one village—proves that stamp scrip will work. What was done in San Zeno, once, on one column, proves the possibility of a craftsman's pride in an unobtrusive structural member. And any thing that is possible can again be. The *Cantos* scan the past for possibilities, but their dynamic is turned toward the future. And they enumerate so many places, so many stones, so many buildings, because nothing is so irrefutable as a stone.

The column on its first appearance in the poem is joined with Ruskin's economic insight:

> Came not by usura Angelico; came not Ambrogio Praedis,
> Came no church of cut stone signed *Adamo me fecit.*

Then:

> Not by usura St Trophime
> Not by usura Saint Hilaire
> (45/230:240)

with the further clarification six cantos later:

> Nor St Trophime its cloisters
> Nor St Hilaire its proportions.
> (51/250:261)

The 12th-century cloisters in St. Trophime at Arles, the intricate stable unornamented arches in St. Hilaire at Poitiers, perfection never for sale, yielding no computable benefit unless by Douglasite computations but enhancing beyond price the minds of generations: these were located in cities first visited for troubadour associations that have left no direct trace. Nor are there traces of Sordello in Mantua, but there is the Gonzaga family portrait on the walls of their palace:

> with usura
> seeth no man Gonzaga his heirs and his concubines
> no picture is made to endure nor to live with
> but it is made to sell and sell quickly.

And once again in Poitiers, where Eleanor of Aquitaine presided over courts of love whereof nothing remains, today in what was once the palace of the Dukes of Aquitaine and Poitou and is now the Hall of Justice we may climb to the Tour Maubergeon, where indirect light suffusing a broad low room is so answered by reflected light from the walls that you can find a point where you are shadowless, while the polite guide waits with his ring of keys. An audacious poetic joined this with a Chou Dynasty ministry charged with

"St Hilaire its proportion" (Poitiers).

"St Trophime its cloisters" (Arles).

making celestial principles blaze through the empire, and to the
Templars' rumored involvement with a religion of light:

> in pochi,
> > causa motuum,
> > > pine seed splitting cliff's edge.
> Only sequoias are slow enough.
> > BinBin "is beauty".
> "Slowness is beauty.":
> > from the   三   San
>
> > > 孤   Ku
> > > to Poictiers.
> The tower wherein, at one point, is no shadow,
> > and Jacques de Molay, is where?
> and the "Section", the proportions,
> > lending, perhaps, not at interest, but resisting.
> Then false fronts, barocco.
> > "We have," said Mencius, "but phenomena."
> monumenta. In nature are signatures
> > needing no verbal tradition
> oak leaf never plane leaf. John Heydon.
> > > (87/572:608)

Slowly now: these are luminous details. (1) *In pochi*, from Machia-
velli's "mankind lives in the few," the epigraph to *Gaudier-Brzeska:
A Memoir*. It rhymes with Yeats's "Nothing affects these people
except our conversation," quoted four cantos previously in the
context of Erigena's "Omnia quae sunt, lumina sunt" and the
attribution of the Tempio bas reliefs to Gemisto's conversation
about gods: intelligence, sculptures, light. (2) Binyon used to say
"Slowness is beauty" at the Wiener Cafe, 1908; Pound has recalled
not believing it then, but being unable to forget it until it yielded its
beauty in slowness. (3) The San Ku he found in the History Classic
(*Chou King*, IV. xx. 6, page 333–4 of Couvreur's edition, where we
read that these three men "font briller l'action productrice du ciel
et de la terre.") (4) Jacques de Molay was the last Grand Master of
the Templars. King and Pope met to suppress that order in Poitiers,
where St. Hilaire exemplifies (5) proportions answerable to *la section*

The room in Poitiers where one can stand casting no shadow, Tour Maubergeon, Palais de Justice.

d'or; and St. Hilaire was "not by usura," whereas (6) Barocco with its detachable ornament, as we learned in the 46th canto, is the type of usurious art. (7) "All who speak of the natures [of things]," said Mencius (IV.ii.26, Legge's version) "have in fact only their phenomena [to reason from], and the value of a phenomenon is in its being natural." Hence the signatures in nature, and the adduction of (8) John Heydon, "secretary of nature," who wrote of "light fighting for speed": and we are to reason in Mencius' way from such phenomena as the sequoia, false fronts, and the tower room at Poitiers. "Our science is from the watching of shadows," we were told in the 85th canto with the same text of Mencius just beyond the mind's scan; which brings us round again to the veneration of light.

Light rains on the sacred places, they sanctify light, light refracted by the crystalline limestone gives its luster to the Rimini

Agostino di Duccio, the luminous Flora, whom annotators of the Tempio Malatestiana call "Botany" because she fits an allegory of the Liberal Arts.

bas reliefs; the figure of Flora ("Botany") in the Tempio, on what may be the most beautiful stone in the world, seems self-luminous from the irradiation of ambient light around the high polish Duccio gave her tranquil gaze. ("Duccio came not by usura," and "The temple is holy / because it is not for sale" 97/676:707.) And another place visited for its troubadour associations, Montségur where their civilization was ended, proved to be the very arcanum and temple of Light.

*   *   *

The exchange value of the pound sterling in 1919 made that a good summer for the impecunious to travel, and Ezra and Dorothy, after five years cooped up in England, met Tom Eliot near Giraut de Bornelh's birthplace, Excideuil. The three headed south, the Pounds finally to Montségur but Eliot on a divagation of his own to inspect nearby cave drawings. That may have been at the Grotte de Niaux. We are to imagine him, rucksacked, deep inside a mountain,

"Mont Ségur, sacred to Helios."

"And in Mt Segur there is wind space and rain space."

individual talent confronted by the Mind of Europe, satisfying himself that art never improves ("but the material of art"—here, bison
"d'un pureté de trait étonnante" drawn with magnesium oxide in
bison grease—"is never quite the same"), while 20 kilometers eastward by crows' flight the Pounds, fortified with chocolate, were
climbing the southwest face of Montségur to the white walls that
ride its summit like a stone ship. It was on or about midsummer
day, a fact to gain meaning in the retrospect of decades. Here
Provençal civilization (in synecdoche) was snuffed out; here, at the
climax of the crusade against the Albigensians, some hundreds of
worshippers of a cosmic dualism were extracted by siege from the
solar temple where they had taken refuge, and two hundred burned
at stakes in the plain below. That was at a March dawn in 1244.
1919's summer seemed to wear a visage in keeping:

> ... and the rain fell all the night long at Ussel
> *cette mauvaiseh venggg* blew over Tolosa
> and in Mt Segur there is wind space and rain space
> no more an altar to Mithras ...
>
> (76/452:480)

Altar to Mithras? A guess, based on regional customs that recall
some bull cult, notably at Arles where they leap between the horns:

> Fell between horns, but up ...
> and the murmur: "salta sin barra,"
> ...
> Mont Ségur, sacred to Helios ...
>
> (87/573:609)

Pound had descended two rows toward the Arles bullring before a
hand on his coattail restrained him from trying that leap ("... with
his eyesight!"). So he lived to ponder, 35 years later, some liaison
between the bull cult and Montségur, "sacred to Helios."

"Sacred to Helios," which must also have been a guess, is now
demonstrable truth, thanks to the patient work of Montségur's
historian Fernand Niel, to whom the *genius loci* also spoke, repeatedly, until he began making measurements. In his published works
on the great white stone enigma, it is clear that every pertinent
measurement somehow entails the sun.

Though books call Montségur a fortress because it was be-
sieged, it was properly a temple across whose unfortified threshold
shadow bounds light diagonally at midsummer noon, and across
whose annexed "cellula" men waiting in darkness at midsummer
dawn could see two slabs of light defined in the dustmotes, entering
by eastern slits and leaving by western, no stone within the stone
box so much as grazed. The cardinal points are traceable on its plan,
and the sunrise directions for each of the 12 days when the sun enters
a new sign of the zodiac. These facts were not known until 1954,
about the time Pound was asserting the relevance of light.

They were back by mid-August at Excideuil, Eliot with seven
blisters. In the castle an old woman lived in a couple of rooms, and
drew no water from the ill-kept well in the courtyard. Ezra bought a
beam to lay across the well-curb (high on the castle bluff; level with
the spire of St.-Thomas), and a chain to go down a long way for the
water: in exchange for which New World enterprise she supplied a
packet of *tilleul*-leaves to make a tea; and Eliot turned there,

> Above him the wave pattern cut in the stone
> Spire-top alevel the well-curb
> And the tower with cut stone above that, saying:
> "I am afraid of the life after death."
> and after a pause:
> "Now, at last, I have shocked him."
>
> (29/145:150)

—"him" being the normally unshockable Ezra Pound, who ten
years later changed Eliot's name to "Arnaut" when he told this
story in the 29th Canto. (At Montségur, where they had the choice
of recanting, they were absolute for death.)

Though Eliot had not yet professed himself an orthodox
Christian, the contrast between his fear of the life after death and the
readiness with which, below Montségur, two hundred embraced
death, spurning the chance to recant, was impressed on Ezra Pound's
mind, a luminous detail; for the men of Montségur were not
Christians by the Church's measure, but heretics. Death, he sensed,
worried Christians and proto-Christians, and he was soon to recall,
in the 13th Canto, that Confucius "said nothing of the life after

Fragment of the wave pattern, Excideuil, now incorporated into a restoration of the entrance archway.

death" and seemed not to be eroded by nameless fears. Another time, at Verona by the arena, where Eliot set forth the program for *The Criterion* (a program "neither published nor followed"— 78/481:512), the sight of a *decaduto*, a decadent fellow with "a little lace at the wrist" prompted Ezra to resume his thrust against Eliotic values:

> And I, "But this beats me,
> "Beats me, I mean that I do not understand it;
> "This love of death that is in them."
> (29/145:150)

And Eliot, years later, as though resuming their talk,

> Whatever we inherit from the fortunate
> We have taken from the defeated
> What they had to leave us—a symbol
> A symbol perfected in death. . . .

"There died a myriad," in the cause of Montségur. Does the raining light remember them?

Barbarians, who have no power over light, obliterated certain things utterly: Lugdunum Convenarum, for example, which comprised 60,000 inhabitants and stretched down from what is now St. Bertrand de Comminges (pop. 318). Four years after Christ was crucified Herod the Tetrarch of Galilee and his wife (Flaubert's and Mallarmé's Hérodiade) were exiled there. The two miles' absence is 100 kilometers west of vacant Montségur. Pound was there that July 12:

> . . . the flat stones of the road, Mt Segur.
> From Val Cabrere, were two miles of roofs to San Bertrand
> so that a cat need not set foot in the road
> where now is an inn, and bare rafters,
> where they scratch six feet deep to reach pavement
> where now is wheat field, and a milestone
> an altar to Terminus, with arms crossed
> back of the stone
> Where sun cuts light against evening;
> where light shaves grass into emerald . . .
>
> (48/243:253)

Light on grass, where there are hardly stones for it to reach; the troubadour song was more durable.

*   *   *

The song came "up out of Spain," (8/32:36) and the hard Pyrenean light fell on singers at Foix, at Toulouse, at Narbonne. Guillaume, "the first troubadour," fetched it as far north as Poitiers, whence Eleanor of Aquitaine went to "spoil in a British climate"— 7/24:28—(she became the shrewish Queen Mother of Shakespeare's *King John*) while Bernart de Ventadorn lamented her passing across the channel waters: he had thereby more pain of love, he averred, than even Tristan for Iseult "la bionda":

> Peitz trai pena d'amor   Que Tristans l'amador
>   Qu'a suffri mainta dolor
>   per Iseutz la bionda.
>
> (93/624:657)

He had asked her previously to intercede at the Chateau of Ventadour with the chatelaine's husband, who very sensibly kept his lady on close leash while Bernart was by. Bernart was no longer by, and we are to imagine him addressing the Queen,

> "Send word I ask you to Eblis
>   you have seen that maker
> "And finder of songs so far afield as this
> "That he may free her,
>   who sheds such light in the air."
>   (6/22:26)

Whether Eblis freed her or not, that place of his is in ruins, one of the few ruins in the *Cantos* (Montségur is roofless but not ruined).

> Where was the wall of Eblis
> At Ventadour, there now are bees
> And in that court, wild grass for their pleasure
> That they carry back to the crevice
> Where loose stone hangs upon stone.
>   (27/132:137)

The bees remain, the song of Bernart remains, and at semiruined Excideuil a wave pattern's lilt in the stone on the high parapet proclaims* an eternal form educed from flux—

> Whither go all the vair and the cisclatons
> and the wave pattern runs in the stone
> on the high parapet (Excideuil)
> Mt Segur and the city of Dioce
> Que tous les mois avons nouvelle lune
>   (80/510:544)

This found its subject-rhyme at Grecian Castalia, the spring near Delphi high above the Corinthian Gulf, which Pound did not visit until 1966, ten years after he had put it into the poem:

> Castalia like the moonlight
> And the waves rise and fall:
>   (90/606:640)

---

* As of 1919. Later the castle crumbled, and still later its restorers fitted stones at random. In 1970 the only discoverable block of the wave pattern had been placed near the top of the left-hand gatepost.

Ruins at Ventadorn, "where loose stone hangs upon stone."

—water gushing with the permanence of the moon's bright trace on Odysseus' unstable sea: a source of eternal flow, resembling Light.

*   *   *

And when Provence was terminated the tradition of light moved east into northern Italy; it was Cavalcanti's *Donna mi Pregha* that sustained notions of Love arising like Light in the region of memory:

> In quella parte
> > dove sta memoria
> prendo su stato
> > si formato
> > > come
> diafana di lume
> > d'una scuritade

Roman sarcophagi, in the long grass, by San Vitale, Ravenna.

Imitation Roman sarcophagi, Tempio Malatestiana, Rimini. The second from
the left contains Gemisto's ashes.

—an image re-enacted by the light over Pisa:

> And the sun high over horizon hidden in cloud bank
> lit saffron the cloud ridge
> dove sta memora
>
> (76/452:480)

And it was Cavalcanti's friend Dante who so commemorated the great troubadours, permitting the greatest, Daniel, to speak his own Provençal whereas even Odysseus must speak Italian, that men centuries later were moved to the curiosity of recovering their form of thought, and students worked through Chaytor's *Troubadours of Dante*. Dante's tomb at Ravenna is ornamented by the same Pietro Lombardo who carved the mermaids in Santa Maria dei Miracoli in Venice—

> . . . Dei Miracoli
> mermaids, that carving
> (83/529:564)

—and ten minutes' walk away by San Vitale the sarcophagi in the long grass from which Sigismundo may have derived the row of tombs down the west side of the Tempio (in one of which lie the ashes of Gemisthus Plethon) line the path to the mausoleum of Galla Placidia, "the blue dome studded with stars," where

> in the gloom the gold
> gathers the light against it.
> (11/51:55)

For the net is drawn tight; each sacred place remembers others. The words about gold in the gloom first enter the *Cantos* when Sigismundo of Rimini is whelmed with disaster but still dangerous:

> And the castelan of Montefiore wrote down
> "You'd better keep him out of the district.
> "When he got back here from Sparta, the people
> "Lit fires, and turned out yelling: 'PANDOLFO'!"
> In the gloom, the gold gathers the light against it.

He is the gold, their torches rhyme with the light. And when these words next appear (Canto 17) their context is Venice; and the third

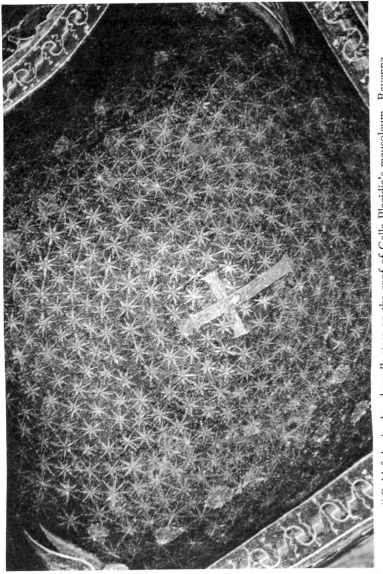

"Gold fades in the gloom": stars on the roof of Galla Placidia's mausoleum, Ravenna.

The Roman arena, Verona.

time (Canto 21) Galla's tomb and the arena of Verona enter a
cluster Venice still dominates:

> Gold fades in the gloom,
>   Under the blue-black roof, Placidia's,
> Of the exarchate; and we sit here
> By the arena, *les gradins* . . .
> And the palazzo, baseless, hangs there in the dawn
> With low mist over the tide-mark;
> And floats there nel tramonto
> With gold mist over the tide-mark.

(21/98:102)

Venice dominates, in part because the ultimate source of the line is a
distich of Pindar's which (remembering Thales) announces that the

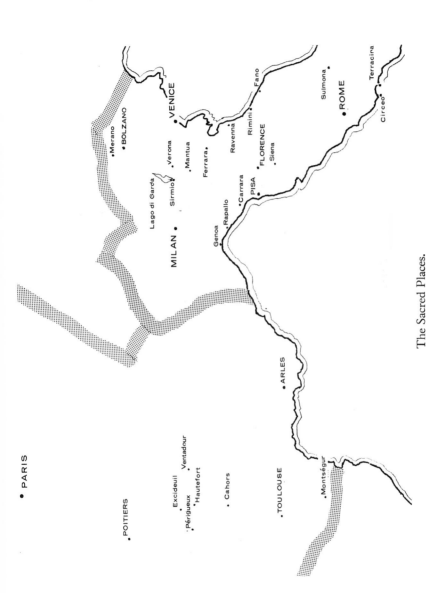

The Sacred Places.

lordliest of things is water; moreover that gold shines forth in the
dark as does fire; (and the sun too, and this Olympic victor . . .):

"Ἄριστον μὲν ὕδωρ

water is chief;

ὁ δὲ χρυσὸς αἰθόμενον πῦρ
ἅτε διαπρέπει νυκτὶ μεγάνορος ἔξοχα πλούτου.

and gold aflame in the night shines beyond other wealth.

Ariston men hudor: this first phrase of Pindar's distich, after so
many commemorations of the rest of it, is acknowledged in the
Canto that begins,

> ὕδωρ
> HUDOR et Pax
> Gemisto stemmed all from Neptune
>   hence the Rimini bas-reliefs
> Sd Mr Yeats (W.B.) "Nothing affects these people
>   Except our conversation"
> lux enim
>   ignis est accidens   and
> wrote the prete in his edition of Scotus
> Hilaritas   the virtue *hilaritas*
>   (83/528:563)

HUDOR, Rimini, and Erigena's light, Pindar's fire the "accident"
of light; but in this Canto the rest of Pindar's distich, so often
formerly echoed, does not appear. Venice however appears—

> . . . Dei Miracoli
> mermaids, that carving
>   (83/529:564)

—concentrated in a Luminous Detail guidebooks ignore; and the
whiteness hidden beneath the sheathes of trees—

> The roots go down to the river's edge
> and the hidden city moves upward
> white ivory under the bark
>   (83/530:565)

"Mermaids, that carving," by Pietro Lombardo, in Santa Maria dei Miracoli, Venice.

performs in natural process the gesture of rising intricately by water, which gesture in earlier Cantos Venice had mimed in stone:

"   There, in the forest of marble,
"   the stone trees—out of water—
"   the arbours of stone—
"   marble leaf, over leaf...
            Stone trees, white and rose-white in the darkness,
        Cypress there by the towers,
            Drift under hulls in the night.
                "In the gloom the gold
        Gathers the light about it." ...

                                    (17/78:82)

For the Venetian light was "not of the sun," and its stone forests not of the order of nature; it is the most complexly ambiguous of all the sacred places, the most wholly an assertion of sheer will, like the will of young Pedro that exhumed the dead Ignez da Castro for her hands to be kissed by the humbled lords who had murdered her, she

                Seated there
                    dead eyes
            Dead hair under the crown
        The King still young there beside her.

                                    (30/148:153)

Venice rose from the waters, a stone Aphrodite; Venice held lordship and its doge wedded the sea; Venice plundered (bronze horses, columns of porphyry, the body of St. Mark); Venetian might was extinguished (a sonnet by Wordsworth); Venice grows old by the sea. By the Piazza San Marco stands a tall brick campanile from the top of which you can see no trace of water except for the Canal Grande, so close do the tile roofs cluster about the hundreds of canals. It is not the original campanile, but a careful restoration. The original campanile, a thousand years old, sifted down one morning into a pyramid of bricks, harming no living thing save one cat. It had seemed indestructible. That was 14 July 1902, 9.55 a.m. Ezra Pound and Aunt Frank were in town that summer. He half-acknowledged the memory, *aetatis suae lxxx*, crossing the square. The Tower of Pisa's summit had shifted three more fingers' breadths in his lifetime.

THE CANTOS—1

Canto One, line one:

And then went down to the ship,

What comes before "And"? In mankind's past, before ever Homer, a foretime; a foretime even before the dark rite of confronting shades which Pound thought *older* than the rest of the *Odyssey*, reclaimed by Homer as he reclaims Homer now. In the *Odyssey*, the ten books that precede. In Ezra Pound's life, the time at Wyncote and Pennsylvania and Hamilton and Wabash, before he took ship for what was not meant as exile. And in the history of the poem, much precedent groping and brooding, out of which mostly unspecifiable darkness the poem as we know it emerges. In that darkness, aided by clues, we can locate a few of the standpoints Pound once occupied, as he pondered a chord that should comprise four of history's beginnings: the earliest English ("Seafarer" rhythms and diction), the earliest Greek (the *Nekuia*), the beginnings of the 20th-century Vortex, and the origins of the Vortex we call the Renaissance, when once before it had seemed pertinent to reaffirm Homer's perpetual freshness.

For what men in those fine times owed to their own glory we

may judge from their efforts to emulate Homer in Latin, the tongue of living thought. From the 1360's prose version follows prose version. By the 1470's Angelo Poliziano, the same whose *Stanzas* afforded Botticelli a program (and perhaps suggested the title of the *Cantos*) was using Vergil much as Pound was to use *The Seafarer*, as a base for idioms and fitting elegances ("that Homeric youth," *Homericum illum adolescentem*, marvelled Ficino). There followed

> cutters of letters
> and printers not vile and vulgar
> (30/148:153)

and Greek Homers printed in massive folios, and at last in the new century the Aldine octavos which men could carry around with them for study. Peripatetic students needed portable help. Hence (Paris, *in officina Christiani Wecheli*, 1538) *Homeri Odyssea ad verbum translata*, the version signed by Andreas Divus Justinopolitanos, who has humbler intentions than had Poliziano. His book is simply an efficient study guide.

When four long Greek words afford Homer a hexameter—

> ʾΗέλιος φαέθων καταδέρκεται ἀκτίνεσσιν
> (XI-16)

then Divus is content with four equivalent Latin words:

> Sol lucidus aspicit radiis

—only ten syllables, and no effort at rhetorical pastiche. (Pound's finding his Latin "even singable" amounts to asserting that Divus by simple fidelity has achieved Renaissance *vers libre*.) His note *Ad Lectorem* stresses the effort to be useful. He has followed the Aldine edition of the Greek page for page; has mapped the text line for line and so far as possible word for word; has had his printer number the lines. Thus whoever is studying the Greek text may open readily to the corresponding Latin, "ut uno intuitu omnia in utroque videre possint." His *Odyssey* is what Pound said it was, a serviceable crib, easily slipped into a pocket.

Now *The Seafarer* corresponds in the same way, line by line with the Anglo-Saxon text (in print about as many years as had been Homer in Divus' time). It corresponds, not, certainly, as a serviceable crib, but as a map. It maps the sound, not the meaning, tacitly judging that local meanings are of secondary importance in that particular poem. In 1959 Pound was still remarking the "sonorities" of the Anglo-Saxon Professor Ibbotson once hammered into him.

> Bitter breast-cares have I abided

plays the doubled long *i* against the triply alliterated *b*, each of six words cut full force into the line. So in Canto 1

> And then went down   to the ship

brackets *then went* between *and* and *down*, two more nasals; releases after the caesura a new sequence of syllables without nasals; and ensures that the last of these, *ship*, shall both terminate the line sharply and supply with its initial sibilant the initial sound of the words that commence and close the line that follows:

> Set keel to breakers, forth on the godly sea, and

—*sea* closing the pattern of sense which *set* initiated, though an *and* repeating the Canto's initial *And* assures us of narrative energies still unexpended. Far from resting in a chink like a bit of mortar, that *and* works like a verb, transmitting force. The emphatic *forth* works verbwise also, and *godly* pervades the sea with animate forces. The words space out. In

> Set keel to breakers, forth on the godly sea . . .

we encounter the shock of separate acts of attention, each crystalline, each enclosed in its identifying sonority. Though the second half of the line moves more smoothly than the first—mimesis of the forward surge after launching—the line's movement does not run the words together because their junctured consonants serve to separate them. *Godly* does not sound godly, but sounds different from—clear and distinct from—*forth* and *sea*. This is not *The Seafarer*, where sounds, not words, get isolated, the consonants ("journey's jargon") zoning off vowels; it is Homer, whose words matter, re-energized in English with the aid of the English *Seafarer*, which Divus' Homer may in fact have suggested.

For Pound published *The Seafarer* in 1911, the year after the visit to America from which he returned with his conviction of an

ODYSSEAE.Λ.HOMERI
COMPOSITIONIS.

Lambda autem, in inferno animabus obuiàm fit Vlyſſes.

AT poſtquàm ad nauem deſcendimus, &
mare,
Nauem quidem primùm deduximus in
mare diuum,
Et malũ poſuimus & uela in naui nigra:
Intrò autem oues accipientes ire fecimus,intrò & ipſi
Iuimus dolentes,huberes lachrymas fundentes: 5
Nobis autem à tergo nauis nigræ proræ
Proſperum uentum imiſit pandentem uelum bonũ amicũ
Circæ benecomata grauis Dea altiloqua.
Nos autem arma ſingula expedientes in naui
Sedebamus. hanc autem uentusq; gubernatorq; dirigebat: 10
Huius ăt per totũ diē extenſa ſunt uela pontũtráſientis:
Occidit tunc Sol,obumbratæ ſunt omnes uiæ:
Hæc autem in fines peruenit profundi Oceani:
Illic autem Cimmeriorũ uirorum populusq; ciuitasq̃;
Vlyſſes ad   Caligine & nebula cooperti,neq; unquam ipſos   15
Cimmerios   Sol lucidus aſpicit radijs,
diuertit.   Neq; quando tendit ad cœlum ſtellatum,
Neq; quando retrò in terram à cœlo uertitur:
Sed nox perniciofa extenditur miſeris hominibus:
Nauem quidem illuc uenientes traximus, extrà aũt oues 20
Accepimus:ipſi autem rurſus apud fluxum Oceani
Iuimus,ut in locum perueniremus quem dixit Circæ:
                                                      Hic

Λ X I. 93

Hic ſacra quidem Perimedes Eurylochuſq̉;
Faciebant: ego autem enſem acutum trahens à fœmore,
25 Foueam ſodi quantum cubiti menſura hinc & inde:
Circum ipſam autē libamina fundimus omnibus mortuis:
Primùm mulſo,poſteà autem dulci uino:
Tertio rurſus aqua,& farinas albas miſcui:
Multùm autem oraui mortuorum infirma capita:
30 Profectus in Ithacam,ſterilem bouem,quæ optima eſſet,
Sacrificare in domibus,pyramq̉; implere bonis:
Tireſiæ autem ſeorſum ouem ſacrificare uoui
Totam nigram,quæ ouibus antecellat noſtris:
Has aūt poſtquā uotis precationibuſq̉; gentes mortuorum
535 Precatus ſum,oues autem accipiens obtruncaui:
In foſſam fluebat autem ſanguis niger, congregatæq̉; ſunt
Animæ ex Erebo cadauerum mortuorum,
Nymphæq̉;,iuuenesq̉;,& multa paſſi ſenes,
Virginesq̉; teneræ,nuper flebilem animum habentes,
40 Multi autem uulnerati æreis lanceis
Viri in bello necati,cruenta arma habentes,
Qui multi àrcum foueam ueniebant aliunde alius
Magno clamore,me autem pallidus timor cepit.
Iam poſteà ſocios hortans iuſſi
45 Pecora,quæ iam iacebant iugulata ſæuo ære,
Excoriantes comburere:ſupplicare autem Dijs,
Fortiq̉; Plutoni,& laudatæ Proſerpinæ.
At ego enſem acutum trahens à fœmore,
Sedi,neq̉; permiſi mortuorum impotentia capita
50 Sanguinem propè ire,antequàm Tireſiam audirem:
Prima autem anima Elpenoris uenit ſocij:
Nondum enim ſepultus erat ſub terra lata,

Inferorum
locus.

Appropea
rant mortu
orū animæ,

Elpenoris
ūbra Vlyſſi
apparet.

Corpus

imminent Renaissance, and we may well wonder if Divus (purchased "1906, 1908 or 1910") supplied the example: a new-Renaissance gesture of mapping one's poetic origins against the idiom of current thought. Did Divus' line-for-line fidelity give Pound the satisfaction of following in the second Renaissance an example from the first?

*   *   *

He wanted—had always wanted—to write a long poem. Memory in later years traced the eventual direction of that impulse to a conversation—say circa 1904-5—with Professor Ibbotson who was teaching him his Anglo-Saxon. "I was in them days contemplatin a jejune trilogy on Marozia.* Which Bib was naive enough to agree wd/ be a man's magnum opus if he pulled it off." Something that might be worth devoting one's life to, early envisaged: every year in every college town 19-year-olds in the dark winter afternoons claim on behalf of such stirrings the leisure of an instructor young enough to understand, old enough to encourage. "Bib" Ibbotson was 35. Somehow his discourse turned to "Bentley's attempt to 'edit' Milton as he had edited, textually, Horace etc." Three decades later Pound thought of the *Cantos* as starting from that talk.

What was "Bib"'s theme? That Milton had slipped into place beside the ancients, inviting from Bentley comparable scholarship? Or that Bentley in finding three hands in *Paradise Lost* had distributed a seeming monologue among three voices? Had he cited that staple of every Milton course, the varied and long-pondered Plans for the Magnum Opus, recorded in the Trinity ms? There is no knowing. But "the CANTOS started in a talk with 'BIB'," and in the complex gesture that now commences the work we

---

* A one-woman Vortex, married to (1) the Emperor Alberic I, a Lombard adventurer who helped expel the Saracens from Italy and was later slain by his subjects; (2) one Guido of Tuscany; (3) Hugh, King of Italy. Her son by Pope Sergius III became Pope John XI; her son by Alberic threw her into prison. She died some time before A.D. 945. Amid a "wilderness of renewals, confusion," Canto XX affords us one glimpse of her:

>   Zoe, Marozia, Zothar,
>   loud over the banners.

may detect a homage to the Rev. Joseph Darlington Ibbotson
(1870–1952).

*   *   *

A few years after that talk we find him in an unpublished
letter assigning the meaning of one poem in *Exultations* (1909) to its
position in the cycle. As early as that, the ultimate unit of composition is the arrangement, embracing component poems, ordering
them. A spectrum, then, an array of moods? Browning's *Men and
Women* stands behind such a conception, Rossetti's *House of Life*, on
a grosser scale Balzac's *Comédie Humaine*. In the adolescent "Hilda's
Book" stammer distracts from a sureness of array, where the
invocation, "Child of the grass . . .", anticipates themes in the
terminal sonnet ("She hath some tree-born spirit of the wood /
About her . . ."). Here and there a still earlier ordering may be
glimpsed, an abandoned sonnet-sequence which the eighth poem of
the typescript he settled for seems once to have initiated.

Arrays comport with the aesthetic of that decade, part of the
Symbolist legacy. Yeats built books with consummate care. Joyce
thought of the poems in *Chamber Music* as ordered vignettes, and
while the book was still incomplete could designate "All day I hear
the noise of waters" as "For the beginning of the second part—the
journey of the soul." The stories in *Dubliners* traversed in sequence
Childhood, Youth, Maturity, Public Life. Henry James made *The
Ambassadors* out of chapters like pictures in a gallery, and when a
publisher transposed two of them pure narrative sequence was so
inconspicuously dislocated that no one noticed the error for years.
In 1913 Pound compared the epic to a temple, the *Commedia* to a
cathedral, and collected short poems to picture galleries, "the
highest symbols of national desire and of our present civilization."
Like galleries, collections are *arranged*, and collections, sequences,
ordered sets, he implies, make today's correspondence with what
Homer or Dante did. Under and through discrete particulars run
the ordered patterns of force they delineate. It was Pound who took
pains, Eliot recalled 40 years later, over the arrangement of *Prufrock
and Other Observations*, and Pound also admonished Margaret
Anderson about pacing *The Little Review's* contents so as to order

and unify the eventual bound volume. "Points," he remarked in
1950, "define a periphery." His attention was on the *Analects*,
which look like Confucius' scattered remarks; he was asking us to
consider that just three points specify a unique circle.

In arraying items to make a tacit statement his first success was
Cathay (1915): a book about the War which employs remote Chinese
wars as reflectors, and places at the beginning, middle, and end three
war poems about remote privations, war poems, moreover, of
graduated starkness. Themes of exile and departure are stated and
resumed between them. One bright chord, "The River Song,"
becomes in this context the token of a better life remembered, a
ceremonious "Tipperary." One alien chord, "The Seafarer,"
rhymes with the adjacent "Exile's Letter." A brief note placed not
with "The Seafarer" but at the beginning of the book assigns its
poet and "Rihaku" to the same century but all the other poets to
earlier times, hinting at another tacit dimension. In the method of
Cathay we have that of the *Cantos* in pencil-sketch, though when he
prepared three Cantos for publication shortly afterward he did not
yet realize this.

*   *   *

Sat down to in earnest at last, the long poem began:

> Hang it all, there can be but the one "Sordello!"

He was talking to Robert Browning, whose *Sordello* occupied the
room a *Marozia* might aspire to.

> ... But say I want to, say I take your whole bag of tricks,
> Let in your quirks and tweeks, and say the thing's an art-form,
> Your *Sordello*, and that the modern world
> Needs such a rag-bag to stuff all its thought in; ...

This was printed in June 1917. A half-century later Pound dated it
"1912." Perhaps he misremembered; or more likely bits of the
Ur-Cantos do date from that year, the year of *Ripostes* and of the
first Imagist formulations.

As inventoried by himself on the opening page of *Sordello*,
Browning's "bag of tricks" includes the calling-up of the dead, the
evocation of remote places, and a knack of impassioned expostulation with the reader. (He says he would prefer to keep out of view

and let "the very man" speak, but the times insist on a motleyed showman. His dramatic monologues came 15 years later.)

Continuing the parley with Browning's shade, Pound notes one impulse, display of wonders one has found. He inverts his ragbag image, no longer a putting-in but a spilling-out:

> Say that I dump my catch, shiny and silvery
> As fresh sardines flapping and slipping on the marginal cobbles?

Some time after 1919, when he was still fussing with this ultimately abandoned Ur-Canto, he scribbled in a copy of its third revised reprinting (*Quia Pauper Amavi*) a note on those cobbles: "where the road runs into the late": meaning to link it with subsequent allusions to the lake around Sirmio, his magic place. He is remembering the sardine-catch he saw dumped in Sirmione, which when they were arranged in boxes a child (whose name happened to be Dante) thought "bella." But here he does not propose boxed symmetries; the *beltà* of the *Cantos* will inhere in the lively fish.

He inventories some; these are nervous passages; the life of each vignette seems to slip away as he sets it down; how much fantasy (it comes over him) has been infused into what was vivid to him! He knew Guido Cavalcanti probably better than Browning knew Sordello; yet

> What have I of this life,
>   Or even of Guido?
>   Sweet lie!—Was I there truly?
> Did I know Or San Michele?*

> Let's believe it.
> Believe the tomb he leapt was Julia Laeta's?
> Friend, I do not even—when he led that street charge—
> I do not even know which sword he'd with him.
> Sweet lie, "I lived!" Sweet lie, "I lived beside him."
> And now it's all but truth and memory
> Dimmed only by the attritions of long time.

* In Cavalcanti's *Sonnet XXXV* "he explains the miracles of the Madonna of Or San Michele, by telling whose image it is:" so Pound's 1910 gloss on "Una figura de la donna mia / S'adora, Guido, a San Michele in Orto." To help him imagine this he used Stefano's painting "Madonna in Hortulo," invoked near the end of Canto IV "As Cavalcanti had seen her."

"by Stefano, Madonna in Hortulo," detail of painting in the Castel Vecchio, Verona. But when Pound saw it in 1912 it was "across the Adige" from San Zeno, i.e. in Palazzo Laveozzola Pompei.

This leads him to:
> No, take it all for lies.
> I have but smelt this life, a whiff of it—
> The box of scented wood
> Recalls cathedrals.

In those elegiac cadences we read the doom of the historical novel, that long intolerance with fragmentary knowledge, that urge to "imagine" and "complete" as Scott imagined Louis XI, as Pound's friend Maurice Hewlett imagined Bertran de Born, encouraging Pound to imagine him, not long before he published this Ur-Canto, in his own image—

> Testing his list of rhymes, a lean man? Bilious?
> With a red straggling beard?
> And the green cat's eye lifts toward Montaignac.

So Browning "imagined" Sordello and Fra Lippo Lippi; so, at the Louvre, they stuck together in the year Walter Scott was knighted the one famous piece of 19th-century sculpture if we except the more ambitious Albert Memorial, a dumpy "Venus" confected for presentation to Louis XVIII from pieces of several statues in different marbles dug from the wreck of a Greek lime-burner's (i.e. statue-junker's) workshop, and vaguely ascribed by the ignorant to a "Milo" of whom nothing else has ever been heard.*

"And half your dates are out"—he says to Browning;

> you mix your eras
> For that great font Sordello sat beside—
> 'Tis an immortal passage, but the font?—
> Is some two centuries outside the picture.

He is quick to add that it doesn't matter, a fusion having been effected by Browning's *virtù*, the urge

> To set out so much thought, so much emotion;
> To paint, more real than any dead Sordello,
> The half or third of your intensest life
> And call that third *Sordello*;

* See R. H. Wilenski, *The Meaning of Modern Sculpture*, 65–6. Milo of course is French for Melos, where the pieces were unearthed, but the writer of the *Encyclopaedia Britannica* article on Dumont d'Urville seems not to have known this.

but what a clutter of distractions attends the self-embodiment! And if we happen to be interested (like Pound) in the true history, what a mad reconstruction! (We should scarcely guess from Browning that this Italian-born master composed in Provençal.)

For Pound, aware that his interests are guided by temperament, nevertheless delights more in their variety than in his temperament's embodiment. The garrulity he's trying out in the Ur-Cantos may emulsify what he knows is miscellaneous. He is trying for a style, and looking for a "Sordello," a focusing hero.

By 1921 the three Ur-Cantos had been extended to seven, the garrulity modified into a mental kaleidoscope (the "phantastikon") which still underlies Cantos 4 to 7 in their present form. The man talking gave place to rapidly dissolving images. Still later, drastically reworking the first three Cantos, he dropped the convention of a man talking completely, though long afterward the convention of a man musing was to govern the 11 Cantos he wrote in Pisa; and for hero he fixed on that slipknot figure Odysseus; and for theme (he now had his theme) the coming and going of vortices in time's river. From wanting to spill out the contents of the mind of Ezra Pound, he had arrived at something as potentially useful as Divus' crib to the *Odyssey*: a "poem including history."

*   *   *

The Ur-canto urge to be present and talking, he seems to have perceived, reflected an anxiety about keeping control; but a structure incorporates its own controls. The final manner of setting element with element relies on that "behavior of whole systems, unpredicted by knowledge of the component parts" which Buckminster Fuller has taught us to call Synergy. Odysseus goes down to where the world's whole past lives, and that the shades may speak, brings them blood: a neat metaphor for translation which we need not be told is a metaphor since it is simply what is in Homer; and if the device for Elpenor's tomb, "A man of no fortune, and with a name to come," summarizes the preface Pound wrote in 1914 for the *Poetical Works of Lionel Johnson*, who was said to have died much as Elpenor did, "By falling from a high stool in a pub," well, very well; and if a voice like that of Odysseus allaying ghosts' importunities says "Lie quiet Divus," why, Divus is a ghostly forerunner like the equally ghostly Browning whom a similar voice addresses on the next page, and none of this needs the showman to "explain" it.

And out of Divus' book, like Browning's Old Yellow Book bought in a Florentine stall, comes more than we'd think; for at the back of Divus' book we find the Homeric Hymns rendered by a certain Cretan (*Hymni Deorum, Georgio Dartona Cretense interprete*). The Second Hymn to Aphrodite supplies the phrases with which the Canto ends;* if we wonder what they are doing there we may discover by later structural analogies how relevant is Aphrodite's appearance from the sea to the feat of syncretism Canto I has performed, and how often such a glimpse culminates such a passage. The very next Hymn, to Dionysus, tells the story of the kidnapped god Canto II takes up, with an Imagist instead of a Seafarer surface, and with Ovid performing the middleman's office of Divus. (An historical light: the Roman Vortex too dealt with Hellenizing impulses.) The previous Hymn, also to Aphrodite, tells the story of her deceiving of Anchises with her yarn about being King Otreus of Phrygia's daughter (Cantos 23, 25); the Hymn before that, to Hermes, the tale of the infant who stole Divine Apollo's cattle (Canto 24). These three, 23, 24, 25, are Renaissance cantos, like Canto I, with the Hymns to the Gods sounding up through their texture. So the "poem including history" works, without insisting. Our notion of the Renaissance alters when we hear those Hymns; so does our notion of the Hymns.

*   *   *

* *Venerandam auream coronam habentem pulchram Venerem*
   Canam, quae totius Cypri munimenta sortita est,

the Cretan commences. Four lines later Pound picked up *hilariter* and turned it to "mirthful"; then *orichalchi* (so spelled by the Cretan, the epithet for her ear-rings); then from

   Collum autem molle, ac pectora argentea
   Monilibus aureis ornabant

he made "golden / Girdles and breast bands," girdles instead of necklaces to alliterate. "Thou with dark eyelids" is based on *Salve nigras habentes palpebras*, apparently a mistake of the Cretan's since the Greek word refers to the eyelids' motion, and "Bearing the golden bough of Argicida" comes from *habens auream virgam Argicida* in the previous hymn, apparently a mistake of Pound's since though Aphrodite is speaking the bearer of that wand is Hermes.

And history in the Pound Era seemed calling for such a poem, expecting it to make a difference. Whatever enters the mind's ecology makes a difference: *Ulysses* has affected our *reportage*. Minds are *in* history. To offer men's minds a reading of historical patterns might consolidate or might alter those patterns, and would anyhow affect the mind's sense of being at home. If we believe that good things have been and will return we can manage to live with bad things. If we believe that the human will is efficacious, we shall want to expedite the bad things' passing away. And the ground for such beliefs was what poets sought in history, writing "poems including history," attentive to that ecology of events in which any detail may be symptomatic of everything else that is happening, and avid to characterize truly massive happenings: cycles, a *bellum perenne*, Yeatsian gyres.

"The gyres, the gyres. . . ." From "any rich dark nothing," Yeats surmised, a whole unfashionable cosmos would regenerate. And to Shelley's millenarian hope—

> The world's great age begins anew
> The golden years return . . .

with its vision of enhanced re-enactments—

> A loftier Argo cleaves the main
> Fraught with a later prize . . .

Yeats posed the possibility that only the paint would be freshened—

> Another Troy must rise and set,
> Another lineage feed the crow,
> Another Argo's painted prow
> Drive to some flashier bauble yet. . . .

—another delusion, to plunge into another extinction, back into the loam. Between Shelley, whose note to his chorus tempers pessimism with a wish that optimism may after all be valid, and Yeats, for whom only the onlooker's "tragic joy" is exempt from propelling illusion, stretched a century everywhere occupied with systems and with cycles, the century that first needed the word "ecology." In Pound's time, inheriting this, men of letters scale the imagination to large works. "Spring, summer, fall and the sea," the story of

Paterson, beginning with "the Delineaments of the Giants;" "Themes have thimes and habit reburns." [*Finnegans Wake*] "To flame in you. . . . Since ancient was our living is in possible to be." "Stetson!" cries Eliot, A.D. 1921: "You who were with me in the ships at Mylae!" (260 B.C.). And

> that the body of light come forth
> from the body of fire
> And that your eyes come to the surface
> from the deep wherein they were sunken,
> Reina—for 300 years,
> and now sunken . . .
> (91/610:644)

—Paradiso linked with explicit historical datelines, since it was 300 years ago that one loss was registered:

> all that Sandro knew, and Jacopo
> and that Velásquez never suspected
> lost in the brown meat of Rembrandt
> and the raw meat of Rubens and Jordaens
> (80/511:546)

These, and more, are "poems including history," offering to read all phenomena as indices to some process larger than the span of lyric attention: to read the eyes of Diana / Aphrodite for instance, actual eyes of some painter's living model: "the eyes of this dead lady" that in Jacopo del Sellaio's Venus still "speak to me," or the "Yeux Glauques" of the girl who stood before Burne-Jones, her sensibility numbed by Victorian London. From what painters report of such eyes we can read a time. And times know, without wholly knowing, their own myths. In the "age of usury" Aphrodite sinks beneath the water, to lure Arnold's Forsaken Merman, to lure Prufrock, to guard the Rhinegold, to summon the last resource of Hemingway's scavenger as she floats drowned beneath the closed porthole of a liner "as big as the whole world" that lies on its side on clear white sand, its bow plates a mere man's height below the surface of the Gulf. "I swam down and took hold of the edge of the port hole with my fingers and held it and hit the glass as hard as I could with the wrench. I could see the woman floated in the water

"All that Sandro knew..." (Detail from Sandro Botticelli, *Venus and Mars*, reproduced by courtesy of the Trustees, National Gallery, London.)

"...and Jacopo ..." (Detail from *Venus Reclining*, once attributed to Jacopo del Sellaio, reproduced by courtesy of the Trustees, National Gallery, London.)

"...and that Velasquez never suspected." (Detail from the *Rokeby Venus*, reproduced by courtesy of the Trustees, National Gallery, London.)

"Yeux Glauques." (Detail from Burne-Jones, *King Cophetua and the Beggar Maid*, courtesy Tate Gallery, London.)

through the glass. Her hair was tied once close to her head and it floated all out in the water. I could see the rings on one of her hands. She was right up close to the port hole and I hit the glass twice and I didn't even crack it. When I came up I thought I wouldn't make it to the top before I'd have to breathe." Lack of heavy tools, loss of his light tools, a nosebleed, all these defeat him, and "the Greeks" strip the wreck clean. The submarine woman with the floating hair is claimed by the sea or the sharks, and her rings by greedy Greeks.

The presence that thus floated so strangely under the waters is expressive of what in the ways of three hundred years men had come to desire. Hers is the head upon which all the senseless movement of the world has beaten, and the eyelids disclose a mortuary stare. She is older than the rocks amid which she drifts, and passes the stages of her age and youth while gossip writers pick her bones in whispers, and beneath a deep sea she keeps the fallen day about her. The Photomat repeats and repeats her lively lifeless image, for Andy Warhol to color by hand erratically, like sheets of homemade stamps.

> Such light is in sea-caves
> e la bella Ciprigna
> where copper throws back the flame
> from pinned eyes, the flames rise to fade
> in green air.
> (93/631:663)

This is she who was Cyprian once, and came adorned in copper (*orichalcum*)

> . . . with the golden crown, Aphrodite
> Cypri munumenta sortita est, mirthful, oricalchi, with golden
> Girdles and breast bands, thou with dark eyelids . . .
> (1/5:9)

So Canto I ended, after talk of seafaring; and to see her now, as the scavenger saw her near Cuba, is to see an overwhelmed time.

For all subjects rhyme. "I suggest that finer and future critics of art will be able to tell from the quality of a painting the degree of tolerance or intolerance of usury extant in the age and milieu that produced it." And "Anyone with Gaudier-Brzeska's eye will see

Greek art as a decadence. The economist will look at their usury. He will find the idea of it mixed up with marine insurance." Usury epitomizes greed for the quick return. The fine line takes much time: "With usura the line grows thick." Men's minds bring at any time the same values to all the variety of their actions.

*　　*　　*

Yet something resists death always, else we should have long been dead. If the 19th century, "the age of usury," battered Burne-Jones's model into near insensibility and showered rewards and a knighthood on Millais after his Pre-Raphaelite craft had accelerated the sales of Sunlight soap, if it drove John Ruskin mad and Dowson to harlots ("cheaper than hotels") and maintained the compliant U. S. Grant in the White House while the W——— company, granted rights to timber it cut for its roadbed,

> cut a road through the forest,
> Two miles wide, an' perfectly legal.
> Who wuz agoin' to stop him!
> (22/101:105)

—if, conniving at such infamies, it herded live minds into inconspicuous occupations, it left them to make it also, unknown to the tabloid press, the great age of correlations, the great age of the collecting of instances to correlate. And positive feedback operated willy-nilly; the *O.E.D.*, that masterpiece of collaborative correlation, both drew on Middle English texts and called editions of them into existence. The *O.E.D.* (of which W. M. Rossetti was an editor) is perhaps the 19th-century epic, as the *History of the Decline and Fall of the Roman Empire* is that of the 18th. (And both, if we stretch the definition of "poem," are "poems including history.") Commerce elicited worldwide navigation, ships and ports and instruments and stores; worldwide navigation carried Charles Darwin from living species to living species round the world, minutely compared alive for the first time. (From island to island, in the Galápagos, finches differed. Why?) The concepts of ecological interaction, with whose aid today we criticize mercantile values, were discovered thanks to mercantile facilities. Events are multivalued, a "poem including history" complex. That was one reason for scrapping the three Ur-cantos; such a poem would not work as a monologue.

* * *

As finches on three isolated islands will slowly change until we have three species of finches, so Latin south of the Alps becomes "Italian," south of the Pyrenees "Spanish." Coherence remains, forms alter. It is not surprising that art in the 20th century should have rediscovered metamorphosis, nor that the metamorphoses in the second Canto should include Aeschylus' grim transformation of the name of Helen, as well as the eyes of Picasso, metamorphoser of vision, peering from beneath a seal's fur hood that conceals a "lithe daughter of Ocean." And it was from under sealskins furnished by such a daughter that Menelaos and his men leaped forth on the beach to bind Proteus. Everything in the Canto is trickily unstable; what is named is not quite what is there.

> The tower like a one-eyed great goose
> cranes up out of the olive-grove
> (2/10:14)

and

> There is a wine-red glow in the shallows,
> a tin flash in the sun-dazzle,
> (2/7:11)

while down through waters deep and crystalline as Time we half-see stirring energies:

> Twisted arms of the sea-god,
> Lithe sinews of water, gripping her, cross-hold,
> And the blue-gray glass of the water tents them,
> Glare azure of water, cold-welter, close cover.
> (2/6:10)

And the style is Imagist. The brevity of Imagist notation seized phenomena just on the point of mutating, as in the most famous example an apparition of faces turns into petals. Misrepresented as a poetic of stasis, it had been a poetic of darting change; for a whole page, in the Canto, perception succeeds perception like frames of film—

And, out of nothing, a breathing,
            hot breath on my ankles,
Beasts like shadows in glass,
            a furred tail upon nothingness.
Lynx-purr, and heathery smell of beasts,
            where tar smell had been,
Sniff and pad-foot of beasts,
            eye-glitter out of black air. . . .
                    (2/8:12)

as the god's vines and his animals emerge on a stopped ship turning into naviform rock. Acoetes, in Ovid's narrative, told this story to King Pentheus who was planning to restrict the rites of Dionysus. Pound wrote this Canto about the time his countrymen were passing the 18th Amendment, outlawing the wine-god. Never having heard of Pentheus, they were courting his fate. Scott Fitzgerald has told the rest.

*   *   *

For the gods persist. James Frazer, later knighted for his insight, published *The Golden Bough* when Eliot was two, Pound five. Christ is Tammuz again; the personnel change, the names of the gods mutate, but the cults have analogous impulses, stubbornly conserving. Eliot specified in the notes to *The Waste Land* not only his poem's indebtedness to that book but his generation's; and viewing at Rapallo every July votive lights set adrift in the Golfo di Tigullio for the festival of the Montallegre Madonna, Pound wove into it cries of "Tammuz! Tammuz!!" and affirmations that Adonis was commemorated still:

But in the pale night the small lamps float seaward
                τὺ   Διώνα
                TU DIONA
καὶ   Μοῖραι   Ἄδονιν
KAI MOIRAI ADONIN
The sea is streaked red with Adonis
The lights flicker red in small jars.
Wheat shoots rise new by the altar,
        flower from the swift seed.
                (47/236:246)

Adonis, a local rite, vegetation cults. And old women in Venice within living memory wore "black shawls for Demeter" (98/685:715).

Creatures, languages, cultures retain vestigial members: the foetal gills, the mute French *e*, the Venetian shawls. Art too, though it "never improves," retains its own past. But art can retain its past in awareness. Against mindless persistence, as when someone thinks it would be nice to write a sonnet, Art places such deliberated gestures as the sonnet diffused through lines 231–48 of *The Waste Land*, to remember, when the young man carbuncular encounters the typist, how Romeo and Juliet exchanged first kisses to the ceremony of a sonnet (I-v-95–112). What process merely recapitulates, what habit merely retains, art will remember. The "Envoi" to *Mauberley* remembers Chaucer's Envoi to his *Troilus*, and remembers the way Waller's verse remembers Waller's rose which admonished a lady, and remembers how a singer of Waller's words in Lawes's setting revived the rose today as another may revive Envoi and rose long hence. Forms remember; Pound worked out the *Cantos'* rite of formal recurrence about 1917–21, his mind on music and on Arnaut Daniel, ritualist of form.

*   *   *

For what other troubadours simply repeat, Arnaut's formal rituals found ways to remember. The words of Guillem de Poitiers, "the first troubadour,"

> Ab la dolchor del temps novel
> foillo li bosc, e li aucel
> chanton, chascus, en lor lati,
> segon lo vers del novel chan . . .*

once fell on delighted ears as they can today; thenceforward troubadour convention repeated these elements, formulaic as a chess opening: the new season, the new leaves, the birds, the proposal to

---

* Semantic map:

> Thanks to the sweetness of the spring
> the wood grows leafy, and the birds
> sing, each one, in their "latin"
> following the meter of a new song . . .

sing of love. And if convention exacted such an opening, good sense moved each new poem quickly away from it . . . into other conventions.

Arnaut however does not move away, but finds means to keep the birds active in the poem. In "Autet e bas" the first onomatopoeia is a little syncopated, coming just *after* the statement that the birds are singing—

> E noi ten mut bec ni gola
> Nuills auzels, anz braia e chanta
> Cadahus
> En son us:
> (More or less: And now are mute nor beak nor throat
>   Of any bird, but cry and sing
>   Each
>   In his speech . . .)

—and thereafter the words that recapitulate this sound, mid-stanza after mid-stanza, are saying nothing about birds at all, merely chancing to sound bird-like while they go about the poem's later business. And our memory of their first onomatopoeic use is all that makes us receive these as bird-like sounds.

Memory evokes, moreover, previous memory. Behind this poem—such is the use of convention—is the entire Provençal past right back to the springtime of the art, two lifetimes previously, when

> Guillaume Poictiers
> had brought the song up out of Spain
> With the singers and viels.
>   (8/32:36)

A polyphony, not of simultaneous elements which are impossible in poetry, but of something chiming from something we remember from earlier, earlier in this poem and out of earlier poems, such is Arnaut's way. It differs from the *leitmotiv*, which as Joyce used it in *Ulysses* requires that an element be quoted verbatim whenever its effect is wanted. It resembles one of the things Joyce did in *Finnegans Wake*, where recurrent phrases using different words are written to the same tune. To distribute rhyme-sounds in Arnaut's way the

length of succeeding stanzas rather than reserve them for local
felicities within the stanza is to make them available at need for such
reactivation of elements. It also suggests a way for the customary six
stanzas to exist not serially but in parallel, bearing a complex
mutual analogy attested to by their carrying the same tune.

W riting of Arabian music in 1920, his most intensive dealing
with Arnaut not long behind him and his *Cantos* beginning to find
their shape, Pound noted how "as in the Provençal metrical
schemes,"

> the effect of the subtler repetitions only becomes apparent in the
> third or fourth strophe, and then culminates in the fifth or sixth, as
> a sort of horizontal instead of perpendicular chord. One might call
> it a "sort of" counterpoint; if one can conceive a counterpoint
> which plays not against a sound newly struck, but against the
> residuum and residua of sounds which hang in the auditory memory.

This "sort of horizontal chord," an "elaboration of echo," had in
Provence and Tuscany achieved great complexity, and had formed
minds fit to delight in it. Arnaut once more, making convention
new, had more than once made of a renewal a consummation.

He commences the *canso* of the radiant *quel remir* detail by
characteristic intentness on worn elements:

> Doutz brais e critz
> Lais e cantars e voutas
> Aug del auzels qu'en lor latin fant precs
> Quecs ab so par . . .

"Sweet chirps and cries, lays and chansons and trills, I hear from
birds which in their latin pray, each to his mate. . . ." Guillaume of
Poitiers also had the birds singing "en lor lati," and so had many a
troubadour after him. It became a cliché to be inherited by Petrarch,
and the lexicons show what becomes of a convention repeated too
often when they give as a meaning for "latin" simply "language."
But Daniel two generations after Guillaume treats the overfamiliar
phrase as Donne treated stock phrases about love's martyrdom: as
if literally. For if birds are singing ritual phrases in Latin, why, they
are singing prayers (*precs*), though not to heaven but to one another
(*quecs ab so par*); and he does not omit the comic onomatopoeia of

precs//quecs broken across a line-ending, like the Elizabethan poet who transcribed a nightingale's "prick-song": *Jug jug jug*. The birds' "prayers" are mating-songs; and when Arnaut continues—

> ... atressi cum nos fam
> A las amigas en cui entendem
>
> [even as we
> To those lief ladies whom our thoughts intend
> —Pound, 1912]

—he has insinuated into the poem, purely by an exercise of attention to what received diction can say, that analogy between divine and courtly love which in other hands is yet another cliché.

And love is accorded its focus. In the second, third, and fourth stanzas we encounter, thrice running, the magical word *midonz*, that technical term for one's lady which carries to modern ears the overtones of *madonna*.

> Lai on estai midonz, don ai gran fam . . .
> Lo jorn quez ieu e midonz noz baisem . . .
> Voilla, si·l platz, qu'ieu e midonz jassam . . .

It is the same word, three times repeated, that Pound invokes at the moment of transubstantiation in his 1912 "Alchemist"—

> Midonz, with the gold of the sun, the leaf of the
>   poplar, by the light of the amber,
> Midonz, daughter of the sun, shaft of the tree,
>   silver of the leaf, light of the yellow of the amber,
> Midonz, gift of the God, gift of the light, gift of the
>   amber of the sun,
>   Give light to the metal.

In Arnaut's poem the word moves, at each of its three appearances, closer to the end of its line, until in the climactic stanza it keys an astonishing prayer the force of which depends on its divergence from all that one prays for in Latin:

> Dieus lo chauzitz
> Per cui foron assoutas
> Las faillidas que fetz Longis lo cecs,
> Voilla, s·il platz, qu'ieu e midonz jassam

En la chambra on amdui nos mandem
Un rics convens don tan gran joi atendi,
Quel seu bel cors baisan rizen discobra
E quel remir contral lum de la lampa.

He asks that God grant him his naked lady, and her envisioned epiphany breaks out of a rich texture of sound: the syllable *joi* climaxing *don tan gran joi* amid two lines that hum with m's and n's; the threefold cymbal celebrating, *quel . . . bel . . . quel . . .* as in lamplight her form is revealed.

> God who did'st rise,
>   And by whom were commuted
> Longinus his blind sin, Thee I beseech
> That we lie in some room communally
> And seal that pact whereon such joys attend,
> There with embraces, and low laughter blending
> Until she give her body to my vision,
> There with the glamour of the light reflected.
>   —Pound, 1912.

Like the birds' Latin, this plays against a convention. The conventions of a Provençal *canso*—the things the poet was expected to do, in a certain order, while making it—seem not to have been inventoried; possibly the list would surprise by its length. Lacking it, we miss many a "horizontal chord." But a little inspection of anthologies indicates that as birds are commonly mentioned in opening strophes, so God is commonly invoked, as here, at about strophe 4 or 5. Again Arnaut invests convention with attentive force. This isn't "Ah God," but the God who on a specific occasion forgave Longinus and granted him sight: on the occasion, moreover, when Longinus had run his spear into the side of God incarnate. Sins augment the wounds of Christ; Arnaut boldly proposes a sin that shall culminate, like Longinus', in vision: and the light, and the paradisal *tan gran joi*, help lend her lovely body, *seu bel cors*, the force of "Hoc est corpus," a revealed miracle, to adore. Nowhere has Donne any effect of such hair-raising power.

All this while, *precs, decs, pecs, cecs,* the chirping has sounded, stanza after stanza; now, refreshed by fruition, substantial birds re-enter.

> Ges rams floritz
> De floretas envoutas
> Cui fan tremblar auzelhon ab lurs becs
> Non es plus frescs . . .

—birds on branches making flowers tremble, flowers no more fresh than she (and flower precedes fruit); and again *frescs* echoing *becs* strikes the ear as do birds' voices, restoring us to the busy fructive world. In bringing the easy gestures of convention so close to the energies of the real and to the marrow of passion, Arnaut not merely observes but fulfills another convention, the one of offering, as he does in his opening stanza, to make a song

> sobre totz de bell' obra
> Que noi aia mot fals ni rima estrampa

—a song surpassing all fine work, wherein no word is false, no rhyme is forced. This time the ritual offer is made good. "Que noi aia mot fals" comes with peculiar aptness within moments of his revivification of the birds' Latin.

"The high mass of poetry," indeed. Applied to "Doutz brais e cris" this phrase is more just than Pound would have guessed in early 1911. In the Latin mass, words said because long tradition has made this or that moment the ritual moment for saying them, nevertheless become efficacious *now*. So here: all those formulae, presenting themselves in order as convention obligates, yet have a bite upon the intense actual, with a bold theological metaphor, firmly grasped—the body offered and transfigured and taken—at the heart of their way of working.

*   *   *

There is little of Arnaut on the surface of the *Cantos*: four or five phrases. The troubadour there drawn on when Provençal qualities are wanted is Bernart de Ventadour, in whose work juicy bits abound. But a structural X-ray tells a different story. From 15 years' work with Arnaut's *canzoni* Pound learned not only to prefer crisp sounds to sleek, but to invest elaborate forms with spoken diction, to make it new, quickening conventions while passing through their forms, and to let structural analogies, reinforced by rhythm, do the work of assertion. When we read, in Canto 91,

> The Princess Ra-Set has climbed

and recognize from Canto 4 the rhythm of

> Thus the light rains, thus pours,

we are not surprised at a further breadth of analogy:

> Light *compenetrans* of the spirits
> The Princess Ra-Set has climbed
>   to the great knees of stone,
> She enters protection
>   the great cloud is about her,
> She has entered the protection of crystal
>   convien che si mova
>   la mente, amando
>   (91/611:645)

reproducing and fulfilling

> Thus the light rains, thus pours, *e lo soleils plovil*
> The liquid and rushing crystal
>   beneath the knees of the gods.
> Ply over ply, thin glitter of water; . . .
> Forked branch-tips, flaming as with lotus.
>   Ply over ply
> The shallow eddying fluid
>   beneath the knees of the gods.
>   (4/15:19)

From "the knees of the gods" to Egypt's "great knees of stone" a mental arc swings, and the Princess climbs to enter "the golden sun boat" that will sail some crystal river. The technique, modified and elaborated as befits its application to a structure of a magnitude Arnaut never envisaged, is derived from those years of studying Arnaut. Fitly, the phrase for the raining sunlight, *e lo soleils plovil,* is borrowed in homage from one of his *canzoni.*

*   *   *

Guillem de Poitiers did not foresee Arnaut; yet a continuity of tradition, guaranteed by repeated acts of attention, allows us to read

"Ab la dolchor del temps novel . . ." and "Doutz brais e critz . . ."
as members of a continuing poetic act, its seedtime and its harvest,
little birds singing Latin all the while. In the same way 30 years
separate

> The liquid and rushing crystal
> > beneath the knees of the gods

from "the great knees of stone" and "the protection of crystal,"
and the earlier need no more have foreseen the later than the Ezra
Pound of 70 *bis* rue Notre Dame des Champs foresaw the prisoner
in the Chestnut Ward at St. Elizabeths Hospital. Like a decades-long
vortex, like a whole literature, like a pine tree, a poem could grow,
ingesting always new nutriment, patterned always by its own past,
provided that primary structures of known integrative power—a
descent to the past of the world, a metamorphosis—furnished
"Gestalt seed." Thus in the first Pisan Canto, as in the first Canto,
Odysseus confronts the past; and in the second Pisan Canto, as in
Canto 2, we behold a metamorphosis, music handed on, chorus to
lute to violin, bird-song all the while ineradicable. Thus Henry
James's device of "A Bundle of Letters" (1880) governs the introduction in Canto 9 of Sigismundo's post-bag (1454), which in turn
is rhymed with the Adams-Jefferson letters of Canto 31 (1787-1814),
a simple citation of the Malatesta motto ("Tempus loquendi,
tempus tacendi") serving to link the latter to the former, as in Canto
21 an Italian phrase had linked a letter of Jefferson's seeking a
musical gardener to a letter of Sigismundo's (Canto 8) seeking to
retain a painter.

Vortices have analogous structures; events, relationships, recur
in history. A poem *about* history, taking note of recurrences, could
go on endlessly, like wallpaper, much as a minor literary tradition
can go on permuting elements for decades, moon, June, soon,
spring, sing. But as the Provençal tradition contained not only birds
and loves but Arnaut, so a poem *including* history will contain not
only elements and recurrences but a perceiving and uniting mind
that can hope one day for a transfiguring vision of order it only
glimpses now, and that in carrying simple themes to a massive
simultaneous orchestration will achieve the poem's end in discovering its own richest powers. Joyce saw *Ulysses* as a whole and worked

at opening and closing episodes simultaneously; Pound hoped to become, while writing the poem in public, the poet capable of ending the *Cantos*.

This is his most tenacious heritage from the 1890's, for it entails one's life being co-extensive with one's work of art. And it entoiled him (though it need not have) in mortal risks, unwilling as he was to perfect his insight and let the world go as it would (that way lay Nietzsche). What does it profit a man, whispered Mauberley's ghost, if he gain his soul and the whole world be lost? What use is a Palace of Art? Hence (in a letter, 1934) "I have, confound it, to forge pokers, to get economic good and evil into verbal manifestation, not abstract, but so that the monetary system is as concrete as fate and *not* an abstraction etc.": such forged iron being meant to dislodge the clinkers in actual grates, and assist the world (even as the poem drew toward a close) to manifest and celebrate ancient flames. They were ancient;

> ... Kung said "Wan ruled with moderation,
> "In his day the State was well kept,
> "And even I can remember ...
>   (13/60:64)

The world, he was convinced, had once known the order it now lacked, and what has been known should not be difficult to recover, a simple matter of reactivating knowledge. And this was implicit in his guiding myth of Odysseus, whose journey through unknown dangers is directed toward his former home. Mussolini seemed to be helping to rebuild Ithaca. All this (and the cage, and the madhouse) lay ahead as he assumed, in the early 1920's, the role of Odysseus and the role, simultaneously, of amanuensis for the mind of Europe, itself Odysseus, in desperate straits (wars, inflations) seeking Ithaca, questing as men always are after lost securities that lie somewhere around the rim of a great circle.

*   *   *

For clearly it was a collective quest. Clearly the mind of Europe in the 19th century is struggling to encompass an intelligible form for its own past and present; clearly the image biologists call ecology—fructive interaction—comes to govern its visions; and as they speak Latin in Rapallo and Barcelona, so our past is alive around us now. And clearly the cycles which guaranteed stability at the cost of local pain (the cycle of trade, the Malthusian cycle of nutriment, the cycle of teacher and taught, rod against buttock, that tortured schoolboys to ensure a learned continuity) yield slowly to some metamorphic analogy as men come to suspect that a Utopia such as their ancestors knew but never really knew may be in fact realizable on Spaceship Earth. Hence, once again, the Poems Including History, their inclusiveness, their paradoxical optimism.

It is paradoxical because we can hope about the future while knowing that a cycle leads nowhere new. (Tennyson fancied an Odysseus bored with Ithaca.) Cycles fascinate the mind; there is security in cycles. The seasons are cyclic; agriculture is cyclic; men (as Eliot wrote)

> long since under earth
> Nourishing the corn

once danced "joined in circles,"

> Keeping the rhythm in their dancing
> As in their living in the living seasons
> The time of the seasons and the constellations
> The time of milking and the time of harvest,
> The time of the coupling of man and woman
> And that of beasts. Feet rising and falling.
> Eating and drinking. Dung and death.

(And "In my beginning is my end.")

For "Cyclic theories of time accomplish for the learned what the mythological rituals of the seasons accomplish for the intellectually unsophisticated. Both mitigate the terror of history, in which events, and most of all man's personal decisions, are set forever in an irreversible pattern." And poems tend to be cyclic, remembering their beginnings; and every act of recognition implies that something like this has been seen before. So the poet of *Four Quartets* drew four elements, four seasons, four places, into a four-part symmetry which closes as it had opened in a transcended garden—

> And the end of all our exploring
> Will be to arrive where we started
> And know the place for the first time

—and only escapes the world's sad repetitions by leaving the world (the river at the end of *Little Gidding* is not a real river, nor the children real children). He had earlier written appreciatively of *The Vanity of Human Wishes*, a work shot through with the post-Augustan conviction that all recurs and nothing can be ameliorated: on which the poet of the *Cantos*, exposing perhaps a deficiency of his own, commented sharply that human wishes are not vain in the least. Pound was working instead from within a poem whose end he did not clearly foresee, in the faith that secular events, and the shape of his own life, would supply a proper finale when it was time. Secular events supplied instead Mussolini hanged by the heels, and a cage and 14 years in a madhouse, and inexorable old age at last in which to reflect how he had "tried to write Paradise."

> ... Do not move.
> Let the wind speak.
> That is Paradise.
> Let the gods forgive what I have made.
> May those I have loved try to forgive
> what I have made.

Yet human misjudgment and the closed curve of human vitality which achieved power at last over the *Cantos* should not in their triumph obliterate the pertinence of his most radical decision: to experience the poem as he wrote it, himself committed to all of which he wrote, himself Odysseus actually *en route*. The mind of Europe, again, had for some decades been adumbrating such a role for someone.

That Newton, who rhymed an apple with a planet, was himself a physical body pulled by the forces he explicated, he and his readers had little need to consider. That Grimm spoke the languages he studied, and that Darwin partook of the animality the descent of whose human form he traced, these are more pertinent matters: Darwin's reader in particular was apt to be horrified at the trend of a book essentially about himself. But it was not Darwin the animal who wrote, and various bishops might well have reflected that it was not in their animal capacity that they could read. The historical and the religious ecologies however—the very stuff of the *Cantos*—

force on their observer some declaration of standpoint, and a wheel is most easily observed from somewhere else. Thus Nietzsche invented his Superman, who like his sibling the Herdsman of Wyndham Lewis is somewhere outside the system on which he comments. ("The terrible processions beneath," runs the Code of a Herdsman, "are not of our making and are without our pity. Our sacred hill is a volcanic heaven. But the result of its violence is peace.") That Sacred Hill is also Yeats's Meru, and is also the mountain carved in lapis lazuli whence his three Chinamen look down "on all the tragic scene" through eyes that are gay; and that gaiety is quite Nietzschean in "The Gyres," where "we that look on but laugh in tragic joy." Gaiety came late; he had earlier been a participant:

> Did that play of mine send out
> Certain men the English shot?

He had also been a theosophist, both inside and outside the religious systems he studied, looking for something to believe, and also in touch with doctrines of reincarnation which allow you to feel yourself both on history's wheel and off it. (With the ant and Achilles I am perpetually reincarnated; unlike them I know it.) Leopold Bloom heard enough of such Dublin talk to explain "metempsychosis" to his wife Molly; what other Greek pentasyllable could he have explained?

Bloom's creator, who was later to use Vico's cycle, used Mme. Blavatsky's with rigorous literalness: *Ulysses* plays on Yeats the immense joke of taking his pet doctrines as naively as John Donne took the idea that lovers are martyrs. For the book's premise must be that Bloom really is Ulysses, though he knows it no more than that wily wandering Greek foresaw being reincarnated as a wandering homebody Jew. Yeats very likely never found this out from a book he found entrancing but did not finish, for Bloom's readers have no more need to know it than does Bloom. Who does know it? Joyce; and the occasional reader whom a commentary, or the title, has guided to insight. And Joyce, is he inside or outside the system he has made?

Why, outside, says his *alter ego* Stephen Dedalus, "like the God of the creation . . . indifferent, paring his fingernails." But wait, is not Stephen Dedalus, that *alter ego*, within? He is, and he exists nowhere else. For Joyce early discovered what it must imply, to write of other people from no experience but one's own. However he may once have hoped to escape imaginary Dublin as he escaped the geographical Dublin's city directory, he settled for concealed roles within it: Stephen has his taste for Dante, Bloom his taste for pork kidneys; he is also Shem the Penman and HCE, and Mr. James Duffy who has translated Hauptmann, and Eveline's Frank who alone knows fully what is happening in what seems to be a tale of impassive pathos. Decade after decade, even with a photograph to help, no one saw him in Frank's yachting cap.

Joyce made the penultimate breakthrough, as Pound and Eliot (and later the Williams of *Paterson*) quickly perceived. On 19 December 1917 Ezra Pound read the first 17 pages of *Ulysses* in typescript. In the next three years he and Eliot gradually came to know half the book as *The Little Review* and *The Egoist* serialized it. In 1921 Eliot wrote *The Waste Land* ("Tiresias, although a mere spectator and not indeed a 'character', is yet the most important personage in the poem, uniting all the rest.") The following year, *Ulysses* at last read as a whole, Pound finally determined what he was doing in the *Cantos*.

All manner of modern preoccupations, it was clear, linguistics, anthropology, biology, folklore, economics, so interrogate present phenomena as to open up tunnels in time, down which we see to an archetypal past whose shadows, under our transparent present, lend weight and nerve and import. And as with Madame Sosostris and her Tarot pack, the seer is inseparable from what is seen. Very early in the poem he sits "on the Dogana's steps," penniless, dreaming of how "Gods float in the azure air." He will be sitting again, in a Pisan tent.

O CITY CITY . . .

The guns of August, and September, and October, the guns of 52 interminable blood-drenched months, destroyed morale, destroyed a generation, destroyed Europe. Everything afterward seems provisional. London was the Capital no longer. No future Whistler or James or Pound would be drawn there. Eliot and Lewis encamped among the ruins of the Vortex, the one to indulge his archaeologist's appetite for decay (shattered columns, moss in the crevices), the other to bombinate in a void for which his affinities were profound. Shades moved about: the Sitwells, Mrs. Woolf, Clive Bell: in certain lights the place seemed almost inhabited.

Unreal City.
Under the brown fog of a winter dawn,
A crowd flowed over London Bridge, so many
I had not thought death had undone so many.
. . . .
What is the city over the mountains
Cracks and reforms and bursts in the violet air
Falling towers
Jerusalem Athens Alexandria
Vienna London
Unreal

—So Eliot; and London "merely shrivels," he wrote in *The Dial*, "like a little bookkeeper grown old."

As for Lewis, he thought he saw hope, being always ready to find chaos hopeful. The febrile but hypersensitive society that shrieked and gibbered when the Vorticists offered it a Renaissance had broken up, and "creatures of a new state of human life, as different from Nineteenth Century England, say, as the Renaissance was from the middle ages" might now seize their old thwarted initiative; might move "forward, and away from the sealed and obstructed past." He wrote of this hope in the first number of *The Tyro* (1921), where he also wrote,

> A phenomenon we meet, and are bound to meet for some time, is the existence of a sort of No Man's Land atmosphere. The dead never rise up, and men will not return to the Past, whatever else they may do. But as yet there is Nothing, or rather the corpse of the past age, and the sprinkling of children of the new. There is no mature authority, outside of creative and active individual man, to support the new and delicate forces bursting forth everywhere today.

But "creative and active individual man" turned out to be in short supply. By the mid-1920's a massive triviality, a failure of will on a truly forbidding scale, was allowing English culture to lapse into shapes characterized by childishness, self-indulgence, utter predictability. Lewis's response was satiric: a painted universe of doll-like figures and columnar totems of equivocal menace, a written universe called *The Man of the World*, a huge fusion of genres, never completed. This would have been a sort of prose Sistine Ceiling on which Goya has collaborated with Cézanne. It ultimately congealed into details which were separately published. Each of these details is several hundred pages in length: *The Art of Being Ruled*, *The Lion and the Fox*, *The Apes of God*, *The Childermass*, *Time and Western Man*. Nowhen, nowhere, the Heaven of *The Childermass* glitters like an assemblage of art movements:

> . . . the upper stages of wicker towers; the helmet-like hoods of tinted stucco; tamarisks; the smaragdine and olive of tropical vegetations; tinselled banners; gigantic grey-green and speckled cones, rising like truncated eggs from a system of profuse nests; and a florid zoological symbolism . . .

—"in the truest sense an asylum," says its proprietor, "and our patients are our children." In the 1950's, blind, near the end of his life, having added a second and third part to this infernal fantasy, he meditated a fourth, left unwritten when he died, to be called *The Trial of Man*.

*   *   *

In the old sense there were no more capitals: no places to which talent repaired as inevitably as young Samuel Johnson (after Oxford) to London. For a while living was cheap in Paris, especially if you had pounds or dollars, and there was the rumor of painting; a generation's scouts drifted to Paris, and young men who simply had to get out of America. Joyce moved there, *Ulysses* was published there, Ford gave parties there and ran his *transatlantic review* for a year; young men, Ernest Hemingway, Basil Bunting, surfaced there; Pound looked in for four years ("The men I knew were Léger and Brancusi and Cocteau and Picabia") and moved on. ("If Paris had been as interesting as Italy in 1924, I would have stayed in Paris.") Robert Menzies McAlmon came to Paris from Nebraska, the inadvertent husband of a millionairess. He published his friends' books; also (1922) *A Hasty Bunch*, meaning stories he did not choose to revise because that would destroy their primal authenticity. ("Gert Northrup was rather a weird looking sort of a specimen, the other girls in town thought.") Bill and Floss Williams were old friends. They came through in 1924. With an eye to some later edition Floss proofread the volume, for what proofreading might be worth when the printers read no English.

It was, if anything, a Printing Vortex. Books were cheap to produce in France. On l'Ile Saint-Louis William Bird's Three Mountains Press published Hemingway, Williams, Pound: notably in 1925 *A Draft of XVI Cantos*, in folio. Nancy Cunard later bought Bird's assets, and in 1930 her Hours Press issued *A Draft of XXX Cantos* (200 copies). Bird's and her printers' vagaries still infest the New Directions edition, for which the Hours Press book once served as copy-text. These were lavish jobs. The economical Maurice Darantiere of Dijon, whose firm had manufactured *Ulysses*, became the printer of avant-garde choice. Williams' *Spring and All*, in McAlmon's Contact Editions, was a Darantiere job. The scrambled, in one case inverted, chapter headings were put there "just to be crazy," but they might have happened anyhow. Nevertheless:

> From the petal's edge a line starts
> that being of steel
> infinitely fine, infinitely
> rigid penetrates
> the Milky Way
> without contact—lifting
> from it—neither hanging
> nor pushing—
> The fragility of the flower
> unbruised
> penetrates spaces

—A laser's freedom (though there were no lasers then) in a time of no time and a place of no place: words written in New Jersey, printed in Dijon, published in Paris, distributed———? Not distributed, really. There were 300 copies, Paris bookshops were not interested, American customs held up shipments for months, American reviewers based 12 miles from Rutherford merely sneered at expatriates when they noticed such books at all. "Nobody ever saw it"—Williams, 35 years later—"it had no circulation at all." . . . The fragility of the flower, unbruised—there was nothing but empty space for it to penetrate.

A mystique of the word—as in Miss Stein's case—is encouraged by the circumstance that one's words will not be read. ("The Revolution of the Word," proclaimed Eugene Jolas, 1927, commencing the serialization, in his *transition*, of what would be *Finnegans Wake*. "Après mot, le déluge," was Joyce's gloss.) Not related to a reader's understanding, the words turn toward one another in a mathematic of mutual connections. "Toasted Susie is my ice cream," wrote Miss Stein, and why not? To so fit and pack and lock and arrange the words that when their capsules are one day broken open—perhaps after 50 years, on an unrecognized planet— they will affirm structured realities, like a watch that should commence ticking as though made yesterday, that seemed the aim and morality of style.

"As birds' wings beat the solid air without which none could fly so words freed by the imagination affirm reality by their flight." This formulation takes account of words, and of realities, but not of readers. They may come by if they choose.

What may words do without readers? They may sound. In Russia, 1913, another readerless time and place, Alexei Kruchenykh had offered

HEIGHTS

(universal language)

```
          e   u   yu
          i   a   o
              o   a
  o   a   e   e   i   e   ya
              o   a
          e   u   i   e   i
              i   e   e
      i   i   y   i   e   i   i   y
```

Williams adduced such Russian precedents but didn't believe in them ("I do not believe that writing is music"); he proceeded to careful statement:

> According to my present theme the writer of imagination would attain closest to the conditions of music not when his words are dissociated from natural objects and specified meanings but when they are liberated from the usual quality of that meaning by transposition into another medium, the imagination.

Attached to meaning, but liberated from meaning's usual quality: perhaps the quality of making verifiable statements. "There is a white bear" invites us to raise our eyes and check the bear's presence. But, remarked Tristram Shandy's father to Corporal Trim, a verbal bear can inhabit a verbal Arctic:

> "A white bear! Very well. Have I ever seen one? Might I ever have seen one? Am I ever to see one? Ought I ever to have seen one? Or can I ever see one?
> "Would I had seen a white bear! (for how can I imagine it?)
> "If I should see a white bear, what should I say? If I should never see a white bear, what then?

"If I never have, can, must or shall see a white bear alive;
have I ever seen the skin of one? Did I ever see one painted?—
described? Have I never dreamed of one?"

Williams found this and quoted it, inviting his ideal reader (one
must be postulated) to "note how the words *alive, skin, painted,
described, dreamed* come into the design of these sentences," with "a
curious immediate quality quite apart from their meanings."

This essay was written, again, in Rutherford, where no one was
listening; printed, again, by an expatriate press (TO publishers,
Toulon: i.e. George Oppen); again, did not find readers. Williams
was the best theorist the Paris decade had, the decade of facilities
but no city, of writers, surrounded by indifferent foreigners, joining
English word to English word. In Rutherford he might as well have
lived in Paris.

In Roussillon in the Vaucluse, 1943 or so, in the evenings of
days he spent passing as a French agricultural laborer while Germans
occupied the north of France, Samuel B. Beckett, M.A., blocked his
remembered English into patterns comparably abstract:

> Well, said Mr Fitzwein, it is always a pleasure for us, for me for
> one for my part, and for my colleagues for two for theirs, to meet a
> moron from a different crawl of life from our crawl, from my
> crawl and from their crawl. . . .

And Pound in 1920, through Spire and DeSouza, located the Abbé
Rousselot, pioneer phonetician, whose apparatus registered on a
smoked cylinder your consonants and vowels as you spoke them:
pitch, duration, and "a double registration of quavering": articulate
human speech reduced to its physical properties, which of course is
one of the levels at which the poet handles it.

*   *   *

The men of Paris were the last Paterians, all art aspiring to the
condition of music. Williams' strength was to know this and then
to reason from it, immune to its romantic blandishments. Ernest
Hemingway developed Pater's proposition in a direction Pater
would have more easily recognized, proposing, since only so many

pulses are given us, to pass swiftly from point to point, "and be present always at the focus where the greatest number of vital forces unite in their purest energy."

"With this sense of the splendour of our experience and of its awful brevity, gathering all we are into one desperate effort to see and touch, we shall hardly have time to make theories about the things we see and touch," and Hemingway's paradigm came to be the bullfighter, who lives in the imminence of death and exquisitely *acts*. Late in life, arguing with himself whether or not to kill himself (an argument he lost), he returned in imagination to the Paris years, when passing moments, simply for those moments' sake, had importuned him to seize them.

A girl came into the café and sat by herself at a table near the window. She was very pretty with a face fresh as a newly minted coin if they minted coins in smooth flesh with rain-freshened skin, and her hair was black as a crow's wing and cut sharply and diagonally across her cheek.

I looked at her and she disturbed me and made me very excited. I wished I could put her in the story, or anywhere, but she had placed herself so she could watch the street and the entry and I knew she was waiting for someone. So I went on writing. . . .

I've seen you, beauty, and you belong to me now, whoever you are waiting for and if I never see you again, I thought. You belong to me and all Paris belongs to me and I belong to this notebook and this pencil.

So romance seeped into the life of art in those years. Thus we are to imagine the Hemingways tramping with the Pounds over battle-grounds at Piombino and Orbetello, where "Hem" imparted strategic expertise on how Sigismundo's campaigns would have been fought; or Hemingway, in love with his wife Hadley, yet feeling entitled to his passion for Pauline Pfeiffer; or Olga Rudge, the concert violinist, finding Ezra Pound, introduced at one of her concerts, the most handsome man she had ever seen, and him reciprocating her regard. She bore his daughter, Mary, in 1925. Dorothy's son, Omar Shakespear Pound, was born the following year. Mary was raised in Gais, in the Italian Tyrol, speaking as her first language a near-German dialect of Homeric starkness. Omar was brought up by Olivia Shakespear in London. An English school was his purgatory. They have their story, which is not this one.

*   *   *

The rumor went about that Pound had abandoned words. He worked at music, an extension of his 1917 work on Arnaut, and welcomed George Antheil as a Vorticist composer come late ("The Vorticist Manifestos of 1913–14 left a blank space for music. . . . There wasn't any vorticist music available.") And Antheil had written, "Sound vibrations are the strongest and most fluid space vibrations capable of a tangible mathematic," an approach which will not lead us near a Pastoral Symphony though it whirls us past the Abbé Rousselot. And struggling to suggest Antheil's world of absolute sound ("a world of steel bars, not of old stone and ivy") Pound drew a distinction and introduced a metaphor:

> The old harmonists made a wire-work, Antheil wants slabs of sound to construct his active time-machines.

Time machines, machines made of compacted time: as indifferent to the auditor as locomotives are. It is an intelligible ideal.

Agnes Bedford, a concert accompanist who had taken over the triangular flat in Kensington, crossed to Paris for a while and went with him afternoons to Natalie Barney's in the Rue Jacob, where a piano was accessible. Outside, beyond the French doors, a gardener worked, his shears snipped, sunlight streamed: Debussy's universe. On the hither side of the glass, in the studio room, Pound and Miss Bedford attended to a young vortex. He beat rhythms, picked out sequences of notes, she transcribed. Villon, so absolute he could not be translated, ("he rhymes on a word meaning 'sausages'") supplied the armature. Against his words, live as a butcher's, remote as Atlantis—

> Dictes moy ou, n'en quel pays,
> Est Flora la belle Rommaine

—Pound angled a rhythm like but subtler than that of café song and specified the variations of pitch. His musical sense, untrained, was of four-dimensional sureness. He dictated part by part a concluding canon for the Ballade of the Hanged, and Miss Bedford was astonished to find that when the parts were transcribed they fitted together. Subsequently Antheil sketched in orchestration. When the *Villon* was performed at the Salle Pleyel, Pound played his own

Dic - tes moi   où   n'en   quel   pays,   Est   Flo   -   ra   la   bel - le Roum - mai - ne

drums. He had watched Cocteau playing a drum in a jazz band, "not with any African fervor but as if it were a very difficult mathematical operation." He had also purchased a Trirbert bassoon, liking its register and its impudent staccato. He chiselled at stone, and left a head half finished, learning in the process what order of craft Gaudier had mastered, much as in 1914 he had spoiled "sheet after sheet of paper in learning just how difficult it is to bring forth a new unit of design." He and Fritz Vanderpyl, whose corner apartment (deuxième étage, with a stone life mask on the balcony) looked down the Rue Royer-Collard to the Luxembourg Gardens, strolled in the Gardens observing official art, notably the statue of Blanche de Castille by Auguste Dumont, 1850, of which they constated the contour in pronouncing it a "beer-bottle on the statue's pediment." As usual he manufactured his furniture, quite as Odysseus would have. In a famous photograph John Quinn, who visited in 1923 and told for Canto XII the Tale of the Honest Sailor, sits with Tammany authority on what seems an improvised electric chair. Years later, when the Pounds had long moved on to Rapallo, that furniture was being used by subsequent tenants of 70 *bis* Rue Notre-Dame des Champs.

That furniture registers a habit of mind. It is nailed together but owes its rigidity to the design, not the nails. (The amateur who puts his faith in nails will find his joints wobble under shifting weight.) At the junction-points of a long worktable which Pound constructed as late as 1958, nails pointing without redundancy in three directions hold snug economical three-way overlaps of impeccable rectilinear geometry. Like Jefferson's plough these junctures can be reproduced by anyone, using wood unmortised just as

"Beer-bottle on the statue's pediment": Luxembourg Gardens, Paris, five minutes from Fritz Vanderpyl's apartment.

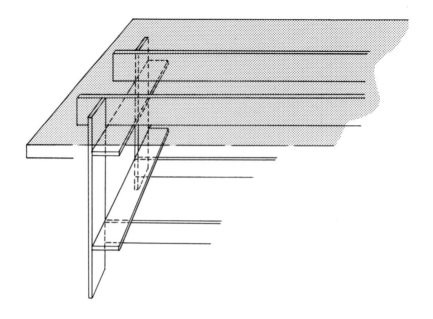

it comes from the lumberyard, and the artifact they sustain is elegant, concealing no secrets. In this homely construction as in the 25th Canto (circa 1927) no visible tricks but a sensibility alert to snug economical structures laid member across member trimly:

> "as the sculptor sees the form in the air . . .
> "as glass seen under water,
> "King Otreus my father . . .
> and saw the waves taking form as crystal,
> notes as facets of air,
> and the mind there, before them, moving,
> so that notes needed not move.
>
> (25/119:124)

These are stable transparent forms, including Aphrodite's, who lulled Anchises' suspicions with a yarn about being the mortal daughter of King Otreus of Phrygia (*First Hymn to Aphrodite*, 111–12). So in a later Canto we read of

> Anchises that laid hold of her flanks of air
> drawing her to him

Cythera potens, Κύθηρα δεινά
no cloud, but the crystal body
the tangent formed in the hand's cup
as live wind in the beech grove
as strong air amid cypress.
(76/456:485)

His mind was also on Guido Cavalcanti, in whose world "thought cuts through thought with a clean edge." After the executioners below Montségur terminated the civilization of Languedoc the tradition moved eastward to upper Italy, still occupied with birdsong and with love, still crisp, but prepared to incorporate an order of formal thought that had been part of the troubadours' weather but was part of the Italians' tool-kit. Guido uses terms like "accident" and "diafan." "Not the idea but the degree of its definition determines its aptitude for reaching to music," Pound was learning to think in those years: thought cutting through thought as musical motifs intersect when harmonic slush does not bedrip their outlines. Guido's "Donna mi Pregha" stands like an elegant geometrized table. Ideally one might assemble it without nails.

A lady asks me
I speak in season
She seeks reason for an affect, wild often
That is so proud he hath Love for a name
Who denies it can hear the truth now . . .
(36/177:182)

for

Donna mi pregha
perch' i volglio dire
D'un accidente
che sovente
é fero
Ed é sí altero
ch'é chiamato amore
Sicche chi l negha
possa il ver sentire . . .

—of which an earlier version had run,

Because a lady asks me, I would tell
Of an affect that comes often and is fell

> And is so overweening: Love by name.
> E'en its deniers can now hear the truth . . .

("I am aware that I have distorted '*accidente*' into '*affect*' but I have done so in order not to lose the tone of my opening by introducing an English word of *double entente*.")

That earlier version, with the Italian text and notes on the versification and with "Mediaevalism" which is perhaps his most pregnant single prose essay, appeared in two installments in *The Dial*, March and July, 1928. They issued from a concentration of work which followed naturally from his work on music, which in turn had arisen from 1917 work on Arnaut, which in turn extricated his still earlier perception of Arnaut from the Pre-Raphaelitism that infested his 1910 version of Cavalcanti's sonnets and ballate. After 18 years he was finally free of that, and well launched on the *Cantos* where thought cuts through thought. In the 25th Canto the lines about the form seen in the air comprise part of a luminous core around which are folded documents from Venetian history: the history of a city where forms were not seen in the air but where the earliest laws repress crapshooters and where decades of committee decisions educed a Pre-Raphaelite dream—

> and the palace hangs there in the dawn, the mist,
> in that dimness
>
> (25/117:122)

—the embellishment of which by the 16th century entailed committee efforts to get Titian painting since Titian having achieved what he wanted, a brokerage, was too busy to paint; while in the 36th Canto (1934) the final version of the "Donna mi pregha" comes between a statement of Venetian rationale ("Undersell, overbuy, maintain defence of the sea route") and Martin Van Buren's efforts against the Bank. All these matters trace trajectories of volition.

*　　*　　*

In 1925 William Bird at his Three Mountains Press had manufactured *A Draft of XVI Cantos* in sumptuous folio, using for the 90 copies paper watermarked "Ezra Pound Cantos": a proper Renaissance gesture beyond the facilities of M. Darantiere. But that vortex was dissipating. The following year Bird's press was sold, and in 1928 the matching deluxe edition of *A Draft of the Cantos 17–27* was manufactured in England, though still on Bird's special paper. By the spring after that the old dreary rows with English firms had resumed. Pound envisioned yet one more deluxe edition, this time of his work on Cavalcanti: text, photographic reproductions of manuscripts ("so the reader could see the difference between a scribe interested in the poem and one trying to make a nice page," he explained *viva voce* three decades later), translations, and critical apparatus. In spring 1929 the Aquila Press in London contracted this expensive work. What happened next is unclear. The bibliographer writes, "After 56 pages had been completed, the Aquila Press failed. The completed sheets (presumably about 470 sets on paper and about 50 on Japanese vellum, plus at least one set on real vellum) were sent to Ezra Pound at Rapallo." His "failed" may be polite; Pound, who had been patient when Swift & Co.'s manager absconded in 1912 just after printing his first Cavalcanti, now growled in print that the British grocer would break a contract for printing Cavalcanti when he would not dream of breaking one for prunes. He salvaged the ruin by paying to have the Italian text and commentary printed in Genoa, the reproductions printed in Germany, and the 56 English pages bound into the whole. There are three different kinds of paper, and the page numbers are jumbled. The University of Pennsylvania received a copy, submitted in lieu of a doctoral thesis. They stipulated further formalities. No degree ensued. The book, piled in the author's storeroom, had little distribution. In Rapallo, where he had moved in 1924, Pound saw every door closing: notably the doors that valved a worldwide flow of currency. Those had slammed, spectacularly, in 1929: a universal disaster comparable to the war that had ended only 11 years before. "Bellum cano perenne." London had been the hub of civilization as recently as when he was 30. He was not yet 45 and there were no more cities. He lived in a salubrious overgrown village now, with mountains and the sea and olive trees and no library but his own.

*   *   *

He had a new reputation, for needless irascibility. On a visit to Paris in 1929 he came upon Joyce holding court and was enraged by what he took to be a climate of sycophancy. Of one slim youth he enquired, in withering tones, whether he might be writing an *Iliad*, or would it be a *Divina Commedia*. One should not say such a humiliating thing to anyone, certainly not to anyone who has done no harm, but it is especially regrettable that he should have said it to Sam Beckett.

SYNTAX IN RUTHERFORD

Any word at all:

cat.

A "noun." And what happens if we affix the article is highly mysterious:

the cat—

for the grammarians' distinction—definite article for the particular, indefinite for the general—is meant to operate between speakers, live persons in a real place who already know, because they are talking about it, which cat is "the cat": "Have you put out the cat?" But typed on a sheet of paper as if to designate some one cat though we cannot identify him, the article performs in pure abstraction a gesture of as-if-specifying: something operative not in the kitchen or the garden but in a language field, where on an invisible string a knot has been tied. (A poem is a machine made out of words.) The invisible string is an infinity of cats; the knot, *the cat.*

Tense the string:

> As the cat

—an exact structure, empty but located, as asymptotes locate a hyperbola. Empty but torqued: the spine braces against an antici-pated swing: there will be two actions, two doings, parallel and related; hence two verbs, the first to be expected immediately.

> As the cat
> climbed over
> the top of
> the jamcloset
> first . . .

—we are braced, now, for the second verb; but the sentence has other business, and we are given instead a distinction:

> first the right
> forefoot

—a clarification, but the verb is still deferred; meanwhile "first" has generated a new substructure for the sentence to complete. First, hence second; do we next encounter "second" or some surrogate? No, we encounter

> carefully

—an adverb as precariously placed as the cat's forefoot. And at last, a structure is acknowledged; "first" receives its answer:

> then

"First the right forefoot, then"—the left?

> then the hind

Though our local foreseeings are inaccurate, we remain attentive, and at last comes the verb we have so long anticipated, even as the cat, once embarked on this expedition, has anticipated, movement by movement, responsive solidities:

> first the right
> forefoot
>
> carefully
> then the hind
> stepped down
>
> into

This ideal cat, this verbal cat, this cat of linguistic torsions has
(though "carefully") stepped down not onto but "into"—

                        into the pit of
worse and worse
                        the empty
—?
                        flowerpot

Verbal flowerpots are as hollow and frangible as verbal cats are
agile. There is no more: we have examined two steps in slow
motion, and if the front foot has been where the hind foot goes, we
can feel as secure in the paradigm as we can in the knowledge that
two subjects are competent to govern one verb. This structure of
27 words commenced off balance—"As"—and closes on a resolution of achievement and precariousness—"flowerpot." It is one
sinuous suspended sentence, feeling its way and never fumbling. Its
gestures raise anticipatory tensions, its economy dislodges nothing.
The cat is as much an emblem of the sentence as the sentence is of
the cat. It is headed "Poem."

                    *   *   *

"Of course it must be understood that writing deals with
words and words only and that all discussions of it deal with single
words and their associations in groups."—William Carlos Williams
in 1923. "Either to write or to comprehend poetry the words must
be recognized to be moving in a direction separate from the jostling
or lack of it which occurs within the piece."

The surfer planes obliquely down a hill that renews itself at
just the rate of his descent. But for encountering the beach he could
glide eternally, leftward and inward and always as if downward, but
never further down: always hung midway on the face of the wave.
He shifts, precarious, through innumerable moments of equilibrium.
And the wave bears him and there is no moving wave: the molecules
of water move not forward at all but only up and down, their forward movement a pattern not a displacement, as his downward
movement is no displacement but a pattern: on and on, self-renew-
ing. So through mere words, renewed by every reader, the cat walks

safely forever. Williams had achieved "Poem" by 1930. Its wave
decades later is undisplaced, unspent, the poem thrown decisively
into the language.

Though Williams seems to have discovered it for himself, the
principle of "Poem" is as old as, say, Ibycus:

῏Ηρι μὲν ἅι τε Κυδώνιαι
. . . though it's in spring that the quinces and . . .

A "men" clause promises a "de" clause ("on the one hand," "on
the other hand"); "Eri men" offers to relate spring happenings to
other sorts ("though quince-time is spring, love assails me at all
seasons"). And a "te" foretells a second "te," paired members;
"te Kydoniai," producing the quinces, engages to produce comparable details (quinces bloom, and vine-shoots bristle). Such a
poem fulfills a syntactic undertaking, purely in a verbal field, as a
picture realizes potentialities of design purely within the flat picture
plane: which is not the world but a place with its own laws, as a
sentence is a governed system of energies, not the world's but its
own. And cats, verbal cats, stalk through poems, verbal quinces
bloom, flowerpots receive delicate steps, Thracian winds blow: all
verbal. As a knot is not rope but a pattern the rope makes visible, so
the poem is not consequent on the cat but precedent to the cat, a
pattern proffered and conceivable as pure syntax, but a pattern which
the cat renders substantial. And renders meaningful: the sentence's
poised "carefully" corresponds to, is substantiated by, the careful
precision of a walking cat. But for the poem, no cat upon the page;
and instead of asking what the poem is all about we may quite as
sensibly ask what an exploring cat is all about, and answer that it is
about the poem.

For consider the two of them as analogous patterns. This,
directed by mental options unimaginable in their intricacy but
limited by the availabilities within a language system, patterns
language which exists only in human minds, and does not dislodge
words. That, directed by neural feedback of intricacy equally unimaginable, but limited by gravitation, equipoise and material
impenetrability, patterns space, apperceived by minds, and does not

dislodge clay pots. Is either prior? As some cat walked before "Poem" was composed—and maybe only in Williams' imagination—so other cats walk after. We can no more imagine what it is like to be a cat than we can imagine what it is like to be a sentence. We think words, we think cats; and though God can imagine, we cannot imagine cats before cats were named, and detached by being named from the "big, blooming, buzzing confusion" Henry James' brother was at pains to stipulate.

* * *

"Which did the child learn first? Did he learn first to isolate 'mama' [*sc.* 'cat'] from the confusion of his sensory world and thereby to think mama first or did he learn the word mama first? The question appears quite impossible to answer. If anything, the word came first and the concept after. Only the word was not really a word till the concept accompanied it. Previously it was just a sound. . . ."
—Walter J. Ong, S.J., *The Presence of the Word*, 143–4.
And:
"Language gives the infant access to hundreds of thousands of years of human experience—millions of man-hours previously spent—developing the concepts with which language furnishes him. It is at least questionable whether anyone would have an effective incentive to think in the absence of a going language, access to the world of sound, and older persons eager to initiate him into the linguistic world. Even if he did have an incentive, he might well never really get his thinking drives off the ground. Instead of forming the concept of mama or man as he is in fact so urgently coached into doing, he might waste his time forming fruitless and relatively unreal categories. He might group together, for example, all upright, brown, smoothish things—chair legs, tree trunks, brown painted oars leaning against houses, and so on. Or he might form a concept grouping all small fuzzy yellow things: dandelions, certain caterpillars (but only certain ones), pieces of fluff from two of his mother's dresses, and other miscellanea."
—*Ibid.*, 144.

And a cat inherits none of this. But thanks to our access to millenia of human experience we can enter the shared world our language creates in our co-lingualists, and draw out of it like needles from a haystack certain trim words to make a mental structure with:

> As the cat
> climbed over
> the . . .

Williams drew, he said, on "the speech of Polish mothers."

*   *   *

Though "Poem," the language-disposing faculty behaving catwise, is unique in its neat suavity, its principle of syntactic leverage is discernible everywhere in Williams' work of the 1920's. At the top of a sheet he types

YOUNG SYCAMORE

then

> I must tell you
> this young tree
> whose round and firm trunk
> between the wet
>
> pavement and the gutter
> (where water
> is trickling) rises
> bodily
>
> into the air with
> one undulant
> thrust half its height—
> and then . . .

—half the poem. It is an effort to stop transcribing, because each phrase reaches forward. From line 3 to line 7 we are drawn past unit after unit of attention by the promise of a verb to fulfill "whose trunk"; then granted that verb but still waiting for the structure initiated by "this young tree" to declare itself, we press on, alerted (by "into the air with") that the dependent clause continues. "And then," a major structural node, undertakes yet a further dependent verb; the poem rushes on—

> and then
>
> dividing and waning
> sending out
> young branches on
> all sides—
>
> hung with cocoons—
> it thins
> till nothing is left of it
> but two
>
> eccentric knotted
> twigs
> bending forward
> hornlike at the top

No full stop, because no termination for the tree's energies; but the poem, an eye's upward scan, is over. We have been carried through it by essentially narrative devices: from "I must tell you" through suspensions and delays to "and then," past vignettes and episodes ("hung with cocoons") to "till nothing is left of it but"; and the terminal episode still secretes hidden force: "bending forward / hornlike at the top." The poem's system is that of a short story.

But the system contains energies left unaccounted, for the main clause it undertook with the words "this young tree" was never completed. Though the whole poem has explicated this young tree, this young tree's syntactic circuit remains open. We may associate this unequilibrated · energy with the poet's headlong generosity ("I must tell you . . ."), as though something had nevertheless escaped the telling. Or we may rhyme it with the failure of the trunk's gesture ("dividing and waning," after the integrated thrust that rose "bodily"). For to rise bodily is to levitate. This levitation was an illusion, the trunk's vigor abetted by the poet's enthusiasm. The tree remains, we discover, tied to earth, toward which it bends back divided. The sentence arches, unarticulated, into ideal space.

The sentence offered, left not really finished, becomes a prime Williams strategy. In "The Sea Elephant" gestures of sentences work like overlapping planes. He wrote poems by dozens, consolidating this discovery.

*   *   *

By 1944, summing up some 20 years' work, Williams had defined a poem as "a small (or large) machine made of words": more like a watch than a shout or an intimate whisper. It seemed important to distinguish a poem from something just being "said," given a public that will make this distinction only when the words are such as no one would say. And for the quick-witted such distinctions slip like sand. Perhaps the jamcloset over which the cat walked will serve to illustrate. A student asked (1969), "What's a jamcloset?"

"Jamcloset" is a word bound in place and time. It pertains to a half-vanished America with cellars (I write this in a ranch house with "crawl space"). Into the cellar every fall went the preserves, after an orgy of home canning, to be carried up jar by jar for winter breakfasts from the cool closet where they were stored. That was the jamcloset. And things unused in winter, like flowerpots, accumulated on jamclosets. They were in dark unvisited parts of basements, well away from the furnace. Naturally a cat would walk there. So any mention of the clutter atop a jamcloset might easily tip into nostalgia, and it is interesting that in "Poem" this does not happen. In that machine made out of words "jamcloset" is a term, not a focus for sentiment; simply a word, the exact and plausible word, not inviting the imagination to linger: an element in the economy of a sentence.

About 1930 a number of men had grasped this principle clearly: Louis Zukofsky, George Oppen, Dr. Williams, Charles Reznikoff, Carl Rakosi, Basil Bunting. Different as the work of each was from that of any other, they were (very loosely) associated as "Objectivists." The Parisian 1920's underlie the term, language as if indifferent to hearers, and an American quality underlies it too, American preference for denotation over etymology, for the cut term over association and the channelled path. Oppen's

The simplest

Words say the grass blade
Hides the blaze
Of a sun
To throw a shadow
In which the bugs crawl
At the roots of the grass . . .

—accords no monosyllable less importance than any other, not
even "a" in two occurrences, and "sun" carries no more intensity
of feeling than "bug." Words "hung with pleasing wraiths of
former masteries" (Williams's phrase) are not found in these poems;
such were the qualities the Objectivists sought to avoid. Miss Moore
was a heroine of theirs; Zukofsky in 1930, noting the Donne-like
quality of her

. . . round glasses spun
To flame as hemispheres of one
Great hourglass dwindling to a stem

implies that her effect does not seek to remind us of Donne, but
resembles the effect Donne can have on a new reader. (So Gaudier
and cave paintings.) On the other hand, he has us distinguish
between Stevens's

. . . Jehovah and the great sea-worm . . .

which is part of a machine made out of words, and Stevens's

Speak and the sleepers in their sleep shall move,
Waken, and watch the moonlight on their floors . . .

which ("climbing the stiles of English influence") stirs memories of
Lycidas (and gets admired).

They worked in utter obscurity, as if in Paris. Williams was
"discovered" only in 1948, when *Paterson I* suddenly attracted
reviews; Zukofsky and Oppen and Bunting not until the 1950's and
1960's, when reprints of work 30 years old began appearing, to
answer tastes a long time forming and still hardly articulate. The
1930's public heard of MacLeish, and Stephen Vincent Benet, and
Robert Frost (now too quickly dismissed as an Eisenhower-poet);

and journalism for which Hart Crane's suicide conferred importance
on *The Bridge* found no way to get interested in Zukofsky's "*A*",
whose author jumped off no boat. Yet *The Bridge* yields only to
nutcrackers, "*A*" to reading:

> "They sang that way in deep Russia"
> He'd say and carry the notes
> Recalling the years
> Fly. Where stemmed
> The Jew among strangers?
> As the hummingbird
> Can fly backwards
> Also forwards—
> How else could it keep going?
> Speech moved to sing
> To echo the stranger
> A tear in an eye
> The quick hand wiped off—
> Casually:
> "I loved to hear them."

—the emotion not stirring older poetic emotions, but new, implicit
in a subtle joinery like music.

    That history is still unwritten. It is a phase of the Pound Era,
contemporaneous with the *Cantos* that arrange citations and draw
intensity from

> "The revolution," said Mr. Adams
> "Took place in the minds of the people."
> (32/157:161)

and also draw feeling from the simplest words, arranged, unpro-
pelled:

> sharp long spikes of the cinnamon,
> a cold tune amid reeds.
> (49/244:255)

Pound was reading them, and they him.

SPECIFICS

Just a few details. We need not follow the 20 years' ins and outs of Douglasite orthodoxy, but Pound's interest in implementation exacts some grasp of what the fiscal reformers he kept in touch with were proposing to do. For the whole point was that something could now be done. What Douglas had to say—so simple, so persuasive—seemed one of those seminal discoveries of the unobtrusive kind whose power to alter the quality of life needs no demonstrating today. It is not naive to foresee great renovations in the working of a simple idea. Newton's laws are very brief, so are Mendel's, so are the electromagnetic equations out of which radio came. And as radio ended age-old isolations, so Douglas seemed to have shown how to end age-old insufficiencies.

To recapitulate: the Douglas hypothesis, that the money distributed by production will not buy the product, means that there is a perpetual shortage of money. This shortage must be made up by creating money. *The money is created as interest-bearing debt:* this, and not any quibble over interest rates, is what Pound means by *usura.*

The money is created without regard to need, but only with an eye to (1) generation of interest, and (2) in case of foreclosure, salability of the security.

Try to get a bank loan to build an unorthodox house: you will encounter the bank's fear that if you cannot meet your payments they will have trouble reselling the house they have seized. Thus the trend toward standardization of houses.

Try to get a loan for a project in which your payments to craftsmen do not enhance the salability of the product to someone unknown. . . . This means: do not hire Duccio to carve your church walls. Buyers (should it come to that) might not like what he would do. (The Franciscans in Rimini still do not like what Sigismundo liked.)

And finally: in a closed system money to meet the cost of borrowing money is most readily segregated by depreciating the product: bread grows worse. Things do not always grow worse because the system is not always closed; in times of capital expansion everyone fares well.

It was in the first glare of the Douglas revelation that Pound wrote *Mauberley*, with its "usury age-old and age-thick" and its "τὸ καλόν decreed in the market-place," its recurrent decline of standards ("Christ follows Dionysius"), its rewards for Mr. Nixon and its proscription of "the stylist," its blasphemy against Eleusis that made "harlots cheaper than hotels," the room alone more expensive than the room and the woman. That poem ended his "aesthetic" period; the "sensitive" man who did not know what was going on he peeled off like a shed skin and called Hugh Selwyn Mauberley. The Ur-Cantos, written before the encounter with Douglas, were put by till he could rethink the long poem's direction. Its scope, when he finally clarified it, was to be nothing less than a vast historical demonstration, enlightened by Douglas' insight; the first 16 Cantos, the first published unit of the poem, march straight from Homer's time, and Aphrodite bedecked in gold, to the World War which came about because gold was misapprehended. But he might expect to see the new age; a single lifetime had seen Clerk Maxwell's equations become Marconi's wireless. And as he and his correspondents concerned themselves with fiscal ideas, they discovered four main foci of interest, all active in the poem as it proceeded and all worth a little attention.

*   *   *

(1) *The Just Price.* Since production was no longer a problem, only distribution, the remedy lay in distributing more purchasing power. As to its source, its source was the community's collective invisible wealth—cultural heritage, increment of association—in which all citizens were shareholders. If I am wealthier as a shareholder in U.S.A. Incorporated than I should be alone on Crusoe's island, then this wealth can be computed and monetized. Distribute, then, from this Social Credit a dividend, its amount computed as all shareholders' dividends are computed.

But would prices not rise, as extra money poured out? They would unless restrained; and Douglas proposed not a freeze, as in wartime, of prices where they happened to be, but a Just Price arrived at season by season, reflecting the extent to which this season's communal consumption is less than this season's augment of communal wealth. At the shopkeeper's counter all prices would be reduced by that official fraction, and the Treasury would reimburse the shopkeeper for the actual discounts he granted on actual sales. Thus purchases would be subsidized at the moment they were made, in such a way as to cancel those unreal "costs" that always pushed prices past incomes. Thus the nation's real wealth, its knowledge, and its corporate will, would lubricate every transaction.

(2) *Stamp scrip.* This was a gadget, not a principle. Orthodox Douglasites disliked it, Pound was fascinated by it. He liked gadgets, and this one might serve as an educational tool. It was simply Silvio Gesell's idea of a self-liquidating currency which it would be useless to hoard under mattresses. Its appeal in a time of economic stagnation is obvious. In addition to firm money there would be circulating money, pound notes or dollar bills to which, at designated intervals, a stamp, say 1%, must be stuck to keep up their face value. It seemed an admirable way to collect taxes, since no one could owe a tax who did not at that moment possess a hundred times the money needed to pay it. It also promised to accelerate circulation, since the cost of servicing money kept inactive would eventually eat it up. (The "income tax" does just the opposite, bleeding value from currency only when it changes hands; thus people refuse transactions their tax accountants say are disadvantageous.) In Wörgl, Austria, July 1932, a mayor who had heard of this scheme issued 1-schilling scrip,

"Bestätiger Arbeitswert," work-certificates, which circulated quickly because they needed periodic stamps, and his town came out of the doldrums. Prosperity lasted (and among other things a bridge was built) until one of the notes attracted official attention by finding its way to a bank in Innsbruck. Pound's telling of the story in the *Pisan Cantos* (74/441 : 468) is for once a model of clarity.

(3) *Banks.* The national wealth derives from what we have and know—the cultural heritage—and from what we can do together but not singly—the increment of association. This naturally conduced to thought in national units,* and the emblematic *fasces*— the axe-handle surrounded by a bundle of sticks you can break one by one but not together—helped Pound suppose that Mussolini's government had its mind on the increment of association. And German and Italian efforts toward economic self-sufficiency seemed to demonstrate, as did Wörgl, that local currency can be generated to meet local needs. A state need not borrow from other nation's banks.

Of Germany and Italy in those years we have two main sorts of general knowledge. We know about their repression of opposition, including the German race-mystique and the miseries inflicted on Jews; and we know about their foreign policies, Hitler's obsession with expansion eastward, Mussolini's dreams of African empire. In his preoccupation with their economic recovery Pound was barely noticing these matters, so he and his critics talked past each other for decades. How the Italian economy really worked, or might have worked but for military aggrandizement, seems an unexplored subject, and to what extent he took slogans for implementations, concepts for intentions, no one can yet say.

We can say why he seemed to talk of nothing but banks. A bank, considered simply as a business, issues purchasing power in the form of debt, this debt, thanks to "interest," greater than the credit issued, and related in no way to the use it has been put to. So

---

* It is easier now to think of worldwide knowledge. Buckminster Fuller observes that metals from around the world—iron, manganese, nickel, molybdenum —plus a shipping industry plus blast furnaces and forges, are drawn on for the head of a common carpenter's hammer. Nationalism—countering his cultural internationalism—may come to seem the most evident imprint of his time on Pound's economic thought.

neither the cultural heritage nor the increment of association governs a reckoning of how much purchasing power is to be supplied, nor to whom nor at what rate: only the bank's calculation of the debt it can hope to recoup. Thus the supply of currency is regulated by merchants of currency, which is as though someone should have a monopoly on oxygen; and the charge made for providing it ("usura") is a tax on everyone's energies.

Congress, the United States Constitution had said as if foreseeing Douglas, shall have power to issue money and to regulate the value thereof. But private banks soon inserted themselves into this potential paradise, and the chance of a new fiscal start in the new world was lost. (Hence the Cantos on J. Q. Adams, Andrew Jackson, Van Buren, Senator Benton).

World trade in turn, and worldwide veneration of gold, made the banking system worldwide; hence those shady figures the International Bankers, at whose whim the world's supply of currency expanded and contracted. They made wars to create debts. They knew, Pound thought, very well what they were about. They became his arch-villains.

(4) *Currency.* Gold first appears in Canto I in Hades, where the golden wand of Tiresias emblematizes a prophetic power as rare and bright and enduring as the royal metal. At the end of the Canto gold ornaments Aphrodite, who is also "orichalci," copper-adorned, and is called the Cyprian ("Cypri munimenta sortita est") because the mines of Cyprus yielded a metal, named, from *Kupros*, copper, that was once as precious as she. Golden coins, the copper pennies Baldy Bacon hoarded in Cuba, these are still current because metals were once used for barter, and gold bars stamped by weight would still serve for barter. ("Pity to stamp save by weight," Pound quotes in Canto 87.)

But when a coin is assigned an arbitrary value, then two values are in potential competition: the value of the metal, the face value of the coin. These can be profitably juggled. Thus in 1724 a certain Wood had a patent to supply Ireland with small coins, on terms according to which every £60 worth of copper became, by fiat, £100 worth of halfpence. The 40% discrepancy was sheer profit, which Wood and the King's influential favorite, the Duchess of

Kendal, proposed to divide between them. Jonathan Swift roused his people against that scheme with six pamphlets, *The Drapier's Letters*, to such effect that Wood's patent was cancelled. This is a simple example of "altering the value," a phrase Pound characteristically arrived at by misunderstanding Aristotle's *metathemenon te ton krumenon.**

We may learn from the Wood episode to think of metals as metals, and not allow them to confuse our talk about monetary supply. "The moment a man realizes that the guinea stamp, not the metal, is the essential component of the coin, he has broken with all materialist philosophies." Sovereignty inheres in the power to issue money, which means the power to affix the guinea stamp. If it is affixed to paper we shall be less distracted by intrinsic values, unless we let ourselves think of the paper currency as a substitute for "real" money.

We may also learn that the profit Wood and the Duchess envisaged depended on a scarcity of small coins in Ireland. In scarcity, not in plenty, lies fiscal opportunity, and if no scarcity exists the way to affluence, Aristotle noted,† is to create one ("Nothing we made . . ."). This is also called cornering the market. Thus Baldy Bacon produced a scarcity of copper pennies, and the late Cantos repeatedly adduce the Portuguese making wealth by uprooting spice trees ("'A common' sez Ari 'custom in trade'"— (92/622:655).

*   *   *

Ezra Pound as a small boy watched his father, at the Philadelphia mint, assaying gold with an incredibly delicate balance, and also looked into crucibles where the dross floated to the top of the royal metal. Gold was romance, was beauty: beauty to adorn

---

* *Politics*, 1257b.16; hence the word *Metathemenon* five times in the *Cantos*. Aristotle was actually talking about the principle that a currency, having only the value assigned to it, becomes valueless (like the Confederate dollar) when its users turn to another. Like so many of the things Pound has mistranslated, this one ultimately does bear on what he intended.

† *Politics*, 1259a, where Thales the Milesian, to show that philosophers can easily be rich if they like, acquired, on margin, all the olive-presses in Chios and Miletus the winter before a large harvest. This device, Aristotle says, "is of universal application."

Aphrodite, its meaning corrupted by a tangle of fiscal ideas. And "What thou lovest well remains," he wrote in Pisa; "the rest is dross." He was thinking of Love as that refining fire.

> What thou lov'st well shall not be reft from thee
> What thou lov'st well is thy true heritage

This is the gold of the mind, which no thief can break through and steal nor any rust corrupt, and "heritage" is Douglas's word for all we know and care about. And no ownership inheres, with its letch toward monopolies (scarcities):

> Whose world, or mine or theirs
> > or is it of none?

This wealth is invisible, the form seen in the air, the pattern projected by the patterning mind:

> First came the seen, then thus the palpable
> > Elysium, though it were in the halls of hell,
>
> What thou lovest well is thy true heritage.
> > (81/521:556)

And against the form in the air he set as always the empty scarcity, the non-arraying of non-forms, vain:

> Pull down thy vanity . . .

These ideas of wealth are not extrinsic to the *Cantos*, but warp and woof. They frequently beat most strongly in the verse when we have no explicit hint of their proximity.

THE CANTOS—2

For 16 years the long poem was inaccessible except in magazine excerpts; the few who purchased the deluxe editions need not have been *readers*. Only in 1933 could a person with $2.50 or 7/6 to spend inspect a continuous sequence of Cantos at leisure, and what he could buy in that year still carried a provisional title: *A Draft of XXX Cantos*. Only then, if his memory or his library ran back that far, could a hypothetical serious reader discover that the three Cantos printed in the American *Lustra* in 1917 were obsolescent though pieces of them survived, and see in what kind of structure the Cantos he might have come across here and there—in *The Criterion,* say, or *The Dial*—were meant to function: this at a time when earnest sensibilities were still struggling to accommodate *The Waste Land* and *Ulysses*.

These had been available, complete, for a whole decade (*Ulysses,* to be sure, not readily available, but for scandalous reasons everybody knew about it). Moreover they are easier to get the hang of. Eliot's poem, about the length of two Cantos, offers a tonal unity and moreover notes, and attracted explication after explication. It is about the right size to explicate satisfyingly. And Joyce's novel, however strange, has the merit of being a novel, with characters and something to paraphrase; it too, moreover, could be approached after 1930 by a book-length exegesis, said to be author-ized. It is understandable, what with other distractions, that still another and much less accessible "difficult" work was not wel-comed, though some enthusiastic things were said about the tone and finish.

Then only a year later there were *Eleven New Cantos*, of which perhaps two might tempt an anthologist; then three years after that *The Fifth Decad of Cantos*, amid great uneasiness about Mussolini; and in another three years—1940—*Cantos LII–LXXI*, with the war against the Axis under way and no one anxious to read of Chinese dynasties, certainly not from that particular author. Not until the 1950's, when controversy over *The Pisan Cantos* had made the topic urgent, did serious discussion commence, and to make its points serious study had to talk as though out of access to a critical tradition that in fact had never existed.

There is no substitute for critical tradition: a continuum of understanding, early commenced. Remy de Gourmont surmised that the *Iliad* discovered today in the ruins of Herculaneum "would produce only some archaeological sensations," interesting exactly as is *The Song of Roland*, illustrative of some vanished civilization. Precisely because William Blake's contemporaries did not know what to make of him, we do not know either, though critic after critic appeases our sense of obligation to his genius by reinventing him. Something analogous is true of Gerard Hopkins, of whom contemporary taste, except for a few correspondents, had no chance to make anything; consequently, it is more of an effort than it should be for us to make of him what we do. In the 1920's, on the other hand, *something* was immediately made of *Ulysses* and *The Waste Land*, and our comfort with both works after 50 years, including our ease at allowing for their age, seems derivable from the fact that they have never been ignored.

But it is reasonably true to say that the first generation of admirers of the *Cantos* is not only alive today, but consists mostly of readers who were not born when the first Cantos were published, and became interested while the last ones were being written. Hence the paradox that an intensely topical poem has become archaic without ever having been contemporary: archaic in an honorific sense, like the gently smiling marbles whose craftsmanship we welcome like Brancusi's though the imaginations that made them escape us wholly.

*   *   *

What might have been noticed, what might we now take for granted, had the enterprise had a normal critical history? For one thing, the relatively simple unity of the first published sequence, *A Draft of XVI. Cantos | for the Beginning of a Poem of some Length.* Homer's world is in the first of these Cantos, the war only eight years ended occupies much of the last one, and if numerous incarnations of Odysseus appear, we may remember that Odysseus was sailing away from a war, and a war from which subsequent Western consciousness dates. Wars, ruins, destructions—a crumbling wall in Mantua, smoke over Troy—these are never far out of mind, and heroes have ill luck, Le Cid proscribed, Malatesta despoiled. This is postwar poetry, as much so as *The Waste Land.* In the seventh Canto today's Paris, today's London are peopled by ghosts, and the eighth, looking back at the seventh, commences by quoting *The Waste Land*: "These fragments you have shelved (shored)."

In these 16 cantos we may also recognize a sketch of Ezra Pound's mental fortunes, from his first going down to the ship to his recent days in Paris, listening to Fernand Léger talk about the War and Lincoln Steffens talk about the Russian Revolution, that decisive sign that a large part of the world had broken with its own past. We find also a compendium of his interests and styles: Seafarer, Imagism, Provençal versions, Chinese poetry, contemporary satires, vision-poems, dramatic monologues, elegies. These styles help us block the sequence into five groups, of which only the third, the Malatesta group, offers a wholly novel rhetoric:

[Overture]

I   Homer: Odysseus and the dead. Glimpse of Aphrodite.   *Greece*

II Metamorphoses: Homeric Hymn to Dionysus, via Ovid.   *Rome*

III "I sat . . ." Declined fortunes of poet, hero, culture; but contains a vision of gods.   *Now*

[Phantastikon Group]

IV Actaeon/Vidal, Greece/Provence. Quivering, flickering.
V   Catullus/Sappho. The murders.
VI Eleanor, Bernart de Ventadorn, Sordello.
VII A present pervaded by ghosts; the dead more alive.

[Malatesta Group]

VIII He concentrates the life of a time. Wars, artists.
IX   The Tempio. The post-bag. (Two emblems of *The Cantos*).
X   His enemies gather forces. The burning in effigy.
XI   His decline (Cf. Le Cid, Canto III). "In the gloom, the gold."

[Moral exempla]

XII Baldy Bacon; "the Honest Sailor." Finance and perverted fertility.
XIII Kung. He says things Greek philosophers don't say.

[Hell Group]

XIV England as Hell, "without dignity, without tragedy."
XV   Exit from Hell, Plotinus aiding.
XVI Visions outside Hell, descent to earthly Paradise, and voices bringing news of the European War.

The apparitions, the blurred identities, the kaleidoscopic glitter of the fourth through seventh cantos may be helpfully referred to Pound's 1912 remarks on the *phantastikon*, a precarious mental state "circumvolved" about its possessor like a soap bubble "reflecting sundry patches of the macrocosmos." "Shall I," he asks in the abandoned version of Canto I,

> Confuse my own phantastikon,
> Or say the filmy shell that circumscribes me
> Contains the actual sun;
>   confuse the thing I see
> With actual gods behind me?

So here in Canto III, sitting on the customhouse steps and gazing across the Grand Canal at splendors he has not the money to visit, he imagines gods floating in the azure air, and indulges (Cantos IV–VII) a kaleidoscope of fancies, visions, glimpses, flickering

From the Dogana's steps, Venice.

wonders that merge into postwar unreality. It is like a compendium
of Pound's early poetry, economically rewritten: then suddenly cut
off and confronted with an order of reality which that early poetry
had always felt it ought to transcend: authentic documents that
survive from the past, commencing with a Malatesta letter of which
the first words are partly obliterated. The Malatesta sequence is the
rappel à l'ordre, as it were real things pasted onto the page (the
cubists used newspaper scraps); it corresponds to the scrap of
authenticity, "Lo Sordels si fo di Mantoana," which ("Hang it all!")
rebuked Robert Browning's *phantastikon*.

But the Malatesta actualities are given in English, an English
moreover that now and again goes out of its way to remind us that
a man in the 1920's is writing it. On a given moment, layered times
converge, as in Canto I the time of the subject (Odysseus), the time
denoted by the style (Seafarer), the present time of writing. And

("Lie quiet Divus") there may often be a fourth, when the subject incorporates some earlier subject: Divus encompassing Homer, Ovid retelling a story he found in the Homeric Hymns, an imagined contemporary of Sigismundo's, chronicling. And a fifth, the time of reading, very evident when the time of writing has itself become history. Canto II's oblique protest against the Prohibition Amendment recalls an America as far removed in 1970 as were Reconstruction days when the Canto was written.

The subject? Vortices and their dissipation. Four of the five groups end with a dying fall: Le Cid proscribed and the poet penniless (3), London become a place of locust-shells (7), Malatesta ruined (11), much of Europe destroyed (16). And near the center, in the ninth Canto, we find two structural models for the poem: Sigismundo's post-bag, Sigismundo's Tempio: the one a clutch of documents proper to one time, the other a deliberate concentration of pieties and traditions, the parts finely crafted (and the structure unfinished).

*   *   *

The "So that" which ended Canto I now opens Canto XVII; the second block, Cantos 17–27, commences with a new metamorphosis, the speaker becoming Dionysus' vinestock, "So that the vines burst from my fingers." We seem to be installed in the classical world, but it is too tidy to be anything but a Renaissance painting:

> ... the cities set in their hills
> And the goddess of the fair knees
> Moving there, with the oak-woods behind her,
> The green slope, with white hounds
> leaping about her ...
> (17/76:80)

And in fact the first sequence began with the Renaissance likewise; the mention of Divus is in part meant to remind us that the Greek and Latin materials are those the mind of the Renaissance was preoccupied with. Once more, in this second sequence, the sweep is from the Renaissance to the Revolution in Russia; from Venice with its "forest of marble" (17) to the chant of "the labours of tovarisch" (27)—

>   These are the labours of tovarisch
>   That tovarisch wrecked the house of the tyrants,
>   And rose, and talked folly on folly,
>   And walked forth, and lay in the earth . . .
>   Saying: . . .
>   Nothing I build
>   And I reap
>   Nothing . . . .
>
>   (27/131:136)

Venice is a place to travel to: this second sequence is full of people journeying, Marco Polo to Cathay, Este to the Holy Land, the young student to see "old Levy," the still younger student ("in my young youth") to phantasmagoric Venice.

Venice is perhaps the central preoccupation of the sequence: not a Tempio, imperfect register of one man's will, but a splendid mortuary place entoiled for centuries with the history of financial practices. The will to splendor built it, feeling its way: banishing "the stink of the dungeons" to another place but not abolishing the dungeons; then finding it unfitting that "the most serene Doge can scarce / stand upright in his bedroom," and finally passing appropriations "for pulchritude of the palace." Each step, registered in Minute Books, had to be formulated as a committee objective, and what emerged was a congeries of gleaming and glancing effects which we are never allowed to see except in mist or by night:

>   Dye-pots in the torch-light,
>   The flash of wave under prows,
>   And the silver beaks rising and crossing.
>   Stone trees, white and rose-white in the darkness,
>   Cypress there by the towers,
>   Drift under hulls in the night.
>
>   (17/78:82)

It was a place to entrance a young man from Wyncote:

>   And
>   I came here in my young youth
>   and lay there under the crocodile

"The crocodile," bestridden by St. Theodore, Venice.

> By the column, looking East on the Friday,
> And I said: Tomorrow I will lie on the South side
> And the day after, south west.
> And at night they sang in the gondolas . . .
>   (26/121:126)

He had proposed to devote one day to gazing at the Palazzo's west façade, another to the panorama across the lagoon, a third to the Salute dome and the Canal. But this is a place where artists were corrupted; we find Titian submitting the low bid for a piece of interior decoration ("the picture of the land battle in the Hall of our Greater Council"), collecting the perquisite, and for 20 years doing nothing.

Here *virtù* is entangled in gain. In the middle of Canto XXV, between the minute-books and the documents concerning the disgraceful behavior of Titian, we find a contrasting *virtù*, that of the Roman poetess Sulpicia:*

> Mist gone.
>   And Sulpicia
> green shoot now, and the wood
> white under new cortex
>   (25/117:122)

—something to set against the "forest of marble," along with her love song ("God does no harm to lovers") and the evocation of the sculptor seeing the form in the air. Venice arose from the water a stone Aphrodite, splendidly dead as the dead Ignez da Castro. This critique will ultimately be developed in Pisa, in the Canto (83) that celebrates water, that begins with Pindar's word "HUDOR" from the distich that supplied "gold in the gloom," and that tells us of natural growth by watercourses:

> The roots go down to the river's edge
> and the hidden city moves upward
> white ivory under the bark.
>   (83/530:565)

---

* What we have of her work is preserved in Tibullus' *Elegies*, as other poets are preserved in the *Cantos*. Pound reactivates the whole motif in the Paradisaic sequence, Canto 93.

"Dryad, thy peace is like water." There are no Dryads in the stone forest of Venice: only Nerea in her cave, "she like a great shell curved," in that place whose aesthetic so answers the aesthetic of the nineties, effects in mist and darkness, "the light not of the sun."

*　　*　　*

Later 1–16 and 17–27 were joined without division, and three more cantos added to make a first block of 30. The span of this no longer reaches from the Renaissance to modern times but makes a closed loop within the Renaissance, with modern extrapolations. We commence with Divus, 1538, and close with the death of Pope Alexander Borgia, 1503: close, moreover, despite this death, on a note of hope, for Hieronymous Soncinus is initiating the kind of printing activity that will bring Divus' Homer into the public domain. Even the wreck of the Malatesta is subsumed: the quotation from Soncinus concludes,

> and as for text we have taken it
> from that of Messire Laurentius
> and from a codex once of the Lords Malatesta . . .
> （30/149:154)

—the grim phrase of the expropriators, "olim de Malatestis," (11/50:54) made into a flourish of accomplishment. They are printing Petrarch's *Rime*. That was the New Birth, we are always told. Looking around at its heritage we may think it was a stillbirth. Why?

*　　*　　*

Pound's heuristic device is always the subject-rhyme. To elucidate the Italian New Birth of circa 1500, he compares it with the American of circa 1770. Specifically, Jefferson and his successors building a nation are rhymed with Malatesta building the Tempio, and a careful structural parallel enforces this rhyme.

Four Malatesta Cantos, 8–11, had been followed by a sharply contrasting pair: Baldy Bacon (12), Kung (13). In *Eleven New Cantos*, four American Cantos (31–34) are followed by a similar sharp contrast: Mitteleuropa (35), Cavalcanti (36). And as when Jefferson first appeared (21) his letter about a musical gardener was linked by an Italian phrase to Sigismundo's letter about a painter

(8), so now the Malatesta family motto, *Tempus loquendi, tempus tacendi*, stands at the head of Canto 31 to rhyme a bundle of Jefferson–Adams letters with Malatesta's post-bag, and by extension a four-canto sequence of documents with the four-canto sequence of Malatestan actualities. Like the Tempio, the nation is being built by minds scrupulous over detail: "screw more effective if placed below surface of water"; "type-founding to which antimony is essential"; "for our model, the Maison Quarrée of Nismes."*

Coming after this, the Cavalcanti Canzone (36) is a model of focused intellection and passion, as its counterpart the *cento* from Kung (13) is a model of practical good sense. One might have expected them to be interchanged, the Canzone d'Amore to comment on the loves of Sigismundo and rebuke the tale of perversion narrated to bankers, the Kung to comment on the Founding Fathers' statecraft and rebuke the Mitteleuropan civic slither. But by transposing them Pound twists these themes together: love, statecraft, order, precision of thought, laconic wisdom, fertility, sound money. Any of these may represent the whole cluster. Thus a Canto (39) of ritual fertility—

> "Fac deum!" "Est factus."
> Ver novum!
>   ver novum!
> Thus made the spring . . .
>
> Dark shoulders have stirred the lightning
> A girl's arms have nested the fire,
> Not I but the handmaid kindled
>   Cantat sic nupta
> I have eaten the flame.
>
> (39/195:204)

—offsets the machinations of bankers and cannon-merchants, and a later Canto (47) of identification with the fructive powers of nature—

> By prong have I entered these hills:
> That the grass grow from my body,
> That I hear the roots speaking together,

---

* Model, that is, for the Virginia capitol: T. Jefferson, architect.

The air is new on my leaf,
The forked boughs shake with the wind.
Is Zephyrus more light on the bough, Apeliota
more light on the almond branch?

                    (47/238:248)

—follows the denunciation of the Bank of England (46) and precedes the account (48) of cadavers being trampled into the ground by a German sergeant "to get the place smooth for the Kaiser." We are deep in fiscal perceptions. Death and life work as metaphors for money; the power of gold, as a metaphor for death and life.

Gold was innocent stuff when we first encountered it, ornamenting Aphrodite at the end of the first Canto, in the citation drawn from Homeric foretime when copper (orichalci) was equally glamorous. But by Canto 2 traders are trying to sell the god ("mad for a little slave money"); by Canto 3 Le Cid, tricky as Odysseus, has realized that a box of sand will pass at the moneylender's for a box of gold so long as he does not open it ("credit" means "he believes"); in Canto 4 Danaë awaits the fructifying golden shower, on "the gilded tower of Ecbatan" which was both King Deioces' treasure-house and the representation of the sun.*

In Canto 12 copper, the Homeric orichalc, reappears in the form of little copper pennies. This Canto consists of three fiscal parables, two long ones grouped round a short one. The first long parable is the story of Francis (Baldy) Bacon, whom the young Pound had met in New York and the middle-aged Pound kept in touch with till the 1940's, another tricksome Odysseus who had discovered that currency might be something to monopolize. He bought up all the little copper pennies in Cuba and released them again at a premium. They were public centavos, but Baldy had the supply cornered. The other long parable is John Quinn's Tale of the Honest Sailor, who rose to the ownership of a "whole line of steamers," all the time supposing the boy he was bringing up had sprung from his belly, begotten by "a rich merchant in Stambouli."

---

* Herodotus, 1.98. The city was built in seven circles, colored to represent the heavenly bodies: hence, at the opening of Canto 74, "the city of Dioce whose terraces are the colour of stars."

This misapprehension rhymes with the sentiments of the bankers
to whom Quinn is talking, bankers who invest

> in new bank buildings
> productive of bank buildings
> And not likely to ease distribution,
> (12/55:59)

and suppose ("quintessential essence of usurers") that some natural
process increases the amount of money they share. So usury rhymes
with sexual perversion.* The unobtrusive story, between these two,
of the Portuguese whose great fortune was founded on the natural
increase of little pigs, anticipates the story (Cantos 42–43) of the
Bank of Siena whose base of credit was

> the abundance of nature
> with the whole folk behind it.
> (52/257:267)

En route to this illumination, we encounter other effects of
money. Money debases the arts and customs of Venice. Madame
Hyle comes

> Clothed with the light of the altar
> And with the price of the candles.
> "Honour? Balls for yr. honour!
> Take two million and swallow it."
> (30/148:153)

Then John Quincy Adams in young America notes

> Banks breaking all over the country,
> Some in a sneaking, some in an impertinent manner ...
> prostrate every principle of economy,
> (34/167:171)

* Hence when we read,

> interest on all it creates out of nothing
> the buggering bank has
> (77/468:497)

we may note the calculation behind the epithet.

and Martin Van Buren discerns the Bank of the United States

> "employing means at the bank's disposal
> in deranging the country's credits, obtaining by panic
> control over public mind" . . .
>
> Bank president controlling government's funds
> to the betrayal of the nation.
>
> (37/184:190)

*　　*　　*

As the *Fifth Decad of Cantos* commences we find the Bank at Siena being founded, the Monte dei Paschi, Mountain of the Grazing Lands, an instrument to monetize the abundance of nature, lending its money

> to whomso can best use it USE it
> (*id est, più utilmente*)
> to good of their houses, to benefit of their business
> as of weaving, the wool trade, the silk trade
>
> (42/210:218)

Unlike Baldy Bacon or the Bank of the United States, this Bank will not prosper by creating shortages. Nor will its profit be the difference between its borrowing and its lending rates; that difference, a mere $\frac{1}{2}\%$, is for bookkeeping expenses. Yet it profits, and distributes communal dividends. The rhetoric, still documentary, shifts toward exultation. Here is something promising, something new. Yet how does it work exactly?

For just here we encounter a kind of difficulty that will bulk larger and larger as the *Cantos* progress. The theme that unites the Monte dei Paschi Cantos to the theme of fertility, and will link the contrasted Bank of England (Canto 46) to themes of perversion and illusion, is easily stated. The Monte's capital did not conceal a bottomless debt for borrowers to fill, but was guaranteed by income from the city's grazing lands toward Grosseto, 10,000 ducats per year, representing the natural increase of the sheep. "And," wrote Pound explaining this in 1935, "the lesson is the very basis of solid banking. The CREDIT rests in *ultimate* on the ABUNDANCE OF NATURE, on the growing grass that can nourish the living sheep."

But it is not explained in the Canto, but in a pamphlet on Social Credit. In the Canto it is virtually hidden amid the picturesque details, and while the facts are all present it is doubtful if an uninstructed reader could be sure he had assembled them correctly.

"Lo Sordels si fo di Mantoana" was quoted against Browning's *Sordello* to imply a discipline: fidelity to one's actual evidence. Thus the visions of Venice are lyric because it takes a lyric softening of focus—

> and the palace hangs there in the dawn, the mist
> in that dimness

—to convey the splendor of which Venetian clutter is capable. On the other hand the accounts of constructive energy are meant to be sharp and bright with phrases emitted as the constructive will encounters immediate actuality:

> And about the silver for the small medal
> (9/39:43)
>
> . . .
>
> Ten slabs best red, seven by 15, by one third
> (9/38:42)
>
> . . .
>
> . . . the aliofants aren't here yet and one can't get the measurements
> for the cornice to the columns that are to rest on the aliofants. . . .
> (9/40:44)

Hence the Malatesta Cantos, the American Cantos, the Sienese Bank Cantos conserve the vigor of actual documents, to convey a *senso morale* and a purpose. But they convey less well what the *senso morale* is engaged on: no description of the Tempio, and no such vivid image for the Sienese bank as the prose pamphlet offers: ". . . on the growing grass that can nourish the living sheep."

These two cases are not quite alike. There is no description of the Tempio in accordance with good Vorticist logic: one art does not attempt what another can do better, and the meaning of the Tempio has been fully explicated on the spot by Agostino di Duccio with his chisel. "If reader don't know what an elefant is, then the word is obscure," Pound told a correspondent; and as the word "elephant" stands for an animal you can go to see, the word

"aliofant" (9/40:44) stands for stone beasts you can visit still in
Rimini, charming creatures whose stone foreheads are smooth from
five centuries' caresses, and the word "Tempio" stands likewise for
a wonder you can see at Rimini or even in photographs. The
austerity that refused to describe it is comprehensible.

But the words "Monte dei Paschi"? What you can go to see
(yes, still: in Siena) looks like any other bank building. That is not
what the words mean in the *Cantos*. What they denote in the *Cantos*
is a perception about the true base of credit (the abundance of nature,
the growing grass that can nourish the living sheep), and this we
need to be told about. Though the facts are in the text we are not
told, except in a retrospective phrase ten Cantos later. So a poetic
opposed to generalizations is thwarting its own didactic purpose.

In *Cathay*, we remember, Pound not infrequently modified
what he found in his sources to yield, if not the authorized sense, a

The "aliofants," Tempio Malatestiana, Rimini.

fit sense which the reader can grasp without the need of notes. The reader of the *Cantos* often wishes for this kind of accommodation. Instead a rigorous morality that will not modify for his comfort but only for its own treats him as Li Po did his Chinese contemporaries who needed no help with what they already knew. ("You allude too much," Basil Bunting used to remonstrate, "and present too little.") *Cathay*, direct in presenting Chinese poetry, was obliquely a little book about the 1914 war. Cantos 42–43, direct in presenting documents, are oblique in apprising us of the true base of credit. It is a curious general fact that the more contemporary Pound's language becomes, the more it is apt to be evasive about its real import.

*   *   *

A Bank, then, to ease distribution and monetize natural increase; after Siena's history has been brought down to Napoleon's time, the great Canto on Usury (45) follows at once:

> . . . Usura slayeth the child in the womb
> It stayeth the young man's courting
> It hath brought palsey to bed, lyeth
> between the young bride and her bridegroom
> CONTRA NATURAM
> They have brought whores for Eleusis
> Corpses are set to banquet
> at behest of usura.
>
> (45/230:240)

And churches are not painted, and stone is not carved. These are far from being mysterious assertions, for nothing will secure a loan unless it has resale value, and "a painted paradise on his church wall" has none, nor a fresco (like Mantegna's "Gonzaga") that cannot be detached from the wall, nor the carvings at St. Trophime intrinsic with the structuring of the cloisters. Such amenities represent nothing but expense.

The Canto that follows the Usury Canto, winding up (since 1919) "seventeen years on this case," offers as the epitome of infamy the Bank that discovered in 1694 how to create money out of nothing and charge interest on the money so created. That was the Bank of England, to which the state had to go for such credit as the bank was disposed to grant. Here originated, we are to suppose, the "clog" Major Douglas diagnosed: the climbing of prices past incomes, the futile production to move which moves wanted goods, the conversion of artists to pieceworkers, the paradigm, in short of that lust for immediate gain that makes things "to sell and sell quickly."

> This case, and with it
> the first part, draws to a conclusion,
> of the first phase of this opus, Mr Marx, Karl, did not
> foresee this conclusion, you have seen a good deal of
> the evidence, not knowing it evidence, is monumentum
> look about you, look, if you can, at St Peter's
> Look at the Manchester slums, look at Brazilian coffee
> or Chilean nitrates. This case is the first case
> Si requiris monumentum?

And

> Wanting TAXES to build St Peter's, thought Luther beneath
> civil notice
> 1527. Thereafter art thickened. Thereafter design went to hell,
> Thereafter barocco, thereafter stone-cutting desisted.
> 'Hic nefas' (narrator) 'commune sepulchrum.'
> (46/234:245)

Whereupon (Canto 47) quiet rituals, very ancient, assert themselves, the lights go down into the water, and the poet's soul enters the hills and the grass, intrinsicate with the rhythms of immemorial time, fructive, waiting.

* * *

He did not need to seek out the glimpses of beauty; they were always near at hand, the sea, the light. It is into Rapallo's bay that the lights are put down; it was in the hillsides around Rapallo that the clicking of looms could once be heard, as though plied by Circe's handmaids; even so, but more literally, Samuel Butler had imagined that "Homer" drew such details from the country around Trapani. (Economic forces never ceased to impinge; Japan's quest for foreign markets hushed all the looms in those hills, "ten thousand after ten thousand," as Pound wrote in the second Usury Canto

[51/250:261], expanding this instance.) It was on an inaccessible Rapallo rooftop that the miraculous cat appeared, as though scouting for Dionysus. There was no way he could have gotten up there, to greet the sunrise from his iron rail. For days the Pounds threw him meat. When he disappeared there was no way he could have gotten down. And after Homer and Isabel Pound retired, it was to Rapallo that they came with their treasures: notably the Chinese picture book which another visitor to Rapallo helped Ezra to translate, and from the texts in which he made the "Seven Lakes" Canto in which the paradigms of natural tranquillity are collected. It is the still point at the heart of the work.

All the soul needs, ran one of his lifelong themes, is at hand, waiting. One need not buy nor own nor import nor burden oneself. One need only hush and look, in a station of the Metro, or from a Rapallo rooftop, or in a prison camp near Pisa where the larks visit, or on the lawn of a madhouse while autumn leaves fall.

*   *   *

And in 1940 the longest installment yet: 167 pages, ten Cantos of Chinese Dynasties, ten Cantos of John Adams. China, though not wholly unprepared for, is a surprise. The preceding volume had ended with two ideographs, the first in the poem:* they denote the Rectification of Names, quoted from Confucius' *Analects* (XIII.iii). Yet it is a long time since we heard of Confucius; that was in Canto 13, less than 60 pages into a work which has now passed its 250th page. Nor has anything else Chinese hitherto appeared except Canto 49, the tranquil vision of the Seven Lakes, with an Emperor's Poem and a People's Poem appended. But now attention swings fully to China. A ritual of the seasons from the *Li Chi* orchestrates the simple instructions Canto 47 transcribed from Hesiod, who had said only to begin ploughing when the Pleiades are set and the cranes fly high. Then the dynastic chronicle commences, from the 3rd millenium B.C. until A.D. 1735 when Kien Long (Ch'ien Lung) ascends the throne and John Adams is born. And Adams is one more Great Emperor.

---

* The one we find at the end of Canto 34 in the current American printing was added 20 years later.

We shall see that this is less arbitrary than it looks; Adams came out of the world that discovered China. Pound's source is the 12-volume *Histoire Générale de la Chine* of Père de Moyriac de Mailla, who, dead by the time his book went through the press in Paris (1777–83), had lived 37 years in Pekin and so far forgotten his French style that much editorial retouching ("fait avec la plus scrupuleuse discrétion") was needed. The Manchu ruled China in de Mailla's time, and he worked from chronicles they had had translated into Manchu (Mongolian): notably the *T'ung-chien kang-mu*, "Outline and Details of the Comprehensive Mirror," which in turn was ("tendentiously") abridged in the late 12th century from the *Tzu-chih t'ung-chien*, "Comprehensive Mirror for Aid in Government," of the strict Confucian historian Ssu-ma Kuang. The abridgment was made by Chu Hsi and his pupils, the same Chu Hsi (1130–1200), inventor of neo-Confucianism, whose ideas may have fertilized the "organicism" Leibniz passed down to Emerson, thus to Fenollosa and to Ezra Pound. Chu Hsi was Arnaut Daniel's contemporary. What power synchronizes such things?

Or protects a poet whose information is sketchy? The *Cantos* by now had used up much of their capital, and were confronting material the author had not known for very long. Pound's use of de Mailla began with page 3 of the first volume, and he worked clear through to the last words of the 11th volume,* "... le génie de ce monarque et son amour pour les lettres," very likely unaware that it was anything but impartial chronicle. No:

> The Confucian historian ... with all his loving feeling for detail, searches for eternal, archetypical situations; the *pastness* of the past (the sense, with all its potentialities for relativism, that the past is not the present) and the *becomingness* of the past (the sense that it is constantly dissolving into the present) are not prominently savored. Confucius establishes this feeling for the paradigm in history, beyond time, since his genius is for moral judgment, a type of absolute, and it necessarily resists the relativities of passing time and change in the human condition.
> —Joseph Levenson and Franz Schurmann, *China: An Interpretive History*, 1969, p. 49.

* The 12th is devoted to appendices and indexes.

The *Cantos'* use of history—witness the Malatesta and Venetian sequences—could not be better described. Nor could the 18th-century way to use history, as the phenomenon of Augustanism may remind us, or the Roman eagle on the American seal. De Mailla had found in China a kind of chronicle thoroughly congenial to his readers, who were eager to know that civilization was possible where the Christian revelation had not been proclaimed. And no volumes could have come more patly than did these to Ezra Pound in Rapallo, 1938, to reactivate the Enlightenment rationalism he had secreted during the first war and was drawing on once more as war clouds darkened. To know clear simple principles in a time of confusion, this is a great resource; to know that statecraft has principles not beyond grasping, that action can be taken and men (Mussolini) found capable of taking it, that history affords paradigm after paradigm. In 1914 he had used China as a mirror for the Great War. Now he would use China again as a mirror of modern Europe, and of eternal principles of government which men before him—men of Voltaire's stature—had been sure the Chinese record contained. China, the Enlightenment, the *Cantos*: it was like the conjunction of three planets. Hence a certain lack of resistance which enabled Pound to write these Cantos quickly despite the formidable problem of finding a style. He wrote, in fact, too many pages for the ultimate good of the poem.

Finding a style, for as usual there are multiple planes of time, one of which had to denote China itself. Skimming and note-taking, then enjambing the notes, gave him elements from which to improvise with great brilliance a "Chinese" idiom moving to gongs and cymbals, conveying the shock of clangorous monosyllables and the contained radiance of luminous details registered in ideograms, ideas with boundaries. Behind the concentrations, the staccato transitions, we sense the Chinese language:

> CHUN, govern
> YU, cultivate,
> The surface is not enough
> > from Chang Ti nothing is hidden.
> > > (53/264:274)

—sheer poetic invention, since the source is a suave French prose:

Tâchez, au contraire [said Tching Tang], d'imiter Kao-Yao &
Heou-tsie, qui furent d'un si grand secours à Chun & à Yu, l'un
dans le gouvernement, & l'autre, en apprenant aux peuples à cultiver
la terre, qui leur fournit les moyens de vivre commodément.
L'extérieur ne suffit pas, le coeur doit y être; des dehors affectés ne
sauroient tromper le Chang-Ti; s'il vous châtie, c'est que vous
l'aurez mérité.

To establish the second plane, the Enlightenment, French
phrases are allowed to break through here and there:

> Chun to the spirit Chang Ti, of heaven
>   moving the sun and stars
>   que vos vers expriment vos intentions
>   et que la musique conforme
>   (53/263:273)

The American poet's idiom breaks through likewise:

> Consider their sweats, the people's
> If you wd/ sit calm on throne
>   (53/265:275)

"Wd/" indeed! There he sits at his typewriter.

That makes three times, three milieux, and the fourth is the
milieu of modern imperial gestures, notably Mussolini's. The term
"Ammassi" (61/335:351) invites us to compare Yong Tching's
policy of collecting grain tithes against famine with what we may be
able to learn about Italian tax proposals of the 1930's. The inter-
polation

> (Pretty manoeuvre but the technicians
> watched with their hair standing on end
>   anno sixteen, Bay of Naples)

is meant to rhyme Han Sieun's festivities for the visiting Tartar
King with the display of synchronized submarining Adolf Hitler
(Tartar King) was shown in 1938. Here and elsewhere the lack of
pertinent information deprives Anglo-American readers of a point.

The question of policy raised by such communicative mishaps

is perhaps insoluble in the abstract. "Ammassi" and the submarines, it is arguable, have escaped our *paideuma* because they are random details. But all specifics, of the kind on which a poetic of immediacy feeds, are random, and yet some are widely remembered: Mr. Roosevelt's dog, Mr. Chamberlain's umbrella. Pound intended the rapid shorthand such details permit, and instead made work for another generation's annotators, which was assuredly the furthest thing from his mind. Short of sticking to the symbols cartoonists validate, which means working within the *idées reçues* of the press, can the present, the public present, be raised to poetic immediacy at all? "The present," wrote Wyndham Lewis resignedly, "cannot be revealed to people until it has become yesterday": an observation more pertinent, if true, than any remark about Pound's political judgment. It poses an unsolved problem throughout the *Cantos*.

THE ANONYMOUS

Eliot at the Garrick, leaning upon a stick, with an undertaker's demeanor; to whom an old friend, Dr. Bard,

"Now do not pretend you are suffering from rheumatism." And Possum:

"I am not pretending that I am suffering from rheumatism. [*con fuoco*] I no longer pretend that I am learned. [*molto con brio*] I no longer pretend I am pretending."

Then: "And what makes you so pleased with life?"

[Should *you* be italicized? To a shipboard acquaintance who thought the white cliffs of Dover scarcely real, Eliot once replied, "Oh, they're real enough," a statement to which four meanings may be attached according as each of the four words in turn is stressed.] Anyhow, at the Garrick, Eliot:

"And what makes you so pleased with life?"

And Dr. Bard, truthfully, "The wonderful horseradish sauce at our club."

And Eliot, with a voice in which "charity and patience with the feeble in mind were wonderfully mixed," "So that is what it is." [Should we italicize *that*? Probably not.] But then, in a whisper, "And what do you eat it with?" And his friend, also in a whisper,

437

"With smoked river trout." And Eliot some weeks later was observed eating smoked trout, and with horseradish sauce. It is nearly a poem.

*   *   *

"I no longer pretend I am pretending": that was his most insidious pretense. The Symbolist poem was meant to seem as if no one had written it, generated by the autonomous language. Discounting the Romantic magic that had entered Symbolism, we may note how what Eliot absorbed from French sources resembles what Pope absorbed from his Augustan ambience. Like Pope he is a habitual imitator, but (being post-Symbolist) a tacit imitator. And as Pope went to Horace, the most neutral manipulator of Latin diction,* so Eliot when he wrote *Burnt Norton* (1935) and the rest of the *Four Quartets* (1940, 1941, 1942) went to the most inconspicuous of English poets, the ones who flourished a generation after Pope and were accustomed to take up a stance in a particularized landscape and meditate. Of all the famous poems that have preceded it *East Coker* most resembles Grey's *Elegy*, with its churches, its tombstone, its hallowed voiceless dead, its rustic intelligences. But more than it resembles a particular poem it derives from a tradition nearly anonymous because little attended to, as Eliot nearly hoped not to be attended to. He was simply pretending to ventriloquize the meditative English Voice.

East Coker opens with a transposed quotation and closes with the same quotation rectified; in passing between these terms it quotes Ecclesiastes and Milton, and imitates a Metaphysical poem, and brushes past many dead men's phrasings, and for several lines appropriates words in antique spelling from the author's ancestor Sir Thomas Elyot's *Boke Named The Governour*. To put an Augustan construction on these facts, we have only to say that the poem, going about its business, passes through certain forms of speech identical with forms of speech previous writers chanced to use, and is at those moments validated by their authority.

Such phrasings slip quietly into their new context exactly as if the man who wrote the surrounding lines had written them also.

---

* Or so at least he seems if, like most students, you have founded your notion of Latin diction on Horace.

["Shun and Wan had a thousand years between them," wrote Pound in 1938, "and when their wills were compared they were as two halves of a tally stick."] When Benson's life of Edward Fitz-Gerald yields the opening words of *Gerontion*—"in a dry month, old and blind, being read to by a country boy, longing for rain"— two situations are not being compared; rather, a grace of expression is being appropriated, the language containing not only the words Eliot found suitable, but for several phrases the very sequence of words. For the language is not a vocabulary, an itemization of vocables. One can make such an itemization; it is called a dictionary. A language is the tradition of what has been decorously said with it: that very tradition which in 1919 we were told could only be acquired by great labor.

To unite in this way a *Symboliste* heritage with an Augustan may have been Eliot's most original act. His way to it lay through *The Waste Land*, which uses the past differently, in a way less close to the vatic than to the grotesque. *The Waste Land* does not pre-suppose the anonymous Language as a sort of simulating device, to be specialized into this or that poem and imply in the process this or that persona. *The Waste Land* presupposes instead that there is something called Poetry, which has come to us from many lands and periods, and consorts with certain elevations of style, and no longer has much meaning. It is packaged like the official Poetry of a time when poetry is dead, complete with numbered lines and foot-notes: a Gilbertian gesture, and a gesture to validate something about the poem itself, which wears its miscellaneousness so jauntily. It is like a parody of a Poem (capital P), which in the course of getting itself written commences where Chaucer commenced, with April, and ends where the Upanishads end, with "Shantih," and manages imitations of Jacobean verse, of Shakespearean set pieces, of Sappho, of Dante, of *vers libre*, of Hindu oracularisms, and of the multilingual play Hieronymo devised to trap the murderer of his son. And it is full of quotations, not unobtrusive ones but ones we are meant to identify.

A parody of a poem? Certainly, a parody of a modern poem, if we are cautious readers in 1922 and have heard what gets said about modern poems. We have really no recourse but to look at the signature. The signature is "T. S. Eliot." Who is he? If we keep up with coterie poetry, he is a modern poet, this time taxing our patience to an extreme. If we move in the City, he is a clerk at Lloyds Bank, of whom it has been discreetly hinted that he may aspire to a branch managership. Signed by a bank clerk, the poem is nearly unintelligible, though it does have the air of having been excogitated at odd moments, in a musty office, on a high stool, with good lines that caught his fancy copied in. If we have the proper connections we may know that T. S. Eliot is the author of anonymous reviews in the *Times Literary Supplement*, very long and dogmatic reviews which employ the pronoun "we" as though on behalf of a pervasive taste and intelligence shared by men who have attended the appropriate schools and lunch with one another. That particular T. S. Eliot might be a younger Sir Edmund Gosse or E. V. Lucas, and a *Waste Land* signed by either of these would be a joke or else an inexplicable mistake.

*   *   *

But Eliot was a great joker. After jugged hare at the Club ("Now there is jugged hare. That is a very English dish. Do you want to be English; or do you want to be safe?"); after the jugged hare and the evasions, he addressed his mind to the next theme. "Now; will you have a sweet; or . . . *cheese?*" Even one not conversant with his letter to the *Times* on the declining estate of Stilton [Nov. 29, 1935, p. 15] would have understood that the countersign was *cheese.* "Why, cheese," said his guest; too lightly; one does not crash in upon the mysteries. There was a touch of reproof in his solicitude: "Are you sure? You can have ice cream, you know." (At the Garrick!)

No, cheese. To which, "Very well. I fancy . . . a fine Stilton." And as the waiter left for the Stilton, Eliot imparted the day's most momentous confidence: "Never commit yourself to a cheese without having first . . . *examined* it."

The Stilton stood encumbered with a swaddling band, girded about with a cincture, scooped out on top like a crater of the moon. It was placed in front of the Critic. ("Analysis and comparison," he had written some 40 years earlier, "Analysis and comparison, methodically, with sensitiveness, intelligence, curiosity, intensity of passion and infinite knowledge: all these are necessary to the great critic.") With the side of his knife blade he commenced tapping the circumference of the cheese, rotating it, his head cocked in a listening posture. It is not possible to swear that he was listening. He then tapped the inner walls of the crater. He then dug about with the point of his knife amid the fragments contained by the crater. He then said, "Rather past its prime. I am afraid I cannot recommend it."

He was not always so. That was one of his Garrick personae. An acquaintance reports that at dinner in Eliot's home "an ordinary Cheddar" was "served without ceremony."

The Stilton vanished. After awing silence the cheese board arrived, an assortment of some half-dozen, a few of them identifiably cheeses only in context. One resembled sponge cake spattered with chocolate sauce. Another, a pockmarked toadstool-yellow, exuded green flecks. Analysis and comparison: he took up again his knife, and each of these candidates he tapped, he prodded, he sounded. At length he segregated a ruddy specimen. "That is a rather fine Red Cheshire . . . which you might enjoy." It was accepted; the decision was not enquired into, nor the intonation of *you* assessed.

His attention was now bent on the toadstool-yellow specimen. This he tapped. This he prodded. This he poked. This he scraped. He then summoned the waiter.

"What is that?"

Apologetic ignorance of the waiter.

"Could we find out?"

Disappearance of the waiter. Two other waiters appear.

"?"

"_____."

He assumed, at this silence, a mask of Holmesian exaltation: "Aha! An Anonymous Cheese!"

He then took the Anonymous Cheese beneath his left hand, and the knife in his right hand, the thumb along the back of the blade as though to pare an apple. He then achieved with aplomb the impossible feat of peeling off a long slice. He ate this, attentively. He then transferred the Anonymous Cheese to the plate before him, and with no further memorable words proceeded without assistance to consume the entire Anonymous Cheese.

That was November 19, 1956. Joyce was dead, Lewis blind, Pound imprisoned; the author of *The Waste Land* not really changed, unless in the intensity of his preference for the anonymous.

*   *   *

And what is one of the things that *The Waste Land* says? It says, repeatedly, that people cry out of a bitter agony that no one heeds, so keen is our attention to nuances of style. Ophelia goes to her melancholy death, and we remember how she sang, and how she chanted "Good night, sweet ladies." We are apt to remember having heard better singing. Baudelaire would reach for the throat of the hypocritical reader, but he can only write words, later a quotation for Eliot's reader to identify. Philomel has her sharp tale of the barbarous king, which no one understands, even when she attempts his name: Tereu. Her song convinces John Keats that she is pouring forth her soul in ecstasy. We suppose that there is no pain, that it is a hoax, or a game, or a mythological puzzle, or a cento of quotations, or an oddly difficult way to produce the cheese.

As for the quotations, a note reminds us of the approach to the Chapel Perilous, and we are to put ourselves in the situation of the Quester, confronted with certain miscellaneous relics about which he was to ask the proper question, What is that? Eliot had once asked a similar question, confronted with a relic much cherished by those around him, a book of 30-odd plays: "Who, for instance, has a first-hand opinion of Shakespeare? Yet I have no doubt that much could be learned by a serious study of that semi-mythical figure." Who, indeed, has a first-hand opinion of Shakespeare? Who, indeed, has a first-hand opinion of literature?

Scholastic knowledge is accessible. *Hamlet* appears to be somebody's revenge-play, imperfectly rewritten in two stages. When that hypothesis was proposed in a book he reviewed in 1919, Eliot approved of it because it displaced from our line of vision the succession of Romantic Hamlets, and restored Elizabethan conditions to view. But he was careful also to specify that the Shakespeare who undertook the revision, and did not complete it satisfactorily, did so with certain private experiences on his mind, concerning which we cannot profitably guess. That is one paradigm for literature: a job with known specifications, undertaken when the psyche's powers are for private reasons rich and strange, and distinguished from journey-work by the infusion of that richness and strangeness. Scrutinize its formalisms and we shall encounter only the specifications of the job. Assess it for its autobiographical content, and we shall encounter not self-revelation but simply the conventions of the kind of work it is. We can only say, there we have been, but we cannot say where. We can say that the language has been mysteriously quickened.

But we (1922) are unwilling to say even that much. We are willing to take an interest in cultural monuments, which like Wren's churches are desirable to have about the city so long as they get in no one's way. We are also willing to feel that when a poet borrows from previous poets, his inspiration (beneath a cunning camouflage) has evidently failed. And we enjoy grumbling about an absence of poets; what can grow out of our stony rubbish?

The situation is plainly impossible; the poem that speaks to it is plainly grotesque. What it set out to do, as a sonnet-writer sets out to write a sonnet, was to assemble the heap of broken images a cultivated person—the kind Virginia Woolf found fit to talk to—would have floating in his head; to make a compendium of these, as certain artisans late in the 18th century made artifacts, to be displayed under glass, of shells and bones and stones and twigs and skulls. Availing itself of existing eloquences, admired eloquences, such as Shakespeare's, it stirred souls, or hoped to stir them, into asking questions: questions we are sure to address to the poem itself —what on earth does it mean?—though the force of such a question ought to strike back to the hallowed materials themselves: what can that song from *The Tempest* mean, which we appreciate so glibly? What did Ophelia mean, when she bade the ladies goodnight? The poem is a grotesquerie, often nearly a parody; Eliot even told Arnold Bennett that yes, the notes were a skit, but not more so than some of the poem itself.

But in time, inevitably, the later Eliot, that great master of the anonymous, appropriated *The Waste Land*, which was after all signed with a name indistinguishable from his. It is a very neo-

Classical poem now, and students are led through it. It failed, apparently, like every other poem, to get poetry taken seriously by the people who quote it, much as *Gulliver's Travels* failed to reform the morals of England. It enacts that attempt and that failure: an enigmatic, nearly comic poem by a poet who had ceased to exist by the time he had written it. For ever afterwards a man named T. S. Eliot lived, like the rest of us, in a world containing, among other curiosities, a poem entitled *The Waste Land*; and the theme of *The Waste Land* had been that there existed (but there ought to) no such poem.

*   *   *

To accept anonymity, that is one heroism; to say you no longer pretend that you are pretending, that is one compensatory amusement. To come to terms with a connoisseurship that will receive nothing you say, so keenly does it cherish only style, that may be either a burden or a relief. Ezra Pound sought to outwit connoisseurship, by devising a style inseparable from what it delivered; the author of "Thirty Days Hath September" did something similar. Seen from his angle, the impersonal Eliot became a richly comic personality. The story of Eliot no longer pretending to pretend was contained in a 1951 letter meant to amuse Pound in his prison. The story of the Stilton Cheese and the Anonymous was told him in Venice in 1965, after silence had descended upon him. He was silent throughout the recital. The recital acquired, in desperation, a coda: how the incident had been narrated, the same day that it happened, to Wyndham Lewis blind in his doomed flat; and how Lewis after listening carefully to the end had commented mordantly. It was at hearing Lewis's comment that Ezra Pound, in his 80th year, threw back his head in laughter. The comment of Lewis had been, "Oh, never mind *him*. He's like that with everybody. But he doesn't come *in here* disguised as Westminster Abbey."

INVENTING
CONFUCIUS

"Aesthetic finish" is apt to mean "covering one's tracks." Pound's habit of not covering them keeps his processes before our eyes, and his reverence for tradition. "Tradition" (*trans* + *dare*) means "handing on." The Japanese names in *Cathay* register such a process: China to Japan to South Kensington. Similarly Divus' name in Canto I registers the existence of a Renaissance Latin Homer, and French phrases in the Chinese History Cantos an Enlightenment intermediary. And in Canto XIII, the Canto about Kung, enough proper names retain French conventions of transliteration to make the immediate source unmistakable: *Les Quatre Livres de Philosophie Morale et Politique de la Chine*, traduits du Chinois par M. G. Pauthier. My copy is dated "Paris, 1841." Pound's, of whatever printing, came to him at the time of *Cathay*, 1914, bringing him a Confucius one could imagine speaking French maxims. The 13th Canto presents such a Confucius:

"When the prince has gathered about him
"All the savants and artists, his riches will be fully employed."

("Savants" acknowledges Pauthier's idiom; "artists" is a link with the Sigismundo of Canto VIII. The authority is Pauthier's *Tchoung-Young*, xx-12: "dès l'instant qu'il aura attiré près de lui tous les savans et les artistes, aussitôt ses richesses seront suffisamment mises en usage.") That was his first Confucius, commonsensical, practical, drawn chiefly from the *Analects* ("Les Entretiens Philosophiques"). It was also, so far as we can tell, the first Confucius known to China.

The *Analects*, despite a proportion of doubtful materials in the last five of its 20 sections, seems on the whole an authentic record of things Confucius said. *The Book of Mencius*, almost as old, seems a pretty reliable record of the thought of a disciple of the disciples of Confucius' grandson. Between them they portray such a sage as Pauthier's idiom could domesticate: "*Sse* dépasse le but; *Chang* ne l'atteint pas," with the question, "Alors *Sse* est-il supérieur à *Chang?*" and the answer, "Dépasser, c'est comme ne pas atteindre;" whence

> And he said
>   "Anyone can run to excesses,
> It is easy to shoot past the mark,
> It is hard to stand firm in the middle."

But here we encounter Chu Hsi once more; for Chu Hsi, the great 12th-century neo-Confucian, detached from the *Li Chi*, that long Han Dynasty compilation on ceremonial usages, two sections which, added to the *Analects* and the *Mencius*, have ever since constituted the Four Books of Confucian China. In so doing Chu Hsi invented the Kung we know. For when the *Ta Hio*, Great Learning ("Great Digest") is added Confucius becomes systematic, and when the *Chung Yung* is added, the Doctrine of the Mean, what Pound was one day to call "The Unwobbling Pivot," he becomes metaphysical.

Pound paid attention to the *Ta Hio* early; not long after writing the Kung Canto he rendered it "into the American language" from Pauthier's French, for publication (1928) by the University of Washington Book Store, Seattle. It was 15 years before the *Chung Yung* seized his attention; during those years his need was for a moralist of statecraft, not a metaphysician.

The *Ta Hio*, meanwhile, was something to believe in. It tells us that the men of old, wishing their kingdoms to benefit by the luminous principle of reason which we receive from the sky, perforce commenced by penetrating and sounding what Pauthier blandly calls "les principes des actions," and moved on through moral knowledge and self-improvement to the rectification of their families and their states; whence peace and "la bonne harmonie" in the world. Though scholars find rhetorical chains of this kind suspiciously post-Confucian, the *Ta Hio* is anyhow very old, and Pound was happy to accept Chu Hsi's judgment that the first seven paragraphs had been written by Kung himself, "on the bo leaves." It was a welcome and authoritative dissent from what he took to be the Christian practice of minding one's neighbor's business before one's own, and it suggested that world harmony would spring from an ethic a single sheet of paper could encompass. On January 28, 1934, he answered Eliot's standing question, "What does Mr. Pound believe?": "I believe the *Ta Hio*."

Still, one would like to know what "les principes des actions" may be, from the investigation of which the wise man must start. Digesting, gisting, such actions as Sigismundo's? That may have been the way to start.

* * *

By 1936 Pound was studying Chinese characters. In that year the "Ideogramic Series" commenced appearing: first Fenollosa's seminal essay, separated for the first time from the out-of-print *Instigations*; then the Pauthier-Pound *Ta Hio*, reprinted; then, as so often, the publisher dissolved his business. The third volume was to have been Williams's *In The American Grain*, inspection of which will indicate what Pound meant by "ideogramic." From the "Notes by a Very Ignorant Man" which he added to the Fenollosa reprint we find that he was searching with sporadic success through the leisurely entries in Morrison's multi-volume dictionary (1815–22), where he found for instance the character 新 the founder of the Shang dynasty (1766 B.C.) inscribed on his bath tub: Make It New. "Renouvelle-toi complètement chaque jour; fais-le de *nouveau*, encore de *nouveau*, et toujours de *nouveau*." In "the American language," 1928, this had yielded "Renovate, dod gast you, renovate," but Morrison's was ampler: "From *hatchet, to erect,* and *wood.* To cut down wood. Fresh, new; to renovate; to renew or improve the state of; to restore or to increase what is good, applied to persons increasing in virtue; and to the daily increase of plants." The axe is at the right of the character, a tree at the bottom left. The full maxim repeats the character twice, with the day sign (sun) twice between; in Canto 53 we find,

> Tching prayed on the mountain and
>   wrote MAKE IT NEW
> on his bath tub
>   Day by day make it new
> cut underbrush
> pile the logs
> keep it growing.

新
日
日
新

Dorothy copied the ideograms with pen and brush, inadvertently picking up two punctuation marks from the *Ta Hio* text; which means that by this time they *had* a Chinese text.

As they had: the Four Books in one volume on thin paper, with an English translation and most elaborate footnotes, anonymous; Commercial Press, Shanghai: a piracy of the great work of James Legge, his two volumes squeezed into one by omitting his Prolegomena and his Indices. The most unlucky omission for Pound's purposes was the comprehensive glossary, which annotates every one of the 2500 characters and distinguishes usages for nearly every occurrence. The student needs a dictionary therefore, and when he used this book in the Pisan camp Pound had a pocket dictionary as well; but on a six-week retreat in the late summer of 1937 he had no dictionary small enough to pack, and simply stared at the ideograms and the crib. "When I disagreed with the crib or was puzzled by it I had only the look of the characters and the radicals to go on from." He went "three times through the whole text," and rose from it with "a better idea of the whole and the unity of the doctrine . . . the constants have been impressed on my eye."

"There are categories of ideogram not indicated as such in the dictionaries, but divided really by the feel of their forms, the twisted as evil, the stunted, the radiant.

"The mountain itself has a 'nature' and that nature is to come forth in trees, though men cut and sheep nibble."

It was the old western dream, a universal language; but expressed in *natural* signs. Gaudier had read some of the radicals at sight. Gaudier's time had been short. Might a man nearing 50, though lacking Gaudier's eye, not make shift to decipher as it were the signatures of things? For this was his belief, which he had from his bones and also from Fenollosa, who had it from Emerson who had it, maybe from Chu Hsi's organicism, that in nature are signatures, that they attest a coherence, that honest man far apart in space and time may therefore read them alike:

> It is of the permanence of nature that honest men, even if endowed with no special brilliance, with no talents above those of straightness and honesty, come repeatedly to the same answers in ethics, without need of borrowing each other's ideas.
>
> Shun and Wan had a thousand years between them and when their wills were compared they were as two halves of a tally stick.
>
> From Kung to Mencius a century, and to St. Ambrose another six or so hundred years, and a thousand years to St. Antonino, and they are as parts of one pattern, as wood of a single tree.
>
> The 'Christian virtues' are there in the emperors who had responsibility in their hearts and willed the good of the people. . . .

And ideograms being pictures of elemental things, in the Chinese written language, however speech had been babelized, the signatures of things lay patent for sages to use. (Never mind that Kung had talked; the written record is what we have.)

Here, then, lay the validation of his syncretism: his faith that honest men—Fenollosa looking at brush strokes, Major Douglas inspecting the books of an aircraft factory, Gaudier eyeing the cone and the cylinder, Cavalcanti attentive to the movement of his heart and of the Italian language—should have perceived a single moral reality: brought to full articulation in the Four Books.

And it would soon be time to tie together the *Cantos*.

* * *

Looking, then, at Legge's Confucius, *Analects* v.vi: "The Master said, 'My doctrines make no way. I will get upon a raft, and float about on the sea. He that will accompany me will be Yû, I dare to say.' Tsze-lû hearing this was glad, upon which the Master said, 'Yû is fonder of daring than I am. He does not exercise his judgment upon matters.'" A picturesque opening, Kung upon a raft; a most lame and impotent conclusion, with a fussy footnote moreover suggesting three alternate lamenesses. Pound looked at the sign for *raft,* 桴 , with the "tree" radical at its left; and looked at the last sign of all, 材 , "tree" radical again; and was illuminated: "For the LOGS are there in the ideogram very clearly" (did he see a tree and a part-tree?): hence "Yu likes danger better than I do. But he wouldn't bother about getting the logs." "Implying I think that logs are used to make rafts. Nevertheless the translator in question talks about 'exercise of judgment,' losing we believe the simple and Lincoln-like humour of the original."

It was a lucky hit; though Legge's glossary would have told him only that what the second character means here is uncertain, we find it in Mathews' dictionary, entry 6661, as "Materials, stuff." In one compound it actually means "Department of Supplies," and combined with the sign for "tree" it means "timber." What Confucius was saying we had best leave to the Confucians, but Pound undeniably picked up something germane.

He was not always that fortunate, but that was thereafter his method: follow the crib, and when it flags, haruspicate the characters. If it flags, something is there to which the crib-maker was inattentive; and since these are natural signs, whatever is there need not take learning to see.

And ideograms began to punctuate the *Cantos.* And by November 1941 he was "making a real translation" of the *Ta Hio,* though into Italian because shut off from English readers; and as to "the luminous principle of reason which descends from the sky," he had at last in January 1940 gotten his hands on the text of Scotus Erigena, for whom "Omnia quae sunt, lumina sunt."

*   *   *

In the 1920's, at work on Cavalcanti, he had read of Erigena in Gilson's *Philosophie au Moyen Age*. He was very nearly the bearer of a secret doctrine: repeatedly condemned,* especially in 1225 and in part for his popularity among the Albigensian connoisseurs of fructive light, yet never extinguished: for centuries, with his neo-Greek theology, a perpetual temptation to the sober Latins. His theopanies—all things low lamps shedding diffuse divinity—shine where the neo-Platonic immateriality is perfused by a text of St. James and a text of St. Paul: "Every good and every perfect gift comes down from the Father of Lights" (James 1.17) and "Omne quod manifestatur, lumen est." (Ephes. v.13). And they rhyme with Bishop Grosseteste's deduction of the whole universe from light: "Lux enim per se in omnem partem se ipsam diffundit," and when it has reached the extreme of its rarefaction, and hence its minimum of luminosity, it is that of which things are made. And Love, said Cavalcanti, takes rise in Memory's locus—"In quella parte dove sta memoria"—and radiates like Light, "himself his own effect unendingly":

> Risplende
> in sè perpetuale effecto.

Brooding on these matters, Pound had written of "the radiant world"

> ... where one thought cuts through another with a clean edge, a world of moving energies '*mezzo oscuro rade*', '*risplende in sè perpetuale effecto*', magnetisms that take form, that are seen, or that border the visible, the matter of Dante's *paradiso*, the glass under water, the form that seems a form seen in a mirror, these realities perceptible to the sense, interacting. ...

—radiant gists, for a while in the 13th century held in many intellects: the self-interfering patterns from which and through which and

---

* During the Albigensian débacle, Canto 36 tells us, "They dug for, and damned Scotus Eriugina." This is metaphorically correct. But when Pound wrote in Pisa (Canto 83) that they "dug up his bones in the time of de Montfort (Simone)" he was confusing him with his disciple Amaury de Bène, whose bones, three years dead, were exhumed and scattered in 1210. They have neighboring chapters in Fiorentino's *Storia della Filosofia*, much underlined by Pound.

into which all corporeality constantly flows. Now might ideograms not represent these?

He assembled a Confucian "Terminology":

示　The light descending (from the sun, moon and stars). To be watched as component in ideograms indicating spirits, rites, ceremonies.

明　The sun and moon, the total light process, the radiation, reception and reflection of light; hence, the intelligence. Bright, brightness, shining. Refer to Scotus Erigena, Grosseteste, and the notes on light in my *Cavalcanti*.

誠　"Sincerity." The precise definition of the word, pictorially the sun's lance coming to rest on the precise spot verbally. The righthand half of this compound means: to perfect, bring to focus. . . .

That the lance should be the sun's, that "perfect" should mean "bring to focus," these are luminous intrusions. 戈 , Mathews 3358, is a spear; 成 , Mathews 379, is "to perfect," by one speculation spear plus cutting edge (at the left) plus man (enclosed): a man able to bear arms, therefore mature. But Pound saw in the convergent gestures to the right of the character rays entering a focus, and did not care that such an etymology was impossible, before there were lenses. Add 言 , a word, and we have 誠 , Mathews 381, a word perfected, hence sincere, true, honest: but in Pound's world of light-philosophers "the sun's lance coming to rest on the precise spot verbally."

Marvelous nonsense? The character occurs some 35 times in the *Ta Hio* and the *Chung Yung*, and 20-odd of its usages in the latter resonate with mysterious intensity which incites Legge to talk of "mystical significance."

> Hence to entire sincerity there belongs ceaselessness.
> Not ceasing, it continues long. Continuing long, it evidences itself.
> Evidencing itself, it reaches far. Reaching far, it becomes large and substantial. Large and substantial, it becomes high and brilliant. . . .

Whatever this "sincerity" may be (the version is Legge's) one cannot wonder that it put Pound in mind of light: "Risplende in sè perpetuale effecto." When he finally tackled the *Chung Yung* in 1945, calling it after the look of its title character, 中 , *L'Asse che non Vacilla, The Unwobbling Pivot*, he made this "sincerity" the attaining of precision of speech with oneself, a "clarifying activity" which starts with discriminating thing from thing, category from category, impulse from impulse, and (like light) "neither stops nor stays." De Gourmont's watchword, "dissociation," is behind this, and Arnaut's consonantal disjunction of word from word, and Cavalcanti's lost world "where one thought cuts through another with a clean edge, a world of moving energies," and Agassiz' reading of natural signatures, distinguishing fish from fish. And as to what Pauthier had called "pénétrer et approfondir les principes des actions," it now means Agassiz' kind of activity: "sorting things into organic categories," in Pound's mature view the primary moral act. ♫♫ is not ♫♫ , he told one enquiring student. Agostino di Duccio is no other stonecutter. Money is not a commodity. A share is not a fixed charge. In the *Pisan Cantos* if not in Cavalcanti, "memora" (verb) is not "memoria" (noun). Which leads us to the operative *virtù* whereby Dick is not John, Ezra not Kung: the characterizing patterned energy.

... Thus justifying, in a poem including history, ten thousand distinct particularities, to be distinguished without end in the faith that they will unify, leaves on one tree, trees in one forest, forests in one world. Throughout his long labor on the *Cantos*, the side of his mind that kept diversifying the poem was balanced by a tacit side that should unify it in due time. Preparing, keeping active, refining what should one day be the unifying force, was a contrapuntal activity, surfacing from time to time in interests the diversity of which bewildered readers. About 1914 he was thinking of his long poem with De Gourmont's "dissociation des idées" and Fenollosa's clustered particulars in mind. In 1917 he was occupied with Arnaut. In the early 1920's the theme was music; in the late 1920's, Cavalcanti; in the early 1930's, credit, an invisible *virtù*; after the mid-

1930's, the dozen or so ideograms by which, he was convinced, Confucian wisdom was shaped. Each led to the next, and all, he postulated, would one day enter his final orchestration. But by 1940 Europe had blown up.

*   *   *

A mystique of ideograms that touch on light had brought him a long way from the commonsense Confucius whose dicta about "order" and "brotherly deference" are recorded in the *Analects*. Such a Confucius, uttering maxims of statecraft, underlies the *Comprehensive Mirror for Aid in Government* which was the ultimate source of the Chinese History Cantos, and the Confucians who arranged the materials from which de Mailla worked saw millenia of history as an oscillation between unifying Kung and disastrous *tao*, the carriers of disintegration always the mystics whom the Cantos teach us to call "taozers."

> ... Down, down! Han is down
> Sung is down
> Hochang, eunuchs, and taozers
> empresses' relatives, came then a founder
> saying nothing superfluous
> cleared out the taozers and grafters, gave grain
> opened the mountains ...
>
> (56/302:315)

Very good, taozers, irresponsible peddlers of the ineffable; their doctrine, as old as Kung's, was as readily perverted toward froth as Kung's toward formalism. There was a vulgarized taoism which instead of cultivating indifference to death offered instead to render death indifferent by brewing an elixir of immortality:

> And there came a taozer babbling of the elixir
> that wd/ make men live without end
> and the taozer died very soon after that.
>
> (54/288:300)

This tended toward alchemy and the transmutation of metals and other opiates for the people:

> another lord seeking elixir
> seeking the transmutation of metals
> seeking a word to make change ...

HOAI of SUNG was nearly ruined by taozers
HIEN of TANG died seeking elixir . . .
(57/313:327)

But the Kung we can set against taozers is not the Kung of the Pivot, the Chung Yung, 中 . This difficulty was not perceived by Pound, who finished his work on these Cantos before he came to grips with the doctrine of the Pivot; and then he was in more trouble than he perhaps knew.

This Pivot is a transcendental norm, not the Aristotelian mean at which we arrive by knowing and avoiding extremes, but the "great root of the universe" to apprehend which is to incorporate a rectificative energy that will never betray one toward extremes. (Hence "the unwobbling pivot," because it is not defined by what it avoids, but stays in one place.) Chu Hsi had brought this concept into Confucian philosophy. And as St. Thomas' theology alters the gospels though their words are unchanged, so such a conception, once brought near the *Analects*, alters the *Analects*; in particular it alters the bearings of a word Confucius used many times, 道 , the way, the path, the course one's action takes. As he uses this word in the *Analects*, it already denotes not any way but *the* Way: ethics is unitive, normative; there is a principle all good conduct follows. In the *Chung Yung*, however, such a principle pervades not only human conduct but the universe. Nature proclaims it, the sun awakens seeds by its efficacy, it is implanted in every human heart. So implanted, it is our rational nature; to cherish it and develop our lives in its manner is The Way (Pound was to call it "the process"). Chu Hsi has a note on this, which Pound in 1945 translated, "The main thing is to illumine the root of the process, a fountain of clear water descending from heaven immutable. The components, the bones of things, the materials, are implicit and prepared in us, abundant and inseparable from us." This "fountain descending from heaven," on the first page of Pound's *Pivot*, like "the tensile light, the Immaculata" on the last page, was conceived by a mind impassioned by Guido's "Risplende in sè perpetuale effecto," by Erigena's "Omnia quae sunt, lumina sunt," by Arnaut's great figure

of the raining light, "lo soleills plovil": a mind intent on the uni-
fication of the *Cantos*, and disposed to perceive their characteristic
imagery in the ideograms. And the brilliance of his language averts
the fact that this clarifying order, this realization of the inborn
transcending nature, for which he found the word *process*, is called

道 : *Tao*. Yes, *tao*. The *Chung Yung* is dense with Taoism.

The neo-Confucianism from which Pound trustingly received
the Four Books was an aspect of Chu Hsi's syncretic mode of
thought. That mode, nominally Confucian, had assimilated much
coloration from 15 centuries of Taoism: from a tradition of thought
that talks of harmony with the universe rather than of modes of
government; that indeed tends toward anarchy in distrusting modes
of government; that is quietist, not active, intuitive not intellective;
that produces as model not the ruler but the hermit. So intrinsic are
such impulses to the long story of China that we cannot sort out
with any plausibility a Confucian orthodoxy which is radically
something other. *Tao*, The Way, Confucius used the term repeatedly; we find it some 80 times in the *Analects* themselves.
Chinese landscape painting, inviting the viewer to enter and lose
himself, is Taoist, so much so that Fenollosa's two-volume *Epochs*
has never a good word to say for Confucianism. The Seven Lakes
Canto, based on poems which accompany pictures, is Taoist in
feeling. The Pound of "The Flame" who imagined his soul rolling
back and growing translucent, consubstantiate with the blue of the
Garda Lake—

> Call not that mirror me, for I have slipped
> Your grasp, I have eluded

—like the earlier Pound of "Hilda's Book" who imagined himself
becoming a tree, and the later Pound of Canto 47 who heard the
"roots speaking together" and the 60-year-old Pound who wrote in
Pisa that "the sage delighteth in water" (and might as well have
written it in China), was Taoist in his deepest impulses, and it is not
surprising that he could respond to places—for instance to Montségur of which he knew so little and guessed so well—with a
geomancer's perception of hill and shade.

Yet hardly had the Seven Lakes Canto been printed when he was steeped in chronicles that inveighed against Taozers.

But do we not know—though Pound likely did not know—that the same Chu Hsi who blended *Tao* with Confucius also stood behind those anti-taoist chronicles? We do; Chu Hsi did; but the Comprehensive Mirror, highly tendentious, uses history, we also remember, to afford paradigms. One of its recurrent paradigms is the folly of trusting anything practical to the likes of, say Henry Thoreau, whose archetypal political action was not to seek office but to get himself symbolically jailed. (Or shall we say, to Ezra Pound, another symbolic prisoner?) A Confucian official might taoize on holiday, painting landscapes; a taoist might not govern; and if this is contrary to the doctrine of the *Chung Yung* in which the luminous clarifying principle will ameliorate the earth, well, it is contrary.

A man can grow committed to incompatible things. Pound's interest in the Fascism he idealized is continuous with his interest in the *Chung Yung*: in the belief that a ruler of sufficient sensibility, sufficiently steady will, could catalyze a whole people's *senso morale*. On the other hand taoist sanctions had been claimed for mere laziness:

> and the country was run by Yang Siun
> while the emperor amused himself in his park
>   had a light car made, harnessed to sheep
> The sheep chose which picnic he went to,
> ended his days as a gourmet. Said Tchang, tartar:
>   Are not all of his protégés flatterers?
>   How can his country keep peace?
> And the Prince Imperial went into the cabaret business
>   and read Lao Tse.
>   (54/282:294)

De Mailla's readers would have recognized that: it is like the court of Marie Antoinette.

Somewhere to the right of such slither, Pound was convinced, but not as far to the right as Robespierre, was a domain where statesman of unitive sensibility brought order without tyranny. He fastened on John Adams, ten Cantos of finely culled citations that are bracing but aesthetically dispersive. Now the poem had to converge. He turned to the *Chung Yung*. But the Chinese History Cantos, which never allow one to suppose that Kung may rigidify as much as Tao may slither, had a one-sidedness difficult to integrate, and it is not surprising that the terminology he settled on in his 1945 version of the *Pivot* tends to interfere with the reader's ever discovering that the word rendered "process" there and in the *Pisan Cantos* is *tao*.*

These matters are not after all irreconcilable, but events were now driving Pound too fast for an overall view. He was hanging on by sheer faith and sheer willpower.

*   *   *

A last ideogram: *hsien:* 顯 : Mathews 2692, to manifest, to display, to be illustrious. On the right, the 181st radical, *the head*. Top left, the *sun*, and below it what was once a picture of silk bobbins and now means *silkworms*. We find it in the Book of Odes, #267, quoted toward the end of the 26th chapter of the *Pivot*, the chapter with which Pound's version closes. Sun held his eye, and silk. Legge is flat: "How illustrious was it, the singleness of the virtue of King Wan!" Legge goes on to add that singleness likewise is unceasing. Once more, an impotent close. But the sun, the silk. And Pound rendered,

> As silky light, King Wen's virtue
> Coming down in the sunlight,
>   what purity!

To which he appended, for the last words of his *Pivot*,

> The *unmixed* functions [in time and in space] without bourne.
> This unmixed is the tensile light, the
>   Immaculata. There is no end
>   to its action.

---

* When Pound learned this himself it is difficult to say. The History Cantos picked up the word *tao* from a French prose with no ideograms; the Legge Confucius on the other hand offers ideograms and translation but no Chinese sounds. The apparent discrepancy between Kung's *tao* and de Mailla's could thus have escaped him for a long time. The dictionary when he turned up the character there would have offered the pronunciation *tao*, but that is not decisive even if he noticed it. Mathew's dictionary for example gives 17 different characters with different meanings, all pronounced *tao*, and he may have supposed for a long time that Kung's *tao* and Lao Tse's were different words.

Sun and silk: the tensile light. Thus in the *Pisan Cantos*,

> Light tensile immaculata
> the sun's cord unspotted
> "sunt lumina" said the Oirishman to King Carolus,
> "OMNIA,
> all things that are are lights"

And above, on the same page,

> ... plowed in the sacred field and unwound the silk worms early
>   in tensile 顯
>   in the light of light is the *virtù*
>   "sunt lumina" said Erigena Scotus
>   as of Shun on Mt Taishan
>   and in the hall of the forebears
>   as from the beginning of wonders
>   the paraclete that was present in Yao, the precision
>   in Shun the compassionate
>   in Yu the guider of waters
>   (74/429:455)

The unspotted sun's cord, the tensile light, Erigena: derived from a character in which no one had ever had the eye to discern such wonders before, That was his forte, the magnificent misreading. In the *Pisan Cantos* splendor on splendor of diction is elicited in this way from characters used as *mantrams*, to invent a Confucius far from the urbane sage of the *Analects*, a light-philosopher and perhaps as much an invention as Chu Hsi's in the 12th century. As in his cloud chamber a physicist sees an electron's trace, so Ezra Pound looking at ideograms in the 1940's was inspecting tracks left, he was thoroughly convinced, by the patterned energies at the roots of phenomena. I raise my eyes from this page and see a jet contrail, very high, luminous pink in the dawn sky. Those who are skilled in fire may read it. It proclaims Newton's third law, action and reaction, and Boyle's law that unites the heat and the volume of gases, and Dalton's discovery that cooling condenses water, and Snell's law of refraction whereby droplets grow luminous when sunlight enters them: self-interfering patterns, written in a lengthening trace in front of which, invisible, a hundred people are being carried through the high air.

THE CAGE

Every night, each man stretched out on his concrete floor, the prisoners relearned the dimensions of their outdoor cages: six feet by six and a half. Each received blankets, general issue, two. The nights are cold on the sea plain, and thick mist rolls in over land as low as the water. None wore shoe laces and none had a belt, lest he pass the time by attempting to hang himself. Deprived of this recreation they existed from today's exercise liberty to tomorrow's, from this meal to the next: the heavy padlock opened, the door swung a little to admit the tin plate and receive the latrine can. Dust settled on the bread as they wolfed it, dust floated everywhere, the chow detail as it marched down the row kicked up dust.

Not all of the worst were exhibited in the ten cages. A troublesome man might be dragged to one of the concrete boxes, to breathe its heat and poke his hands occasionally out of the roof port. It was said that within two weeks he would be lifted out dead. These were the "death cells," efficacious without an executioner. Executions on a proper gallows entailed a journey to another town, though an impromptu version by Browning Automatic Rifle might occasionally be witnessed from the cages when some maddened group making a break for it was mowed down in the drill field by marksmen in the four towers at the four corners of the camp. Had the guns been tardy the escapees would have had barbed wire to climb, and then met an obstacle, overhead barbed wire, supported on offset arms that projected from each fence post and, silhouetted in the morning mist, gave the Training Center the look of being surrounded by gibbets.

The guns were seldom tardy. One summer day eight out of eight escapees from the Special Company (mental cases) were freed of their delusions just a few feet from the cages. Another time, unaccountably, the guns despatched only seven of a party of ten, but the unscathed three were recaptured "within 20 minutes." No one ever escaped and was not recaptured.

This was, the guards said, "the arse hole of the army," Lt. Col. John L. Steele of St. Johnsbury, Vermont, commanding ("Steele that is one awful name" said a "cheerful reflective" prisoner, perhaps in pity). Under Lt. Col. Steele's command were guards and drill instructors and medics, the usual functionaries of a table of organization, and 3,600 "trainees," all of them under sentence (five years to life) for something—AWOL, desertion, theft, rape, murder—but here by great mercy allowed to work out the sentence in one terrible year of 14 hours' drill per day not counting close-order punishment by night, after which they might be privileged to re-enter the army. Every week the camp's peristalsis discharged some 150, while jeeps brought 150 more, manacled, to its processing stockade. The army's small intestine was always full.

The men in the cages were incorrigibles. The man in the tenth cage of the ten was different: older than they, and bearded: (Dr.) Pound, E. L.: no rank, no serial number. He was in a cage because he was very dangerous, as witness the heavy air-strip that was welded over his galvanized mesh, with so many welds the acetylene torches blazed blue a full 36 hours. Some of the inner mesh was then cut off, for no clear reason unless 50-odd jagged spikes (what to do but count them?) were an invitation (as he thought) to slash his wrists. He was sometimes tempted. A tough customer, clearly: he alone was never led outside for exercise. By day he walked in the cage, two paces, two paces, or slouched, or sat. By night a special reflector poured light on his cage alone, so he kept his head under the blanket. There were always two guards, with strict orders not to speak to him. Everyone, including the incorrigibles, had orders not to speak to him.

Short of a turn in the death cells, there seemed no way to prevent the prisoner speaking to the guards. He sat stroking his amber beard and talking, talking, as the sentry paced and pivoted, paced and pivoted. Five years later one sentry, a leathery Texan ("specially trained" as were all the DTC personnel to a toughness that would turn ordinary topkicks white) sat reflective in a Los Angeles bar near a gaggle of law-students talking law-student talk. "You guys been to college," muttered the Texan. "Think you know everything. I never been to college, and I know more'n you'll ever know." He then told the students of the Chinese Written Character, of Sigismund Malatesta and Isotta, of similar actualities. When that story was relayed to Dr. Pound, E. L., by then installed in the District of Columbia madhouse, he pronounced it, yes, a romance, though the emphasis, he recalled, had been on more modern history. Alas, people remember only what alerts them, and neither Mr. Roosevelt's derelictions nor those of the Rothschilds apparently alerted "Pistol-packing Jones."

This prisoner's status was irregular in many ways. Being in his 60th year (hence "Uncle Ez") he was permitted four extra blankets. After a drenching rain they came round to see how he had survived, and opened his door wide enough to insert a military cot. This kept him off the concrete but took up space. More rain, and a pup tent was bundled into the cage. Being a longtime handyman he put it up himself, in various improvised geometries, and took it down every morning. Then there was the book. He should really not have had a book. Only military and religious reading matter were permitted, edicts from the C-i-C's amanuenses, and from Jehovah's. He had brought the book there in his pocket, on the jeep from Genoa. Perhaps he told them it was the book of his religion. It contained no pinups or comics. Someone let him keep it, and moreover the Chinese Dictionary he used with it. He also had the eucalyptus pip. Probably no one saw that.

Book, cot, pup tent, despite these amenities in about three weeks he collapsed: claustrophobia, partial amnesia, bouts of hysteria and terror. The "top of his head" felt "empty," and "his eyebrows were constantly taut in a raised position, due to the heat and glare." They moved him to a tent in the Medical Compound. The other incorrigibles stayed behind in their cages. He was to remember one lying on his back like an ape, singing "O sweet and lovely, O lady be good": name of Bullington. Whether, to return it to conformity with specifications, they then unwelded the airstrip from the special cage is not known. It had served a purpose.

*   *   *

Before he came there in the jeep, handcuffed to a man accused of rape and murder, he had been for some years in a frenzy of exacerbation. In April 1939 he had sailed on the *Rex* out of Genoa to his homeland, and attempted to reach Mr. Roosevelt, who was "too busy" even for Congressman T. C. Pound's grandson. He did manage to explain economic principles to Agriculture Secretary Henry Wallace, who later forgot what they were. Senator Bankhead told him the President was "stubborn as a mule," and Senator Borah didn't know "what a man like you would find to *do* here." He returned to Europe in frustration, and the long-dreaded war came, only 21 years after the last one had ended, to confirm his views of the 1930's as clearly as the economic crash had confirmed Douglas's views of the 1920's. "This war" (he wrote for Italian readers, 1944) "is a chapter in the long and bloody tragedy which began with the foundation of the Bank of England in far-away 1694": when the power to create money, thus to guide policy, ceased to be the prerogative of governments.

In the 1930's he had begun to veer from Douglasite orthodoxy, which concentrated on mechanisms to distribute purchasing power while holding prices down. *The Bankers' Conspiracy* of Edison's onetime associate Arthur Kitson (London, 1933) caught his attention, and *The Natural Economic Order* of Silvio Gesell (English translation, 1934). While the Douglas of *Economic Democracy*, a book that does not go into fiscal detail, remained his moral philosopher in these realms, the specifics that interested him had to do increasingly with banks and money, and with the men behind them, bankers and usurers. *The Fifth Decad of Cantos* (1937) with the great

Usury Canto at its heart, is polarized between two kinds of bank: the Monte dei Paschi which monetized natural increase, and the Bank of England which coined currency when it chose, on condition that more be repaid than had been coined. And where Douglas in 1919 had argued that humanity was being impoverished by a mistaken accounting system that inflated prices by including false costs in them, Pound by 1938 was convinced that the mistaken economic system masked conscious evil, willed by elusive men who had gathered into their hands the power to issue what everyone else went into debt to borrow, and into still deeper debt to repay. And Germany and Italy had demonstrated the fraudulence of their premise by managing economic recovery without their aid.

The misuses of monopoly had exercised him at least since Mr. Prothero in 1915 closed the *Quarterly Review* to an ally of Lewis and Gaudier. How came it that Mr. Prothero, otherwise unimportant, should determine which writers should eat? What larger evil might that Luminous Detail signify? For Confucius taught the diagnostic force of details ("He puts up with that," said Confucius of a lax ruler, "What won't he put up with?") Four years later Douglas was suggesting that the false accounting system stimulated the production of all manner of trash. One might apply this to intellectual production: on every publisher's list the few books of interest float on gallons of swill that permit large-scale, hence "efficient," operation. It was soon easy for Pound to discern a self-perpetuating system which kept everyone capable of criticizing it too busy at staying alive to marshal his attack. (In France the very newspapers were subsidized by the Comité des Forges.) And after he had read Van Buren's *Autobiography* (noting that it had stayed—been kept?—in manuscript from 1854 to 1920), and learned that Nicholas Biddle's cohorts knew exactly what they were up to, he could no longer think of the system impersonally. Not only did galactic Baldy Bacons expand and contract the currency on international money marts, they knew that they were doing this and that they were depressing the quality of life, and periodically making wars to create debts. The Rothschilds, who had defeated Napoleon, were long-standing archetypes: despised outsiders who had come to master those who snubbed them, even as the boy who became Sir Basil Zaharoff (the

"Metevsky" of the *Cantos*) was to hate the British all his life because a Britisher kicked him in Constantinople (18/80:84). Hitler jailed no Rothschilds, and Pound thought that the poor Jews whom German resentment drove into concentration camps* were suffering for the sins of their inaccessible coreligionists.

> Stinkschuld sin drawing vengeance, poor yitts paying for
> Stinkschuld
> paying for a few big jews' vendetta on goyim

he wrote on the first page of Canto 52, and went on to excoriate "the international racket, spécialité of the Stinkschuld," with further remarks on their infuriating conduct. The ideograms for calling things by their names appear on the last page of the preceding Canto, and fury at not being able to print "Rothschild" betrayed his style. Even pseudonymized the words were held libellous. Though the thick black lines that replace them are more eloquent, it is a pity Pound's distinction between the financiers and the rest of Jewry was not allowed to be emphasized while he was still in the habit of making it.† Correctly or not, it attempted a diagnosis, and one tending rather to decrease than to encourage anti-Semitism. "Race prejudice," he wrote in 1937, "is a red herring."

By January 1941 he was recording talks for broadcast on Rome Radio's American Hour, at 350 lire a time, with Vivaldi recordings, by his stipulation, played before and after. He thought the Vivaldis should be heard in America, and enjoyed them himself, on his couch in Rapallo, listening to playbacks. He found his own voice strange.

As it was. The details are violent, the rhetoric disordered, the phraseology intemperate. The war was outrageous; in particular

---

* Places not yet (1938) committed to a policy of extermination. News of that policy, when it was instituted, no more reached Rapallo than it did most of Germany.

† Since the New Directions edition of this installment was set from a copy of the Faber, it repeats the black lines and the unusually copious misspellings, the proofs in wartime not having had the benefit of even Pound's erratic reading. More commonly the British and American publishers were upset by different things; thus in 1933 we find the New York firm going to the expense of inserting a cancel leaf to get rid of one letter in a four-letter word which the British publishers in the same year printed in full three times: the same British publishers who 16 years later would not permit the *Pisan Cantos* to report Cocteau's comparison of Maritain to "un curé déguisé."

"For the United States to be making war on Italy and on Europe is just plain damn nonsense," and session after session he attempted in a few minutes to explain from halfway round the world to his countrymen how this nonsense had come about. Unlike the propagandist who says what he is told to, he was offering his own highly specialized account, so crammed with apparently unrelated allegations that some Italian officials are said to have wondered if he were transmitting code under their noses. The man who had had such trouble, and at leisure, in focusing the Monte Dei Paschi Canto clearly, was still less successful, under these conditions, in manifesting a semblance of calm. Exacerbations needled him. In particular, the principles of fiscal and civic order were difficult to talk about because they were so simple. He had to assume that people who didn't understand them were simply not interested. But a man in power would be by definition interested, and could be enlightened in, say, 15 minutes? That was why he had wanted to talk to Roosevelt. Had he been able to counsel Stalin, "but one point" would have sufficed: "You need not": need not, that is, take over the means of production, since production is not the root of the problem. He seems never to have doubted that powerful men wanted anything but their countries' good.

Back in Washington, for the first time in his life, he was being paid attention to; might he be saying something for which he should be hanged? After Pearl Harbor, transcripts were made. The transcribers were insufficiently competent (writing for instance "confusion" for "Confucian") and the reception often bad.

> And if you'll say that this day teaches a lesson, all that the Reverent Eliot (Haston) more natural language, you who think you'll get through hell in a hurry, huh, ah, that day how those cloud over his (horizon) and for three days snow clouds over the sea, banked like a line of mountains.

—thus a detail for 12 February 1942, as transcribed. The script was Canto 46:

> And if you will say that this tale teaches
> a lesson, or that the Reverend Eliot
> has found a more natural language . . . you who think you will

get through   hell   in   a   hurry . . .
That day there was cloud over Zoagli
And for three days snow cloud over the sea
Banked like a line of mountains.

By July 1943 a Grand Jury in the District of Columbia had returned a true bill indicting him of treason. He heard of this indirectly, and on August 4 wrote Attorney General Biddle a civil, temperate, and lucid letter:

> . . . I do not believe that the simple fact of speaking over the radio, wherever placed, can in itself constitute treason. I think that must depend on what is said, and on the motives for speaking.
>
> I obtained the concession to speak over Rome Radio with the following proviso. Namely that nothing should be asked of me contrary to my conscience or contrary to my duties as an American citizen. . . .
>
> I have not spoken with regard to *this* war, but in protest against a system which creates one war after another. I have not spoken to the troops, and have not suggested that the troops should mutiny or revolt.
>
> The whole basis of democratic or majority government assumes that the citizen shall be informed of the facts. I have not claimed to know all the facts, but I have claimed to know some of the facts which are an essential part of the total that should be known to the people. . . .
>
> We have not the right to drift into another error similar to that of the Versailles Treaty. . . . The ruin of markets, the perversion of trade routes, in fact all the matters on which my talks have been based is of importance to the American citizen; [whom] neither you nor I should betray either in time of war *or* peace. . . .
>
> At any rate a man's duties increase with his knowledge. A war between the U.S. and Italy is monstrous and should not have occurred. And a peace without justice is no peace but merely a prelude to future wars. Someone must take count of these things. And having taken count must act on his knowledge; admitting that his knowledge is partial and his judgment subject to error.

So, we must assume, ran his intentions, formed in the still center of his mind where majesty of language had long gathered: intentions almost routinely betrayed at the microphone as the persona of a folk Isaiah slipped into place, denouncing.

* * *

The debacle of late fall 1943—invaders sweeping northward—caught him in Rome. At his old friend Degli Uberti's he left his Borsalino, borrowed a pair of heavy boots, and joined the exodus northward: a long miserable trip by train and on foot to Gais in the mountains almost at the Austrian border where Mary was staying among the people who had raised her. The boots blistered his feet. "Grüss Gott!" went up the cry as he staggered into the village: "Der Herr!"—barely recognizable as the handsome man who had first come there bringing a baby 19 years ago in a miraculous car. He had always been Der Herr, from some other world. And "Tatile" —Papa—"ist gekommen," (78/478:509) a cry to Mary. The two talked long; he thought it might be their last meeting. And after the blisters were healed, though villagers hinted at a pass over the Alps, he headed back toward Rapallo and perhaps other last meetings.

The waterfront was evacuated and the beach studded with tank traps. He and Dorothy were exiled from Via Marsala 12. On its rooftop black tarpaper covered the Gaudier stone. In Miss Rudge's Casa Seicenta in the hills by Sant' Ambrogio, with an olive press on the ground floor, the three coexisted. Though it had been a marital stipulation of Dorothy's that she should not be required to cook—hence in part Ezra's expertise with restaurants, and his

> Some cook, some do not cook
> Some things cannot be altered

—she and Olga shared cooking there.

Pound's immediate people had become the Italians. He had had streamers run off by a job printer to be posted:

COSI' VIVERE CHE I TUOI FIGLI E I
LORO DISCENDENTI TI RINGRAZINO

—so live that your children and their descendants will be grateful. In spring 1944 he had offered the Italians three pamphlets on the true monetary root of their miseries; two of these, printed in Venice, attempted to explain to them that fiscal fraud ran through the history of the Americans who were bombing their way up the peninsula. Did either party understand it, they were victimized by the same enemy and fighting on the same side of the real (not the manifest) war. In July his *Testamento di Confucio* (an Italian *Ta Hio*) was reissued, in September a collection of *Orientamenti* printed, in December an Italian rewriting of his ten-year-old comparison of Jefferson and Mussolini, the following February (1945) his *Ciung Iung: L'Asse che non Vacilla*. ("Better gift can no man make to a nation / than the sense of Kung fu Tseu"). Cantos 72 and 73 were written chiefly in Italian,* and he started translating his "poem including history" into the language of the people among whom he lived, using the occasion to try a written idiom based on what he took to be their linguistic strength: Dante's tongue, and the spoken regional dialects. The modern literary language he regarded as no more capable than Oxford English of handling gristly actualities.

No one saw the Italian Cantos, *Orientamenti* and *Jefferson e Mussolini* were destroyed soon after printing as inopportunely controversial, and the Allies when they got their hands on Confucius' Unwavering Axis burned the edition unread out of prior knowledge of what the word "Axis" must mean. Who saw, who read the other utterances in distracted and collapsing Italy it is impossible to say. At Salò by the Lago di Garda a powerless Mussolini was reading the *Republic* of Plato and administering a Republic of Italy actual only in his dreams: seeing, it must be supposed, the form in the air. Pound made his way there more than once, talked to the Minister of Foreign Affairs, hoped to bring fiscal enlightenment into the dream, sat at nearby Gardone with the Prefect Gioacchino Nicoletti where in sight of a mountain that looked like Fujiyama a quiet cat stalked a railing and quiet water moved southward:

> and the water was still on the West side
> flowing toward the Villa Catullo
> where with sound ever moving
> > in diminutive poluphloisboios

* And never published. The gap left by their absence has now become part of the poem: a fault line, record of shifting masses.

in the stillness outlasting all wars
"La Donna" said Nicoletti
                    "la donna,
                        la donna!"
                        (74/427:453)
—a rare vision, a rare moment of stillness as the times crumbled.

*　　*　　*

The sky was lighted by the bombardment of Genoa, though the mountains cut off its sound. Bombs sometimes fell at random; nearby Zoagli had been reduced when the smoke lifted to two old women and one cat. Then the Americans occupied Rapallo. Ezra Pound, formally dressed, went down from Sant' Ambrogio into the town to make his knowledge of modern Italy available. A solitary black GI, out of touch with his unit, neither understood what he was talking about nor knew that the man before him should be detained under a Washington Grand Jury indictment. He merely tried to sell his interrogator the bicycle on which he was mounted. Pound walked back up the hill.

The next day, 2 May 1945, two armed men rapped on the door of Casa Seicenta. Everyone was denouncing everyone; there were rumors of a half-million-lire bounty. Olga Rudge had gone into town to buy a paper; Dorothy was paying her weekly visit to Ezra's old mother. Ezra, his Legge *Four Books* spread open on the table, was typing at a version of Mencius. It is said that the gun butts sounded, then "Ci segua, traditore." He thrust the Confucius and the dictionary into his pocket and preceded them down the path, past the eucalyptus tree where he stooped to gather the pip.

Olga Rudge returned to an empty cottage. Anita, on the floor with the olive press, had the key he had given her before he left, and could report that it had been no ordinary leaving. Olga dashed after them. At six o'clock Dorothy returned from Rapallo to the utter emptiness. Nothing to be done. She wrote in her diary, "They took him away today." She need not have reflected that it was banal, really. Such things happened everywhere.

A polite man named Amprim called and confiscated the typewriter with the misaligned "t" and the page of Mencius still in it.

It has not been seen again. Amprim was an American; there was involvement at last with officials who knew about the indictment. As the daughter of a solicitor, Dorothy knew the rights of a prisoner's wife. She could not be interrogated. The questions were hers. Where was Ezra? He was "in a room." There was plenty of coffee, Amprim said. Soon, though no one told Dorothy, he was in a cage. She did not know for weeks whether he might not be dead.

The partigiani had taken their prisoner to their HQ in Chiavari, where he was soon released as possessing no interest. He had then demanded to be taken to the Americans, and was driven to the U.S. command post in Lavagna to turn himself in. The following day MP's drove him to the CICHQ in Genoa, where the FBI commenced interrogation.

*   *   *

The Detention Training Center, Mediterranean Theater of Operations, United States Army, lay north of Pisa on the coastal plain, near the village of Metato, by the Via Aurelia which for 17 centuries has run along the sea from the Palatine Gate through Pisa, Viareggio, Carrara, Rapallo, Genoa, all the way to Arles. White oxen now shared the Aurelian Way with jeeps, and down a side road past the camp moved more traffic than the road builders had envisaged, raising slow clouds of dry dust. A half-mile square of barbed wire enclosed the place; birds settled on the strands, the prisoner was to observe, like notes of a silent music. North and east stretched mountains, one cone-shaped above delicate trees (he named it Taishan, for China's sacred peak), two to the left of it low and hemispherical (he named them the Breasts of Helen). Pisa lay south; peering through dangling laundry on clear days one could see the Tower. Sun and moon rose over the mountains, set over the invisible sea. Lizards basked in the heat; grass clung to friable earth; one could watch a wasp building her nest, or ants marching or crickets singing, or men at the Obstacle Fence working out the 14-hour days and looking uncommonly like figures at the grape arbor in the Schifanoia frescoes in Ferrara. He was in a tent in the medical section of the compound, regaining his wits, wits as always

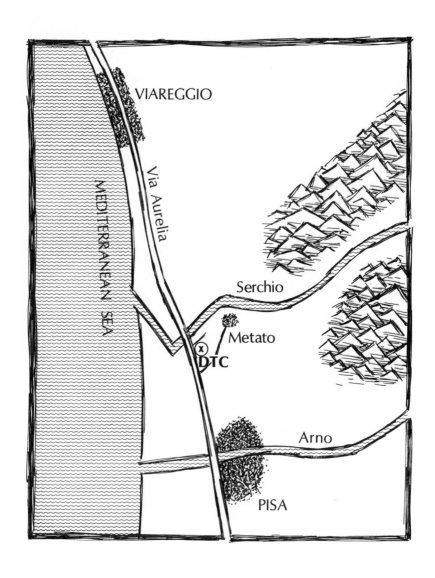

"Taishan at Pisa," as seen from the direction of the DTC.

Francesco del Cossa, detail of "March" panel, Schifanoia Palace, Ferrara. The Obstacle Fence at the DTC apparently resembled this grape arbor.

shaped by myth: a man of no fortune and with a name to come, Odysseus in the Cyclops' den.

*   *   *

He might even have reflected, though probably he did not, that Eliot also, a quarter-century before, had written a masterpiece in a "decayed hole among the mountains," recuperating from a nervous breakdown.

He had begged notebooks, and folded them down the center to make them pocket-size; with a very sharp pencil in a careful hand he wrote fair copies of new Cantos on the right half of the right-hand page, the half to the left of the fold kept for second thoughts. When he chose to work at Confucius he turned the book around, so that the left-hand page became the right. So the *Pisan Cantos* run through the notebooks in one direction, the *Great Digest* and *Unwobbling Pivot* in the other. Legge's text, as its binding disintegrated, was mended with medical tape, and no one seemed to mind if he pounded the dispensary Remington in the evening, making carbons on flimsy paper.

*   *   *

The Confucius is a dialogue with Legge; the *Pisan Cantos* compose a peace with himself, the great poet forcing the angry propagandist to surrender all but a few cragged redoubts. Plucked out of the world where he had been so desperately busy, the world of the typewriter pounded six hours a day, the world of ten thousand letters, some calm, some furious, of radio scripts and economic tracts, of histories condensed in frantic haste; enclosed by barbed wire in a timelessness ("now there are no more days") around which the great world itself seemed to have stopped, he welcomed all of himself that he had excluded for so long—ever since London—to aid in recovering what had been lost in the cage.

"The Master said, 'Is it not pleasant to learn with a constant perseverance and application?'": so Legge, opening the *Analects*, which then go on to speak of indifference to not being noticed. But undergoing his

> nox animae magna from the tent under Taishan
> amid what was termed the a. h. of the army
> the guards holding opinion

> (74/437:464)

Pound felt a perfusing urgency, something more than the obligation of "constant perseverance." 時 , *always*; 習 , *perseverance*; Legge's footnote on this latter character calls attention to "the rapid and frequent motion of the wings of a bird in flying, used for 'to repeat,' 'to practise'." Pound noticed beneath these wings the radical 白 , *white*, and the normal meaning of 時 is *time*:

> To study with the white wings of time passing
> is not that our delight
>
> (74/437;464)

—Kung's calm suffused with his own plight in which time passed and might soon have passed for ever. These ingenuities kept his mind alive.

"For forty years," he had written some months before, "I have schooled myself . . . to write an epic poem which begins "in the Dark Forest," crosses the Purgatory of human error, and ends in the light, 'fra i maestri di color che sanno'." And the time had come to write his "Paradise": here: "Elysium, though it were in the halls of hell" (81/521:556). He lacked time and strength to think it wholly into the poem; the *Digest* and *Pivot*, running through the same notebooks as the *Pisan Cantos*, register the act of faith that now sustained him: that a sage was thinkable in whose syncretic vision *i maestri* and their sundry worlds might be as one: Dante, Erigena, Homer, and the rest, perfused by light. That visionary Kung is an extraordinary invention, talking of a clarifying activity that neither stops nor stays and is identical in the sage's mind and in the mind of the Universe.

> This earth that bears you up is a handful of sand, but in its weight and dusky large, it holds The Flower Mount and Dog Mountain without feeling the weight of them; Hoang Ho, the river, and the oceans surge and the earth loses not a drop of their waters, holding them in their beds, containing the multitude of their creatures. . . .

To grasp a handful of sand is to grasp all that; men's knowing is a synecdoche, so are men's poems; attend to the bits, they cohere. However much of this sage may have been Chu Hsi's invention, however much Pound's, it was necessary to posit his historicity;

then one man's Paradise, existing only in fragments ("the smell of mint, for example") might tend toward the sage's vision as toward an asymptote.

The one man's resources were relatively meager. He had carried Kung's text here in the jeep. On an outhouse seat he found *The Pocket Book of Verse*. And Holy Writ was supplied, as conducive to reformation; during his six Pisan months he read it through, the only man, he later remarked, to read the Bible *after* translating Confucius (the former translators had been missionaries). Beyond these, his resources were his thoughts; and what filled the office of Divus or De Mailla, coming between present immediacy (camp, guards, prisoners) and the elements of the Paradise, could only be Memory. Very well, Paradise is what is loved; and Love (Cavalcanti) arises "dove sta memoria." And "the Muses are daughters of Memory."

Present immediacy also furnished four elements, earth, air, water, light. Water receives a whole Canto, the body's union with earth culminates another, forms crystallize from air, the tensile light is pervasive:

> nor is it for nothing that the chrysalids mate in the air
> color di luce
> green splendour and as the sun thru pale fingers
> Lordly men are to earth o'ergiven ...
>
> (74/432:459)

That last line is from *The Seafarer* (London, 1911); he was constantly drawn back to London, not least by the memory of having invented there, and discarded as a false start, the form he was now employing, free-running monologue. It was the right form now for memory.

*   *   *

Memory brought strange phantasms into the dusty place. Rain altars, what might they be like? Kung walks in their vicinity, *Analects* xii-21, but subjoined to their mention is the character denoting "under." Under the altars? Legge conjectures, under the trees about them.

as he had walked under the rain altars
>or under the trees of their grove
>or would it be under their parapets
in his moving was stillness

(80/512:547)

—whereupon memory brought flashing the elucidative scene: the old cemetery at Arles, *Elysii Campi*, a name worn down to Alyscamps: trees, and a long row of visually plausible rain-altars:

as grey stone in the Aliscans

—a rhyme of a scene imagined with a place remembered.
"In his moving was stillness," two Greek words a few lines

"Under Abelard's bridges," Paris.

earlier having recalled that all things flow even though some seem still (there are tranquil vortices):

> for those trees are Elysium
>   for serenity
>   under Abélard's bridges   πάντα 'ρεῖ
>   for those trees are serenity

—a rhyme of a stillness felt with a setting remembered; and the trees, like the Arles graves, are called Elysian.

The trees by L'Ile St. Louis were remembered in turn out of the background of Lévy-Dhurmer's portrait of Georges Rodenbach, reproduced in the poet's *Choix de poésies*: a portrait in an inventory of modern portraits, prompted by thoughts of a sequence of Venuses; and Venus, dread Cythera, *Kuthera deina*, in sound very nearly

Lévy-Dhurmer's portrait of Rodenbach. (Courtesy Musées Nationaux, Paris.)

"The moon barge": Duccio figure of Diana in the Tempio Malatestiana.

Diana, might be seen in the Pisan moon as Duccio carved Diana "in the moon barge":

> with the veil of faint cloud before her
> Κύθηρα δεινά as a leaf borne in the current
> pale eyes as if without fire
>
> (80/511:546)

—a rhyme of a goddess envisioned and a carving remembered.

Change and permanence, the flux and the pattern: a theme for elegy now that bombs had fractured the Tempio's stones and smashed the Osservanza above Siena ("and the best Della Robbia busted to flinders"—80/497:530), "all that Sandro knew" moreover lost in Rubens' "raw meat," (80/511:546) but the permanences "in the mind indestructible": in one vulnerable mind getting down with a lifetime's craft the feel of it all, a bullet perhaps in waiting, or a noose.

The goddess however will survive any one mind, and nature's signatures will survive this year's leaves. Wasps are intricate patterned energies making intricate patterns. Each generation without being taught will build its four-room house of mud, "swallow system," and each little wasp enact the chthonic rite:

> The infant has descended,
> from mud on the tent roof to Tellus,
> like to like colour he goes amid grass-blades
> greeting them that dwell under XTHONOS ΧΘΟΝΟΣ
> ΟΙ ΧΘΟΝΙΟΙ; to carry our news
> εἰς χθονίους to them that dwell under the earth,
> begotten of air, that shall sing in the bower
> of Kore, Περσεφόνεια
> and have speech with Tiresias, Thebae
>
> (83/533:568)

To this breath-taking passage, its minute tenderness rhymed with Canto I's heroic vigors, we find subjoined, "and that day I wrote no further." Paolo and Francesca one fatal day "read no further," lost in their guilty ecstasy; so now Ezra Pound, lost in the fatigue he next designates? More likely in exaltation at seeing that tiny

Odysseus; "it is not man," he had written a few pages previously, "made courage, or made order, or made grace."

* * *

The stream of reminiscence and perception encounters periodically some phrase ("Tiresias, Thebae") that serves for shorthand: here of "Tiresias Theban" in Canto I, with his prophecy of Odysseus, "man of ill star," come to disaster, losing all companions. The phrase as link is a well-tried device in the *Cantos*. In the *Pisan Cantos* however it is often extended, when a dozen such luminous motes circle one another, each one a concentration, drawing many large motifs into a tight cluster. In the passage that terminates Canto 74 one might annotate almost every word:

> Serenely in the crystal jet
>   as the bright ball that the fountain tosses
> (Verlaine) as diamond clearness
>   How soft the wind under Taishan
>   where the sea is remembered
>   out of hell, the pit
>   out of the dust and glare evil
>   Zephyrus / Apeliota
> This liquid is certainly a
>   property of the mind
> nec accidens est   but an element
>   in the mind's make-up
> est agens and functions   dust to a fountain pan otherwise
>   Hast 'ou seen the rose in the steel dust
>   (or swansdown ever?)
> so light is the urging, so ordered the dark petals of iron
> we who have passed over Lethe.
>
>   (74/449:477)

Thus "crystal" takes us back to Canto 4's raining light, "liquid and rushing"; to Canto 23's waves, "holding their form" and mentioned with Aphrodite, mentioned again in Canto 25 along with musical "notes as facets of air," also with the sculptor seeing the form in the air as Acoetes in Canto 2 saw "beasts like shadows in glass," manifested by Dionysiac energy. The one word "Verlaine" assembles "crystal" and "jet" and sculptor under the sign of his "Clair de

Lune" which closes with great ecstatic fountains among statues
("les grands jets d'eau sveltes parmi les marbres").

> out of hell, the pit
> out of the dust and glare evil

rhymes with the emergence, Plotinus' mirror aiding, from the political hell of Canto 15, where we read of "the dern evil" (*dern*: dark;
"evil," there as here, is the noun; *dust and glare*, like *dern*, adjec-
tival). The named winds are moving energies; so is the force that
makes the rose in the steel dust, rhymed with the flowers Botticelli
painted springing forth in the breath of embodied winds; rhymed
too with the divine Rose of *Paradiso* xxx, whose petals appear amid
clustered white points of light, the souls of the Redeemed. And
"swansdown ever"? Ben Jonson wrote it, John Dowland set it,
Arnold Dolmetsch published the setting:

> Have you seen but a bright Lillie grow,
> > Before rude hands have touch'd it?
> Ha' you marked but the fall o' the Snow
> > Before the soyle hath smutch'd it?
> Ha' you felt the wooll o' the Bever?
> > Or Swans Downe ever?
> Or have smelt o' the bud o' the Brier?
> > Or the Nard in the fire?
> Or have tasted the bag of the Bee?
> O so white! O so soft! O so sweet is she!

As, glimpsed through Latin phrases, a vision of Aphrodite climaxed
Canto I, so one quoted phrase annexes Jonson's stanza to bring this
lady, barely seen, into being at the end of the first Pisan Canto.
Jonson assembled his homage to the lady out of discrete elements
patterned by syntactic ritual. Pound's homage to the mind implies a
lady because all his invocations of the flux yielding form imply
Aphrodite; and the essay on "Mediaevalism" which celebrating
"magnetisms that take form, that are seen, that border the visible,"
had invoked the rose a magnet makes in iron filings (and also "the
plant brain . . . filled with . . . a persistent notion of pattern") was
part of a commentary on Cavalcanti's Canzone of Love.

* * *

The mind is a fountain, sculptured water, not frozen but sustained by ceaseless flowing. What confers a fountain's form? "Who am I?" Pound's earliest poems had asked and asked. And one, not reprinted after 1910, had affirmed that he might at times literally be some dead master:

> ... Thus am I Dante for a space and am
> One Francois Villon, ballad-lord and thief...
> ... And as the clear space is not if a form's
> Imposed thereon,
> So cease we from all being for the time,
> And these, the Masters of the Soul, live on.

In 1911 he had become the Seafarer-poet long enough to write *The Seafarer*, which, pedantry assures us, is not at all "a translation."

> —wuniað þa wacran ond þas woruld healdaþ
> —Waneth the watch, but the world holdeth.

But stop, *healdaþ* is plural and *woruld* accusative; *wacran* isn't "watch" but "weaker" [sc. folk]; *wuniað* isn't "wane" but (cf. Ger. *wohnen*) "dwell": "A weaker sort survive and possess the earth." Similarly Pound's splendid phrase "The blade is layed low" derives from a phrase ("Blæd is genæged") which sounds as if it ought to treat of blades, but means "glory is humbled." He was interested chiefly in the 9th-century sounds.

—Interested, that is, beyond philology, in how the bard breathed: in the gestures of tongue and expulsions of breath that mimed, about A.D. 850, the emotions of exile. And if emotions are psychic, *psyche* means "breath," and meter is breath measured. By rhythm and gesture, by rhythmic gesture: so, according to Aristotle, do the flute-player and the dancer imitate emotion. Bring both the dance and the flute within the body, and we have the bard in the grip of his emotion, extemporizing. To develop his sense was the least of the Seafarer-bard's concerns; the meanings of the words fit in somehow, vessels to receive his longing, as the structure of sound is built up, prolonged, modulated. And Pound in response made a similar English poem, so far as possible breathing as it breathed, intoning as it intoned, letting plausible words fall throughout the incomparable performance:

> May I for my own self song's truth reckon,
> Journey's jargon, how I in harsh days
> Hardship endured oft. . . .

His interest dwelt on how the bard's throat shapes air: his cadence (cadenza): his breath, literally his *psyche*. (*Psyché te ménos te*, says Homer, equating the two: his breath and strength, all that it is to be alive.) Pound liked to quote what Yeats said of a poem, "I made it out of a mouthful of air": a physical reality for the Irish poet who paced the downstairs room at Stone Cottage, intoning

> that had made a great Peeeeacock
>   in the proide ov his oiye
>   had made a great peeeeeeecock in the . . .
> made a great peacock
>   in the proide of his oyyee
> proide ov his oy-ee;
>
>   (83/534:569)

and Homer as we now think composed only aloud, building the *Iliad* out of mouthfuls of air, the Muse singing as his chest contracted, his breath governing the line, his heart beating against the stresses.

Now "to break the pentameter, that was the first heave," Canto 81 recalls; for

> . . . as Jo Bard says: they never speak to each other,
>   if it is baker and concierge visibly
>   it is La Rochefoucauld and de Maintenon audibly.
>
>   (81/518:553)

This means that as courtly diction encysts French speech, so iambic pentameter imposed on English an arbitrary measure, alien to the bardic way of being alive. Pound's own early cadences were Greek, and almost from the first own a personal signature, a spondee terminating the line:

> Eyes, dreams, lips and the níght góes   (1909)

> . . .

> And was her daughter líke thát;
> Black as Demeter's gown,
>   eýes, háir?
> Dis' bride, Queen over Phlegethon,
>   girls faint as mist abóut hér?   (1959)

Though it carries one man's signature, the line lies open to many
voices: Homer's:

> Thus with stretched sail, we went over sea till dáy's énd.

Sappho's:

> Fades light from séa crést

Kung's:

> If a man have not order withín hím
> He can not spread order abóut hím.

Who am I? A way of breathing. That spondee is himself. And not
the least strange of the Pisan adventures was the invasion of the
great dead, to speak through him and receive his signature on their
cadences. There are eerie moments in the *Pisan Cantos* when he
suddenly becomes some other.

*   *   *

For instance, Whitman, who in 1905 was still "man of no
fortune and with a name to come." Four miles from Camden, where
Whitman had died 13 years earlier, Professor Riethmuller cried
indignantly, "Fvy! in Tdaenmarck efen dh'beasantz gnow him!"
Canto 82 remembers that; the act of remembering is the propitiatory
ritual, blood for Walt's ghost; and suddenly the poem commences
to speak as it were from Walt's mind:

> "O troubled reflection
> "O Throat, O throbbing heart"
> How drawn, O GEA TERRA
>   what draws as thou drawest
>   till one sink into thee by an arm's width
>   embracing thee. . . .
> Where I lie let the thyme rise
>   and basilicum
>   let the herbs rise in April abundant . . .
>   (82/526:561)

Gea Terra is not part of Whitman's pantheon, but the opening
words are his, abridged from two lines he had put into "Out of the
Cradle Endlessly Rocking":

> (O troubled reflection in the sea!
> O throat! O throbbing heart!)

This poem of Whitman's recalls a bird singing night after night "in the moonlight on Paumanok's gray beach," calling for his lost mate; and the young Whitman (who "treasur'd every note") stealing down to the shore to listen, and discovering in the process his poet's vocation; and the ultimate word given young Whitman by the whispering sea, which word is "death." And now singing through Ezra Pound as the bird had sung through him, the gray shade undertakes a reprise, thyme and basilicum standing for Leaves of Grass, Whitman supplying the motifs and Pound the language. The longed-for mate becomes the earth-bride, *connubium terrae*. The sea-wind blowing along Paumanok's shore ("I wait and I wait till you blow my mate to me") gives the Canto

> wind: ἐμὸν τὸν ἄνδρα

the words of Theocritus' woman at the charm-wheel calling her man back to her house. For dead poets can be of mutual service, the voice of one bereaved singer supplying in courtesy words for another. Then Whitman's sea, with its "low and delicious" message,

> . . . death, death, death, death,

—this sea, "rustling at my feet, / Creeping thence steadily up to my ears and laving me softly all over") finds austere articulation as

> fluid *XΘΟΝΟΣ*, strong as the undertow
> of the wave receding,

touched by which, Pound says,

> the loneliness of death came upon me
> (at 3 P.M., for an instant);

and as the voices fade, Whitman's bird, tripled, presides over the terminal cadence:

> three solemn half notes
>   their white downy chests black-rimmed
> on the middle wire
>   periplum

This extraordinary homage, a structural X-ray of Whitman's intricate poem, in articulating itself has stirred into life many voices; we can identify Theocritus, Nicolas Este, Aeschylus, Kipling, Mencius who invoked the "two halves of the tally."* Whitman himself states the principle, recalling how he had cried to the bird,

> Now in a moment I know what I am for, I awake.
> And already a thousand singers, a thousand songs,
>   clearer, louder and more sorrowful than yours,
> A thousand warbling echoes have started to life
>   within me, never to die.

The resources in the Canto are Pound's, as are those of Canto I. Yet as behind Canto I are the voices of Divus and Homer, so behind the last page of Canto 82 is the voice, the spirit, of Whitman: *anima*: psyche.

> We have one sap and one root,

Pound had written 32 years before, making compact with Whitman;

> Let there be commerce between us.

*   *   *

In the Canto before this one something still stranger is transacted, a courtship with the eponymous English decasyllabic itself, since Chaucer the language's most pervasive measure. This time the "masters of the soul" are innumerable, and have been thronging since Canto 80, where we hear the voice of Browning ("Oh to be in England...") and the Elizabethan throat that shaped "Let backe and side go bare," then Bertran de Born for eight Provençal words ("Si tuit li dolh elh plor elh marrimen") and 12 lines shaped by the shade of Edward FitzGerald:

> Tudor indeed is gone and every rose,
> Blood-red, blanch-white that in the sunset glows...
>   (80/516:551)

---

*Pound was looking at Legge's note to Mencius IV.ii.1, which explains how split bamboo sticks were once used as a test of identity: whence, "man, earth: two halves of the tally." And tally sticks in Greek are σύμβολα, whence 'symbols.'

("Iram indeed is gone with all his rose," FitzGerald had written,
"And Jamshyd's Sev'n-ring'd Cup where no one knows.")*

These stirrings, as toward the climax of a séance, suggest some major possession to come; and Bertrans and FitzGerald have in fact introduced into the poem two related measures not formerly at home in it, the decasyllabic and the pentametric. Within a page comes the reminder that "the first heave" was "to break the pentameter," which Pound heard as a thickening (based on five stresses) of the Italian hendecasyllabic (based on 11 syllables). He worked hard to break it when he made, about 1910, his first versions of Cavalcanti:

> I síng how I lóst a tréasure by desíre
> And léft all vírtue and am lów descénded

—not pentameters, but four-stressed lines of 11 syllables. Of such verse there is much in Pound's published volumes, though very little in the *Cantos*. He always treated it as an archaic form, through which Italian or Provençal voices may speak; virtually abandoned it when he left the *Canzoni* behind in 1911; and in the 1929 essay "Guido's Relations" discussed its anomalous English life. There the matter rested till Pisa.

But in Pisa, Bertrans and FitzGerald nudged that old metrical motif into the *Cantos*, FitzGerald's example recalling a long, specifically English tradition. And three pages later Cavalier songwriters suddenly help reassert Englishness, as a cadence ends,

> at my grates no Althea.

Richard Lovelace, writing "To Althea, from Prison" has entered the flow of another prison-poet's reminiscence; Pound is recalling

> When Love with unconfined wings
> Hovers within my Gates;
> And my divine Althea brings
> To whisper at the Grates . . .

* And "Nor seeks the carmine petal to infer . . ." seems prompted by a line of FitzGerald's friend Tennyson: "Now sleeps the crimson petal, now the white."

It is the 17th century, and time has flowed out like a great wave, to leave him possessed by the eponymous spirit (spiritus:psyche:air) that used clear-cut lute-sound and viol-sound:

> Has he tempered the viol's wood
> To enforce   both the grave   and the acute?
> Has he curved us the bowl of the lute?
>
> (81/520:555)

He is undergoing, it seems, in the "aureate sky," some interrogation as to his worthiness; following which (is it some inaugural rite?) he suddenly finds himself speaking words of Chaucer's:

> Your eyen two wol sleye me sodenly
> I may the beauté of hem nat susteyne:

lines addressed by Chaucer to "Merciles Beauté" and by Pound through him to the eternal Aphrodite, known always in the *Cantos* by the emblem of her eyes. And these pure English decasyllabics are followed by the contemporary speaking voice:

> And for 180 years almost nothing.

Then decasyllabic reasserts itself, in the tongue of Dante whom Chaucer read and paraphrased:

> Ed ascoltando al leggier mormorio*

"And listening to the gentle murmur"—of many voices, none yet dominant—

> there came new subtlety of eyes into my tent
> whether of spirit or hypostasis

—one line spoken, one line measured, and the measured line the decasyllabic once more, its third occurrence, modern English this time, though dealing in Tuscan precisions of terminology. Then three more irregular lines; then, *then*, the anonymous genius of English asserts itself:

> Sáw but the eýes and stánce betwéen the eýes

---

* "Not a quotation," Pound answered an inquiry, "merely the author using handy language."

—a full-blooded iambic pentameter, not simply ten syllables but five unmistakable stresses. He continues to muse, in short irregular lines; another iambic pentameter rises as from the deeps—

> cásting but sháde beyónd the óther líghts

—to be countered by three lines of Imagism, school of 1912:

> sky's clear
> night's sea
> green of the mountain pool

And these three Imagist lines total ten syllables. The English main-stream measure is slipping past the defenses of the years when the pentameter was "broken." But not slipping past unaltered; for the decasyllabic line to which the Imagist lines add up is by no stretch of mensuration pentametric, or even iambic:

> ský's cléar / níght's séa / gréen of the móuntàin póol

This is a line composed, as the third Imagist canon had it, "in the sequence of the musical phrase, not in the sequence of a metronome." And it is followed, this ghost line, by a line clearly printed as decasyllabic, not iambic pentameter at all but a ten-syllable line with stresses heavily grouped, closing in the paired (indeed here tripled) stress that is Ezra Pound's key signature:

> shone from the unmasked eyes in hálf-másk's spáce.

A process has traversed in half a page the history of English versifi-cation from Chaucer to 1945, decasyllabic becoming pentameter, pentameter encountering Imagist resistance, and metamorphosing into the idiosyncratically stressed line that carries Pound's hallmark.

And now the attainment of his honorable truce opens the poem to many anonymous masters, an English tradition of weighty moral utterance, of grave didacticism, that finally returns to paraphrased Chaucer as to its tonic. It announces its presence with the sonorous lines on Love, a Poundian decasyllabic moving unresisted, line after line after line:

> What thou lov'st well shall not be reft from thee
> What thou lov'st well is thy true heritage
> Whose world, or mine or theirs
> > or is it of none?

Then the Bible he had been reading supplies Vanity and the Ant (*Eccles.* I.2; *Prov.* vi.6), lending this mounting utterance the authority of the translators commissioned by King James:

> The ant's a centaur in his dragon world.
> Pull down thy vanity, it is not man
> Made courage, or made order, or made grace,

—Greece with its centaur and China with its dragon enlisted with the ant in a triple alliance. Again and again the Poundian double stress terminates a line:

> . . . nót mán
> . . . máde gráce
> . . . púll dówn
> . . . thý pláce

Yet sustaining idiosyncrasy the decasyllabics march on, generally end-stopped, varied by resources—anaphora, internal rhyme, witty diction ("scaled invention," said of a beetle) that so delight the mind as virtually to conceal the didactic reiteration.

Chaucer paraphrased ("Master thyself, then others shall thee beare"*) terminates the passage as Chaucer quoted had opened it; decasyllabics break into halves

> A swollen magpie in a fitful sun,
> Half black half white
> Nor knowst'ou wing from tail;

and four trisyllabled rhymes—

> Fostered in falsity,
>   Pull down thy vanity,
> Rathe to destroy, niggard in charity,
> Pull down thy vanity,
>   I say pull down

—terminate the cadence.

---

* "Reule wel thyself, that other folk canst rede"—*Balade de Bon Conseyl.* *The Pocket Book of Verse* offers Henry Van Dyke's modernization, "Work well thyself to counsel others clear," and could Ezra Pound have resisted improving Van Dyke?

Still, so considerable is the decasyllabic momentum that it asserts itself twice more in the nine-line coda to this Canto, and even manages to open the Canto that follows:

> When with his hunting-dog I see a cloud

—the measure, as it might be, of an American Wordsworth. But the real world intervenes:

> "Guten Morgen, Mein Herr" yells the black boy
> from the jo-cart

—a voice from the camp, innocent of iambs; and the camp roll-call commences:

> (Jeffers, Lovell and Harley
> also Mr Walls who has lent me a razor
> Persha, Nadasky and Harbell)

The ghosts are scattered. Speech, unless the speakers are reciting Shakespeare, will not sustain the measure into which English craft has recast so much speech; and Pound's mind, his metrical adventure behind him, returns to thoughts of Swinburne who had labored to bring Greek meters into Tennyson's England.

Is there another passage in literature that can number among the protagonists in its drama the meter itself? Swinburne hauled out of the sea by French fishermen, reciting them Greek ("might have been Aeschylus") provides a faint parallel; the Greek language itself, falling on astonished unlearned ears, entered *that* drama. Pound dwells for a few lines on the vivid incident. What did they drag from the sea? They dragged as it were Arion; or as it were Odysseus; a queer fish, from a world where the sphere of adventure is the imagination, and where mastery achieved by labor may open the mind to possession by minds past. So Odysseus took sheep with him in the black ship, that he might provide blood for ghosts. The soldiers who guarded Pound had an equally strange catch, to wall up under the tireless lights, and the ditch they dug round his cage "lest the damp gnaw through my bones" (74/429:455) recalls the fosse in which sheep's blood flowed in Hades. Their barbed wire did not wholly a prison make: not enough to exclude the Masters of the Soul.

*   *   *

So he passed the long summer and the chill fall. To dusty earth, timeless air, the tensile light, the skies contributed the fourth element, water, evoking memories of

              ... Dei Miracoli:
    mermaids, that carving

For small treasures survived Europe's wreck, and a mind that cherished them; a mind that remembered how

        ... Tullio Romano carved the sirenes
              as the old custode says: so that since
    then no one has been able to carve them
        for the jewel box, Santa Maria Dei Miracoli ....
                        (76/460:489)

For

    ... the drama is wholly subjective
    stone knowing the form which the carver imparts it
    the stone knows the form
                ... in Santa Maria dei Miracoli
        where Pietro Romano has fashioned the bases
                        (74/430:457)

The stone remembers the form, the mind misremembers the men; for the carvers of the miraculous bases and mermaids in Venice the water-city were not Romanos but Lombardos, Pietro and Tullio, father and son. The mind plays tricks, the stones live.

At times, during that ordeal, the mind "hung by a grass blade." In November they flew him to Washington. In December four psychiatrists characterized the defendant, "a voluntary expatriate for nearly 40 years ... making an uncertain living by writing poetry and criticism," as "eccentric, querulous, and egocentric." He insisted that his broadcasts were not treasonable, and moreover exhibited "discursiveness." In February he was judged unfit to stand trial, and confined to St. Elizabeths Hospital until such time as his condition should improve, which, the doctors told his attorney, "would never happen." For a year he stayed in a barred cell in the criminal ward ("Problem now is not to go stark screaming

hysteric"). From that cell, late in January 1946, came the coda to
the *Pisan Cantos*, a single scribbled sheet to his man of law:

Dungeon

Dementia

mental torture
constitution a religion
a world lost
grey mist barrier impassible
    ignorance absolute

anonyme

futility of might have been
coherent areas

constantly

invaded

    aiuto

Pound

Aiuto: "Help."

THE LAST
EUROPEAN

Lewis spent the war years in Canada, of all places. Things were passably normal for middle-class Canadians, though cars ran on rationed fuel till patched tires gave out, and intercollegiate football had been suspended. At the University of Toronto a freshman member of the class that would graduate, Hitler permitting, in 1945 could watch black squirrels scamper beneath great elms while Wyndham Lewis was completing his first year's stock-taking of Toronto as a city of exile (". . . Things have come to an awful pass here: if I don't do something to break out of the net, I shall end my days in a Toronto flophouse.") While the freshman listened to lectures on historiography and Shakespearean compassion the author of *Time and Western Man* and *The Lion and the Fox* was enduring the social chill and the central heating in a room "twenty-five feet by twelve" at the Hotel Tudor a half-hour's stroll away. The sophomore year coincided with Lewis's third ("We are freezing out here slowly, in this icebox of a country. This hotel burned down six weeks ago, all but the annexe. I am living in the ruins.") By the time the junior curriculum had commenced its annual dealings with Roman satirists, English Augustans,

French Cartesians, the author of *The Apes of God* had moved 220 miles west-southwest to a flat city called Windsor with a hospitable little Catholic college.

The point of this synchronicity is that it has no point. Lewis saw no students, students were not told of Lewis. There was no conspiracy to prevent them from finding out he existed. Such of their mentors as had heard his name didn't seem to think it mattered, and a 1945 alumnus can identify only in retrospect, as a remote little space-time convolution, two years lived not a mile from a Titan.

*   *   *

When he crossed the Atlantic he left behind what he lived on: his reputation, such as it was. Such as it was, it had gotten him portrait commissions, though never as many as fell to Augustus John, all of whose portraits look alike. Chiefly he lived on advances for books, also obtained by pledging his reputation. Some were books he cared about, some he would not have elected to write but for necessity. Either kind drew on meditations nearly habitual with him, concerning fame, illusion, groundless belief, and the manipulability of these. No wonder he wrote so much about politics.

Painting can be a fantastically lucrative vocation, though it never was for Lewis, and if a painter have Lewis's gifts, and Lewis's lack of income, he is likely to give thought to what it is that people who buy pictures, when they do buy them, think they are paying for. These reflections are apt to reinforce any interest he may take in voids and vacua. A picture-buyer, Lewis had known since the days of the Vortex, pays only for fame (*fama:* rumor), acquiring an example of work to each example of which, by agreement, great value may be affixed. The agreement will possibly one day collapse, as in the case of Millais, and the market deflate. Meanwhile the living painter, needing to eat, will hope for such an accretion of public imponderables as will set on new examples of his work the price commanded by a reputation.

Will hope; will strive? Possibly. And if he is gifted, like Lewis, with word-skills also, he will set them to work too, in the interest of making himself better known. Rossetti, an indifferent

Ezra Pound, Sant' Ambrogio, 1965.

painter, did this, and Whistler, an excellent one, both profitably. In England Wyndham Lewis too had a public existence, compounded, like all public existence, of rumor and noise and gallery talk and press cuttings (a delimited void, laced with tracer bullets): a less potent existence than John's or Picasso's or Klee's but sufficient to foster, here and there, the feeling that "a Lewis" on one's wall might be something more than x square inches of pigment: might be, in fact, a whiff of heady "reality," worth an outlay. That was partly what the books were *for*. It was also (hence their lasting interest) what they tended to be *about*: the nature of public identity, the identity of a person, a movement, an idea. All these, Lewis thought, were corrupted once they went into action. But in action, entoiled with the contingent, they brought in groceries, and men of the intellect need groceries.

*   *   *

He meditated best with his hand, and notably about 1938, in a series of remarkable portraits of men doomed to be themselves. T. S. Eliot is discerned with astringent, minute attention, trapped in

Wyndham Lewis, *Portrait of Ezra Pound*, 1938. (Courtesy Mrs. Wyndham Lewis and the Tate Gallery, London.)

poethood, a little slouched before a hospital-green panel to the left and right of which a loamy riot of jungle-forms (Philomel; history's echo chamber) discloses to careful inspection coy nested birds: quiet, and the poet's averted eyes are quiet, but the posture is tense. Or Ezra Pound, apparently asleep, reclines before Odysseus' vast sea, but a painted sea, explicitly a painting, nailheads to hold a canvas to its stretcher running metrically down its edge. A folded newspaper denotes his concern with newspaper events, and three *objets d'art*—unused ashtrays, one crystalline, one with a dragon-emblem—imply glazes and translucencies polarized toward the unpretentious and the oriental. Amid artifacts, since nothing but an art-world is visible, he dreams, drawn into "the obscure reveries of the inward gaze," the face at ease but intent, caught in his dream ("a man in love with the past") and clearly more to be reckoned with than other men awake. Each man is enclosed in the visible embodiment of a lifetime's habits: Yeats said, a Body of Fate. That is what it means to exist for a public: you are enclosed like that. The act of depicting such manifestations so immediately and with so stark a geometry Lewis called "burying Euclid deep in the living flesh." What might have been a career of performing such miracles was aborted in 1939 by a war, as an earlier war had aborted his Vorticist career. The capacity to paint unpainted pictures, spun out of the analogy between their subjects' burden of fructive nothing-ness and his own serviceable réclame (that brought him, for in-stance, £250 for the Eliot portrait, from the Municipal Gallery of Durban, South Africa), evaporated, alas, as he crossed the water. For in North America, in New York at first and for three long years in Toronto, his own réclame ceased to be at his disposal. He was simply a man who could paint pictures, if you liked the kind of pictures he painted, and could also write, with forceful word-joinery, deploying ideas not reassuringly continuous with the other ideas that were going round in those years, installed at the age of 60 in a world where nobody knew who he was. "Wyndham Lewis" had ceased to exist. Devoid of an identity, he was reduced to a nervous system. No wonder everything Torontonian got on his nerves: the heat, the cold, the plumbing, the ventilation, the liquor regulations, the intellectuals.

*   *   *

He began his North American experience by finishing a novel—*The Vulgar Streak*—about a man who discards his own identity and makes a new one supported by a new trade, that of counterfeiter. He finished with that experience by recreating it from a decade's distance, back in London, in another novel—*Self Con-demned*—about a man who discards his identity (that of British professor) and exists in Momaco, Canada, as an exacerbated nervous system merely, until after some years, claiming a new identity (American professor) he is free to carry on "insect-like activity" in a "Cemetery of Shells." His Canadian years, his years as a nervous system, expose him to shock and psychic reduction and tragedy. Canada, projected from Lewis's experience there, is *Self Condemned*'s synecdoche for limbo, a frigid province remote from a forgotten sun.

His sight failed about 1951, and he was blind when he wrote *Self Condemned*. He wrote it longhand, the ball-point scrawling its way till it bumped off the edge of the pad on his lap, then commencing a new line three finger-breadths below the previous one, a sheet with five or six wandering lines at last torn off and dropped on the floor to be retrieved by Mrs. Lewis and typed. In his private mind he anchored the career of his René Harding explicitly to the fortunes of the Vortex: the odd-shaped Harding flat of the opening chapters is Ezra Pound's old triangular flat at 5 Holland Place Chambers, sketchily but exactly described: the flat in which Lewis had first seen Eliot "growling out melodiously his apt and bright answers" to the red-bearded collector of geniuses, the flat in which *Propertius* and *Mauberley* were typed on an exiguous table also triangular. Agnes Bedford moved into the flat after the Pounds left for Paris, and Lewis somewhat intensified what she much later told him of its wartime fortunes:

> ... the cellar was full of dead leaves and a wild cat had established its home there, a brood of wild kittens springing about among the leaves. This wild cat so terrorized the tenants that they dared not go down to their trash bins just outside the cellar door.

So Europe: a "House that Jack Built," derelict, with a wild cat in the cellar. And the New World?

A cold "as impossible to keep out as radium," cold that "walked through your heart, it dissolved your kidney, it flashed down your marrow and made an icicle of your coccyx"; a morning light that "seems to bang you in the face, as it glares in at the window"; a newspaper clipping about a boy's eyeball pierced by a splinter of ice; tears caught by the wind "as they came over the rim of the eyeball" and dashed against the wayfarer's shoulder: a climate not indifferently *there*, but actively malevolent, corresponds in the book to Lewis's sense that he was menaced. He was menaced, there, by annihilation. By a mere change of state, by translation in wartime across a body of water, Wyndham Lewis, painter, satirist, pamphleteer, Enemy, had been reduced to virtual non-existence.

There could have been no better demonstration of his lifelong thesis that the human world, identity itself, is precarious, provisional: for imagine that unsleeping intellect, that acetylene will, still blazing but rendered irrelevant, disregarded by professional custodians of the life of the mind, leafing their lecture-notes among the elms and the squirrels a mile away! So little does it take—a mere switching-off of attention—to annihilate worlds. And René Harding, nobody, nowhere, come out of nowhere, unknown, finds that in such a plight anything at all that can touch your attention does so with uncanny aggressiveness. Thus a squirrel like the Varsity squirrels is suddenly perceived staring "with one large pop-eye through the window, his head, like a neolithic axe-head, pressed against the glass, standing on his hind legs": an alarming apparition that does not recur. Such moments of hallucinatory encounter belong to dreams, and *Self Condemned* is like an immense bad dream, implacable, engulfing, unnervingly paced, voices and blurs and acts of madness and over and over those moments of eerily heightened awareness, so randomly related to what is there to be aware of: the vertigo of a man without an identity on which he can rely.

But something of more moment was going forward than one ignored painter's privations. Midway through his first summer in Toronto Lewis wrote to T. Sturge Moore:

> How calm those days were before the epoch of wars and social revolution, when you used to sit on one side of your work-table and I on the other, and we would talk—with trees and creepers of the placid Hampstead domesticity beyond the windows, and you used to grunt with a philosophic despondence I greatly enjoyed. It was the last days of the Victorian world of artificial peacefulness—of the R.S.P.C.A. and London Bobbies, of "slumming" and Buzzards cakes. As at that time I had never heard of anything else, it seemed to my young mind in the order of nature. You—I suppose—knew it was all like the stunt of an illusionist. You taught me many things. But you never taught me *that*. I first discovered about it in 1914—with growing surprise and disgust.

"It was all like the stunt of an illusionist," ready, as Yeats said, to "vanish on the instant if the mind but change its theme," or if one is dropped among minds that have always known different themes. So when René Harding near the end of the novel is shown his wife on a morgue slab he sees her much as the squirrel had been seen:

> Topmost was the bloodstained head of Hester, lying on its side. The poor hair was full of mud, which flattened it upon the skull.

Her eye protruded: it was strange it should still have the strength to
go on peering on in the darkness.

This nauseous intensity of random detail, so expressive of René's
shock, fits the texture of much else in the book. In fitting, it clarifies
the intent of the book's less lurid passages: they document the
continuous disorientation of the political prisoner, the man displaced, the survivor (there have been millions) of a community
elsewhere in space or mislaid in time. Everyone alive today knows
something about this. The breakup of familiar order transposes
whole peoples into a sort of lifelong Toronto. Momaco, the slow-
motion city of *Self Condemned,* was made out of Lewis's experience
of Toronto, as later Third City in *The Human Age* was made out of
his experience of postwar London. Both are places of exile constructed by the imagination out of inhabited places, as though the
imagination were insisting that exile, since the wars, has entered into
the very stuff of human experience.

*   *   *

Meanwhile the New World went on providing, it supposed,
access to all that man's heart can desire: mountains and fir trees,
water and wheat and sunlight. Do men need men? Do they need
cities? The New World inclines to think not. Her sage is Thoreau.
She feels that her cities are her problem areas; that some economic
process, no doubt related to the concentrations of capital, makes
them exist and metabolize thought and wealth; but that they turn
cancerous.

But Europe is a place of cities, and the reliance of a Wyndham
Lewis on his city is so complex that a city on a lower plane of
organization than the old London's deprived him virtually of existence. (In that respect postwar London was like Toronto.) He was
not one of the millions whose gratitude has confirmed the New
World in its hypotheses, who deprived in Europe took life and hope
from the gift of elements in an elemental continent. It was not for
elements Lewis hungered but for community: for all that can cross
neither frontiers nor oceans: the web of relationships, indescribably
fragile, that made his career possible. Even his enmities were such
relationships.

After *Self Condemned* Lewis generalized the case of René Harding and reapplied it. He repeated the fictive experiment of cutting a man loose from Europe, but this time set him in alliance with the centers of power, for access to which René Harding had hungered. The centers of power were successively the Bailiff and the Lord Sammael, proprietors of worlds that come after this one, and the book was *The Human Age.* And power does the hero of that book no good at all. Theological issues then opened up which Lewis was still expecting to confront in 1956. In 1957 he died.

René in Momaco, Pullman in Third City and Dis, are beings abstracted from accustomed spaces and times. In the world in which we read these books little symptomatic adjustments occur. The arts turn anonymous, as we learn that the TV commercial, not the play with a known author or the painting validated by someone's signature, is the imaginative focus of our culture. The bicycle chain swings in a suburban street. An eye is gouged out. Crowds walk past death indifferently. And the New World's century is under way.

*   *   *

On the lawn of St. Elizabeths Hospital on summer afternoons, while Lewis in London was writing *The Human Age,* Ezra Pound swung a peanut on a stout cord to entice a patrolling squirrel. It came closer and closer with nervous flicks and darts, clutched the bait, and found itself hauled kicking into the lap of the eminent Confucian ("Come on, you little devil.") He untied the peanut and the squirrel scrambled off with it. He then re-baited the string for another squirrel. This was his recreation while he educated people who knew nothing, and mistaking his vitamin supplements for the meal, were apt to suppose that Latin literature consisted of Sextus Propertius, or that Aristotle was reducible to a phrase or two about currency. Pound had always presupposed an excellent formal education which he proceeded to modify. His signs of satisfaction with some of his Washington auditors suggest that he did not really reflect that he presupposed this. And when there was nothing to modify, the formulae of modification became a few crankish notions to rattle in some fervent void. That was his postwar milieu, much of the time. To some extent it is everybody's.

Pound thought, rightly, that *Self Condemned* deserved the Nobel Prize. The Nobel Prize, however, takes no heed of such books. Its formula of endowment speaks of "idealism." After it was announced Pound's acquaintance Allen Upward devoted an incredulous volume to assaying this word. He cited the semantic intricacies of *glaux* as the sort of detail a sanctioned "idealist" could be counted on to miss. Lewis of "the harsh and hirsute, the enemies of the rose," evaded no spiky detail.

THE JERSEY
PAIDEUMA

Each morning 24 hours lay ahead. The assignment was "to get through them without cracking." Around him milled the criminal lunatics. The need for "15 minutes *sane* conversation daily" was occasionally met by a doctor ("Olson saved my life"). There was also, improbably, a Dr. Kaffka.

Eventually he was moved from the prison ward to the Chestnut Ward, second floor. A visitor, once registered in a book labelled "Ezra Pound's Company," climbed an outside spiral stair and was admitted through a door that was locked behind him. Slippered men drifted along linoleum floors. Across a window alcove at the junction of two corridors an exiguous screen suggested that they pass without intruding. The denizens of Chestnut Ward were mostly suggestible, and seldom intruded on the alcove tête-à-têtes: Ezra, Dorothy, a visitor or two. Incursions from the illimitable sepsis "outside" distressed a blank-faced microbiophobe. The story went that when Possum Eliot arrived, all alarms jangled in the microbiophobe's psyche: the weskit, the umbrella, the ample tailored fabrics, these harbored, plainly, microbes by the billion. A sweeper was plied about the Possum's chair. Third-hand retellings of the story had Eliot sitting with his feet aloft while the floor in front of his chair was madly abraded. Anyhow it became the custom to draw the chairs in close, confining rare kibitzers to the periphery.

"Well, since you are younger and more vigorous than I, perhaps you will not mind if I sit *here* . . ."—in the reclining chair with the aluminum frame: rituals make ease: in ten minutes one was half-expecting tea to be served.

And letters were once more pouring out: pencilled ones through the hospital censor, who initialled the flap; typed ones mailed from Dorothy's flat. The typed letters were never signed; "Strictly Anonymous Communication," they were frequently headed, and the understood convention was that Dorothy had typed them, though the typing was a Gestalt of idiosyncrasies. They always mentioned "E. P." in the third person.

Marianne Moore visited, seeking help with LaFontaine. Cummings visited. Bill Williams visited. Eliot (Nobel Prize for Literature, 1948) visited and was lectured about the Times Slithery Souplement and about Faber and Faber's obligation to launch the documents of a real *paideuma*, Kung for example. Eliot felt no enthusiasm for Kung. And was there no one to translate the seven volumes of Frobenius's *Erlebte Erdteile?* Eliot was made uncomfortable by Frobenius. ("How you gwine ter keep deh Possum in his feedbox," Pound had written a Faber partner in 1937, "when I brings in deh Chinas and blackmen??")

Joseph Bard had put him onto Frobenius der Geheimrat in 1928, and when the anthropologist met the poet some years later each was astonished by his physical resemblance to the other. And what Frobenius meant by a *paideuma*—a people's whole congeries of patterned energies, from their "ideas" down to the things they know in their bones, not a *Zeitgeist* before which minds are passive —validated the *Cantos* and underwrote Pound's notion that the *Cantos* were "the tale of the tribe." And ("naturally") no anthropology department in America seemed to have heard of Frobenius, and no publisher ever underwrote a translation.

Leo Frobenius (1873–1938) had begun leading expeditions into Africa at the turn of the century, paleolithic cave paintings, then newly discovered, having suggested to him the sweep of a continuous civilization from Africa up into Europe. This is *Kulturmorphologie*; Gaudier with his migrating Vortices had a similar intuition. So, perhaps, did Picasso, who visited the Altamira cave in 1902 and put African masks into a famous painting in 1907. The Frobenius expeditions brought back such masks; Pound saw them at the Frobenius Institute in Frankfort, and remembered them looking at a fine African face in Pisa.

The natives also observed Frobenius. In Biembe, so we read in the *Erlebte Erdteile*, the apparition of white strangers set the Babunda tribesmen to beating ominous drums and drinking palm wine. But late in the night a drenching, flashing storm persuaded them to leave the white strangers in peace; their *paideuma* joined natural and human events so intimately that a few gestures they had seen Frobenius make were evidently what brought on the storm. Later he found he had left a knife among them, and the jungle-drum telegraph beat out plans for restoring it to a man it was sufficient to identify as (in German translation) "Der Weisse, der in Biembe das Gewitter gemacht hat": the white man who made the tempest in Biembe. By this honorific he is known in the *Cantos*; it is like a Homeric designation, and the adventure is like a scrap from a proto-Odyssey.*

Wanting evidence of *Kulturmorphologie*, Frobenius gathered folktales, the role of which in preserving knowledge deepened Pound's understanding of Ovid and the Chinese *Odes*. In *African Genesis* (1938) we may read the tale of the lute song of Gassire he took down in 1909 from a Djerma bard at Togo, with its "Hoooh Fasa" refrain and its city, Wagadu, four times remade. The lute would not sound until sufferers' blood had been spilled on it, one reason Pound remembered the tale at Pisa, blending its "four gates mid-wall" with the layout of the DTC and reflecting Frobenius' remark that Wagadu "ist mehr 'Idee' als Realität" with his "now in the mind indestructible."

> 4 times was the city rebuilded, Hooo Fasa
> Gassir, Hooo Fasa dell' Italia tradita

---

* The phrase first appears in Canto 38 (1933), though with a characteristic error, never corrected: "Baluba," from the preceding volume of *Erlebte Erdteile*, for "Beimbe." The story is in Vol. V, 49–53.

now in the mind indestructible, Gassir, Hooo Fasa,
With the four giants at the four corners
and four gates mid-wall Hooo Fasa
and a terrace the colour of stars
pale as the dawn cloud, la luna
    thin as Demeter's hair
Hooo Fasa, and in a dance the renewal
  with two larks in contrappunto
      at sunset
        ch'intenerisce
          (74/430:457)

But he did not give up hope of inflecting "Realität." Old friends came to "St Liz," new friends came, bluestockings came, the unfledged came, cranks came. He tended to be vulnerable to the cranks because they were prepared to *act*, and sometimes their actions could be guided. It was not an established publisher that finally issued Confucius at a dollar, bound with Fenollosa's Essay; it was John Kasper and David Horton, bringing to the service of a man who had struggled with printers all his life the discovery that the cheap new offset process made it unnecessary to set type anew. At moments when everyone was jumpy about "public opinion" his association with Kasper did Pound no good at all, but the "Square Dollar" Fenollosa (with *Pivot* and *Digest*) and the "Square Dollar" *Analects* (offset from *The Hudson Review*) were the only editions of these texts a person could buy for years and years. They were meant to go into the new *paideuma*. So were the Englished *Odes*, in the *Classic Anthology Defined by Confucius*. So was Sophocles' *Women of Trachis*, which he half-conceived as a Noh play. So was Pound's last St. Elizabeths project, an anthology, *Confucius to Cummings*, meant for use in classrooms. He persisted in his overestimation of classrooms.

*   *   *

Back in Rutherford, a stunned *paideuma* was occupying a man who knew it intimately. As the four parts of *Paterson* came out, 1946, 1948, 1949, 1951, literati who were just conceding the existence of the *Cantos* had also to accommodate that of Dr. Williams ("a

New Jersey pediatrician," one journal identified him, "who versifies between cases").

The long work surprised everyone but Williams, who had gestured toward it in 1914 ("The Wanderer") and thought of it seriously ever since *The Dial* published his 85-line poem called "Paterson" in 1927. "Say it, no ideas but in things," we read in that draft:

> —Say it, no ideas but in things—
> nothing but the blank faces of the houses
> and cylindrical trees
> bent, forked by preconception and accident
> split, furrowed, creased, mottled, stained
> secret—into the body of the light—

—lines embedded verbatim in *Paterson I* two decades later. "No ideas but in things" was his motto for at least that long.

"No ideas but in things" is an epistemology (what you can know is in front of you). It is a statement of American limitation (things are multiple in their opaque thinghood, no Duccio having transfigured the local stone). And it is a poetic, to rhyme with the "Lo Sordels si fo di Mantoana" Pound had set against the cult of "recreation" (what is actually to hand, put that on the page and that only). "Blocked," he wrote in Book II:

> Blocked.
>   (Make a song out of that; concretely)

"The thing that saves your work is *opacity*," Pound had written him in 1917, "and don't you forget it. Opacity is NOT an American quality. Fizz, swish, gabble of verbiage, these are echt Amerikanisch." Opacity:

> —an old barn
> is peaked there also, fatefully,
> against the sky. And there it is
> and we can't shift it or change
> it or parse it or alter it
> in any way.

And:

> There it is and
> we'd better acknowledge it and
> write it down that way, not otherwise.
> Not twist the words to mean
> What we should have said, but to mean
> —what cannot be escaped: the
> mountain riding the afternoon as
> it does, the grass matted green,
> green underfoot and the air—
> rotten wood.
>
> —"A Unison," 1946.

Since "things" comprise unobtrusive lilt and lift, it is permissible to say that the mountain rides the afternoon, and that the old barn is peaked "fatefully." One may even insert, as Williams did, eight words between these blocks—

> Listen! do you not hear
> them?   the singing?

—one of the things we'd better acknowledge and write down, on the same plane of reality as the old barn and the matted grass, though no microphone would pick up that song ("Hear! Hear them! / the Undying"). And what affirms their song in this place? The disposition of the place:

> a grove of gnarled
> maples centering the bare pasture,
> sacred, surely—for what reason?
> I cannot say. Idyllic!
> a shrine cinctured there by
> the trees, a certainty of music!

—that, and a 9-year-old's gravestone. Not Henry James, the connoisseur of absences, ever read an abandoned orchard more delicately.

For the grove is as much a statement as the stone. As someone carved the stone, so someone in clearing the pastureland left those trees, feeling something, meaning something. The temple at Delphi was built out of such geomantic sensitivities. Of Delphi a poet might write with some assurance, since it gathered an articulated cult. The American poet ("no ideas but in things") can only note the mysterious grove of trees, and writing for them the chorale they would enunciate, call his poem "A Unison."

("... The discreet voice of the air," wrote Henry James of Connecticut, "—which quavered away, for me, into still other admissions." In more than 400 pages without dialogue, *The American Scene* has no ideas but in things.)

"You need a poet," Williams mused (1957), "otherwise it would all die voiceless." He was looking across the Park on Garret Mountain, another mute statement. On May 2, 1880, according to an account transcribed in *Paterson II*, the German Singing Societies of Paterson understood that statement one way, and a man named William Dalzell understood it differently:

> ... However the meeting of 1880 proved a fatal day, when William Dalzell, who owned a piece of property near the scene of the festivities, shot John Joseph Van Houten. Dalzell claimed that the visitors had in previous years walked over his garden and was determined that this year he would stop them from crossing any part of his grounds.
>
> Immediately after the shot the quiet group of singers was turned into an infuriated mob who would take Dalzell into their own hands. The mob then proceeded to burn the barn into which Dalzell had retreated from the angry group.
>
> Dalzell fired at the approaching mob from a window in the barn and one of the bullets struck a little girl in the cheek. ...

That too was a dialogue. Below their babble of sound—

> Take the Pelham Bay Park Branch
> of the Lexington Ave. (East Side)
> Line and you are there in a few
> minutes

or

> Her milk don't seem to ..
> She's always hungry but ..
> She seems to *gain* all right,
> I don't know.

or (on the telephone, about a baby)

I, I, I don't think it's brEAthin'

—below this, around this, Americans are saying little of all they feel pressed to say, the *paideuma* intense but tacit. No one knows this better than the physician, confronting someone who wants an interview badly enough to have paid for it, and then cannot get beyond "She's always hungry but . . . / . . . I don't know." He learns to rely chiefly on physical signs. And if he is of Williams's generation he has no antibiotics to prescribe. He fends off despair while the body cures itself.

*   *   *

Paterson, New Jersey. "Paterson," the *London Times* explained on page 13 of its 7 Jan. 1965 issue, "is an imaginary town in New Jersey which Williams created as his symbol of America, and the poem is a mosaic of lyrical and narrative fragments about the people of this town, interspersed with fascinating newspaper clippings and letters." We may choose to take "imaginary town" as a testimonial to Williams's art. Paterson (pop. 139,423 in 1950, one third of them foreign-born whites) surrounds a waterfall on the Passaic River, 13 miles north of Newark and 17 miles northwest of New York City. When Williams was writing his poem a census disclosed 722 manufacturing establishments employing 27,700 people, 2582 retail outlets, some 700 wholesale houses. It was built by fiat in the 1790's, a planned community. L'Enfant the planner of Washington was engaged, but his plans were "more magnificent than practical," and cheaper ones were used.

A planned community, a System designed to incorporate human beings: that was a time's novelty (Pantisocracy, Oneida): an application of the new discovery, Systems. Newton's system, timeless because eventless, was no longer as interesting as Adam Smith's, through which coins circulate like heavenly bodies, both modelling and facilitating the transactions by which men sustain their lives and also improve them. Since the flow of currency, and the augmentation of its quantity, might ideally model an abundance stemming from nature, Smith was on the brink of envisaging ecology; but, Scotsman among hard people in a hard land, he was primarily aware of brute *work*. One is unaware of the abundance of nature when there is never quite enough to go round, and scarcity became an Invisible Hand, working a valve to keep the market self-regulating.

Adam Smith's younger contemporary James Watt modelled one cyclic system in his engine, water to steam to water to steam again, and incorporated another system, self-regulating, in the cycle of work for the sake of which the engine was worth building. His chief invention, the governor, supplied more steam when the engine was taxed and slowed down, less steam when it speeded up. In the next overlapping generation Thomas Malthus proposed a Food and Hunger Cycle, for which scarcity was once more the governor, producing homeostasis by starvation. When the land was over-grazed population would drop; as it dropped, food would regenerate.

But nothing was scarce in America, not even Power; those falls would not wear out. In 1791 Alexander Hamilton of the exploiter's eye helped charter the Society for Establishing Useful Manufactures, which still owns the Paterson falls. It was to have tapped their power to supply the colonies with manufactured goods —all the "cotton, cassimeres, wall papers, books, felt and straw hats, shoes, carriages, pottery, bricks, pots, pans and buttons needed in the United States." At one time water diverted around the falls drove 247 undershot waterwheels. The Society included the new town's population in its feedback loop, but homeostasis soon had to be preserved by clubs and guns, the wealth distributed by the act of production being (C. H. Douglas would have said) insufficient to buy the product. Within three years the S.U.M. was party to the first American lockout, and three decades later to the first American strike. It was bad for the people, the economy, and the landscape. Today "the falls themselves are a dry cleft in the rock, except when the river is in flood." At one time travellers thought they rivalled Niagara. Williams saw the landscape as a comatose giant:

> Eternally asleep
> his dreams walk about the city where he persists
> incognito. Butterflies settle on his stone ear.
> Immortal he neither moves nor rouses and is seldom

seen, though he breathes and the subtleties of his machinations
drawing their substance from the noise of the pouring river
animate a thousand automatons.

Are these automatons the machines? No, they are the people,

> Who because they
> neither know their sources nor the sills of their
> disappointments walk outside their bodies aimlessly
> for the most part
> locked and forgot in their desires—unroused.

A familiar kind of story; and having looked across the Hudson at
such bleakness in 1910 and again in 1939, Ezra Pound saw in a
drizzling Pisan dawn

> the lights of the penal area
> as some Jersey City by Lethe.

* * *

Paterson may be described, along one of its axes, as Pound's
30 years' war applied to a local case. So Williams rhymes Hamilton's
scheme (which ruined the falls) with excerpts from a pamphlet
against the Federal Reserve System ("a Legalized National Usury
System, whose Customer No. 1 is our Government, the richest
country in the world.") He collected stifled invectives written by
cranks, instances of the pressure toward cogent speech of which
his governing image is the roar of the falls, a babble out of which
meaning must be combed:

> A false language. A true. A false language pouring—a
> language (misunderstood) pouring (misinterpreted) without
> dignity, without minister, crashing upon a stone ear.

As for the poet,

> Caught (in mind)
> beside the water he looks down, listens!
> But discovers, still, no syllable in the confused
> uproar: missing the sense (though he tries)
> untaught but listening, shakes with the intensity
> of his listening .

And when his listening has been rewarded, they say

> We're so proud of you!

> A wonderful gift! How *do*
> you find the time for it in

> your busy life? It must be a great
> thing to have such a pastime. . . .

> Or, Geeze, Doc, I guess it's all right
> but what the hell does it mean?

—with which Williams juxtaposed an account of an Indian ritual:

> Whereupon, as the smoke ascends on high, the sacrificer
> crying with a loud voice, *Kännakä, Kännakä!* or sometimes *Hoo,
> Hoo!* turns his face towards the east.
> While some are silent during the sacrifice, certain make a
> ridiculous speech, while others imitate the cock, the squirrel and
> other animals, and make all kinds of noises. . . .

No ideas but in things, no words but in local words.

> —of this, make it of *this*, this
> this, this, this, this   .

* * *

Two boys went to Harvard. One stayed home afterward, and became an insurance executive. The other went abroad, and became a banker and publisher. Both wrote poetry.

Two boys went to Penn. One stayed home afterward and became a physician. The other went abroad, and became Ezra Pound.

Stevens: Eliot. Williams: Pound. It is as neat as a laboratory experiment. And Williams, the intensely local, was often in Europe, whereas Stevens, the exotic, never went there.

One evening on the Chestnut Ward TV Ezra Pound heard of Stevens's death. "*Poetry* owes him a memorial issue," was his immediate response; and would someone, preferably ol Doc Wms, take the occasion to say what it was that Wallace Stevens's work had been all about? The request was passed on to Williams, and he wrote a feeling obituary but did not venture to answer the question.

Of the four, Stevens alone concerned himself not at all with a *paideuma*: rather with

> Pure coruscations, that lie beyond
> The imagination, intact
> And unattained,

in fact,

> the ithy oonts and long-haired
> Plomets

—an Edward Lear poetic, pushed toward all limits.

THE LAST VORTEX

He had turned 20 in Pennsylvania,
30 in London, 40 not long after leaving Paris, 50 in Rapallo, 60 in
the Detention Training Center "in sight of Mount Taishan at
Pisa"; now 70 in the madhouse, by which time, 30 October 1955,
the canon had acquired three major additions: a full version of the
Chinese *Odes*, a version of Sophocles' least known play, and a new
block of Cantos.

The *Odes* fulfill a resolve he had implied in Rapallo with only
Legge's English version ("an infamy") and Père Lacharme's
18th-century Latin to go by: "Dust on my head, that I trod the
earth 50 years and have not read them in the original." Here
Washington offered opportunities: visitors who could read the
Chinese aloud to him, and answer questions, and call his attention to
Karlgren's immensely learned notes and transcriptions (which he
worked through, annotating). And one could buy a Harvard reprint
of Mathews' Dictionary, which alphabetizes the characters by their
romanized sounds, thus encouraging the frequent seeker to bear
sounds in mind. (This is why, commencing with Canto 85, pronunciations and tone numbers appear in the *Cantos* as well as
ideograms.) He was in a position for the first time in his life to

satisfy some of his old curiosity about Chinese sonorities, and sustained by his new resources he performed intermittent wonders,
letting for instance the sound of *yu tsai yu tsai* suggest "lute sound
in lute sound is caught" at a different place in the same Ode (#1),

or reproducing the Chinese eye-rhyme 磬 聲 *ch'ing*, "a

musical stone" and *sheng*, "a sound" with an English ear-rhyme,
"the stone's tone under it all." (#301). And as always he etymologized *ad libitum*. When the words Karlgren maps for #259—

> Lofty is the sacred mountain, grandly it reaches to heaven; the
> Sacred Mountain sent down a Spirit who bore (the princes of) Fu
> and Shen; (the princes of) Fu and Shen became the supports of
> Chou; the states of the four (quarters) they went to (fence, be a
> fence to =) protect, the (states of) the four quarters they went to
> (wall, be a wall to =) defend

become, in Pound's text,

> High, pine-covered peak full of echos,
> Proud ridge-pole of Heaven, roof-tree
> whence descended the whirl of spirits
> begetters of Fu and Shen,
> Out of the echoing height, whirling spirits of air
>   descended.
> To sires of Chou were given in vassalage, bulwarks
> under the bright wings of the sun
> a square kingdom against invasion,
> Strong as the chamber of winds,

the recreator has found uses for the 山 *mountain* and 松

pine-tree components in the name of the sacred mountain, *Sung*,

崧 ; and espied 言 *a word* enclosed in the character 嶽

high mountain, hence "peak full of echoes"; and extracted *wings*
羽 and 日 *sun* from 翰 *support* (in the phrase "the
supports of Chou") to generate a whole line, "under the bright
wings of the sun." This last is not an autodidactic quarrel with the
dictionary meaning of the character, since "bulwarks" stands for
that meaning. It is one device among many for getting more

resonance out of this stanza than the dictionary will yield. The justification of all these devices is the ceremonious result.

Pound once called the *Odes* "China's epic," meaning in part "a poem including history," in part the corpus of tested wisdom Kung and Mencius drew on as Socrates drew on Homer, in part the variegated *paideuma* sprung from the folk and millenially active in China. No comparable reservoir of impulses feeds English poetry, so often have languages and traditions changed. His version, touched by the mannerisms of the main English modes since the Miracle Plays, was meant to suggest how such an English tradition might feel if it existed: a service to readers of English, not to students of Chinese. And a unity come out of seeming miscellany would give the *Cantos* one more precedent. Much tensile light unknown to sinology shines through the ceremonial Odes at the end of the volume, extracted from ideograms in St Liz as once in Pisa, and in the last line of the last poem the sign 成 (*perfected, achieved*) activated his cherished heretical etymology "focus" to yield a triumphant finale:

> They went up the King mountain,
> straight trunks of pine and cypress
> they cut and brought here,
> hewed pillars and rafters
> carved beam-horns ornate
> contrived pillars and sockets
> to the inner shrine, perfect
> that his ray come to point in this quiet.

*   *   *

A man of 70 may be conceded the right to deeds which raise more questions than they can answer. Pound's *Classic Anthology Defined by Confucius* is not the *Shi Ching* (Book of Odes) Chinese readers know, let alone the somewhat different field of attention scholars of Chinese know, for the evident reason that it is a book of poems in English.

習   習   谷   風

hsi   *hsi*   *ku*   *feng* ...

Hsi (it is the "white wings" ideogram we encountered near Pisa) means "repeated practice," and *ku* means "valley," and *feng* means "wind." But *ku feng* means "east wind," a compound in which "valley" seems more relevant, but perhaps is no more active, than the "butter" in "butterfly." Though the degree of the valley's presence is not for a westerner to guess at, he may guess that it is tricky for a native scholar, etymological lore and linguistic response being so often separable vectors. And *hsi* with "east wind" means something quite different from "repeated practice," it means "gentle," a meaning Mathews' Dictionary illustrates only from the line before us, the first line of Ode #201, a line perhaps 3000 years old and long proverbial. We are deep in the whispering forest of all traditional poetries ("Who, for instance, has a first-hand opinion of Shakespeare?"), where the very words to which millions of minds respond have helped form the minds that respond to them. You and I and Ezra Pound are attending to them for the first time, with Mathews' and Karlgren's help. Follow Pound, put "East Wind" for your title, write

> Soft wind of the vale
> that brings the turning rain,

and you stir the whispers of a different forest, the one in which English sensibilities have learned to feel that "vale" is less topo-graphic than "valley" (indeed "chiefly poetic," says the *O.E.D.*, citing Wordsworthian slumbers stealing o'er vale and mountain, and Shakespeare's vale of years); where moreover soft winds when they blow through very short lines of verse animate a lyric tradition so nearly anonymous that it is rather an air in the mind than a cluster of examples. This English tradition has never, unlike the Chinese, been annexed to moral directives that will not forget Kung's "ruler like the wind over grass" nor suffer *feng* to lose touch with pervasive custom, a climate emanating from the ruler. For no more than a Christian can dissociate lying down by still waters from the Good Shepherd, can a Chinese be expected to isolate *feng*, the wind, in these Odes, from generations of moral commentary. There is no way to translate all this.

... As Pound seems to have realized when he plotted so many

points of analogy between this and that Ode, this and that recognizable English voice, Browning's, Chaucer's, Pope's, the Bible's, even
Joel Chandler Harris's. Only a whole mobilized tradition, he implies, can hope to match this one. It can't, really, so differently are
the traditions structured. And the unanswerable question remains,
what would English literature be like, what on earth would it be
like, could the whole *Shi Ching* be somehow annexed to it? There are
traditional ways of imagining how one's literature might be enriched by the presence of something equally exotic, the epic of the
Homeridae of Chios. Vergil tried to imagine this for one language,
Milton for another. But neither Latin nor English contains "the
epic" as a result; they contain *The Aeneid* and *Paradise Lost,*
eccentric, seminal donations. It is not because Pound did less well
with some poems than with others, or because he ignored scholarly
caution so often, or even because his own English decorum sometimes broke down, that the *Classic Anthology* is not the *Shi Ching* in
English. It might have been more fully what it is, but there was no
way for it to be more than it is, an eccentric donation, possibly
seminal.

*   *   *

More: what on earth, in any vernacular, would a Greek
tragedy be? What would we do with it? Act it? How? Where?
Choruses, declamations, stichomythia, what would we make of
them, reading? There is not even, as there is with the epic, a continuous tradition of attempts to find out, and tragedy seems embedded as is no other ancient genre in a time, a place, and a culture:
Ancient Greek Theater, radically unlike any other. Men have never
thought of the *Iliad* in that way as Ancient Greek Poetry. Even our
own Formulaic Homer is manifestly our own, a modern being
unknown to Bentley or Jowett, let alone Aristotle, extrapolated by
20th-century minds from 20th-century researches in Yugoslavia.
There is no Sophokles we call our own. There are "translations,"
poor things we call our own, consisting of rant intermixed with
naivete, the rant scaled down, the naivete stepped through with
imperturbable pedagogy, "O suitably attired in leather boots" as
Housman imperishably phrased the process.

What we do possess with regard to the tragedies is a record of their recurrent discovery by poets in crisis, the very pedantry of the form permitting the indulgence of self-expression. Thus H. D., forcing every occasion to dilate on her preferred imagery of weeds and sandy shores, turned choruses from Euripides into statements of her own impassioned sterility. Milton's play about Samson was written a decade after the rout of the Protectorate in which he had been an official, and when we read in its bitter opening speech,

> Ask for this great Deliverer now, and find him
> Eyeless in *Gaza* at the Mill with slaves,

we know with whose agony we are in touch; and comparably, when we read in Pound's *Women of Trachis* words written in a Washington madhouse though ascribed to "Herakles (*in the mask of divine agony*)" we cannot doubt that the mask is Pound's *persona*, strange, remote, primitive enough to voice things the high decorums of China had forbidden:

> Holy Kanea, where they build holy altars,
> done yourself proud, you have,
> nice return for a sacrifice:
>> messing me up.
> I could have done without these advantages
> And the spectacle of madness in flower,
>> incurable, oh yes.
> Get some one to make a song for it,
> Or some chiropractor to cure it.
> A dirty pest,
>> take God a'mighty to cure it and
> I'd be surprised to see Him
>> coming this far...

(And who but Ezra Pound, wanting an ultimate in iatric futility, would have let *cheirotechnes* supply him with "chiropractor"?)

As this diction suggests, the play also belongs to the story of its author's 40 years' dialogue with T. S. Eliot, with perhaps for informal epigraph the opening of Canto 46:

> And if you will say that this tale teaches...
> a lesson, or that the Reverend Eliot
> has found a more natural language... you who think you will
> get through   hell   in   a   hurry...

Eliot's "more natural language" came with unforeseen acclaim to Broadway in 1950, in *The Cocktail Party*, another tacit self-revelation and—as Pound may have learned before the public did the next year—another play about Herakles.

Vivien Eliot, long deranged, had died in 1947. During 1948 T. S. Eliot began and brought to nearly final form his unsettling drawing-room comedy, with its psychiatrist-Herakles, a bold lift from the *Alcestis* of Euripides, offering to bring back a lost wife from a place we cannot imagine. Eliot's Sir Henry Harcourt-Reilly is as suavely elusive a figure as his creator. If we are never told he is Herakles, we are never told that he is a psychiatrist either, much as we are tempted to think so. He drinks a great deal (gin and water), breaks into song, dispenses oracular wisdom, traffics in supernatural rites. Though his drawing-room manners are impeccable, he is meant to disorient the securities of a drawing-room play; as Alec Guinness played him, equivocally smiling, he fascinated Edinburgh and Broadway audiences, who had no idea either that the playwright was exposing private agonies or that they were looking at a Greek play transposed; or that its theology was (somehow) Christian, or— in all cases anyhow—that it was written in verse (one Edinburgh reviewer mentioned "deathless prose" repeatedly).

So much dam' evasiveness, and Christian to boot; it was quite enough to send Ezra Pound back to "the *real* Greeks" he and his subtle collaborator had both tried to renovate back in the *Waste Land* period. Eliot had sent an attempt at the *Agamemnon*, or part of it. Pound had tried to improve it; had "twisted, turned, tried every ellipsis and elimination. . . . made the watchman talk nigger, and by the time you had taken out the remplissage, there was no play left on one's page." And now Eliot had demonstrated that you could hold the commercial stage by removing from a Greek play everything identifiably Greek. Responding as of old, *il miglior fabbro* made no such concessions to prudence. He drew on his unbetterable grand manner—

> TORN between griefs, which grief shall I lament
> which first? Which last, in heavy argument?
> One wretchedness to me in double load.

DEATH'S in the house,
> and death comes by the road;

his old semantic vigor—

> ... the Hydra in Lerna
> and those unsociable bardots, half man and half horse,
> the whole gang of them all together
> arrogant, lawless, surpassing strong,
> and the Eurymanthian animal, and that three-headed pup
> from Hell down under, the Echidna's nursling
> brought up by an out-size viper,
> and the dragon-guard of the golden apples
> at the end of the world;

and an intricacy, learned long ago from Arnaut, of assonance and internal rhyme—

> ... The great weight silent
> for no man can say
> If sleep but feign
> or Death reign instantly.

As for what should be done with this, it should be staged. He specified musical effects, invented *opsis*, hinted that *Noh* players might add it to their repertoire. These are hints, not really thought out, that might stimulate a director. (Here Eliot had the advantage of a producer working with him closely upon the text. Eliot was patient, and was not in prison.) What Pound did think out was an overarching form, making the play run "from the dawn blaze to sunset," from the opening of the first Chorus,

> Phoebus, Phoebus, ere thou slay
> and lay flaked Night upon her blazing pyre

to the pyre that will consume "Herakles, the solar vitality" when Hyllos has done his bidding at the end. And the line about comprehending the Oracle's words, in which a footnote invites us to find "the key phrase, for which the rest of the play exists," runs in Greek

> ταῦτ' οὖν ἐπειδὴ λαμπρὰ συμβαίνει, τέκνον

"Since, then, my son, those words are clearly finding their fulfilment," and in Pound's English,

> come at it that way, my boy, what
> SPLENDOUR,
>   IT ALL COHERES.

For *lampra*, which the construing mind reads "clearly," at root means "radiantly." Pound saw the flames of the pyre and the inflammation of the Nessus shirt subsumed at this moment by intellectual light, the body of light coming forth from the body of fire. In Canto 87, lifting a word from the first Chorus, he calls it "The play shaped from φλογιζόμενον" (blazing), and claiming to have made it new, sets above this line the axe-tree-woodpile "Make It New" ideogram, and the ideogram of the sun (87/571:607).

The inert lexicographic reverence that normally kills Greek plays in English does not touch these pages thanks to that governing vision. Vision controls the details like a magnetic field, turning, for instance, *lampra* into "splendour" and supplying, out of hints in the Greek words, the "blazing pyre" on which dawn consumes night. Recurrent lapses, unhappily, beset the often brilliant execution, all of one kind but very troublesome for actors. The messenger who says "'Arf a mo' Ma'am!'" says a moment later "Jus' lis'en a bit," forcing the player to mediate between Putney and Chicago. The Queen's diction includes "Put it on the line" and "Well, my dears, I been thinking 'bout that," and a Chorus whose repertoire extends to "Aye, thou art keen, as is the lightning blaze" must find a convincing way to say "Nope." That dialogue should be colloquial is in keeping, but not colloquial written like a foreign language, single words patched in without regard for idiom. *Spoken* colloquial is highly formalized, as Mark Twain knew when he structured five dialects in *Huckleberry Finn*, and as Pound in the past, though without Twain's virtuosity, had also shown he knew. Noting similar but rarer lapses in the *Odes*, we may reflect that for the first time in decades he was surrounded by American speech, not of uniform quality. His environment contained guards and lunatics, who spoke coherently, and visitors, who often did not.

*   *   *

He was feeding what he hoped would be a novelist, out of Sealtight containers from the hospital kitchen. "X is silent on two occasions. When he is eating; and when I am talking." (And, "Pound," he would say, "an enclosure for stray animals.") He was sparring with the great lady of classical studies, aged 85 years, Edith Hamilton. She had heard of a great Confucian who wrote a letter, such that only one other man in all China could understand. "That is not very democratic, I'm afraid. That is aristocratic, like you, Mr. Pound."

"But it is democratic as long as it provides that any one may have the opportunity to learn enough to read that letter."

He was recalling efforts to spring Basil Bunting from a Paris jail: ". . . And the officer learning that I was a man of letters, and concerned with the welfare of another man of letters, produced from his pocket a poem of his own, with the lady's name running in acrostic down the initial letters, and when I had read it said in a tone of apology, 'Ça plait beaucoup aux dames'." . . . [A long silence, the head thrown back, the eyes closed. Then, starting suddenly forward:] "Sometimes the guards ask *me* . . . to write poems . . . for them to give their sweethearts." "And do you?" "Why, yes!" The guards could discern a pro. So could Shakespeare's clientele: the sonnets, Pound thought, and notably the "advice to the young man" (83/534:569) were the work of "a public letter writer." And in St Liz there was also the inmate who wanted his name typewritten on a handkerchief; for writers have divers functions, meet divers demands.

Hemingway, one learned from full-page advertisements, endorsed—a beer, was it? Also a fountain pen. "Hem always believed that you should get yours *in*side the system." And when *The Old Man and the Sea* had appeared in *Life*, "One of the fellows in my ward . . . thinks it's a pretty good job." Dorothy laughed; her back, she said, had been stiff, when she finished the story, from all the rowing. Ezra's mind was on Bob McAlmon, who was never inside the system. "When McAlmon met me his very first words were, 'I think I should tell you that I do not admire your work'. And whereas Hem would polish . . . and polish . . . [polishing gestures] . . . McAlmon would rip the sketch off and start a new one. Because McAlmon was curious about human variants. Whereas Hem . . . never knew one human being from another . . . and never much cared."

But he would permit this kind of talk about his old friends from no one else, and when a seeming decrease in Eliot's sense of fun was remarked, his response was severe: "When a man has had to turn his home for years into a private madhouse . . . that is not conducive to a sense of humor."

*   *   *

The best talk in St Liz was the monologue. Had he listened so much, in Rapallo, to the sound of his own voice? Possibly not. And the best writing that came out of his Washington vortex was contained in the new Cantos, which he did not have to accommodate to surrounding idioms, Chinese or Greek or American, because he had the freedom of a poem which he alone owned and operated. In 1955 *Section: Rock-Drill. 85–95 de los Cantares* took its title from the heading ("The Rock Drill") of Lewis's review of Pound's *Letters* in the 7 April 1951 *New Statesman and Nation*. The rock-splitter in these Cantos is persistent growth: as the "hidden city" of trees challenged the Venetian "forest of marble," so now we are to think of "pine seed splitting cliff's edge," and reflect, prompted by the flyleaf of Pound's *Analects*, on "the kind of intelligence that enables grass seed to grow grass; the cherry-stone to make cherries." The word "roots" is emphatic as early as line 3 of the text; a dynasty grows massively when "a great sensibility" roots it. On the second page we find the sun and the sheltered grass; and

> Not led of lusting, not of contriving
> > but is as the grass and tree
> eccellenza
> > not led of lusting
> > not of the worm, contriving.

Next we learn of Rapallo peasants bringing cocoons to Easter mass under their aprons,

> That you lean 'gainst the tree of heaven
> > and know Ygdrasail

—the Norse heaven-tree; an organicism contrasted with the cult of

> This "leader", gouged pumpkin
> that they hoist on a pole

—such dicta twined round a full 104 ideograms in the first *Rock-Drill* Canto alone, ideograms taken from the History Classic, *Chou King* (Couvreur's edition with Latin and French translations), and represented as the millennial seeds from which imperishable China grew: in a later phrase, "Gestalt seed." As once before, China is followed by America, the chief source being Senator ("old bullion") Benton's *Thirty Years in the U.S. Senate*, during the time of the Bank Wars. And as China and America (52–71) had been followed by the retrospect of Pisa, so now China and America juxtaposed introduce vision and concealed retrospection.

For as in Pisa, his mind ran back. He had thought long ago of building the *Cantos* round the legend of the twin pines of Takasago and Sumiyoshi, which were the visible forms of the spirits of a man and a woman, and in their rhyming growth in places remote from each other (nearly as remote, in ancient Japan, as China and America now) enacted the unity of these spirits, and the pervasion of the universe by poetry, and the auspices of an orderly reign. The story of Baucis and Philemon is cognate; so is the heaven-tree; so is the very first poem in *Personae*, one he had written in his youth for Hilda; so are the self-interfering patterns of "wood alive, of stone alive" in the 1912 essay on Psychology and the Troubadours that was printed in G. R. S. Mead's *Quest* and is now chapter six of *The Spirit of Romance*. He wrote to Dublin for W. B. Yeats's copy of John Heydon's *Holy Guide*, mention of which had dropped out of the poem long ago when the Ur-Cantos were suppressed, and though he was to grumble to Mrs. Yeats that there was less in it than he had remembered, he extracted congenial details from the "Secretary of Nature's" strange treatise on sympathetic medicine and the use of herbs and metals. And he recalled from the days with Mead a sage whose life Mead had written, Apollonius of Tyana, and worked through the two Loeb volumes of Philostratus' Life of Apollonius, extracting phrases, as "that the universe is alive." He wanted materials for a rhyming and harmonized cosmos pervaded by respect for

orderly growth, something very like the universe of Buckminster
Fuller, one of whose pupils came to visit him: the full Confucian
"process" which the Great Digest tells us commences from an
activity which Pauthier had evasively called "investigating the
principles of actions," but which Pound had finally called "sorting
things into organic categories." (And in the 18th century, by
contrast, they had "only the alphabet for a filing system.") "This
completion of knowledge is rooted in sorting things into organic
categories"—so *The Great Digest*, 1945, Pisa. That is where everything starts: where, we are to remember, Agassiz started: it may
ignore inherited categories. And noting the words "rooted" and
"organic," we need not be surprised at the leap in Canto 90 from
ordered empiricism to great holy trees:

> "From the colour the nature
> > & by the nature the sign!"
> Beatific spirits welding together
> > as in one ash-tree in Ygdrasail.
> > Baucis, Philemon.
> > > (90/605:639)

—whereupon the upward sweep becomes that of a fountain—

> Castalia is the name of that fount in the hill's fold,
> > the sea below,
> > > narrow beach.

—and (Greek temples being stone enactments of pillar'd trees)

> Templum aedificans, not yet marble,
> > "Amphion!"

—Amphion, who made Theban walls rise to music; and we move
(via China) to another building,

> the room in Poitiers where one can stand
> > casting no shadow.

Cantos 90, 91, 92, 93, four visionary Cantos, present a syncretic
exaltation nowhere previously present in the poem. Then it fades,
and we find him gazing at a leaf:

> The autumn leaves blow from my hand,
> > agitante calescimus . . .
> > and the wind cools toward autumn.

> Lux in diafana,
>> Creatrix,
>>> oro. . . .

> For me nothing. But that the child
>> walk in peace in her basilica,
> the light there almost solid.
>> (93/628:661)

(So the clear mountain light had been when he came footsore, 1943, to visit his child in Gais.) Botticelli's petal'd air (Mauberley's "aerial flowers," Kung's blowing apricot blossoms in Canto 13, the "live tradition" to be "gathered from the air" in Pisa) come into the vision—

> Came then Flora Castalia
>> "Air hath no petals now,
>> where shall come leaf on bough
>>> naught is but air.
>>> "pone metum, Cerinthe,
> Nec deus laedit . . .
>> (93/630:663)

"—Lay aside fear, the god does not harm lovers": the words Sulpicia spoke in Canto 25 with her flute in her hand, that tube of empty air. And finally:

> Flora Castalia, your petals drift thru the air,
>> the wind is ½ lighted with pollen
>>> diafana
> e Monna Vanna . . . tu mi fai rimembrar.
>> (93/632:665)

"Tu mi fai rimembrar": you call to mind (Dante says) where and what Proserpine was, when her mother lost her and she lost the spring flowers:

>> nel tempo che perdette
> la madre lei, ed ella primavera.
>> —*Purgatorio* xxviii, 49–51.

The flowers gone, we turn back to books: Apollonius, and finally Homer's account of the raft of Odysseus, blown upon "as it were

thistle-down" until Leucothoe gave him her miraculous garment
the *kredemnon* ("my bikini is worth your raft") to bear him to the
shore of the Phaeacians where men will hear his tales: as under those
Washington elms, amid those squirrels.

*   *   *

Each group of Cantos, it grows clear, has its special plane of
attention: the first 16, we may say, perspective, all things in the mind
simultaneous; the next group, journeyings; 31–41, letters and documents; 42–51, money and fertility; 52–71, history and biography;
the Pisan sequence, memory; 85–95, vegetable growth; and finally,
Thrones, 96–109, philology. For there is nothing elsewhere in the
poem to match the concern of this last full block Pound completed
for individual terms, precisions, distinctions, correlations.

As Joyce progressed from tidy narrative to verbal phantasmagoria, so the *Cantos*. In *Thrones* the words, as never before, are
exhibited.

> Remy's word was "milésiennes"
> William's: monoceros,
> vide his book plate.
> (104/742:768)

In Tibet one may hear

> Na Khi talk made out of wind noise,
>   And North Khi, not to be heard amid sounds of the forest
> but to fit in with them unperceived by the game.
> (104/738:764)

Elsewhere,

> the sheep on Rham plains have different names
> according to colour,
> nouns, not one noun plus an adjective.
> (105/747:772)

Anselm develops "a clear line on the Trinity" "by sheer grammar"
(105/750:775). There are even pages of Byzantine lexicography, at
one point given ideographic cognates. Ford is quoted on learning
the meaning of words (98/689:719), and Frobenius on the German

pupil who "took the Z for the tail of the KatZe" (102/729:755), and Dr. Nicole is detected committing the Pound-like "error" of letting the look of a Greek word suggest a French one:

> ... rather nice use of *aveu*, Professor
> though you were looking at ἄνευ.
> (96/667:698)

Like the talking oak at Dodona, nature has voices.

> The cat talks μάω
> (mao) with a Greek inflection,
> (102/729:745)

—*mao* (in a rising tone) being Chinese for cat, and μάω Greek for what the cat says, "I am hunting." Dictionaries merely sample this profusion. A Chinese name is cited as "not in Mathews" (96/653:685) and the Byzantine vocabulary is "not Dr. Liddell's" (96/658:690). There is delight in linguistic accidents, the pairing of θῖνα θαλάσσης (the sea shore) with "thinning their oar-blades" (98/684:714), or the splendid opportunism that can pair the ideo-gram of the tensile light with the ideal music of the Pythagoreans—

> by the silk cords of the sunlight
> Chords of the sunlight (*Pitagora*)
> non si disuna (xiii)
> (98/693:723)

—the last phrase Dante's (*Paradiso* xiii.56) for the light which emanates from its source but (like a stretched thread) does not leave its source behind.

For words build laws, which extend through time like those cords. We follow Edward Coke picking through the words of ancient statutes:

> Cope is a hill
> dene: a valley, arundinetum
> drus is a thicket
> Si nomina nescis perit rerum cognitio
> nemo artifex nascitur
> (109/772:796)

"If you do not know names the knowledge of things disappears"; and (a turn on Nero's "Qualis artifex pereo!" as well as a rebuke

to "poeta nascitur non fit") "No one is born a master." Hence
Ford's advice, "Get a dictionary;" and

> I shall have to learn a little greek to keep up with this
> but so will you, drratt you
>
> (105/750:775)

With the aid of a little Greek and a little Chinese we are led through
the terminology of the *Eparchikon Biblion*, that of Coke, and that
of Wang the "commissioner of the salt-works" who rendered the
Sacred Edict in the vulgar tongue. For "thought is built out of
Sagetrieb,"* and we find "The meaning of the Emperor" juxtaposed
with "ten thousand years heart's-tone-think-say" (98/691:721). In
the parts of the Sacred Edict Pound has excerpted we are to discern
the wisdom that arose from the people being returned to them,
codified.

   Good humor is conspicuous in these Cantos ("Gemisto: 'Are
Gods by hilaritas'"—98/685:715). Pound takes huge enjoyment in
his lexicographic high jinks, teases the presumably impatient
reader—

> Patience, I will come to the Commissioner of the Salt Works
> in due course
>
> (98/685:715)

—and closes the sequence with a shout over his shoulder:

> You in the dinghey (piccioletta) astern there!
>
> (109/774:798)

—"you in the dinghey" being the reader once more, following
Odysseus' great bark through this foam of language as the reader of
Dante ("o voi che siete in piccioletta barca") followed his singing
keel (*Paradiso* ii.1). Turn back, calls Dante to the casual follower,
for if you lose me you will be left to wander, but as for you other
few, *voi altri pochi*, why, follow.

* * *

* A lexicographic puzzle, not in the German dictionaries. "Saying-force"? In
Canto 90 it is paired with "tradition," but its etymology suggests paideumic energies,
not passive inheritance. Pound ascribes the word to Frobenius, in whose text it has
not to my knowledge so far been found, though Frobenius (*Erlebte Erdteile*, IV)
has much to say about the inborn urge to make one's tradition into poetry.

"Follow": where? Canto 117, ran the rumor, would be the termination; and one day, having been challenged on his capacity to devise an ending, Pound produced under the elms a sheet of paper— "That is for the last Canto"—bearing 16 ideograms blocked into a square. "That is my first Chinese quatrain." Would there be a translation? No, only the pronunciations. "It consists of the sixteen ideograms I find most interesting." Chinese has advantages; you cannot make an English poem out of the 16 words you find most interesting.

They included, of course, *hsien*[3], the sun's silk, "manifest," and *chien*[4], the luminous eye with its legs, and *ching*[4] which we are told on the flyleaf of the *Analects* means reverence for seminal intelligence. Here, the early Cantos' great blocks having been ground into *Thrones'* luminous particles, all threads were to converge like sun-silk into 16 terms; and as he had begun the voyage a half-century before, bringing blood to Homer's ghosts, now in Ithaca he was to dispose luminosities each pregnant with intrinsic racial experience, and make a new poem by manipulating the oldest written signs still used in the world. From translating to creating, but

> it is not man
> Made courage, or made order, or made grace,

and the poet does not make the meanings he releases. It was an astonishing arc to contemplate. Its completion was but a few Cantos off, and notebooks held drafts of the convergences to come. He had less working time left than he knew.

* * *

On 18 April 1958 he heard himself described in a Federal courtroom as permanently, incurably insane, so that there was no point in holding him under indictment. He was therefore free. Being formally incompetent, he could not sign a contract or a check. Robert Frost, who had said to Richard Wilbur, "To hell with him, he's where he belongs," claimed credit for this event, and drew attention to its magnanimity. Much more credit, it would seem, belongs to Archibald MacLeish, who drafted the letter Frost signed, to Harry Meacham of Richmond, whose tireless letters let no one's attention wander, to Congressman Burdick of Idaho, who demanded that the case be investigated, and to H. A. Sieber of the Library of Congress, whose report, putting on record so many Pisan details, may have inhibited Congressional denunciations. No one man needs the credit. Moving a government is like moving a brontosaur, whose centers of consciousness are distributed through innumerable ganglia. Thus enquirers at the Library of Congress will be told that the Sieber Report is kept in the strictest confidence, whereas browsers in the *Congressional Record* may find it there, as read into the record by Congressman Burdick.

Pound went to the Atlantic coast and gazed at the sea, huddled in blankets. He went to Wyncote once more, and kissed Dorothy under the apple tree in the backyard of his boyhood house. He was photographed by Richard Avedon, eyes shut against the sun like blind Tiresias. He told the press that Ovid had had it worse, in the long years at Pontus, a statement the press was unprepared to evaluate. Under a sky now receiving dust from artificial satellites, he went down to the ship for the last time. The *Cristoforo Colombo* set forth on the godly sea, toward Italy. He had spent one quarter of his working life in confinement.

ENDINGS

Rome kept watch up the valley of the Athesis down which transalpine barbarians were likely to pour toward Lombardy. Latin became Italian, and the Athesis the Adige. On the foundations of the watchtowers feudal barons raised castles. Many are ruins today, and some inhabited. They cling to spurs, they dominate the sweep of the great curving valley. Austrian and German vacationers stump along paths, leaf guidebooks, stare up at grey walls. *Gasthöfe*, not Alberghi, in the high villages offer them maps, clean beds, and sauerbraten. Villagers quote lire prices in dialect German. Only the lire and the road signs sustain the convention that the visitor is in Italy.

The massive land is restless. Subterranean water jets and pours down hillsides. Springs gave a name to one castle built in 1244 on Roman foundations above a sheer drop where the valley widens: the Castle at the Well, Castel Fontana, Schloss Brunnenburg. A land bridge, and, legend says, a tunnel, once joined it to another castle still higher, but the bridge has collapsed, tradition says by earthquake, leaving a boulder-strewn saddle. Castle Brunnenburg was to lapse slowly too, inhabited, neglected, for centuries. Fire brought down wooden beams, and walls fell with them. "Estrema decadenza," says a regional history of its state at the opening of our century, when a certain Herr Schwickert acquired it. Herr Schwickert had noble ambitions, and a bride, less alluring, tradition hints, than his pretty young niece. In 1904, while Henry James was gazing at ruined New Hampshire orchards, stone masons from the village of Tirolo were making it new once more atop its spur: a warren of serene rooms at many levels; a square central tower, square room above square room above square room; an adjacent round tower up which coils a dizzying stone stair; a dark enclosed court; a minute garden with pines. The site is high, the surrounding peaks are higher; on a misty day they whelm it with menace. Tradition has Frau Schwickert plunging—pushed?—from a balcony outside one long sunlit room, down past sheer walls, down past sheer cliffs, down to the lesser spurs that slope into Merano.

Franz Kafka came to Merano in 1920, a bleak year in which his diary has but two entries. (Later he wrote *The Castle*. Nothing should be made of this. His Bohemian homeland abounds in castles.) The Austro-Hungarian Empire had just dissolved, and that side of the Tirol had just become nominally Italian, so Kafka was technically a foreign visitor, one of the first.

Mussolini dictated Italian speech, but German went on being spoken. "Das heis' Walterplatz," Ezra Pound once heard someone say in Bolzano (Bozen), making this point (83/535:571). During the Axis war the Tiroleans felt little pull toward either partner. In Bruneck, where an *alpino*'s statue eyed the mountains, a valise was set at his feet to suggest that the foreigners he represented— the Italians—might think about packing up and leaving (77/470: 500). The natives had their own concerns. At Gais, not far from Brunnenburg by map but an intricate journey by road,

> Herr Bacher's father made Madonnas still in the tradition
> carved wood as you might have found it in any cathedral
>   and another Bacher still cut intaglios
>   such as Salustio's in the time of Ixotta,
> where the masks come from, in the Tirol,
>   in the winter season
>   searching every house to drive out the demons.
>   (74/448:476)

When Ezra Pound stumbled up there in 1943 he was simply a foreigner, someone out of the south. They nearly executed him. He is said to have been saved by Herr Bacher's eye for his facial planes. Protestors' dynamite still explodes now and then. Pairs of soldiers with slung rifles patrol the platform of each railway station.

Brunnenburg, with vine terraces on its slopes, with a family in its farmhouse to work its modest lands, belonged by the 1950's to Prince Boris de Rachewiltz, an Italian Egyptologist whose *Massime degli antichi Egiziani* led to the hieroglyphs we find in *Rock-Drill*. His correspondence with Ezra Pound commenced because he had married Pound's daughter (broad-browed, amber-headed, her father's image). And Brunnenburg, in July 1958, was the poet's place of return from his Washington exile. He was installed in the tower room below the top one; the archives came up from Rapallo; the Gaudier sketch went on the wall; the Gaudier head was carried by strong men into the garden; he made chairs, shelves, a long table; he set to work on the final typescript of *Thrones*; he drafted bits for

Brunnenburg, 1965.

the last run of *Cantos*; and eyes sharpened by having traversed the *Odes* character by character went once more through Ernest Fenollosa's yellowing notebooks, annotating, extracting the gists of Mori's lectures. He felt good, he estimated, for 20 more years. "At last I have found a setting."

On clear days you could see 50 miles. Below, the Adige wound through Merano, curved eastward out of sight toward Bolzano: thence toward sacred places: south past Lake Garda to Verona, then east toward the Adriatic sea, whose grey-green waters it enters a little below Venice, a little above Ravenna and Rimini. Pound thought the castle might be self-sufficient if it had maple syrup for sale, but the maple trees he ordered from America, like the vinestocks Jefferson brought to Virginia from France, refused to survive (but are said to have brought poison ivy into Italy). The seasons turned, the castle bottled its wine. A ham came from Harry Meacham in Richmond ("THAT HAM is kulchur, THAT ham is civilization," he had written of a previous Virginia offering). Geoffrey Bridson, whose verse had been in the *Active Anthology* (1933), came with a BBC crew and made a 14-minute film and nearly three hours' worth of edited sound recording, with for climax Ezra reading in congenial dialect "The Tar Baby Story" from *Uncle Remus* to his grandchildren. (It was his rendition of a dialect Canto excerpt, from XVI by one account or from XXXV by another, that Mussolini had once pronounced "divertente"—41/202:210).

But he was chronically short of breath in the high air, and arthritis was inconveniencing his upper vertebrae. There was also trouble about a female disciple. By spring 1959 he was in Rapallo ("sea air doin me good"), by July the last Cantos—now to reach 124; he was not "hypnotized by a number"—were requiring more energy than he had; by the following spring he was "stuck." On 11 Aug. 1960,

> ... the plain fact is that my head just doesn't WORK.
> Stretches when it just doesn't work.

Surgery followed. Letters ceased. In the clinic he looked "very handsome and white." And, in a great weariness, silence descended.

*　　*　　*

"Ezra—*silent?*" said Floss Williams. Could anyone believe it. He and Bill "used to fight like kittens." Bill was in slow decline, two bloods fighting within him: the susceptibility of the male line to strokes, the invulnerability of his mother's people. So he incurred the strokes, but survived them. His speech halted, his right arm hung, the strong gentleness to turn an emerging baby's head no longer his hand's to command. Up at dawn, he typed, letter by letter, the left hand guiding and letting fall the right over an electrified keyboard. His eyes followed a line of type with ease but had trouble finding the start of the next line; the three-step indentation he came to favor was in part a way of making a page he could reread. After *Paterson V*—finished on Ezra's birthday, 1957, the 36th anniversary to the day of Joyce's end to *Ulysses*—he had started "a loosely assembled essay on poetic measure." His hands between his knees and his ear inclined, he listened to Floss read out of Chapman's Homer, the *Iliad,* the *Odyssey,* written for the ear. (Who last *listened* to those measures?) Although nothing gave him more trouble than abstract statement, although he could no longer read and could barely type, yet there was a large topic whose outlines he wanted to set down, its elements accessible less to his head than to neuromuscular systems a lifetime schooled. "A blind old man," he called Homer,

> whose bones
> have the movement
> of the sea.

And Homer's deepest knowledge was like his own, as he thought of himself

> —learning with age to sleep my life away:
> saying .
> The measure intervenes, to measure is all we know,
> a choice among the measures . .
> the measured dance
> "unless the scent of a rose
> startle us anew"

He struggled with the essay on Measure, could not subdue its roughness, abandoned it finally for greatly edited publication. An iambic pentameter civilization had ended: that was the principle he

wanted to entrap, down among history's slow currents. In the
essay, as elsewhere, he spoke of "the American idiom," a phrase
whose *virtù* he had discovered late in life, and of "the variable foot"
which seems like a rubber inch. Such terms do not deliver meaning;
they are points for meditation. Take his three-ply line; take the
remarkable passage in which he had first come upon it:

> The descent beckons
> > as the ascent beckoned.
> > > Memory is a kind
> of accomplishment,
> > a sort of renewal
> > > even
> an initiation, since the spaces it opens are new places
> > inhabited by hordes
> > > heretofore unrealized,
> of new kinds—
> > since their movements
> > > are toward new objectives
> (even though formerly they were abandoned).

—Did he mean, for instance, each line to take up the same time? He
at once said, Yes; then he said, More or less. The Abbé Rousselot's
machine might have resolved something, or perhaps not;* his was
neuromuscular knowledge, *psyche te menos te,* breath and strength,
the way of being alive. Only the poems record it.

> . . . Look at
> > what passes for the new.
> You will not find it there but in
> > despised poems.
> > > It is difficult
> to get the news from poems
> > yet men die miserably every day
> > > for lack
> of what is found there.

* Robert de Souza concluded from Rousselot's data that "Le rythme est
une ordonnance variable de l'espace ou du temps dont les coups plus ou moins
équivalents et rapprochées—qui, dans la parole, dépendant de notre émotion—n'ont
entre elles que peu ou point d'égalité temporelle, numérique, intensive."—*Du
Rythme en Française,* 1912, 29.

Thinking to enlighten by example, he entitled a late poem

EXERCISE IN TIMING

> Oh
> the sumac died
> it's
> the first time
> I
> noticed it

—inviting us to hear the movement die if we amalgamate lines 3, 4, 5, or even lines 4, 5. (No one would propose amalgamating 5, 6; we have all come *that* far.) And the last poem in the posthumous *Pictures from Breughel*—

> Sooner or later
> we must come to the end
> of striving
>
> to re-establish
> the image the image of
> the rose . . .

conceals a loose iambic pentameter ground:

> Sóoner or láter we must cóme to the énd of stríving
> to re-estáblish the ímage, the ímage óf the róse
> but not yet, you say, extending the time indefinitely
> by your love until a whole spring rekindle
> the violet to the very lady's-slipper,
> and so by your love the very sun itself
> is revived

Printed as he prints it, and unpunctuated, the delicacies this scansion obliterates are set out for the mind to discover, the run of live breath checked by eager nerves, played against the units of attention. Make it new; its last word is "revived."

He had said he would not outlive the sick elm in the front yard at 9 Ridge Road that had always been his Tree. A visitor in the summer of 1962 found "no guile in him" during two hours' talk: "all raw honesty, utter lack of polish (bless him); all the squirming bashfulness of adolescence still there, laced with a countrified slyness." He died at 79, in 1963, on the 4th of March; trees were gripping down and beginning to awaken.

*   *   *

"I believe in an ultimate and absolute rhythm"—Pound, 1910—for "the perception of the intellect is given in the word, that of the emotions in the cadence." And "Rhythm"—1934—"is a form cut into TIME." This means that the poet, cutting forms into time, is the amanuensis of harmonies like those the Pythagoreans discerned in the cosmos, their recorder and preserver. "Song keeps the word forever," he wrote in his tower room at the castle opposite a Chinese quatrain in the Fenollosa notes,

> Sound is moulded to mean this
> And the measure moulds sound.

The firm rhythms this implies seem a long way from Williams's delicate notations of speech; and yet not so long; for his measure, uncounterfeitable, is the poet's own, the speaking man's, *psyche te menos te*, his breath and strength, and it will have its larger meaning only because he is himself part of something larger: the human community that confers language, and "the universe of fluid force" and "the germinal universe of wood alive, of stone alive." Thus Williams drew on "the speech of Polish mothers" and on the persistence of Jersey trees and flowers. *Ling²* with its dancers below, its rain falling above, its ritual engaging by harmony cosmic process, the "great sensibility" by which dynasties are generated, may serve as emblem for the poet's role, making the dance, questing for the right and absolute rhythm to mime with his blood and breath some greater process: whether the speech of mothers with sick babies, or the energies locked in some alien ancient poem, or the fingers of recurrent dawn.

More and more a web of silent rhythms held Ezra Pound's ear, as though he was no longer noticing the voices around him. He told a friend that the *Cantos* would end with everything caught up into music. Long ago in Paris, absorbed for a time in music, he had been rumored to have given up language. Now he had the Dolmetsch clavichord repaired, and in the tower room the strange sound, half humming, half singing, he was accustomed to make while he gestated verse—soldiers in Pisa had remarked it—accompanied a quest for the rhythmic nuances of a poem from the Fenollosa notes to which he would not have paid attention in 1914, a poem without people in it, a poem about estranged stars, the "drawing ox star" and the "weaving girl star" with a river—is it the Milky Way?—between them. One version:

> She weaves and ends no pattern to day
>   Milky way girl
> and the heavy ox pulls and pulls
> to the end of the day no pattern
> Via lactea clear and shallow
> far from each other
>   one wide river to cross

Another:

> By the river of stars, its brightness
>   the ox herd far from star-girl
> her white hand on the shuttle
>   and at day's end no pattern yet made
>
> a rain of tears for their distance
>   tho the river is clear and shallow
>   they cannot cross it;
>
>   nor their pulse beat, come into words.

"Knowledge is to know men," he had quoted from Confucius 20 years before, commencing the *Guide to Kulchur*; but Odysseus' voyage was back to where he began, and as in *A Lume Spento* the personalities he donned as masks had looked past other persons, barely noticed, toward "the star fields of Arcturus" and

> Green of the wood-moss and flower colors
> And coolness beneath the trees

and restless leaves and winds and dawn, as Cino turning his mind away from "women in three cities" resolved instead to

> sing of the white birds
> In the blue waters of heaven,
> The clouds that are spray to its sea,

so now, remote, Ezra Pound dwelt on the courage and the order and the grace no man had made, on sky, clouds, pines, on minute living things. He was driven down the west side of his beloved Lago di Garda, through the 70 tunnels and over the 56 bridges of a spectacular engineering achievement of *l'era fascista*, and saw the lake waves "Canaletto'd" and "the rock layers arc'd as with a compass." Nature had achieved such things before Canaletto or any geometer. Canaletto and the compass do not impose the human, they simply give us eyes, teach us to see.

Words he had written himself also gave him eyes. A St. Elizabeths line from a *Thrones* Canto (106)—"And in thy mind beauty, O Artemis"—spun new wonders out of the sight of the Gardasee:

> And in thy mind beauty, O Artemis
> > as of mountain lakes in the dawn,
> Foam and silk are thy fingers,
> > > Kuanon,
> and the long suavity of her moving,
> > > > willow and olive reflected . . .
> > > > > (110/778:8)

(And the word "olive" reflects the word "willow" as though in rippled water.) Ease, ease of movement, such as never before. Old words brought to old places now seen as new after so long, this might make the terminal music. Venice—

> Hast'ou seen boat's wake on sea-wall,
> > > how crests it?
> What panache?
> > > paw-flap, wave-tap,
> > > > that is gaiety.
> > > > > (110/777:7)

The Tirol—

> Yet to walk with Mozart, Agassiz and Linnaeus
> > 'neath overhanging air under sun-beat
> Here take thy mind's space
> > > (113/787:16)

.   .   .

> In mountain air with grass frozen emerald
> and with the mind set on that light
> saffron, emerald,
> seeping.
> (113/789:19)

He went to the place north of Pisa where the cage had been. There was no more asphalt, but still much dust; still a wire fence, but modest, topped by a barbed strand, to keep prowlers out of a rose nursery ("Rose Barni," on the sign facing the Via Aurelia). And back of the rose garden, still (and still were after yet another decade, in October 1969) two grey cans, "Trash Only. U.S. Army." Men fish in a quarry. Their cars have U.S. plates, and a sign, "Off Limits," interdicts enquiry. "Taishan" still etches the skyline. Not only were the guards and prisoners gone, and all trace of their habitation, but the tree—Pound looked for it—which he had used to see from his tent. In all his life there had never not been trees. St. Elizabeths' grounds were once an arboretum.

"God's eye art 'ou, do not surrender perception," he mused half to the sun and half to himself. "Some hall of mirrors" (eight words after "my mind"); and

> to reign, to dance in a maze,
> To live a thousand years in a wink.
> (114/793:23)

The sheer landscape was invading him; light and order and beauty simply there; what was there to say?

> I have brought the great ball of crystal;
> who can lift it?
> Can you enter the great acorn of light?
> But the beauty is not the madness
> Tho' my errors and wrecks lie about me.
> And I am not a demigod,
> I cannot make it cohere.
> (116/795:25)

He grew gentle, and slowly frail, and the struggle against his failing body came to seem a struggle against the quiet of nature, the abashment of sheer will to utter by all that utters itself. To utter is to invade?

> the verb is "see," not "walk on"
> i.e. it coheres all right
>   even if my notes do not cohere.
>   (116/797:27)

Amid attention's intermittences he seemed to become slowly what he had dreamed of being a long 50 years before, "*simplex naturae,*" "at peace and trans-sentient as a wood pool," merely one with what lives. Does Baucis, or Philemon, presume to inject poems into the cosmos? "Sky," said Kung, "what words does the sky use?"

There were counter-currents. In the last, by date of sanctioned publication, of all his poems that we have, the persona is Horace, the text *Odes* III.30—

> This monument will outlast metal and I made it
> More durable than the king's seat, higher than pyramids.
> Gnaw of the wind and rain?
>   Impotent
> The flow of the years to break it, however many.
> Bits of me, many bits, will dodge all funeral . . .

"Many bits" for "non omnis moriar"—that is Pound, not Horace, remembering his many years' cunning attention to details. The poem ends, "My hair, Delphic laurel." But more typically, as in four lines designated for Canto cxv, he is content to fade into nature's anonymity:

> A blown husk that is finished
>   but the light sings eternal
> a pale flare over marshes
>   where the salt hay whispers to tide's change.
>   (115/794:24)

He was grasping many straws. Let the mind not stop. "Do not surrender perception." (Yet what to do with the mind save simply perceive?) Lewis, "Old Vort," the arch-Vorticist, had not grown placid but had affirmed, affirmed.

> Wyndham Lewis chose blindness
> rather than have his mind stop.
> (115/794:24)

*   *   *

A tumor had pressed on the chiasmus of the optic nerves, constricting their transmission as it grew. Lewis declined surgery—a risk, at his age—and watched the seen world fade. In May 1951 he informed readers of *The Listener* why he could no longer serve as their art critic: "I can no longer see a picture." "Pushed into an unlighted room, the door banged and locked for ever, I shall then have to light a lamp of aggressive voltage in my mind to keep at bay the night." In the next five years he wrote seven books, longhand.

The flat overlooking Notting Hill Gate had an almost invisible entrance between two shops. One climbed stairs and pursued corridors at oblique angles until utterly disoriented concerning the bearings of the inner fastness, the door to which was answered only after disquieting delay. On his last birthday, 18 November 1956, the festivities were curtailed. He had recently been taken ill. There was champagne, there was pheasant ("Life is too short not to travel first class") but Lewis showed little interest in either. His massive form stooped, his sparse silvery hair curling at the collar, he acquiesced in the ritual of shuffling on his wife's arm to the dinner table, but it was only back in the blue armchair that he seemed remotely comfortable. The drawing board and the huge pad of paper he wrote on stood propped beside it. Somewhere nearby dust thickened in the locked studio. It was never alluded to. No one had entered it in the half-decade since Lewis had conceded he was blind.

Still the most magnetic figure in London, he seemed not to be surrounded by London but by a trackless void. His own best books seemed to him thin and remote; he painstakingly identified *Time and Western Man*: "That's a book of mine." His paintings did not interest him. The very flat was condemned, due to be razed any day to make room for a deluxe tube station. This fact, however outrageous, so bespoke the world's norm of abnormality that Lewis indicated no effort to move. The bell-pushes in the hallways downstairs had been disconnected, coils of wire hanging loose over illegible nameplates. Amid imminent decay he maintained his daily orbit, bed to armchair to dinner table to telephone to armchair again, with the fixed determination of a body in outer space, his features reposed in a disquieting smile, his mind steadily arranging words with unexampled vigor. "The greatest prose master of style of my generation," Eliot had written recently, "perhaps the only one to have invented a new style."

His last words, in a hospital four months later, are said to have been "Mind your own business!" addressed to an enquirer after the state of his bowels. Friends got to the studio just before the wreckers' ball. Pictures, a profusion, piles of them, littered the floor: of "a world that will never be seen except in pictures."

A few weeks before that last birthday he suffered a journalist to put newspaper questions; as, did he intend to write any more novels? To which, with steely acerbity, "You insult me. I am still alive. I shall work till midnight if I feel like it."

*   *   *

Joyce had been the first to go of the "Men of 1914," struck down just short of his 59th birthday by a perforated ulcer. Pound paid tribute to his memory on Rome radio ("May his spirit meet with Rabelais' ghost at Chinon and may the glasses never be empty"). Having been delivered while his country was still neutral, this does not figure on the roster of his treasonable utterances. Sixteen years later he left unanswered all requests for some memorial tribute to "Old Vort." That was a complex silence, one of its components doubtless exasperation at being asked, a non-person, to adorn a public occasion. And the sense that their time was ending, that would have assailed him too. That was in the spring of 1957, when his imprisonment still seemed unendable, though a year later it was suddenly over.

But in 1965, Eliot; and in London, for the service at Westminster Abbey, a white-bearded ghost deplaned, frail, with piercing mobile eyes. He had not seen the Eliot of the last years, weakened by emphysema beneath the invincible sartorial armor (the lapels a shade wide, the suit in fact somehow *massive*; and the fountain pen a size larger than customary, and the watch chain suggesting anchorage for a cruiser. "Remarkable man, Mr. Eliot," said a tailor he patronized. "Very good taste. Nothing ever quite in excess." There has been no more accurate insight.)

"Up and down," said the dwindling Eliot of his condition; "or rather"—always the precisian—"down and up." And he remembered how Pound had chosen and arranged the poems for *Prufrock and Other Observations*; in fact affirmed—explicitly—that he owed "everything" to Pound. Whereas Joyce—"concerned with nothing except his own writings"—was the most egocentric of all the men he had known; was Ezra's polar opposite. And Wyndham Lewis—"sweeter after his blindness"—if Lewis had not quarrelled so. . . . Compressed air exercised Eliot's slack lungs. His memory was vivid for remote things.

His ashes went to East Coker. It was to a memorial service of some grandeur, a month after his death, that Ezra Pound came, an astonishment to journalists. He did not live in the past, though he came from the past. He did not live in the modern world which, he had told an Italian interviewer, "does not exist." ("Because nothing exists which does not understand its past or its future.") The mind of Europe, a mind "which changes" but "abandons nothing *en route*," not Homer, nor the rock drawing of the Magdalenian draughtsmen, still lived, doubtless, in crannies it was not incumbent on a man of 79 to locate. Enough for him to accept the blank which public distractions and unceasing wars had made of their own great effort to render the working of that mind a public possession.

They were born within a six-year span: Joyce and Lewis, 1882; Williams, 1883; Pound, 1885; Eliot, 1888. (And Picasso, for that matter, 1881, and Stravinsky, 1882.) And how remote those dates seem! The lanes of London were still scavenged by municipal goats. *Marius the Epicurean* was published in the year of Ezra Pound's birth. Browning and Ruskin were active. Wagner was but two years dead, Jesse James but three.

When those men were children the *Symbolistes* were active, so their heritage included those dark worlds, that succulent craftsmanship, in which urbanized post-Romanticism sought satiety: Yeats's

> When my arms wrap you round I press
> My heart upon the loveliness
> That has long faded from the world

or Arthur Symons'

> I am Yseult and Helen, I have seen
> Troy burn, and the most loving knight lie dead.
> The world has been my mirror, time has been
> My breath upon the glass . . .

or Mallarmé's

> Oui, c'est pour moi, pour moi, que je fleuris, déserte!
> Vous le savez, jardins d'améthyste, enfouis
> Sans fin dans de savants abîmes éblouis,
> Ors ignorés, gardant votre antique lumière
> Sous le sombre sommeil d'une terre première . . .

—telling glittering equivocal golden beads in gloom.

To give over all that: to recover the gods, Pound had called it, or to free (said Lewis) faculties "older than the fish," to achieve (Eliot) "the new, the really new" which should be fit company for an Altamira bison, these had been the intentions of their vortex, dragging a dark world up into the light, forging an ecumenical reality where all times could meet without the romance of time, as jewelry perhaps Helen's had hung around Sophie Schliemann's neck for a photograph to be made by daylight, like Dublin daylight. An exactness of perception like an archaeologist's, brought to bear upon faces in the La Concorde Métro station; a pattern-making faculty like Uccello's or a hymenopter's, to accommodate iron girders and Shakespeare's Timon; an idiom (Williams) unself-conscious alike in the presence of a rose or the merry-faced coroner's children: such had been the aspirations of 1913. Gaudier (22, merely perfecting his alphabet) on one stone restored Egyptian sculpture, and could catch with a fountain pen an animal's gesture as though at Lascaux, or work stone—he should have had jade—like the men of Chou.

> Worlds we have, how many worlds we have . . .
> And from these like we guess a soul for man
> And built him full of aery populations. . . .

—so a cancelled passage about a cancelled time, when "the creative eye," as Eliot said dismissing Gilbert Murray's pastiche, could see the past as different from the present, "yet so lively that it shall be as present to us as the present."

They had come of age to commence that revolution, and been old enough after Europe blew up instead to know what had been lost in that vast amnesia. Yeats's generation, Ford's, for whom they were "les jeunes," was too old to make the transition, Auden's too young to know what needed transferring. There was no more Vortex after 1919, and they went each his own way from that common memory.

Joyce, his subject always the stories people tell themselves, followed his account of the fragmented mind of Europe by day with *Finnegans Wake*, the mind of Europe in shock, babbling a long dream, stirring, swooning. Lewis turned to satire, visual and verbal: the socio-politics of gargantuan dolls. Eliot, like an early Christian remembering Roman forms after the Vandals, hoped to make do with what was there against a time when there should be more there: hence his plays in the manner of such attenuated theater as London offered, and his meditative poems making use of the landscape and the past and the stance of Thomas Gray ("... But of old stones that cannot be deciphered." ...) His *Criterion*, a sort of veterans' hospital, maintained a practice arena for young skirmishers. They could at least monitor the quarter's solemnities. So Eliot coexisted with treacly minds, Clive Bell's and Mrs. Woolf's, and with Miss Sitwell, the Amy Lowell of poetry.

Eliot dead now, "Who is there for me to share a joke with?" Pound was photographed silent in London—the press tried to make an incident out of his snubbing Stephen Spender, whom he simply had not recognized—and left by air for Dublin and Mrs. Yeats. It was also the year of the Yeats centenary. In Texas men were rehearsing what they should do on the moon.

And he was photographed in Zürich leaning on his cane, contemplating a jaunty bronze grasshopper-Joyce with opaque bronze spectacles, newly set by admirers over the new joint grave of Jim and Nora. Until this dual plot could be acquired, Joyce had lain for a quarter-century filed away by accession number in a narrow space some distance from Nora's narrow space, and a stone's throw from the massive memorial to La Famille Blum. It became a characteristic image in European picture papers, Ezra Pound silent, communing with the silent dead.

> No man can see his own end.
> The Gods have not returned. "They have never left us."
> They have not returned.
>
> (113/787:17)

*   *   *

The gods have never left us. Nothing we know the mind to have known has ever left us. Quickened by hints, the mind can know it again, and make it new. Romantic Time no longer thickens our sight, time receding, bearing visions away. Our books of cave paintings are the emblems of its abolition, perhaps the Pound Era's chief theme, and the literary consolidation of that theme stands as the era's achievement. Translation, for instance, after Ezra Pound, aims neither at dim ritual nor at lexicographic lockstep, but at seeming transparency, the vigors of the great original—Homer, Kung—not remote but at touching distance, though only to be touched with the help of all that we know. Robert Fitzgerald's *Odyssey*—

> Of these adventures, Muse, daughter of Zeus,
> Tell us in our time; lift the great song again

—is greatly told and in, exactly, our time; and the translator learned the meaning of certain words by using his eyes, on a boat in the Aegean, at dawn. (Only the arcanely skilled may deeply read.) And 50 years after the dismal fuss about Pound's *Propertius*, we read in Christopher Logue's variations on the *Iliad* how Achilles, inspecting armor "Made in Heaven" "Spun the holy tungsten like a star between his knees"; read them, moreover, printed and commended, in a learned journal devoted to the classics, though in that line for instance not one word stands for a word of Homer's.

To write so goes with reading so. We read differently now, though the only possible evidence is the way we write. So reading, we have kept the classics alive. Whereas 30 years ago the classical languages were near death, undergraduates today demand to be taught Greek to read a Homer they first glimpsed in some lame version read, maybe, at the behest of *Ulysses* or the *Cantos*. And poetic language characteristically strives today for intricacy and immediacy together, and often prose does too.

The men of the Vortex achieved all that and more. We will never know how much of our minds they prepared. In other ways Pound's terminal mood was just; in other ways their careers were majestic failures. What cost all of them so much lost effort was not being "wrong from the start": it was the dissipation of the Vortex: the necessity, all the latter part of their lives, of working alone. Each in his own place, after the disaster, they went each his own way. The age was divisive. Having attacked what he took to be its principle of divisiveness, having succumbed to frenzies during that attack, Pound when he had outlived frenzy looked back on his long career as though it had contained little else.

*   *   *

Why had he done so poorly with his great theme, fiscal scarcity as the engine of history-makers? Such exposition need not resist verse. W. S. Gilbert had been deft and deadly—

> Some seven men form an Association
> (If possible, all Peers and Baronets),
> They start off with a public declaration
> To what extent they mean to pay their debts.
> That's called their Capital: . . .

Not Homer, but it got its tweezers on the subject; though even with Sullivan's music the opera (*Utopia Limited*, 1893) did not hold the stage. Swift did still better. He achieved the pamphleteer's dream, efficacy, making the iniquities of Wood's Halfpence so vivid to his countrymen that the patent was cancelled. Swift concentrated on the immediate case, the unbacked coin rung on the counter, and the King himself capitulated. But Pound managed only to sound like a crank professor, with his Emperor Tching Tang opening the copper mine and his documents from the Monte dei Paschi: always the long way round to get home. In that he was most like Odysseus. He had fetched, via Fenollosa's notes, transcendentalism from China, and made a Kung out of hints from Scotus Erigena.

And his violences? He wrote various old acquaintances to regret his harshness of dissent from them ("A bad sign," Eliot had said when he opened such a letter.) His life's work, like Vergil or Kafka, he pushed from him ("I botched it"). The magazine *Epoca* printed an interview to that effect. It was quoted around the world. The Yahoo press was delighted. *Poetry* named him the 50th anniversary recipient of the Harriet Monroe Memorial Prize ("The editor only wishes that all choices could be made with such transparent justice, and with the effect of so precise a testimony"); Pound's letter of acceptance claimed remembrance only as "a minor satirist."

In Paris he was moved by Beckett's *Fin de Partie*, with its emptily eloquent blind man and its old man confined to a trash can ("C'est moi dans la poubelle," he whispered). Later he and Beckett were moved by each other's proximity. Pound crossed to a seat next the playwright, and they embraced wordlessly on parting, with likely no memory on Pound's part of that miserable first encounter, 1929. Still later Beckett's Nobel Prize delighted him. They should have been friends.

Where had he gone wrong? What had been his root error? "That stupid, suburban anti-semitic prejudice"? He rummaged, sleepless, in a senescent cave. To seek the root error is an American habit. He had also sought it in history, and for a while equated the founding of the Bank of England with original sin; but that sin is not in time. To look back over one's path, and all its branches, and speculate on what might have been otherwise at each rejected path, that is an exhausting pastime. He should perhaps never have left America, or he should have returned there. He should not have buried himself in an Italian town, remote from the vectors of the world, and gone on excoriating American universities as though they were still indistinguishable from the Wabash of 1907; and lost touch with the speech he loved and preserved and gradually parodied, always under the impression he was utilizing its immediacies.

> That I lost my center
>   fighting the world.
> The dreams clash
>   and are shattered—

> and that I tried to make a paradiso
>> terrestre.
>> (117/802:32)

Terrestre: on earth. But "in the mind indestructible"? Fragments. He pushed his book away.

So Sigismundo, his fortunes wrecked and no hope of finishing his Tempio, sat one day on a bit of stone "hunched up and noting what was done wrong"—Duccio's statues of the Virtues crowding the niches Matteo de' Pasti had designed for Gothic slenderness, or Flora in the chapel of the Arts, so cunning had grown Duccio's hand and so tranquil his vision, transcending and making seem tricky the vigors of the divinities in his earlier chapel of the Planets.

> And an old woman came in and giggled to see him
>> sitting there in the dark.
>> (11/50:54)

Yet the Tempio can still evoke and brave ecclesiastical disesteem ("Non è un Tempio, è un' ecclesia," a priest retorted, 1964), and still repay a visitor's many hours, the affirmation triumphant over centuries and over its incompleteness and its defects and over Sigismundo's despair. So the Pound effort stands, repaying the attention it exacts, gathering into a possible unity much, much that might have been lost or forever scattered. (A thing is lost when men can find no way to relate their interest in it to other interests; that is how Sappho and Catullus were lost.) The craft is timeless; the work, with its errors and defects, an anthology of rightnesses; we can scarcely distinguish what Pound instigated from what he simply saw before it was obvious. A generation in America and Europe has validated his interest in the east, and can learn from him how not to discard the west. A time whose engrossing activity is teaching may discern that he was right in restoring to poetry its ancient didactic function. His open forms, we may feel, belong to our future. Credit—the Latin word means "he believes"—touches on a central theme, men's mutual trust; an age that built banks like temples gives way to an age that finds bankers' suspicions anomalous. His music awaits rediscovery. For a TV sound track a group called The Improved Sound Ltd. elicited from part of his 1920 *Villon* the vigors proper to 1969, drums and rhythms and quasi-Arab admixtures; German papers referred wonderingly to the Pound Sound. He is very likely, in ways controversy still hides, the contemporary of our grandchildren. To note, as he did in old age, things he had missed is but to respect the nature of his mind, branching and connecting. We do not dwell on what self-contained poets missed.

In Rapallo he had missed American giants: Fuller, Frank Lloyd Wright. Wright knew Pound's early work, down to *Cathay* and *Mauberley*, but then lost track, as so many did, in the 1920's. Wright (92) wanted to invite him to Taliesin, but learned he was kept in a madhouse ("It figures": Wright thought America intent on stifling its uncommon men. It would learn, he said, that it couldn't live without them.)

Fuller's realities were less romantic, and in not encountering them Pound had missed much more. Rapallo hid industrialization from him: hence the sharpest limit on his economic perceptions. Always he referred wealth to the soil—the sun, the grass, the sheep, the olive trees—in a time when increasingly its source was the mind. It may one day seem that he missed, in his isolation, the major historical event of his time, the *de facto* transfer of the basis of capital from matter to understanding, from work to design, gold to credit: a transfer he of all men was disposed to celebrate. But in Rapallo, as though in an earlier America, he remained an old-fashioned populist, his folk sage such a man as the *pharmacien* who noted the disparity between the prices of toilet paper and the *Divine Comedy*. So he aged, a relic.

He could walk up the *salita* from Rapallo to that eucalyptus tree, and on up to Sant' Ambrogio without stopping for breath, visitors half his age panting. In a book-lined room looking over the Gulf lay an open notebook, two lines legible—

> That I should manifest some fragment of manhood
> and cleave to it

(The strenuous Yankee conscience. Yet what else had he ever done?) The sky yellowed before a rainstorm. He gazed at it a moment, and sank back quiet.

Or, from Miss Rudge's apartment whose walls before the war

had displayed Tami Kume's huge baffling painting, "Tami's dream" (76/462:491) now lost, he could set out across Venice, known stone by stone, past the window overlooking

the Squero where Ogni Santi
meets San Trovaso

(76/462:491)

where he had drunk in the Venetian beauty and affirmed that no man had the right to tarnish his portrayal thereof with notions of ownership (jejune didacticism for his own eyes, in a notebook); past the canal where he had taken lessons from a gondolier, across little bridges and through little lanes to the Scuola degli Schiavoni, there to sit hunched, contemplating, while friends marvelled at the Carpaccios (St. Jerome and his little dog; the lion disrupting the monastery; St. George and the Place of Skulls); one afternoon to the Biennale, where the lady at the American pavilion recognized the great revenant and proudly showed off pop sculpture, Red Grooms' *Chicago* bestridden by a wooden pipe-smoking Hugh Hefner, grimaced over by a mask-like Mayor Daley (what did he think of it? The friend of Gaudier and of Brancusi said "I've seen worse"); another time by the Giardini Publici, where on a plinth adorned with pelican bas-reliefs a stone head of Richard Wagner confronted the lagoon:

"Ezra!" (the American voice of Miss Rudge, custodian of the oracle) "Why is Wagner's bust here?"

(In slow remote tones) "He died here."

"Ezra! What on earth do young pelicans tearing at the old bird's entrails have to do with Wagner?"

(A short pause. The imperial moment:) "Toujours les tripes."

He listened to a lengthy exposition of the Homer *de nos jours,* the formulaic Homer of Milman Parry and Lord, a Homer improvising with interchangeable parts, a wealth of formulae to fill out the meter; and replied with a wicked twinkle, "But that doesn't explain why Homer is so much better than everyone else." As it doesn't.

And at last, in October 1970, just weeks before he was to turn 85, he heard Buckminster Fuller lecture in Venice at the International University of Art; and part of Fuller's subject was Ezra Pound. He returned; he listened to four long Fuller discourses; the two men talked; a copy of Fuller's Nehru Memorial Lecture changed hands; Pound listened to it, sitting up late at night. Men are impoverished, it says, by an accounting system "anchored exclusively to the value of metals." But all wealth comes "from the wealth of the minds of world man."

*   *   *

The Fenollosa notebooks were boxed at the castle. Up there, each morning, the stone Gaudier eyes watched the counter-dawn break on the peak called "Ziel" (aim). As its weight tilted its tree-stump pedestal, its eyes were slowly shifting toward "Mut" (courage). The volumes of Adams and De Mailla stood on a low shelf, occasionally consulted when visitors were judged to have proper business with them. Among the Egyptian artifacts Mary worked at an Italian text of her father's *Cantos*, to go *en face* with a cleaned-up English text. Dorothy, who could remember Henry James's red waistcoat, wintered in Rapallo, summered in England. He needed far more care than she had strength for.

("You ordered that for me?"

"Yes, Ezra. Eat it.")

Now in Venice, now in Sant' Ambrogio, the Great Instigator was slowly closing doors. He read Cantos into a home recorder, pausing when Miss Rudge left the room to see to the soup ("Some cook..."). He marked the 500th anniversary of Shakespeare's birth by recording "They that have power to hurt and will do none." He read with startling vigor Kit Smart's "I will remember my cat...". These were private utterings only. He turned up suddenly in unexpected places: at Delphi, where donkeys drink at a trough fed from Castalia; at Hamilton College for graduation day, autographing copies of the *Drafts and Fragments* that formally marked his abandonment of the *Cantos*; in New York, where he and Marianne Moore held court, the last survivors. He thought of Hailey, but did not go there. And once at a concert in Sigismundo's Rimini, applauded and asked to speak, he would say only, "Tempus loquendi, tempus tacendi."

His mind on Carpaccio, on cats and stones, on butterflies ("gasping," "milkweed the sustenance"), on the conversation frequent visitors brought, on faces present and gone, on his own past; shrunken, slight, no more weight than he had had half-grown, long ago, in Wyncote, he shouldered the weariness of 85 years, his resource memory within memory within memory. At Wyncote, last, a summer night in 1958, St Elizabeths freshly behind him, in bed in his old house for the last time (and aged 72), he had somehow wakened—always a brief sleeper; genius enjoys long days—and tiptoed downstairs in his pajamas, out into the dark street, and down to the Presbyterian Church, to sit on its steps looking over the moonlit lawns of great estates: sitting where a boy had sat 60 years before, his eye on trees before dawn, his mind on a poet's destiny, which should be that of dreaming old men's silences; the old man's memory now in turn accessible to the still older man in Venice, to be guessed at but never experienced by any comer. "Shall two know the same in their knowing?" Thought is a labyrinth.

NOTES

Source material is cited by means of selected catch phrases in the order of their occurrence on a particular page. Pound's short poems are referred to by title, his published Letters by number, Confucian citations by chapter and verse, and various random details by chapter number of the work, to circumvent confusion arising from the varying pagination of reprints.

Locations of unpublished mss. are indicated and those who furnished unpublished information are named. Such information may be deemed to have been given in conversation unless a specific letter is designated. The conversations cover a period of 22 years and may not always be accurately dated.

Quotations are generally cited from the most accessible reprint. Those wishing to locate first references may do so with the aid of Gallup (see below).

Abbreviations for material frequently cited within a single chapter are given in a headnote to that chapter. The following abbreviations are used throughout:

Gallup: Donald Gallup, *A Bibliography of Ezra Pound* (1963).
G-B: *Gaudier-Brzeska: A Memoir* (1960 reprint).
GK: *Guide to Kulchur* (any edition).
LE: *The Literary Essays of Ezra Pound* (1954 or subsequent printings).
Letters: *The Letters of Ezra Pound,* ed. D. D. Paige.
Personae: Pound's collected shorter poems (1926 edition and reprintings; not the 1909 volume).
SR: *The Spirit of Romance* (1953 reprint with revisions and inserted chapter).
Translations: *The Translations of Ezra Pound* (enlarged edition, 1963).

GHOSTS AND BENEDICTIONS

3–5   Encounter with James described by Dorothy Pound, 1964.
   3   He had assured her mother: James *Letters,* ed. Lubbock, ii, 363.
   4   "May be imagination": letter from DP, 14 July 1964.

4   Woman from Bangor, man from Boston: in "A Bundle of Letters."
4   "Ear for stilled voices": James, *Sense of the Past*, 41.
4   Wetting of lips, *Sense of the Past*, 54.
6   Legal citizenship: according to American law then in force. It saved DP from Italian internment in 1940.
6   Forage of horses: Barbara Tuchman, *The Guns of August*, end of ch. 5.
6   Without passports, 20-franc pieces: EP, letter to HK, undated.
6   Order to sharpen swords: *Guns of August*, ch. 12.
6   Sharpened on August 7: assuming the order was carried out, though Mrs. Tuchman (1969) recalled no evidence that it was.
6   "The wind of its passage": Alistair Horne, *The Price of Glory*, ch. 1.
7   Jottings on endpapers: copy of *Cathay* now in Univ. of Texas library. For the poem see "Moeurs Contemporaines."
7   "Men of my time," *GK*, 82.
7   Met only in gardens: Prof. Leon Edel (letter to HK, 22 Apr. 1965) states that Pound was never at Rye and that no extant James letter mentions him.
7   "Have met HJ again": EP to his mother, Letter #241 in Yale Library.
8   And he said: "Oh! Abelard!": "Moeurs Contemporaines," vii.
8   Caricatured by Max: in *The Poets' Corner*, 1904.
8   Lydia Yavorska: see *Time's Chariot* by her eventual husband Sir John Pollock, 205–11, and photograph at 208; reference from Prof. Edel.
10 Older than James had been: letter to HK, 1956.
11 "Ex*act*ly": on the lawn at St. Elizabeths, Sept. 1952.
11 The massive head: *LE*, 295; cf. 7/24:28.
11 Scarcity of congressmen: *The American Scene*, 340.
12 "So Mr. Eliot": EP, Sept. 1952.
13 Confucius on style: *Analects*, XV, xl. For the characters see 79/486:518, Pound's phantom sheep apparent in the upper right.
13 Detail of the *Pisan Cantos*: "to take the sheep out to pasture," 80/499:533.
13 Celebrities will belaud: *Homage to Sextus Propertius*, I, XII, II.
14 "Phantom with weighted motion": 7/24:28.
14 Tsang-kié: so spelled in de Mailla, *Histoire Générale de la Chine*, I, 19. Etymologies from a letter from Mr. Wai-Lim Yip to HK, and cf. L. Weiger, *Chinese Characters*, 1927, 182.
15 "Our dynasty": opening line of *Rock-Drill* (1955), 85/543:579.
15 EP's early opinion of Mao: from Eva Hesse, 1969. Later promotion of the Square Dollar Confucius (a Pound enterprise) alleged the banning of these texts in Red China.
15 "Where we have got to": 87/576:612.
15 By association: see first page of Canto 85, where the "point of rest" ideogram (*chih*3) is placed just beneath *ling*.
16 "Attempt to condense the James novel": *Letters*, #189.
16 "Hands that can grasp": Marianne Moore, "Poetry."
16 The reddish: "Spring and All," WCW, *Collected Earlier Poems*, 241.
16 "Blocked": *Paterson*, II, ii, opening.
16 To lead you: "Prufrock," of course.
17 Drifted: "Hugh Selwyn Mauberley," second sequence, II.
17 "A society trying": *American Scene*, 159.
17 "An impression so documentary": *American Scene*, 69.
17 The touching appeal: *American Scene*, 21.

18 They have "run down": *American Scene*, 17.
18 "Say it, no ideas but in things": *Paterson*, I. i.
18 "It was an adventure": *American Scene*, 7.
18 "Oh, yes; we were awfully dear": *American Scene*, 8.
19 The most as yet accomplished": *American Scene*, 9.
19 The pure products": WCW, *Collected Earlier Poems*, 270.
19 James visited the Penn campus: *American Scene*, 299.
19 In 1958 he asked: conversation with HK.
19 James meditated in Harvard Yard: *American Scene*, 70
20 Member of the Agassiz Club: Carlos Baker, *Ernest Hemingway, a Life Story*, 1969, 6.
20 A street James mentions [Rutgers Street]: *American Scene*, 133; and cf. Zukofsky's "*A*" *1–12*, 154–5.
20 A visiting lecturer: L. W. Chisholm, *Fenollosa, the Far East and American Culture*, 1963, 156.
21 "Must I declare them dirty": *The Letters of Wyndham Lewis*, 16.
21 "I have absolutely no boots": *Letters of James Joyce*, II, 59.
21 "The immodesty": *American Scene*, 33.
21 "Artless need": *American Scene*, 114.
21 "The amiable side": *American Scene*, 115.
22 "A ghost / Is that part": Eli Siegel, *James and the Children*, 1968, the sharpest single look into James's mind in *The Turn of the Screw*.

SPACE-CRAFT

26 His words came feebly: Wordsworth, "Resolution and Independence."
28 Pater and *La Gioconda*: the Leonardo da Vinci chapter (1869) of *The Renaissance*.
28 Though my house: *Homage to Sextus Propertius*, I.
31 Heliads lift the mist: 83/530: 566.
31 "Is it likely": 24/114: 119.
31 For Botticelli's procedures see H. Ruhemann, *The Cleaning of Paintings*, 1968, 115.
31 An *Aphrodite Anadyomene* of Apelles: the sources are Pliny, *Nat. Hist.*, xxxv, 91; Ovid, *Am.*, I, 14, 35; Strabo XIV, 657; Ovid, *Ars Am.*, III, 401 ff., Ovid, *Ep. Pont.*, IV, 1, 30, Cicero, *Epist. ad Atticum*, XIII, 590.
32 Lewis on EP and time: *Time and Western Man*, 1927, I, ix, xv.
34 Joyce published in the *Irish Homestead*: "Eveline," now of course in *Dubliners*.
38 "A chapter in the moral history": *Letters of James Joyce*, II, 134.
39 Yeats as chairman of the Coinage Commission, D. R. Pearce, ed., *The Senate Speeches of W. B. Yeats*, 1960, 161–7.

RENAISSANCE II

41 "Excessively cobwebbed": *LE*, 311.
42 Red poppies: go and look.
42 "A pair of outsize ladies' drawers": *Ulysses*, late in the "Ithaca" section (Vintage ed., 730).
43 *Euknēmides* has acquired particularization: Denys Page, *History and the Homeric Iliad*, 1959, 245.

44 "Few things were as convincing": Sir John L. Myres, *Homer and his Critics*, 1958, 191–2.

44 His *Les Phéniciens*: for Joyce's use of Bérard see Stuart Gilbert, *James Joyce's Ulysses*, index.

44 As a boy: see A. Walton Litz, *The Art of James Joyce*, 1961, 1–3.

44 Pound on Paris *quai*: *LE*, 259. Stock's surmise (*Life of Ezra Pound*, 1970, 116) that it was one of the books he bought in May 1912 I find unconvincing.

45 "Reached for his six-shooter": *Letters*, #292.

45 Allen Upward had ventured: in *The New Word*, quoted by Pound in *The New Age*, 23 April 1914, 779–80.

45 "The property of the glaux": *Letters*, #290; cf. 74/438: 466.

45 Should Dublin be destroyed: Frank Budgen, *James Joyce and the Making of Ulysses*, 67–8.

46 Literature in the subsequent decades: for a summary see Myres, *Homer and His Critics*, 163 ff.

48 "Did not like inventing": Butler, *Authoress of the Odyssey*, 202.

48 "No artist": Butler, 208.

49 "He is a very bold man": *Letters of James Joyce*, II, 134.

51 "Commenting on machines": *G-B*, 116.

THE MUSE IN TATTERS

54 Professor Schubart published in a German journal: *Sitzungsberichte der Akademie der Wissenschaften*, 1902, 195–206.

54 A reconsidered deciphering: *Berliner Klassikertexte*, V-2.

55 Paul Shorey "wouldn't stand for it": letter and Pound's reply, unpublished, in Harriet Monroe Collection, Univ. of Chicago Library.

55 Pound reaffirmed his admiration: *Egoist*, V (Nov.–Dec. 1918), 130.

56 A torn beginning: the standard edition is Lobel & Page, *Poetarum Lesbiorum Fragmenta*, 1955, #96, but quotations in this book are from the *Classical Review* version Pound used.

56 "Homeric" simile: see Phillip Damon, *Modes of Analogy in Ancient and Mediaeval Verse*, 1961, 272–80.

57 Aldington's version: in *Des Imagistes*, 1914, 19.

59 Accessible collections: the first was Wolf's, 1733, but scholarly interest and proliferated editions did not peak for another century.

60 Swinburne's slow-motion re-enactment: in *Songs of the Springtides*, 1880.

61 Reduced "the whole art": *Letters*, #103.

61 Drew Miss Barry's attention: *Letters*, #104.

61 Mathews and his printer balked: see Forrest Read, ed., *Pound/Joyce*, 1967, Appendix A, and Gallup, item A-11.

63 Cavalcanti's five strophes: *Translations*, 116–17.

65 In the tenth line: i.e. by Edmonds' numbering, which counts a hypothetical opening line he supplied. Aldington picked up the name "Mnasidika" from it.

67 Eliot on Byron: in *On Poetry and Poets*, 1957, 201.

67 A translator of Sappho: see Guy Davenport, *Sappho: Poems and Fragments*, 1965, poem 43.

68 Aeschylus nearly agglutinative: *LE*, 273.

68 Moncli and Audierna: *Translations*, 424.

69 Who, in some such perfect moment: quoted in Barbara Charlesworth, *Dark Passages*, 1965, 44.
70 As one who devoutly practiced: Charlesworth, 110.
71 Nothing but death: 80/494: 527.
71 "Have a care against spondee": *Letters*, #281.
72 In 1949 Pound could not say: conversation with HK.

MOTZ EL SON

77 Favorable reviews of Hewlett's novel: sampled in a publisher's advertisement at the back of Hewlett's *The Queen's Quair*.
77 Five-leaf clover: DP, letter to HK, 16 Jan. 1970.
78 R. P. Blackmur: in his "Masks of Ezra Pound," often reprinted.
78 Lectured on Cavalcanti at Oxford: Stock, *Life of Ezra Pound*, 1970, 131–2.
78 Green shirt: Frank MacShane, *The Life and Work of Ford Madox Ford*, 1965, 89.
79 "High mass of poetry": deleted page in proof-sheets of *Canzoni*, Univ. of Texas Library.
79 Salvaged from Wyncote adolescence: i.e. from "Hilda's Book," at Harvard.
79 "Bits of coral like human brains": quoted by MacShane, 89.
80 Hottest summer since 1453: Ford's hyperbole; but Marianne Moore, in Paris with her mother, remembered that heat for 50 years. "One of the hottest summers the world has ever known," *Paris Review*, 26, Summer–Fall 1961, 46.
80 Ford rolled on the floor: Pound, "Ford Madox (Hueffer) Ford: Obit," *Nineteenth Century and After*, Aug. 1939, 178–81.
80 "Canzone a la Sonata": in Ford's *High Germany*.
80 "The common verse of Britain": *LE*, 205.
80 Ford's preface: reprinted at the end of his 1936 *Collected Poems*.
81 "Nothing, *nothing*": *Letters*, #60.
82 Quan lo rossinhols escria: in Carl Appel, *Provenzalische Chrestomathie*, 3d ed., 1907, #54.
83 Pound's imitation: see "Langue D'Oc" in *Personae*.
83 Never satisfied him: *Letters*, #189.
84 A swallow for shuttle: *Translations*, 447.
84 "Birds of the air": *Confucian Odes*, #242.
85 "A 'song'": *Antheil*, 73.
85 "The Pye-ano": *Antheil*, 85.
85 "At its birth": *Antheil*, 87: all cited from *New Age* music reviews.
85 Homage to Dolmetsch: 81/520: 555.
86 A frail hand: Symons' version of Verlaine's "Le piano que baise une main frêle," *Ariettes Oubliées*, v.
86 Pound shouted in the Greek theater: *LE*, 205.
86 Autet e bas: text in *LE*, 124.
86 Lanquand li iorn, Appel, #14.
87 When he cited it: *SR*, 42–4.
87 One modern commentator: Phillip Damon, *Modes of Analogy in Ancient and Mediaeval Verse*, 1961, 308.
87 The Pound of 1912: *New Age*, 11 Jan. 1912, 249–51.
87 "The chatter of birds": *LE*, 127.
87 "Arnaut breaks the flow": *LE*, 123.

87 Four separate times: *SR*, 28, 35; *New Age*, 11 Jan. 1912; *LE*, 123, 127; *ABC of Reading*, 39–40. These span a quarter-century.

87 "Bird Witted": collected in *What Are Years?* (1941) and all subsequent collections.

87 Arnaut from life as it is: *New Age*, 21 Dec. 1911, 178–80.

89 Arnaut loves: *LE*, 126; Provençal on facing page.

90 Ezra Pound typewrites: Facsimile in N. Stock, ed., *Ezra Pound: Perspectives*, 1965, 208. The spelling of "Paquin" was later emended.

91 "The beauty proper": Blake, *Poetry & Prose*, ed. Keynes, 1941, 611.

91 "Distinct, sharp, and wirey" *Blake*, 617.

91 Discussing French decadence: *Criterion*, xviii (Jan. 1939), 227.

91 On another occasion: *GK*, 368.

92 "Listened to incense": *Noh*, 1960 reprint, 4.

92 The Homeric simile rhymes: example suggested by Alan Stephens.

92 "The Dead" and the *Iliad*: parallel noted by Phillip Damon.

93 The pine-tree in mist: *G-B*, ch. XIII.

93 A house of good stone rhymes: Canto 45.

THE INVENTION OF LANGUAGE

94 "Forloyn": see also *Translations* 71, 1910 version of Cavalcanti's 23rd Sonnet, where the word is used and glossed; and cf. *Letters*, #188.

95 Swahili components: Jack Dalton, "Kiswahili Words in *Finnegans Wake*," in Hart & Senn, eds., *A Wake Digest*, 1968, 43–7.

95 *Erhebung:* in "Burnt Norton," II.

96 "The cords of all": *Ulysses*, "Proteus" episode.

97 "How can you have 'PROSE',": *LE*, 198.

97 "That was the real way": *American Scene*, 309.

97 "Quiet fields": Ford, *A Man Could Stand Up*, II. ii. (*Parade's End*, Knopf combined ed., 1950, 566).

98 "As far as I have gone": Williams, *The Great American Novel*, 1923, 47.

98 So much depends: Williams, *Collected Earlier Poems*, 277.

98 Stephen Dedalus heard the Dean: *Portrait of the Artist as a Young Man*, ch. v.

99 Stephen Hero read Skeat: Joyce, *Stephen Hero*, 1955, 26.

100 View him with scornful: "Epistle to Dr. Arbuthnot," lines 193 ff.

100 Vindicate the ways of God: "Essay on Man," I, 16.

101 Speech of Panamanian Indians: Clyde Kluckhohn, "The Gift of Tongues," in his *Mirror for Man*, 1949.

101 First part of the *New English Dictionary*: for the dates of the part publications, M. M. Mathews, *A Survey of English Dictionaries*, 1933, 101–4.

102 To assist its sub-editors: *N.E.D.*, vol. I, Introduction.

102 There survives a card: P. Hutchins, *James Joyce's World*, 1957, 169.

102 "Gave the first impulse": *Encyclopaedia Britannica*, s. v. "Trench."

103 Defined in 1851: R. C. Trench, *On the Study of Words*, Lecture I.

103 "The kind of intelligence": flyleaf to his version of the *Analects*.

103 Trying to persuade Santayana: Daniel Cory, "Ezra Pound: A Memoir," *Encounter*, xxx.5 (May 1968), 34.

103 Morrison's Chinese Dictionary: Macao, 1815–22, 6 vols, bound as 7, bought by DP about 1914; at Brunnenburg, 1970, copiously annotated by Pound. On

one flyleaf he wrote, "In all vols. notes are to be considered simple query or conjecture—not based."

103 "All men": *Chung Yung* (*Unwobbling Pivot*), I.iv.2.

104 "L'uomo nel Ideogramma": unpublished ms. on what seems to be wartime paper, at Brunnenburg, 1969.

104 "To *spark*": Richardson, I, 49.

105 "May not the *blue*": Richardson, s.v. Blue.

105 "To Etymology": Richardson, I, 43.

105 "And if that be etymology": Tooke, *Diversions of Purley*, II, 135.

105 Borrowed from the Boston Library: K. W. Cameron, *Emerson the Essayist*, 1945, II, 167.

105 Every word, a metaphor: Fenollosa, unpublished draft of "The Chinese Written Character"; notebook at Brunnenburg, 1969.

106 "A radiant node": *G.-B.*, 92.

106 "From every sounding being": Herder, "Essay on the Origin of Language," tr. Alexander Gode in *On the Origin of Language*, 1966, 132.

106 Hence Stephen Dedalus: *Ulysses*, the "Proteus" episode.

107 Le Maître: Mallarmé, "Toast Funèbre," 32–5.

107 "Priest of the eternal imagination": Joyce's phrase in *A Portrait of the Artist as a Young Man*.

107 When Pound noted: *LE*, 53.

108 Barnes: see Austin Warren, "Instress of Inscape," in *Gerard Manley Hopkins, by the Kenyon Critics*, 1945, 83. My assertion of Doughty's indebtedness to Barnes is conjectural.

109 "Hourly communicate": "Preface" to *Lyrical Ballads*.

109 *Sensorium commune*: "Origins of Language," sec. iii. Lightning example in Gode, 141–2.

109 "Eine Sammlung": quoted in Hans Aarsleff, *The Study of Language in England, 1780–1860*, 1967, 151.

109 700 basic Bengalese roots: Aarsleff, 153.

109 Sir William Jones: Aarsleff, 119 ff.

110 "May be those in which the dead poets": "Tradition and the Individual Talent," second paragraph.

110 "Network of tentacular roots": "Ben Jonson," tenth paragraph.

110 Friedrich Diez: *Encyclopaedia Britannica*, s.v. "Diez."

111 And does "Doutz brais . . .": see variant readings in U. A. Canello, *La Vita e le Opere del Trovatore Arnaldo Daniello*, 1883.

111 Gradual differentiation of Latin: Jespersen, *Language*, 1922, 85.

112 "Ways of speaking Latin": *SR*, 12.

113 Not quite in Homer: *Od.* XII–44 comes a little closer than the line I cite.

113 The viel: users of the U.S. edition should correct the misprint "veil."

114 Two sides of a 14th-century page: reproduced in G. Toja. ed., *Arnaut Daniel: Canzoni*, 1960.

114 "Old Levy": so spelled (correctly) in *SR*, 23, and *LE*, 115, but in the Canto "Lévy," apparently to indicate that he used the French pronunciation.

115 Vermeil, green, blue: version in *LE*, 139.

116 Signor Canello speculated: p. 240 of his edition.

116 Lavaud's 1910 edition: in *Annales du Midi*, XXII, 1910, 17–55, 162–79; 300–39; 446–66; XXIII, 1911, 5–31. Cited by Pound in *LE*, 115.

116 "Quasi-allegorical descriptions": *LE*, 139.

118   Three separate translations: *SR*, 34; *New Age*, 22 Feb. 1912; *LE*, 137.
119   "But the great thing": unpublished Fenollosa draft.
119   Perhaps the wife: the *raʒo* on Daniel's life names just one lady: "Et amet una auta dompna de Guascoigna, moiller d'en Guillem de Bouvila." Hence Pound's "Lamplight at Bouvilla," 7/26:30.
119   Ovid's scarlet curtain: *Metamorph*. X, 596.
120   "Very often": *SR*, 26.

WORDS SET FREE

121   Fear no more: *Cymbeline*, IV.ii.
122   A visitor to Warwickshire: W. Arrowsmith, reported by Guy Davenport.
123   "Genuine poetry": third paragraph of his "Dante" essay.
124   Components of Burgon's line identified by Guy Davenport.
124   Age of Time was quite definite: Glyn Daniel, *The Idea of Prehistory*, 1962, beginning of ch. 3.
124   Guy Davenport remarks: in his *Sappho: Poems and Fragments*, 1965, xviii.
125   Take from them: W. B. Yeats, "The Symbolism of Poetry," II.
125   For what Greek forgot: suggested by Marion M. Miller's 1925 translation, 130.
126   Mr. Walker and Dr. Johnson: reported by Boswell.
126   *Donner un sens plus pur:* Mallarmé, "Le Tombeau d'Edgar Poe."
126   "Really it is not I": Eugene Jolas, "My Friend James Joyce," in S. Givens, ed., *James Joyce, Two Decades of Criticism*, 1948, 13.
127   "I am less alarmed": Eliot, "That Poetry is Made of Words," *New English Weekly*, 27 Apr. 1939, 28.
127   *"As well written as prose":* *Letters*, #60.
127   And Wyndham Lewis: recalled by Mrs. Lewis, 1965.
127   Has she eaten: WCW, "Two Pendants: for the Ears," *Collected Later Poems*, 227–8.
130   Certain remarks of Mallarmé's: e.g. those cited in Arthur Symons' *The Symbolist Movement in Literature*.
133   An American classroom handbook: never mind, the editors corrected it and have earned anonymity.
133   Under the sign of Mallarmé: an unpublished essay by Miss Toni Clark underlies this sentence.
134   "The form in which": Eliot, "Introduction" to *Eʒra Pound: Selected Poems*.
134   "Strictly correct": this and subsequent quotations from the "Laforgue" chapter of *The Symbolist Movement in Literature*.
135   "Perfectly plain statements": *Letters*, #103.
138   Lord God of heaven: *A Lume Spento*, 1965 reprint, 13.
142   Which John Quinn tried to correct: B. L. Reid, *The Man from New York: John Quinn and his Friends*, 1968, 282.
142   "So hast du ganz": see "Translations and Adaptations from Heine," II, in *Personae*.

KNOT AND VORTEX

145   He grasps and tenses: R. Buckminster Fuller, lecturing at the University of California, Santa Barbara, December 1967. Cf. his *No More Secondhand God*, 1963, 102 ff.
146   "Things," wrote Fenollosa: all Fenollosa quotations from "The Chinese Written Character as a Medium for Poetry," often reprinted.

146 "A radiant node": *G-B*, 92.

146 "Our kinship to the vital": *SR*, 92.

146 "Energy creates pattern": "Affirmations, IV," *The New Age*, 28 Jan. 1915, 349.

146 "Emotion is an organizer of form": *ibid.*, 350.

146 "Order and vitality": "Affirmations, II," *The New Age*, 14 Jan. 1915, 277.

147 "Art never improves": Eliot, "Tradition and the Individual Talent," I.

147 Pound wrote in 1935: *Letters*, #296.

148 "In the year of grace": *LE*, 259.

150 "I'd like to see a 'rewrite'": *Letters*, #292.

150 "Don't bother about the WORDS": Michael Reck, *Ezra Pound: a Close-up*, 1967, facsimiles preceding p. 99.

150 "Don't translate what I wrote": reported by Eva Hesse.

150 "A bust of Mozart": *Polite Essays*, 193.

150 "Too trivial to believe": paraphrased from letter to HK.

150 A retouched version in 1932: corrected *New Age* tear sheets, prepared for TO Publishers' *Prolegomena* series, seen at Brunnenburg, 1965.

151 "I have sought": *New Age*, 7 Dec. 1911, 131.

152 But when in Burckhardt: *ibid.* The installment is headed, "A Rather Dull Introduction."

152 In the history: *ibid.*

153 "And that the universe": 94/637:670.

154 "As we or mother Dana": *Ulysses*, "Scylla and Charybdis" episode.

154 We might come to believe: *LE*, 49.

155 "To gather the latent energy": *New Age*, 21 Dec. 1911, 178–80.

155 The donative author: *ibid.*

156 "Antennae of the race": *LE*, 58.

156 It is by reason of this *virtù*: *New Age*, 4 Jan. 1912, 224–5. For Catullus and Propertius, cf. 5/17:21 and 7/25:29.

157 For Emerson analogies see "The Poet," 1844, and part iv of "Nature," 1836.

157 In Nature there are no terminations: "The Method of Nature," 1841.

157 "Nature is a symbol": "The Poet."

158 The wealth of the Indies, "The American Scholar."

158 "Big essay on verbs": *Letters*, #95.

158 Rose, sunset, cherry blossom: Fenollosa's synthetic example, later mistaken by Pound for an etymology of the "red" ideogram; cf. *ABC of Reading*, 8.

158 Left the *Osiris* series behind him: *Pound/Joyce*, 118.

159 "A wet leaf": "Liu Ch'e," in *Personae*.

160 Words like great hollow cones: *New Age*, 25 Jan. 1912, 297–9.

160 Analysis of Chinese line courtesy of Mr. Wai-Lim Yip.

161 Fuller watching bubbles: reported by Calvin Tompkins, *The New Yorker*, 8 Jan. 1966.

162 A Red Army poster artist: Marie Seton, *Sergei M. Eisenstein*, 1960, 37, and cf. 81. Eisenstein's 1929 essay "The Cinematographic Principle and the Ideograph," is in his *Film Form*, trans. & ed. Jay Leyda, 1949, 28–44.

162 "Heisenberg said": conversation, Dec. 1967.

TRANSFORMATIONS

163 "The forces which produce": Fenollosa, "Chinese Written Character."

163 "The pattern-making faculty": *New Age*, 14 Jan. 1915, 278.

163   Generative grammar: cf. Noam Chomsky, *Syntactic Structures*, 1957, and Bibliography therein.

164   "O body swayed": Yeats, "Among School Children."

164   "Sailing to Byzantium" and Keats: perceived by Prof. D. R. Pearce.

164   "When we actually try": Chomsky, *Syntactic Structures*, 80.

164   Subject and object are also verbs: Horne Tooke on the contrary tried to make every verb a noun, encountered discrepancies, and burnt the ms. of his third volume. See H. Aarsleff, *The Study of Language in England, 1780–1860*, 1967, 67–8.

165   Dr. Williams was to perceive: cf. *Paterson*, 206–10.

165   "There are few fallacies": *New Age*, 15 Feb. 1912, 370.

165   "If a book reveal": *New Age*, 4 Jan. 1912, 224–5.

165   "For order to persist": "Tradition and the Individual Talent."

167   Vesicles almost entirely: Guy Davenport, ed., *The Intelligence of Louis Agassiz*, 1963, 10.

167   Snapping in the same fierce manner: *ibid.*, 178.

167   The grasses: J. Kasper, ed., *Gists from Agassiz*, 1953, 68.

167   The cells are stellate: D'Arcy W. Thompson, *On Growth and Form*, ed. 2, 1942, 547.

167   "Hearken" and "oftentimes": *ibid.*, 8.

167   Un vieux piano: "Un Coeur Simple," fourth paragraph. Cf. 7/24:28.

168   "An anthology of transit": Williams, *Selected Essays*, 123.

169   "A typical Scaroid fish": *On Growth and Form*, 1062 (figs. 519–20).

170   Gilbert Murray presented Hamlet: G. Murray, *The Classical Tradition in Poetry*, 1930, ch. viii.

170   "That prehistoric and world-wide": *ibid.*, 234.

170   Müller's edition: identified by J. P. Sullivan, *Ezra Pound and Sextus Propertius*, 1964, 95–6.

170   "Almost thirty pages": *Letters*, #189.

170   "Certain emotions": *Letters*, #246.

171   Cellulose tension network: cf. Buckminster Fuller, "Conceptuality of Fundamental Structures," in G. Kepes, ed., *Structure in Art and Science*, 1965, 85–6.

172   "Eucalyptus that is for memory": 74/435:463.

IMAGISM

174   By one account: unpublished memoir by H. D., in keeping of Prof. Norman H. Pearson. (And my thanks to Mr. Robert Duncan.)

174   "Laconic speech": EP to Harriet Monroe, *Letters*, #7; but I follow the punctuation of the original (Harriet Monroe Collection, Univ. of Chicago Library).

174   The trees, books, readings, from H. D.'s memoir.

175   "Hilda's Book": now at Houghton Library, Harvard; described and copied for me by Mr. Laurence Scott.

175   "Tall, blond": phrases and anecdotes from WCW, *Autobiography*, 67–70.

177   "The whole affair": EP to Harriet Monroe, letter in Univ. of Chicago Library.

177   "A chorus in the Hippolytus": Aldington to Amy Lowell, 20 Nov. 1917, quoted in Charles Norman, *Ezra Pound*, 1960, 89.

177   "A pig-headed fool": from the full version of *Letters*, #60, Univ. of Chicago.

178 "I made the word": EP to Magaret Anderson, 17 Nov. 1917, Univ. of Wisconsin, Milwaukee, library.

178 Flint's article: "Contemporary French Poetry," *Poetry Review*, Aug. 1912, 355–414. For the succeeding quotations, see 394, 380, 394, 398, 408, 367.

181 "On a Marsh Road": Ford Madox Ford, *Collected Poems*, 1936, 199. This source for "dim lands of peace" was noted by N. Christoph de Nagy, *Ezra Pound's Poetics and Literary Tradition*, 1966, 58.

182 "Simply for those moments' sake": Pater, "Conclusion" to *The Renaissance*, final sentence.

184 On a visit to Paris: see *G-B*, 86–9. Pound first told the story in *T.P's Weekly* (6 June 1913), 707.

185 "'lords' over fact": *G-B*, 91–2.

185 "An 'Image' is that which presents": *LE*, 4.

185 "Radiant node or cluster": *G-B*, 92.

185 "Real because we know it directly": *G-B*, 86.

186 "Luminous detail": cf. *New Age*, 7 Dec. 1911, 130.

191 "Translating at sight": Yeats, "Introduction" to *The Oxford Book of Modern Verse*, section X.

191 "I defined the vortex": *G-B*, 81.

THE INVENTION OF CHINA

I inspected all the Fenollosa notebooks at Brunnenburg, October 1969. I regret that an earlier draft of this chapter, based on the microfilmed sampling of the notebooks at the Univ. of Virginia Library, misled Mr. Wai-Lim Yip (*Ezra Pound's 'Cathay,'* 1969) into correlating two of Pound's versions with notes he didn't use. Neither of us then knew how enormously superior were the notes Fenollosa did with Mori to the notes he did with anyone else. Mr. Yip's book, which contains guides to all the Chinese originals, remains the indispensable commentary on *Cathay*.

192 "It must be pointed out": Eliot, "Introduction" to *Selected Poems of Ezra Pound*.

194 Giles, *History of Chinese Literature*, 1901, 97.

195 "So-called 'free verse'": Henry H. Hart, *The Hundred Names*, 1933, 29.

195 Fletcher has recalled: J. G. Fletcher, "The Orient and Contemporary Poetry," in A. E. Christy, ed., *The Asian Legacy and American Life*, 1945, 145–74.

196 The sound of rustling silk: Giles, 100.

196 The rustling of the silk: "Liu Ch'e," in *Personae*. Achilles Fang, "Fenollosa and Pound," *Harvard Journal of Asiatic Studies*, 20 (1957), 236, has the "indefatigable poet" turning to Giles because he had exhausted Fenollosa. But (Gallup, 140) the Giles versions were mailed to New York before the Fenollosa notebooks were received.

197 No indication that Pound supposed: when he wrote a year later (*G-B*, 83) that Ibycus and Liu Ch'e "presented the 'Image'," memory had apparently replaced what was findable in Giles with his own rescription.

197 Instructed Harriet Monroe: undated letter in Harriet Monroe Collection, Univ of Chicago. In the *Poetry* printing we find another space, after 'black': perhaps indicated in proof.

197 *Contemporania* group: Tenzone; The Condolence; The Garret; The Garden;

Ortus; Dance Figure; Salutation; Salutation the Second; Pax Saturni; Commission; A Pact; In a Station of the Metro. All but "Pax Saturni" now in *Personae*.

198   Some in London, some later: one wrapper survives, with a London postmark and undecipherable date; a letter dated 25 Nov. [apparently 1913] accompanied the books sent from America. Information from Eva Hesse.

199   Single line the unit of composition: see Donald Davie, *Ezra Pound; Poet as Sculptor*, 1964, 41–6.

199   (Lo! this thing: "And Thus in Nineveh," 1909.

199   (I have known: "A Song of the Degrees," 1913.

199   (My love is lovelier: "Canzon: The Spear," 1910.

202   "I keep the book": *G-B*, 68.

202   "A sight worthy of Dante": *G-B*, 58–9.

203   The rain has stopped: letter to John Cournos, 27 Dec. 1914.

203   Canonical list: e.g. Achilles Fang, "Fenollosa and Pound," *Harvard Journal of Asiatic Studies*, 20 (1957).

204   Chaucer in much the same way: line 2281 and Robinson's note. Alan Stephens suggested this example.

206   "Closer than the Rubaiyat": *Letters*, #71.

206   Waley found this judgment ridiculous: Arthur Waley, "The Poet Li Po, A.D. 701–762," paper read Nov. 1918 and published in 1919.

208   Some 30 of which he used only two: the other was the epigraph to "Four Poems of Departure." There are also notes for "Lament of the Frontier Guard" and "South Folk in Cold Country," but Pound used the better notes dictated by Mori. Fang's "Soon Pound came to the end of Ernest Fenollosa's notes" ("Fenollosa and Pound," 236) may pass, at Harvard, for literary history.

209   The lingering clouds: Waley, *170 Chinese Poems*, 1919, 115; this is actually a version of the second stanza.

209   Lowering, lowering: William Acker, *T'ao the Hermit*, 1952, 135; this scrupulously dead version is a useful guide to the way the poem comes out character by character.

210   How fair, the lingering clouds: Lily Pao-Hu Chang and Marjorie Sinclair, *The Poems of T'ao Ch'ien*, 1915, 11.

213   Making contact with the notes: Pound's habit from *The Seafarer* on. The contact is often no more than a finger's touch.

214   "Talking about each other's lives": in this paragraph I follow the discourse of Mrs. Alice Leng of the University of Virginia. Mr. Yip (230) has "to talk about past and present"; the discrepancy is a good instance of the leeway between ideograms and western languages.

215   I am told: again by Mrs. Leng; and Mr. Yip has "Not that there is no one around." And they are explicitly not in disagreement.

215   Indications of number, of tense: See for instance James J. Y. Liu, *The Art of Chinese Poetry*, 1962, chs. i, ii, iv, and Wai-Lim Yip, *Ezra Pound's 'Cathay'*, ch. i.

215   In a prose poem: translated by Arthur Waley, *170 Chinese Poems*, 41, as "The Man-Wind and the Woman-Wind."

216   An expert gloss: Roy E. Teele, *Through a Glass Darkly, A Study of English Translations of Chinese Poetry*, 1949, 34–5. Teele also glosses "The Beautiful Toilet," 29–31.

217   W. H. D. Rouse surmised: "Homer's Words," annexed to his version of the *Odyssey*.

217   Complaining of inaccuracy: as they will when they notice the cognate note on *oinos aithiops*; "the gloss, probably, not the colour": 97/675:706.

217   Mr. Auden has described: "Auden on Poetry," *The Atlantic*, Aug. 1966, 98.

218   The luckless scholar: see John Chadwick, *The Decipherment of Linear B*, 28–9. And "storehouse inventories" has more recently been challenged.

219   Clear hand and quaint English: for Ariga's version (mistakenly identified as Fenollosa's) see Lawrence W. Chisholm, *Fenollosa; the Far East and American Culture*, 1963, 252.

220   Pound finished his version: date written into the notebook; a rare happening.

222   South Folk in Cold Country: see Donald Davie's discussion of the prosody of this version, in *Ezra Pound: Poet as Sculptor*, 41–2.

THE PERSISTENT EAST

223   Bacon on Chinese characters: *Advancement of Learning*, VI-i.

223   As numerous as were the classes created by God: hence Wilkins, *Essay Toward a Real Character and a Universal Language*, 1667, 450–1, thought there were 120,000 of them. Karlgren (*Philology and Ancient China*, 1926, 51) says 50,000 would be a high estimate, and 12–14,000 would comprise "the most important words in Chinese literature." The *Four Books* of Confucius and Mencius use only 2,500.

224   To construct ideal languages: for a survey, see Paul Cornelius, *Languages in 17th and Early 18th Century Imaginary Voyages*, 1965, chs. ii, iv.

224   In Lagado, *Gulliver's Travels*, III–v.

225   Fenollosa set out to refute: in "The Chinese Written Character as a Medium for Poetry," often reprinted.

225   Leibniz: see Joseph Needham, *Science and Civilization in China*, II, 1956: for Boole and *De Arte Combinatoria*, 497; for *Book of Changes*, 340–5.

226   [Footnote] primitive sounds: unpublished Fenollosa ms. Pound edited the Essay heavily to elicit an Ars Poetica from Fenollosa's drafts of a lecture confined to Chinese.

226   "I now doubt if it was inferior": "Terminal Note" to the Arrow Editions reprint [Gallup B-36], 1936. Cf. "Note to Plate I": "We will remain bestially ignorant of Chinese poetry so long as we insist on reading and *speaking* their short vowels instead of taking time to sing them with observance of the sequence of vowels."

227   *Fang*: see Karlgren, *Sound and Symbol in Chinese*, 1923, 55, and *Philology in Ancient China*, 1926, 36.

228   Principle clearly explained: Fenollosa notebook, at Brunnenburg, 1969; Pound has marked the passage with a blue crayon slash.

229   Leibniz in the 1670's: Cornelius, 97–103. His speculation about ideograms is summarized, 101: "If they were based upon a philosophy of things, and represented the simple and composite natures of things, he thought that they might well serve as 'universal characteristics' for the entire world."

230   Teaching Emerson: L. W. Chisholm, *Fenollosa: the Far East and American Culture*, 1963, 218.

230   Emerson, Mailla, Thoreau: see Arthur Christy, *The Orient in American Transcendentalism*, 1932, 321, 319, 196.

231 Needham's remarkable hypothesis: Needham, II, 291–3, 496–505.

VORTEX LEWIS

234 "Arguably the greatest": Edmund Gray, "Wyndham Lewis and the Modern Crisis in Painting," *Agenda*, Autumn-Winter 1969–70, 90.

236 "Starting a new Futurist": *Pound/Joyce*, 26.

238 Electrified cones, *New Age*, 25 Jan. 1912, 297–9.

238 "A vortex, drawing strength": *New Age*, 30 Jan. 1913, 300.

239 "We do not desire": *Blast* #1, G.-B. 90.

239 Gaudier postulated: his "Vortex" is reprinted in *GK*, 63–8, and in *G-B*, 20–24.

239 "A universal scheme": Fenollosa, *Epochs of Chinese and Japanese Art*, xxiv.

240 "Caruso tenor-instincts": Michel & Fox, eds., *Wyndham Lewis on Art*, 1969, 156.

240 "Throats iron eternities": R. Rosenthal, ed., *Wyndham Lewis: A Soldier of Humor and Selected Writings*, 1966, 80.

240 Chinese Geomancy: Lewis, "Feng Shui and Contemporary Form." in *Wyndham Lewis on Art*, 1969, 41–2.

241 "What I, personally, did": *Wyndham Lewis on Art*, 451.

241 "Matter that has not sufficient mind": Lewis, "Code of a Herdsman," *Little Review*, IV.3 (July 1917), 5.

241 Our Vortex: *Wyndham Lewis on Art*, 53.

241 "Lets Life know its Place": *ibid.*

242 "Do not allow yourself": Lewis, "Code of a Herdsman," *Little Review*, IV.3 (July 1917), 3.

242 "It makes Bergson look like a gnat": EP to Margaret Anderson, 22 June 1917, Univ. of Wisconsin (Milwaukee) library.

242 Beauty is an icy douche: "Inferior Religions," VIII. Accessible in Lewis, *The Wild Body*, 1928, and in R. Rosenthal, ed., *Wyndham Lewis: A Soldier of Humor and Selected Writings*, 1966, 67–73.

243 "Cemetery of shells": Lewis, *Self Condemned*, last chapter.

243 "Belief in public's intelligence": *Letters*, #9.

243 "Save the public's soul": *Letters*, #10.

243 Prothero's letter: *LE*, 357–8.

244 Able to earn in the next 12 months: *Letters*, #278.

244 "The sinews": *Letters*, #278.

244 "Mr. Nixon": *Mauberley*, IX.

244 Lewis decorated a fireplace: D. Goldring, *South Lodge*, (1943), 13.

245 Gaudier "obtained a clerkship": *G-B*, 43.

245 "Convert the King": *Wyndham Lewis on Art*, 26.

246 "Unwatered moon": Lewis, *Demon of Progress in the Arts*, 1954, 3.

246 Anecdote of *Blast* in the rain from a Pound broadcast in O. Rudge, ed., *If This be Treason*, Siena, 1948, 31.

247 "Kept his melodic sense": *ABC of Reading*, 34–5.

247 "Caught as was the custom": *GK*, frontispiece caption.

247 Typewriter and two carvings: *Letters*, #31.

THE STONE

248 We left the platform: Lewis, *Blasting and Bombardiering*, 1967, 108.

248 Imagine a dull dawn: *G-B*, 70.

249 Today is magnificent: *ibid.*

249 He was the first sculptor: Guy Davenport, *Ezra's Bowmen of Shu*, privately printed artifact, 1965.

250 "It was done": *G-B*, 141

250 "Definitely a visionary": *G-B*, 67, footnote.

250 Accustomed to the company of the aloof cat: John Quinn bought the "Cat" in August 1916 (B. L. Reid, *The Man from New York*, 1968, 251). After Quinn's death (1924) the Pounds reacquired it.

250 He could see the horse: *G-B*, 46; *ABC of Reading*, 7.

251 Münch and Chinese dictionary: Pound in conversation, 1952.

251 "Cubism has not decayed": *G-B*, 143.

251 "Large house full of plush furniture": *G-B*, 80.

251 "Inundated with rain": *G-B*, 40.

252 Threepenny bus fare: Bridson interview, *New Directions 17*, 163.

252 Cost all of three pounds: *ibid.*, 160.

252 "No finer moment": *G-B*, 48.

252 "Ten acre lot": 9/37:41.

252 "Pale eyes": 80/511:546.

252 "Stemmed all from Neptune": 83/528:563

255 Some hundred drawings: *New Directions 17*, 160.

255 Sigfried Giedion confirmed: in his *The Eternal Present: the Beginnings of Architecture*, 1964, Part XI.

255 Man succeeded: *G-B*, 21; *GK*, 64.

256 "Great passive vulva": "Postscript to *The Natural Philosophy of Love*," in *Pavannes and Divagations*, 204.

256 Structure, not impression: cf. R. H. Wilenski, *The Meaning of Modern Sculpture*, V.l.ii.

256 "It will not look like you": *G-B*, 50.

256 Notebook rejection of Michelangelo: *G-B*, 42.

256 "Line an imaginary thing": *ibid.*, my translation.

256 I SHALL DERIVE: *G-B*, 28.

258 Father of their spokesman: i.e. of the "Herr Bacher" of 74/448:476.

258 Shape of a Mauser rifle: *G-B*, 28.

259 "An ideal for super-aesthetes": *Egoist*, 16 Feb. 1914, 67.

259 "The Greeks, the caressable": *Egoist*, 16 Mar. 1914, 117.

259 "Plastic moving toward coitus": *LE*, 150.

259 Died, a myriad: *Mauberley*, V.

260 Required to be shrouded: Dorothy Pound, 1964.

260 Occupied with the pre-dawn: see Hugh Witemeyer, *The Poetry of Ezra Pound: Forms and Renewal, 1908–1920*, 1969, 56–7. For the turning of the bust, see *New Directions 17*, 184, where we learn that Pound also intended an allusion to the 11th of his "Dialogues of Fontenelle" (*Pavannes and Divagations*, 135).

260 Henry Moore: David Sylvester, *Henry Moore*, 1968, 1.

PRIVACIES

263 Lawrence professed: A. W. Lawrence, ed., *T. E. Lawrence*, by His Friends, 1937, 330. I owe this detail to Achilles Fang's unpublished Harvard dissertation.

263 "In ermine": reported, Aug. 1965, by Mrs. Gatter, present inhabitant of the Wyncote, Pa., house.

264 O Summer time: oral tradition indeed; my memory of an informant's memory of a Pound classmate's memory.

264 The voice of Monsieur Fouquet: 74/447:475.

264 Tree houses, tennis: unpublished paper by Carl Gatter.

265 Sequence of tranquil scenes: at Brunnenburg in 1965. Cf. Daniel Pearlman, *The Barb of Time*, 1969, Appendix B.

266 She hath called me: "La Fraisne" in *Personae*.

266 I have tried: "Canto 120," in *Anonym* #4, Buffalo, N.Y., 1969.

266 Brancusi's bird: incident in May 1964.

267 "Expect to be carried": *Letters*, #270.

267 "Wipe your feet": *Letters*, #50.

267 "Any change in any art": *New Age*, 14 Jan. 1915, 277.

267 "give a long list": W. B. Stanford, *The Ulysses Theme*, 2d ed., 1964, 247.

268 "Yourself must be your caste": Lewis. "Code of a Herdsman," *Little Review*, IV.3 (July 1917), 4.

268 "I have allowed": *Time and Western Man*, 1927, Preface to Book I.

268 "What an entangled Absalom": Ursula Bridge, ed., *W. B. Yeats and T. Sturge Moore, Their Correspondence*, 1953, 115.

268 "Older than the fish": "The Caliph's Design," in Michel and Fox, edd., *Wyndham Lewis on Art*, 1969, 152.

269 The creation: *ibid.*

269 "The music of *Carmen*": *ibid.*, 155.

269 "As to the wing mechanism": *ibid.*, 153.

269 "Thought of the modern": *Egoist*, Sept. 1918, 106.

269 Fabre had described: *Wyndham Lewis on Art*, 153.

270 D'Arcy Thompson explained: *On Growth and Form*, 2d ed., 1942, 1010–11.

270 "Life, simply"; stones: *Wyndham Lewis on Art*, 155.

270 A young woman deciding: Dorothy Pound.

270 "Do not send yourself": "Code of a Herdsman."

271 "Burying Euclid": *Wyndham Lewis on Art*, 330.

271 "My Dear Job": *Pound/Joyce*, 121.

271 The last survivor of his college generation: Constantine P. Curran, *James Joyce Remembered*, 1968.

271 "Hell Opened to Christians": James R. Thrane, "Joyce's Sermon on Hell: Its Sources and Its Backgrounds," in M. Magalaner, ed., *James Joyce Miscellany, Third Series*, 1962, 33–78.

271 Anglo-Irish Dublin: Donald Davie noted its absence from Joyce in a 1956 conversation.

274 "It has always struck me": *Pound/Joyce*, 92.

275 They reminded Eliot: Marshall McLuhan told me this years ago.

276 "Poetry is not a turning loose": "Tradition and the Individual Talent."

276 Or when, under ether: *East Coker*, III.

276 Penchant for ether-sniffing: reported by Aldous Huxley, 1960.

SCATTER

279 The woman who had grubstaked [Kate Lechmere]: Lewis, *Letters*, 69.

279 "Ended with 185 subscribers": *Letters*, #278.

280 Arthur Waugh mentioned: see *Pound/Joyce*, 87.
280 At Coney Island: B. L. Reid, *The Man from New York: John Quinn and his Friends*, 86; cf. 80/507: 542.
280 Early in March 1915: Reid, 198.
280 If a patron: Reid, 199–200.
281 He rallied: copies of four telegrams in John Quinn archive, New York Public Library.
281 "Roosevelt to write": JQ to EP, letter in New York Public Library.
281 Pound transmitted long lists: in letters to Margaret Anderson, Univ. of Wisconsin (Milwaukee) Library.
281 "Undependable volition": EP to Margaret Anderson, 6 June 1917.
282 But the world has glory: unpublished Fenollosa notebook, at Brunnenburg, 1969. I have not seen the other *Noh* notebooks.
282 The world's glory: Pound & Fenollosa, *The Classic Noh Theatre of Japan*, 1959 reprint, 127.
283 "If I don't finish": EP to Margaret Anderson, 3 Apr. 1917.
284 His long poem's theme: sentence in headnote sent with Canto typescript, but cancelled by Pound after typing. Harriet Monroe Collection, Univ. of Chicago Library.
284 Preserves one allusion: or possibly quotation; I have not seen the Fenollosa text of this play. In the accessible text (*Japanese Noh Drama*, Tokyo, 1955, Japanese Classics Translation Committee) the other pine is at Sumiyoshi.
284 He spent a guinea: EP to Margaret Anderson, 17 May 1917.
284 "Religio": *Pavannes and Divagations*, 96–8.
285 "Carried his lucidity": *Pavannes and Divagations*, 116.
286 "Print the left foot": EP to Harriet Monroe, Univ. of Chicago Library.
286 "Cat-piss and porcupines": letter in Univ. of Chicago Library.
288 Mrs. Eliot reported: EP to Margaret Anderson, 21 June 1917.

MAO⁴, OR PRESUMPTION

Damon: S. Foster Damon, *Amy Lowell, a Chronicle*, 1935.
Gregory: Horace Gregory, *Amy Lowell, Portrait of the Poet in Her Time*, 1958.
F/A: H. F. MacNair, ed., *Florence Ayscough and Amy Lowell—Correspondence of a Friendship*, 1945.
Fir-Flower: *Fir-Flower Tablets*, Poems translated from the Chinese by Florence Ayscough, English Versions by Amy Lowell, 1921.

289 Fenollosa quotations from drafts, mostly unpublished, at Brunnenburg, 1969.
291 "Tumbling through rocks abrupt": Thomson, "Winter"; example suggested by Prof. Thomas Steiner.
291 Winter of 1914–15: since in the first printing the wording of a footnote places Gaudier at the battlefront, but alive.
291 "Adamantine stupidity": *Letters*, #71.
291 Fenollosa's big essay on verbs: *Letters*, #95.
291 Tried *Seven Arts*: *Letters*, #115.
291 Sandburg on Amy: *F/A*, 19.
292 Pound on Percy Lowell: EP to Margaret Anderson, 20 Aug. 1917, letter at Univ. of Wisconsin (Milwaukee).
292 Amy's first poem: Damon, 147–8.

292 "I too am an *Imagiste*": Damon, 196.
292 Maroon-clad chauffeur: Damon, 226.
292 Ezra looked "terribly ill": Gregory, 125.
292 Model campaign: detailed in Damon, 197–252.
292 "He does not work enough": *F/A*, 255.
293 Mr. Miyaoka: Damon, 55.
293 "Japanese prints": *F/A*, 20.
293 "Lacquer Prints," hara-kiri: *F/A*, 21–22.
293 "Rings of intrigue": *F/A*, 196.
293 "Knock a hole": *F/A*, 43.
293 "Not Chinese in the first place": *F/A*, 43–44.
293 We were at work: *F/A*, 26.
294 "I have made a discovery": *F/A*, 251.
294 My son is ill: *Fir-Flower*, 163.
294 "Awful study of cadence": *F/A*, 252.
294 "I wrote back": *F/A*, 37.
295 "Shanghai pidgin to her servants": Gregory, 187.
295 "That root theory of ours": *F/A*, 38.
295 Typescript had gathered Illinois dust: several references in the Pound–Anderson correspondence, Univ. of Wisconsin (Milwaukee).
295 Eliot on Amy: *Egoist*, V.4 (Apr. 1918), 55.
295 "I will only try": *F/A*, 39.
295 How stupid: *F/A*, 68.
295 "Oh, dear me": *F/A*, 65.
295 Misinformation, apologies: *F/A*, 91.
295 "Perfectly foolish": *F/A*, 103.
296 Florence in the early months: paragraph gleaned from *F/A*, 40–52.
296 "I will in that case": EP to Margaret Anderson, 7 July 1918, letter at Univ. of Wisconsin (Milwaukee).
297 "Poor Ezra": *F/A*, 256.
298 Britannic Commissioner: *F/A*, 80, 140.
298 What whiteness: 74/425: 451.
298 She sounded him out: *F/A*, 140.
298 L. C. Hopkins, 1854–1952. See *The Six Scripts, or the Principles of Chinese Writing, by Tai T'ung*. A Translation by L. C. Hopkins, with a memoir of the translator by W. Percival Yetts, Cambridge Univ. Press, 1954. The translation first appeared in 1881. Hopkins was Consul General at Tientsin until 1908.
298 "Poorest way of saying things": *F/A*, 227.
298 "A baker's dozen": *Fir-Flower*, xc.
298 I bid goodbye: *Fir-Flower*, 52.
298 One ought not to use the word "Chinamen": *F/A*, 201.

DOUGLAS

ED: C. H. Douglas, *Economic Democracy*, 1920.

301 During the war money could be found: H. T. N. Gaitskell, in G. D. H. Cole, ed., *What Everybody Wants to Know about Money*, 1933, 347. Since Gaitskell's refutation of Douglas, itself refuted by Gorham Munson, *Aladdin's Lamp*, 1945, 146–8, is often regarded as classic, his later experiences as Chancellor of the Exchequer are not without irony.

301 "More uniformly high": *ED*, 94.
302 "Orage taught Douglas": Pound, quoted in Wallace Martin, *The New Age Under Orage*, 1967, 171
302 More than once he complains: e.g. letter in *Pound/Joyce*, 30.
302 "What I had written as free agent": *Polite Essays*, 100.
304 "Waste is not less waste": *ED*, 66.
304 "If by wealth we mean": *ED*, 69.
304 The "fittest": *ED*, 8–9.
305 "Absolutely no virtue": *ED*, 45.
305 "'Labour-saving' machinery": *ED*, 15.
305 "Ever-increasing complexity": *ED*, 15–16.
306 "An orthodox economist": 22/102:106. He is said to have been Keynes.
306 Toilet paper and *Divine Comedy*: *Letters*, #248.
307 [Footnote] Munson's exposition: Gorham Munson, *Aladdin's Lamp*, 1945, 150.
307 "The sum of the wages": *ED*, 120.
307 "Unequal distribution of wealth": *ED*, 54.
308 "Real unit of the world's currency": *ED*, 100.
309 "The quantity of currency in circulation": Martin, *The New Age Under Orage*, 271.
311 Charlie Mordecai: so called, from Marx's pre-baptismal family name, in 72/420:443.
311 "Masses of congealed labour time": Marx, *Capital*, ch. i (Everyman ed., p. 8).
311 "The fallacy that labour produces": *ED*, 91.
311 To build Stonehenge: computations in ch. iv of Gerald S. Hawkins, *Stonehenge Decoded*, 1965.
312 Sheer mind, sheer intellection: students of Buckminster Fuller will note his independent arrival at a similar economic vision: *Nine Chains to the Moon*, 1938, ch. 9; *Operating Manual for Spaceship Earth*, 1969, *passim*.
312 "Misdirected effort which appears in cost": *ED*, 66.
313 "The whole argument": *ED*, 64.
313 "If production stops," *ED*, 74.
313 A Canadian Economist: Lorne T. Morgan, *The Permanent War, or, Homo the Sap*, Toronto, circa 1943.
313 "The tawdry ornament": *ED*, 78.
315 Fallacy that value is related to demand: *ED*, 106.
315 Paying a man by piecework: *ED*, 101, 108.
316 Whoever sets men a little freer: *ED*, 110–11.
316 Possibly three hours a day: *ED*, 102.
316 "It must be perfectly obvious": *ED*, 124.
316 "Real credit is a measure": *ED*, 121.
317 "Co-operation of reasoned assent": *ED*, 8.

THE SACRED PLACES

Much of this chapter based on inspection of sites, 1958–70.

318 Balloon frames: Sigfried Giedion, *Space, Time and Architecture*, 3d ed., 1954, 345–53.
319 Not the branches: Louis Zukofsky, *All (1956–64)*, 44.
319 The lines of this new song: Zukofsky, *All (1923–58)*, 97.
319 "Distaste for lingering": Williams, *Selected Essays*, 121.

320　"A portable substitute": *LE*, 16.

320　Dante in New England: see Angelina La Piana, *Dante's American Pilgrimage*, 1948.

320　"Lying in bed": Herbert Howarth, *Notes on Some Figures Behind T. S. Eliot*, 1964, 74.

321　Tissue-paper packets of green tea: *Pavannes and Divagations*, 9.

322　Shall I claim: scrapped version of Canto I, in *Quia Pauper Amavi*, 1919, 22.

323　In germ: Louis Zukofsky, *All* (*1923–58*), 145.

330　Pound has recalled: *Letters*, #275.

333　The exchange value of the pound sterling: details of this trip from Dorothy Pound, conversation, 1969, and letter, 16 Jan. 1970.

333　Grotte de Niaux: the painted cave nearest Montségur; but it may have been some other cave he visited. The region boasts many.

335　Fernand Niel: see his *Montségur, Temple et Forteresse des Cathares d'Occitanie*, Grenoble, 1967.

336　Eliot with seven blisters: postcard from EP to DP, 18 Aug. 1919.

338　Pound was there that July 12: date from a postcard to Olivia Shakespear, courtesy Mr. O. S. Pound.

346　*Ariston men hudor*: Pindar, *First Olympic*, 1–2.

THE CANTOS—1

350　Poliziano's Homer: see specimens, with James Hynd's commentary, in *Arion*, VI.3 (Autumn 1967), 325–35.

351　"Sonorities" of the Anglo-Saxon: H. Meacham, *The Caged Panther*, 40.

351　Sounds, not words: pointed out to me by Mr. John Reid.

354　Purchased "1906, 1908 or 1910": *LE* 259.

354　"I was in them days": quoted in Charles Norman, *Ezra Pound*, 356.

355　In an unpublished letter: at Yale.

355　"For the beginning of the second part": Richard Ellmann, *James Joyce*, 119.

355　In 1913 Pound compared: *New Age*, 9 Oct. 1913, 694–6.

355　Pound arranged *Prufrock*: Eliot, *viva voce*, May 1964.

356　"Points define a periphery": headnote to his version of the *Analects*.

356　A half-century later: in his foreword to the *Selected Cantos*, 1967.

357　Scribbled in a copy: now in the Univ. of Texas library.

357　Whose name happened to be Dante: see *Personae*, "The Study in Aesthetics."

360　A "poem including history": Pound's definition of an epic in, e.g., *LE*, 86.

363　"Age of usury": *GK*, 96, quoting La Tour du Pin.

363　"I swam down and took hold": Ernest Hemingway, "After the Storm," from *Winner Take Nothing*, 1932.

365　"I suggest that finer and future critics": *GK*, 27.

365　"Anyone with Gaudier-Brzeska's eye": *GK*, 33.

366　Worldwide navigation: see Walter J. Ong, S.J., *Darwin's Vision and Christian Perspectives*, 1960, 3–6.

367　Menelaos and his men: *Odyssey*, iv.

368　TU DIONA: Bion's "Lament for Adonis," of which the texts are in disarray and the Canto citations also. I follow the Budé edition, which is very close to Pound's wording.

371　The effect of the subtler repetitions: *Antheil*, 95.

372　[even as we: Pound's 1912 version is in *The New Age*, 22 Feb. 1912, 393.

375 One of his *canzoni*: the 4th, "Lancan son passat li giure," of which it is the final phrase.

377 "I have, confound it": *Letters*, #279.

378 "Cyclic theories of time": Walter J. Ong, S.J., *Darwin's Vision and Christian Perspectives*, 1960, 134–5.

379 He had earlier written: T. S. Eliot, "Introductory Essay" to *London: A Poem and The Vanity of Human Wishes*, 1930.

379 Commented sharply: *GK*, 180.

379 Do not move, "Canto 120," in *Anonym #4*, Buffalo, N.Y., 1969.

380 Yeats did not finish: Richard Ellmann, *James Joyce*, 545.

O CITY CITY...

383 London "merely shrivels": Eliot, "London Letter," *The Dial*, May 1922, 510.

383 The upper stages: *The Childermass*, 1928, 7.

384 "In the truest sense an asylum": *The Childermass*, 224.

384 "If Paris had been as interesting": interview with D. G. Bridson, *New Directions 17*, 1961, 170.

384 Robert Menzies McAlmon: see R. E. Knoll, *Robert McAlmon, Expatriate Publisher and Writer*, 1957.

384 "Gert Northrup was": *A Hasty Bunch*, 1922, 1.

384 Floss proofread: Florence H. Williams letter to HK, 1970.

384 Nancy Cunard later bought: Knoll, *Robert McAlmon*, 35.

385 "Just to be crazy": WCW in conversation, 1957.

385 From the petal's edge: *Spring and All*, 1923, 32; in *Collected Earlier Poems*, 250, the last word is "space."

385 "Nobody ever saw it": WCW and Edith Heal, *I Wanted to Write a Poem*, 1958, 36.

385 "Après mot": Richard Ellmann, *James Joyce*, 600.

386 "As birds' wings beat": *Spring and All*, 91.

386 Alexei Kruchenykh: in V. Markov, *Russian Futurism*, 1968, 121.

386 According to my present theme: *Spring and All*, 92.

386 "a white bear": quoted in WCW, *Selected Essays*, 114.

387 Well, said Mr Fitzwein: Samuel Beckett, *Watt*, 181.

387 Abbé Rousselot: *Polite Essays*, 129–30.

388 Pater quotations from the Conclusion to *The Renaissance*.

388 A girl came into the café: Hemingway, *A Moveable Feast*, 1964, 5.

388 The Hemingways tramping with the Pounds: Carlos Baker, *Ernest Hemingway*, 1969, 107.

389 "The Vorticist Manifestoes": *Antheil*, 44.

389 "Sound vibrations": *Antheil*, 44.

389 The old harmonists: *Antheil*, 47.

389 Information about how the *Villon* was composed from Agnes Bedford, 1965.

389 "Word meaning 'sausages'": *ABC of Reading*, 104; see *Le Testament*, line 524.

390 "Not with any African fervor": *New Directions 17*, 170.

390 Bassoon, stone head: both at Brunnenburg.

390 "Sheet after sheet": *Egoist*, 15 June 1914, 233.

390 "Beer-bottle": 7/25:29.

390 Famous photograph: reproduced, e.g. in Herbert Gorman, *James Joyce*, 1939, opposite p. 315.

393   "Not the idea": *LE*, 71.
394   "I am aware": *LE*, 159.
395   The bibliographer writes: Gallup, 158.
395   the British grocer: *Polite Essays*, 143.
395   "Bellum cano perenne": 86/28:604
396   SB to HK, conversations, 1964

SYNTAX IN RUTHERFORD

397   Williams's cat-poem: *Collected Earlier Poems*, 340.
399   "Of course it must be understood": *Spring and All*, 85–6.
399   The surfer: based on Buckminster Fuller, *No More Secondhand God*, 98–9.
402   Young Sycamore: *Collected Earlier Poems*, 332.
404   "A small (or large) machine": WCW, *Selected Essays*, 256.
405   The simplest: George Oppen, *This is Which*, 1965, 68.
405   "Hung with pleasing wraiths": WCW, *In The American Grain*, 221.
405   Zukofsky in 1930: L. Zukofsky, *Prepositions*, 1967, 137.
405   He has us distinguish between: *Prepositions*, 130–1.
406   "They sang that way": L. Zukofsky, *"A"* 1–12, 156–7.

SPECIFICS

This chapter draws chiefly on Gorham Munson's *Aladdin's Lamp*, and Douglas's first two books, *Economic Democracy* and *Credit-Power and Democracy*, read with an eye made selective by Pound's "Money-Pamphlets" and by the *Cantos*. The exposition being purposely condensed to a minimum, it seems pointless to tease detailed "sources" back out of it.

409   *The Just Price:* see Munson, 172–7.
410   [Footnote] Buckminster Fuller observes: *Ideas and Integrities*, 1963, 38.
412   Ezra Pound as a small boy: *Pavannes and Divagations*, 49–50.

THE CANTOS—2

415   Book-length exegesis: Stuart Gilbert, *James Joyce's 'Ulysses.'*
415   Enthusiastic things were said: e.g. Allen Tate, *Collected Essays*, 1959, 350–7. This 1931 review of *XXX Cantos* is notable in having preceded the trade edition by two years. It was based on one of the merely 210 copies of the Hours Press edition.
415   Remy de Gourmont surmised: *Selected Writings*, tr. and ed. Glenn S. Burne, 1966, 97.
417   Pound's 1912 remarks: *SR*, 92.
427   "And," wrote Pound: *Social Credit, an Impact*, I, iv.
428   "If reader don't know": *Letters*, #268.
430   "You allude too much": remonstrance recalled by Bunting, 1968.
433   De Mailla's sources are indicated in Achilles Fang, *Materials for the Study of Pound's Cantos*, unpub. dissertation, Harvard, 1958. See also Needham, *Science and Society in China*, I, 75.
435   Tâchez, au contraire: de Mailla, I, 173.
435   Que vos vers: de Mailla, I, 93, where Chun is appointing a superintendent of music: "... Que vos vers expriment votre intention, & que la musique y soit

analogue. . . ." And at I, 99 Pound marked the footnote, "On voit par ces textes [of the Chou-King] que la musique et les vers avoient une relation étroite au gouvernement, *Éditeur*."

435 Italian tax proposals: see e.g. *What Is Money For?*, 1939, 4th item of the Appendix: "Rossoni, Italian Minister, indicates the policy of *ammassi*, or assemblages of grain with possibilities of a totally different tax system in kind."

435 Synchronized submarining: see my fuller account in Stock, ed., *Ezra Pound: Perspectives*, 1965, 34–5.

436 "The present," wrote Wyndham Lewis: quoted from a memory at least 15 years old.

THE ANONYMOUS

437 Eliot at the Garrick: letter from Joseph Bard to EP, 26 Aug. 1951; copy furnished me by Dr. Bard.

437 To a shipboard acquaintance: this was Mr. John Reid, in 1938.

439 "Shun and Wan": *Impact*, 1960, 130, and *Criterion*, July 1938, 615.

442 "Who, for instance": Eliot, "Observations," *Egoist*, May 1918, 69.

442 In a book he reviewed in 1919: *The Problem of 'Hamlet'*, by the Rt. Hon. J. M. Robertson. Eliot's review is in *Selected Essays*.

443 Eliot even told Arnold Bennett: Bennett's *Journal*, 10 Sept. 1924.

INVENTING CONFUCIUS

Creel: H. G. Creel, *Confucius: the Man and the Myth*, 1949 (reprint entitled *Confucius and the Chinese Way*).

L & S: J. R. Levenson and F. Schurmann, *China, an Interpretative History*, 1969.

"Mencius": Ezra Pound's essay "Mang Tsze (The Ethics of Mencius)", *Criterion*, July 1938, 603–25, and *Impact*, 1960, 118–41. In dual page references below, *Criterion* always precedes.

445 At the time of *Cathay*: "Dedication" to the Calcutta edition of his version (Gallup A58b). *Gaudier-Brzeska* (written 1915) has an epigraph from Pauthier.

446 Proportion of doubtful materials: Creel, 291–3. *Analects* XIII.iii, on purifying terminology, long a key passage for Pound, appears to be inauthentic (Creel 221, and 321 note 13).

446 But here we encounter: L & S, 58; Creel, 243–4.

446 For publication (1928): Gallup, 66.

447 On January 28, 1934: *LE*, 86; for the date, *Make It New*, 3.

447 "Ideogramic Series": Gallup, 165.

447 "Renouvelle-toi": Pauthier, *La Grande Étude*, II.1.

448 Dorothy copied the ideograms: her account, 1965.

448 The Four Books in one volume: *Letters*, #331. Pound's working copy being (1969) inaccessible, Mr. Omar S. Pound showed me a duplicate.

448 A pocket dictionary: unidentified, but existence vouched for.

448 A six-week retreat: "Mencius," 604/119.

448 "Three times through the whole text": "Mencius," 609/124.

449 "There are categories": "Mencius," 620/136.

449 It is of the permanence: "Mencius," 615/130.

450   Looking, then, at Legge's Confucius: "Mencius," 605/120.
450   "A real translation": Gallup, 172.
450   He had at last in January: *Letters*, #336, 337.
451   In the 1920's: this paragraph leans on an unpublished essay by Mr. Walter Michaels.
451   [Footnote] confusing him with his disciple: first suggested, without benefit of the Fiorentino confirmation, by Achilles Fang, *Materials for the Study of Pound's Cantos*, unpub. Harvard dissertation, 1958.
451   Where one thought: *LE*, 154.
452   he assembled a Confucian "Terminology": prefixed to his 1945 version of the *Great Digest*.
452   By one speculation: R. B. Blakney, *A Course in the Analysis of Chinese Characters*, 1926, 105.
453   He told one enquiring student: *Letters*, #273.
453   "Memora" (verb) is not "memoria"(noun): EP to HK, letter, 1951, reproving an effort to regularize.
454   There was a vulgarized taoism: L & S, 127.
455   A word Confucius used many times: Creel, 122–3.
456   Chinese landscape painting: L & S, 112.
456   "The sage delighteth in water": 83/529:564. See *Analects* VI.xxi.
457   To afford paradigms: L & S, 49.
457   Might taoize on holiday: L & S 110–18, a most clarifying discussion.
459   Plowed in the sacred field: early New Directions printings had the wrong ideogram here, and the Faber still has.

THE CAGE

Sources for the DTC are in constant conflict over details, official accounts, guards' accounts and prisoners' accounts being shaped by different emotions and also using different terminology (thus it is unclear whether the "death cells" were the cages or the concrete boxes). While I have invented nothing, I cannot be sure that these pages contain no folklore. Principal sources:

Julian Cornell, *The Trial of Ezra Pound*, 1966: cited as "Cornell."
Hofman, Sgt. Norbert, "G.I. Reform School," *Yank*, IV-21 (1945), 16–17, clipping from Meacham files, Univ. of Virginia. A detailed "official" version.
David Park Williams, "The Background of the Pisan Cantos," and Robert L. Allen, "The Cage," both in O'Connor & Stone, eds., *A Casebook on Ezra Pound*, 33–43. Guards' accounts.
Notes by Prof. G. Giovannini on a conversation with Pound, supplied me by H. M. Meacham.
Dorothy Pound on two visits to her husband (conversation, 1965) and Mary de Rachewiltz on a visit to her father (conversation, 1969).
The Pisan Cantos.
Visits to the site, 1968 and 1969. Barbed wire now encloses a rose nursery. The mountains and dust are unchanged.

461   "Steele one awful name": 78/479:510.
461   Five years later one sentry: anecdote from Mr. Gordon Ringer, Los Angeles.
462   Four extra blankets, cot, pup tent: handwritten note by Pound, Meacham files, Univ. of Virginia.

463 "Top of his head" felt "empty": Cornell, 30–1.

463 "O sweet and lovely": 74/439:466.

463 Washington visit: Charles Norman, *Ezra Pound*, 1960, 359–61.

463 "Stubborn as a mule": 84/537:572.

463 "This war" (he wrote: *Gold and Work*, 1951 English reprint, 9 [Gallup A52c].

464 Mr. Prothero in 1915: *LE*, 357–8.

464 "He puts up with that": paraphrased from *Analects*, III.i.

464 (In France the very newspapers: 38/192:199, and *Letters*, #257.

465 Stinkschuld: blanks in Canto 52 filled in from typescripts examined at Brunnenburg by Eva Hesse.

465 "Race prejudice a red herring": *GK*, 242. Cf. *New English Weekly*, 14 Nov. 1935, 85–6, "anti-semitism, a red herring if ever was one."

465 350 lire a time: Norman, 1960, 384.

465 Vivaldi recordings, strangeness of hearing his own voice: related by Pound *viva voce*, 1952.

466 "For the United States": 16 Apr. 1942, quoted by Norman, 391.

466 If he were transmitting code: Norman, 387.

466 Had he been able to counsel Stalin: 74/426:452.

466 And if you'll say: Library of Congress microfilm.

467 Letter to Attorney General, Norman, 389–90.

468 At his old friend Degli Uberti's: Dorothy Pound, 1965.

468 Grüss Gott!: anecdote from Mary de Rachewiltz; cf. 78/478:509.

468 Streamers run off by a job printer: copies at Brunnenburg.

468 Three pamphlets: *L'America, Roosevelt e la Cause della Guerra Presente; Oro e Lavoro; Introduzione alla Natura Economica degli S.U.A.* See Gallup, 93–7.

469 "Better gift can no man": 76/454:482.

469 What he took to be their linguistic strength: Mary de Rachewiltz, 1969.

469 Mussolini reading *The Republic*: according to his secretary Giovanni Dolfin, cited in Achilles Fang, unpub. dissertation.

470 Nearby Zoagli: Dorothy Pound's anecdote, perhaps folklore.

470 A solitary black GI: turned up by Eva Hesse's researches.

470 The arrest is surrounded by folklore, those who talk about it not having been there. The gun butts are dramatic but improbable. For Dorothy Pound's recollections of that day, see her letter in Meacham, *The Caged Panther*, 25.

470 "They took him away today": reported by Omar S. Pound, 1969.

470 Amprim confiscated typewriter: Dorothy Pound, 1965.

474 Notebooks: seen by me, 1949.

474 Legge's text mended with medical tape: detail from Omar S. Pound.

474 "Now there are no more days": 80/499:532.

475 "For forty years": *Introduction to the Economic Nature of the United States*, opening sentences.

475 This earth that bears you up: *Unwobbling Pivot*, XXVI.9.

476 "The smell of mint": 74/438:465.

476 The only man, he later remarked: conversation, 1949.

481 Paolo and Francesca: *Inferno*, V, 138.

483 Arnold Dolmetsch published: *Pathways of Song*, 1938, 6.

484 Thus am I Dante: "Histrion," *A Lume Spento*, 1965 reprint, 108.

484 According to Aristotle: *Poetics*, 1447a.

485 *Psyche te menos te: Iliad* v–296; viii–123, 315.

485 Eyes, dreams, lips: "Cino," in *Personae*.

485 And was her daughter: 106/762:777.
489 I sing how I lost: Cavalcanti, Ballata I, *Translations*, 99.
489 "Guido's Relations": *LE*, 191–200.
494 "A voluntary expatriate": Cornell, 37.
494 "Would never happen": Cornell, 46.
495 "Problem now": Cornell, 71.
495 Single scribbled sheet: Cornell, 75.

THE LAST EUROPEAN

496 "Things have come to an awful pass": Lewis, *Letters*, 297.
496 "Twenty-five feet by twelve": *Self Condemned*, ch. xi.
496 "We are freezing out here": Lewis, *Letters*, 352.
497 Lived on advances for books: Mrs. Lewis, conversation, 1965.
498 "The obscure reveries": *Hugh Selwyn Mauberley*, II.
498 "A man in love with the past": Lewis, *Time and Western Man*, ch. xv.
500 "Burying Euclid' : Michel & Fox, eds., *Wyndham Lewis on Art*, 1969, 330.
501 The odd-shaped Harding flat: information from Agnes Bedford, 1965.
501 "Growling out melodiously": H. Kenner, ed., *T. S. Eliot, a Collection of Critical Essays*, 1962, 29.
501 The cellar was full: *Self Condemned*, end of ch. i.
501 A cold: phrases gleaned from *Self Condemned*.
502 Lewis wrote to T. Sturge Moore: Lewis, *Letters*, 291–3.
505 An incredulous volume: Allen Upward, *The New Word*.

THE JERSEY PAIDEUMA

506 "To get through them": Pound, *viva voce*, 1948.
506 "15 minutes *sane* conversation": Cornell, 72.
506 Dr. Kaffka: reported by Mr. Richard G. Stern.
507 "How you gwine ter keep": *Letters*, #318.
507 Joseph Bard had put him: Joseph Bard, conversation, 1964.
508 Remembered them: 81/519:554.
508 In *African Genesis*: Leo Frobenius and Douglas C. Fox, *African Genesis*, 1938, 109–10.
508 "Ist mehr 'Idee'": *Erlebte Erdteile*, VI, 59.
510 "A New Jersey pediatrician": *Time*, 20 Feb. 1950, 100.
510 His 85-line poem: *Collected Earlier Poems*, 233–5.
510 "The thing that saves your work": *Letters*, #137.
512 "The discreet voice of the air": *American Scene*, 42.
512 "You need a poet": WCW, October 1957.
512 However the meeting: *Paterson*, 60.
512 Take the Pelham Bay Park branch: *Collected Earlier Poems*, 283.
512 Her milk don't seem to: *Collected Earlier Poems*, 427.
513 I, I, I: *Collected Later Poems*, 230.
513 No one knows this better: see *Autobiography*, 359.
513 No antibiotics: Dr. Gael Turnbull has remarked that Williams had at his disposal just two efficacious drugs, morphine and digitalis.
513 Paterson statistics from *Encyclopaedia Britannica*.
514 S.U.M. details from George Zabriskie, "The Geography of 'Paterson'," *Perspective*, vi.4 (Autumn-Winter 1953), 201–16.

514 Eternally asleep: *Paterson*, 14.
515 The lights of the penal area: unused detail for Canto 84, from papers in the keeping of James Laughlin.
515 Pamphlet against the Federal Reserve: *Paterson*, 90–1.
515 A false language: *Paterson*, 24.
515 Caught (in mind): *Paterson*, 100.
515 We're so proud of you: *Paterson*, 138.
516 Whereupon, as the smoke: *Paterson*, 139.
516 Of this, make it of *this*: *Paterson*, 168.
516 "*Poetry* owes him": EP letter to HK, then Contributing Editor of *Poetry*.
517 Pure coruscations: "Analysis of a Theme," Stevens, *Collected Poems*, 348–9.

THE LAST VORTEX

518 The *Odes* fulfill a resolve: *GK*, 214–6.
518 Worked through Karlgren: i.e. Bulletins 14–18 of the Museum of Far Eastern Antiquities, Stockholm, 1942–6. Mr. David M. Gordon showed me one of these volumes, heavily annotated by Pound.
519 Pound's etymologies reconstructed from Karlgren and Mathews.
520 "China's epic": quoted by W. McNaughton, *Texas Quarterly*, X.4 (Winter 1967), 55.
520 Mannerisms of the main English modes: see H. Kenner, "Faces to the Wall," *Gnomon*, 1958, 80–100.
521 *Feng:* see L. S. Dembo, *The Confucian Odes of Ezra Pound*, 1963, 9.
524 During 1948 Eliot began: E. Martin Browne, *The Making of T. S. Eliot's Plays*, 1969, ch. 6.
524 Eliot had sent an attempt: *GK*, 92–3.
526 "Since, then, my son": translation in the Jebb bilingual edition, almost certainly the one Pound used.
527 Sparring with Edith Hamilton: E. Mullins, *This Difficult Individual, Ezra Pound*, 1963, 307–9. Other incidents in this section observed by me.
527 Name typewritten on a handkerchief: 100/724:742.
529 He wrote to Dublin: recounted by Mrs. Yeats, *viva voce*, 1956.
530 One of whose pupils: recalled by Pound, 1964, but unidentified. Fuller is mentioned at 97/680:711, where the spelling "Buckie" (for Bucky) indicates that Pound got the name by ear.
530 "Only the alphabet": *Impact*, 177 (written 1937).
531 So the clear mountain light: Mary de Rachewiltz in 1964 recalled that day of solid light.
535 On 18 April: Cornell, 134.
535 Robert Frost to Richard Wilbur: reported by Wilbur to H. M. Meacham, and by Meacham to G. Giovannini, letter 31 Dec. 1958, Meacham files, Univ. of Virginia Library.
536 See Mullins, ch. 14, and Meacham, *passim*. And the story is not complete yet.
536 *Congressional Record*, Appendix, 29 April 1958, *et seq.*

ENDINGS

537 Castle built in 1244: *Guido dei Castelli dell' Alto Adige*, a cura di Dott. Marcello Caminiti, 1955, 156–8. This book being of sporadic reliability, I have taken most of my lore from the conversation of Mary de Rachewiltz.

540   Said to have brought poison ivy: Hubert Creekmore, *Daffodils are Dangerous*, 1966, 216.

540   "THAT HAM is kulchur": Meacham, *The Caged Panther*, 74.

540   It was his rendition: Guy Davenport, who heard Pound discuss the incident, thinks it obvious that whatever the content of the reading, what amused Mussolini was the performance.

540   "Sea air": Meacham, 173.

540   Head just doesn't WORK, Meacham, 189.

540   "Handsome and white": DP to Harry Meacham, in Meacham, 190.

541   "Fight like kittens": conversation, 1962.

541   Finished on Ezra's birthday: I was there.

541   "A loosely assembled essay": *Spectrum*, III.3 (Fall 1959), 131–57. *Inter alia* this reprints from the October 1957 *Poetry* his observations on Chapman's Homer.

541   "A blind old man": *Pictures from Breughel*, 166.

541   Learning with age: *Paterson*, 277–8.

542   The descent beckons: *Paterson*, 96. Cf. WCW, *Selected Letters*, 334.

542   He at once said, Yes: conversation, Oct. 1957.

542   Look at what passes for the new: *Pictures from Breughel*, 161.

543   Exercise in Timing: *Pictures from Breughel*, 47.

543   Sooner or later: *Pictures from Breughel*, 70.

543   A visitor: Guy Davenport, letter to HK.

544   "I believe": *Translations*, 23.

544   "Rhythm is a form": *ABC of Reading*, 188.

544   "Universe of fluid force": *Spirit of Romance*, 92.

544   "Speech of Polish mothers": *Autobiography*, 311.

544   He told a friend: David McCall Gordon, who imparted it to me in July 1962.

545   She weaves: Brunnenburg ms.

545   By the river of stars: Brunnenburg ms. Entitled "Baijo's Poem in the Koshigen" and with different indentations, it is printed in *1889* [per i 70 anno di Giovanni Scheiwiller], 1959, 58.

545   "The star fields of Arcturus": "In Tempore Senectutis," *A Lume Spento*, 1965 reprint, 33.

545   Green of the wood-moss: "The Cry of the Eyes," *A Lume Spento*, 37.

545   Sing of the white birds: "Cino," fourth poem in *Personae*.

547   The tree—Pound looked for it: DP, conversation, 1969.

548   "*Simplex naturae*": "Note Precedent to 'La Fraisne'," *A Lume Spento*, 14.

548   "Sky," said Kung: *Analects*, XVII.xix.3.

548   This monument: *Translations*, 407, dated 1964.

549   "Life is too short": recalled by Mrs. Lewis, 1965.

550   "The greatest prose master": T. S. Eliot, "A Note on *Monstre Gai*," *Hudson Review*, VII.4 (Winter 1955), 526.

550   Friends got to the studio: Michael and Elizabeth Ayrton.

550   "A world that will never be seen": Lewis, *Rotting Hill*, Chicago, 1952, 222.

550   "May his spirit": *Pound/Joyce*, 271.

550   A tailor he patronized: Cyril Langley, then of Albemarle Street; the remark was made in November 1956.

551   "Up and down": conversation, May 1964.

551   He had told an Italian interviewer: *Epoca*, 50:652, 1963.

551   When my arms: "He Remembers Forgotten Beauty."

552 I am Yseult: "Modern Beauty."
552 Oui, c'est pour moi: "Hérodiade: Scène."
552 Worlds we have: Canto I, cancelled version, *Quia Pauper Amavi*, 22–3.
553 "Who is there for me": in Allen Tate, ed., *T. S. Eliot, the Man and his Work*, 1966, 89.
554 In a learned journal: *Arion*, VII–1, 143.
556 "A bad sign": imparted by Mrs. Eliot, 1969.
556 "I botched it": frequently reported by Daniel Cory.
556 "The editor only wishes": *Poetry*, Nov. 1962,
556 "A minor satirist": EP to Henry Rago, who sent me a copy.
556 "C'est moi dans la poubelle": reported by James Laughlin.
556 Meeting with Beckett: SB to HK.
556 "Stupid, suburban": quoted in Michael Reck, "A Conversation Between Ezra Pound and Allen Ginsberg," *Evergreen Review* #55 (June 1968), 26–29, 84.
557 "Non è un Tempio": to Guy Davenport, 1964.
557 Frank Lloyd Wright on EP: Mrs. Lorraine C. Reid to HK, 6 July 1963.
558 Set out across Venice: glimpses from three visits, 1964–8.
559 No man had the right: his autograph end-note to "Venetian Night Litany," in *Iconografia Italiana di Ezra Pound*, 1955, plate 4.
560 "Mut" (courage): so local lore, but the accurate Eva Hesse insists that they do not say "der Mut" (= courage) but "die Mut" (= customs post). Alas.
561 Down to the Presbyterian Church: recounted by Mrs. Gatter to Guy Davenport.
561 "Shall two know the same": 93/631:664.

INDEX